CW00538522

Reading Revelation

Tympanum of images from Revelation by Marie-Hellen Geoffroy,
cut by scalpel on black and white papers.

Reading Revelation

A Thematic Approach

W. Gordon Campbell

James Clarke and Co

James Clarke and Co
P.O. Box 60
Cambridge
CB1 2NT

www.jamesclarke.co
publishing@jamesclarke.co

ISBN: 978 0 227 17383 1

British Library Cataloguing in Publication Data
A record is available from the British Library

Copyright © W. Gordon Campbell, 2012

First Published, 2012

All rights reserved. No part of this edition may be reproduced, stored
electronically or in any retrieval system, or transmitted in any form or
by any means, electronic, mechanical, photocopying, recording, or
otherwise, without prior written permission from the Publisher
(permissions@jamesclarke.co).

Contents

Part Three: When God and Humanity meet

Foreword to the English Edition

I am especially pleased to commend the treatment of the Apocalypse of John by Gordon Campbell in this book. As readers pick up and read through the following analysis of Revelation, I believe they will find a lively engagement with the text that puts the interpretation of John's enigmatic visions on a new footing. The literary narrative method adopted by Campbell is not entirely new; such an approach to the Apocalypse has been taken up for nearly 30 years. It is, instead, rather *how* Campbell uses his chosen method that helps put the book of Revelation in a new light.

As Campbell is aware, the study of Revelation has been dominated by a number of approaches; these approaches are often so narrowly applied that other, complementary ways of considering the book are left aside. Of course, the *way into the text* of the book will frequently determine what one ultimately extracts from it as valuable for the communities of faith who consider it authoritative. While the present volume is no exception, the way Campbell reads Revelation serves as a splendid example of the use of a particular reading strategy without, at the same time, doing away with the value of others.

Among the many interpretations of Revelation during the last several decades, two approaches – broadly defined – continue to be influential among larger numbers of readers, academic and otherwise. One is to regard the book as a predictive prophecy, and the other is to regard it as a source for how Christians were coming to terms near the end of the first century CE with their emerging religious identity in the Mediterranean world. With the present volume in mind, we can reflect briefly on these two interpretative strategies.

First, there is the understanding of Revelation as prophecy chiefly concerned with predicting the future. Is the Apocalypse of John to be thought of as a book written by someone who, whether from his own vantage point or in relation to Christians then and now, charted a map of future events by drawing on a wealth of symbols that those who are discerning can decode? How one answers this question is bound up with how one addresses a number of related issues that include one or more of the following: (1) Is an 'apocalypse' – the book designates itself as 'the apocalypse of Jesus Christ' (Rev. 1.1) – by definition going to be a work that focuses on the eschatological future as the end and goal of history? (2) Is interest in an eschatological resolution to history necessarily shaped by a pessimistic outlook that questions whether the power structures of this world can actually be transformed into institutions that embody the will and the purpose of God? Related to this, does Revelation essentially speak best to a context of persecution, whether then or now, in which people have no recourse but to hope for divine intervention? (3) Is the future, referred to in Revelation as what will happen 'soon' (1.1; 22.6; cf. 1.19; 4.1; 22.10), an imminent or a distant reality? Given the passing of nearly 2,000 years since the composition of Revelation, to what degree is it appropriate for interpreters to find ways to make an ancient prediction relate to contemporary events? (4) If an eschatological reading of Revelation is combined with the assumption that it is concerned with 'us' as contemporary readers, what purpose might there be, if at all, to search for or speculate on the historical allusions in the book? To what extent is it appropriate to read Revelation as a fund of symbols to be deciphered and matched to people and events that readers may be able to recognize? (5) In the end, how well does a futuristic interpretation of Revelation help us make sense of the book as a whole? Readers will notice that Campbell does not frequently use terms such as 'future', 'eschatology', or 'prediction' in his analysis. His narrative treatment of Revelation adopts a view that its message is ultimately bigger and grander than eschatology.

Another influential approach to Revelation that the present volume avoids without being able to dispense with it altogether is 'historical'. Seen and read in its ancient context, the text is explained as arising from and responding to *external* stimuli. Essential to reading the Apocalypse is the study of source material from the Greco-Roman and Jewish antiquity that can be said to lie underneath, behind, and around the text. Campbell's wish in this volume is not to ignore this dimension as a way to help make sense of Revelation. However, a one-sided focus on the identification of factors *outside* the text neglects the possibility, if not the likelihood, that such a richly symbolic work may in fact go a long way in providing its own 'text-immanent' terms for interpretation. The discernment of correspondences between the text and details that come to us through ancient sources about life in Asia Minor towards the end of the first century CE may, in principle, anchor the book within the time, space and ideology of a certain context. However, what does this approach offer to readers of the twenty-first century? Campbell's literary analysis adopts a perspective that renders the search for meaning in the book of Revelation as involving something bigger than the sum of its historically contingent parts.

New Testament scholars have had little problem referring to Paul and, indeed, the writers of each of the four canonical Gospels as theological thinkers. By contrast, there is more hesitation in many communities of faith to regard John of Revelation as a theologian in his own right. Campbell offers us a way to read the book as more than simply a glimpse into the future, as more than a response to circumstances faced by the Christian communities of Asia Minor, or as more than a creative interpretation of biblical tradition. In Revelation we are to see something of *John as a theologian* who consciously thought about several issues that are crucial to an understanding of a Christian identity: John assigned a central place to Jesus the Lamb within the God of Israel's redemptive purpose for the cosmos; John modeled discipleship on Christology and, to some extent, Christology on discipleship; John thought about what it means to worship God while at the same time accommodating a figure like Jesus in a way that does not undermine faithfulness to God alone; and John, perhaps more radically than any of his Christian contemporaries, posited a tension between a casual participation in social, economic and political spheres of life and the unswerving loyalty to God. For these underlying theological convictions the text of Revelation offers its own terms of reference, and therein we may discern both the promise and challenge of the book, not only for audiences who first heard it read aloud in the first century but also for faith communities today.

I hope that in this respect, readers will benefit from the present volume by Gordon Campbell as much as I have already.

Loren Stuckenbruck
Shavu'ot 2012
Jerusalem

Preface to the English edition

When the French original of this book appeared in 2007, it was my intention that it should also be published in due course in my mother tongue. Much of the first draft in English was, in fact, already complete by that time. Sparse reaction from scholars to the French edition, especially beyond the francophone context, has been somewhat frustrating: it may be attributable to the partial eclipse of French in Biblical Studies, amid a growing trend towards the exclusive use of English. Therefore, perhaps by its very accessibility this edition will excite greater interest among Revelation scholars and others. Where specialists with whom I engaged in the French edition have published relevant work in the five years since it appeared, I have attempted to recognise this in the footnotes and bibliography.

It took me more time than anticipated to find an English-language publisher willing to take on so substantial a project as this, in today's climate. I am therefore delighted by the interest that James Clarke and Co. have shown in my work since first it came to their notice, and I wish to record my gratitude both for the help they have given and the speed with which they have done so.

For many reasons, the only satisfactory way I could imagine making the French original available to readers of English was to translate the book myself. As both translator and author, I faced the temptation on almost every page to revisit whatever point was being made and – as time passed – to update the material accordingly. Whilst this enticement was resisted, for the final draft I nonetheless felt free to correct any mistakes which remained in the French edition, or to improve on the clarity or the force of the argument wherever this seemed appropriate. I am very grateful to my secretary, Renée McCracken, for her invaluable help with the indices and to my children Myriam and Stuart Campbell for their contribution. Any remaining obscurities can only be my fault! In agreement with James Clarke & Co., this English edition also uses endnotes instead of footnotes. It is hoped that this change will help readers focus on the main task – reading Revelation.

In the foreword to the French edition I expressed my indebtedness to Alain Martin. Following protracted ill health, Alain passed away in Spring 2011. I wish to take this opportunity to mark his passing by expressing my profound gratitude to God for his life and ministry.

The stance which I have adopted in this study mainly reflects the context of teaching and research in which it was undertaken – in the Academy – but also that of the Church. Since the French original was published I have continued greatly to value interaction on Revelation with theology students in general and with those preparing for ordination in particular, whether in Aix-en-Provence, Belfast or Riga. In so far as my book is an invitation to my readers to read John's Revelation with new eyes, I hope this may result in an enhanced appreciation of the Book by scholars and a renewed influence for it in the worship and the witness of the Church. In light of this, I am especially grateful to Prof. Loren Stuckenbruck for his assessment in the foreword to the English edition and enthusiasm which he expresses there.

What was first said in French has now been repeated in English. Accordingly, like the French original this English edition is dedicated to my wife Sandra and to our children Aimée, Myriam, Stuart and Marc – with all my love.

Foreword to the French edition

To write a foreword is a difficult art. On the one hand, it should show thorough familiarity with the author's intentions and respect for them. On the other, it should help and facilitate readers by putting across an independent view of the book. Although it is rather like trying to square the circle, I will endeavour to take up this considerable challenge. In a foreword, there is a limit to what may be said, but the bottom line is this: to make readers want to read Gordon Campbell's work, devoted to the biblical book of Revelation.

They will not find here a verse-by-verse commentary of the book. Nor will they find the classic explanations of historical context by which those who take Revelation to be a coded message attempt to decipher it. For Campbell such pursuits are a pretext; they too quickly supply a key, blurring just as quickly what the biblical book itself intended. Accordingly, he stands back somewhat from historical-critical methodology, picking up instead where structural or narrative approaches left off and going beyond them.

However, it would be wrong to restrict Campbell's intention merely to a question of method. What he tries to do is to take the text on its own terms, with a view to discovering the primary purpose for which it was written.

The foundation for his thinking is a *thematic reading*, approaching Revelation through the study of a number of themes which run right through this book. Among the unifying themes which Gordon Campbell identifies are pseudo-divinity, bogus messiahship, false worship, humanity struggling against propaganda, faithful or unfaithful bride-cities and covenant. This enumeration is admittedly too terse, since behind it lies a wealth of themes which intermingle and correlate with one another.

For instance, it is not long before the importance of parody comes to light. Thus the forces of evil (the two monsters, the devil) do not attempt to attack God head-on, but rather try to take his place by imitation. Revelation describes a parody of the Trinity, of the Messiah or again, of the Lord's Supper. Propaganda is a parody of the Word of God, a 'lies factory' as Paul Claudel put it. I might add that in other biblical passages there is similar parody to be found, as in what some call the Synoptic Apocalypse: 'false messiahs and false prophets will arise and perform signs and wonders so that even the elect, if possible, might be led astray'(Mark 13.22).

For Campbell, the whole history of Israel is taken up into Revelation from the start; this process is underway right from the letters to the seven Churches, which are not to be separated from the rest of the book. He sees Babylon, in chapter 18, not as a description of the economic life of Rome but of the corruption of Jerusalem, as depicted by the prophets. Revelation is the (hi)story behind history. The chaos of history hides the reality of the purposes of God, where the Messiah takes his place. Revelation's Christ-Lamb is most definitely the Jesus Christ of the Gospel. Revelation is not the New Testament's last and difficult book, which no one quite knows how to handle – like Luther or Calvin, both of whom found it too difficult and refrained from writing a commentary on it. It is no post-script either, which had difficulty getting into the Canon. Rather, as a book it represents the crowning achievement of the Scriptures. The coherence of these Scriptures, when taken together, is affirmed by Gordon Campbell not just through frequent quotation from the Old Testament, or by rooting so many of its elements in the history of Israel, but also by recalling the work of Jesus Christ.

To use an expression coined by Oscar Cullmann, 'it is in salvation history that Revelation firmly belongs'. This explains why the book has been so relevant to readers in times of persecution; as the testimony of Irenaeus of Lyons suggests, this may already have been so in the Roman era, although this ought not to be made into an interpretative key. Nearer to our own time, Revelation nourished the faith of Christians struggling against Nazi totalitarianism.

What, then, of us today? Without a doubt Revelation summons us to resist propaganda, advertising, slogans of the day – anything, in fact, which devalues or perverts the spoken word. Humanity is taken in by the attempts of the forces of evil to imitate God's actions. Evil is not the opposite of good but that which would substitute itself for good. In Genesis 3, the error of humankind was not opposing God but wanting to regard itself as God.

Gordon Campbell puts it very nicely: 'If God has the last word in this story, it is because he had the first word'. In every age readers are encouraged to distinguish where the unadulterated Word of God may be heard. He goes on: 'our author never fails to underline the obligations and responsibilities incumbent on faithful partners in their relationship to God, under the new covenant sealed by the blood of Christ'. For Campbell, Revelation is not to be used for satisfying whatever more or less unhealthy curiosity we may have. Instead, it is for disabusing us of our false illusions, diverting our attention away from values which we may find hypnotic and towards the one true God, who alone is able to save us.

These several reflections, which are far from complete, do not mirror at all adequately the wealth found in Gordon Campbell's work. However, if they make readers want to immerse themselves in this demanding but immensely rich book, then this foreword will have achieved its goal.

The work depends on an extensive bibliography comprised of English, German and French-speaking authors. Among the latter Allo, Brütsch and (for the liturgical dimension) Prigent may be mentioned, but especially Jacques Ellul, some of whose insights are once more found in Campbell, particularly where propaganda is concerned.

The results of Gordon Campbell's research were first presented within a university setting. We owe this Irishman our gratitude for making them available here to the wider French-speaking public. Personally, I am always filled with admiration for English-speaking friends like him, whose grasp of our language is so good.   Alain G. Martin

Preface to the French edition

Publication of this book is the result of a research project which goes back more than fifteen years and originates in my doctoral studies. During those years, spent living in France, it was my joy to serve first as a minister of the Reformed Church of France (ERF), in the department of Charente and later Marseilles, then as Professor of New Testament at the Faculté libre de théologie réformee (FLTR/FJC)[1] in Aix-en-Provence. Despite having returned to Ireland with my family in 2005, I was keen to make available to the French-speaking public, in the first instance, the fruit of my time spent in the company of Revelation. It is my prayer that French-speaking exegetes I have encountered, but especially ministers and Church members, might find this a useful tool for reading John's Revelation, deriving benefit from it and sharing its message with others.

Various Churches and institutions, together with several individuals, helped and encouraged me as I undertook this work. In this foreword, I particularly want to express my profound gratitude towards them.

That my wish to write in French was granted is due, in no small measure, to the Academic Council of Queen's University, Belfast (QUB), in Northern Ireland. Through application of the criterion of professional development, I was allowed to write my doctoral dissertation in the language of John Calvin. That thesis, submitted and accepted in 2002, was reworked and expanded for the present work, as well as being transformed with a wider readership in view.

The faithful support of two individuals helped me complete my research culminating in the award of a PhD in 2002. The first is my supervisor Professor Cecil McCullough, a minister of the Presbyterian Church in Ireland, Principal of Union Theological College (UTC) at the time and Professor of New Testament within the QUB Institute of Theology. His contribution was particularly helpful in terms of my methodology. The second is Professor Alain-Georges Martin, a retired ERF minister and Emeritus Professor of New Testament in FJC. Right up until the completion of my doctoral work, he remained a trusty consultant, especially where my French expression is concerned. In spite of their valuable contributions, I alone am responsible for any defects that remain.

My former colleagues on the Faculty of FJC supported my work through their encouragement and prayers whilst the College's governing body was of practical help on a number of occasions, notably by granting me study leave. I hope they will not be disappointed by the 'result'. Several groups of students who followed my lectures or other occasional papers on John's Revelation should, from time to time, find their questions, comments and especially their enthusiasm reflected in these pages. The same goes for their opposite numbers at UTC in Belfast.

Without the backing of the Presbyterian Church in Ireland, of which I am a minister, and especially of two successive Executive Secretaries of her Board of Mission Overseas (which employs me) – Rev. Terry McMullan and Rev. Uel Marrs – I would never have been able to set aside the time needed for serious research on Revelation and for writing the present book. I am very grateful to them both.

Last of all, I should like to express my heartfelt thanks to the publishers, *Excelsis*, for accepting this piece of work and including it in their *Biblical Theology* series.

With much love and gratitude, I dedicate this work to my wife Sandra, who faithfully sustained me through the ups and downs of work on such a scale, as well as to our children Aimée, Myriam, Stuart and Marc, for all the patience they have shown me.

Notes

1   Recently renamed Faculté Jean Calvin (FJC).

Methodological introduction

'There is something dreadfully presumptuous, forbidding and uncalled-for about writing anything at all on the subject of Revelation' (J. Ellul).[1]

In spite of J. Ellul's disclaimer, which still remains spot on today, here I am undertaking my own quest for the meaning of the Book of Revelation over thirty years later. As Ellul set about his task then, he thought it a good idea to leave behind more well-trodden paths of interpretation. My own proposal also represents a desire to break new ground and accordingly the study which follows is a *thematic reading* of Revelation – the first of its kind, as far as I know.

The reader must be giving me the benefit of the doubt to some degree by even opening this book, but you are likely wondering what it will contain and just as keen to learn, as quickly as possible, *what a thematic reading is*. Ultimately, it will take me a whole book to answer that very legitimate question! A preliminary sketch of what it entails will nonetheless be provided in the second part of this introduction.

First, we need to face two facts. One is that – as widely agreed – Revelation is a difficult biblical book to read. The other is that my approach to Revelation here will be unfamiliar. It is my conviction that a thematic reading will contribute towards a better understanding of this challenging biblical text, complementing the more familiar commentaries on Revelation. However, it will help my readers at the outset if I provide some orientation by justifying the method adopted and explaining what is at stake. Whilst this may seem like a detour, I think it is the best way to broach our subject.

Why undertake a thematic reading?

The interpretative climate

In 2001, in a specialist article published in a biblical journal, I already supplied the groundwork for the *why* of the approach I have adopted.[2] At the time, my objective was to give some prior indication of results arising from an investigation being undertaken for my doctoral dissertation, as well as providing necessary advance justification for the thematic approach I am now using here. For the purposes of the dissertation,[3] I reflected on several methodological issues requiring clarification, all of them fundamental. In the conclusion to the article, I expressed a twofold conviction: concerning the way Revelation is put together, I affirmed that the Book's thematic materials make a major contribution to its linguistic and narrative unity. As a consequence, I suggested that interpreters ought to be making it their priority to explore in detail the way these materials are deployed and developed, in order that Revelation scholarship might expand the rather rudimentary literary appreciation which we then had of the Book as a complex unity.[4]

Because of the state of play in biblical exegesis, this enterprise seemed to me to be a matter of some urgency. Let me briefly outline a situation which non-theologians among my readers will likely find surprising. If we were to survey the considerable body of exegetical work on John's Revelation published in the West around the turn of the third Christian millennium, we would be forced to conclude that the vast majority of interpreters are not, in fact, really interested in getting to grips with Revelation in its final form, as it appears today in our Bibles. And this would be true not only of journal articles – which, by definition, can have only a limited scope – but also of longer works devoted to examining this biblical book as a whole.

Exactly what, then, *is* the main interest of specialists of the last book of the Bible, whose works will fill my footnotes and bibliography? Generally speaking, they focus on Revelation's relationship to the context in which it was produced, as viewed from the standpoints of history, politics, sociology and religion. Thus, my main dialogue partners understand the act of interpretation to involve, in particular, the investigation of that to which Revelation might refer, beyond itself. Their goal is constantly to improve our understanding of the way Revelation fits into the public history of the century it came from, as reconstructed by historians striving to use the tools of their trade. Unlike the present author, a majority of researchers are not primarily interested in the text of the Book of Revelation *as such*; instead, they focus on the context that lies behind the text – that is, its hypothetical original circumstances (often called its *Sitz im Leben*, from the German).[5] That, we could say, is how the prevailing exegetical wind has been blowing. In contrast, the present study attempts to give an account of Revelation's complex unity or its narrative coherence by using a thematic reading. Straightaway, the question arises as to whether the thematic reading of Revelation found in these pages represents, by implication, a kind of cross-wind.

Admittedly, to take an interest in the themes of a book of the Bible is nothing new in and of itself, even if interpreters who have had recourse to such a method – sporadically, it has to be said – have insufficiently thought through what might be meant by themes.[6] Yet my own efforts here at exploring Revelation's complex thematic materials in a thoroughgoing way, by means of both analysis and synthesis, are nonetheless definitely new and indeed unheard-of in the history of the Book's interpretation. The same goes for my methodology, a sort of 'reasoned eclecticism'[7] which combines literary and theological readings whilst leaving aside the historical approach. In the worst-case scenario, this originality of approach might look like naivety, making my efforts in this book just another case of hermeneutical rashness of which the history of exegesis has already produced too many. In the best-case scenario, my chosen methodology (supposing it were justifiable) would, at the very least, require satisfactory explanation. The question posed a moment ago is therefore inescapable: Why undertake a thematic reading at all?

Originally, my research had another aim than the one being pursued here; this was to study, as systematically and fully as possible, the 'fundamental antithesis'[8] which underlies the composition of John's Revelation. This objective led me to undertake an exhaustive preliminary exploration of Revelation aimed at finding anything that might be indicative of a deliberate intention, on the author's part, to describe the world, its history and human beings as having two, antithetically parallel sides to them. I was soon faced with a major methodological challenge. How could the large amount of data from Revelation relevant to the study be both listed and correlated, without getting lost on the way in the welter of detail? My solution to this problem was to innovate, by examining the Book's antithetical parallelism via the detailed description of its principal themes – something no one had ever attempted. I did this on the basis that these themes, as will be shown in the present book, were arranged in contrasting pairs of negative and positive elements.

What was originally a *means to an end* – a thematic approach to the textual data, using both analysis and synthesis – has for present purposes now become *the end in itself*. In this book my goal is to give an account of Revelation's major literary-theological themes; to what extent these major themes are arranged antithetically – or clustered around corresponding negative and positive poles – will emerge incidentally as I am able, in ensuing chapters, to analyse and synthesise their configurations.

Turning things around, in this way, for publication should not diminish the contribution which I hope my research will make to scientific study of John's Revelation – quite the opposite. The first reason for this is negative: adequate refutation, by the results presented here, of what could be called *the apocalyptic colour hypothesis*. It was long thought by commentators that Revelation's frequent literary contrasts, which wrench the text more or less abruptly back and forth, were simply the mark of a banal literary characteristic, typical of apocalyptic genre. It will no longer do to make such a gross approximation or merely to credit the author with a mental framework liable to reduce everything to a fundamental conflict consisting of 'for and against'.[9]

The second reason is positive. I show how Revelation's ever-present use of antithesis is solidly established to be hermeneutically significant by three hard facts:

a) We are dealing, here, with a skilfully woven part of Revelation's compositional web.

b) The Book's numerous antithetical phrases, figures and images are carefully interlinked within its complex narrative.

c) These very motifs, with their positive and negative poles, both regulate and punctuate the developing narrative.

At the same time, I believe I am justified in reworking the outcome of my research so as to provide a full-blown thematic reading of Revelation. For after all, it does not ultimately matter to a reader that Revelation abounds in sophisticated contrasts which are seen to be cleverly connected in the final composition as we have it – even if this is true, and worthy of emphasis. No, what matters is the Book's message and meaning. By inviting readers to engage with the full substance of Revelation's various major themes which, as I hope to demonstrate in detail, are carefully conditioned by antithetical parallelism, I mean to draw attention to those very themes as key vehicles of meaning and accordingly to derive from them constant implications for the interpretation of Revelation.

What about historical research?

But back to the cross-wind. Given the domination of historical questions in the study of Revelation, as just noted, there is an issue that simply cannot be dodged. Does my proposal to undertake a thematic reading of Revelation, for which historical research as such is to be set aside, entail denying the importance of the historical dimension of biblical books? Since the emergence of structuralism, it is certainly the case that synchronic approaches to literary texts which assert in principle the immanence of the text do, quite openly, abandon two traditional objectives of exegesis. One of these is investigation of the author's intentions; dispensing with this can lead, in some cases, to all interest being focused on readers in their subjectivity and on what they may find relevant in the text they are reading.[10] The other is location of a text in its context of origin; for new literary criticism, a text is in no way anchored to this context and cannot refer to it in any 'ostensive' manner (that is, a text is judged to be incapable of breaking free of its own textual confines into some alleged external context lying beyond its own limits).[11]

Let me state clearly, with no disclaimers that, whenever explanation of Revelation's difficulties is called for in this study, I will always give preference to solutions found within the parameters of the text, rather than have recourse to factors beyond it. This is because I refuse, in principle, to do damage to the text as a self-contained narrative by presuming to sever its content from its form. However, it would be quite wrong to interpret this as a desire, on my part, to call into question ordinary exegetical work, whose historical questioning seeks a fuller understanding of biblical books through due consideration of their original historical milieu. In fact, the opposite is the case. For even if the present book makes resolute use of an altogether different method, I take it as self-evident that a book's frame of reference ought to be investigated.

There are two clear reasons for this. First, and from an explicitly Christian point of view, it is beyond dispute for me that 'God has revealed himself in the history of human beings and . . . his revelation, [as] recorded . . . in the Old and New Testament[s], is itself historical [in nature]'.[12] Confining myself to the New Testament, that means that in historical terms Jesus of Nazareth and the phenomenon of emerging Christianity, as described in its writings (including Revelation), are deeply rooted in the history of the first century of our era. From this standpoint, it is clear that the various representations of Christ in Revelation's narrative – among them 'one like a Son of man'[13] (1.13; 14.14), the Lamb (5.6, *etc*.), or the messianic warrior (19.11*ff*) – each refer, in their own way, to the historical figure of Jesus, crucified under Pontius Pilate, and to God's acts in history in raising him from the dead, exalting him and calling forth a Church to confess his name (in Roman Asia or elsewhere).[14] Without such history or the events that comprise it – notably Christ's redemptive death – Revelation would simply lack the historical and extra-linguistic 'moment' to which the Book's linguistic narrative so obviously bears witness. Revelation refers to extra-textual happenings in the remembered past which continue to be relevant in the lived-in present where the Book came about. Jesus' coming upon the human scene has left its trace or mark in this text which, together with the New Testament's other documents, now represents that past history, stands for it and is equivalent to it.[15]

Yet a gulf in time separates us from that world, so different from our own, and this fact renders our access to it at best indirect and incomplete. This means, secondly, that if we are to understand and interpret as successfully as possible a writing originating in a communicative setting that is foreign to us, and if we are to treat that setting with due respect, it is (and will remain) absolutely vital that we take into account the historical context being presupposed. The question of how exactly a particular biblical book corresponds to a given frame of reference, requires thorough exploration. Correspondingly, historical research must remain a privileged arrow in the exegete's quiver. Although the tools of historical investigation are certainly always capable of refinement, and whilst its methods are only means to an end and not ends in themselves,[16] biblical research cannot do without historical inquiry. In the pages that follow, therefore, I will not be ignoring completely the historical question of Revelation's original *Sitz im Leben*. How this or that part of the narrative has been handled throughout the history of exegesis will, from time to time, necessitate a short historical detour or, at the very least, discussion of historical issues in the footnotes.[17]

John's Revelation and 'History'

Nevertheless, it is one thing to reject the assumption made by semiotics in its pure form when it is asserted that we can know nothing about the circumstances in which the act of writing occurred, and do nothing to try to shed light on them.[18] It is quite another to conceive, theoretically, how one might adequately research, and then critically reconstruct, the original communicative situation for such a complex book as Revelation.

Elucidating the relationship of John's Revelation to history is a task whose real difficulty ought not to be underestimated. As far as its author's intentions are concerned, the point of the Book does not seem to be fundamentally historiographical in nature – as is the case, for example, with Luke's work. It is therefore far from clear how this relationship should be understood or even, what sort of 'history' might be involved. Of mixed narrative genre, Revelation requires its would-be interpreter to reckon with the very complex way its apocalyptic, prophetic-visionary and epistolary characteristics merge together into one single account.[19] As far as 'history' is concerned, this already means we are dealing with an intermingling of several possible modes of reference, or correspondence, to extra-textual realities located in the domain of *Weltgeschichte* (the history of the world, or public history).

Nor is it immediately obvious what segment of the real-life experience of its first readers to which Revelation might be referring. Bearing in mind that Revelation's narrative gives so prominent a place to the worship of God and the Lamb – an activity which plainly enjoys great importance for both author and addressees – any extrapolation to a supposed original context would have to take full account of the Book's cultic atmosphere and episodes depicting worship, along with their liturgical elements. Accordingly, we might ask whether today's readers (like those before them) are not in fact invited, through the act of reading, to become participants in this worship and to get involved as actors alongside the Risen One in contemporising a kind of Christusgeschichte (or [hi]story of the living Christ).

Alternatively, might the centuries-long career of God's people, of which John and the Christians of Asia believe themselves to be members, not constitute the historical context to which Revelation, in the final analysis, makes reference? For in constantly alluding to the Old Testament, the text of Revelation invokes its own sub-text, or collection of constant inter-textual references, which mould from start to finish the story it recounts.[20] The difficult task of reconstructing the circumstances in which Revelation could have been written and read therefore demands that consideration be given to just such a historical backdrop: to *Heilsgeschichte* (or salvation history). For it is as if the issue which is at stake in Revelation's narrative, and our successful explication of it, is that of the correct interpretation of the Hebrew Scriptures and of the historical tale they combine to tell.[21]

In consequence of all of this, as I have written elsewhere,

> It is a hazardous enterprise for the interpreter of Revelation, at a distance of two millennia, to attempt to piece together the historical circumstances reflected in the story told by an ancient apocalyptic book. In extrapolating from the poetic and highly symbolic world of the text to the real world, how is one to avoid imposing an alien

interpretative framework upon the apocalyptic narrative? Exactly how any corresponding socio-religious context in first-century Asia Minor is to be inferred from this apocalyptic story is far from apparent.[22]

Yet there is no shortage of books and articles in which, undaunted, scholars still profess to be able to move in more or less direct fashion from the textual data of Revelation to their alleged 'real' frame of reference. Supposing for a moment (for sake of argument) that there is no problem here, and that my warning to readers of Revelation is actually groundless, we must still acknowledge the very fragmentary nature of our current awareness of the socio-religious context of the Churches of first-century Asia Minor. And this dictates that whenever Revelation is read in this way, great caution should be exercised in any effort to recover and fit together pieces of historical data that might be taken in combination to reflect the context of its production.[23] For in spite of the current preponderance of scholarly reconstructions that posit a Roman backdrop for Revelation, it remains more natural (from a strictly historical point of view) to presuppose that if there is historical light to be shed on Revelation, as on the New Testament as a whole, then such illumination will derive especially from the context of Second Temple Judaism – one which, moreover, has bequeathed to us other Jewish apocalypses. Clearly, such a line of reasoning would entail me breaking with the current consensus.[24]

As a result of my research, that is precisely where my own reading of Revelation has ultimately been taking me. As the present study progresses, we will see reflected in Revelation's narrative not, as is usually assumed, a rhetorical position fundamentally at loggerheads, politically or religiously, with the ancient Roman status quo, but instead manifestations of a distinctly inner-Jewish debate, conducted on the basis of rival readings of the Old Testament current at the time. Consequently, a provisional reconstruction of the cognitive and rhetorical situation that gave rise to Revelation would suggest a context linked to the synagogues of the Jewish Diaspora.[25]

Historical method and the world behind the text

However, there is more to be aware of, here, than merely the considerable difficulties which beset all efforts to locate Revelation in the context in which it was produced and that it addressed, or the consequent unreliability of historical reconstructions as commonly proposed. In its theoretical dimension, it is the historical-critical method itself which proves to be fundamentally problematic. Here, I must call a spade a spade. The historical-critical method born of the Enlightenment, as customarily understood and practised, tasks the interpreter not with attending to the text, as such, but with uncovering something else to which the text is thought to grant access. Its object lies *behind* the text (to use a spatial metaphor) or is considered to be *prior* to the text (in temporal terms, relating to the genesis of the document concerned).

Such an approach places priority upon the text's historicity or better, its anchorage within history. This is why it is true to say that 'historical-critical methodology operates particularly at the level of a text's archaeology and development, trying… to get back to the original text as written by a specific author'.[26] At their best, exegetes do of course return in the end from this extra-textual inquiry to focus on the text of a biblical book in its final form. However, this does not alter the fact that in their application of the method to the business of interpretation, whatever meaning and significance can reasonably be apportioned to the text will depend, above all else, upon the results of prior investigation of its historical origins.

Notice that through the bracketing-out of the text in its final form, the real point of the exercise is not to read the text in and for itself, but instead critically to reconstruct the historical backdrop. In other words, the aim is to go beyond the text, *ad fontes*. It is crucial to grasp the extent of the influence of such an approach, because:

> Modern hermeneutics since the Enlightenment has made 'reference'
> the key to meaning, with the meaning of a narrative dependent on
> one's perception of that to which the narrative referred rather than
> living in the story world of the narrative itself.[27]

It is well beyond the scope of my present purpose to explore the ins and outs of this characteristic historical-critical preoccupation with the world behind the text and with a description of the hypothetical context of origin of a given biblical book. To do so would require, at the very least:

a) Shedding light on the atheistic move which, in the name of a faith resting on human reason, set in motion the whole enterprise of depriving the Scriptures of the Old and New Testaments of their status as revelation (as though God did not exist or at any rate, had nothing to say);

b) Responding to the pluralism which has resulted from the drive to be emancipated from any and all Church or faith-based readings (and their dogmatic premises), when it demands that biblical books be read exactly like any other texts from Antiquity, whether religious or profane;[28]

c) Taking stock of the combined 'disciplines of the historical-critical era'[29] which began with the Enlightenment and tracing the particular influence exercised on scientific interpretation of the Pentateuch or the Gospels[30] by the principle of methodical Cartesian doubt and its by-product, that hermeneutical suspicion which has targeted the final form of texts as they have come down to us; and most of all,

d) Investigating much more fully than I can here 'the subtle transformation of historical consciousness which began in the eighteenth and nineteenth centuries and persists to the present [and which] mistakenly succeeded in identifying or equating the meaning of a narrative with its ostensive reference[31] – a situation whose result was the imprisonment of scientific interpretation of the Bible in an empirical straitjacket.[32]

World of the text, or reconstructed world?

What readers must be aware of, at this point, are certain consequences of a historical-critical approach to Revelation that would embark upon a sometimes obsessive search for the Book's hypothetical context of origin. Whenever the decision is made to disregard a text's textuality or final state in favour of its archaeology and transmission history, this tends to reduce the text to a vehicle for entering a world that lies behind it, and even leads to its being commandeered for this sole purpose. In this way of looking at texts, only penultimate value is accorded to that which the text as a literary work conveys, as though this content offered a mere threshold to be crossed as swiftly as possible. Scholars taking this view subordinate the text's description of the world to their own account of an extra-textual world to which (they believe) the text refers – a first-century socio-cultural world, as scientifically reconstructed by their efforts. Fundamentally, this interpretative approach disparages the text's capacity to shed its own light, preferring another, artificial light-source of scholars' making that purports to shine independently somewhere beyond the text.

One wonders what happens, in such cases, to 'the universal rule of interpretation . . . that a text can be read and understood and expounded only with reference to and in the light of its [own] theme'.[33] It would seem that, for this approach, texts in their final form cannot ultimately have anything 'true' to say, or any claim to be 'realistic'; only scientific reconstructions of their alleged historical origins can. Somewhere upstream, in the current of textual prehistory connecting a text's conception to the acquisition of its final form, the historical-critical researcher hunts for some original 'reality' to which the finished work is deemed, somehow, no longer to conform. For this method, the specialist's first task is to write the history of the biblical text in question, in other words, to make sense of the diachronic historical processes (the changes over time) undergone by a text en route to its final form. Via this archaeological quest, the aim is to attain to the full 'truth' and 'reality' of the world from which the text came.[34]

We have to ask, *what does this entire enterprise do to texts?* The answer, in fact, is that it transforms them into *data banks to be searched*. By way of ricochet, concentration upon the extra-textual situation in which texts arose leads to them being thought of as quarries from which to mine and extract precious historical nuggets for critical examination. The text becomes equivalent to a sort of stratified deposit in which assorted artefacts, originating in various extra-textual contexts, now lie encrusted; these historically valuable remnants and traces are to be identified and then removed from the seam, in the finished text, where they now lie haphazardly embedded. For, according to the method, these textual data are witnesses to a more or less protracted process of textual sedimentation, a movement which can be reconstructed by tracing back to its source the current that transported and deposited them there. The text itself is seen as filled with faults and fractures which betray internal tensions or even contradictions. Explicitly or implicitly, the text in its final form is understood as the artificial agglomeration of its constituent parts. The recovery of the raw materials (or even, the prior texts) from which texts were formed, in the course of their prehistory, is reckoned to necessitate and legitimise the dismantling and dismembering of texts undertaken by interpreters whose attention is centred on the parts of a text[35] and on smaller and smaller isolated units of a text.[36]

Historical extrapolation and forsaking the text

A method which, from start to finish, shows itself unable or unwilling to respect the inviolable nature of the biblical text in its final form, simply cannot take seriously the complex literary unity which characterises several New Testament books – the Gospels, the Acts of the Apostles and in the present instance, John's Revelation. Is this assessment over-hasty and too excessive? Or, is its relevance limited to certain types of research once applied to the Gospels, but now abandoned?

Admittedly, it is rare enough to find contemporary Revelation specialists commandeering the text and its data in quite the way I have described whenever they seek to piece together a world behind it. Nevertheless, the real influence still exerted by the archaeological and genealogical quest outlined above, together with researchers' appetite for exploiting Revelation to historical ends, are still seen and felt everywhere in contemporary exegesis of the Book. This is somewhat surprising given that interpreters have had at their disposal, for more than thirty years now, newer tools for reading texts. These were forged and honed with the declared intent of centring attention once more on texts, studying what narratives are made of (and how they convey their meaning) whilst deferring, fully, to the final narrative form they take. I will come back to this. Yet the grand design of scientifically reconstructing worlds behind the text continues to prove attractive. Although in principle exegetes may be committed to the idea that Revelation is an indivisible whole – one thinks of commentators, for example[37] – whenever this stimulating Bible book obliges them to try to overcome interpretative difficulties, they regularly beat a methodological retreat and head, in spite of themselves, for an emergency exit marked *historical extrapolation* where they may hope to find reassuring extra-textual space in which to manoeuvre.[38]

Why must we forever turn and run, like this, from the text? The reason for such flight, if not the justification, may be the fact that Revelation does not possess the 'narrative lifelikeness'[39] which normally characterises narrative in general. Instead, by its unusual and difficult narrative logic, where chronology or cause and effect proceed in disconcerting ways, Revelation tends to disorientate readers. And so exegetes, knocked off-balance both by problems of comprehension and by the added risk of adding to the vagaries of interpretation of this book – of which there are already too many – can yield to temptation and turn from the text in search of some external interpretative safety lever.

As already intimated, I have chosen in principle, for the purposes of the present study, *not* to resort to extra-textual reconstructions whenever the text of Revelation has presented problems of interpretation requiring viable exegetical solutions. This course of action is my way of overcoming what I perceive to be a twofold exegetical temptation: First of all, the enticement of taking every interpretative challenge thrown down by Revelation's narrative as an obstacle blocking the route to meaning, like a huge boulder on a road. And second, the allure of historical extrapolation as a systematic strategy for getting around the perceived obstruction. By resisting these influences, I am attempting to apply my own principle, already enunciated in a published article:

> To figure out one or another of Revelation's mysteries, and before having recourse to explanations of a realistic kind (which may, on occasion, be quite legitimate), exegetes ought to be at pains to explore the means provided *by the text itself* for helping its first readers draw out its meaning.[40]

Those who do not see boulders barring their way feel no corresponding obligation to look for ways around them. Therefore, in the course of this reading I will be offering other solutions to problems that arise. They will be of two kinds. Some are *inner-textual*: taking account of Revelation's narrative logic as a whole, I will be letting Revelation act as its own interpreter. Others will be inter-textual in nature: to the extent that the Old Testament serves as Revelation's sub-text from start to finish, it will frequently provide us with indispensable interpretative keys.[41]

Before leaving the issue of the world behind the text, I should make one final point – a theological one, this time. For Bible reading undertaken in a Church context, or for the work of biblical scholars who submit to the authority of Scripture, it would surely be a fundamental hermeneutical error to countenance using an exegetical method which stubbornly transfers to some extra-textual context of its own invention the very 'realism' it invariably expects the texts themselves to reveal. The community of believers and every one of its readers, whether they are experts or not, take the biblical text lying open before them to be the locus of a divine revelation, whose impact is felt through their reading and whose interpretation is conducted with the aid of the Holy Spirit. How, then, could they ever be satisfied with, let alone lend credence to, the extra-textual reconstructions offered by the historical-critical method? Or how could they ever assent to the claim that such moves deserve pride of place among the procedures of biblical interpretation?

A thematic reading? Why not!

I now come back to the newer tools for reading texts alluded to earlier and used by interpreters in recent years. It must be acknowledged that in our day, a new exegetical wind is certainly blowing across the Bible's narrative texts. So in such a climate, why not have a thematic reading that endeavours to study and explain the complex interweaving and the thematic correlation of Revelation's textual data! This is, after all, the era of new literary criticism with its interest in the cohesion of narrative discourse in its rhetorical, poetic and narrative dimensions. Biblical scholars now have to hand an impressive tool-kit assembled by two pragmatic approaches to texts: narrative criticism, which investigates the characteristics and workings of narratives; and rhetorical criticism, which concerns itself with the analysis of discourse.[42]

No more than for the historical-critical paradigm briefly examined above can I do justice, at this point, to these newer methods which have exchanged a focus on the world behind the text for a long, hard look at the text itself. Before them, of course, came structuralism and semiotics,[43] which had already made this interpretative move. However, unlike these latter approaches – both of them committed to the autonomous text – narrative and rhetorical criticism each understand the literary works they study to be the result of a deliberate exercise in communication and, as such, to have effects upon readers that can and should be examined.

Restoring the primacy of the text

Since detailed discussion is impossible here, it will be sufficient for present purposes to outline what a pragmatic approach might achieve in practice, using narrative criticism and its operations as an example. In its simplest terms, such an approach essentially treats Revelation as a self-contained narrative, told by a narrator, which undertakes a communication strategy aimed at specific recipients.[44] Each of its statements or episodes is in their relation to others, linked both by chronology (or temporal sequence) and by causation. Within the overall narrative, covering all of Revelation from 1.1 to 22.21, the various micro-narratives that develop their own episodic plots are probed. In the larger macro-narrative, where a unifying plot is set in motion, the various round or flat characters that interact with one another are studied with an eye on how they, and the events which involve them, come across: the inner realities of the characters themselves are considered, but also how the narrator intrudes into the narrative. Within this unfolding plot it would be necessary to investigate how time is managed, in terms both of order (past-present-future) and rhythm. Order might be found to be fixed and linear, *i.e.* chronological, or provided by narrative time (including both flashbacks and foreshadowings). Rhythm, meanwhile, would be dictated by the pace at which the narrative moves. Throughout the reading process, the space-time framework, and the socio-historical context into which everything is set, would be borne in mind. Finally, due account is taken of explicit or implicit comment from the narrator concerning the action taking place, since this conveys certain values and betrays an identifiable point of view.

In my own research, two pioneering narrative-critical studies of Revelation have proved very useful,[45] for example in my attention to the Book's plot. It is worthwhile giving a brief outline, here, of the manner in which one of these studies analyses Revelation's developing plot. At the start, initial stability reigns on earth; this then gives way to terrestrial instability, but as seen from a heavenly perspective; finally, stability returns both to heaven and to earth.[46] The initially stable state of affairs is a product of the order placed in the cosmos by God, who is the instigator of all that is revealed or transpires upon the earth (Rev. 1), over which he rules from heaven (Rev. 4–5). The oracles septet – a kind of plot in miniature – anticipates the fortunate and unfortunate events which will occur subsequently, in a world where chaos seems to reign (chapter 6–19); the Churches thereby discover that it is the Christ who is the guarantor of their stability and the wholly reliable source of their life. By the same token they learn that the temptation to unfaithfulness which harasses them could threaten their very status as Churches. From Rev. 17 onwards, as the step-by-step destruction of evil's forces is recounted, the plot begins to move towards a renewed stable situation on earth (achieved in Rev. 20) as well as in the new heaven and earth of the finale (Rev. 21–22). Thus, in Revelation, whilst the pendulum swings away from stable beginnings, where the salvation of believers is made secure in advance and where all glory belongs to God (1.5-6), whenever disobedience and idolatry complicate matters it starts to swing back again, towards God's triumph and the rewarding of his faithful people, to which heavenly Jerusalem will give particular shape at the end.

By directing its attention, in a sustained way, to the phenomena that make up a narrative text like Revelation, such a method can only help restore respect for the Book's textuality and, in so doing, gladden those who have been waiting so long for its eclipse to end. As stated previously, the exegetical wind does seem to be turning. Despite some hesitation, Revelation is now indeed being read – as I have dared hope – as an integrated whole and viewed as a carefully crafted literary work that ought not to be dismembered.[47] Instead of carving up the narrative and obtaining correspondingly discrete results – as the historical-critical approach has characteristically done – here and there scholars are attempting 'literary appreciation of Revelation which resolutely addresses the book's coherence'[48] as part of a new interest in its internal configurations and literary developments.

As part of this exploration, for the present study I have chosen not to cross-section the text vertically, as commentaries habitually do, because that would have run the risk of fracturing the text artificially. Instead, I have opted for a more dynamic approach, alert to the forward movement of Revelation and to the ups and downs of its plot whereby successive scenes and pictures take us from the opening state of affairs to the eventual outcome.

The text, the whole text . . . and the text as a whole

Although I welcome and endorse the intrinsic worth of the pioneering narrative-critical studies mentioned so far,[49] their methodology remains inadequate for what I am attempting in this book. For the task I have set myself, some tools are unfortunately missing. Among narrative criticism's characteristic operations none, curiously, aims to correlate textual data in their diversity in order to determine how they fit together. Rather, like students forgetful of old advice from their professors of literature, narrative criticism in its appreciation of literary works may consider how locales change, characters evolve or plot advances, yet it strangely neglects to take any interest in how themes develop.[50] Unlike literary criticism in its classic form, narrative criticism does not reserve any consideration for the phenomenon of integrative themes – including the various sub-themes and minor motifs they may display – whenever it sets about explaining texts (typically) by the study of characters, the tracing of plot or the examination of settings.

Since the tools and techniques of narrative-critical methodology have only just begun to be applied to the study of Revelation, further work of this kind remains indispensable and is to be heartily encouraged. Nonetheless, the exploration of Revelation's inner-textual world must not stop at *analysis*; it must then go on to provide a *synthesis* of how, by means of sophisticated compositional strategies, the author has conferred upon the welter of detail in this text a complex literary unity and, consequently, its meaning. Since, in my perspective, Revelation's internal thematic organisation is responsible for giving the Book significant trajectories of meaning, which run through its narrative, it is crucially important that these be taken into account from the start and that the way Revelation's various thematic components undergo development be duly investigated. After all,

> Everything tends to become progressively more explicit as Revelation's visions and auditions proliferate and complement each other. Meaning gradually becomes clearer, much as a fund might progressively grow richer.[51]

What a thematic reading cannot be

To reiterate: from the question I have been addressing– *why undertake a thematic reading?* – has emerged the fact that, in this study, I wish (negatively speaking) to fall into neither of two traps, thus avoiding both the devil and the deep blue sea.

First, I decline to work from the premise that Revelation's meaning is only (or even, primarily) to be explained through an elucidation of that to which it supposedly refers, namely, a world situated somewhere behind the text and deemed to be 'real' or 'true'. Speaking positively on this same point, I will make Revelation's internal literary coherence my preoccupation (in contrast to the historical-critical enterprise) and treat the text as the vehicle for its own message, leaving it free to create its own significance as it opens up its own textual universe to the reader.

Second, because this undertaking commits us to looking into the plethora of narrative and rhetorical elements which make up Revelation's inner-textual world, another duty follows. In contrast to new literary criticism as commonly practised, a thematic reading will entail striving to describe and account for a profound organic linguistic unity detectable at the level of Revelation's macro-narrative.[52] This unity is not merely artistic or aesthetic, as a product we might say of the author's genius; it is also theological. It comes from a grand narrative which undergirds everything: the Gospel story, comprising the ministry of Jesus as well as the life of the Church it brought about, and also the story of Israel as read in the whole Old Testament by Jesus, then by his apostles and, specifically, by Revelation throughout its twenty-two chapters.

With these preliminaries completed, we may now move on from the *why* of my chosen method of interpretation and focus on the *what*.

What is a thematic reading?

Reading Revelation: where do we start?

In the following few paragraphs, I aim to familiarise readers with the approach taken in this book. In my estimation, Revelation's author engineers dynamic communication with us, his hearers/readers, artfully attuning our ears to his wavelength as it were. His message even commits us to more than one hearing, for his text – which was explicitly designed for being read aloud in public (1.3) and originally conceived for oral performance – constantly makes demands on the capacities of its intended audience for cognitive appreciation: we are to hear, see and understand, and go on doing so.[53] Accordingly, many passages in Revelation only yield their meaning to a close reading/hearing of the text and to prolonged reflexion upon it which, in the longer term, the target readership is willing to undertake. What I mean is that Revelation is essentially a book to read and re-read, with a view to appreciating all its nuances progressively. Apparently intended for study, it is a book whose implied readership closely resembles the one that seems to lie behind the Gospel of John.

Fundamentally, a thematic reading takes account of this and is therefore a sustained literary/auditory approach. Since I myself have been frequenting the Book over time, the reading I will be putting forward is a result of the time I have spent in its company. More specifically, and as already mentioned, this is an *inner-textual reading* which has involved patiently tracing and marking out the main paths followed by the Book's themes and unifying ideas, as well as mapping (we could say) the complex ways they merge, endeavouring to be alert and alive to the criss-cross of meaning that results.

I ought to make clear, in passing, that my treatment of Revelation as a literary phenomenon should not be interpreted as a devaluation or denial of either the visionary experience out of which the book originated, according to the narrative itself, or what that experience implies – namely, that the living God has revealed himself. My point is, rather, that the only way for Revelation's very first hearers/readers to see and hear what John heard and saw was by listening to the revelation read aloud in Asia's Churches, in the course of Sunday worship. For us as contemporary readers – whether individually or in groups – reading remains our means of access to Revelation. In either case, it is through a book that the God who chose to reveal himself to John (as to other biblical authors) is happy to be known, still, by those who continue to read their works.

Equally as fundamental, the present book is an *inter-textual reading*. This is because Revelation constantly takes readers back to the Hebrew Scriptures and assumes their thorough familiarity with these. In Part Three of this study in particular (though not exclusively) we will be able to gauge the extent of the influence exerted by the Old Testament upon the composition of Revelation as well as upon its message. To be more precise, we will see how Revelation's thematic materials draw constantly upon the Old Testament for motifs and figures, characters and events, texts and contexts, redeploying each of them in light of the all-important coming of Messiah Jesus. By means of what is nothing short of a Bible memory lesson, Revelation offers a subtle re-reading of holy history which is teleological, *i.e.* which takes its understanding from the end-point at which its decisive last stage is reached, when Messiah Jesus dies a redemptive death for Israel and the Gentiles. Through the narrated plot-line, everything in Revelation witnesses to the fact that the God of Israel has at last revealed himself, as never before, in the person of Jesus Christ crucified and risen, who is chiefly depicted as a slain but standing Lamb.

It follows, then, that my thematic reading is fundamentally also an effort in *biblical theology*. Every theme we will study bears the imprint of prior revelation and, at the same time, shows traces of the footsteps of Jesus of Nazareth and of all that flowed from his appearance in human history. In both text and notes, readers will find themselves being directed to various prophetic or other books of the Old Testament canon, but also and especially to the writings of the apostolic tradition (whether Gospels and Acts, or Epistles) – itself thoroughly Jewish – as found deposited in the New Testament. In addition, we will have to reckon with inter-testamental writings and, among these, particularly with the apocalyptic books. From time to time it will be this literature which affords an analogy, or provides a link, that will allow a better connection between particular themes from the Gospels or Revelation and their antecedents in the Old Testament.

Literary art and beauty

In our Bibles, Revelation crowns the canon both of the New Testament and of the Bible as a whole. To my mind, this is indeed the Book's rightful place, for it is a true masterpiece whose interpreter must learn to marry art and science, intellect and intuition, faith and imagination. Methodologically speaking, a reading-strategy is required which is capable of letting Revelation speak to us in all its dimensions. Exegetes must be able to show full respect for the unique and unbreakable combination of form, content and function manifested by Revelation. They must also be able to ascribe full value to the Book's combined literary and theological qualities, neither stripping it of any of its power nor imposing upon it any interpretative yoke that would be alien to it. The degree of complexity and indeed refinement observable in Revelation's composition requires interpreters to conceive of the interpretative task in a way that takes adequate account of how, within the Book's textual universe, certain aesthetic processes are responsible for conveying meaning.

It is widely acknowledged that, throughout the history of its interpretation and even today, Revelation has often been treated to rough handling. Personally, I hope to honour Revelation as a work of art, and not to deface it under any circumstances. Of course, I happily acknowledge in principle that *several* literary-theological readings like the one I am proposing here – and indeed, other kinds of readings besides – might, in their own way, do equal justice to the logic of the book as a whole. Let me therefore make something quite clear right away: whatever hermeneutical gain may accrue from the present literary-theological study of Revelation's thematic materials (which, I argue, are antithetically arranged within the text) – and readers will be the judge of that gain – I am certainly not claiming for the category of *theme* the status of *sole* structuring device for the Book. Nor am I suggesting that analysis of theme constitutes *the* interpretative key for unlocking Revelation. My book's proposal is in reality much more modest. What I hope to demonstrate, and affirm, is simply that:

> One factor in Revelation's broad cohesion as a text, aiding the complex
> organisation or articulation of its parts into a whole, is theme.[54]

Throughout this book, I will be conducting a literary-theological study which understands Revelation to be a coherently organised totality. By treating Revelation as a complex unified entity, my aim will be to search tirelessly for its total meaning, out of respect for its integrity as a text. Instead of setting about unravelling the astonishing unity which arises out of the interpenetration and correlation of its diverse materials, I will endeavour to follow and keep pace with Revelation's overall dynamic. This dynamic is the very thing that allows the narrative, from start to finish, to develop its own themes and to bind these to one another progressively.[55] We will find ourselves having to move back and forth through Revelation's complex, mazy narrative, endeavouring to run alongside multiple thematic vectors as they wind their way throughout its plot.[56]

To summarise the approach taken in coming chapters, among other things it will mean the following:

a) paying attention to how Revelation's narrative as a whole progresses, although without skating over the mass of detail found in its various pictures and scenes;

b) simultaneously taking into account subtle changes in perspective which occur every time familiar elements, met earlier in the text, appear again and so cause the text to update itself;[57] or

c) doing justice, at every step of an essentially linear reading process, to the spiralling evolution of different leading ideas as they progressively shape the developing plot.

Three parts, seven thematic trajectories

My goal, in the present study, is to plot the main thematic trajectories which, individually and as a network, lend Revelation as a whole its literary and theological cohesion. Those studied here seem to me to be irreducible and I do not think any have been omitted, even if it has not been possible to explore every meander taken by every motif. The study is comprised of three parts, each prefaced with a short introduction and brought to a conclusion by the briefest of syntheses. In each introduction I say briefly what the relevant part of the study aims to do and what each of the thematic trajectories to be explored essentially consists of. The role of the corresponding conclusion, once the investigation is over and done, is to restate succinctly the key elements explored by each pathway that has been followed. Parts One and Two contain three chapters each while Part Three has only one – giving a reading in seven sections of varying length.

Any exegete who shares my esteem for Revelation's linguistic unity and inner cohesion might give his or her own account of those principal thematic vectors which carry the Book's meaning and provide a set of results that considerably disagree with my account of Revelation's themes. Thus, whilst I stand by my work, I freely admit that there is nothing definitive about the number of thematic trajectories I have explored (seven). The same goes for the fact that each is arranged as a binary unit made up of two corresponding and contrasting halves, or that they all combine into one in the final part of the book. Readers could easily imagine other ways of fitting the parts into a whole and so must make up their own minds as to whether my way of describing and arranging Revelation's thematic treasures succeeds or fails. In doing so I hope all readers will also familiarise themselves quickly with the substantial thematic index I have provided, and will find it helpful. It is a kind of pick-and-choose facility, designed to allow readers to explore for themselves the many sub-themes and motifs of Revelation which I have tried to cover in these pages.

Because it is impossible to take in everything at one look, the chapters which follow invite readers to go on what I would call a cumulative series of guided tours of Revelation. This is a fine narrative 'which acquires its meaning and significance even as it proceeds',[58] so each new thematic itinerary that we will follow aims to familiarise the reader with the logic behind its composition.

In Part One (*God reveals himself*), three separate pathways will take us in turn through the text of Revelation. Predominantly *theo*-logical, each will open up contrasting themes relating to the God who reveals himself and to what is found to be in opposition to him. The respective titles for these itineraries are: *Divinity and pseudo-divinity; True sovereignty and usurped claims;* and *Legitimate adoration and bogus worship.* In combination they will bring into focus the negative and positive poles of Revelation's testimony to the one Sovereign God who is worthy of praise and who is known through the slain but standing Lamb.

In Part Two (*Humanity finds itself*), three fresh routes will be followed. Predominantly *anthropo*-logical this time, they will all address in their own way the issue of human beings' self-discovery whereby, in light of God's self-disclosure, they either run from or draw near to him. These three explorations are entitled: *Genuine testimony and counter-proclamation; Faithful belonging and counter-allegiance;* and *Bride-city and whore-city.* One after another, they will lay bare humanity's real calling and true identity, together with God's plans for human beings as embodied in Messiah Jesus; and in all of them this Good News will have a counterpoise in the disclosure of what becomes of humanity without God.

In Part Three (*When God and humanity meet*) a single, final pathway will involve bringing the combined results of Parts One and Two to bear upon a journey through Revelation's story of the disrupted or, contrariwise, restored relationship between sinful humanity and God. The title in this case is: *Broken covenant and new covenant.* This investigation will demonstrate both how Revelation sees human beings' rebellion against God and how a possible relationship between man and God may nevertheless be envisaged, based on the covenant sealed in the blood of the Lamb. Here, in this third and final part, the six individual trails followed previously in Parts One and Two will all converge and merge into a single, holistic thematic reading which – I would venture to suggest – amounts to more than the sum total of the parts.

Notes

1   J. Ellul, *L'Apocalypse. Architecture en mouvement*, Paris, Desclée, 1975, p.5 (my translation).

2   G. Campbell, 'How to say what. Story and interpretation in the Book of Revelation', *Irish Biblical Studies* 23, 2001, pp.111-34.

3   G. Campbell, *Parody in the Apocalypse. A literary-theological study of convergent antithetical themes in John's Revelation.* This was the English title; written in French, but within the Institute of Theology at *Queen's University Belfast*, it was accepted for the award of a PhD, following a viva in Strasbourg, in 2002.

4   G. Campbell, 'How to say what', pp.133-34.

5   To be convinced of this it would be enough to note the vast number of studies or articles which continue to address the historical question in one way or another. For one recent example, the article by T.B. Slater, 'On the Social Setting of the Revelation to John', *New Testament Studies* 44, 1998, pp.232-56, could be read.

6 Once again, see G. Campbell, 'How to say what', pp.132-33. More often than not what are called 'themes' are actually categories, borrowed from systematic theology, into which the interpreter has slotted the subject matter extracted from the narrative, involving a separation of content from form rather like ore might be separated from slag. Yet dissociating form and content in a narrative is quite simply a violation of what narrative is. For one recent instance of this all-too-common error, see the commentary by J. Knight, *Revelation*, Sheffield, Sheffield Academic Press, 1999, pp.156-68, 'Themes of the Apocalypse'.

7 I am borrowing this terminology from G. Guthrie, 'Boats in the Bay. Reflections on the Use of Linguistics and Literary Analysis in Biblical Studies', in S.E. Porter & D.A. Carson, *Linguistics and the New Testament*, Sheffield, Sheffield Academic Press, 1999, p.35.

8 E.-B. Allo, *St. Jean, l'Apocalypse*, Paris, Gabalda, 1933, 4th edn, lxxxvi. Allo had put his finger on a 'principle of constant antithesis' which, he thought, shaped the entire Book of Revelation. The discovery of his inklings in this area helped me formulate my own approach which, as far as my doctoral dissertation was concerned, led me to mine the deposit which Allo located but which subsequent exegesis completely abandoned, either forgetful or ignorant of his contribution – until, that is, similar inklings surfaced (independently, it seems) in the little commentary of J. Roloff (English version *The Revelation of John*, Minneapolis, Augsburg Fortress, 1993). Roloff in fact speaks, on p.155, of '*a parody approach*' (Ger. *Parodieverfahren*) which, in his view, is a determining factor behind the composition of ch. 13–22 of Revelation. And in a later article he applies to the section ch. 17–22 the category of *Gegensatz-Schema* (system of contrasts); see 'Neuschöpfung in der Offenbarung des Johannes', in *Schöpfung und Neuschöpfung*, Neukirchen-Vluyn, Neukirchener Verlag, 1990, p.131. As I see it, the parody approach which Roloff detected in the second half of Revelation is made intelligible for the reader only thanks to careful prior preparation of it in ch. 1–12.

9 See G. Campbell, 'Un procédé de composition négligé de l'Apocalypse de Jean', *Etudes théologiques et religieuses* 77, 2002/4, pp.494-95.

10 On This, see D. Marguerat, 'L'exégèse biblique à l'heure du lecteur', in *La Bible en récits*, Geneva, Labor et Fides, 2005, notably pp.13-22.

11 It was Paul Ricœur who initiated theoretical discussion of the semantic autonomy of texts; see P. Ricœur, *Interpretation Theory: Discourse and the Surplus of Meaning*, Fort Worth, Texas Christian University Press, 1976, p.30.

12 P. Guillemette and M. Brisebois, *Introduction aux méthodes historico-critiques*, Montreal, Fides, 1987, p.9 (my translation), who write from a Roman Catholic point of view.

13 Unless otherwise stated, quotations of the text of Revelation incorporate my own translation from the Greek.

14 For determining the meaning of the story which Revelation recounts, its reference to this intervention by God in human history is indispensable. On this matter see M.E. Boring, 'Narrative Christology in the Apocalypse', *Catholic Biblical Quarterly* 54/4, 1992, p.722.

15 For a theoretical conception of what is involved in the historical enterprise, historiography and the literary representation of past historical facts, see P. Ricœur, 'Philosophies Critiques de l'Histoire: Recherche, Explication, Ecriture', in G. Fløistad (ed.), *Philosophical Problems Today I*, Dordrecht, Kluwer Academic Press, 1994, pp.27-51 and especially, by the same author, *La Mémoire, l'Histoire, l'Oubli*, Paris, Seuil, 2000.

16   H. Conzelmann and A. Lindemann, *Interpreting the New Testament: An Introduction to the Principles and Methods of N.T. Exegesis,* Peabody, Hendrickson, 1988, p.2. Two hundred years of historical research into the biblical text also show that historians can never escape their own historical contexts. From the very start of this quest, they may be seen drawing inspiration for their task from Hegel's philosophy of history, for example, or more recently from overtly existentialist philosophy. This raises the issue of an exegete's own subjectivity and of his or her particular way of approaching the text.

17   For readers wishing to discover or use the basic tools and procedures of a historical-grammatical exegesis which remains faithful to Scripture, three fine examples (among many others) may be given here. 1. Four articles taken from the *Expositor's Bible Commentary* and published in a little guide entitled *Biblical Criticism: Historical, Literary and Textual,* Grand Rapids, Zondervan, 1978, written by two Old Testament and two New Testament specialists (for each of whom the biblical text is the Word of God). 2. A manual for exegesis written by one of them, G.D. Fee, *New Testament Exegesis. A Handbook for Students and Pastors,* Louisville, Westminster/John Knox, 1993. A respected biblical scholar, Fee is an Evangelical; significantly, the American editor of this edition of the manual is not. The excellent introduction to New Testament studies by H.-W. Neudorfer and E.J. Schnabel (eds), *Das Studium des Neuen Testaments. Eine Einführung in die Methoden der Exegese* (vol. 1), Wuppertal, R. Brockhaus, 2000. This book brings together specialists from the NT working-group of Germany's *Fellowship of Evangelical Theologians (AfET)*; a two-volume work, it offers readers with a grasp of German an excellent initiation to the disciplines of NT study.

18   When semiotics insists that texts are autonomous, there are in fact several ripostes which can be made. Two methods which refuse, in different ways, to disconnect a text from the communicative act and situation that originally produced it, and which take a keen interest in the author-reader relation, are *narrative criticism*, which studies the outworkings of the language of a given text, and *relevance theory*, which investigates the communicative or rhetorical dimension of a text, from the angle of its relevance to the reader. For more, see later in this chapter.

19   I have more to say about this in points one and two of my article 'Apocalypse de Jean', in *Grand Dictionnaire de la Bible,* Cléon d'Andran, Excelsis, 2004, pp.87-89 (the augmented French adaptation of the *New Bible Dictionary,* Leicester, IVP, 1996, 3rd edn). Here, readers of French will also find what I would wish to say by way of general introduction to Revelation.

20   The notion of a sub-text is to be clearly distinguished from what lies behind or beyond a text (see below).

21   This very issue is fundamental for Jewish apocalyptic, with its interest in theodicy and the fate of the righteous whose lot it is, despite the reign of God, to suffer in this world.

22   G. Campbell, 'Apocalypse de Jean', p.91. The very same comment can be made in relation to the quest for a suitable historical context for *1 Enoch, 2 Baruch, 4 Ezra* or the *Sibylline Oracles.*

23   Scholarship has wanted to locate Revelation's production in one of two decades of the first century: either in its closing decade, under Domitian (this was the twentieth-century consensus), or in the sixties around the time of Nero's death (according to a dating that prevailed in the nineteenth century). My reservations apply to either variant of this 'Roman' hypothesis.

24   G. Campbell, 'Apocalypse de Jean', p.91 (there is more detail in paragraph III of
     this article). Nevertheless, consensus does not mean unanimity. In the dictionary
     article's bibliographical note, I include a recent study which, like my own, sets
     Revelation in the context of ancient Judaism: J.W. Marshall, *Parables of War. Reading
     John's Jewish Apocalypse* (Studies in Christianity and Judaism 10), Waterloo (Canada),
     Wilfred Laurier University Press, 2001. Readers may compare the standpoint of
     A.J.P. Garrow, *Revelation*, London & New York, Routledge, 1997, p.120.

25   For consideration of the impact Revelation may have had on inner-Jewish
     controversy concerning the interpretation of the Scriptures, see the epilogue to
     this book.

26   P. Guillemette and M. Brisebois, *Introduction*, p.10 (my translation).

27   Boring, 'Narrative Christology', *op. cit.*, p.723. Here, Boring, himself a Revelation
     specialist, is using a summary version of Hans Frei's thesis in *The Eclipse of
     Biblical Narrative: A Study in Eighteenth and Nineteenth Century Hermeneutics*, New
     Haven/London, Yale University Press, 1974.

28   According to this vision of things, inspired by theological relativism and by
     a desire to conform to secular definitions of what might be 'scientific', the
     University ought to take no account of the canonical status of Bible books or
     of their authority.

29   M.-A. Chevallier, *L'Exégèse du Nouveau Testament. Initiation à la méthode*, Geneva,
     Labor et Fides, 1985, p.8 (my translation). This would be a task of formidable
     scope entailing, at the very least, that geographical and cultural variants within
     the historical-critical paradigm be distinguished, so as to speak of German,
     Scandinavian, British or American schools of thought (each with its own history,
     particularities and range of approaches). The same would hold for French-
     language research, with its own geography and culture, special commitments
     and ties.

30   Where (for example) the archaeological quest for what is true and real behind
     the Gospels is concerned, the current form of the Gospel texts, with its story
     of Jesus, would represent the crust. Thanks to historical questioning, this crust,
     once breached, would permit access to three successive strata: first, to the one
     with which the Evangelist or the final redactor is credited, considered to be the
     most recent (explored using redaction criticism); second, to another deeper layer
     in which lie deposits of the traditions inherited by the Evangelist (examined by
     form criticism); and last, to a stratum farthest from the surface in which are
     preserved the fragments of real deeds and actual words of the Jesus of history
     (opened up by historical Jesus research). For more detail, see F. Watson, *Text
     and Truth. Redefining Biblical Theology*, Edinburgh, T&T Clark, 1997, ch. 1 and 2,
     'History and Difference', pp.37-41.

31   J. Fodor, *Christian Hermeneutics. Paul Ricœur and the Reconfiguring of Theology*, Oxford,
     Clarendon Press, 1995, p.262. As Fodor helpfully explains, the implicitly realistic
     character of biblical narratives, their quality as narratives which recount history-
     like events, was lost from view during a divorce which historicism brought
     about, that is, the disjunction of narrative *form* (seen as a vehicle for recounting),
     which now became devalued, from its narrative *content* (conceived of as referring
     to external historical realities). Higher criticism focused its attention upon this
     content, whilst at the same time suspecting it of a lack of historical factuality
     or reliability. In opposition to this, defenders of the historicity of biblical texts
     mounted a defence of the historical credentials of this same content.

32 I can pause only briefly to address this problem. Anyone wishing to delve deeper, from the standpoint of a faith-based reading, into what is at stake theologically in the act of reading biblical texts, may profitably turn as I have to an excellent collection of essays. Thanks to these, it has now become possible to consider, from an avowedly Christian point of view, how biblical scholars committed to the authority of Scripture might overcome the hermeneutical and epistemological problems posed by the historical-critical method: see C. Bartholomew *et.al.* (ed.), *'Behind' the Text: History and Biblical Interpretation* (Scripture & Hermeneutics Series, vol. 4), Grand Rapids/Carlisle, Zondervan/Paternoster, 2003.

33 K. Barth, *Church Dogmatics*, Edinburgh, T&T Clark, 1956-69, vol. I, ch. 2 (written in 1938), pp.492-94. According to Barth, the task of reading, understanding and expounding the Bible cannot be construed as *bypassing* biblical texts with a view to accessing facts situated behind them. To do so, in the name of a fascination for antiquities, would for Barth mean giving in to the temptation to dissociate the form and content of the biblical text. Barth was probably the first, in the twentieth century, to work for the reinstatement of readings which take the Bible seriously as a realistic narrative in its own right.

34 It should be underlined that this very obsession with an original text differentiates historical-critical exegetes from historians in the strict sense. The latter, whose business is history as such, happily work with ancient documents in their final form.

35 On the problem of the parts and the whole, see F. Watson, *Text, Church and World. Biblical Interpretation in Theological Perspective*, London/New York, Continuum, 2004, p.34. For Watson, giving priority to alleged diachronic relationships that link parts of a text over their synchronic inter-relationship is to construe the text 'as an assemblage of originally discrete parts related to one another in an artful or artificial manner by a final redactor whose activity is always belated and secondary'.

36 Neudorfer and Schnabel, *Einführung, op. cit.*, p.21, speak of the *atomising* of biblical texts.

37 Even writers of commentaries do not always hold the final form of Revelation in high regard. In his influential commentary R.H. Charles, *The Revelation of St. John* (vol. 1), Edinburgh, T&T Clark, 1920, IV 'The Editor of the Apocalypse', could still famously postulate that, in the finished product, a collection of disparate components had been thrown together, in an unintelligible way, by a hypothetical stupid redactor, or find in Rev. 20.4*ff* (for example) intellectual confusion that could no longer be resolved and a tissue of irreconcilable contradictions. While we can immediately detect the heyday of source criticism in such remarks, in the 1970s the commentaries by H. Kraft, *Die Offenbarung des Johannes*, Mohr, Tübingen, 1974, or J.M. Ford, *Revelation*, Doubleday, Garden City, 1975, could still presuppose that Revelation was a composite work. Quite recently, the scholarly, three-volume *magnum opus* by D.E. Aune has sought to dust off this hypothesis once more (*Revelation 1-5*, Dallas, Word, 1997; *Revelation 6-16*, Nashville, Nelson, 1998; and *Revelation 17-22*, Nashville, Nelson, 1998).

Despite this swan-song, Charles's hypothesis was already being adequately refuted, just after it appeared, from 1921 onwards by E.-B. Allo, *Apocalypse, op. cit*. Allo's commentary already approaches Revelation as a complex but unified composition; yet more than eighty years later, whereas Revelation's narrative unity is now established and undeniable, exegetical exploration *of its complex narrative* has, in a real sense, only just begun.

38   As Fodor says, *Christian Hermeneutics*, p.265, it is by no means easy for modern interpreters to break free from their reliance upon – or sometimes, their enslavement to – notions of historicity, factuality, truth and meaning bequeathed to them by the Enlightenment, or to take measures to counteract that which these notions may instil, namely a lack of respect for the text being interpreted.

39   This is my translation of 'vraisemblable narratif'; I borrow this expression from J. Calloud, J. Delorme and J.-P. Duplantier, 'L'Apocalypse de Jean. Propositions pour une analyse structurale', in L. Monloubou (ed.), *Apocalypses et théologie de l'espérance*, Paris, Cerf, 1977, p.366.

40   G. Campbell, 'Procédé', p.515. In 'How to say what', *op. cit.*, pp.124-25, I considered the over-hasty and premature recourse to extrapolation by one commentator nonetheless convinced of Revelation's organic unity.

41   It will of course be up to readers to judge whether I have held to these methodological principles, and how satisfactory or otherwise are the exegetical solutions I propose.

42   Readers of French seeking help with reading biblical narrative have available to them two books edited by D. Marguerat, and two more co-authored by him: the first of them, which has been published in English – D. Marguerat and Y. Bourquin, *How to Read Bible stories: An Introduction to Narrative Criticism*, London (tr. SCM Press), 1999 – explains the methodology in a very accessible way. The others are D. Marguerat (ed.), *Quand la Bible se raconte*, Paris, Cerf, 2003; D. Marguerat, A. Wénin & B. Escaffre, *Autour des récits bibliques* (Cahier Evangile 127), Paris, Cerf, 2004; and D. Marguerat (ed.), *La Bible en récits* (2005), *op. cit.* The 2003 and 2005 volumes present exegetical work on a range of Bible texts; it has to be admitted, though, that John's Revelation is conspicuously absent. For rhetorical analysis of texts, readers of French may turn especially to two manuals by R. Meynet, *Initiation à la rhétorique biblique: qui donc est le plus grand?* (2 vols.), Paris, Cerf, 1982, and *L'analyse rhétorique. Une nouvelle méthode pour comprendre la Bible*, Paris, Cerf, 1989, as well as to the fine introduction to the method provided in his *Lire la Bible*, Paris, Flammarion, 2003.

       For readers of English, the best place to start is J.L. Resseguie, *Narrative Criticism of the New Testament*, Grand Rapids, Baker, 2005; there is an excellent themed bibliography, including a section on rhetorical criticism. Since the publication of the French original of the present book, Resseguie has also published a narrative commentary on Revelation itself, *The Revelation of John*, Grand Rapids, Baker, 2009.

43   It so happens that semioticians have devoted time to Revelation: Calloud, Delorme and Duplantier, 'Propositions pour une analyse structurale', *op. cit.*, p.367, analysed apocalyptic narratives from a 'semiological' point of view. According to their findings, such narratives have twin poles and travelling between these always involves a triple movement beginning with an affirmation, then moving to a negation and finally arriving at a second affirmation.

44   For further detail see D. Marguerat, *Quand la Bible . . .* , pp.23-28. Of particular interest for our present needs (see below) is Resseguie's proposal, in *Narrative Criticism*, for reading Revelation's overall plot (pp.213-240), where he reworks a schema already set out in J.L. Resseguie, *Revelation Unsealed. A Narrative-Critical Approach to John's Apocalypse*, Leiden/Boston/Cologne, Brill, 1998, pp.166-192.

45   To Resseguie's study, already noted, can be added another done by D. Barr, *Tales of the End. A Narrative Commentary on the Book of Revelation*, Santa Rosa, Polebridge Press, 1998.

46   Resseguie, especially in the first two books. Two weaknesses of this proposal
     do need to be pointed out. Firstly, the way he conceives the joint role played
     by heaven and earth requires modification. Between 4.1 and the point
     (in the closing vision) when the frontier separating the two is abolished,
     Revelation in fact connects these two places in deliberately ambiguous ways
     – as I have already asserted in 'How to say what', p.129. Secondly, thinking
     of the structure of the plot as a u-shape, descending from a stable order
     of things (Rev. 1, 4, 5) into instability or imbalance (Rev. 2–3, 6–19) before
     at last regaining a stable footing (Rev. 20–22), has the unfortunate result of
     forcing Resseguie to reject all notion of recapitulation in Revelation and
     to see nothing but linear development there, even though the presence of
     recapitulation in the book has been recognised since Victorinus wrote the
     earliest extant commentary (in the third century of our era). Father Allo,
     Apocalypse, lxxxvi, was right to insist, on the contrary, that one cannot do any
     justice to Revelation without recourse to recapitulation theory. In my own
     view, the way Revelation's action moves is both recapitulatory (or circular)
     and linear. The plot progresses (in a linear way) but it also goes back over
     the same ground more than once (by recapitulation), never simply repeating
     itself but always, as it were, describing things from farther up or deeper in.
     This kind of plot development might be suitably represented in the form of
     an ascending, three-dimensional spiral – on this see E. Schüssler-Fiorenza,
     The Book of Revelation: Justice and Judgment, Philadelphia, Fortress, 1985, pp.3-
     5, 171-73.
          In spite of my twin reservations, Resseguie's proposal remains interesting in
     general terms.

47   Once more, I am only repeating here what J. Ellul has already said in *Architecture*,
     p.7: 'I am committed to reading Revelation in one piece, where each part takes
     its meaning from the Whole. In other words, Revelation is not to be understood
     verse by verse' (my translation).

48   G. Campbell, 'Procédé', p.515.

49   See my comments in 'How to say what', pp.126-27 (on Barr) and pp.128-29 (on
     Resseguie).

50   For more detail on this, see once more 'How to say what', p.133.

51   G. Campbell, 'Procédé', p.492.

52   This makes Revelation, in and of itself, a complete and irreducible whole;
     compare G. Campbell, 'Procédé', *idem*.

53   Thinking of Revelation, A. Paul, *Jésus-Christ, la rupture: Essai sur la naissance
     du christianisme*, Paris, Bayard, 2001, p.266, speaks of 'the infinite power of
     its language where linguistic signs, visual signs and even auditory signs are
     articulated together' (my translation).

54   G. Campbell, 'How to say what', p.133. I am now supplying the evidence for the
     earlier claim.

55   Compare K. Strand, '"Overcomer": A Study in the Macrodynamic of Theme
     Development in the Book of Revelation', *Andrews University Seminary Studies* 28,
     1990, p.237. Strand is particularly attentive to the way his chosen motif of the
     'overcomer' is progressively developed through successive visions. He argues
     that the necessary preparation for this is made in the first septet, that a first
     outcome is achieved in 11.19–14.20 (p.246), and that the motif then crosses the
     second part of the Book before reaching a climax in 21.5–22.5.

56   Work which recognises the importance of Revelation's themes is rare, but not
     altogether non-existent. I will give two examples. First, an article by K. Miller,
     of limited scope, entitled 'The Nuptial Eschatology of Revelation 19-22',
     Catholic Biblical Quarterly 60, 1998, pp.301-18. Miller looks at the narrative unity
     of 19.5–22.9 from the angle of the nuptial reign, which he understands as a
     not yet fully realised, eschatological victory by which the Church has a part in
     Christ's victory. And second, the more significant article (already referred to) by
     Strand, 'Overcomer', pp.237-54 (see the previous note), where some thought
     is also given to how one might study themes which are present throughout
     Revelation.
57   The idea is J. Ellul's, *L'Apocalypse*, p.51. His exact phrase is 'réactualisation du
     texte par le texte'.
58   G. Campbell, 'Procédé', p.492.

Part One
God Reveals Himself

Introduction

The object of inquiry in Part One will be the question of God, as Revelation frames it, together with the answers which the Book provides. Given that all of the Book's major themes are shaped fundamentally by antithesis, Revelation's story of God and the Lamb provokes another parallel story – its caricature – which concerns their adversaries.

Divinity and pseudo-divinity

My task in the first chapter will be that of attempting to describe both *who God is* and *what he is not*, according to Revelation. Throughout the Book, that which anti-god forces *appear to be* is correlated in a relationship of appearances to reality with who God *is*. As is the case with every subsequent theme, two things are at stake in this: recognising the one true God, who only reveals himself in the Lamb, and consequently, identifying and eliminating any and every pretender.

True sovereignty and usurped claims

My second chapter complements the first. Its focus will be on *what God does* in Revelation as well as on any attempts to fake his activity. What God desires and intends for his fallen creation gives rise, in the course of the plot, to a counter-plan governed by another logic altogether. So our attention will be directed both at the actions of God who alone saves, reigns and is victorious, through his Messiah, and also at each and every imitation of this activity to which we are alerted by the text.

Legitimate adoration and bogus worship

Finally, we will turn in a third chapter to the topic of legitimate worship in celebration of the person and work of God and the Lamb, and of the rival false worship which is craved by their enemies the dragon and the other monsters. Here, the issue at stake is the exclusive worship of the One who alone is worthy of glorification, together with the exposure of all idolatry.

1. Divinity and Pseudo-divinity

'The book of Revelation is not only theocentric; it is also theological. In other words, it does not take for granted who God is; it embodies profound reflection on who God is . . . No one who shares Revelation's vision of God and understands who this God really is could ever again be tempted to worship the beast'.[1]

(R. Bauckham)

In the Book of Revelation, God reveals himself. This happens progressively in the course of an account of the story of God and the Lamb and of their adversaries. In the two chapters which follow this one, I will concentrate my attention first on the activity of each of these characters, whether divine or pseudo-divine (chapter 2), turning subsequently to the true worship deserved by the former and to the idolatry inspired by the latter (chapter 3). For an initial reading of this story-line, however, the current chapter aims to provide an introductory character study of the various protagonists and antagonists, doing so within the framework of a dual theme which is here explored: the divinity which God and the Lamb share; and the rival, pseudo-divinity which a dragon and two associate monsters claim.

Since this will be readers' first thematic journey through the whole of Revelation, I suggest that it is best undertaken (because it can thereby be substantiated) with the text of Revelation open in front of you. The same goes for forthcoming chapters. Throughout, sub-titles indicating the relevant chapter(s) of Revelation should help readers keep their bearings.

Revelation 1

Right from its opening sentence Revelation asks its reader to take note of an intimate relationship between God, who makes the revelation, and Jesus Christ who receives it. Quite soon (in 4.1–5.14), twin pictures will give to this relationship a magnificently dramatic shape, depicting first the Seated One on the throne – the transcendent God and Creator, who has in his right hand the book of his will (4.1-11) – and then, emerging from that same throne, the Lamb who is Revelation's principal figure for Jesus Christ, the Redeemer capable of receiving the scroll from the hand of the Eternal One (5.1-14). Farther on in the complex story, Revelation will narrate how personified forces will come forth to oppose the Lamb and the Seated One on the throne, showing traits, intentions and behaviour which are systematically modelled on those that characterise their divine adversaries. It is barely an exaggeration to describe Revelation as 'an allegory of God and of his work, nothing more!'[2] Everything related to God or to Jesus Christ, in the Book, will be also the object of one take-off after another: various aspects of the benevolent project of God and his Christ, on behalf of human beings, will be matched by a series of contrary indicators of malevolence that are satanic in inspiration and whose aim is to mimic the divine to the point of outright caricature. Thus, for a time God and his Lamb will be parodied, in detail after detail, by the anti-god dragon of chapter twelve and by the monstrous anti-christs which appear, like Siamese twins, in 13.1 and 13.11 respectively.

This double dramatisation of positive divine attributes and actions on the one hand and of their negative caricature on the other, begins to be seen in all its originality right from Revelation's opening chapter. Our author wastes no time in establishing a very close association between the two great positive figures that will be the focus of chapters. 4 and 5: the sovereignly-enthroned but somewhat passive divinity, and the One who is presented as the executor of his will, a slain but standing Lamb (Christ); throughout the plot these characters share one reign and deserve joint worship. Here at the outset the seven Churches to whom the revelation is sent are immediately greeted jointly by Jesus Christ, by the seven spirits and by God (1.4-5). In a theological variation upon the divine tetragram of Exod 3.14[3], God is described by means of a strange and original formula whose very repetition indicates its importance (1.4,8). Literally translatable using verbal nouns, as 'The Is, the Was and the Coming (One)', this bizarre expression makes an obvious grammatical error by being in the nominative, despite following a Greek preposition (*apo*, *on the part of*) that clearly takes the genitive case. But this is no faux pas. Instead, it is a deliberate stratagem for spelling out a key fact: God, and only God, can be the real subject; therefore, he is invariably nominative and his predicates, in defiance of grammar, are indeclinable!

The importance of this striking theological nominative should not be underestimated, given the extremely subtle role it will play later on. The formula recurs in 4.8, in what can be called a chronologically corrected version – 'The Was, the Is and the Coming (One)' – which serves to echo another designation, 'thrice holy'. After that, it reappears in 11.17 alongside several references to God's almightiness, in a binary variant 'the Is and the Was' which seems to indicate that, by this juncture of the plot, God no longer needs to be designated as 'coming'. We meet it one last time in 16.5, in the form 'the Is, the Was [and] the Holy (One)', intelligible because 'the Holy (One)' has already been introduced in the interim (in 15.4). As if this positive new usage for designating God were not already striking enough, as a variable three-part phrase it will subsequently undergo an astonishing distortion that transforms it into a number of negative tri-partite formulae, all of which audaciously parody God. We will return to this later at some length.

First, though, we need to take note of the occurrence (in 1.5) of another three-part theological nominative, again following the preposition *apo*, which is set in obvious parallel to the previous one – this time, in order to qualify Jesus Christ: he is 'the Faithful Witness, the First-born from among the dead and the Sovereign over earth's kings'. This parallelism between 1.4 and 1.5 adds a new dimension. Not only can the name of the God of the covenant, as revealed to Moses at the burning bush (Exod 3.14-15) and rendered by the Septuagint 'I am the Is', be paraphrased as 'the Is, the Was and the Coming (One)'. It may also be interpreted using three titles of Christ, who is called Witness, Risen One and Lord. Thus the 'Coming (One)' of 1.4 finds an exact correspondence in Jesus Christ who 'is coming' (1.7). As a result, when Exod 3.14 is once more evoked in 1.8 – this time borrowing from Exod 3.15 'the Lord God' – there is a certain ambiguity, for we aren't quite sure if only God is speaking or if in fact the Christ now speaks in concert with him; the latter possibility could certainly be inferred from the equivalence expressed in the very next verse, in the phrase 'the Word of God and the Testimony of Jesus' (1.9).

As chapter one proceeds, still more titles are used to reinforce, for readers, the great degree of proximity or even identity between God and Christ which the rest of the book will take for granted. In 1.8 two additional appellations for God occur: 'the Alpha and the Omega' and 'the Almighty'. The first of these will be picked up again in 21.6, when God is also described as 'the Beginning and the End'. The second is one of Revelation's favourite ways of talking about God (4.8; 11.17; 15.3; 16.7,14; 19.6,15; 21.22). In 1.17 'the Alpha and the Omega' is paired with a synonymous formula which the Risen One uses to refer to himself and which will be used of no one else in the entire Book: '(I am) the First and the Last'. It leaps out at us from the page that this is a formal parallel with 'I am the Alpha and the Omega' (in 1.8). We should also realise that these equivalent ways of referring to God are not John's invention but something he has inherited from his predecessors, in particular Isaiah (Isa 44.6; 48.12, LXX; cf. 41.4; 43.11 and Deut 32.39). In Rev 22.13, where what was said about God from the start is repeated at the end of the book, the three equivalent binary expressions found in 1.8,17 and 21.6 are climactically combined to comprise a triple designation which describes Christ alone: 'I am the Alpha and the Omega, the First and the Last, the Beginning and the End.'

A preliminary conclusion is in order. From the moment the curtain rises and until it falls, the Christ of Revelation is conspicuously presented as sharing God's identity. It will be important not to forget this, whenever other twosomes that appear in the course of the plot directly parody this privileged relationship without ever actually managing to reproduce it.

Assimilation of the Risen One to the divinity can be further seen in the way the stunning opening vision characterises him (1.9-20). The description takes the form of a theophany in which John, like Moses or Elijah before him, finds it unbearable to be in the presence of a figure with clearly divine attributes; this establishes the high dignity which the Christ shares with God and which will receive prolonged focus later in the twin-panelled picture of the Creator and the Redeemer (4.11; 5.2,4,9,12). In 1.13-16 the elegant depiction of the figure of the Risen One suggests someone who possesses heavenly glory and who resembles God himself,[4] thus further expanding the parallelism, in use from the start,[5] between the ways of designating God (1.4) and Christ (1.5, perhaps also 1.8). A major given of the narrative, in all that follows, will be the strict unity that exists between God and his Christ – again something that this grandiose inaugural vision underlines. Whenever anti-christ figures try, in forthcoming episodes, to parody Christ in who he is or what he says and does, it is this very first representation of the real Christ, which also seems to be the most complete found anywhere in the Book,[6] that will enable the reader to observe how none of the counterfeits ever succeeds in bringing together more than a few of the elements which characterise him here on the threshold.

In 1.17-18 a few supplementary titular items are introduced by an 'I am' which balances that of 1.8 and once more recalls the 'I am' of Exod 3.14. By specifying that Christ possesses the keys of death and Hades, in other words that he rules over the very powers which he wrested from their grasp (Rom 14.8-9), the word-picture is asserting his prior domination of these same powers that will later be personified (in 6.8). To this first attribute others are then added. The 'Living One' conveys an implicit contrast with the dead or inanimate gods of paganism – for God is frequently described as 'the Living One' in both the Old Testament (Josh 3.10; Pss. 42.2; 84.3, etc.) and the New Testament (Mt 16.16; Ac 14.15; Rom 9.26, etc.) – while at the same time anticipating the sea monster's apparent immortality which, in reality, is a sham (13.3,5). Then comes 'I was dead and look, I am the Living One from everlasting to everlasting'. This is a way of re-echoing deliverance through shed blood (in 1.5) spelling out what, in the apocalyptic plot, the slain but standing Lamb will soon embody and the wounded but healed beast will only disfigure. We should note, here, how the message to Smyrna incorporates a short but significant version of this portrayal of the Risen One ('who was dead but came to life', 2.8).[7]

One final element of the first chapter deserves our full attention. In 1.19 we find the expression 'what you see and what is and what will come about after that'. Noticing how the command to write (in 1.11) is here repeated and reasoning that 1.19 might therefore offer an explanation for what is to be written, many exegetes have thought that this verse provides a kind of table of contents which sheds light prospectively on the structure and contents of the Book as a whole. To my mind, however, this tri-partite construction is governed by another logic altogether, which also supplies its meaning. Modelled on the previous three-part formula in 1.4,8, but here 1.18 adding to the scope of Christ's titles in 1.18 (as in 1.5), this key expression is an invitation to the reader to take it as self-evident that God (and Christ) who is, was and is coming will remain present throughout Revelation's intrigues. Such a presupposition will be of vital importance for understanding the highs and lows of the plot. For example, however disturbing the reader might find the dragon and the monsters to be when they burst onto the scene, or however impressive might appear the claims to independence that they make, at no point in their short career will they ever escape the divine sovereignty which covers all eventualities. Ultimate proof that this is indeed how we should read 1.19 will come in the shape of the triple titles given to Christ when he makes his final appearance at the very end of the book (22.13).

Revelation 2.1–3.22

So much, then, for the opening chapter. At this stage we will take only the briefest account of the septet of oracles to Churches (in 2.1–3.22), since I will come back to them at greater length later. In their headers, all seven oracles pick up from the opening vision (1.9-20) this or that characteristic of the Risen One who presides over the seven lampstands much as the OT priest watched over the menorah in the Temple. Accordingly, the introductions to the oracles to Churches are shot through with christological attributes. We may take the last of them (to Laodicea) as our example. In 3.14 mention of the Christ speaking as 'the Faithful Witness' directs our gaze not so much towards the splendid figure of the vision in 1.13*ff* as towards the Witness introduced from the very start (1.2,5)[8]. This is an *inclusio* marking the close of the first septet. After this, a different representation of the Risen One as the slain but standing Lamb will occupy centre stage from chapter 5 onwards. This in turn will provoke the emergence of a dark, blasphemous and ridiculous version of itself, split into two – in the form of two monsters which both undergo pseudo-healing plus their own fictive death and resurrection (13.3,12).

Arising out of the visions or auditions of 4.1-11 and 5.1-14 is the close association between God and the Lamb; this is in preparation right from the end of the communication to Laodicea. We have already taken note of the linkage of the two figures (in 1.4-5), but it is the developed treatment which this receives in chapters 4 and 5 that will elucidate for us the various inversely parallel combinations between the dragon and the twin monsters in chapters 12 and 13. In 3.21 the Victor *par excellence* declares how his death has entitled him to sit down with his Father on his throne; it is worth reminding ourselves that a statement made by Jesus before his death, in Lk 22.30,[9] parallels this promise of the Risen One. Things become more explicit still in 5.6,9 and the idea of sharing the same throne – 'God's throne and the Lamb's throne', as 22.1,3 will put it several times over – will again be called to mind in 7.10.[10] We may also note, in passing, how the notion of God and Christ sharing one throne will provide the blueprint for the joint enthronement of Christ and his followers. The throne seals Jesus's participation in the divine identity. As such, it is a cipher for a high christology and one of several elements which powerfully symbolise equivalence and which help explain why both God and the Lamb are worshipped in Revelation.[11] Their joint reign is consolidated in 21.22-23, where together God and the Lamb replace the Temple and shed their combined light on the holy city whose glory and illumination they are.

Revelation 4.1–5.14

At the very instant when our gaze leaves the Creator and catches sight of the Redeemer (4.11), the kingdom of the world is said to belong to God and, implicitly, to his Christ. To hear this stated explicitly we will have to await 11.15, but we can already detect it in the doxologies of 5.9,12 which hail the Lamb and correspond to the acclamation of God in 4.11.[12] This declaration is especially important since, as the plot proceeds, the whole universe will be put massively out of joint. Yet there is never any doubt that its only origin is in God, even though cosmic renewal and the descent of New Jerusalem are delayed until the denouement, as is the establishment of the divine presence with human beings once and for all (21.1-3).

From the moment the seer locks his gaze onto the Lamb emerging from the very centre of the throne (5.6), from the heart of the divinity who governs the universe, a certain pictorial tension takes hold at the core of the narrative. On the one hand there is a representation of equality, as symbolised by the throne shared by God and the Lamb (*cf.* 14.4), or by the Lord God and the Lamb (21.22). On the other, a certain pre-eminence is given to Christ dead and risen. Tension, here, does not however mean material contradiction and readers who know the Gospels are reminded of similar incongruity between Messiah sitting at God's right hand (Mt 22.41-46; 26.64) and his enjoyment of an unheard-of entitlement to act as Judge,[13] which Jesus will do as Son of Man (Mt 25.31*ff*). Another similar juxtaposition comes in Rev 6.16, where God looking out from his throne, or the Lamb showing anger, amount to the same thing – not that this identification prevents the reappearance of one like a Son of Man (1.13*ff*) for a second time, in 14.14.

When we take a closer look at this tension to see what creates it, it turns out first and foremost to be a simple matter of place. The reason is that the real arena for the action of the book, what we could call its topographic centre, is at the heart of the throne which functions as the epicentre of a universe that God fills with his presence.[14] Around this centre are clustered the various locations for the Book's successive scenes, some of them positioned *on earth* (in the cities of Roman Asia, on a mountain, outside the walls of Jerusalem or 'Babylon',[15] inside New Jerusalem . . .), some of them *in heaven* (in the celestial court, or Temple, or in front of its altar . . .) and even, as we move from one vision or audition to another, *alternately in heaven and on earth*. This space at the centre of all things, where the divine throne stands, provides the reader with an additional component for an interpretative framework into which to fit the various activities of maleficent forces that will appear later. These powers are deprived of any proximity to God and so, for anybody with eyes to see, what they perform are basically anti-actions played out, by the fake heroes they are, before a very peripheral *pseudo*-throne which they are ultimately forced to abandon.

Revelation 4 in counterpoint with Revelation 12

How do chapters 4 and 5 anticipate and prepare for the appearance, in due course, of these parodic entities?[16] The answer is, meticulously; it is now our task to explore this. We must first take cognisance of fundamental structural parallelism here. Chapter 4, with heaven opened, describes God in his otherness and underlines, much as the Jewish Scriptures do, that the Creator is ineffable and invisible. Chapter 12 then responds and corresponds to this with another celestial sign, namely that of a dragon with quasi-divine and quasi-messianic characteristics that antithetically reflect the shared traits of God and the Lamb. By extension, the description 'seven heads and ten horns and on its heads seven diadems' (in 12.3), will recur once the narrative needs to delineate the monster's attributes (in 13.1, where all the traits from 12.3 are re-used); at that point there is just a slight change of word order, with the addition 'and on its heads blasphemous names'. Clearly, the intention is to try to pair the dragon and the monster(s) to the same degree that God and the Lamb are united together. As far as the plot goes, the dragon and the sea monster make up a diabolical duo whose precise role is to act as the counterpart and, above all, the counterfeit of God and the Lamb.[17] Of course, even as their hellish alliance is inaugurated, the description of the dragon's failure in heaven (12.7-9) and its subsequent inability to destroy the woman or her male child on earth (12.13-17) together spell out for us that this is nothing but a show. Our ears are meant to pick up the little acclamation of God and his Christ carefully slipped in between the two incidents (12.10), that is, before ever the dragon can recruit two other monsters to whom to delegate its power (13.2,12). What this little hymn serves to recall is the invincible divine partnership which the ridiculous tandem of monsters may try to resemble but can only hope (in vain) to replace.

In short, a rival rears its head before God with a throne that parodies his, while Christ is confronted by another monster that shares the dragon's throne even as he, the Lamb, shares God's. The equivalence is striking, yet it is also simply without substance. The reader well knows that only the true Messiah may rise up to God and his throne (12.5), whereas the accuser and everything related to it has already been dashed into the abyss (12.10) – a locale that is home to the first monster which had proleptically emerged from it (in 11.7) and now reappears from the wings to take centre stage. Having fallen from heaven (12.12) the devil is now obliged, as we have seen, to seek assistance from a sea monster (13.1) followed by another from the land (13.11). In this way is constituted a sort of satanic anti-trinity which lays claims to a sovereignty over heaven, earth and sea (10.6) that belongs only to the Creator (chapter 4) and to his plenipotentiary, the Lamb (chapter 5). The correspondences between these two opposing 'teams' stretch to even the smallest details, as a few examples will easily demonstrate. First of all, when applied to malevolent forces 'seven' always parodies the divine.[18] Second, when the dragon casts stars onto the earth this activity is intended as an imitation, however vain, of what God does. Thirdly, the blasphemous names in 13.1 are to be clearly distinguished from the hitherto unknown name of the royal Messiah (19.12) or from the title that no one can miss, 'King of kings and Lord of lords' (19.16). The elaborate antithetical parallelism in the description of these monsters, where everything opposes them to God and his Christ, hands us an interpretative key which helps us understand them as parodic entities. It explains the partial attempts at imitation by the one 'resembling a lamb'[19] (13.11), for in reality there is only One in the whole universe in whose person God's infiniteness and human finitude may or do come together: in the slain but standing Crucified One.

Revelation 5 in counterpoint with Revelation 13

The second part of our investigation brings us to chapter 5 and to its echo in chapter 13, where the same structural parallelism that we have just seen remains operative. Like every other motif of significance deployed here, the sealed book which the Lamb receives is a borrowing from Daniel 7.[20] The various elements are nonetheless adapted to a new context where the 'one like a Son of Man' (in the text that provides the model) has now been transformed into a Lamb. In Dn 7, 'one like a Son of Man' – implicitly a created being – presented himself before the Ancient of Days for an investiture to the messianic work that awaited him. Here, by contrast, it is obvious that the Lamb is endowed with patently divine attributes from the instant he makes his appearance. His place of origin can be located nowhere in the created universe, whether in heaven, earth or under the earth (5.3), for he emerges instead from the midst of the throne. The task that awaits him, and only him – involving the opening of a book – is beyond what any created being could undertake: we must conclude that his status and dignity are those of Lord of all creation and that, by taking the book, 'he emphasises that whatever he does, God does . . . from now on for knowing God, we will have to know the Lamb'.[21]

To sum up, then, several elements of the Lamb's characterisation from the moment he makes his entrance have been borrowed from a source text in prior revelation. That being said, what has exerted the most decisive influence on the description, at this point, is something brand new: the key designation 'standing there as if slain' (5.6).[22] To comprehend this we need to fast forward to the point (in 13.8) where the very same expression is used again, unchanged, to qualify the first of the dragon's subversive sidekicks and thus to set it in flagrant opposition to the Lamb. Within the confines of the literary world created by Revelation, we will see this monster mimic, in every respect, the Lamb already encountered. Its characterisation as anti-christ or anti-god results from the author's sophisticated use of a process of literary parody. The Lamb's portrait in 5.6 is therefore a skilful literary anticipation of his future antagonists' mimicry, before ever their satanic hijacking actually occurs in the later plot. Consequently, it makes perfect sense to see the traits that define the anti-god squad of chapter 12 or the anti-lamb brigade in chapters 13 and 17 as having been 'chosen to correspond, in antithetical fashion, to Christ's portrait'.[23] Their only significance is negative because their only value is antithetical; in an artfully written work like this they serve to guarantee, from 5.6 onwards, that once readers encounter this partial caricature of God and the Lamb they will find it fully legible.

Quite possibly the ten diadems in 13.1 redeploy the image of the crowns in 9.7. At any rate they obviously pick up on those worn by the dragon usurper (12.3) as well as anticipating, in contrary fashion, the many diadems of the Rider-Messiah and true King of kings (19.6,12). Also borrowed from 12.3 are the monster's seven heads. As for the 'blasphemous names' by which their adversaries are known, they can only be corrupted divine epithets that testify to diabolical pretensions of divinity: only God and his Christ represent ultimate reality. I am reminded of how Jesus spotted this claim during the temptations he overcame at the outset of his ministry; in Lk 4.8 and Mt 4.10 we hear him retort using a quotation from Deut 6.13.[24] In the present context, the same blasphemy also provokes a riposte in the form of an assertion that true names of dignity will belong, in the final analysis, to Christ alone (19.11-12,16). All this being so, it is clear that 13.1 is the starting-point for a description conditioned, in a sustained way, by factors of mimicry and impersonation; we are face to face with a real parody of Christ[25] which the text's later insistence on the monster's blasphemies will only serve to underline.[26] The flood of blasphemies spewing out from the monster's maw is an attack on the supreme name, the heavenly dwelling and the angel-servants of God (13.6); in other words, an assault respectively on the dignity, presence and entourage of God and the Lamb, as previously evoked in the worship scene of 5.1-14.

The next thing to have an impact on ear and eye, because of its perfect symmetry with the Lamb 'as though slain' (5.6),[27] is a head 'as though slain' (13.3), mortally wounded (with its throat cut, like the Lamb's) and yet miraculously healed. Such is its importance that this detail will merit repetition twice more (13.12,14; see further 17.8,11). As Christ's death and resurrection, which are being parodied here, had generated the 'new song' of 5.9, so they now conjure up no less than a pseudo-risen one whose caricature of a healed wound suggests deliberate satanic imitation of Christ's death. The history of exegesis shows that it has not been difficult to detect this very thing: beginning with Hippolytus in the Early Church, commentators have indeed spotted it easily.[28] However, it may be the case here that the wound which disfigures the monster is actually caused by the stigmata of the Crucified One, in the sense that the latter's death deals a death-blow to the powers of evil in general and, as chapter 12 of Revelation testifies, to the serpent in particular.[29] If this were true, the link from cause to effect would only sharpen a parody that is already very pointed; if the monster's congenital wound, healed in appearance only, had been occasioned by the honourable stigmata of the Christ who gave his own life, the caricature could only be further underscored.

Keeping all these points in mind, it becomes clear that it is the death of Christ, whose importance is underlined for the reader from the very start (in 1.5-7 and then 5.9,12), that continues to be of first importance in chapter 13. What has changed is that now it comes clothed in a new, parodic garb.[30] Christ is the Risen One so the monster, too, comes back to life in a deceptive pseudo-resurrection[31] by which the earth is bewitched and pressed into its service. The reader, however, is not fooled. Irony tinges the whole affair from start to finish, for although the monster may hope to discredit Jesus Christ's work of salvation, what actually transpires is the opposite and it is the monster that looks ridiculous! In the plot, the monster's trickery is about passing off its defeat as a great victory. The resurrection of the two witnesses (11.11-12), akin to that of the Crucified One himself, probably provides the monster with a second anchor point for its own resuscitation. Its so-called death and resurrection make the sea monster a sham saviour, hard to distinguish from the true Messiah. Jesus had warned his disciples against misleading appearances (Mt 24.5,11,24) and now, in a similar way, John seems to do all in his power to make his readers just as vigilant. Once forewarned they will not fall into the same trap as the credulous peoples or hoodwinked inhabitants of the earth (13.4,8). The devil, as Martin Luther used to say, might want to be God's ape but has never ceased to be his devil, held firmly on a leash.

With the appearance of the second monster, the ongoing caricature develops further. Characteristic of the activity of this sidekick is its powerful speech (13.11 'would speak', 13.14 'saying . . .' and 13.15 'it was permitted . . . to make the image speak . . .'). However, its speech is just sweet talking which contrasts with what the witnesses say (11.3 'they will prophesy'; 11.5 'fire will come out of their mouths') and which parodies the strong Word of the Risen One (2.16, compare 19.11,15). Every time it reappears the second monster will be dubbed 'false prophet' (16.13; 19.20; 20.10): this appellation is justified in that it provides a clear link to the pseudo-christs and false prophets, opposed to the true Messiah, whom Jesus expected in the end-time (Mt 24.24) and to which he referred, in advance, as wolves in sheep's clothing (Mt 7.15). So the incongruity of a monster that looks like a lamb but sounds like a dragon is hardly surprising at this point. The story of this unleashed monster, whose every trait makes it an anti-incarnation of the Crucified and Risen Christ, has a firm anchor at the core of the account of the witnesses in chapter 11, which tells of their faithfulness, death and resurrection – in other words, of their passion.[32] Once their testimony has been delivered the monster's victory is allowed to ensue, with express 'permission' for it not unlike that which led to the Son's crucifixion by the Romans. Not until 20.10 will this antagonist's anti-christ career finally come to an end.

Now that the dragon and the sea monster have been joined by the land monster, a counterfeit trinity is assembled and ready to reign over its baleful kingdom, with the third member fulfilling a role comparable to that of the Holy Spirit under God's rule. With its coming on the scene an indivisible group of three adversaries is set up (16.13); three being the number of divinity, as of its counterfeit, it is opposed in its number and its function to the divine Trinity.[33] When we see the second monster, from the moment it enters the scene, making use of the authority delegated to it by insuring the universal worship of the first monster (13.12), this is nothing if not striking. The first monster's resemblance to the Lamb is explicitly re-echoed in two distinct but equivalent formulae, each of them a caricature: first, 'whose mortal wound was healed' (v.12) – and we may note in passing that the monster is now healed in its entirety (and no longer just its head); then, 'who[34] has a sword wound and came back to life' (v.14).

Bestowal on the second monster of an authority capable of prompting earth's inhabitants to worship the first monster (13.12) is tantamount to being delegated a kind of pseudo-apostolic authority. Taking over its master's 'ministry' this underling relies on a wonder – the so-called 'resurrection' of the first – for promulgating its veneration more effectively, performing signs and wonders of its own to lend false credence to its proclamation. All this resembles 'a sort of anti-Pentecost'.[35] Impressive though the three-member anti-team might look at first sight, it is actually as ridiculous a triumvirate as we could find see. Had not the satan pretentiously claimed, in the desert, to possess and to command the kingdoms of the world, only to be obliged to concede defeat to God's Anointed One (Mt 4.9; Lk 4.6)? So, when Revelation's dragon has to be content with manufacturing its 'lamb' in two bits, we can only smile. At the end of the day, the close parallels between the monsters and the true Lamb convey a veiled compliment made, in spite of it all, to God.

Let us take a closer look at the second monster. Just as the Spirit has a relation to the Risen Christ and speaks with his voice (2.1, 2.7 and the rest of the oracles to Churches; cf. 5.6), so the rival false prophet resembles Christ in externals but gives itself away by its devil-dragon voice (13.11). When the second monster promotes (13.12) the superstitious worship which the first demands (13.4), this is an obviously diabolical imitation of the Spirit's speech. According to Jn 16.14, the Spirit draws from the dead and risen Son whatever will glorify the Son. The dragon and first monster desire, in their own way, to replicate the close relationship and community of goods which exist between the Father and the Son (13.2 ; cf. Jn 16.15 and Mt 11.27), simulating it in their own collaboration.

The interpretative ambiguity surrounding the infamous '666' (see on 13.18 below) is well known. Whatever might be the value of 666 if it were to be unscrambled – a puzzle that remains unresolved even after a long history of successive attempts at deciphering it – the veil is lifted ever so slightly by what we have just seen: this mysterious number represents still

-- GIFT RECEIPT --

Faith Mission Bookshops

Magowan Buildings
028 3833 4123

READING REVELATION A THE
9780227173831

Operator Gillian	18/12/2020 11:00:08
VAT No GB268515632	Portadown Shop

Thank you for calling.

18|19|202012181100
e98ba925-cf8b-4c52-9234-4b11aeb42d1e

one more attempt at deriding divinity.[36] As will become clearer later, readers
– wise and intelligent as John takes them to be (13.18) – are supposed to get
behind the number to the scheming monster's motives which it symbolises
and perceive, there, an effort which (when it all comes down) is doomed to
failure.

A consequence of this is that we now understand better the absence of
the true Lamb, invisible since the end of the account of the opening of
the seals (in 8.2) where he had been the central figure. This invisibility was
not, after all, his eclipse; and so the eruption onto the scene of a second
beast that simulates a lamb so well (13.11) should not destabilise readers
to the point that they forget to whom, alone, primacy can belong: to the
Redeemer and Son, in accordance with the Father's will (7.9-17). While it is
true that the victory of the anti-god forces appears assured at the end of
chapter 13 and that the universal reign of the evil one seems to have become
established at the centre of human history, these are nothing but illusions.

Revelation 14.1-5

Any remaining doubt is dispelled, in any case, by the next episode. The
curtain rises on the Lamb's comeback as he stands, in the victory of his
death and resurrection, erect on the mountainside in the company of those
he has redeemed.[37] A dragon, a false lamb and a pseudo-prophet have been
enacting a weak parody of the divine economy, but all of this now evaporates
completely and these liars must give way to the Lamb's followers who have
remained true to the genuine Word and who live lives beyond reproach
(14.5). As in chapters 4 and 5, a hymn is perfectly appropriate at this point.
It is brand new and rings out both before the throne and on earth (14.3), in
acknowledgement of God's omnipresence. In sum, the standing Lamb, alive
for eternity since his resurrection, offers a curt rejoinder to the sea monster's
so-called resurrection (13.3), literally countering it here and now by its very
appearing,[38] whilst his position 'standing on the mountain' (14.1) is also a
put-down to the dragon 'posted on the sand by the sea' (12.18).[39]

Revelation 16.13-14

Nevertheless, the parenthesis of evil is not yet definitively closed. Many more
scenes in Revelation still await discovery and readers have not yet seen the
last movements of the diabolical triumvirate made up of the dragon and two
monsters. Which is why, after we lose sight of them for a while, the pendulum
swings back and they reappear as a 'hellish trio'[40] in 16.13-14, for the outpouring
of the sixth bowl. On this occasion they spit forth three impure or demonic
spirits; functionaries[41] tasked with charming the kings of the earth, these
spirits offer an arresting contrast to the three angels of 14.6*ff* whose role is to
carry out God's designs. We are not to be fooled by this abortive comeback,
however, for it will have no effect whatsoever on the ultimate fate of this team
from hell, which will founder in the lake of fire.

Revelation 17.8-11

Before that happens, in 17.8a,8b,11 our author comes up with three new castings for a monster that *was, is not and will come* (or go). To do this he picks up and re-sizes the three variations on a wounded-but-healed monster (or monstrous head) which we met already in 13.3,12,14. Ought we to identify the 'monster you saw' (17.8) as the same one the seer previously showed us? That is precisely what the earth-dwellers' astonishment (13.3), which is worldwide, appears to point to,[42] linking as it does the beasts of chapter 13 to the scarlet monster of 17.3.[43] Should the identity of the monsters, then, extend also to the *events* in which they are implicated in the two contexts? This question is difficult to answer with any certainty.[44] However, we can be attentive to just how perfectly the present description does balance the triple parody of the Lamb's wounds which we studied earlier (13.3,12,14). Moreover, we can take note of how, in this fresh context (in 17.8a,8b,10-11), John creates several subtle new variations to the key designation for God already examined above (in 4.8, *cf.* 1.4,8): 'the Was, the Is and the Coming (One)'.

In 17.8, it is especially remarkable to find the recurrence of a formula used from the very start of the book to circumscribe divinity. It designates two distinct monstrous caricatures. These two new versions of it – the second of which is the shorter – are each as twisted as the other. In the first of them, the monster 'was and no longer is and will come up from the abyss and go off to perdition' (17.8a). In the second, with parallelism that covers two phrases out of three, it is immediately stated that it 'was and no longer is and will come back' (17.8b). Here, 'will come back' rounds off the monster's destiny just as the parousia represents the ultimate phase in Messiah's story.

More significant still, however, than this dualling of the parodic formula observed in 17.8 is the artful re-working of both variants in 17.10-11, in two further expressions. The textual data here, as I understand them, warrant the following triple observation:

a)   Firstly, the formula 'was and no longer is and will come up from the abyss and go off to perdition' (in 17.8a) serves to orientate our interpretation of the two expressions which follow it, *i.e.* 'of five which are fallen, one is, the other has not yet come, and when he has come he must remain for a short while' (17.10), together with 'the monster which was and no longer is and which is itself an eighth and is one of the seven and will go off to perdition' (17.11). Both expressions amplify the first one.

b)   Secondly and as a result, the spectacle of a monster which although *eighth* cannot escape the *fate of the seven* – for they are all, in any case, destined to fall – is to be understood as yet another parody of the resurrection (see 13.3).

These first two points are not original to me; in their essential details, they are the fruit of recent exegesis.[45] In my opinion, however, they have yet to receive all the attention they deserve. More often than not, exegetes continue regarding 17.10-11 as a kind of brain-teaser which may only be solved by importing data gleaned from elsewhere. Generally speaking, they have recourse to a reconstruction of attitudes which John and/or his addressees are supposed to have adopted towards contemporary political and social realities believed to underlie the text. However, treating 17.10-11 as an enigma to be resolved only by the reconstruction of historical references behind the text is a move that need only be made when all attempts at finding an appropriate interpretation of the text as it stands have proved fruitless.

This is patently not the case. What is reputed to be an unintelligible text becomes its own interpreter once proper account is taken of a third point, which adds to the import of the previous two:

c)   17.8-11 deliberately repeats, in the form of four variants, the series of texts examined above, including not only the triple formulae in 1.4,8 and 4.8 but equally the binary version 'the Is and the Was' (in 16.5) that picks up on the interim occurrence in 11.17.

Before substantiating this third remark, as I must do, it will be helpful at this point to bring together in tabular form every variant of the initial three-part formula (introduced in 1.4) which was catalogued and studied earlier. The table on p.57 will allow us to take in at a glance the extraordinary antithetical parallelism which links the four instances noted in 17.8-11 to the previous ones, helping us observe straightaway the parodic value that characterises all these claims to pseudo-divinity.

When taking in these assembled parallels the eye is immediately struck by the juxtaposition and contrast between two sorts of time, namely God's time (or his eternity) – presupposed from the moment Revelation opens – and a parody of time which comes about in the course of narration.[46] God is eternal but, as the second element in each of the formulae in 17.8 shows, the monster by contrast can cease to be through temporary non-existence. And when it does return, this will usher in no eternal reign or establish any sovereignty whatever. The verb *erchomai* (come) does not appear in the third element of the relevant expression, no doubt to distinguish the monster's reappearance from Christ's eschatological coming (2.5,16; 3.11; 16.15; 22.6,12,22; *cf.* 3.3). Yet the use of a synonym, *parerchomai*, does seem to imply a sort of parousia (17.8b) even if Revelation, unlike other New Testament writings, never uses such terminology for the return of Christ (compare 1 Cor 15.23; 1 Th 2.19; 1 Jn 2.28; and so on). The *manner* of the return is also different,[47] for the monster comes up from the abyss (17.8a) – a place where all evil is found (9.1,2,11; 20.1), equivalent to the sea from which the dragon summoned it (13.1) – whereas Christ comes down from heaven (19.11). When, finally, the monster goes off to perdition (17.11) this fate will match its destiny perfectly (11.17).

Antithetical Parallels in 17.8-11

(God)	'the Is	and the Was	and the Coming (One)'	1.4
	'the Is	and the Was	and the Coming (One)'	1.8
	'the Was	and the Is	and the Coming (One)'	4.8
	'the Is	and the Was'		11.17
	'the Is	and the Was	[and] the Holy (One)'	16.5
Jesus Christ	'The Faithful Witness	The First-born from the dead	and the Sovereign over earth's kings'	1.5
'Write …	what you saw	and what is	and what is going to happen next'	1.19
(the monster)	'was	and no longer is	and will come up from the abyss and go off to perdition'	17.8a
	'was	and no longer is	and will come back'	17.8b
	'of five which are fallen, one is	the other has not yet come	and when he has come he must remain for a short while'	17.10
	'the monster which was	and no longer is	and which is itself an eighth and is one of the seven and will go off to perdition'	17.11

What is novel about 17.8*ff* is the fact that it finds words to convey yet another imitation or forgery of God or Christ's work.[48] The monster glimpsed by the seer at this juncture (17.3,6,8) recalls both the dragon of chapter 12 and, simultaneously, the first monster of chapter 13. Particular note should be taken of how the same three-stage chronology affects both monsters, beginning with a position of power, moving through a heavy defeat and on to a spectacular recovery which, being only illusory, simply hastens final annihilation.[49] That the abyss is a location either to come out of or go back to (17.8a) is something the reader already knows (9.1; 11.7); here, there is added the notion of a place of final destination or fate ('and go off to perdition', 17.8a), a supplementary detail which reinforces the parody of the third and last element of the description in which God, quintessentially, is the 'Coming (One)' (1.4,8; 4.8).

The stress laid on the monster's destruction – it no longer 'is' (or, it is no longer there)[50] and although it returns, it has no future (or future coming)[51] – corresponds exactly to what is underlined in the formula used for describing God. The name of devotion given him just prior to the scarlet monster's appearance, in 16.5, had become bi-partite only, 'the Is and the Was', implying that he no longer need come (having already come definitively). So instead of, and in apposition to 'the Coming (One)', we find 'the Holy (One)'. As for the monster, its coming back only to go off to definitive perdition leads to the conclusion that, in contrast to the eternally Living One, it is no more than the *definitively destroyed* one!

Bearing in mind that christological parody was established at the very moment the first and second monsters appeared (in chapter 13), it is immediately apparent that the description in 17.8-11 functions as a renewed parody of the Christ-Lamb who died, was raised and now lives forever. Each of the four versions of the tri-partite phrase, and all of them together, present the antithesis of a crucially important divine appellation (1.8/4.8/11.17/16.5). Equally, and perhaps more especially, they contrast the tri-partite formula in 1.18a, which refers to Messiah as 'the Living (One), I was dead and look, I am the Living (One) from everlasting to everlasting' or another formula, in 2.8, which recapitulates this in shortened form: 'the First and the Last, who was dead and came back to life'.[52]

More significant still is the frankly ironic import of the expression 'and go off to perdition' (17.11). As a modification of the third element in the phrase, this contrasts with another from 11.17. By a similar process 'the Coming (One)' of 1.4,8 had been replaced, there, by a complex formula 'the Almighty, you showed your great power and you began to reign', putting down a marker and an anticipation of the final state of things. Consequently, 'go off to perdition' (17.11) – a re-expanded formula reinforcing the phrase found in 17.8a and repeated, in concertina fashion, in 17.8b – contrasts this coming with a going, or departure, that will be just as final. These considerations warrant the endorsement of a conclusion reached, half a century ago, by C. Brütsch at this point in his commentary: 'The 'beast' was, then no longer is, only to reappear and in the end destroy itself. The parody of Christ's birth, death and resurrection shows through. Whereas the latter comes from the Father and goes to the Father, after having been made nothing at the cross, the beast emerges from nothingness only to languish there again once all is said and done'.[53]

It is time to try to summarise these findings. Taking the tale of the monster in chapter 13 as his template, our author has managed through the variations in chapter 17 to conceive a story for the monster comprising successive phases. The result is an antagonist for Christ which experiences its own parallel death, resurrection and parousia. Aping the way Christ's resurrection and parousia compensate for his apparent defeat at the cross (1.5,7) the monster, once killed, attempts to hoodwink the world by feigning its own deceitful resurrection and arranging its own return – even if this leads only to its definitive removal from the scene. By paralleling the corresponding events in Christ's life, the so-called death and resurrection of the monster forcefully raises the question of what is truly divine. To those who might be tempted to worship the monster for its apparent victory, which is a lie, the narrative says in no uncertain terms that they should worship the true God, acquitting themselves like the martyrs whose ostensible failure, as was the case for Christ their master, is in reality an unqualified triumph.

Revelation 20.1-2

The story of the dragon and its henchmen reaches its climax in the events of 20.1ff, an extremely important section for the climax of Revelation's plot.[54] What the reader witnesses here, in spite of its last-ditch pirouettes, is the satan's demise as an active subject, implacably opposed to God. This finality is rather skilfully reflected in the titles used to describe the dragon, with nomenclature which is a more compact but almost word-for-word retrieval of that found, essentially, in 12.9. It is important not to miss how the description (literally 'the ancient serpent, which is devil and the satan', 20.2) is couched in the nominative whereas grammatically an accusative is required in Greek. Notwithstanding the inattention of virtually all commentators at this point,[55] we ought to see this as a hugely significant phenomenon. As we noticed when reading 1.4-5, the titles applied to God and to Christ are themselves systematically formulated as nominatives: accordingly, 20.2 confronts us with an ultimate case of antithetical parallelism. The nominative is a smokescreen: final punishment of the primordial enemy sets a seal upon the failure of the satanic anti-trinity's attempts at lording it over creation in place of the Creator or at forging a bride in imitation of Christ[56] and at silencing the Word and the comfort it brings. Evil's total rout means that it will no longer find any room where God dwells with human beings. A previously cursed humanity, meanwhile, will no longer be excluded from a right relationship with God (cf. Gen 3.16-19) but be able, from now on, to see his face (21.4,27; 22.3) and to bear his name on the brow (22.3-4).

By condensing into one aggregate designation all the anti-titles applied to the satan in Revelation, 20.2 gathers together everything said about it at previous stages of the plot while at the same time giving expression, for one last time, to what competes with the true Messiah's titles. His own self-referring three-part title, in 22.13, will forever erase the adversary's three titles: 'I am the Alpha and Omega, the First and the Last, the Beginning and the End'. The monster may have arrogated to itself divine *predicates*, but only the Christ who is one with the Father enjoys the true *attributes*!

Revelation 21–22

In Revelation's closing vision, the characterisation of God and the Lamb developed throughout the narrative is completed and crowned. Here, I want to draw attention to its salient points. In 21.22 comes an expression of remarkably high theological density: descending Jerusalem has no Temple. It is a surprising phrase, given the Temple's importance in the main source text John is referring to here, that is to say Ezekiel's prophecy. However, the Temple's material absence is accounted for and justified by a corresponding double presence[57], since 'the Lord God, the Almighty (*cf.* 1.8), is its Temple, as is the Lamb'. In Israel, the Tent of Meeting and later the Temple were symbols of the inroads made by a holy God into the world of human beings, in order to be really present with his sinful people (albeit to a limited extent). But now, in the end-time city of salvation, what is holy has been expanded[58] and universalised to cover everything,[59] and what was symbolic of the Holy Place is redeployed to signify the presence of both the almighty God and at the same time the slain Lamb.[60] An utterance of Jesus in Jn 2.19-21 spontaneously comes to mind, in which substitutes his presence for that of Jerusalem's Temple. By such a juxtaposition of God and the Lamb at the close of the tale it tells, Revelation distils into ten words or so the very essence of chapters 4 and 5. What the anti-lamb of chapter 13 had tried in vain to parody, never managing *to be* but always obliged *to appear to be*, is now fully accomplished in the work of salvation wrought by the true Lamb, who *is* even as God is.

In continuation of this, in 21.23, God and the Lamb are closely associated together once again, this time through the metaphor of light. The glorious divine light which illuminates the city as it previously had the Temple (Rev 15.8, no doubt harking back to Isa 60.19-20), corresponds to the description of the Lamb as 'its lamp'.[61] Probably this expression makes more explicit the reference to 'his radiance' in 21.11: The Temple may disappear, but the Risen One in contrast shines with the glory of God. The combined splendour of God and the Lamb matches the abolition of the two light sources whose roles they assume, the sun and the moon whose creation was recounted in Gen 1.14-18. For the reader this is still another image of their close association, even if the phrase 'the Lord God will illuminate them' (in 22.5) seems to respect the Father's pre-eminence. The fundamentally reciprocal nature of their light-bearing, in reflection of their shared identity, is a final retort aimed at the imitative duo comprising the monster and the dragon. Finally, the light they jointly shed is paralleled by two mentions of the 'throne of God and the Lamb' (in 22.1,3), a joint session already announced (we may recall) to the Church at Laodicea (3.21). Finding God and the enthroned Christ present now, with human beings, on the new earth would appear to indicate a transposition of what, in chapters 4 and 5, had had its setting in heaven.[62] The narrative cause of this lies in the irrevocable eradication of the parodic throne and thereby, of its capacity to cause any further harm.[63]

Notes

1   R. Bauckham, 'God in the Book of Revelation', *Proceedings of the Irish Biblical Association* 18, 1995, p.42.

2   According to the rather categorical but nonetheless quite plausible view of J. Ellul, *Architecture, op. cit.*, p.75 (my translation).

3   Compare J.-P. Prévost, *L'Apocalypse*, Paris, Bayard, 1995, p.26. In this formula D.E. Aune, *Revelation 1-5* (vol. 1), p.30-33,59, sees a unique combination of a) Jewish divine names drawn from the OT and from certain traditions in the Targums with b) Graeco-Roman appellations occurring frequently since Homer – *cf.* the inscription on a statue of Isis according to Plutarch, *De Iside et Oriside* 9, or the song of the Peliades (or doves) at Dodona, in Pausanias's *Descriptio* x.12.10, which call out 'Zeus was, Zeus is, Zeus will be'. On this way of thinking, our author might have minted this designation for God so as to oppose the one found on Roman coins, which celebrated the emperor's *aeternitas*. Whatever the truth of this, we should note how the expected 'will be' has been replaced by the less static designation 'will come' – on which subject it is worth consulting, at this point in his commentary, J.P.M. Sweet, *Revelation*, London, SCM Press, 1979.

4   Compare G. Beasley-Murray, *The Book of Revelation*, London, Eerdmans, 1974, p.66.

5   That is, if the absence of an article before 'Lord God' in 1.8 (for which Jn 21.7 offers a comparison) signifies that Jesus, and not God, is speaking here.

6   As Eugenio Corsini says, *The Apocalypse. The Perennial Revelation of Jesus Christ* (Good News Study no. 5), Dublin (tr. Veritas), 1983, p.85, each of the christological figures still to come in the Book – the Lamb, the Son of Man coming on the clouds or the Logos on horseback – will, by comparison, be less 'supreme and final' in scope.

7   For Colin Hemer, *The Letters to the Seven Churches of Asia in their Local Setting*, Sheffield, JSOT Press, 1986, pp.61-64, dying and coming back to life further reflects Smyrna's destruction by the Lydians in 600 B.C.E. and its renaissance, as a Greek city, under Antigone in 290 B.C.E.

8   In reference to 3.14, C. Rowland, *Revelation*, London, Methodist Publishing House, 1993, p.38, states that the key to reading Revelation correctly lies in the person of Christ, in such a way that his faithful testimony should unlock the Book for us as we read.

9   In Luke, as also here, access to this throne is via suffering and death. Matthew has a form of the same saying; however, it occurs in another context (Mt 19.28).

10 Elsewhere I have studied in much greater detail how Revelation understands the notion of the reign of God (or indeed of the Messiah) and its outworking in the experience of Christ's disciples; see my article 'La royauté de Dieu, de l'Agneau et des siens', *Revue Réformée* 233, 2005/3, pp.44-61.

11 Concerning the NT's own christological categories, see the point of view of R. Bauckham, *God Crucified: Monotheism and Christology in the New Testament*, Carlisle/ Grand Rapids, Paternoster/Eerdmans, 1998, p.77. His thesis is that the NT authors (among them John, in Revelation) include Jesus in the unique *identity* of the God of Israel. I think he is quite right.

12 As S. Moyise remarks, *The Old Testament in the Book of Revelation*, Sheffield, JSNTSS, 1995, p.128, God and the Lamb are here set side by side in their particular dignity, in a creative tension which is left unexplained.

13 For a study which places the sovereignty assumed by God and the Lamb at the heart of Revelation's plot, it is worth consulting, in German, 'Die theologische Mitte der Weltgerichtsvisionen in der Johannesapokalypse',*Trierer Theologische Zeitschrift* 77, 1968, pp.1-16.

14 For R. Bauckham, *The Theology of the Book of Revelation*, Cambridge, CUP, 1993, pp.141-42, this is the Book's central symbol in which both political and cultic imagery coalesce. A similar view is taken by L.L. Thompson, 'Mapping an Apocalyptic World', in J. Scott and P. Simpson-Housley (eds), *Sacred Places and Profane Spaces. Essays in the Geographies of Judaism, Christianity and Islam*, Westport, Greenwood Press, 1991, pp.117-18. This author draws attention to the fact that as the Book's plot reaches its climax, the throne (a spatial element) and eschatological Jerusalem (a temporal element) merge with one another like the twin centres of a parabola.

15 In this and subsequent chapters, reference to 'Babylon' in inverted commas is deliberate, so as to draw attention to the symbolic significance of the name as used in Revelation (*i.e.* as meaning more than just historical Babel/Babylon); this expanded meaning will be explored in due course. However, Babylon without inverted commas is used when simply quoting the English text of Revelation itself, when referring to OT Babylon and to OT texts, or in compounds (like Babylon-the-whore).

16 For the 'parodic' see R. Bauckham, *The Climax of Prophecy*, Edinburgh, T&T Clark, 1993, pp.284. Father Allo, *Apocalypse*, p.202, had already noticed how the satan's defeat in ch. 12 balances God's glory in ch. 4, with God in heaven and the satan, as the world's virtually dispossessed prince, found on earth.

17 For an influential suggestion concerning the source from which John drew his inspiration here, see the article by D.E. Aune, 'The Influence of Roman Court Ceremonial on the Apocalypse of John', *Biblical Research* 38, 1983, p.5.

18 Bauckham, *Climax*, p.36, who notes a similar parodic use of 'three' in 16.13. W. Hendriksen, *More Than Conquerors*, London, Tyndale Press, 1962, p.136, wonders about the difference (in 12.3) between 'diadems' and 'crowns', finding the latter to be signs of victory and the former to be the crowns of usurped authority. Usually very sharp, at this point Hendriksen has failed to take account of one of Revelation's literary techniques, which is to re-use the very words which designate God or the Lamb in order to parody them. So when, in 19.12, the Messiah in turn sports 'many diadems', this is the very same phenomenon working in reverse!

19 As is noticed by Prévost, *L'Apocalypse*, p.72, this is the only one of the twenty-nine references to a lamb, in Revelation, to be 'applied, in ironical fashion, to the beast'.

20 For Bauckham, *Climax*, p.424, the constant recourse to Dn 7 is to be explained by the fact that Dn depicts one of Revelation's eschatological hopes, namely that the kingdom of this world should one day become the kingdom of the Lord and of his Christ (Rev 11.15).

21 M. Carrez, 'Le déploiement de la christologie de l'Agneau dans l'Apocalypse', *Revue d'Histoire et de Philosophie Religieuses* 79, 1999, p.10 (my translation). For C.H. Giblin, *The Book of Revelation: The Open Book of Prophecy*, Collegeville, Liturgical Press, 1991, p.76, the scene in 5.6-14 serves to clarify the role and unique status of the divine Redeemer, whose task it is to finish God's creation by redeeming for God a universal people.

22 As I have already suggested in 'Procédé', *op. cit.*, p.502. I am freely using the article in question for what follows on the subject of the two monsters in ch. 13.

23 H. Kraft, *Offenbarung*, p.107, who is following W. Bousset in speaking of an 'analogy', and who wonders whether the various antagonists in chs. 12, 13 and 17 have not had an influence on the present case. This is of some significance, given that Kraft had previously warned against identifying the satan too precisely as the Lamb's antagonist.

In spite of these considerations, exegetes have been particularly preoccupied with the *historical identity* of the first monster. Their main proposals have been either a) the expected anti-christ (already the preferred option for Irenaeus of Lyons, *Adversus Haereses* 5.30.33), for which a link between 2 Thes 2.4*ff* and the *Ascension of Isaiah* 4.7 proves decisive, or b) the Roman Empire, as most commentators in the modern era have thought. As an example of the latter we may point to Aune's excursus on Messiah's eschatological adversary, *Revelation 6-16* (vol. 2), p.752-55, which envisages the historical backdrop to be the international myth about cosmic combatants. Interestingly Aune thinks it virtually inevitable that the Christian doctrine of the incarnation should have given rise, in a Christian eschatological perspective, to the figure of a satanic counterpart whose most prominent characteristic would have been a claim to divinity. However, this commentator remains oddly silent about both the uncanny resemblance that there is, *in Revelation itself*, between the Christ and his opponent(s) and what this phenomenon might betray concerning its author's intentions.

24 The second retort in Luke's version and the third in Matthew's account. Traditionally, Revelation exegetes have set these pretentions against a backcloth of the blasphemous titles which, according to Suetonius, an emperor like Domitian could arrogate to himself: god, divine, august (or venerable), son of god, saviour and lord.

25 Several commentators are aware that parody is at work from as early as 13.1 onwards, especially A. Pohl, *Die Offenbarung des Johannes*, Wuppertal, Brockhaus, 1983 (vol. 2), pp.119-121. The gist of his commentary is worth reproducing: 'The other sets itself up as Christ's rival, with a coming which copies his . . . the prefix 'anti-' points, above all, to total and irreducible opposition . . . as a result, in almost all the references to the antichrist the imitation motif plays a crucial role – the antichrist as a disfigured image of Christ, as Christ in appearance only with a message of salvation, a wound and worship that rival the authentic ones. This imitation motif contains a backhanded compliment to the real Christ' (my translation).

26 E. Cothenet, *Le message de l'Apocalypse*, Mesnil-sur-l'Estrée, Mame/Plon, 1995, p.116, is representative of many exegetes who take the blasphemies to be a reference to the imperial cultus. For Roloff, *Revelation*, p.156-59, the crown

and the blasphemous name combine to represent the Roman Empire and the Caesar cultus, which together arrogate to themselves the honour due to God and usurp a power that belongs to Jesus Christ alone.

27 This is already noticed by R.H. Charles, *The Revelation of St. John*, Edinburgh, T&T Clark, 1920 (vol. 1), pp.349-50. Following Bousset, he finds that this wound makes the monster the antitype of the Lamb, marking it (or rather, one of its heads) out as a satanic counterpart of Christ.

28 Ought one also see a reference to Nero, here? Having committed suicide by a dagger-blow to the throat, Nero, according to popular versions of the legend, would return to haunt an Empire which had too quickly thought it was rid of him. Like many others P. Prigent, *Commentary on the Apocalypse of St. John*, Tübingen, Mohr Siebeck, 2004, p.406, finds it virtually certain that Revelation's first readers would have spotted a reference to the Nero *redivivus* legend here. Nonetheless, I find this interpretation to be secondary. What remains primary, in my view – shared by Giblin, *Revelation*, p.132 – is the *literary* parody of the slain Lamb, reinforced as it is by deliberate evocation of a parody of the slain Lamb in 13.8. As was already stated by C. Brütsch, *Clarté de l'Apocalypse*, Geneva (tr. Labor et Fides), 1955, p.223, 'whether or not we see a precise allusion, here, to the critical times the Empire went through at Nero's death, the miraculously healed mortal wound constitutes a parody of Christ who died and rose' (my translation).

29 For Allo, p.205, the serpent is crushed before its vassal, the first beast, is even born. We might add that this can be seen in the *gospel before the Gospel* that is Gen 3.15c.

30 Thus, F. Grünzweig, *Johannesoffenbarung* (vol. 2), Neuhausen-Stuttgart, Hänssler Verlag, 1981-82, p.337, sees the first monster as a saviour without cross or wounds (p.340), as a 'satanic distortion of the death and resurrection of Christ' intended to bewitch. Later (p.390) this author dubs the first monster 'pseudo-prince of Easter, God's adversary, whose actions feign and ridicule those of Jesus' (my translation). Similarly, H. Ritt, *Offenbarung des Johannes*, Würzburg, 1986, p.70, finds the aim of the satanic project to be that of pouring out ridicule.

31 G.R. Beasley-Murray, *Revelation*, p.210, casts a glance in the direction of the Gospels at this point, where Mt 28.13*ff* shows how the true resurrection, ironically, could be passed off as a lie and explained by the theory of a stolen corpse!

32 So, too, Beasley-Murray, *Revelation*, ibid., p.185.

33 See *e.g.* Brütsch, *Clarté*, p.228, n.3, who endorses a comment from D.T. Niles, *As Seeing the Invisible*, New York, 1961, p.165. 'Evil is a trinity . . . The followers of the beast bear a mark even as do the followers of the Lamb. The mystery of iniquity is as much a mystery as the mystery of redemption . . . man is made for worship and if he will not worship God, he will worship some other power that claims his absolute obedience'. I agree with G.K. Beale, *The Book of Revelation*, Grand Rapids/Cambridge, Eerdmans, 1999, p.691, who finds the organic parallels, which the text of Revelation establishes between Christ and the monster, to be closer than those which might link the monster to any extra-biblical parallels. This gives priority to the internal literary relationships and, whilst possible historical or mythical antecedents for the duo of monsters may be interesting, they have only secondary significance for the interpretation of the text. Any reader interested in source criticism should nonetheless refer

to Aune's updating of the history of traditions and of the stages by which disparate elements could have been fused together, *Revelation 6-16* (vol. 2), pp.728-29. I must say that this kind of textual archaeology offers very minimal interpretative gain: Aune's short concluding paragraph devoted to the final form of the scene in Rev 12.18–13.1 (p.726) proves to be very disappointing. Finally, on the question of fusion between the traditional combat myth and the Nero *redux* or *redivivus* legend, the benchmark study remains that of G.C. Jenks, *The Origins and Early Development of the Antichrist Myth*, Berlin, 1991.

34   This 'who' is a masculine, an anomaly which recalls another: John personifies the monster here in the same way as Mark, in his Gospel, personifies the abomination of desolation by qualifying a neuter noun with a masculine adjective. In Revelation, two things are going on in conjunction: on the one hand, evil (or, the evil one) is being given a parodic personified characterisation; on the other, the Crucified and Risen One, through the Lamb, is being *animalised*.

35   J.-P. Charlier, *Comprendre l'Apocalypse*, Paris, Cerf, 1991 (vol. 1), p.287 (my translation). A little later (p.288) the same author alludes to 'a counterfeit of the Christian Pentecost' (also my translation).

36   This was already suggested in my article 'Procédé', p.511.

37   Compare Prévost, *Apocalypse*, p.116: 'John abandons the beast and his acolytes, who were allowed to rage against the saints for a time on *earth*, and moves yet again to another, *heavenly* plane, where in opposition to them he sets the Lamb and the multitude which accompanies and acclaims him' (my translation).

38   I develop this point more fully in 'Procédé', p.513-14. E. Schüssler-Fiorenza, *Justice and Judgment*, pp.82,88, reads the image of the Lamb standing on Mt Zion as the anti-image of the wild beast from the sea.

39   As was already noticed by Swete, *Revelation*, p.177.

40   The expression is from Prévost, *Apocalypse*, *in loc* (my translation).

41   Thus Kraft, *Offenbarung*, p.186: 'If the anti-god trio assembles its retinue on Har Mageddon, the adherents of the divine trio – God, the Lamb and the Holy Spirit, for whom the prophets served as spokesmen – come together on Mount Zion' (my translation).

42   See A. Yarbro-Collins, *The Apocalypse*, Dublin/Wilmington, 1979, pp.185-86.

43   In defence of such an identification, see Bauckham, 'Christological Parody', *Climax*, pp.431-41. For an interesting dialogue with Bauckham's view, see further Beale, *Revelation*, pp.864-78, especially the note on p.877.

44   Against exegetes whose tendency it is to assimilate the 'return' of 17.8 to that in 13.3, as if both were a parody of Christ's resurrection, R. Bauckham, *Climax*, p. 435, insists that these are distinct events. Whilst it is true, as Bauckham says, that in their respective commentaries Farrer, Yarbro-Collins or Sweet have all *noticed* the second parody in ch. 17, it remains the case that this has scarcely been explored in their work. It is my intention, here, to remedy this.

45   For an appreciation of the symbolical significance which John attached to the numbers he uses, see especially Bauckham, *Climax*, p.32. For this exegete, like many others, the best interpretative option on offer is the story of Nero with the legends about him that were in circulation. I must point out, however, that trying to find the precise identity of the seven kings in 17.10 (most frequently understood as successive Roman emperors, Nero among them) or to locate geographically the seven hills of 17.9 (regularly interpreted as indicating Rome, the *urbs septicollis*), is to indulge in speculation. In a passage about a *monster*, why

fail to recognise the especially symbolical value of its seven heads? After all, had not the mythological Leviathan always had seven heads? It seems clear to me that an approach much better suited to the rhetorical purpose of such a text is that taken by Resseguie, *Revelation Unsealed*, p.60, when he says, 'the beast is an eighth: it is resurrected as Christ was resurrected [NB – if the procedure called *gematria* is followed, the name Jesus would yield the value 888] the beast claims to be a fresh and distinct alternative like Christ. The power of the beast lies in the deception that it is an eighth as Christ is an eighth, but John unmasks the deception here, showing that the beast is really like the seven'. See also now his *Revelation of John (op.cit.)*, pp.224-25.

46 To see this is to give renewed airing to an ancient interpretation, suggested by Hippolytus, whereby the five 'fallen' might refer to the five demons who presided over five millennia of fallen humanity's history which preceded Christ's coming; the sixth which 'is' to the era inaugurated by Messiah; the king of the seventh millennium is one whose power would be curtailed by the establishment of Christ's reign.

47 For this return, see Bauckham's discussion, *Climax*, pp.435-37.

48 A few exegetes have devoted their attention, in this text, to the parody directed at God or at Christ. Thus, for example P. Prigent, *Apocalypse*, p.480, who combines parody with a reference to the Roman Empire: 'it is certain that the formula 'was, is not, will return' was conceived as symmetrically opposed to the formula which describes God as he who was, is and is coming . . . the empire . . . is truly the rival of God, the anti-God. A pathetic rival, for he is headed for perdition'.

49 Prigent, *ibid.*, p.478; *cf.* also p.560. Grünzweig, *Johannes-Offenbarung, op. cit.* (vol. 2), p.130, appears correct in affirming that the information supplied about the monster builds on what we know already from 13.1*ff.*

50 This translation depends on the fact that, according to 17.8, the monster withdrew for a time to the abyss; it seems to go back to M. Rissi, *Alpha und Omega: eine Deutung der Johannesoffenbarung*, Basle, Friedrich Reinhardt Verlag, 1966, p.83.

51 For Ellul, *Architecture*, p.209, this means that although the beast may imagine that it makes history, it no longer has any future to look forward to.

52 Following Beale, *Revelation*, p.864. Ritt, *Offenbarung*, p.72, shares this view and picks up on an explicit parody of Jesus's life journey.

53 (My translation). In similar vein, see more recently Pohl, *Offenbarung* (vol. 2), p.206.

54 For a discussion of this passage, see part three of my article 'Royauté', p.55*ff*, entitled 'l'Apocalypse et le règne de mille ans' (Revelation and the thousand-year reign).

55 However, see Prigent, *Apocalypse*, p.565. The re-use in 20.2, in identical fashion, of the epithets from 12.9 (dragon-ancient serpent-devil-satan) is reinforced by the parallel between 'the one who leads astray' (12.9) and 'so that he may no longer lead astray' (20.3). These details confirm a more general correspondence between the accounts in Rev 12 and 20, on which see *e.g.* Beale, *Revelation*, p.994.

56 A theme we will have occasion to study below, in ch. 6.

57 U. Vanni, 'La dimension christologique de la Jérusalem nouvelle', *Revue d'Histoire et de Philosophie Religieuses* 79 (1999), p.130, offers a judicious interpretation: 'There is nothing astonishing [about the absence of a temple] since . . . the real communion between the bride-city and God through the Christ-Lamb

makes its presence superfluous' (my translation). Beale, *Revelation*, p.1091, finds this role to be anticipated in the Risen One's inaugural appearance right in the Temple (1.12*ff*); see further his excursus *The Worldwide Extent of the Paradisal City-Temple* (pp.1109-11) and compare Aune, *Revelation 17-22* (vol. 3), pp.1166-68, as well as the latter's two excurses 21A, *Jerusalem and the Temple in Early Judaism and Early Christianity*, pp.1188-91 and 21B, *Ancient Utopias and the Paradise Myth* (pp.1191-94).

58   As it is well put by the commentator G.B. Caird, *The Revelation of St. John the Divine*, London, 1966.

59   From now on, instead of measuring a temple (11.1-2) there is measurement of a whole city (21.15-17), where worship has become universalised. For R.J. McKelvey, *The New Temple. The Church in the New Testament*, Oxford, 1969, p.161ss., John in ch. 4–20 shows no interest in the celestial Temple as such because its meaning is synonymous with that of New Jerusalem, itself equivalent to the new heavens and new earth (pp.161, 167-68, 171).

60   For W. Thüsing, 'Die Vision des 'Neuen Jerusalem' (Apk 21,1-22,5) als Verheissung und Gottesverkündigung', *Trierer Theologische Zeitschrift* 77, 1968, p.24*ff*, the absence of a temple may be explained by the coming into force of a personal relationship with God, expressed pictorially in New Jerusalem. See also D. Georgi, 'Die Visionen vom himmlischen Jerusalem in Apk 21 und 22', in D. Lührmann and G. Strecker (eds), *Kirche. Festschrift für Günther Bornkamm zum 75. Geburtstag*, Tübingen, 1980, p.368.

61   In the sense of its 'light-bearer', I am following U. Vanni, 'Dimension christologique', *in loc*. Perhaps this 'lamp' is meant to evoke the *menorah* in the Holy of holies in the Jerusalem Temple, as is the meaning in the great majority of cases in the LXX. For this view see Charlier, *Comprendre* (vol. 2), p.235: 'In the Risen Christ all the glory of God is revealed and made manifest, to the extent that the Lamb is the permanent lamp of his presence' (my translation).

62   Compare J. Fekkes, *Isaiah and Prophetic Traditions in the Book of Revelation: Visionary Antecedents and Their Development*, Sheffield, JSOT Press, 1994, p.101, and more recently (and independently) S.J. Friesen, *Imperial Cults and the Apocalypse of John. Reading Revelation in the Ruins*, New York, Oxford University Press, 2001, pp.163-64.

63   E. Schüssler-Fiorenza, *Justice and Judgment*, p.120, for whom the throne constitutes Revelation's central theological motif, finds that the Book espouses a *limited dualism* which grants demonic powers room for manoeuvre within certain temporal limits. To my mind, it is better to speak of an *absolute optimism*, with G. Stemberger, *Le symbolisme du bien et du mal selon saint Jean*, Paris, Seuil, 1970, pp.239-40. Although his remarks apply to the Fourth Gospel, their relevance to Revelation is none the less evident: 'John does not conceive of two worlds set side by side in some static way; on the contrary, here are two worlds that are joined in battle and since only one of them, God's world, world of good, is a reality or enjoys real existence, the struggle [results] in God's victory' (my translation).

2. True sovereignty and usurped Claims

'A great contrast in Revelation is between the throne of God and the throne of
the beast, ultimately the throne of the dragon (12.14). The question is all about
authority; more especially, the exercise of authority' (W. Harrington)[1].

In the previous chapter, we began examining the developed literary antithesis
which shapes all Revelation's main themes. From the angle of our first twin-
faceted theme, which oscillated between divinity and pseudo-divinity, we
were able to circumscribe Revelation's plot in its main thrust: God in the
Person of Jesus Christ reveals himself to his people, but 'anti-forces' aim to
match his true divinity by trying (though in vain) to take his place and to forge
their own relationship with humanity. We have also become acquainted with
the Book's main protagonists and antagonists: first, the Creator, a character
who presides over everything while playing a rather passive role, and then
his plenipotentiary, the Messiah – the Risen One endowed with divine traits
but figured especially as a Lamb which, though killed, has also been restored
to life. We also encountered the pseudo-divine adversaries of both which
form a hellish triumvirate made up of the dragon, the sea monster and the
land monster (the last of which finds reinforcement in the scarlet monster
of chapter 17).

Building on all this I intend, in this chapter, to look again at the Book's
characterisation of God and the Lamb and their antagonists. We will go into
considerably greater detail, delving deeper into their story and anti-story.
To do this will entail following every meander of a second, related, double
theme. This theme establishes the supremacy of the Seated One on the
throne (or, of the God of the covenant) and of the Lamb his Mediator,
while simultaneously telling the parallel tale of another usurped lordship
whose 'successes' – by which, for a long time, most of humanity is taken in
– are set over against a victory which the Lamb has already won.

Revelation 1

A programmatic declaration unites together God, the seven spirits and
Jesus Christ as Lord over earth's kings (1.5). From this point onwards
the theme of the lordship and victory of God and his Messiah occupies
a privileged position at the heart of Revelation's narrative. A few clues
carefully inserted in the text serve the purpose of helping readers perceive,
behind and beyond any event of substance that may transpire, the reign

of the Almighty without the permission of whom nothing at all could take place. But his government will not go undisputed. The trials of life in this world constantly throw up the pressing question: *who reigns?* Its corollary, in Revelation, is a plot which grows up around the desire of the dragon and its side-kicks to arrogate to themselves this sovereignty over human beings, producing a project in which they appear to succeed (temporarily, at least). In particular, the handing over of powers by God to the Lamb will find a strict counterpart in the granting of authority to the first monster by the dragon, whilst the Lamb's enthronement as Lord will again be the object of a detailed parody through which the monster enjoys a rival anti-investiture.

We return immediately to the Lord-Christ to whom Revelation's opening paragraphs refer. The three-part designation for Jesus Christ in 1.5 – 'the Faithful Witness, the First-Born from among the dead and the Sovereign over earth's kings' – is a remarkable condensation of his entire career, showing his life given up to death, his triumph over death and his entry into his reign.[2] This tri-partite phrase is an initial thematic anticipation[3] of roles which the Messiah will take on in the ensuing action and which will, in turn, provoke an imitation. To see how such anticipatory writing can work for readers we can take the last of these three appellations. If we are alert from the start to the designation 'Sovereign over earth's kings', it will arm us in preparation for the sight of the first monster with its ten diadems (in 13.1*ff*); we will therefore not let ourselves be dazzled by what is clearly a parody of this lordship and remember, instead, that there is only One who is considered 'Sovereign' from the very start. Later on, the very same recollection will enable us to recognise that the One who comes forth wearing many diadems (19.12) is none other than the One who has been Lord from the very beginning.

Another example serves to illustrate how Revelation highlights the sovereignty of God and Christ at its positive pole and their parody at its negative pole. Thus in the sequence by which the seals are broken open, the kings of the earth become afraid when faced with their only true Sovereign (6.15); but in their fear there is also irony since, in reality, Jesus Christ who is not powerful in worldly terms does not instil fear. Instead, as described in Mt 20.25 (par. Mk 10.42 & Lk 22.25), Jesus says: 'the rulers of the nations lord it over them and those who are great impose their authority on them'. For him, by contrast, to reign and to exercise authority means to serve and to give one's life (Mt 20.28 and parallels). Analogous with this power expressed through weakness, in Revelation is the paradox whereby supreme royalty is symbolised by means of a slaughtered but upright Lamb (as replacement for the Lion of Judah), a representation that centres attention on the cross and takes as its focus a king who reigns through his shed blood.[4] The martyrdom of Antipas in Pergamum (2.13) appears to be an illustration of the same point, while the monstrous reproduction of Christ's stigmata, in the form of a healed mortal wound (13.3, *etc.*), is in imitation of this suffering royalty. All this allows us to say that where power is concerned – be it legitimate or usurped – 'we are at the heart of a debate which is central to Revelation'.[5]

As for the two remaining descriptive terms employed for Jesus Christ in 1.5, each in turn inspires a caricature. As 'First-Born from among the dead' he will find himself being aped by a rival who survives a sword-wound (13.14); this simulated crucifixion and resurrection is a negative way of throwing the real events into sharper relief. The import of his death and resurrection is reinforced in 1.7 where, as in Jn 19.34,37, the notion of being 'pierced' (a detail borrowed from Zech 12.10) is applied to the sufferings of Christ; in Matthew's Passion narrative (Mt 24.30) a similar combination is to be observed comprising echoes of a coming on the clouds (Dn 7.13) and the lamentation of the peoples (Zech 12.10).

Similar issues arise in respect of 'Lord God' (1.8). Exegetes explain the use of 'Almighty', here, in two ways. Either it is viewed in relation to prior revelation, by taking it to be equivalent to 'Lord of hosts' (which is how the Septuagint, except in the case of Isaiah, translates 'YHWH[6] Sabaoth' in the Hebrew Bible). Or else John is thought to be deliberately wresting from the Roman emperor one of his coveted titles, thus reserving it for God alone. In my own view, Revelation's constant allusion to the Jewish Scriptures makes the first option preferable, but either way the important thing is that Revelation reserves the term 'Almighty' for the One who holds all things and in whom all power resides. Usually, this is in the context of prayer and praise, with its occurrence in 21.22 as the only exception to this rule.[7] The vision of an open heaven in chapter 4 once more uses this designation of almightiness (4.8), certifying that God is Sovereign Lord over all and Creator of all things (4.11). A forceful reminder of this fact will come in 19.16 in the title 'King of kings, Lord of lords'.

Meanwhile, however, the dragon and its subversives would very much like to arrogate this almightiness to themselves (13.2*ff*), despite the fact that what power they may have has been given to them (13.7); whenever the satan causes suffering, he is merely exercising prior permission to do so (2.9-10). The power it *purports* to have is thus a caricature, recalling the genuine almightiness of God and the unquestionable sovereignty of Messiah as signified by the iron sceptre placed in his hands by the Father (2.27; *cf.* 19.15); this, the dragon will never manage to snatch from him.[8] The dragon and beast hope for better but their pretensions are in vain since it is clear from the outset that 'supremacy[9] for ever [and ever]' (1.6) belongs to Jesus Christ, not to them, and that sevenfold sovereignty (over the stars in his right hand, 1.20) is his, not theirs. For the Greeks stars were gods and for the Jews they were angels; the way they are used here, as a description for Churches that come under the aegis of Christ, suggests that in this vision the Churches are themselves being elevated to the rank and dignity of such powers.

Revelation 2.1–3.22

Revelation's first recipients – members of the Church living in Roman Asia – are addressed as the conquerors in Christ they are expected to be. From the beginning, the author sets about giving them assurance that they have a share in the sovereignty and judicial authority which only Christ possesses, according to the promise to the victor carried by the central oracle to Thyatira, 'I will give him authority over the nations' (2.26). Such reassurance will enable them, in the forthcoming visions, to adopt a critical stance towards the various attempts of the maleficent powers to make power over the nations their own. Before ever any such usurping takes place, the sole legitimacy of divine sovereignty is established as a pre-requisite. The victory hymn of 12.10 functions in a similar way, since to sing 'our God's salvation and power and royalty, and his Messiah's authority' is tantamount to disputing the authority to which the monsters lay claim for their empty actions (13.2,4-5,7,12), before they have even taken place!

From the word go, the Christian conquerors who appear in the apocalyptic plot are armed, through their communion with God and through the death and resurrection of his Christ, with a series of promises (2.7,10-11,17,28; 3.3-5,12,21) which will be recalled and revisited in 21.1–22.5.[10] All seven proclamations taken separately, as well as the seven rolled into one, are a representation in miniature of Revelation as a whole and of the Church in her entirety, because each word to the victor gives reinforcement to one message and one only: keep on fighting the fight and staying faithful, for you will be rewarded and the hour of judgment is already sounding. On the strength of these encouraging words believers will be able to brave the dragon's persistent attacks (12.17) or the short-lived triumphs of the wild beasts (13.7,15), safe in the knowledge that it is through their witness that the redeemed will gain their inheritance.[11] By finding words for addressing ahead of time, the difficulties and tensions which affect the communities themselves, these oracles to Churches anticipate the cosmic opposition which will line up against God, his Messiah and believers in the ensuing plot.

Historical detour 1:
Is knowledge of daily life in Asia's cities accessible?

At this point, a brief historical detour is necessary. A quite customary move, in exegesis of the oracles in 2.1–3.22, entails interpreting the textual data which relate to each of the seven local Churches mentioned there by comparing them to what is known (or capable of being reconstructed) concerning the historical situation of the cities in question, in its social, political or religious aspects. Without going into details, the procedure is the same as that habitually adopted, with varying degrees of success, for the purpose of shedding light on the life situation of the recipients of one of Paul's letters.[12] By analogy with the way a commentator, say, of Paul's

Epistle to the Philippians might present the Roman colony of Philippi, in Macedonia, most commentaries on Revelation offer their readers detailed information concerning what is known of day-to-day life, towards the end of the first century CE, for example at Pergamum in Mysia, or at Philadelphia in Asia. The assumption is made that the elements which comprise the oracles to Churches allude directly to hard facts that were part of actual experience in the cities in question; commentators then explain and account for this or that utterance in the text by linking them to reference points drawn from such historical research.

I must point out that reading Revelation 2–3 historically, like this, runs into several difficulties. The first of these is the curious absence of any oracles dispatched to important contemporary Churches which, we know, existed at the time at Miletus (south of Ephesus) or at Colossae and Hierapolis (in the same district as Laodicea). How is this silence to be explained? From a *literary* perspective, nothing at all prevents us from interpreting this as a first clear signal to readers that the situation of each Church is not meant to be taken as a direct reflection of historical data, whether known (by independent means) or simply conjectured. When posed from an historical point of view, however, the same question yields no satisfactory answer; this is because the application of historical questioning to exegesis of Revelation is fundamentally problematic, however commonplace it may be in practice.

Revelation is a prophetic-apocalyptic narrative, which like all narratives, sets about creating, in a very sophisticated fashion, its own literary world of meaning. In such a textual universe, within a narrated world which is figurative in character, the 'real' world situated outside the text – the world in which Revelation is supposed to have originated, and about which it may be supposed to offer a particular perspective – never appears *as it really is*. The same goes for the real experience of Jesus's hearers in the Galilee of the time, which is never reproduced *as it really is*, either, in one of his parables in the gospels – however 'realistic' they might otherwise be. This raises the question of whether we are at all warranted in thinking that poetic data from the literary world which Revelation depicts can provide so many historical clues that somehow directly reflect a given religious, political or social situation. Can historians in fact utilise such data, as they stand, for their work of historical reconstruction and extrapolation? May commentators in their turn use these results for explaining the text?

The only way to answer these questions is in the negative. Where the interpretation of the seven oracles is concerned 'it is not certain that the [historical] import of the cities is anything more than circumstantial, incidental or secondary; their worth is not simply something to calculate [in historical terms], it is also representative and symbolic'.[13]

It should be quite clear, from what I have said in the introduction to this book, that I regard historical inquiry as such, and the detachment from the world of the text which it enables, as something quite crucial. However difficult may be the question of Revelation's relationship to history, it is an issue that simply must be addressed.[14] Just as crucially, however, it must also be admitted that the socio-literary and rhetorical relationship between an apocalypse – as a literary production with its origins in apocalyptic thought – and the 'real' world of historical thinking and reconstructions is not at all plain to see. How, exactly, the phenomenon known as apocalyptic relates to space and time remains a matter of some controversy for academic study: in any event, this relationship can only be indirect or better, parabolical. Readers of the present study should note the consequence of this: when approaching the discourse of the oracles to Churches, or anything else that follows in the later narrative, I am assuming as a matter of first importance that Revelation, through its story, creates its own rich and complex symbolic universe which deserves to be explored with all the attention, effort and patience that interpreters are able to devote to the task. Later in this chapter, when faced with the sea monster, I will need to come back to the problem of Revelation's relationship to history.

Back to the text: Revelation 2.1–3.22

From start to finish the first septet of oracles is shot through with a contrast between the vicissitudes of salvation, as experienced by God's people in the melting-pot of history, and the faithful promises of restoration concentrated in the person of their victorious Messiah. Truly 'new Jerusalem begins here and now',[15] at Ephesus, Sardis or even Laodicea, as is evidenced by a breath-taking promise which resounds in the ears of Laodicea's would-be conquerors (3.21): 'To the victor I will grant [the right] to sit next to me on my throne'. Yet 'to conquer', here, remains a paradoxical term since the enthroned Messiah himself gained access to his reign by undergoing death and resurrection. We should take note, in passing, of another similar use of the idea of 'conquering' in *4 Ezra* 7.127-29, a writing which shares some of Revelation's characteristics and which may come from a milieu itself impacted by prophetic movements.[16] In the course of the following chapters we will have reason to return, a number of times, to these oracles to Churches; so many of the elements which will be developed throughout the apocalyptic drama are rooted precisely here.[17]

Revelation 4.1–5.14

When the cosmos is renewed and New Jerusalem descends in the very last vision of the Book, divine presence in the midst of human beings is definitively established (21.1-3). However, this triumphal denouement is anticipated, on the same cosmic scale,[18] by chapters 4 and 5. Here, the divine glory is made manifest and the Lamb enjoys an investiture, or enthronement,[19] to which (unsurprisingly, for discerning readers) will correspond the anti-investiture undergone by the monster. As far as the plot goes, it is between this cosmic prelude (in chapters 4 and 5) and the eschatological fulfilment of all things that evil, as a force already clearly identified and judged in the oracles to Churches of the opening septet, will burst on the scene and attempt to prevent this divine plan from happening. In other words, there is a parenthesis of evil whose so-called victory, won by the dragon's henchmen, is not what it appears to be; temporary disruption only is caused to the unstoppable progress of the reign of God and the Lamb, whose full establishment none can prevent.

The visions of chapters 4 and 5 are dominated both by the heavenly throne, glimpsed in 1.4, and in parallel by thrones promised to victors by the final oracle (3.21), which are the seats of a shared reign (4.2-6,9-10; 5.1,6-7,11,13[20]). Farther on, at the beginning of the millennial reign, thrones of judgment will reappear (20.4) – perhaps reminding us of the role of coadjutor to be given, according to 1 Cor 6.2, to elect saints – once the interim tale of an *anti*-throne has been told (13.2; 16.10; *cf.* 2.13).[21] Reading the Gospel makes us receptive to these motifs already: in Mt 19.28 Jesus speaks of the enthronement of the Son of Man as judge, promising that those who have been his followers will sit on twelve thrones for judging the twelve tribes of Israel; here in Rev 4.4 this provision seems to have been doubled, for now that the new covenant is fulfilled, there have to be twenty-four thrones. Again, the idea of judging the nations from the throne is also found in Mt 25.31-32.

In Revelation, the divine throne virtually acquires the personified status of an emplotted character. At the same time, from a spatial perspective, it constitutes the main space opened up by the narrative. A central throne is absent from only four out of the twenty-two chapters; to focus upon it is a way of putting God himself at the centre,[22] of symbolising in a manner tantamount to personification the One who is seated there (4.2), the God whose life and whose activity are those of One who reigns. Given all that we have seen so far, it would be no surprise if a throne of such significance attracted a parodic counterpart in the story, as other entities have done. This is indeed what will happen. I hope that my comments about the throne, in what follows, will not be too prosaic, either flattening or trivialising an important symbol of divine sovereignty which possesses inherent metaphorical power and which makes a significant contribution to Revelation's image-filled rhetoric.

At the heart of the oracles septet, the throne of the satan in Pergamum (2.13) implicitly raises the question asked by every believer who is buffeted by life's trials: *who reigns?* Now there comes an immediate and hugely decisive answer, given that nineteen of Revelation's forty-seven references to one or more thrones are clustered here in chapters 4 and 5 (4.2, twice; 4.3 ; 4.4, three times; 4.5, twice; 4.6, three times; 4.9; 4.10, twice; 5.1 ; 5.6 ; 5.7 ; 5.11 ; 5.13).[23] Then at the denouement of the plot, when all else has disappeared, only one throne will remain (20.11; 22.1,3), still standing for absolute divine sovereignty at the end as it has from the start. As 'a figure symbolising [God's] Reign' it is essentially an image whose 'literary role is that of a character with elusive traits, but definite effects'.[24] Meanwhile, as I said before, a rebel bound for perdition – the sea monster, that is (13.2) – will try to usurp God's place by occupying a throne granted to it by the dragon, in a parody of God. Without a doubt this is a developed version of the scenario outlined in 2 Th 2.3-4. However, this throne will be judged, symbolically shrouded in darkness and then neutralised when the fifth bowl of retribution is poured out ('and the fifth [angel] poured out its bowl upon the monster's throne, plunging its reign into darkness', 16.10);[25] the Enthroned One, the slain-but-standing Lamb, is responsible for this out-poured draught. From that point on the throne of God and the Lamb is the only one remaining (22.1); their joint presiding had in fact been the foundation for the promise to Laodicea's victors (3.21).

The throne of glory in Rev 4–5 takes further a way of representing God's power and justice which is common in the Old Testament, as seen particularly in Jer 14.21. A rich store of antecedents for a throne of cosmic dimensions may be found not just in the Old Testament but equally in the inter-testamental writings.[26] Heaven serves as God's throne, as is asserted by Mt 5.34 where Jesus is likely referring to Isa 66.1ff. Yet it is not the throne as such which is of interest to our author but rather the One who comes to sit on it, for the syntax with *epi* + accusative (*cf.* 5.7 and 20.11) connotes not so much sitting as the movement whereby God comes to take his place of majesty and almightiness and reign over the whole creation. In the ensuing scenes this reality will not be altered in the slightest by any lack of acknowledgement of this sovereignty from the 'earth-dwellers', or by any opposition shown to it by maleficent forces.

In the next part of the vision, in chapter 5, it is from the one true throne that there emerges a Lamb. Although it has been killed, it stands erect and it has the right to receive a scroll from the hand of the Seated One on the throne, and to open its seals. This means that the sovereign God who sees, knows and is able to do all things has shown his power at the cross, where he offers his forgiveness and salvation through the blood of the Lamb. Indeed, it is especially at the cross that God's presence among humanity is made manifest. It is this event 'in human historicality which becomes the source of what happens in heaven, in the world of the powers and the angels, [for] ' God's (hi)story ' has taken place on earth [and]... the divine sphere has been totally defined and transformed by the crucifixion' – so stated Jacques Ellul.[27] From now on the power to carry out God's hidden designs lies with his Messiah and it is the Redeemer (4.5; 5.6) to whom belong not only the seven spirits of God's creative activity but the angelic world besides (something already glimpsed in 1.16 and 2.1). As for the throng which worshipped the Creator, it now adores the Lamb. From this point onwards the Lamb's reign is identical to that of God, a fact which will enable the plot to keep a certain tension between the sharing and the handing-over of powers until, at the end of the Book, God and the Lamb together become 'all in all' (1 Cor 15.28). So, while the throne, here, is shared between the Seated One and the Lamb, there is also a handover of powers from God to his Christ: for designating the Risen One as 'having the key of David, being the one who opens, so that no one may shut, and who closes, so that no-one may open' (3.7, echoing Isa 22.22) does in fact imply a passing on of powers.[28]

Revelation 5 in counterpoint with Revelation 13

The theological importance of this delegation of lordship will be underlined in red for us when it is feigned by a dragon that shares its own throne and powers with the first (13.2) and then, by extension, the second of its henchmen (13.12). The 'throne of the satan' at Pergamum (2.13), a place where a plethora of pagan cults flourished at the time, clearly prefigures this hellish throne set in opposition to the one true seat of divine power.[29] Using correspondences as antithetical as they are grotesque, John in chapter 13 will create a scenario given over to the developing actions of the dragon and two monsters in strict parallel to the granting of lordship to the Lamb by the Seated One on the throne. In both cases, these parallel authorisation scenes each present an agent, the authorisation of that agent and the action which results from this.[30]

Thus, the declaration that 'the dragon gave it its power and its throne and great authority' (13.2b) could hardly make it clearer that, what we have here, is a parody of the prior grant, by God to the Messiah, of the very same privileges. For readers of the Gospels this is a familiar scenario. Had the tempter not said he could give to whom he wished the authority that had been entrusted to him (Lk 4.6)? In the last chapter, we saw how the first monster aped the Lamb; by its actions here, the dragon shows itself to be impersonating God.[31] Just as God, source of all good, acts through Christ while remaining invisible himself, so also in opposition the dragon, source of all evil, delegates its own corresponding authority to the rivals of Messiah, the two monsters, behind which it then hides. And so the aping continues, for not only does the first monster seek to arrogate to itself the sovereignty which God shares with his Christ when granting him his power and obtaining, as he should, the human submission due to him; in order to establish its own relationship to the dragon this monster will also try to be lord itself and to reign, in sham self-sacrifice, by means of its imitative scars.

Not that these goings on will stop it from being a phantom monster with loathsome markings and fake stigmata, or conceal the fact that its reign is a mere pretence. It should be as clear as day that all this is none other than a parodic mockery of the cross and resurrection of Jesus. If we bear in mind that every other 'sore' or 'plague' in Revelation will be a punishment handed out by God the Judge, this fatal wound becomes an eloquent testimony to the monster's defeat, even as the Lamb's immolation paradoxically signifies his victory. Admittedly, readers may be tempted, at first sight, to interpret the exploits of the monsters in chapter 13 in terms of the absence and silence of God. Yet God is no less ready and waiting; and the monsters' pirouettes are in reality no more than *pretence* at autonomy. God 'is even secretly directing the game'[32] as is confirmed by a phrase, reiterated on several occasions, which says that the monster 'was given [power]' (13.5,7,14). This is a discreet but insistent signal to readers that God remains in charge, despite the activism of a second monster whose frenzied activity is underlined no fewer than eight times (in 13.12-16). Though the beast's subordinate role does point to the dragon, which it obeys, its remit rests particularly on that divine permission for which the dragon's delegation of powers to the monsters is no more than a poor parody.[33] Rendered intelligible because of authentic power, as exercised by God and the Lamb, the counterfeiting in chapter 13 will keep on the agenda, in negative fashion, a question already implied in chapters 4 and 5: *who is God?*

Revelation 12 once more

Because the God of Revelation, in his otherness, hides (as it were) behind his minister the Messiah, the job of offering a riposte to the monsters' blasphemous and presumptuous claims to sovereignty is given to Christ in the unfolding action. He responds as the many-diademed conqueror (19.12), identified from 1.5 onwards (we should recall) as being the only one who possesses unlimited sovereignty. Therefore anything done by the dragon, the monsters of chapter 13 or the scarlet monster with identical traits ridden by the whore (17.3), will be no more than a diabolical imitation of this transcendent majesty and sovereignty, shared by God and the Lamb,[34] or a fruitless attempt at squaring up to the true Lord of the world.[35] In other words, Revelation rigorously presupposes, throughout, that God reigns.

For any readers who know their Jewish Scriptures, a description of evil as *what is not God*, or as *what speaks or acts against God*, has a familiarity about it, even if the way these motifs are dramatised in Revelation remains something quite new. If readers pay enough attention, they will easily pick up the entirely empty ring to the claims made by the antagonists of God and the Lamb. For instance, the exaltation 'to God and to his throne' which snatches the Messiah-child from the dragon's claws and foils its plot to devour him (12.5) is a victory about which the dragon can do nothing. Its limited room for manoeuvre is underscored by verbs in the passive: 'was snatched' (12.5), on the one hand, or 'was (twice)/were thrown down' (12.9) on the other, together indicate how God is covertly dictating the game and continuing to work for his own will to be accomplished. The dragon will try to change these passives into an active ('he came down', 12.12), but in vain, for at no time will it succeed in turning 'heavenly defeat into an earthly offensive.'[36]

The Gospels, too, help us know what to look for. A 'birth' which, though under threat, is also given protection recalls the beginning of Jesus's ministry in the wilderness, when the satan tempted him in vain (Mt 4.1-11 and Lk 4.1-

13; Mk 1.13 is content with a reference). From the beginning, well before the Passion narrative, the evil one's failure to put a stop to the messianic mission hints at who it is that will truly triumph, and over whom. As for Revelation, what is presupposed in the figure of a Lamb invested, from chapter 5 onwards, with all powers is in fact the entire, victorious ministry of Jesus up to and including the empty cross and tomb.

The most spectacular of the Book's images for reflecting God's sovereign victory will be the new creation (21.1*ff*), another theme already familiar from the Jewish Bible (*e.g.* Isa 65.17-18). Prior to its use the narrative will recount evil's total rout and the dragon's ultimate defeat by Jesus Christ, the dragon-slayer, and relate a decisive battle pitting archangel against fallen archangel and heavenly army against hellish horde. Jesus had expressed what needed to be said about the fate of the devil and his angels in Mt 25.41. Although we will have to await Rev 20.10 before seeing the outcome of this conflict, already in 12.7-8[37] the victory is in fact won by Michael (*cf.* Dn 10.13,21; 12.1[38]).

Believers' expectation of help in their struggle against evil was given a voice in the cry of 6.10. In an apparent response to this, it is stated in 12.8 that the self-deluded dragon 'did not triumph' in its attempt to take God's place by challenging the One whose name means 'who is like God?' Later, the monster will also be caught (19.20). Before the satan-accuser can set about any action whatever on earth, or even the reign of God and his Messiah is established there, this 'dragon' finds itself already expelled from heaven.[39] Its being hurled down corresponds to and countermands the desire of the demoniacal forces for exaltation and enthronement. Our author will underline this fact no fewer than four times, echoing the judgment and fall of the 'ruler of the world' mentioned in Jn 12.31 and 16.11. The honours which the enemy coveted, meanwhile, are aptly matched by ironic anti-titles in 12.9-10 (picked up again in 20.2) which are anything but honorific: 'in being diametrically opposed to the Creator of all things the dragon, for all its efforts at creating, will have managed only to destroy, in conformity with its nature, as the names Abaddon and Apollyon [already] betray (in 9.11) since they mean 'destruction' in both Hebrew and Greek'.[40] 11.18 had already confirmed this, via a prophecy concerning the elimination of these destructive forces.

There is now no place left in heaven for the would-be usurper of God's sovereignty and it will therefore not be long before the same thing happens on earth, whatever trouble the beast may cause (11.7). So now that all judgment has passed into Messiah's hands, why have any fear of what can no longer bring any accusation against humanity before the heavenly court (12.10)? Should Christian consciences still be exercised by another question – *how long must we wait?* – again, Revelation will not fail to spell out how few opportunities remain for the hurled-down devil (12.12). In the way Revelation depicts a demoniacal parody of the divine economy, it both dramatises and, in so doing, plays down the importance of all the urgent existential questions to be asked: *who reigns? who is God? when will he triumph?*

Even if, to the fight of faith, evil may appear to have some depth to it, it is in reality only deep in the sense of being profoundly hollow!

Further confirmation of just how hollow, how doomed-to-failure this caricature of divine lordship is, comes from the heavenly acclamation which greets this defeat (12.10-12a) and echoes the praise of 4.11. Before ever the hurled-down satan comes to stalk the earth, this ceaseless heavenly praise is his defeat. The present imperative 'rejoice, heavens' in 12.12 means that deliverance from the oppressive presence of the satan has already been obtained, a deliverance grounded on the reality of the salvation, power and universal domain of God and his Christ. The heavenly adoration is chorused by the prayer, on earth, of the saints obedient to the divine will (8.3-5), who will gain their own victory over these maleficent cosmic powers and all their vain efforts to take God's place. 'The salvation and power and royalty of our God and the authority of his Messiah' remind us of that reign of God which has been taking shape since the Lamb earned the right to open the seals through his death on the cross.

It is true that the earth (and the sea) onto which the dragon is hurled down are as yet unable to participate in all this jubilation (12.12b),[41] even if the earth to which the evil one has been cast down is the very place where Messiah's earthly ministry will combat and defeat it. A certain ambivalence surrounds the value to be set upon the earth, given that it is both a place for meeting God and at the same time a theatre of evil and a refuge for demons. The dragon takes its stand on the sand of the sea (12.18), while a mountain can either be somewhere for the elect to gather (14.1) or else for a demoniacal horde to assemble for the last battle (16.14,16; 19.19-21). Similarly a desert can offer the woman protection (12.6,14), whilst the abyss can harbour demons (*e.g.* 20.3).[42]

By means of a device not dissimilar, in function, to irony as deployed in the Gospel of John, Revelation brings the logic of salvation inescapably to bear on every incident that involves forces inimical to God and the Lamb. Thus, the defeat of the hurled-down dragon is in reality the same event as the Lamb's triumph: 'the resounding failure of the devil is the decisive victory of Christ'.[43] The death of Christ is the hurling down of the dragon, with the blood of the Lamb sacrificially given (12.11) sealing the victory.[44] In the scenario of Rev 12.1-6 this triumph is pictured as the exaltation to God and to his throne (12.5) of the woman's son, an image for the ascension which crowns Messiah's career in contrast to the defenestration (12.9) of a dragon whose diadems (12.3) clearly amount to nothing at all.[45] Having enjoyed great authority and occupied an exalted position, only to be dispossessed of it, is to enjoy no reputation at all – as Jesus had seen (Lk 10.18; *cf.* Job 1.6-12; 2.1-7; Zech 3.1-5). By contrast, the One who had humbled himself ascends to the throne. In the Christ, the satan must recognise its master.

The heavenly war in 12.7-8 will only detain us briefly. Michael and his angels have been regarded as the heavenly projection of Messiah and of

Messiah's community, as implicated in salvation history on earth.[46] Michael's
triumph in heaven could also stand for the victory of the true defence
counsel over the accuser or bogus prosecutor, as a heavenly counterpart to
the triumph of Christ won at the bar of Jewish and Roman justice (*i.e.*, at
the cross), as both defence counsel (1 Jn 2.1-2) and intercessor (Heb 7.25).
In the doxology of 12.10-11 there is mention of the saints' triumph over
the accuser 'thanks to the blood of the Lamb,' which suggests a link to the
pardon obtained by Christ's sacrifice. As a result of this, from now on the
satan's accusations will have neither weight nor foundation or keep a single
believer from God's presence.

One remaining scenario involving the dragon (12.13-18) requires
examination at this point. Given its eviction from heaven, the dragon's
terrible anger is understandable (12.12,17); but like its allotted time this will
not last: the primeval enemy is now a vanquished foe which will taste its
own finiteness in place of hoped-for everlastingness. This can be seen in
its renewed efforts at destroying the woman and the male child (which take
up and extend the story of 12.4b-6) and in the woman's successful flight.
Even as it intensifies its actions, the dragon finds itself frustrated at every
step. Eagles' wings for escape 'were given' to the woman (12.14 – compare
the 'were given' relative to the trumpets in 8.2): like each of the uses of
'was given' in the singular, starting with the series of six between 6.2 and
7.2, the plural is used here as a discreet way of referring to the true cause
behind this action, that is, the activity of God who has remained in charge.
Evil's power is derivative only; it has been granted, as it also depends, on the
foreknowledge and permission of God alone. Hence the dragon, here, is
unable to resist God's power. When it spews forth a river (12.15) to engulf
the woman (the 'river of the water of life' in 22.1 will be its counterpart),
the earth which God created comes to her aid (12.16). Although the dragon
does not concede defeat on earth straightaway, its determined pursuit of the
woman's offspring will serve only to hasten that very outcome. Taking up a
position on the sea ('posted there', 12.18) will in no way allow it to supplant
the Lamb who is slain but 'standing there' on the mountain (14.1), indeed
who has been 'standing' since his first appearance in the midst of the divine
throne (5.6).

Revelation 5 and 13.1-10 (continued)

With the benefit in particular of the previous chapter of this study, we are
now quite familiar with the antithetical correspondences that link the Lamb
as a character, in chapter 5, to his rivals the two monsters of 13.1-10 and
13.11-18. At the risk of repeating myself from time to time, I will now
examine, in detail, the characterisation of these figures and their allotted
roles in the plot, approaching this from the angle of the Lamb's victorious
lordship and of his adversaries' claims. Whilst everything in chapter 5 takes
place, as in chapter 4, in the presence of the Seated One on the throne

(5.1,7,13), two further references to the throne as the place where the Lamb comes from (5.6) and where the praise of the whole assembled creation is focused (5.11), confirm the exalted status of this new Christ-figure. Earlier I mentioned the Lamb's investiture (see especially note 18) and this event centres, in a dramatic way, on the reception of a scroll.[47] The scenario comprises four elements in all:

a) A twofold problem spelt out by the repeated expression 'no one could... open the book or look inside' (5.3-4);

b) the inability of John, who 'wept and wept', and potentially of readers (who see what he sees) to bear the fact that nobody, anywhere in the entire cosmos, is seemingly qualified to open what God will not himself unseal (5.4);

c) the command 'do not weep', which nevertheless hints at a happy resolution of the problem (5.5a); and finally,

d) description of the One who, when all is said and done, will prove able to open the book (5.5b).

All the dramatic tension is skilfully concentrated here in one small but bothersome question (5.2) of paradoxically cosmic proportions – *who is worthy?* – and with it the reassuring response made in 5.9, which involves acclamation of the Lamb: 'you are worthy.' Or put another way, the response is in fact a respondent. The answer is a person, 'a Lamb standing but as though slaughtered' (5.6), and a newcomer to readers when he makes his appearance. Unexpectedly, and without explanation, he replaces the anticipated lion with its traditional messianic traits.[48] Given its seven horns symbolising omnipotence, as in Dn 7.7,20,24 (*cf.* Deut 33.17; 1 Ki 22.11; Ps 112.9), one wonders whether this Lamb is not a transformed lion. It is as though where the Old Testament said *lion* (Gen 49.9), Revelation – in a metaphor for power cloaked in weakness[49] – will now say *leonine Lamb*, or messianic lion metamorphosed into a lamb. Other animals, or rather monsters, will burst upon the scene later sporting their own imitative horns, but only the one true Lamb will have seven of them.[50] Added to his universal power are his 'seven eyes'; these connote a wisdom of equal extent (compare Zech 4.10), which is breathed on him by the sevenfold Spirit who fills the whole earth (4.5). This effusion makes the Lamb God's ambassador.

From a literary point of view, a Lamb bearing the scars of its immolation, yet still standing and ready for action, is a means of representing almightiness by powerlessness and absolute sovereignty by complete acquiescence.[51] So daring an innovation needs to be acknowledged for all it is worth. Whatever may have been the precise elements which Revelation borrowed from various source texts – the main suggestions being Exod 12.3*ff*; Isa 53.7, *cf.* 1 Cor 5.7; Jer 11.18; Dn 7; *1 Enoch*; and *The Testament of Joseph* 19.8-9)[52] – and put to good use in fashioning its Lamb, a thoroughly novel way of representing the sacrificial death and resurrection triumph of Messiah Jesus is the outcome of their synthesis here, in which I take the Exodus paschal lamb to have exercised most influence. The only analogy we possess is the little reference in 1 Pet 1.19 to 'Christ, like a lamb pure and without defect.'

The caricature which the monsters represent only enhances, albeit negatively, the significance of the strong-yet-weak figure of the slain Lamb, as Crucified Messiah. The first element in the satanic imitation of the Lamb's prior power (5.6) is provided by their horns, whether two for one head or ten for several heads, dragon's horns initially (12.3) or the monster's subsequently (13.1). It is to him that belong the *seven horns for one head*, in token of his impregnable lordship: the government to which they lay claim is his, and when all is said and done no one will wrest it from him! We might say that if the lion is a Lamb, then the monsters are ferocious wolves which, as we well know, try to appear lamb-like (Mt 7.15). Our author does a marvellous job, here, of playing on the relationship between appearance and reality.

To see this more clearly still it is enough to pay careful attention to the way a sustained contrast is created, at point after point, between a grotesque antagonist (the sea monster) and its original (the Lamb), a protagonist for which it is nothing but a hopeless caricature. Take for example the 'ten diadems' of the sea monster (13.1). This picture, which may re-use that of the 'crowns [that were] something like gold' from earlier (9.7), allows two things to be achieved: picking up on the ten diadems of the dragon (12.3), already known to be a usurper; and, later on, spotting how these entitlements lose all value when compared to the contrasting 'many diadems' of the Rider-Messiah, the true King of kings (19.12,16). Or, take the way 12.3 is being exploited yet again when the 'seven heads' are mentioned. While still other contrasting traits await our discovery, these few are sufficient for showing us what to look for: a monster which will be a travesty of the Lamb, as we already know for a fact. But now, this also means that the Lamb presented to us in 5.5-6 is to be understood – with the benefit of hindsight – as conqueror of a sea monster that is no more than a deformed reproduction of itself. It follows that such a monster can have no significance of its own: its many characteristics are a counterfeit which simply disfigures the divine reality of God and the Lamb; its only reason for existence is to give the illusion of being a perfect adversary of Christ,[53] while its actions are no more than a distorted copy of the Lamb's.

Historical detour 2:
Is the sea monster decipherable?

Before adding flesh to the bones of this sketch, we must return to the problem of Revelation's relationship to history. Recourse has frequently been made to the historical method in interpreting this sea monster. The characters whose growth takes place within the confines of Revelation's developing literary plot, like the actions related there, have been held to represent identifiable events or actors from the external social and political theatre of Roman Asia. Thus, many exegetes have taken the monster of 13.1-10 to be a cipher for Rome or for her empire. Emperor worship, in the context of Asia's flourishing paganism, together with the allegedly widespread persecution of Christians by Rome's oppressive and degenerate regime (under the emperor Domitian) are two factors thought to have inspired the author of Revelation to express what is interpreted as implacable criticism of the dominant political ideology. Some find, in his writing, a response to the suffering and persecution of Christians in Asia, in the form of a robust message of hope and consolation whose objective would have been to strengthen and mobilise them for ongoing obedience.[54] Others think that the author went one of two ways: either, he rejected the road of protest in favour of an escapist avenue where time and the sufferings that time brings are suspended (or even, abolished), leaving the way open to millennial happiness somewhere outside this world; or, he took his readers in their imagination to a place where, through a process of reflection, they could resolve their present crisis in a cognitive-emotional experience of *catharsis* or purgation.[55]

It is a flimsy hypothesis which sees Revelation's author as being motivated, more than anything, by political concern.[56] Leaving that aside, there is no justification for extrapolating from the story of a crisis instigated by a dragon and two monsters – knowing, as we do, how commonplace such crises are in apocalyptic writings – any 'real' social and political situation in which privation or hostility suffered by Christians might be capable of description. How are we even to begin to clear away the ambiguity from the alleged historical references of a writing whose suprahistorical or even cosmic dimensions so obviously expand them?[57]

Even if the ten horns and seven heads of the sea monster, crowned by diadems (13.1), might *conceivably* refer to Rome, the horn here is to be seen primarily as the symbol of power – power to the power ten and therefore absolute power – while the head should be interpreted as the symbol of control or, when sevenfold (as here), of an authority which claims blasphemously to equal God and to take his place. The diadems are emblematic of royalty and simply underline all this.[58]

Back to the text: Revelation 5 and 13.1-10

Since we have already started to look at the characteristics of the monster from the sea, the drawing of any conclusions concerning its historical referent(s) ought to be postponed until we have first enumerated every trait by which this sea monster conveys its profound travesty of the Lamb – for which I will set out the main correspondences, in a series of points – and secondly, explored the more important of these in some detail.[59]

a) By diadems on its horns and by its blasphemous names the monster arrogates to itself honour that is due to God and to his Christ (13.1).

b) From the dragon, which has hidden itself away, the monster receives power, a throne and authority (13.2), just as the Lamb with sevenfold powers who came from the throne (5.6) had received a book (5.7) and power (5.12) from the enthroned and invisible God.

c) Almightiness is claimed for the monster (13.4) by means of two questions that twist those of Ps 89.7 or 113.5, whereas another question framed by an angel had prepared readers for the Lamb's own share in God's almightiness (5.2).

d) Prior permission renders the monster capable of action (13.5) as it apes the work of the Lamb whose victory on the cross enables him to open God's book (5.5) and its seals (6.1*ff*); the room for manoeuvre granted to it is for a strictly limited period only (13.5), whereas the authority which the Lamb receives from God knows neither spatial nor temporal limits (5.13).

e) Its arrogant speech dissembles the fact that it knows or does only what it has permission for (13.5), whereas the Lamb with the seven eyes enjoys fullness of wisdom and knowledge (5.6).

f) The monster would dearly love to reign over tribes, peoples, languages and nations (13.7), because the Lamb reigns over a universal people bought by his death (5.9-10 and 1.6; see, too, 7.9 and 14.6).

g) The monster goes to war and defeats its adversaries (13.7), in imitation of Christ's victory (which is his dignity, 5.5).

h) It finds an accomplice in the second monster (13.11), whose two horns betray another kind of anti-lamb with a dragon's voice and make it diametrically opposed to the Lamb with the seven horns of universal power (5.6).

This series of correspondences calls for some further remarks. It is patently obvious how much the sea monster desires to be 'worthy', like the Lamb, while remaining unable to be so. The Lamb is worthy because he is Lord of creation; the monster, by contrast, is a mere creature. For this reason, the dragon's delegation or handover of powers to the first monster is a calculated move to reign through another, an attempt to rival the grant of powers from God to his Messiah.[60] This is nothing short of ridiculous and irony strongly tinges the double characterisation of an anti-christ – a grotesque inverted amalgam of the four beasts in Daniel 7 – and of an already dethroned and hurled-down dragon which passes on to the monster its so-called authority.

None of this means that Revelation underestimates evil or encourages its readers to do likewise. Actually, the opposite is true since, in the plot, a whole world is taken in by its machinations, leaving readers to ponder their gullibility. Yet it remains the case that a monster which the dragon thinks fit to become its accredited agent does not cease to be a poor mockery of the Lamb acclaimed worthy of 'power, wealth, wisdom, strength, honour, glory and praise' (5.12). As for the dragon, it never shakes off its fetters but instead, as a result of its fall, has to hide away and do its business by proxy, through henchmen invested with its powers. The dragon being forced to relinquish its power in this way actually prefigures the shackling inflicted on it by an angel with greater power (20.1-2).[61] Whatever it may 'give' (13.4) to its marionnette remains within boundaries set, first of all, by five passives of divine action that are as discreet as they are effective – 'it was given [power]' (13.5 twice, 13.7 twice; *cf.* 13.15)[62] – and then by the strictures imposed on its dealings (forty-two months).[63] The contrast is obvious with the boundless supremacy enjoyed by God and the Lamb (5.13). God's permission similarly characterises the Gospel scenario where the tempter, face to face with Jesus, admits to possessing a kind of universal dominion that is nevertheless a grant (Lk 4.6). The dragon's viceroy in Rev 13 might appear to be reigning but its allotted time-scale is nothing in comparison with the thousand-year reign of the righteous which precedes Christ's eternal reign.

In spite of the perspective that I have just identified, a very real dilemma is played out *within the narrative action itself*. For when the power, throne and authority of the dragon's first satellite rival what the Risen One possesses (2.28; 3.21), the world in its blindness unfortunately looks to the dragon as its god, as 'the god of this age' (2 Cor 4.4) or as its prince, 'the prince of this world' (Jn 12.31). For this a monstrous smokescreen is to blame, caused by an adversary referred to elsewhere as a 'liar and father (of liars)' (Jn 8.44). The Jesus of the Synoptic Gospels had stood up to him (Mt 4/ Lk 4), refusing to receive from the satan's hand what would one day be given to him by God, whose throne (according to Revelation) he shares (Rev 3.21). Even if these cautionary texts from elsewhere in the New Testament were unknown to readers of Revelation, we would still see what the poor 'earth-dwellers' of the plot cannot, duped as they are by various wiles, and would still recognise the ridicule which the text spectacularly heaps on these diabolical schemes, by which they are made comical.

What energises the idolatry to which virtually the whole earth succumbs, at this point, is the monster's arrogant attack on God and on his dwelling-place (13.5-6): '*all* earth's inhabitants' are involved[64] here (and only here, among the many always negative uses of this expression); this is no doubt because the monster hankers for the diversity (5.9-10) and the vast number (5.11) characteristic of true worshippers, in imitation of that universality reflected in the formula 'every creature in heaven, on earth, under the earth and in the sea, with everything they contain' (5.13). Moreover, the monster's inordinate pride reflects the figures found in Dn 7 and 8, on which its characterisation may well be modelled.[65]

In terms of the developing plot, the sea monster's apparent terrestrial success represents an attack on the order over which God presides from his throne. At first sight, the defeat of God's worshippers (13.7) seems to crown it with success, but in reality, this is of only secondary importance. We ought not to forget who it was that declared war, from 6.1 onwards, by opening the seals: the Lamb, whom we know to be victorious (5.5). In Revelation evil never has the initiative; its lot is only ever to react and so whenever the conflict appears to intensify, this does nothing to alter its outcome. Yes, the monster's retort to a redemption which encompasses human beings 'from every tribe, every language, every people and all nations' (5.9) is destruction, whose intention is to confirm its own rival authority over 'every tribe, every people, every language and every nation' (13.7). But such success is only partial, for the name of the vanquished saints who are destined for eternal life can never in any circumstances be blotted out of the book of life (13.8, picking up 3.5).

Therefore, their death is not the consolidation of any supremacy for or consecration of a universal reign of evil. Instead, their martyrdom will, by a turn-around, become the means of defying their enemy. The anti-god consensus among earth's inhabitants will turn out to be every bit as illusory: in line with robust Christian hope, which receives its classic apostolic expression in Phil 2.10-11, the nations set free from the monster's yoke will find God to be their light.[66] So the decisive thing is not at all the war waged on the saints by the monster (13.7), but their own endurance and faith (13.10), since the victory of the Lamb whom they follow everywhere proves to be an irrevocable triumph for them, too. There is all the difference in the world between 'he has conquered' (5.5), betokening the paradoxical victory of the cross (as the final victory) and the ironic divine passive 'it was given [power] . . . to conquer' (13.7) which, although it may be a riposte of sorts, represents no more than a partial, penultimate and ephemeral little success. This monster only *seems* to conquer and can do no more than parody the work of salvation performed by Messiah, who is crowned with glory in recognition of his triumph.

It is true that our author does make use of this monster whose morphology is just like the dragon's, from the moment it appears, to concoct a scene where enemies square up, empire against empire, and that this allows him to re-open the question: *who rules the world?* Yet for all that, this pretender's 'authority', which is repeated four times (13.2,4-5,7), can never displace divine power as symbolised in 5.13 by its 'supremacy'. There remains only one valid answer to the question, namely *God is on the throne, and so is his Christ.* It is the Lamb, slain but raised up, whose actions really count, as is shown by the fact that he personally opens the seven seals (6.1–8.1). He may have rivals, but he has no equal. Therefore, what was implicit in the vision of chapter 5 now becomes explicit: from start to finish, the story of the dragon and the other monsters is a tale of failure. It is Revelation's fundamental view of things that only God is King and that humanity owes its obedience to him alone.

What is to be said about the sea monster (13.1-10) finally boils down to this. Its every trait is characteristic of a travesty of the Crucified and Risen One in whose genuine victory truly legitimate power over the universe is exercised, in the name of the Sovereign God. As an anti-messiah which caricatures the Lamb in various ways, this monster is merely a usurper able only to make a show of counterfeiting the true Christ's royalty. Blinded by what looks like the monster's supreme power and imprisoned as they are by a perspective from below, earth's inhabitants for their part find it to be invincible (13.4); theirs may be the very temptation into which Revelation's first readers were about to fall, as some interpreters think.[67]

As I see it, this parody of Messiah gave the believers of Asia the wherewithal to adopt (or maybe, keep hold of) a perspective from above. In light of Christ's true victory via defeat, they could take a second look at whatever reverses they had endured on their road of faith and obedience, seeing them in the final analysis as setbacks only. Indeed, from the instant the Lamb lets himself be glimpsed in triumph before the throne (5.6), in anticipation of the moment, at his parousia, when all his prerogatives are fulfilled (19.11-21), believers are aware in principle that any victories for the monstrous adversaries must be victories in appearance only. What counts is how they see things or more precisely, how they interpret what they see.

Historical detour 3:
Is christological parody decodable?

At this juncture, I should refer to an influential view which I cannot share. This is the idea that by parodying a Crucified and Risen Messiah, Revelation's author made his sea monster correspond 'to real features of the history of the empire, to the character of the imperial cult, and to contemporary expectations of the future of the empire.'[68] On this view the christological parody is inspired by some religio-political entity which deified power in an oppressive fashion and which John and his addressees could recognise from their experience. For a century or more, attention has been drawn to polemical parallelism thought to link *emperor worship* and *Christian worship* (or, in its more elaborate version, taken to oppose *Christ's empire* to that of Rome, with all its trappings).[69] There is no lack of recent contributions which persist in reading Revelation's christological parody as the expression of political dissent.[70] My reply is a question: is it not, rather, the thoroughly theological orientation of Revelation's author which shapes the message of his Book?[71]

Back to the text: Revelation 13.11-18

In 13.11 the land monster appears. For the purposes of Revelation's plot, it would seem that one monster trying to imitate the Lamb is simply not enough:[72] thus, Irenaeus of Lyons called the second monster its predecessor's 'squire'.[73] We should notice how 13.11 harks back not only to 13.1 but also to 5.6, for this new land monster comes complete with a dragon's voice and a young ram's horns. These characteristics make it, like the dragon and sea monster before it, a new antagonist for God and the Lamb. Two questions immediately spring to mind. Why would the plot have a second monster burst on the scene, at this point, to replicate a caricature already established by the first? Knowing that the first is anti-christ, and an ape for Messiah, what might be the template for this assistant that now joins forces with it?

To answer the second question first, the fact that 13.1-10 re-reads Dn 7 allows us to notice the influence, in 13.11*ff*, of the twin-horned ram of Dn 8.3-4 which seems to have been reworked here;[74] the upshot is a second pseudo-lamb, made in the same mould, which is explicitly said to have 'two horns like a lamb'. As for the first question, any monster which tries 'in its own way, and from another angle than the sea beast, to resemble Christ'[75] is bound to behave in ways that are inseparable from those of the first monster. This very fact is hammered home on no fewer than eight occasions in 13.12-17. Unaided, the slaughtered-but-standing Lamb was able to break open the scroll's seals and to unleash their series of judgments. By contrast, this wounded-but-healed monster, for all its frenetic activity, requires ancillary help: seven times, in 13.12-16, mention is made of what its henchman 'does' or undertakes and we are reminded of the dragon, unable to do anything on earth without its (two) helpers. Just as the Son does nothing without the Father (Jn 5.19), so this monster defers to the first and does everything 'in its presence'. In short, rivalling the Lamb requires the support of a second monster able to do a better job of mimicking lamb-like features.[76]

A second reason[77] behind the creation of this tandem of monsters is the advance duo formed by the two prophetic witnesses of chapter 11. As trustees of the message given to them by God (11.3), they may very well personify 'the Word of God and the Testimony of Jesus' (1.2).[78] Already their joint resurrection (11.11-12) has been the original on which the first monster's pseudo-resurrection was based (13.3, referred to again here in 13.14), and its allotted time for action is the same as theirs (forty-two months, 13.5; 11.2-3). Now, a single antagonist glimpsed as it emerged from the abyss (11.7) then further described in 13.1-10, itself metamorphoses into a hellish duo. There are other corresponding features which confirm the influence exerted by the scenario of chapter 11 on the one in chapter 13; these are the war waged on the saints (11.7; 13.7), humanity's involvement on an almost universal scale (11.9; 13.7) and the ability to put opposition to death (11.5; 13.15) and to elicit others' respect (11.13; 13.4).

Finally, we should note how the seductive 'great signs' performed by the assistant monster (13.13) are copied from the witnesses' earlier miracles (11.5-6). Such miracles were expected to break out as a corollary of the arrival of the anti-christ (Mk 13.22; 2 Thes 2.9; compare *Ascension of Isaiah* 4.10). In a far-off past, divine fire had accompanied God's Anointed One; one thinks of Elijah (1 Kgs 18.38)[79] and of the grand signs performed before Pharaoh by Moses, in validation of his prophetic authority (Exod 4.17,30; 10.2; 11.10). Fire is also alluded to at Jesus's baptism (Lk 3.16), whilst tongues of fire accompanied the speech in other languages of the first Pentecost (Ac 2.3-4). Overall, the way the land monster is described makes it a parallel or counterpart to the first, whose power it shares. Their actions are joint and complementary; intimately linked to one another, they are powers whose only strength is the fact that they never act independently.

At the same time, the land monster relates to the sea monster in the same way as the sea monster depends on the dragon. The resulting three-in-one hegemony brings to fulfilment the woe that was predicted for the sea and the land when the dragon fell from heaven (12.12). In claiming the same almightiness and universal sway over land and sea (10.2) – in other words, over the whole earth (Exod 20.4,11; Ps 69.35) – this trio is seeking to rival God. Thus, the dragon ejected from heaven, the sea monster and the land monster, together parody the Creator of heaven, land and sea[80] (10.6), the sevenfold Spirit and Jesus Christ, who have been in association since the revelation began (1.4-5).[81]

This being so, the triple six of the mysterious number 666 (13.18), briefly referred to in the previous chapter, functions as a metaphor or cipher for this triple domination. Moreover, by parodying the divine Trinity[82] the entity it describes seeks (though, in vain) to set itself up on the earth as God, in competition with him and with what he has done in Jesus Christ. For what God has done in Jesus Christ, according to Revelation, is the only thing that counts on earth. That it is justifiable to read 666 like this is confirmed in two ways. First, there is the fact that, in what follows, the maleficent forces retain their irreducibly tri-partite characteristic: in 15.2, a text which refers back summarily to 13.15-18, 'conquering' means defeating 'the monster, its image and the number of its name' while farther on, in 16.13-14, the anti-trinity surfaces once again, in transformed guise, as a triad of unclean spirits which lead an insurgent army against God. Second, there is the immediate juxtaposition of this number-name, inscribed on foreheads (13.17-18), with the name of the Lamb inscribed on his own forehead (14.1), in patent opposition to this number from hell and in immediate confirmation of its fundamental value as an anti-number.[83]

Another look at Revelation 6.16-17 and 7.9-17

Before we devote any more attention to chapter 14 the time has come to backtrack so that two scenes involving the Lamb which have until now been passed over in silence (6.16-17 and 7.9-17) can be integrated into our theme of lordship and victory. The sequence whereby the Lamb breaks the first six seals open comes to its close in a scene where humanity, subdivided into various categories, tries to hide from 'the wrath of the Lamb' (6.16). This striking and extremely terse expression merits our attention.

By talking of the Lamb's wrath, at this point, Revelation is both crediting the one who opened the seals and set their judgments in motion with the right of demonstrating God's wrath on evil – for judging evil is a divine prerogative – and also anticipating the victorious Lamb of chapter 14.

To interpret 'the wrath of the Lamb' correctly we must not forget who Revelation's first recipients would have taken the slain but standing Lamb to be. Notwithstanding the fact that the exercise of judgment is given to the Lamb (chapter 5) and that his appearance will strike terror into his enemies (19.11-21), it remains true that it is through the cross that he has conquered (12.11). Speaking of his 'wrath' is a paradoxical way of combining a verdict of imminent condemnation for the wicked with the good news of vindication for the Lamb's own. His wrath, which is explicit, and his grace, which is implied, together model the two covenant categories that correspond to the blessings of salvation to be enjoyed by his followers and to the curses that will condemn those who have rejected him. By way of conclusion, it can be said that this shock phrase (6.16) and the rhetorical question that flows from it (6.17) sum up the Lamb's executive role in divine judgment, given to him in chapter 5 and already exercised by him in the breaking of the seals.

This brings us to the second text, 7.9-17, where the action takes place 'before the throne' (7.10,15) and 'in the presence of the Lamb' (7.10). Standing exactly 'in the midst of the throne' (7.17) the Lamb is back where he first appeared (5.6). From 1.4 but especially the pivotal chapters 4 and 5 onwards, Revelation's epicentre is this very place or – if temporal terms are used instead of spatial ones – 'moment' for revelation or for divine action. Here we encounter a vast innumerable throng (7.9) of universal origin, drawn 'from all nations and tribes, all peoples and languages'. This is the first variation on the fourfold phrase first used in 5.9 to qualify the redeemed; it modifies the order of the four terms and by pluralising them, puts stress on the immensity of their number as a complement to their universality. Although the tribulation from which they are set free is 'great' (7.14), in apparent opposition to the more negative trial undergone by 'Jezebel'[84] (2.22), this is no more than what customarily befalls all those who belong to Jesus (1.9; 2.9) and thus no different from the ordinary experience of those slaughtered like the Faithful Witness, according to the picture of the fifth seal (6.9, recalled later in 18.24).

Following an exchange between one of the elders and the seer about the identity of the throng, (7.13*ff*), 7.14b says explicitly that 'they have washed their robes and made them white in the blood of the Lamb'. This detail confirms that those concerned are the same as those redeemed through blood in 5.9 (not forgetting 1.5). The somewhat paradoxical image of blood that make the robes white means sacrificial blood that purifies (Heb 9.22; 1 Jn 1.7; a similar, equally striking image is found in Gen 49.11-12, in the prophecy concerning Judah). Later the garment soaked in the blood of the chief Rider and the pure white linen of his co-riders will be differentiated (Rev 19.13-14). The notion of white robes (7.9,14) comes from the fifth seal but also occurred previously in the vision of the twenty-four elders (4.4) and earlier still in the promises given to Sardis (3.4-5).

We should also note, at this point, a shift in the characterisation of the Lamb which makes him into a Lamb-Shepherd (7.17). The paradox of a lamb that can care for the flock incorporates the promise to the victor in 2.27 – repeated concerning the male child (in 12.5) and the rider (in 19.15) – as well as including, by way of reinforcement, a pastoral element drawn from Ps 23.2 (finding water for the sheep). Thanks to Jn 10.3-4 we are already familiar with this paradox, which also appears in *1 Enoch* and in the *Testament of Joseph*. It draws in part on the imagery of Ps 2, leaving aside the strike-power of the iron sceptre. The juxtaposition of lamb and shepherd is a reminder that we ought not to separate into neat, logically distinct categories Revelation's various ways of characterising the dead-but-risen Messiah who presides over his people. In sum, this is a text where the Lamb is at all times coordinated with the divine throne and the Seated One upon it (7.9-10; *cf.* 5.13). Their proximity is underscored here by the way pastoral Lamb and consoling God are united together (7.17).

What is the gain, for readers, from this backward glance at 6.16-17 and 7.9-17? Essentially, an even clearer grasp of how the two monsters are apes, and of how ridiculous are their antics. Now we see that the parodic nature of what these beasts are and do is not merely to be seen in their imitation of the traits of the Lamb who came on stage in chapter 5. Thanks also to the scenes that separate the seals and trumpets, what was already asserted in 5.12 appears even more true: truly it is the Lamb who is worthy, both as the One who received the Book from God's hand (referred to again in 13.8) and as the shepherd who shed his blood. In 7.9-17, the success of his mediation is obvious, in anticipation of the ultimate happiness of 21.3-4 when all tears will be forever wiped away and when God will be present with humanity, never to leave. Thus it is the entire intervening depiction of pretend government by a triumvirate made up of the dragon and its sidekicks which is forestalled by our sight of the real and true sovereignty of the Lamb who already broke open all the seals (6.1,3,5,7,9,12; 8.1).

Indeed, his victory through his blood (7.14), expressly tied to his messianic office (12.10-11), had been declared to be the reason for, and the cause behind, the hurling out of heaven of the evil one by whatever name, of that 'huge dragon, ancient serpent, the one called devil and satan, that leads the inhabited world completely astray' (12.9) and that 'accuser of our brothers' (12.10). The hurled-down dragon then got help from two allies on earth. But once this maleficent trio had done all it could do and, as it were, 'conquered', this all turned out to be no more than a fake victory with no effect whatsoever on the Lamb's universal sovereignty or on the unassailable salvation he had won for his own. Before or after the episodes involving these anti-powers, nothing will have happened but the redemption of their supposed victims: before or after their pseudo-investiture, the enthronement of the Crucified and Risen One will have been the only One that really counts.

Revelation 14.1-11

Just as the scenes in 6.16-17 and 7.9-17 prepare, in their own way, for the opening of the parenthesis of the dragon and the monsters with their claims of lordship, so the scenario of 14.1-5 constitutes its closing again. Before ever, as readers, we watch these adversaries break loose in chapters 12 and 13, we know that God will have the last word in vindicating his witnesses (11.11*ff*) and in having his Christ reign over the universe (11.15). Admittedly the apparent success of the monsters' anti-project does leave some room for doubt in the narrative, but God and the Lamb's lordship must prevail in the end. In spite of the havoc caused, the dethroned prince of this world (*cf.* Jn 14.30) can do nothing against God or prevent him in any way from establishing his reign (11.17). Between two mentions of the fact that the Almighty, the Is and the Was, is no longer the 'Coming One' (11.17; 16.5; see 1.8 and 4.8) – in other words, he no longer needs to come and reign *de facto* because he already does *de jure*[85] – there is placed, in 14.1-5, a vision of the victorious Lamb which erases all foregoing pictures given over to the monsters and which restores the logic in play in chapters 4 and 5.[86] The monsters have done what they could, but now 'if we might put it like this God draws more and more aces from the pack' in order to have all peoples come back to him (15.4); it is as though the activities of his adversaries 'force God to bring out his big guns.'[87]

We could say that those redeemed by the Lamb immolated at Golgotha find themselves, in this scene on Mount Zion, in the company of the Lamb resurrected from the tomb. They hear the proclamation of an eternal gospel whose scope is just as universal as was the empty propaganda of the anti-gospel (14.6, to be compared with 13.14). The Faithful Witness, reputation intact, offers a contrast with the infamous liar, now condemned. For readers of the Gospels, when evil lost the first battle and the Word triumphed over lying words (Mt 4.3-10; Lk 4.3-12) this skirmish heralded total defeat: right at the outset of Jesus's prophetic ministry the devil could only withdraw and await a moment for revenge (Lk 4.13). But Revelation's readers now discover that no such opportune moment ever came, not even when the Crucified One was abandoned and left in human hands at the mercy of evil powers.

Unlike the many characters within the course of the narrative who are taken in and bewitched by the monster's so-called power, Revelation's first recipients like its contemporary readers are wise to this. In principle, they can see that they belong with believers in the Lamb, whose obedience is vindicated here in 14.2*ff* in an acclamation of universal scope that rehearses the fine promises made in 7.16-17. In anticipation of both 17.16 and 19.3, 14.8-11 spells out the disastrous consequences that will flow from following the monster. This result, where everything is played out 'before the Lamb' (14.10), trumps whatever had transpired previously 'before the monster' (13.14) and confirms as quite illusory all its supposed accomplishments. A biting two-part parody in 14.11 reinforces this: for the monster's slaves, being struck by God's fury will mean that 'the smoke of their torment will rise up eternally' and that 'they will have rest neither day nor night', in flagrant contrast to the eternal rest from their suffering enjoyed by those who died in the Lamb (14.13).

Glimpsing the end of the road

There is another reason why the scene on Mount Zion is of capital importance. It sets the direction for our reading of what follows, where other episodes in the story of the adversaries of God and the Lamb are yet to be discovered. We can now briefly survey these in a preliminary way. In 16.13-14, first of all, there will be a brief reappearance by the threesome of the dragon and two monsters, for a battle which will do nothing to change the projected victory of God through the death of his Christ. Indeed, there is something ironic about these kings of the East joining forces against God and his Messiah here, when one recalls how (according to Matthean tradition) magi-kings had in their time welcomed Messiah! Secondly, in 17.3 one of the monsters will return alone in a new role. But neither this comeback, nor that of the seven or ten kings (in 17.10,12ff), can alter the fact that the "royal pretensions of the beast,"[88] as expressed in chapter 13, have already been undone, making sure that this new manifestation can only be bathed in an ironic light. The monster and its assistant will not fail to end up together in the lake of fire (19.20), where the dragon will also eventually join them (20.10). This outcome can be foreseen from the moment the fifth bowl, sent from God's throne, is poured out against the monster's throne, plunging its realm into darkness (16.10-11).

Revelation 17.8-18

Chapter 13 had depicted the monster's apparent public victory. Cut down, then restored by a miracle which seemed to vindicate its claim to divinity, it had got the better of Messiah's followers – or at least, it had conquered them from its own point of view (since there is another way of looking at this, in 15.2). Yet now, in chapter 17, what becomes visible is the monster's certain failure. Its resurrection might have seemed to achieve something but its return will lead only to destruction. From now on public victory lies with the returning Christ, while those who receive vindication are the wild beast's victims (17.14). This resurgent monster may wish to tread a path that rivals the road taken by God who came in Christ, but in its impotence it continually falls foul of the lordship of the Lamb (17.14); accordingly, its inescapable perdition is twice underlined (17.8,11). What we have known from the very beginning of the plot is now being trumpeted, namely that the victors are the Lamb and his followers. Only he is Lord and King and this makes those who follow him, who are 'called, chosen and faithful', just as unassailable. This is said with a simplicity designed to give wise hearers and deep-thinking spectators (17.9) confidence, allowing them to attach appropriate significance to the leitmotif of the victory of the Lamb and his followers. The plot constantly assumes this and directs its development mainly towards it.

In chapter 17 further light is shed on the matter of lordship, not only by the story of the re-emergent monster – which we explored in detail in the previous chapter – but also by the coming onto the scene of the kings, whose historical identification has so preoccupied interpreters. Their identity is not what counts for readers, however; what matters is the precariousness of their status as mere kinglets for an hour (17.12),[89] involving them in a silly alliance under the aegis of a monster assembled to fight against the One called 'King of kings and Lord of lords' (17.14, picking up 'Sovereign over earth's kings' from 1.5). The high dignity of his name (19.16) hints at how the rather unequal combat will turn out (19.19*ff*): only Christ is King, so any victory for the monster (13.7) is bound to be completely hollow; the kings whom the monster has massed can do nothing to thwart God's designs (17.17).

Revelation 19.11-18

It is in the logic of any tale well told – Revelation, in this case – that a confrontation should eventually arise between the hero (the Lamb-Messiah) and everything that opposes him. Our author will not disappoint his readers on this score. In order to recount this final showdown, however, Revelation will no longer have recourse to the figure of the Lamb with his attributes 'as diverse as they are many'.[90] Instead, preference will be given to a substitute figure, a Rider mounted on a white horse.[91] On the cards since chapter 14,[92] this decisive clash takes Revelation's plot beyond the incidents in 16.13*ff* and 17.13-14, pitting the Messiah in whom true lordship resides against those usurping forces of evil desperate to wrench it from him (19.11*ff*). In a less well-developed form, this scenario appears frequently in the rest of the New Testament, with a vision of the Messiah victorious in combat over evil underlying both John and the Synoptics. 'The New Testament shows Christ struggling against the forces of evil whose annihilation, with the destruction of sin, is accomplished in Jesus's death: Christ wins the victory precisely when he seems defeated. From the start Jesus's public life is already characterised by combat, when Jesus faces up to Satan in temptation'.[93] Revelation's originality lies in its powerful symbolic dramatisation of this widespread theme.

It so happens that the description of the Rider in 19.11 is identical to that of the rider on a white mount in 6.2, who also went out 'conquering and to conquer'. This raises the question of the relationship between these two figures, and the interpretation of the first of them is a famous crux which surfaces from time to time in the secondary literature. As I see it, the resemblance between the first rider, conjured up by the Lamb (6.1-2), and the present Rider-Messiah that looks so like him (19.11), conforms to the logic of antithesis: the white coloration of the first is a camouflage which, like his imitative crown, is simply designed to deceive; his bow meanwhile, borrowed from the mythical king of Gog (Ezek 39.3,6,17-20), confirms that he has the status of an adversary.[94] The only way it is possible to set the white horse against the three others (and then to see it as already signifying Messiah's mount) is to break the indivisible fourfold parallelism of the series of four riders (6.2,4-5,8) and do some violence to the text.[95]

By the plethora of titles and traits, emblematic of royalty, given to this Rider, we can understand that the moment of victory, so often foreshadowed up to this point, has at last arrived. According to the Gospel, Jesus Christ had declined the diadem offered to him by the tempter (Mt 4.9); here, the Rider-Messiah wears 'many diadems', since the One who is 'King of kings and Lord of lords' must, of course, have more crowns than any other! By a deliberate antithetical correlation these diadems cancel out the ones which crown his adversaries alternately with seven diadems, betokening a claim to universal power (as with the dragon, in 12.3), or with ten diadems (like the sea monster, in 13.1). It is quite evident that this Rider is the incarnation of the royalty which the monsters had tried in vain to imitate.

We can now take a closer look at the impressive succession of names by which the Rider or his behaviour is described. The title 'King of kings and Lord of lords' (19.16, a variant of 17.14) has already been examined: here we may add that it could well correspond, through the logic of contrast, to 666 in 13.18.[96] Like the titles 'Witness' (19.11; cf. 1.5; 3.14), 'Unknown One' (19.12) and 'Word' (19.13), which signify great trouble for his enemies, this one is clearly set over against those that refer to the activity of the dragon and its assistants as a retort to their blasphemous claims. So cumulative a set of appellations marks a decisive appearance of Christ – the fifth, so far, in the Book – and one which, after those found in chapters 1, 5, 12 and 14, amounts to a revelation of some fullness. Yet his name can neither be known nor understood (19.12), taking up the 'name that no-one knows' from 2.17 (whilst omitting 'new'), showing that these epithets are nevertheless not exhaustive, and bringing to mind the one who is above every name (Phil 2.9). This is the opposite of the accumulation of names to call the dragon, when it was hurled down (12.9) or again when it is bound (20.2) which I commented on in the previous chapter; these are names which say all there is to say and leave no doubt whatever concerning the inevitability of its defeat. Together, the Rider's traits convey the same message: Messiah possesses universal sovereignty and, like the Lamb in the preceding conflict scenario (17.14), in consequence he must win. All this knocks on the head the first monster's claims, for its very 'successes' arise out of prior permission (13.7).

In this account, God, to put it bluntly, wins the last battle, as is only to be expected. Confirmation of this comes in the confident and threatening tone of the angel's invitation to the slaughterhouse banquet (19.17-18). We should take note, however, of the way the apocalyptic motif of a victory won by an ostensibly belligerent Messiah is subverted or at the very least, transformed. For clearly, this figure fights armed only with his unopposed Word. The symbolic war he has waged is barely even described as having occurred and is not narrated as such; like the angels in the inaugural conflict of Mt 4.6 and Lk 4.10-11, the heavenly armies on apparent standby do not even play a part in it (19.14). Most of all, there is blood on Messiah's cloak from before the battle is joined: could this be his own, poured out at the cross? The point is ambiguous, to say the least, given the ironic value attached to blood poured out in conquest (5.5*ff*; *cf*. 12.11).[97] Just as the Lion became the Lamb, so also 'conquer' becomes 'die'. From his first appearance (5.5), the Lamb is simultaneously a conqueror and conquered, being slain from the foundation of the world (13.8). Thus the militant and triumphant King of 19.11-16 is, in reality, Jesus the crucified man of Nazareth whose death, according to the Gospel, is a victory. As we will see in part two of this study his disciples, too, will 'conquer' by the blood of the Lamb, disarming evil with only perseverance as their weapon.

Revelation 19.19–20.10

As in the whole of the New Testament so, here, what matters about the fight fought by Messiah is simply its outcome: a just and anticipated victory over the monster and its slaves, contrasting with the unjust war they had waged on the saints. The adversaries' defeat happens in two stages, with the undoing of the two monsters occurring first (19.20-21) followed by the last exploits, defeat and final destruction of their master (20.1-10). I will examine each of these in turn. As happens also to death and Hades (20.13-14; *cf*. 6.7-8), these antagonists are finished off in strictly reverse order to their arrival on the scene. This sequence of appearance and disappearance has been represented in the form of a chiasm whose structure, in its simplest form, is like this[98]:

A = Dragon (12.3)
    B = Sea monster (13.1)
        C = Land monster or false prophet (13.11)
            D = Babylon (14.8)
                E = Worshippers of the monster (14.9-11)
                E' = Worshippers of the monster (16.2)
            D' = Babylon (16.19)
        C' = Land monster or false prophet (19.20)
    B' = Sea monster (19.20)
A' = Dragon (20.2)

From this presentation we can see straightaway how ironic is the fate of these forces opposed to God and the Lamb. Although evil's power appears to grow spectacularly during its universal campaign, its defeat has already been secured and therefore good will triumph in the end. Elegant though this attempt to cover the entire career of the forces of evil in Revelation may be, from a literary point of view, as a scheme it does admittedly have one glaring defect: the diptych of chapters 17 and 18 is passed over in total silence, with the episode of the scarlet monster totally forgotten; this makes for an incomplete proposal. If, instead, full account is taken of the episodes which arise in Rev 17 and 18, the result is a more adequate summary of the main stages of the progressive rout of evil, from our initial glimpse of the first monster (in 11.7) to the abolition of the triad of monsters (in 19.20, then 20.10). The whole sequence would then read as follows:

a) The satan is unable to prevent the preaching and resurrection of the Witnesses (chapter 11).

b) Further failure is twofold, first when attempting to kill the Son of God and then when pursuing his people (chapter 12).

c) Gaining the world and defeating believers outwardly, through the two monsters, proves to be a victory without substance (chapter 13), for despite everything Christ and his own still endure (chapter 14).

d) God is able freely to pursue his plan for the nations (chapter 15), which produces a final series of warning plagues (in chapter 16) greater in severity than the previous ones.

e) In the defeat suffered by the curious coalition of the scarlet-coated monster and Babylon-the-whore, in chapters 17 and 18, 'evil's headquarters collapses'.[99]

f) Finally, one last satanically-inspired international gathering tries to mount an attack on God, only to suffer a crushing defeat (chapter 19).

Once the horde rallied by the monster has been overcome (19.19), the dragon's two henchmen are caught and their final punishment is meted out. Since this was expected, it happens swiftly (19.20). No resistance can be offered to the sharp sword (19.15), which disposes of any opposition (19.21). Now at last an answer is given to the naive question posed, in 13.4, by the blinded 'earth-dwellers': *who can fight against it?* Readers are briefly reminded of the propaganda spewed out by the second monster and of all its great signs, but since these are no more than empty manoeuvres (19.20) they must vanish.

Sharing the same four-stage fate as its lieutenants (20.10), the dragon which came on the scene as the first member of the team from hell will be the last to leave it again, via a defeat, a short-lived upturn and then neutralisation. Deception was its characteristic activity but now it is shut away in the abyss 'to keep it from deceiving' (20.3), before being released once more to go on deceiving (20.8); then, when the countdown reaches the very last divine passive of a long list ('was hurled', 20.10), it is consigned to the fire. In these events, readers should have no difficulty spotting that the tale recounted in 12.7-11 is being retold. In the interim, there is even less to be said since no mention is now made, in chapter 20, of the satan's role as accuser: that has already been abolished (12.10). The pendulum of justice has swung back, for now the perpetual accuser of the saints before God the Judge will have to endure its own perpetual sentence, night and day (20.10). In the final analysis the career of the dragon and monsters, having lurched from one defeat to another, turns out to have been nothing but a kind of anti-story shaped around the true Messiah's career. His reign and the satan's chains exactly coincide, just as in chapter 12 the dragon's banishment had corresponded to Messiah's 'birth' or, in chapter 13, the monster's wound had been a retort to the wounds of the slain but standing Lamb.

Although all these adversaries have been active since chapter 12, once their frenzy has ceased and the parenthesis of their activity has come to an end, a simple but terse expression is all that is needed to say what God will now do. With one creative Word that seems to repeat that of Gen 1.3 he declares: 'I am making everything new' (21.5).[100] Clearly, 20.1*ff* simply brings us to the final phase of evil's ruin as told, already, by 12.9-10,13. This is related once more in 20.2-3, using a series of verbs that describe the five unstoppable actions of the angel who grabs the dragon, binds it, hurls it into the abyss, locks it away and seals it up. Its temporary release in 20.4 should cause no alarm since (from 9.1 onwards) readers are fully aware of the limits set, by God, on the hurled-down star.

Known from when time began (Gen 3), this adversary had been the first to dare to oppose God and the One responsible for the circumstances of the curse that had weighed heavily on humanity since the Fall. However, after having been forced since the cross to do its work through substitutes, it like them will now be eliminated. Glimpsed all together in 16.13, they are again seen reunited in 20.10, but only for their eternal punishment without resurrection. The dragon's imprisonment (20.3) is equivalent to its fall or to its defeat by Michael (12.7-8), or again to the fulfilment of salvation and the securing of the victory sealed by the blood of the Lamb (12.10-11): as ever in Revelation, the victory of the cross remains the preliminary to everything (1.5). Hurled out of heaven there, the dragon is of course hounded from the earth here; but the reasons for rejoicing at this now (20.6) may simply be added to those emphasised earlier (12.12). 20.4-6 represents the earthly counterpart to the heavenly event of 12.7*ff*; then, the accuser of the brothers had been banished from the heavenly court (12.10), and all restricted access to God lifted, whereas now on earth the satan is bound before being let loose temporarily (20.2 and 20.7).

If God has the last word in this story, it is because he had the first word. The stories of the dragon and monsters have spiralled downwards in inverse parallel to the Lamb's ascent. The parenthesis of evil comes to its close, now that 'the devil has been put completely out of business'[101] and now that Messiah reigns together with his own (20.4). In chapter 12 the satan's two attacks (12.1-6; 12.13-17) had been separated, and in consequence robbed of their import, by the intervening account of its defeat in heaven (12.7-12). Here, this same sandwiching technique is cleverly inverted so that the Church's victory (20.4-6) provides perspective both on the satan's initial defeat (20.1-3) and on the ultimate fate which this anticipates (20.7-10).

Readers need not have worried. When the ancient adversary gets a short reprieve (20.7*ff*) in preparation for a final showdown, two verbs in the passive – 'are over', 'will be released' (20.7) – confirm that this is to be interpreted as only a fleeting re-emergence of evil, probably inspired by Ezek 38–39, in the face of which 'God . . . decides, on his own terms, as though he were making the Dragon his plaything.'[102] When fire falls from heaven (20.9) and more verbs in the passive complete the account – 'was hurled', 'will be tormented' (20.10), which correspond exactly to those of 20.7 – then all is said and done: 'this time, ruin for the satan and its allies is total'.[103] Their last assault on God (20.7*ff*) fails miserably and the devil and its allies are consigned to the second death, a point of no return (20.14). This had been anticipated in the death of Jesus, by means of which the plan of salvation was finally accomplished.

We should notice, here, that identical logic (involving death, healing and a return) applies to the satan as had previously been the case for its two servants (13.3; 17.8-11). That is to say, final destruction at the hand of God must befall it, too. The hostility, here, is not to be thought of as 'fundamental, eternal, heavenly'[104] in nature – which a dualistic view of things might suggest – but is rather an earthly, partial and temporary kind of opposition by means of which a creature had sought in vain to defy its Creator. So the people of God, knowing that he will ultimately have the victory over evil in all its guises, have the wherewithal to stay faithful (to the death, if necessary) because, in their reign together with Messiah, they find concrete proof of the dragon's certain defeat. Ironically, even its apparent victory brings them closer to heaven where they will forever be beyond reach.

Revelation 21.1–22.5

Throughout Revelation's final vision, the consequences of the eradication of the forces of evil, in the lake of fire, make themselves felt. As they disappear, so too the elements of the old order are dissolved, yielding to the new creation in which evil is no longer to find a haven. One after another, the former things fade away: the first heaven and earth, and the sea (21.1); death, and with it, mourning, tears and suffering (21.4); the ancient curse (22.3); night and, by implication, the sun or the moon (21.23; 22.5). It is as though the dis-creation of the satan removes the last obstacle to the re-creation of a universe in which all memory of Adam and Eve's conquest by the serpent is erased once and for all. God's victory has established a renewed covenant (21.3b-4; 22.3b-4), whose Mediator, the conqueror of sin and death, bequeaths to his co-victors a relationship of filial closeness to their God (21.7).

Several references to the triumph of divine lordship, in 22.1-5, bring aptly to its conclusion the major theme I have tried to trace throughout this chapter. In New Jerusalem is to be found the very 'throne of God and of the Lamb' (22.1,3) which, on page after page, has so often held our attention. Repeatedly, it is the question of 'who reigns?' that has been asked and the only answer that fits is the one we find underscored here for the very last time: *God and the Lamb*. Then it is stated that the vassals of God and the Lamb 'will reign forever and ever' (22.5). What is fulfilled here, as the plot finds its denouement, is the promise made in 3.21, the icing on the cake of assurances already given by the Risen One to Asian Christians, throughout the septet of oracles. Ever since the cross the victorious Lamb has had a share, in principle, in the Father's throne (*cf.* 1.4b-5; 3.21b); now, however, in a scenario which recalls the one described to Peter by Jesus in Mt 19.28, the new world is brought to completion, the Lamb is seated in glory and those who have followed him are seated next to him.

Being 'seated' can also be explained as serving or worshipping him (22.3c; *cf.* 7.15). That is why my next chapter begins where this one ends, as we move on to discover a third main facet of the way God is represented in Revelation: true adoration of God and the Lamb, together with its caricature, bogus worship.

Notes

1 W. Harrington, *Revelation*, Collegeville, Michael Glazier, 1993, p.32.

2 Exactly how this career should be divided into three parts is a matter for debate. A. Schlatter, *Die Briefe und Offenbarung des Johannes*, Stuttgart, 1938, *in loc*, made the three designations correspond to the three distinct moments of the incarnation, resurrection and return of Christ. Picking up on this idea, Beasley-Murray, *Revelation*, p.56, nevertheless prefers to see in them the three phases of his death, resurrection and ascension.

3 Similarly J.W. Mealy, *After the Thousand Years: Resurrection and Judgment in Revelation 20*, Sheffield, JSNTSS, 1992, p.72.

4 Specialists who have given thought to the way Jesus's royalty is characterised in Revelation are few and far between. For this reason, it is well worth consulting the discussion in L.L. Thompson, *The Book of Revelation: Apocalypse and Empire*, Oxford/New York, Oxford University Press, 1990, especially pp.189 and 200. Also, see now my own article 'Royauté' and the literature cited there.

5 Prévost, *Apocalypse*, p.49 (my translation). For a detailed discussion of the linguistic problem caused by the translation of the verb *poimanein* (shepherd; shatter), I refer readers to Aune, *Revelation 1-5* (vol. 1), pp.210-11.

6 This is how the divine name will be rendered throughout this book.

7 See Aune, *ibid.*, p.306.

8 Similarly, in 12.5, 'all nations' modifies the very same allusion.

9 *Kratos* may be translated in various ways. E.g. Ellul, *Architecture*, p.253, proposes victory, government, triumph and reign.

10 For a helpful presentation, in tabular form, of these parallels see Celia Deutsch, on page 124 of her article 'Transformation of Symbols: The New Jerusalem in Rev 21.1-22.5', *Zeitschrift für die neutestamentliche Wissenschaft* 78, 1987, pp.106-26. The question has been taken up by Beale, *Revelation*, pp.134-35 and pp.1057-58.

11 On this, compare Mealy, *Thousand Years*, pp.80-81, 89.

12 As for example Prévost, *Apocalypse*, p.36, whose suggestive reading identifies three 'fronts'. A first front line is traced through the communities themselves (true or false apostles; appeals for discernment). Another front involves facing up to the practices and institutions of Judaism (meat offered to idols; 'synagogue of the satan'). Finally, a third front is directed against Roman power ('throne of the satan'; death of Antipas; persecution for ten days). See my own remarks on this subject in A. Kuen, *Introduction au Nouveau Testament: L'Apocalypse*, St.-Légier, 1997, ch. 4. 'Les Eglises destinataires', p.39, n.1.

13 G. Campbell, in some correspondence alluded to by Kuen, *Introduction*, p.39, n. 1. I will be dealing with the specific problem of the interpretation of Revelation's cities in ch. 6 of the present book.

14 See for example my article 'Pour lire l'Apocalypse de Jean: l'intérêt d'une approche thématique', *Revue Réformée* 224 (2003/4), p.63, where I formulate four types of historical questioning which are suggested by the findings of my work on the theme of worship and liturgy. All four points are reproduced in full below – see Historical Detour 5 in the next chapter, 'Legitimate adoration and bogus worship'.

15 Prévost, *Apocalypse*, p.39 (my translation).

16 On this point, see the remarks of Schüssler-Fiorenza, *Justice and Judgment*, pp.47-48.

17 It is not only the promises to victors which anticipate the later narrative but, as Thompson points out, *Apocalypse*, p.179, its symbols, images and metaphors will also recur farther on. For H. Ulland, *Die Vision als Radikaliserung der Wirklichkeit in der Apokalypse des Johannes*, Tübingen/Basle, Francke Verlag, 1997, p.324, the visionary drama of Rev 4–21 actually rests upon the analyses, values and demands laid down in the oracles. For G.K. Beale, too, *John's Use of the Old Testament in Revelation*, Sheffield, 1998, pp.315-16, the two parts of the Book interpret one another; in a similar manner to parables, the symbolical visions of ch. 4–22 seem to develop the propositions (exhortations, warnings and promises) of ch. 2–3. Although I agree with Beale that chs. 4–22 do elaborate on what is sketched in the first septet, in contrast to him I find the oracles to be every bit as symbolical or parabolical as what follows them.

Some exegetes consider 22.6*ff*, like ch. 1–3, to have been written later than 4.1–22.5. On this view, everything which links the first septet, in an organic way, to the rest of Revelation, would be the upshot of a powerful *distillation*. Alternatively, if the oracles septet provides the outline from which the remaining septets are worked out, and the fabric from which they are all woven, we would be talking about a splendid *orchestration* of leitmotifs introduced in the first septet. As I see it, the second option is better at explaining how, in chs. 12–13 alone (for example), fifty or so items encountered in Rev 1–3 (according to Ulland's list, p.327) reappear. It is easier to imagine how these chapters could have given pictorial development to so many elements from the first septet than it is to postulate, on the opposite view, some later process of abstraction.

18 For discussion of this cosmic framework, see J. Fekkes, *Visionary Antecedents*, p.143.

19 Exegetes have put forward three possible lines of interpretation for what is happening when the Lamb receives the scroll from the hand of God. One is an *investiture*. Another is an *enthronement* (or, a coronation), accompanied by court ceremonial for which Dn 4.34-37 or *1 Enoch* offer analogies. The third is a *dispatch*,

which either authorises its bearer to answer a question or else corresponds
to other anticipated eventualities. In an excursus Aune, *Revelation 1-5* (vol. 1),
pp.332-37, makes his choice by calling the scene an *investiture*, by analogy with
Dan 7.9-18, Ezek 1–2 and above all Ezek 2.9-10 (where the scroll comes from),
as well as mentioning reminiscences of 1 Kgs 22 and Isa 6. However, this leads
him into incoherence later on regarding 13.2, in *Revelation 6-16* (vol. 2), p.735,
when he calls *enthronement* the obviously antithetical handover of power by the
dragon to the first monster!

It is preferable to acknowledge the presence, in this text, of elements drawn
simultaneously from all three, an *investiture*, an *enthronement* and a *dispatch*. Due
weight should also be given to the imprint of the theme of royalty (with five
references to the throne) upon the slaughtered Lamb who, notwithstanding his
weakness and wounds, comes to God and finds acceptance from him as true
Sovereign over earth's kings (*cf.* 1.5). 5.12 confirms that when the Lamb receives
the scroll, what is meant is that he receives power and honour. I might add that
the Lamb, here, does not receive his own status or dignity. For Revelation, that
is something he already possesses from the start by virtue of the victory he has
already won at the cross. This is the prerequisite which allows him to receive
all honours, as was stated by W.C. van Unnik, '"Worthy is the Lamb" - the
background of Apoc 5', in *Mélanges Bida Rigaux*, Gembloux, 1970, pp.445-61.

20 A comparison may be drawn, in the OT, with the installation among the
powerful which is promised to the poor in Hannah's Song (1 Sam 2.8).

21 At this point, I am further developing the presentation of the throne theme in
my article 'Royauté', especially pp.50-52.

22 Compare Friesen, *Cults*, p.163.

23 Like John M. Court, *Reading the New Testament*, London, 1997, I have found 47
occurrences; here is the complete list of these references: 1.4; 2.13; 3.21 (2x); 4.2-
4 (3x), 4.5 (2x), 4.6 (3x), 4.9-10 (2x); 5.1,6,7,11,13; 6.16; 7.9-11(2x), 7.15 (2x), 7.17;
8.3; 11.16; 12.5; 13.2; 14.3; 16.10,17; 19.4-5; 20.4,11-12; 21.3,5; 22.1,3. I would draw
the same conclusion as E. Cothenet, *Message*, p.63: 'the theme of power underlies
the entire unfolding of these two scenes. This is how John's vision answers a
question underlying the entire Book, namely, who is it that really exercises power
in a world where the forces of evil appear to triumph?' (my translation).

24 As M. Carrez puts it so well, 'Déploiement', p.5 (my translation). What does this
throne fundamentally mean? For Beasley-Murray, *Revelation*, p.112, the throne
signifies the sovereign power of God whilst God's work consists precisely in the
fact that he reigns.

25 D.E. Aune, *Revelation 6-16* (vol. 2), p.736, draws attention to a parallel in the
second *Apocalypse of Enoch* 29.4, where the satan's attempt to establish its throne
near to God's provokes its expulsion, as happens similarly in the *Apocalypse of
Moses* 39.2 (or, *of Adam and Eve*, 47.3).

26 On the matter of Old Testament antecedents, see especially the recent study by
H.-D. Neef, *Gottes himmlischer Thronrat. Hintergrund und Bedeutung von sôd JHWH
im Alten Testament*, Stuttgart, Calwer, 1994, pp.62-67, 'Neutestamentlicher
Ausblick: Gottes himmlischer Thronrat in Apk 4,1-11'. As for inter-testamental
literature, the short and recent article by M. Philonenko, 'Une voix sortit du
trône qui disait . . . (Apocalypse 19,5a)', *Revue d'Histoire et de Philosophie Religieuses*
79, 1999, pp.83-89, is a profitable read. It evaluates the current situation or
'new context' (p.85) opened up, for exegesis of Revelation, by Jewish *merkaba*

mysticism and in particular the *Hêkhâlôt* in which similar formulae for speaking of God's throne are to be found, together with discussions of the voice issuing from the throne. 'The voice coming from the throne, he says, is the voice of the personified throne. The johannine formula is a simple copy of the Jewish formula' (p.88, my translation). Philonenko mentions five scenes which particularly have to do with the throne (p.83: 4.2–6.17; 11.15-19; 14.1-5; 15.2-8; 19.1-8); to these should also be added a crucial final one which for some reason he omits, involving the great white throne (20.11).

27 *Architecture*, p.48 (my translation).

28 The French *Traduction œcuménique de la Bible* understands this expression 'in a messianic sense: it signifies how the Christ has received total authority and how his judgment cannot be appealed' (my translation of the relevant note).

29 Numerous commentators have linked this throne to the Temple of Zeus; others have read into it the Pergamum acropolis understood as an anti-mountain of God symbolising false worship (including that given to the emperor); still others have thought that the Temple dedicated to the emperor, which was the city's most imposing sacred building, best explains this 'throne'. Nothing in the text can either confirm or disallow any of these suggestions.

30 I am presupposing, here, very close correspondence between Rev 4 and 5 on the one hand and chs. 12 and 13 on the other. This was established by E.-B. Allo and confirmed by the thesis of H.-P. Müller, *Formgeschichtliche Untersuchungen zu Apok.4f*, Heidelberg, 1962, whose work was taken up in turn by G.K. Beale, *The Use of Daniel in Jewish Apocalyptic Literature and in the Revelation of John*, Lanham, University Press of America, 1984.

31 In similar vein, L. Lafont, *L'Apocalypse de Saint Jean*, Paris, Téqui, 1975, p.54, says this: 'Satan, God's ape, calls forth the sea monster as God had called forth his Messiah' (my translation).

32 Quoting Brütsch, *Clarté*, p.224 (my translation) in a note which picks up a comment of A. Schlatter, *Die Offenbarung des Johannes*, Stuttgart, Calwer, 1910, p.145.

3 R.H. Mounce also reads it this way, *The Book of Revelation*, Grand Rapids, Eerdmans, 1998, 2nd edn, p.251.

34 It is correct to say with E. Stauffer, *Die Theologie des Neuen Testaments*, Stuttgart, Kohlhammer, 1948, p.51, that the New Testament has no theology which does not also include demonology, but that it is the former which always has the last word. The satan cannot escape the parameters set for it as a creature and imposed on it by the Creator. This is the context into which Revelation's parody of things divine should be set. On this question see M. Rissi, *Was ist und was geschehen soll danach. Die Zeit und Geschichtsauffassung der Offenbarung des Johannes*, Zurich/Stuttgart, Zwingli Verlag, 1965, p.67.

35 In his study *Revelation Unsealed*, p.103*ff*, Resseguie classifies Revelation's principal and secondary characters, together with the Book's various images, into two antithetical categories which pit 'apocalyptic' characters or images (we could also call them 'idealised') against others which he dubs 'counterfeit' or 'demonic'; see his table on p. 104 and the accompanying commentary (pp.103-5). On this matter we can compare Barr, *Tales*, pp.106-14, who develops a double typology which differentiates *antagonists* (as characters that generate destruction) from *protagonists* (as agents of preservation or passive recipients of its benefits). For Barr, this double typology only becomes operative after Rev 11.19*ff* where he locates the beginning of the Book's third story-within-a-story. However, this

is to misread the Book's compositional logic, which as we have seen, arms spectator-readers with what they will need *later* for detecting, just beneath the surface of the conflict they will encounter, how God still triumphs.

36 Brütsch, *Clarté*, p.211 (my translation).

37 For an examination of the parallelism between the scenarios in 12.7-11 and 20.1-10, see again my article 'Royauté', p.57-59. Exegetes have largely concentrated on the origins of the dragon's story and taken it to be a creative association of diverse mythological elements. For example, it has been regarded as a free adaptation of the widespread Leto/Apollo/Python myth, well known in Asia Minor, or as a combination of the story of the Python's defeat and the ancient Semitic myth of the victory over Leviathan. In Prigent's view, *Apocalypse*, p.381, following M. Kiddle, *The Revelation of St. John*, London, Hodder and Stoughton, 1940, p.228, the delta dragon, standing for the Pharaoh of the Exodus with whom God joins battle (in Ezek 29.3 and Ezek 32), could be the primary reference for the text of Rev here.

38 As the French *Traduction œcuménique de la Bible* notes at this point, Michael's significance (for Judaism) as Israel's intercessor and as opponent of the satan-accuser, rests on these texts from Dn.

39 For Ellul, *Architecture*, p.261, it is in the incarnation that God 'came in on man's side, in a covenant so deep that there will no longer be any accuser or any accusation before God' (my translation). Through the new beginning that is the incarnation, the forces of evil have lost their power; they can no longer win even if they may still accuse human beings and bring them to destruction.

40 G. Campbell, 'Royauté', p.56.

41 Prigent, *Apocalypse*, p.392, following Swete, *Apocalypse*, p156, at this point.

42 For a study (wider in its scope than just Revelation) of the ambivalence of place as well as of time, readers should consult O. Böcher, *Das Neue Testament und die dämonischen Mächte*, Stuttgart, 1972, ch. 2 'Ort und Zeit der Dämonen', p.22*ff.* This author shows just how ambivalent can be each of the elements fire, water, air and of course earth – comprising desert, mountain or abyss – as well as time (particularly night and darkness).

43 C. Brütsch, *Clarté*, p.207 (my translation).

44 For R. Bauckham, *Climax*, pp.185-86, the originality of the picture painted here by John is the way evil's decisive defeat, in the blood of the Lamb, is depicted as the fall of a great red dragon already conquered in the past, in heaven, before having to take its chances on earth.

45 On this point, compare R.W. Wall, *Revelation*, Peabody, Hendrickson, 1991, p.161.

46 So Kraft, *Offenbarung*, p.172.

47 For an exhaustive look at the interpretations of this book suggested by exegetes, see the discussion in Aune, *Revelation 1-5* (vol. 1), pp.338-46.

48 Moyise, *Old Testament*, p.133, thinks our author is leaving unresolved, at this point, what could be called a *dialogical tension*, by setting in dialogue elements of his work which appear at first sight to be irreconcilable (lion and lamb). The same concept was used by J.P. Ruiz, *Ezekiel in the Apocalypse: The Transformation of Prophetic Language in Revelation 16.17-19.10*, Frankfurt, Peter Lang, 1989, p.104.

49 An examination of the metaphor 'power through weakness' can be found in the study by H. Giesen, 'Symbole und mythische Aussagen in der Johannesapokalypse und ihre theologische Bedeutung', in *Metaphorik und Mythos im Neuen Testament*, Freiburg/Basle/Vienna, Herder, 1990, p.260.

50 Similarly Prigent, *Apocalypse*, p.252.

51 On this matter, see the excursus 'Der Sieg des Lammes' by Pohl, *Offenbarung* (vol. 1), p.178.

52 For a brief discussion of various possible antecedents, see my article 'Procédé', pp.501-2.

53 For a theoretical treatment of how image and anti-image correspond in Revelation, see P. Trummer, *Aufsätze zum Neuen Testament*, Graz, Eigenverlag, 1987, ch. 6 'Offenbarung in Bildern: zur Bildersprache der Apokalypse. Eine Skizze', §4 'Gegenbilder', pp.192-203. According to Trummer, there are several variants to the anti-image of the Lamb. G. Glonner, *Zur Bildersprache der Johannes von Patmos. Untersuchung der Johannesapokalypse anhand einer um Elemente der Bilderinterpretation erweiterten historisch-kritischen Methode*, Münster, Aschendorff, 1999, takes Trummer's work farther and suggests that the power of the imagery in ch. 13 be attributed to the way traits which might distinguish the Lamb from the monsters are all but eradicated (p.264).

54 For example, E. Schüssler-Fiorenza, *Justice and Judgment*, p.129, for whom Revelation offers its target readership the vision of another world, with a view to improving morale and strengthening resistance in the face of a threat, posed to them by Babylon/Rome, that could rob them of life's essentials or even of life itself.

55 L.L. Thompson, *Apocalypse*, p.175, notes these two variations; they correspond to the points of view of J. Gager and A. Yarbro-Collins respectively.

56 See further the penetrating critique by Thompson, *ibid.*, pp.174-75, who locates the logic of conflict that can be detected in Revelation, not in the vicissitudes which John and his addressees have experienced but rather, in a theological vision of society for which 'Church' and 'world' represent antagonistic forces.

57 In this connection Thompson, 'Mapping', p.120*ff*, speaks of *passports between the mythical and the historical*: 'the throne/city centers the mythic dimension of John's world, while Asian cities center the historical dimension of his world . . . the mythic, cosmic throne/city is an extension or expansion of the historical. A boundary exists between the mythic and the historical . . . a transformational boundary, a point of crossing or passing through'.

58 I am happy to adopt, at this point, the wise and measured approaches to the monster's characteristics (in 13.1-7) taken by Ellul, *Architecture*, pp.92-94.

59 For a more developed analysis of what I present here, readers should again consult my article 'Procédé', pp.503-9.

60 For understanding the dragon's dispatch of its monster as a parody of God sending his Son, see for example A. Pohl, *Offenbarung* (vol. 2), p.124.

61 Corsini, *Apocalypse*, p.365, for whom the satan's defeat, here, is not to be read as future but as already past, as having been accomplished at the cross.

62 Although I do not share it, C. Rowland's interpretation may be mentioned here (*Revelation*, p.113). He prefers to read these passives not as divine permission but rather as (tacit) human acquiescence: if ever Caesar or Mammon should succeed in usurping what belongs to God alone, it will have been *our* fault.

63 This definite period of time corresponds exactly to the one during which the Church is afflicted or protected, *i.e.* one thousand two hundred and sixty days or three-and-a-half years (11.2; 12.6,14). It follows that the monster cannot escape the rules which govern all human history between the moment the new covenant was inaugurated and its consummation one day.

64 6.10; 8.13; 11.10 twice; 13.8; 3.14 twice; 17.8; and finally, with variations, in 13.12; 14.6; 17.2. Aune, *Revelation 1-5* (vol. 1), p.240, cannot see the antithetical parallel and so is content to gloss the expression with the rather lame paraphrase 'non-Christian persecutors of Christians'.

65 Similarly Beale, *Revelation*, p.698.

66 In ch. 5 I will return to Revelation's optimism about what the success which faithful proclamation of the gospel will encounter.

67 This is Bauckham's view, *Climax*, pp.233-35. His discussion presupposes that John's Revelation is a Christian adaptation of a war scroll. Christians, he argues, found themselves impotent in the face of the irresistible power of Rome and of pagan society (the monster); for them, resisting compromise could only mean victimisation. Revelation allowed them to see their own faithful witness as the means of combatting and defeating the monster: as re-read in light of the suffering of the slain-but-standing Lamb, their own suffering would then be the way to have a victory over political or military might.

   Aside from the question of whether it is in fact a legitimate move to decode the sea monster as standing for Rome or pagan society, the problem with this proposal leaps from the page. It assumes that believers in the Crucified and Risen One living, at the close of the first century (according to the dating to which Bauckham subscribes), in Asia – a territory sown with the seed of Paul's gospel – did not grasp the cruciform shape of their lives, as followers of the Crucified One, until they read this in Revelation's message!

68 Bauckham, *Climax*, p.451.

69 A. Deissmann, *Light from the Ancient East*, New York/London, 1910, p.346; E. Stauffer, *Christ and the Caesars*, London (tr. SCM Press), 1955, ch.10 'Domitian and John', especially pp.175-77, 191. See also, more recently, P. Barnett, 'Polemical Parallelism: Some Further Reflections on the Apocalypse', *Journal for the Study of the New Testament* 35, 1989, pp.111-20.

70 In a rubric entitled 'Either God, or Satan', F. Vouga, *Geschichte des frühen Christentums*, Tübingen/Basle, Francke Verlag, 1994, pp.261-62, proposes to find the clearest example of the theme of political dissent in Rev 12.1–13.18. For this exegete, John drew from the well of radical apocalyptic tradition what he needed for expressing a critique of Roman totalitarianism. His aim was to counter a certain legitimacy given, in the Churches of Asia, to the Roman state and to combat a desire for passive co-existence with it by a rejoinder which was a broadside that demonised the state. For S. Friesen, *Cults*, even if Rev 11 ought not to be squeezed to extract the juice of historical references (p.143), ch. 13–19 would indeed seem to allude to forms of emperor worship (pp.145-47) and therefore contribute a criticism levelled, by John, not just at worship or institutions of society, but at the whole imperial system and way of life (p.151). Lastly, and in similar vein, E. Cuvillier, in 'Christ ressuscité ou bête immortelle? Proclamation pascale et propagande impériale dans l'Apocalypse de Jean', in D. Marguerat and O. Mainville (ed.), *Résurrection. L'après-mort dans le monde ancien et le Nouveau Testament*, Geneva/Montreal, Labor et Fides/MediasPaul, 2001, thinks the sea monster's 'resurrection' is designed to show the invincibility and immortality of imperial power whereas, for John, God has sovereignly raised up a crucified man as Lord.

71 So F. Mussner, ,'Weltherrschaft' als eschatologisches Thema der Johannesapokalypse', in E. Grässer and O. Merk, *Glaube und Eschatologie: Festschrift W.G. Kümmel*, Tübingen, Mohr, 1985, for example pp.219-22.

72 I am taking what follows mainly from my presentation of a 'second back-up anti-lamb' in my article 'Procédé', pp.509-10.

73 Prigent, *Apocalypse*, p.399, attributes this to Irenaeus, without giving a precise reference to his writings.

74 For Beasley-Murray, *Revelation*, p.216, this re-use is a touch of genius on the part of the author of Revelation.

75 Allo, *Apocalypse*, p.210 (my translation).

76 For a good summary of the correspondences between the Lamb and the two monsters, see Thompson, *Revelation*, pp.81-82. I cannot follow this author, however, when he suggests that these correspondences tend to blur or make hazy the distinction between good and evil. Quite the contrary: in my view, wherever this might have happened they show, instead, just where the frontiers lie! F.J. Murphy, *Fallen is Babylon: The Revelation to John*, Harrisburg, Morehouse, 1998, p.196, also sees it this way; so, more recently still, does Friesen, *Cults*, p.162.

77 For this paragraph, I am once more using the corresponding features suggested in my article 'Procédé', p.510.

78 This is how K.A. Strand reads it, 'The Two Witnesses of Rev 11.3-12', *Andrews University Seminary Studies* 19, 1981, pp.127-35.

79 For Bauckham, *Climax*, p.447, this second monster is the satanic counterpart of Elijah.

80 The dragon figure is an anti-creator; so V.S. Poythress, 'Counterfeiting in the Book of Revelation as a Perspective on Non-Christian culture', *Journal of the Evangelical Theological Society* 40, 1997, pp.411-12.

81 Instead of being seen as an anti-trinity, here, this triple alliance is occasionally set against a pagan backdrop (Zeus-Poseidon-Hades), as Böcher does in *Mächte*, p.32.

82 Aune, *Revelation 6-16* (vol. 2), pp.771-73 – *cf.* Prigent, *Apocalypse*, pp.423-7 – reviews three approaches: 1) Multiple interprétations of 666 which rely on gematria, a procedure that involves adding up (in Hebrew or Greek) the numerical value of letters so as to decipher a hidden name; 2) Solutions which are based on triangular numbers; 3) Various ways, lastly, of reading the number symbolically. Aune himself favours solving the enigma 666 by gematria. However, it has to be admitted with Beale, *Revelation*, pp.718-28, that any such identification of the name is simply irretrievable today. More fundamentally, it is my firm conviction (against many commentators, I must admit) that it is quite simply wrong to interpret 13.18's call for discernment, from ancient or contemporary readers, as an invitation to engage in deciphering or decoding.

83 For Ellul, *Architecture*, pp.97-98, 666 admirably conveys an oppositional element. It is a cipher for imperfection (or accumulated imperfections), triply opposed to the number of perfection (777) which it is always trying to attain, but without ever reaching.

84 In this and subsequent chapters, reference to 'Jezebel' in inverted commas is deliberate, so as to draw attention to the symbolic significance of the name as used here in Revelation (*i.e.* as evoking connotations that derive from historical OT Jezebel).

85 Brütsch, *Clarté*, p.192.

86 For Kraft, *Offenbarung*, p.161, the accession ritual of chs. 4 and 5 only comes to an end at this point, when the acclamations of 4.11 and 5.9,12, anticipating a reign worthy of God, turn into thanksgivings for his successfully completed work.

87 Brütsch, *Clarté*, pp.265-66 (my translation).

88 Prévost, *Apocalypse*, p.125 (my translation).

89 I have already suggested this corrective in my article 'Royauté', p.53; see my discussion there, including note 14.

90 The expression comes from Comblin, *Christ*, p.20 (my translation).

91 In the following pages, given over mainly to the triumph of the rider (in 19.11-16) and to the end of both the monsters and dragon (19.19-20.10), I am again drawing inspiration mainly from my discussion already published in 'Royauté', pp.53-59.

92 See Mealy, *Thousand Years*, p.70.

93 As G. Stemberger puts it so well in *Symbolisme*, p.191 (my translation).

94 See, for example, A. Pohl, *Offenbarung* (vol. 1), pp.195-97. For another well-argued viewpoint which sees the first rider as a triumphal victor with a positive role, compare H. Giesen, *Im Dienst der Weltherrschaft Gottes und des Lammes: Die vier apokalyptischen Reiter (Offb 6.1-8)*, Stuttgart, SNTU, 1997, pp.92-109. Also, for a recent exchange on the subjet see M. Bachmann, 'Noch ein Blick auf den ersten apokalyptischen Reiter (von Apk. 6.1-2)', *New Testament Studies* 44, 1998, pp.257-78. In response, J.C. Poirier, 'The First Rider', *New Testament Studies* 45, 1999, pp.257-62, as well as (in the same issue, pp.230-249) the study by J. Herzer, 'Der erste apokalyptische Reiter und der König der Könige. Ein Beitrag zur Christologie der Johannes-apokalypse'.

95 In Beale, *Revelation*, pp.375-79, can be found a list of seven reasons which are nevertheless put forward in defence of this exegetical option, together with eight further considerations listed as supporting the stance I adopt here.

96 In his article 'King of kings, Lord of lords (Apoc.19.16)', *Catholic Biblical Quarterly* 10, 1948, p.398, Patrick Skehan notes the intriguing fact that the consonants that make up this title, when translated into Aramaic, have a value of 777 (by gematria) – a worthy counterpart to 666!

97 Although Revelation borrows its *form* from its source at this point (Isaiah 63), enabling the painting of a picture of God winning the last battle and putting an end to his enemies, it gives this a new *content*. On this see, for instance, Harrington, *Revelation*, pp.193-95, or more recently C. Koester, *Revelation And The End Of All Things*, Grand Rapids/Cambridge, Eerdmans, 2001, p.176. Beale, *Revelation*, pp.958-59, argues for the judicial import of Messiah's blood, since he is the agent of divine judgment, whilst acknowledging the ironic value of blood that is shed in victory (5.5*ff* and 12.11).

98 This proposal comes from W. Shea, 'The Parallel Literary Structure of Revelation 12 and 20', *Andrews University Seminary Studies* 23, 1985, pp.37-54, who takes over a chiasm suggested by his colleague K.A. Strand, 'Chiasmic Structure and Some Motifs in the Book of Revelation', *Andrews University Seminary Studies* 16, 1978, p.403.

99 Brütsch, *Clarté*, p.320 (my translation); my summary follows his at this precise point.

100 Charlier, *Comprendre* (vol. 2), p.207, puts it well: 'God only has to be 'doing' one deed and this is enough to cause the new world, God's world, to break forth! There is a sharp contrast, here, with the Sea Monster's two 'doings' and the Land Monster's eight' (my translation).

101 This good way of putting it is from Brütsch, *Clarté*, p.322 (my translation).

102 Charlier, *Comprendre* (vol. 2), p.178 (my translation).

103 Prévost, *Apocalypse*, p.160 (my translation).

104 I am borrowing these well-chosen epithets from Prigent, *Apocalypse*, p.575.

3. Legitimate adoration and bogus worship

'If we were allowed only one key to the understanding of Revelation, we should have to choose "worship"' (C. Le Moignan).[1]

The data in Revelation which relate to the story of God and the Lamb and their antagonists have been assembled and analysed in two stages, in the course of the two previous chapters. In chapter 1, first, we went in search of characters and anti-characters characterised by divinity and pseudo-divinity. Our special interest was identity and we took particular note of how the characteristics of the protagonists – the Seated One on the throne, the Risen One/Lamb/Messianic Rider, and the Spirit or seven spirits – were caricatured by those of their antagonists the dragon, the sea monster, the land monster or false prophet and the monster with the scarlet pelt. The legitimate lordship of the former and the rival usurping claims of the latter were explored in chapter 2, as we delved deeper into the question of how God and the Lamb preside over a plan of salvation, brought into effect by a victory of cosmic proportions and, in tandem with this, how their adversaries engage in activities that will lead, in the end, to nothing but their own fall and ruin.

In order to complete Part One of our study – *God reveals himself* – we now need to factor in the liturgical and cultic colouring which Revelation gives to its presentation of this story.[2] Whilst, Revelation specialists now generally acknowledge the importance of the liturgical register of the Book and especially of its hymnic material, a more exhaustive study will be attempted here.[3] This will take us off the beaten track as we follow every twist and turn of the contrasting theme which comprises both worship (of God and the Lamb) and its counterfeit. We will be concerned, on the one hand, with the true adoration through which humanity is transported to heaven into the presence of the God it worships, and on the other hand by bogus worship which catapults humanity down into the abyss where the dragon dwells. This is a thematic vector which will take us into the heart of Revelation, since 'a major theme of this book is the distinction between true worship and idolatry.'[4]

As I sought to map out, as extensively as possible, the developing trajectory of true worship and its bogus counterpart in Revelation, I found myself face-to-face with a specific problem. It was not enough to study scattered hymnic fragments or a variety of moments with a distinctly cultic character: to trace out this theme I would need to cast the net more widely (as it were) and take full account of a phenomenon not visible to the eye in the text of Revelation as normally set out in our Bibles. I am referring to the constantly alternating use of narrative and direct speech throughout the Book, and to the fact that material of relevance to true worship or to its caricature are to be found in both. I therefore faced the practical difficulty that readers would need to see what their open Bibles generally fail to make clear.

My solution is that this chapter will systematically present readers both with my commentary and with the relevant texts themselves. My starting-point is the *New Revised Standard Version*, although I modify its renderings in many cases; I have included all the passages in question and I use a type-setting which allows readers to distinguish narration from speech at every point: all the narrative materials appear in italics, whilst all passages in direct speech are both non-italic and indented. Finally, the whole is set out in such a way as to facilitate reading aloud.[5]

Revelation 1.1-8

From the beginning of the narrative and until its close, the action of Revelation's plot is cast in a carefully crafted liturgical framework. It opens with a conditional benediction or beatitude, spoken first over the liturgist or reader whose task it will be to undertake a public reading of this prophecy, and then over the assembled worshippers who hear it read. Straight away, it is clear that for all those present that such a hearing must result in their obedience (1.3). Next, there comes an epistolary greeting from the seer, 'John', who puts into words an opening benediction that finds its triple source in God, the seven spirits of his presence and Messiah Jesus (v.4-5a). This is extended by means of speech involving dialogue, where the 'we/us' of 1.5b-6 connotes the worship assembly to which the revelation is sent, together with their liturgist(s) and perhaps John himself. A doxology focusing on the fruits of redemption won by the One 'who loves us' is followed by a first 'amen' (v.5b-6). Then, in terms borrowed from Zech 12.10 and Dn 7.13, comes testimony which anticipates the imminent coming in glory of the exalted Christ, complete with a dual 'yes/amen' (in Greek and Hebrew) by way of conclusion (v.7). Finally, God himself, 'the Alpha and Omega', from whom the revelation is ultimately derived (*cf.* 1.1), begins to speak (v.8) – just as, a little later and in parallel fashion, the Risen One will also address his Church and describe himself in his turn as, among other things, the 'First and Last' (*cf.* 1.11-12,17-19).[6]

It is difficult to identify with certainty each distinct utterance that makes a contribution to the opening liturgical dialogue, or to say just how many speakers or voices are involved – whether the seer, one or more liturgist(s) or the gathered assembly, and whether they speak alone or in unison. Nevertheless, the following is one possible arrangement of the various statements that make up the prologue (1.1-8), with the descriptive elements in italics. I have tried to bring out the prologue's antiphonal character.

Revelation of Jesus Christ
. . . which God gave him to show his slaves what must soon take place
and which he made known by sending his angel to his slave John . . .
Word of God and Testimony of Jesus Christ,
seen by John, who has testified [to it].

Blessed is the public reader
And those who hear the words of the prophecy
And who keep what is written in it!

For the time is near!

John, to the seven churches that are in Asia:
Grace to you and peace
From the Is, the Was and the Coming [One]
And from the seven spirits who are before his throne,
And from Jesus Christ, the Faithful Witness,
The First-born of the dead
And the Sovereign over earth's kings!

To Him who loved us,
Who freed us from our sins by his blood
And made us to be a kingdom,
Priests serving his God and Father,
To him [be] glory and dominion forever and ever!

Amen!

Look! He is coming with the clouds!
Every eye will see him, even those who pierced him,
And on his account all the tribes of the earth will wail!

Yes, amen!

'I am the Alpha and the Omega,'
says the Lord God
The Is, the Was and the Coming [One], the Almighty!

At its climax, Revelation will culminate in another antiphonal dialogue of a more elaborate nature than this opening one and the Lord Jesus himself will participate in it, more than once. It will feature two beatitudes, several attestations as to the authenticity of the prophetic Word and (once again) various exhortations to be faithful; we will come back to this at the close of the present chapter.

Such a cultic framework is perfectly suited to a self-disclosure where God makes himself known in Jesus Christ (1.1) who is, was and is coming (1.4,8). As will be made explicit in due course we find ourselves gathered on the Lord's Day (1.10). Sunday, the first day of the week, was between his resurrection and ascension, the moment when the Risen Jesus made himself present with his disciples (*cf.* Mt 28.1,9-10 ; Lk 24.1,13,15*ff*,36*ff*; Jn 20.*14ff*,19*ff*,26*ff*). Under the new covenant instituted by the Risen Messiah, this day of resurrection came quite naturally to replace the Sabbath as the day when the Churches linked to Paul would meet (*cf.* Troas on the coast, Ac 20.7 or Corinth, 1 Cor 16.2); visibly, this remains the case here inland in Asia, where the apostle had also laboured. On Sundays, therefore, the company of believers would come together to meet with their Lord and hear his Word revealed in the Jewish Scriptures and in the apostolic testimony. In the present instance such a message reaches the Churches in the form of a prophetic writing (Rev 1.2-3,10-11) which serves to communicate an account of the vision-audition of the Risen One received by John.

Once this revelatory encounter comes to an end – in other words, at the close of worship – the Lord's coming will be invoked once more. This is because in liturgical time, governed as it is by the cycle of weekly encounters in worship, the God of the covenant returns again and again to his worshipping people (22.17,20) in such a way that what believers expect him to do, in days to come, is already experienced by them at the present day, as the hour of worship begins.[7] What could be more important for the seer or for those to whom his Book is addressed than this relationship to God through Jesus Christ, as structured by the worship service? Texts shaped by worship punctuate Revelation throughout and, no matter which of them we will examine below, one basic issue essentially will arise in them all: the unique status and dignity of God and the Lamb, shared by no one else, entail that they should be worshipped.

This is already the case, for instance, in 1.5-6 where every predicate used to describe Jesus Christ is pressed into the service of praise. How fundamentally important such adoration is for Revelation will be confirmed as we go on to discover, amid the ups and downs of the story being told, that bogus worship also exists and that it hopes to rival the true. The same antithetical parallelism, which we have found to govern the two thematic trajectories previously examined, will also drive this one, creating in the ensuing narrative an exact caricature of this worship of the God of the covenant. Thus, the giving of legitimate glory to God is bound to provoke rival *pseudo*-glorification; readers will discover in the plot a simply frenetic idolatry at work. It will of course turn out to be derisory in the end: the One who alone is God (the object of our first investigation in chapter 1) and Lord (the focus for our exploration in chapter 2), will share his glory with no one, because as we shall see all glory belongs to Jesus Christ and to God his Father.

In the previous chapter, I devoted several paragraphs to the triple designation for Christ in 1.5, 'Faithful Witness, Firstborn from among the dead, Sovereign over earth's kings'; there is no need to repeat myself here. As for 1.6, its attribution of glory to Christ anticipates the praises of which the Lamb will later be the object in 5.8-10,12-14, thus inaugurating an important motif for Revelation: giving glory to God who is worthy of high praise, or refusing to do so. Since God indwells the praises of his people, Christian worship, as Revelation amply testifies, is understood as the place above all others where glory is to be attributed to the Father and to Christ and where heaven's ceaseless adoration of God is mirrored on earth. The involvement of John and the believers of the Churches of Asia in this true worship is taken for granted; the repeated communitarian 'we' of 1.5-6 commits them to participation and, along with them, every reader who identifies with their experience.

In sum, 1.4-8 incorporates both an epistolary address and, at the same time, a significant opening liturgical salutation which prepares us for every other doxological moment to come in Revelation, including any counterfeit liturgy that may arise later.

Revelation 2.1–3.22

According to the twin injunctions of 1.11,19, the seer must send to the Churches of Asia a written transcript of what has been revealed to him. In the septet of oracles to Churches a cultic orientation for these Asian communities is clearly reinforced. A good place to begin exploring the literary context is the atmosphere created by the places, objects or furnishings of worship referred to throughout this opening septet. With every Church being represented by its golden menorah (1.12,19), in recollection of the seven-branched candlestick in the Temple, the Risen One without further ado makes clear to the first of them – and therefore, to all seven of them – that he 'walks amid the golden lampstands' (2.1, picking up on 1.13). And should there be no repentance in response, his threat is precisely the removal of this lamp stand (2.5) as a way of designating its loss of the status as a true Church of Messiah Jesus, met to hear his Word before dispersing for witness and for spreading his love.

In the oracles to Smyrna and to Philadelphia rival assemblies – 'synagogues of the satan' in which so-called Jews come together (2.9; 3.9) – are identified as a grouping whose abuses and lies are not to be feared. To the conqueror at Pergamum is promised 'hidden manna', which would seem to refer to the small portion of manna preserved before the Lord (Exod 16.32-34), and also a mysterious 'white stone', which might be an entrance token possessed only by true worshippers. As for victors in Philadelphia, they will each be a 'pillar in the Temple of my God' (3.12). The 'door' in the Laodicean oracle appears to open onto a space where the God of the covenant may be encountered, whether this be at Church – as the believer opens and the Risen One enters, 3.20 – or else at 'God's place' (we could say), in which case the door opens onto heaven and the seer goes into God's very presence (4.1), accompanied by believers as they share in his vision. One is reminded of the Holy of Holies, to which access is now granted. Given that the throne is mentioned just after this (in 3.21), it would probably be a mistake *not* to think by association of another throne, namely the mercy seat found represented on the lid of the Ark of the Covenant placed in the Temple.

To these furnishings of worship we may now add, secondly, specifically liturgical or religious activities also alluded to in the oracles, beginning with those which smack of false worship. At Pergamum, there are those in the community engaged in idolatry, eating sacrificial meat and involved in debauchery (2.14) or adhering to what is called the false doctrine 'of the Nicolaitans' (2.15). Similar abuses typify the behaviour of some in Thyatira, but this time as tutored by 'that woman Jezebel, who calls herself a prophet' (2.20) and whose very name is enough to conjure up the legendary apostasy that Elijah had to face. As a counterpart to such excesses, however, mention is made of signs of true piety such as the rejection of the Nicolaitans' works at Ephesus, persevering faith in Pergamum (2.13), certain people's fidelity to wholesome teaching in Thyatira (2.24,26) or obedience in Philadelphia to the Word and especially to the command to keep on going (3.8,10). Finally, the way in which the lukewarm Laodiceans, in the last of the seven Churches, are urged earnestly to repent (3.19) corresponds to the repentance already required of the first of them (2.5), as of both Pergamum (2.16) and Sardis (3.3) but which, in spite of all warnings, was found wanting in the behaviour of the stubborn idolaters of Thyatira (2.21-22).

This accumulation of disparate elements gleaned from the various oracles, all of which have to do with the practice of worship or piety, is sufficient for grounding our third major theme at the very heart of this first septet. Equally, this cultic register itself benefits from the way the first septet is arranged and especially from the parallel structure which governs the seven oracles as a whole. As already alluded to above (1.10), we find ourselves on the Lord's Day: the day when the seer, in the Spirit, had received the revelation and Asia's believers, gathered in their Churches, had themselves heard it read.[8] This means that the context in which the message intended for them is both transmitted and framed is a liturgical one. This is in perfect harmony with the context already established on the Book's threshold (1.4-8) before its further development by the vision and audition of the Risen One: it is he who issues the order to write the prophecy down and to dispatch it to the Churches (1.11,19) and it is he, in person, who now addresses each of the Churches through the medium of what is written.

As for the parallel structuring of the oracles, which we will have cause to examine closely when pursuing the final thematic trajectory presented in this book, it can already be said at this point that each oracle constitutes a mini-liturgy of the Word, set out in three broad stages. Each time without fail the sequence begins with an address to the angel-star (*cf.* 1.20), where this or that characteristic of the Risen One is drawn from the inaugural vision and audition (1.13*ff*). In each case there follows a verdict on the spiritual life of the Church in question, accompanied by a word of approval or censure (or even both) and, wherever appropriate, by an injunction to repent. Finally, the culmination is always a promise to those who hold firm combined with an exhortation to take to heart 'what the Spirit is saying to the Churches'.

Here is a short synopsis of the various formulae, occurring in the direct speech, which lend structure to the oracles to Churches as a whole (2.1–3.22). Since the audit arrived at for each Church can be positive, negative, or mixed, these elements are not all present in every oracle:

> To the angel of the Church at xxx, write!
> These are the words of him who . . .
> I know your works . . .
> I well know how . . .
> You have this in your favour . . .
> However, I have this against you . . .
> Remember, therefore . . .
> Change radically, or else I will come . . .
> To the victor I will give . . .
>
> Let anyone who has an ear listen
> To what the Spirit is saying to the churches!

For interpreting such a scenario, and such comments from the Risen One to his Church gathered in worship on the day of his resurrection, it may be helpful to think of an analogy from another Johannine scene. During his earthly ministry, Jesus finds himself, on one occasion, at the well of Sychar where he puts into words the conviction that soon true worshippers will undertake their worship in Spirit and in truth (Jn 4.23-24). According to the testimony of the Fourth Gospel, 'Jesus' (Jn 4.7,10,13,16,21,26) as 'Master' (Jn 4.11,15,19) reveals this to the Samaritan woman who is now herself a worshipper. In an analogous way, I would suggest, the Living One here (Rev 1.18) unveils God to the Asian communities at worship. Whereas the Gospel recounts the response of the woman to this transforming word, together with what followed in Samaria (Jn 4.28-42), and the incident represents a key stage in the unveiling to readers of the One who reveals the Father, Revelation first encourages readers of these oracles to imagine how the Churches of Asia met in Lord's Day worship might have reacted, before having us join them via the liturgy of chapters 4 and 5 in their worship of the Creator and Redeemer.

Revelation 4.1–5.14

When heaven opens, in 4.1, the seer is told 'come up here, and I will show you what must take place after this'; along with him the worshippers in the seven congregations of Asia are transported, on the wings of their praise (as we might say), to where may be found the throne on which God sits and from which Christ will emerge. They have just been promised participation in God's reign (3.21) and the promises to the 'victors' in the Churches have just referred explicitly to thrones and to the white garments and crowns (3.4-5,11,21), worn by the people of God of both covenants, suitable for glorifying the Creator (chapter 4) and the Redeemer (chapter 5). John had received his revelation in the Spirit on the Lord's Day: assembled now on that same day, from the opening liturgical dialogue onwards the Christians of Asia, in turn, hear the same things and gaze on them in their mind's eye. Carried, as it were, on the praises formed by the lips of the first recipients in the seven Churches, readers also go with John and with their worshipping brothers and sisters into the very place where God's purposes are conceived, there to share in worship sung before the throne. This worship consists mainly of two distinct liturgical moments (4.8-11; 5.8-14);[9] after the opening of six of the seals it will be prolonged by still further adoration coming, this time, from the lips of those who have persevered through the great afflictions of 7.15 (on this, see below).

In the order of events as Revelation recounts them this cultic access to the divine throne signals a start to the fulfilment of the promises previously made to the Churches. Here the people of God of both covenants, as symbolised by the twenty-four elders, are already beginning to receive their inheritance and to start joining in a glorification of the Creator and Redeemer, which will reach a climax in the Book's very last vision. In this context the phrase 'what must take place after this' (4.1) does not signal something chronological but states something theological which will prepare the next part of the story in the light of what has gone before. Instead of heralding a pre-programmed future, however, these words illuminate in advance how readers who are called to follow Jesus Christ ought to interpret everything they are about to see; how to react, for example, once a monster bursts alarmingly on the scene and kills the two witnesses (11.7), or what to think about the impressive rise of the triumvirate of evil powers that they will experience in chapters 12 and 13. Prior to such developments, this worship declares the legitimacy of hailing as Sovereign the invisible God who, through his Messiah, presides over the course of world history and intervenes in it in his benevolence. Any forthcoming rebellion[10] is therefore to be set against the horizon of prior celebration of the certain accomplishment of God's own will for the world (5.2-5).

In this twin-panelled picture of heavenly worship, joint homage is paid to God and the Lamb. No one else may receive the acclamation 'worthy are you!' (4.11; 5.9),[11] because to them alone belongs the absolute primacy which it expresses. This praise is sounded out representatively by the four living creatures (4.8*ff*) and then by God's people (4.11), before being relayed again by the same characters, joined by others, in the second panel of the diptych (5.9-10). By then the song has swelled and on the lips of a vast choir of heavenly origin it becomes a proclamation of Christ's divinity in seven propositions (5.12). A theological crescendo[12] brings us finally to the apotheosis of praise which, at last, is carried on both in *excelsis* and *de profundis*.

Here now are the two hymnic pieces which require our attention in chapter 4, together with their immediate context:

> *The four living creatures* . . . without ceasing sing,
> Holy, holy, holy [is]
> The Lord God, the Almighty,
> The Was and the Is and the Coming [One]!   (4.8)

> *And whenever the living creatures will give*[13] *glory and honour and thanks*
> *To the Seated One on the throne, to the forever Living One,*
> *The twenty-four elders will fall before the Seated One on the throne and on their*
> *faces before The forever and ever Living One and they will cast their crowns before*
> *the throne, singing,*
> Worthy are you, our Lord and our God,
> To receive glory and honour and power,
> For you have created all things,
> And by your will they existed and were created!   (4.9-11)

In chapter 4, in the first panel of the diptych, the Seated One on the throne is the worship's only object; the same can be observed once more in the case of Revelation's final hymns in chapter 19. With the verbs in v.9-10 as the exception, almost everything here is expressed in the present tense. While this undoubtedly refers to heaven's ceaseless adoration, it equally reflects liturgical time – which is always in the present tense[14] – and the rhythm it gives, Sunday by Sunday, to the life of the Church on earth which is transported, here, to the heavenly realms. Two praises – a *tersanctus* and a *dignus* – acclaim the Lord God. The first picks up (from 1.4,8) titles which betoken his eternity (*cf.* 4.9-10), while the second particularly celebrates his dignity and sovereignty as Creator. Two groups of worshippers carry on these praises, in inverted order to that of their appearance (4.4,6). First, there are those already familiar to us thanks mainly to the visions of Isa 6 and Ezek 1, who are to be found in the greatest closeness to God's throne. Next come the twenty-four enthroned elders whose appropriate action, in worship, provides an echo of the promise of a throne which they have just heard (in 3.21), as well as giving material shape to it for the benefit of John and his brothers and sisters. In yet more worship scenes, the very next one included (5.8,14), this very same tandem of worshippers will figure; on occasion, others will swell their company (*cf.* 7.11; 14.3; 19.4).

The principal praises to be heard in chapter 5 still centre, as earlier (in 4.11), upon someone 'worthy' – in this case, on the Lamb. Equally, the double 'worthy are you!' (5.9,12) also represents a response both to the question posed by the angel in 5.2 ('who is worthy . . . ?') and to the seer's tears at the insufferable thought that the entire universe might contain no one 'worthy' (5.4). Before this double acclamation is formulated the living creatures and elders fall on their faces a first time (5.8, *cf.* v.14). One of their number speaks up in order to deprive John of his reason for weeping

(5.5), presenting him with the One who 'can' (or, put another way, who is 'worthy'), that is the slain-but-standing Lamb (5.6).

With such preparation, worship of the Lamb can ensue once he takes possession of the Book (5.7) with a gesture that signifies his performance of God's will. This praise comprises several stages. First of all, it is offered by the living creatures and twenty-four elders, in concert with the Church purchased by the blood of the Lamb and made up of priest-kings (5.8-10). This initial cultic action essentially involves celebrating new creation and new covenant by the singing of a new song, accompanied by the elders on their harps (*cf.* 14.2; 15.2); stringed instruments had habitually accompanied Israel's hymns (*e.g.* Pss 43.4; 81.2; 98.5; 150.3-4). As part of this event, important objects in cultic use appear, such as golden bowls (*cf.* Exod 25.29; 37.16). Only here, in Revelation, do they connote something other than plagues of judgment, for their contents at this stage are not (as later) divine wrath (*cf.* 15.7, *etc.*) but metaphorical incense, 'the prayers of the saints'. The next development is adoration offered by the living beings and the elders, in which the 'saints' by their prayers have a share ; it will swell as the voices of numberless angels become associated with it (5.11-12) and as all creation adds its own complement (5.13).

Here is the new song itself, together with the two pieces and amen which echo it, all in their immediate context:

> And they sing a new song,
> You are worthy to take the scroll
> And to open its seals!
> For you were slaughtered
> And by your blood you have ransomed for God
> [Those] from every tribe and language and people and nation,
> And you have made them to be a kingdom and priests serving our God,
> And they will reign on earth!

> *Then I looked, and I heard the voice of many angels . . . and the living creatures*
> *and the elders . . . singing with full voice,*
> Worthy is the Lamb that was slain to receive
> Power and wealth and wisdom and might
> And honour and glory and blessing!

> *Then every creature in heaven and on earth and under the earth and in the sea –*
> *All that is in them I heard singing,*
> To the one seated on the throne and to the Lamb [be]
> Blessing and honour and glory and supremacy
> Forever and ever!

> *And the four living creatures said,*
> Amen!

> *And the elders fell down and fell on their faces.*   *(5.9-14)*

The first two songs celebrate the Lamb. In the prior adoration of the Creator, the declaration 'worthy are you' (4.11) represented the high-point of the sequence; here the same confession, addressed to the Lamb who receives the scroll, constitutes the point of departure for the praises (5.9) and through repetition it even becomes an indirect third-person refrain: 'worthy is [he]' (5.12). Important, for the way the scene is set, are things as various as the cultic instruments and objects mentioned, the rather developed words of the new song, the way stress is put on the immensity of the number of earthly and heavenly worshippers and how sevenfold honours are attributed to the Lamb.[15] Taking account of all of these, we come to realise what important theological statement underlies the text: if the Lamb is to be found at God's side (5.6,13), and if the redemption he has accomplished (or the community so redeemed) is for God (5.9-10), then it is his own person and mediating work which, under the renewed covenant and via the 'new song', deserve all the worship that angels and human beings can give. In short, although an angel can later twice give the order that God alone is to be adored (in 19.10 and 22.9), Revelation's message is also to insist, 'fall on your face before the Lamb!' In this there is no material contradiction with worship given to God alone; see my discussion of 7.12 below.

In the third item of praise, where God and the Lamb are acclaimed together, we may note the way that creation is referred to by its *fourness*, since four stands for what is universal: 'every creature in heaven and on earth and under the earth and in the sea – all that is in them'(5.13a). Accordingly, the praise they express is itself composed of the four corresponding terms 'praise, honour, glory and power' (5.13b).[16] This is now the third in a series of imputations of honour: in 4.9 the description spoke almost incidentally of glory, honour and thanksgiving attributed to the Seated One on the throne, whilst in 5.12 as we have just seen it is the Lamb who receives every honour.

As for the amen which brings the heavenly worship to a close (in 5.14a), it is spoken aloud by the same four living creatures responsible for setting in motion the liturgy from the heart of the throne (in 4.8), while the prostration of the elders accompanying this conclusion (5.14b) is a terse echo of their similar opening gesture in 4.10. In this way, too, the text sharpens our hearing as we listen to the hymns, and directs our gaze as spectators to the liturgical actions which, in the contribution they make to the two sequences in 4.8*ff* and 5.9*ff*, orientate us and help us interpret them as forming one single cultic 'moment' that takes place before the throne of God and the Lamb.

Thus the praise of 5.9-14, by the way it completes that voiced in 4.8-11, firmly establishes the double adoration offered in Revelation to the Creator God and to Christ. All creation is summoned, not only to chant the benefits of the One who formed it, as for instance the twenty-four elders had done in 4.11, but also to celebrate the work of the One who had redeemed it and by so doing, recreated it. Already in 1.5 there was acclamation of the One 'who freed us from our sins by his blood'; now this very redemption – 'by your blood you have ransomed [people] for God' (5.9) – is said to be of equal dimensions to the original creation which it sets free. The newness of the hymn offered to the Lamb and of the one sung later by his followers on Mount Zion (14.3-4), picks up a leitmotif from the Psalms (Pss 33.3; 40.4; 98.1; 149.1), which early Judaism linked to the Servant's new song (Isa 42.10) by applying it to Messiah's advent in the world to come.[17] As in Ps 33, this 'new hymn' in Revelation is sung in respect of both the Creator and Saviour. Its newness undoubtedly lies in the fact that it celebrates the decisive changes brought about by the death and resurrection of the last and greatest Mediator.

In chapters 1 and 2 of the present book, our charting of the previous two major themes enabled us to look very closely at a parody of this redemption conveyed by the imitative traits of the first monster – a false mediator. Similar compositional logic ties the universal concert to which the praises of Rev 4–5, which lead to the caricature of rival worship that the monster provokes. Hijacked praise will very soon be directed at the monsters, when the dragon and its sidekicks demand universal false worship from humanity (in 13.4,14). That will be our cue to recognise, for what it is, a blasphemous counterfeit already anticipated here and so disqualified, in advance, by the only true adoration possible. Emanating from all that dwells in heaven, earth, sea and even the abyss (5.13, and in spite of Isa 38.18!), it is transmitted by the multitude that has fallen on its face from the beginning before God and the Lamb.

Here, genuine adoration wells up even from the chaos of the sea – the first monster's domain (13.1). This suggests that the caricature of praise is somehow caused by the prior concert of real praise. Similarly the ritual prostration of the elders, as an appropriate self-abasement following the 'amen' in 5.14, somehow calls forth the idolatry of anti-liturgies yet to come (as in 13.4). In any case, when human beings do not worship God they necessarily fall on their faces before evil powers, which is why almost all earth's inhabitants, bar those whose names are written where God is (13.8), will offer to their idols deformed worship woven from blasphemies (13.1,5-6). I will return later to this anti-liturgy when examining 13.4 in its context, but for the moment, it is sufficient to note how the genuine worship in chapters 4 and 5 forestalls this frenetic but incomplete and ultimately useless activity. The bogus worship, which Revelation will reveal in the later plot, can only be copied from the real thing, which in that sense appears as a self-conscious anticipation of its false counterpart.[18] We can verify this by looking at one correspondence overlaid with irony: genuine adoration never ceases (4.8), since the work of divine providence which it celebrates – a work of creation and re-creation – is similarly incessant; correspondingly unceasing is a cry of woe that will sound from the lips of the monster's luckless slaves (14.11). We will take a closer look at this once we have occasion to examine 14.9-12 below.

By giving a liturgical focus to the activities of the One who is, was and will always be the Almighty (4.8), Revelation is also anticipating in the manner of a prelude those actions which will accomplish the work of justice to be done – a task given to the Lamb who will break open the seals (6.1*ff*). A similar sequence can be observed later in 15.3-4, when renewed liturgical acclamation celebrates the Almighty's exploits ('great and amazing [are] your deeds, Lord God the Almighty') in anticipation of the outbreak of his sovereign judgments, through the outpoured bowls. Against this temporary resistance only will manifest itself, from antagonists that will emerge during the parenthesis that is chapters 17 and 18.

Historical Detour 4:
Is political parody detectable?

Before leaving the diptych of chapters 4 and 5, we must stop a moment longer to consider a phrase about which much ink has been spilt – the title 'Lord our God' (4.11). For many exegetes this title constitutes a valuable historical reference. Rather than belonging to the context of Jewish monotheism, where to say 'Lord our God' might be a way of underscoring the lordship of YHWH alone, this expression is said to refer to the blasphemous claim that could be found on the lips of the emperor Domitian.[19] Accordingly, Revelation's intent at this point is taken to be the proclamation of God alone as lord, using terms which would ordinarily be reserved for describing Alexander, the Seleucids or the Caesars (in a pagan context). Whatever we make of this hypothesis of the rehabilitation of pagan language, it seems to me that the text means something different: that the entire creation – symbolically four (4.8*ff*), then twenty-four with the scope of a people that is first universal (4.10), then innumerable (5.11) and finally, fully complete (5.13) – sings the holiness and otherness of the ineffable God described characteristically, in a simple but allusive way, as the 'Seated One' (*cf.* 1.4).

Back to the text: Revelation 6.1–7.17

The living beings remain associated with the Lamb for the opening of the first four seals, summoning each of the horses and riders with a peremptory 'come!' However, we have to wait until the interlude in the breaking open of seals six and seven, by the Lamb, before we see these living creatures once again joining with angels and the twenty-four elders in adoration centred on the throne. Nonetheless, the opening of the fifth and sixth seals is the occasion for three prior moments when we hear, in turn, the martyrs' complaint from under the altar (6.10), supplications inspired by Hos 10.8 (*cf.* Lk 23.30) from the earth-dwellers trying to flee the Lamb's wrath (6.16-17) and the cry of an innumerable throng before the throne, drawn from the whole of humanity, as it acclaims the triumph of God and the Lamb (7.10). The function of each of these three declarations, in reacting to the ongoing narrative, is exactly the same as for the other speech events whose character is more obviously liturgical. We can examine them in order, along with their contexts:

When he opened the fifth seal, I saw under the altar the souls of those who had been
slain for the word of God and for the testimony they had given;
They cried out with a loud voice,
Sovereign Lord, holy and true,
How long will it be before you judge
And avenge our blood on the inhabitants of the earth?
They were each given a white robe and told to rest a little longer . . . (6.9-11)

At a basic level this plea addressed to the Sovereign God, or 'despot', arises amid a situation of oppression (like the one in Ac 4.24) and is a demand that a wrong endured be justly avenged. On a more literary level, however, the cry simply brings on the next phase of the narrative: the seal judgments that have already begun to be followed by the trumpets and bowls with increasing severity, will constitute what could be called both the plot's response to their plea and, at the same time, the answer to their prayer and consequently the proof that, in his holiness and truth, God has already triumphed and will do so again.

Ought we then to view the cosmic dislocation described in the next scene as the beginning of an answer to their prayer? Furthermore, in some of the categories of human beings glimpsed at the breaking of this seal should we see a representation – at least in part – of the oppressors of these victims? Here is the text:

When he opened the sixth seal, I looked . . .
Then the kings of the earth and the magnates and the generals and the rich
And the powerful, and everyone, slave and free,
Hid in the caves and among the rocks of the mountains,
Calling to the mountains and rocks,
Fall on us and hide us
From the face of the Seated One on the throne
And from the wrath of the Lamb!
For the great day of their wrath has come,
And who is able to stand?   (6.12,15-17)

Seven categories of the wicked are listed here in hierarchical fashion. In so far as they plead with the earth for protection from a face-to-face meeting with God and the Lamb, just as faithless Israel did in Hosea's prophecy, these human beings could be the enemies of God's people and form a sort of avant-garde of false worshippers. Yet their more open words in the second couplet suggest that they might come to their senses and, sooner or later, truly repent. At this stage, readers simply do not know whether these judgments will have the effect of converting, or hardening, those who endure them.

As for the next group (7.9), who cry out to God for deliverance, their clothing identifies its members as being truly 'freedmen':

After this I looked, and there was a great multitude that no one could count,
From every nation, from all tribes and peoples and languages,
Standing before the throne and before the Lamb,
Robed in white, with palm branches in their hands.
They cried out in a loud voice, saying,
Salvation belongs to our God, to the Seated One on the throne,
And to the Lamb!   (7.9-10)

This same 'salvation' will recur in 12.10 as the first of four terms used for welcoming the satan's expulsion from heaven while in 19.1, following a hallelujah, 'salvation' will introduce two other words for singing the justice of a God who, having sentenced the whore, has won redress for those she had cheated (19.2). When we combine other elements with the palm branches found here, then as with those of Jn 12.13 there may be an allusion to the ritual of the Feast of Booths (*cf.* Lev 23.40),[20] when celebration of Israel's deliverance from Egypt by YHWH included prayer for such 'salvation' to be renewed and re-enacted (*cf.* Ps 118.24-27).

This brings us to the praise of 7.12, when the same doxology ascribed to the Lamb in 5.12 is now addressed to God:

And all the angels stood around the throne
And around the elders and the four living creatures,
And they fell on their faces before the throne and worshipped God, singing,
Amen!
Blessing and glory and wisdom and thanksgiving
And honour and power and might
[Be] to our God forever and ever!
Amen!   (7.11-12)

Six out of seven of the terms used in this doxology come from the one previously addressed to the Lamb. 'Wealth'or 'abundance' there is replaced by 'thanksgiving' here, but even this piece of changed vocabulary is borrowed from the praise of the Creator already put into words by the four living creatures in 4.9. Thus whenever Revelation says 'God and the Lamb', it is remaining resolutely monotheist. A solemn 'amen' sounds forth once more (*cf.* 5.14) except that this time, it is said twice and in such a way as to frame the doxology liturgically (something we heard already in 1.6-7). Unlike 5.8-14, nothing here distinguishes the three groups of creatures, elders and angels from one another, with the result that their common praise and joy are expressed with the same unison that found prior expression in chapter 4. We could say that, here, the God of the covenant is thanked for the work of salvation and redemption which he handed over to the slain-but-upright Lamb, a work which seems to have set in motion a huge unending festival anticipated in the Jewish Scriptures. From this point on in Revelation, this 'service' (*cf.* 22.3) of true adoration which goes on 'day and night', like the Feast of Booths (7.15),[21] will be offered up to God alone as is confirmed in 15.3-4.

Then one of the elders addressed me, saying,
Who are these, robed in white,
And where have they come from?
I said to him,
Sir, you are the one that knows!
Then he said to me,
These are they who have come out of the great ordeal!
They have washed their robes and made them white
In the blood of the Lamb!
For this reason they are before the throne of God,
And worship him day and night within his temple!
And the Seated One on the throne will tabernacle with them.
They will hunger no more, and thirst no more;
The sun will not strike them, nor any scorching heat!
For the Lamb at the centre of the throne will be their shepherd,
And he will guide them to springs of the water of life,
And God will wipe away every tear from their eyes!   (7.13-17)

7.9-17 is an episode where various elements of chapters 4 and 5 are skilfully consolidated and reinforced. The first thing to notice is how the character development of the Lamb, introduced in 5.6, takes place in the same liturgical mode. Although on this occasion the Crucified and Risen One is not described explicitly as stabbed-but-standing, the depiction does underline the importance of three things: his active role in salvation, for which he is praised (7.10); his redeeming blood (7.14), which will be briefly alluded to once more in 12.11; and the way he leads and cares for the vast people assembled before God (7.17). With the reminder that the Lamb is to be found 'in the midst of the throne' (*cf.* 5.6), renewed stress is placed on his exalted role as the plenipotentiary through whom God comes to the aid of his people and in whom the people recognise God at work to save them. From now on, the divine throne is shared by God and the Lamb (*cf.* 21.22-23; 22.1,3).

And now similar universal adoration continues before the throne, becoming nothing short of a truly ceaseless liturgy in which there is a remarkable double allusion to the Temple and to the God who will 'tabernacle' forever with the covenant people (7.15, *cf.* 21.22; 22.3). The way these worshippers are characterised anticipates the state of blessedness which the very last vision will describe, referring in turn to their washed clothing (7.14, *cf.* 22.14), God's dwelling with them (7.15, *cf.* 21.3), the worship they give him (7.15, *cf.* 22.3), the water that slakes their thirst (7.17, *cf.* 21.6; 22.1,17) and their tears, which are definitively wiped away (7.17, *cf.* 21.4). The unending praises to which they give expression (*cf.* 4.8) provide advance protection for us, their hearers, against being fooled, later in the plot, by the monstrous sight of human beings singing a monster's praises!

Revelation 8.1-5

Through the opening of the seventh seal (8.1) and the accompanying prelude to the trumpets septet (8.2-5), Revelation's readers are drawn into two moments, which are both rather unusual, from a liturgical point of view. The woes unleashed by the horsemen of the first four seals, the martyrs' cry in the fifth or the cataclysmic bangs and crashes of the sixth seal, together with everything we have heard in chapter 7, would lead us to expect that when the time comes to break open the seventh seal – subject to delay, so far – a real end will be reached and the process of judgment, presided over by the Lamb, will at last be completed. Instead, after the unbroken heavenly din of endless praises in chapters 4, 5 and 7, or the plagues of the previous six seals, there comes 'silence in heaven for about half an hour'. Because this is unexpected, it is nothing if not dramatic![22] Ever since exegesis of Revelation began, there has been a preoccupation throughout with the meaning of this pause.[23]

Silence can connote various things in the Jewish Scriptures. Nowhere is more silent than the place where the dead sojourn (Ps 115.17)! Someone may be reduced to silence through fear (cf. Isa 23.2), or may fall silent when some revelation is to be heard (Isa 41.1) or keep silence when there is judgment to be undergone (Isa 47.5; Lam 2.10). More important, without doubt, for the present instance is the silence of Israel when the Lord takes up their cause in judgment against Egypt (Exod 14.14) – a silence which is in liturgical counterpoint to the Song of Moses (Exod 15.1-18) – and, in particular, the reverential silence which several of the Minor Prophets order their hearers to adopt in the context of the Day of the Lord – a day when woes will break out and the end will have come, but also when it may be anticipated that the covenant, flouted for so long, will at last be renewed.

'Silence!'   (Am 8.3)
'The Lord is in his holy temple. Silence before him, all the earth!'
(Hab 2.20)
'Silence before the Lord God! For the day of the Lord is at hand'
(Zeph 1.7a)
'Silence before the Lord, all people! For he has roused himself from his holy dwelling'.   (Zech 2.17)

We may conclude that whenever silence is required in Israel, it is because either God has done something for his people or is about to do so. Silence, whether beforehand or afterwards, is a suitable response to his active presence and for this reason is fully appropriate whenever worship celebrates his acts. By anticipating the ultimate silence with which, when it happens,[24] the end to all things should be greeted, liturgical silence is always what we might call penultimate. Therefore, it would be wrong to think that nothing is going on during such a silence: although there is nothing to be heard, there may very

well be things to see. At the very least, the silence of 8.1 signals the end of
an audition which allows a transition to vision mode and carries with it the
invitation to use our eyes instead of our ears.

So, what is it that John sees, here, and what do we (in our turn) see
through his eyes? What seems to be happening during this time of silence is
cultic action involving twin censers. First, the prayers of the saints – already
called 'incense' in 5.8 – are mingled with incense and offered up on the altar
(whether altar of incense or of sacrifice is unclear),[25] before the throne (cf.
6.9); from here they rise up to God's nostrils (8.2-4) like a fragrant evening
offering (cf. Ps 141.2). Second, another censer spreads fire from the altar
onto the earth; for the spectator this seems to bring the silence to an end,
since renewed noisy disruption now takes place (8.5; cf. 4.5; 6.12ff; thereafter
11.19; 16.18). The first censer is employed by an angel to whom 'was given
a great quantity of incense to offer.' In this offering, the combined prayers
of the saints, which are acceptable to God, are their sacrificial service which
constitutes a pleasing aroma offered up in imitation of the Messiah who had
given himself as 'a fragrant offering and sacrifice to God' (Eph 5.2). With
the second censer comes proof that their sacrifice has found acceptance and
their prayer has been heard, for 'there is a correlation between the prayers of
the faithful and the fire thrown down upon the earth'.[26] Fire hurled down in
this way (cf. Ezek 10.2) is in fact the divine response to their demand in 6.10.

Revelation 10.1–11.19

In parallel fashion to the interlude that separated the last two seals, there
is a significant caesura between the plagues unleashed by the sixth trumpet
(9.13-21) and the sounding of the seventh and last in the series (11.15). It
consists of two intimately related major episodes (10.1-11; 11.1-13),[27] which
together greatly enrich our theme of encounter with God in worship. An
initial three-part scenario centres on a little scroll open, no doubt, because
all its seals have now been broken: it seems to herald a fuller revelation.
A majestic angel who has come down from heaven[28] holds the scroll and
when he gives a shout, seven thunders are the result. Curiously, the seer
is forbidden to reveal or even describe their contents, which looks like an
abortive revelation (10.1-4). Despite this, however, the angel continues
speaking his solemn declaration and anticipates the sounding of the seventh
trumpet as the moment for 'the mystery of God' (cf. Col 2.2) to reach
its climax; this is 'good news' that has been progressively revealed to the
prophets and, in the final analysis, it is inseparable from the person and
work of Messiah Jesus (10.5-7; cf. 5.9-10). Lastly, addressing the seer in direct
speech, the angel's words invite him to eat and digest the scroll in question
and, by so doing, to have his own prophetic mandate renewed (10.8-11).
This means that there will, after all, be a revelation of universal proportions;
by swallowing the scroll, the seer will be actively associated with it much as
Ezekiel was before him (Ezek 2.8–3.3).

A lot of exegetical work has been devoted to interpreting the detail of the next brief episode (11.1-2), which draws on Ezek 40.3*ff* for its inspiration. For our purposes, the thing to be noted is that every one of its metaphors (Temple, altar, worshippers, outer court, holy city) relates to worship which, for God's people, is centred on the Jerusalem Temple and on its ritual. As in the source text, the worshippers benefit from a symbolically protective act of measuring; although this does not spare them trials caused by oppression at the hands of the nations (*cf.* Lk 21.24), as conveyed by the fate that befalls the unmeasured zone, it nevertheless preserves them. Yet in what follows the focus falls not on what is said *to* God, as in a liturgy of approach addressed to him, but instead on a corresponding act of communication – of prophetic testimony, in fact – which speaks *of* God and reflects the liturgy of the Word. What the prophetic witnesses will have to proclaim (11.3-13) is, no doubt, the Gospel of 10.7; and in whatever they utter, God is heard to speak (v.3). Their testimony directed at human beings is not, however, to be separated from praise addressed to God. The cultic tenor of the scene is sustained through the image of the menorah (v.4) and the fire of God's verdict (v.5), but especially through the sacrifice of the prophetic witnesses (v.7-9); their resurrection (v.11) and ascension (v.12) testify that their sacrifice is as acceptable and pleasing to God as was their Master's.

In their malevolent glee the 'earth-dwellers' (v.10) anticipate the emergence of counterfeit anti-worship later on. By contrast, the earthquake which follows the witnesses' ascension elicits from the survivors, at long last, a positive response to a judgment designed to reform them and, in consequence, have them give glory to the God of heaven (v.13). Now it is time for the seventh trumpet: unlike the last of the seals, this one does not bring silence; instead, on this occasion, a great moment of praise (11.15-19) is set in motion by a choir:

> *And there were loud voices in heaven, saying,*
> The kingdom of the world has become
> The kingdom of our Lord
> And of his Messiah,
> And he will reign forever and ever.   (11.15)

G.F. Handel made the most of this first leitmotif in his famous *Messiah*, turning it into a powerful aria on the lips of a heavenly multitude (*cf.* 4.8; 5.11-12 and perhaps 7.9-10). Where Revelation is concerned, the choreography once more involves appropriate prostration, while the elders of chapters 4 or 7 sing a thanksgiving hymn:

> *Then the twenty-four elders who sit on their thrones before God*
> *Fell on their faces and worshipped God, singing,*
> We give you thanks, Lord God Almighty,
> The Is and the Was,

For you have taken your great power
And begun to reign
The nations raged,
But your wrath has come,
And the time for judging the dead,
For rewarding your servants, the prophets
And the saints and all who fear your name,
Both the small and the great,
And for destroying the earth's destroyers!   (11.16-18)

Introduced by a unique liturgical formula ('we give you thanks'), which reminds us of the collective 'we' of the assembled Church in 1.5-6, this hymn corresponds to the earlier one in 7.9-12 and complements it. The God who, in his sovereignty, has conquered evil is now no longer celebrated as the Coming One, for the consummation of his reign has already begun. We could therefore entitle this song The Time Has Come and see it as another answer to the 'when?' of 6.10. At any rate it celebrates that opportune moment when all those who recognised in the Lord and Messiah their King – whether they are dead or living, prophets or saints, small or great – are justified and recompensed, and when 'the earth's destroyers' are paid back by divine wrath; God's wrath against the nations, here, recalls the Lamb's in 6.16.

In its turn, this hymn sets in motion three events in one, all of them revelatory in character:

Then God's temple in heaven was opened,
And the ark of his covenant was seen within his temple;
And there were flashes of lightning, rumblings, peals of thunder, an earthquake,
and heavy hail   (11.19)

Throughout this intermezzo (10.1–11.19), John is on earth in the holy city, in front of the Temple. Although the earthly Temple had been destroyed in the past along with all its furnishings (2 Kgs 25.8-10), and although here the trampling of at least a section of its courts is in view (11.2), the vision of the heavenly model, its Ark of the Covenant intact, nonetheless bears witness to God's accessibility as 'God of covenant and of encounter'.[29] As for the five cosmic manifestations described here and elsewhere, they show figuratively that he is present (cf. 4.5; 8.5 and farther on, 16.18). Like the seer before us, we reader-spectators no longer find ourselves for these scenes before the throne, where perfect and unending adoration was put into words. Yet in spite of this, there is encouragement to believers to keep on celebrating his sovereignty, his salvation and his reign – whose full accomplishment will be recounted in the remainder of the narrative – from the mere glimpse of the Ark in the heavenly Temple, which serves to confirm God's faithfulness to his covenant with his people on earth.

Revelation 12.1–13.18

All this begins to take concrete shape in the early episodes of a sequence which separates the trumpets from the septet of bowls. The first narrated event is Messiah's rescue, effected by an ascent to heaven to be with God whose throne he shares (12.5; *cf.* chapters 4–5). In what follows, it does indeed appear that the Lamb may have abandoned the whole stage (from chapter 13) to the monsters; we will have to come back to this later. His rescue nevertheless signifies his defeat of the dragon which is unable to eradicate Messiah's ministry as it had hoped (12.3-6) or to do anything to prevent its being hurled down once and for all (12.7-9). In the interval between the moment the hurled-down dragon starts roaming the earth (12.9) and the juncture when, mad with rage (12.12), it starts pursuing the woman and her offspring (12.13-17), a vitally important hymn is inserted which bursts forth from heaven and announces how those brothers and sisters who had stood accused now conquer this enemy by their testimony (12.11). Thus, the vacuum left behind in heaven by the evicted accuser is instantly filled.

This praise echoes that of the earth when the Church, met on the first day of the week, sings its psalms. In heaven, the dragon will no longer be able to accuse anyone before God (12.10) while on earth those whom it had previously accused now conquer it by the blood of the Lamb and by their own testimony (12.11). Here is the song in question, together with the narrative that anticipates it:

> *The great dragon was hurled down,*
> *That ancient serpent, which is called the devil and the satan,*
> *The deceiver of the whole inhabited world –*
> *It was hurled down to the earth, and its angels were hurled down with it.*
> *Then I heard a loud voice in heaven, proclaiming,*
> Now have come the salvation and the power and the kingdom of our God
> And the authority of his Messiah!
> For the accuser of our comrades has been hurled down,
> Who accuses them day and night before our God.
> But they have conquered it by the blood of the Lamb
> And by the word of their testimony.
> For they did not cling to life even in the face of death.
> Rejoice then, you heavens
> And those who dwell in them!
> But woe to the earth and the sea,
> For the devil has come down to you
> With great wrath, because it knows that its time is short!   (12.9-12)

By expressing the reality of the salvation, power and empire of God and the Lamb, which have now been put in place (12.10-12), this hymn takes farther the previous acclamation of God's victory. The hurling down will mean woe for the earth (12.12), but that woe is put in perspective by heavenly rejoicing which offers a retort to the malevolent exultation that had greeted the death of the witnesses (in 11.10) and shows it to have been premature. Like all the hymns which have punctuated the text of Revelation up to now, this one also assumes that the divine reign has already been established; in so doing, it removes in advance any credence for the apparent success of the monsters when, subsequently, they try to take the Lamb's place. The accusing counsel, in other words the satan (*cf.* Job 1-2; Zech 3), has fallen; by contrast the slain Lamb, the Defence Counsel (*cf.* Heb 7.25; 1 Jn 2.1-2), stands upright. For believers, therefore, everything has changed. There is now no one to contradict their testimony and nothing to take away from their victory. Although they cannot see the Lamb, hidden as he seems to be by the three monsters of this sequence, he is no less present and victorious: their redemption, obtained by his spilt blood (1.5; 5.9; 7.14), therefore remains fully efficacious for them. It is this 'liturgical support from the Lamb'[30] which we should keep firmly in mind when, as already anticipated, we hear the 'earth-dwellers' pronounce their competing anti-liturgy.

For what faces readers, here, is a real 'conflict of worship.'[31] When a first monster appears, miraculously cured of its wound, the entire earth is bewitched and throws itself into idolatry:

> *And I saw a monster rising out of the sea having ten horns and seven heads . . .*
> *One of its heads seemed to have received a death-blow,*
> *But its mortal wound had been healed.*
> *In amazement the whole earth followed the monster.*
> They worshipped the dragon . . .
> And they worshipped the monster, saying,
> Who is like the beast,
> And who can fight against it?   (13.1-4)

The 'earth-dwellers' who fall on their faces before the monster and offer it praise through their false worship (13.4) provide a distorted version of the homage given by the heavenly creatures, in the name of all creation, to the Lamb who is to be adored for the redemption his death and resurrection have achieved (5.9,12). Before pausing to examine the only anti-hymn, *per se*, which Revelation is willing to depict, we can go a little farther. The monster is itself a blasphemer, denigrating God and everything to do with God:

> *The monster was given a mouth uttering haughty and blasphemous words . . .*
> *Against God, blaspheming his name and his dwelling . . .*
> *It was allowed to make war on the saints and to conquer them.*
> *It was given authority over every tribe and people and language and nation,*
> *And all the inhabitants of the earth will fall down before it,*
> *Everyone whose name has not been written from the foundation of the world*
> *In the book of life of the Lamb that was slain.*   (13.5-8)

In spite of the monster's ability to federate human beings in its cause, based on this text it is not quite true that 'the whole earth' falls into line behind it. Since those with their names in the book of life do not bend the knee to it, it is quasi-universal adoration only that the monster actually receives (13.8), making its caricature of genuine Christian hope, at best, partial. One day, every knee will bow in acclamation of the Lamb (5.8,13; *cf.* Phil 2.10)! In the meantime, we should not simply believe what we see . . .

> If anyone has ears to hear, he should listen up!
> If anyone is to be taken captive, into captivity he will go;
> If anyone kills with the sword, with the sword he must be killed.

> This calls for perseverance and faithfulness from the saints![32]   (13.9-10)
> [*cf.* This calls for wisdom! 13.18]

In the earthly theatre of operations those whom the monster seeks to subdue, but cannot, must resist it with endurance and faith (13.10) in the knowledge that, in spite of everything, their prayers go before them into the immediate presence of God, to whom they belong (5.8).

We return to the praise of the monster placed on the lips of its worshippers. In one brief sentence, this praise succeeds in parodying both the liturgical acknowledgement of the transfer of authority from God to his Christ (5.9) and the legitimate prostration which accompanied it. The result is a look-alike of believers submitting to the authority of their Lord. This imitation latches on to the rhetorical style and diction of several psalms, hymns and praises from the Old Testament in which, at the heart of Israel's worship – and in the context of polemics against the false gods and idols of surrounding peoples – the question is put 'who may be compared to YHWH?' The corresponding question on the lips of idolaters, here, is a diabolical adaptation of 'oh Lord, who is like you ?' as found on the lips of Moses (Exod 15.11) or the Psalmists (Pss 89.8; 113.5; *cf.* 18.31; 35.10; 71.19; 82.1; 93.5).[33]

Short though this anti-hymn may be, with its vocabulary 'modelled on the prayers and praise addressed to the one true God by his followers,'[34] we ought not to underestimate the considerable strike-power it must have had on the ear of members of the Churches of Asia, accustomed as they were to the praises of Israel. By daring to call 'incomparable' anyone other than the God of the covenant (13.5), it must have sounded like the worst of blasphemies. In terms of the Book's plot, such an idolatrous song is not to be tolerated but demands an answer. Precisely such an answer is not long in making itself heard, as a new song is sung by those whom the Lamb has redeemed from the earth (14.3): this genuine worship will swiftly erase the bogus worship of the pseudo-hymn.

Before examining that pseudo-hymn, however, there is some more light to be shed on the reason why Revelation would even allow this sole fragment of false worship in the Book to be heard We know that in ancient Jewish writings, from the Book of Daniel onwards, the anti-christ demanded worship;[35] if we are looking for a source of inspiration external to Revelation, perhaps this was of influence in the present instance. If, however, we ask what it is first and foremost – within the text of Revelation itself – that causes this unnatural worship, the answer is quite explicitly the supernatural healing of the first monster (13.3,12), which makes a deep impression on the whole earth. It is the second monster that organises such worship (13.12-15): as false prophet and misleader, it seeks to promote the adoration of the dragon *and* of its understudy; in so doing, it apes the Spirit-Paraclete who leads believers to worship God and the Lamb.

The hymn in reverence of the monster (13.4) is a diabolical chant that celebrates the satan's victory over God's saints (13.7). Its counterpoint is the genuine praise which sang of God and the Lamb. Just as the heavenly court had seen the enthronement of Christ and had fallen down in worship, so now in their turn human beings on the earth are constrained, when they set eyes on its counterfeit, to offer their worship. Designed as a travesty of the twin liturgies of chapters 4 and 5, it does not manage to be other than idolatry (13.14-15) of the most vain and hollow sort. As a hymn it is colourless, in no way equalling the new song of 5.9-10 which deserves to be called a *magnificat*, justifying the Lamb's right to assume eschatological sovereignty over the world on three accounts: his death; the redemption won thereby; and the reign of God instituted by this sacrifice.[36]

One after another, admiration (13.3), prostration (twice in 13.4, then 13.8) and blasphemy designate the false adoration which emanates from the earth and its inhabitants. This is the first occasion in Revelation when 'fall down in worship' has referred to prostration before idols; it will be used in this way on one further occasion, although in the future tense (in 13.12).[37] The monster hopes its power will be deified, while the idolaters who fall down before it remind us of how the four creatures and twenty-four elders also 'fell down' in acclamation of the Lamb (5.8), or 'fell down and fell on their faces' (5.14). In similar fashion the blasphemies proffered by the monster and then taken up by those fervent in their false worship of it (13.5-6,8) correspond to the prayers and songs chorused by the innumerable voices before the heavenly throne (5.8-9).

After this point no more detail will be given of the practices linked to this false worship, although in what follows allusion will regularly be made to it (13.8,12,15; 14.9,11; 16.2; 20.4). This is no surprise: Revelation's author, like most psalmists or prophets before him, is content to denounce idolatry without actually describing it. Exegetes, for their part, may have invested great effort in the precise identification of this false worship and of those who practised it;[38] but for Revelation itself this is of only passing interest and the Book's recipients are therefore given no information about the exact form these idols or false gods may have taken.

Revelation 14

By this point, the issue for the story is this: genuine worship, which is to be offered to God alone, has been hijacked; genuine praise must now therefore repel this sustained assault by the forces of evil on divine glory and majesty. This is exactly what happens in the next episode; here are its essential contents:

> *Then I looked, and there was the Lamb . . .*
> *And with him were one hundred and forty-four thousand . . .*
> *And I heard a voice from heaven like the sound of many waters*
> *And like the sound of loud thunder;*
> *The voice I heard was like the sound of harpists playing on their harps,*
> *And they sing a new song*
> *Before the throne and before the four living creatures and before the elders.*
> No one could learn that song except the one hundred and forty-four
> thousand
> Who have been redeemed from the earth . . .
> These follow the Lamb wherever he goes.
> They have been redeemed from humankind
> As first fruits for God and the Lamb,
> And in their mouth no lie was found; they are blameless . . .   (14.1-5)

The Lamb's victory, presupposed from 5.5 onwards, will be confirmed in 15.2. At this stage, the text is anticipating the future defeat of the monster from chapter 13 and of everything it controls. The signal for this is the double use of the word 'redeem' (in 14.3-4, borrowed from 5.9) by the new victory song in which it is precisely the 'redeemed' who take the places of the living beings and the elders in the earlier text. French-language exegesis has not been slow to notice the important contrast introduced in 14.1: instead of 'servile vociferations'[39] or 'insolent hymns by the monster's slaves'[40] (13.4), what now rings out is a song rich with the accent of heaven. The fact that the contents of this 'new song' are known in advance (ever since 5.8-10) has already had the effect of silencing, before they were even uttered, the blasphemous and slanderous words of the second monster.[41] Now, at the very moment when the idolatrous refrains need to be answered by a sharp retort, this effect is repeated and reinforced: 'there is something apparently deliberate about the contrast between the second monster, a lamblike caricature that speaks like a dragon, and the powerful but harmonious voice heard here'.[42] The very fact that there is anyone available to learn and then sing this new song exposes as a lie the monster's apparent victory, which is hereby erased (13.7). Now that the bogus worship which had been addressed to it (13.8; *cf.* Rom 1.18-23) has been purged of its idolatrous strains, God may become the object of adoration (14.7) through worship which celebrates, in a suitable way, both his victory and the monster's defeat. This song from the earth's redeemed (14.3) puts a complete stop to the blasphemous adoration of chapter 13.

Nevertheless, the idolaters' behaviour still calls for God's judgment. This is proclaimed, or should we say shouted, by angels as 'an eternal gospel' intended for the entire earth (cf. Mt 24.14), and by this means God gives his enemies their answer. For all of humanity (cf. 4.11) this verdict provides a new reason for reverent adoration:

Fear God and give him glory,
For the hour of his judgment has come!
And fall down before the Creator
Of heaven and earth, the sea and the springs of water!   (14.7)

In two further liturgical passages (15.4; 19.5), we find the same concerns as those raised in this universal gospel, namely fearing God and at the same time glorifying him (cf. Ps 96 / 1 Chr 16.23-33). As for the present allusion to the arrival of the appointed moment when his 'judgment' will take place, three other references to it will follow (cf. 16.7; 18.10; 19.2).

The scene is prolonged as two further angels fly where the first one already soared. An insistent announcement from the first of them – 'fallen, fallen is Babylon the great' (14.8) – is in anticipation of an event on which chapter 18 will focus at length. As for the last declaration in the series, it condemns outright everything that chapter 13 has just recounted, at the core of which was the false worship given to the monster:

Those who worship the beast and its image,
And receive a mark on their foreheads or on their hands,
They will also drink the wine of God's wrath . . .
They will be tormented with fire and sulphur
In the presence of the holy angels and in the presence of the Lamb!

And the smoke of their torment goes up forever and ever.
There is no rest day or night
For those who worship the beast and its image
And for anyone who receives the mark of its name!
Here is a call for the endurance of the saints,
Those who keep the commandments of God
And hold fast to the faith of Jesus!   (14.9b-12)

The verdict made public by this angel reaches those branded with the mark of this covenant, i.e. everyone who has had a part in false worship. How important this is can be seen in the way the reference to those tattooed, and to their prostration, is repeated with only slight modification (14.9b,11). The true nature of these idolaters and of their bogus worship, parodying true worship offered to God, is thereby unmasked and judged: its practitioners, who despise God's grace, will have to face his wrath (14.10) and suffer a punishment as unending (14.11) as the adoration undertaken by the living beings in 4.8.

Here, in fact, we should take note of a very effective literary device whose function is to repeat, with variations, particularly meaningful

phrases. It is immediately apparent when 14.11,13 is re-read in light of
4.8-9: the expression 'there is no rest day or night', preceded by 'forever
and ever' (in 14.11), takes over from 4.8-9 'day or night… there is no rest',
a phrase itself reinforced by 'forever and ever'. As regards the second
of these contexts, the worshippers of the monsters never have any rest
(14.11), just as it is punishment without respite that awaits the monsters
themselves, in 20.10; this is in contrast to the martyrs who have been
waiting since 6.11 but who will take their rest (14.13). Then, comparison
between the two texts shows how the lack of rest day or night, which
afflicts worshippers of the monster (14.11), corresponds antithetically
to the equally unceasing activity of the four living creatures engaged
in perpetual adoration of God in heaven (4.8). This contrast is further
reinforced by 'the smoke of their torment' which rises up eternally, like
that of the city in flames later on (19.3). Resting on the formal parallelism
established, as we saw earlier, between worship given to God and worship
directed at the monster, this device sets in place for readers a material
contrast between ceaseless activity by worshippers of God, inspired as
they are by endless joy, and lack of rest for worshippers of the monster,
which signifies their unbroken torment.[43]

Just before three further angels appear or make a proclamation, a short
dialogue is inserted which is as significant as it is brief:

> *And I heard a voice from heaven saying,*
> Write this!
> Blessed are the dead who from now on die in the Lord.
> Yes!
> *says the Spirit,*
> They will rest from their labours,
> For their deeds follow them.   (14.13)

This verse 'is of the utmost importance'.[44] In respect of the contribution it
makes to the major theme we are currently studying, there are three pertinent
things to note. The first is the order to write: the order is given, on this
occasion, by an anonymous heavenly voice which may be assimilated to the
Risen One's voice.[45] The seer has not heard such an order since the unveiling
began (1.11,19) or since messages were addressed to the Churches (2.1, *etc.*);
there will be another recurrence in 19.9, where a comforting beatitude is
again dictated, and still another order given in 21.5. The second thing is the
first mention of the Spirit since the septet of oracles to Churches: he even
utters some words, decreeing rest for believers, and will play no more part
until late in the final dialogue of 22.17. The third and last thing is the 'now'
which qualifies the blessing announced here; it suggests, as in 12.10 earlier
on, that salvation is already a present reality for those who must persevere
continually (14.12): this is so because a verdict in their favour has already
been obtained by the Messiah.

Over and above the importance of such content, what is significant about this latest piece of heavenly dialogue is the fact that we are obliged (in my opinion) to see it as liturgical not just in its function but, especially, in its force. For it is surely characteristic of any cultic act that it should re-enact, through the medium of celebration, the blessings of grace which a faithful God gives to those who belong to him.

In what follows the context remains that of heavenly worship, since the last three angels in the series of six all emerge from the heavenly Temple or from its altar. The meaning of what each one says or does derives from the presence of a figure 'like a son of man' who wears a crown, carries a sickle and is seated on a cloud (14.14). This character is exhorted by the first angel to harvest the earth in an act of judgment, while in parallel a second angel (under encouragement from a third) harvests earth's grapes and treads them. In both cases, their advocacy takes a similar form:

> Use your sickle and reap!
> For the hour to reap has come,
> Because the harvest of the earth is fully ripe!   (14.15b)

> Use your sharp sickle and gather
> The clusters of the vine of the earth,
> For its grapes are ripe!   (14.18b)

Three angels had proclaimed an 'eternal gospel' with its consequences; now three more angels have hastened the hour when its promise of judgment and salvation will be fulfilled.

Revelation 15

Several times already, we have taken preliminary note of 15.1-5 — a text which acts as a prelude to the septet of bowl plagues.[46] The time has come for examining it more closely. It is another section whose meaning may be illuminated by the play on true and false worship. The author still has in mind, here, the act of liberation that was the Exodus, as sung by the Song of Moses (*cf.* Ps 74.13-14). This is an event which demonstrates, in the face of the monster's idolatrous claims, that the God who redeemed his people from Egypt has no equal. For Revelation the New Exodus of Christ's death and resurrection allows God to reveal his peerless divinity to the nations. Consequently, there can be nothing remotely fortuitous about the same strophe of the same Song of Moses as was previously parodied in 13.4 being adapted, now, for this new 'Song of Moses and of the Lamb'.

The song is placed on the lips of those who have conquered the monster (15.2). If we mistakenly thought there were only victims (13.7), this proves that there are those who have remained unbending before the land monster's coercion, refusing to worship the sea monster's image. Their victory gives them the right to stand on the heavenly sea (*cf.* 4.6), an expanse

which extends to the throne of divinity and which replaces that other sea
of trials. In 13.4 the sea monster's restoration, in spite of its mortal wound,
was supposed to be a testimony to its invincibility; in fact, the Lamb's death
and resurrection have neutralised any pretentions arising from the healing of
that fatal wound: the divinity of the one and only true God can therefore be
invoked (15.2-4). Choristers take up and recapitulate the praises of chapters
4 to 12, thereby erasing the idolatrous song sung by the peoples in their
blindness. By celebrating now a New Exodus that will one day concern all
nations, they also point forward to a unanimous adoration yet to come. The
anti-hymn of 13.4 had commandeered elements of Old Testament tradition;
now the hymn of 15.3-4 borrows from prior revelation in a positive way. Its
theme of God's righteous acts comes from the hymn in Deut 32 (v.4), with
other echoes drawn from acclamations found in various psalms (Pss 86.9-
10; 111.2; 139.14; 145.17). Adoration originally expressed by the prophetic
oracle of Jer 10.6-7 is also put to new use, as is the greeting reserved for the
Almighty Lord found in Am 3.13 and 4.13.[47] Here is the song in question,
together with the narrative that introduces it:

And I saw… those who had conquered the beast and its image and the number of
its name, Standing beside the sea of glass [mixed with fire] with harps of God in
their hands.
And they sing the song of Moses, the servant of God,
And the song of the Lamb:
Great and amazing [are] your deeds,
Lord God the Almighty!
Just and true [are] your ways,
King of the nations!
Lord, who will *not* fear
And glorify your name?
For you alone are holy!
All nations will come
And fall down before you,
For your righteous acts have been revealed!   (15.2-4)

Prior to the outpouring of the bowls, which comes next, this song
celebrates the deeds – 'your works' (15.3); 'your righteous acts' (15.4) – of
the God who lives eternally (15.7). By analogy with 4.6 the sea of glass,
although mixed with fire this time, must be located in front of the heavenly
throne. The compact expression 'those who had conquered the beast and
its image and the number of its name' (15.2) reiterates the victory of
those who have experienced the triumph of the true power of God over
that illusory, defeated power which had opposed it. Here the reverence
inspired, *among the nations*, by the blessings which God their King has
bestowed (15.3; *cf.* 21.24,26) offers a retort to the astonishment of pagans
bedazzled by the sea monster (13.3). The double rhetorical question,

so typical of biblical hymns,[48] 'who will *not* fear and glorify your name' implies only one answer: no one! There must be universal acclamation of the One who is Lord of everything and everyone. It is expected that the nations will come to worship him (*e.g.* Ps 86.9-10) and under the new covenant, through the blood of Jesus, his faithful ones do indeed hail from all nations. His 'righteous acts' (15.4), which were already the focus of the oracles, seals and trumpets and which will soon find renewed expression in the outpoured bowls, are fundamentally salvific in character and so are a worthy theme for song.

As already happened in 11.19 (see my commentary above), it is to similar effect that the heavenly Temple now opens to the seer's gaze. This time it is designated the 'Tent of Testimony', as it was during the wilderness wanderings (*e.g.* Exod 38.26; 40.34); this makes it equivalent to the way the earlier text mentions the Ark that housed the covenant documents. Out of the Temple, in other words out from the presence of the God of glory and power himself – hidden though he is by smoke (15.8; *cf.* e.g. Exod 40.34-35; Isa 6.1-4; Ezek 10.1-5) – come the seven bowl-angels clad in linen like heavenly priests. Their bowls of wrath containing 'seven plagues, which are the last', were referred to in 15.1 and again (though without 'last') in 15.6. Now, by a ritual action, the four living creatures implicated at the very centre of the heavenly worship (4.6; 7.11; 14.3; *cf.* 19.4 later) hand each of them a golden bowl set apart for the service of the heavenly altar (*cf.* Exod 27.3; 38.3). The wrath that these contain is no doubt the counterpart of the prayer incense offered up to God in 5.8, now transformed by him, here, into judgment. It is a beverage originating with the one 'who lives forever and ever': this liturgical formula reminds us, should we need reminding, that what we are witnessing here is an enactment of worship in heaven that stands in an organic relation to adoration on earth.

Revelation 16

However, neither the vision of universal acclamation offered to the Lord nor indeed that of a service in the heavenly Temple (which follows it) bring the blasphemers' treachery to an end – not as yet. On the contrary, even worse blasphemies are to come in 16.21. But when that happens we will be ready, for the inaugural bowl in the series quite explicitly affects 'those who had the mark of the beast and who worshipped its image' (16.2). So then, the blasphemies and misdirected praise expressed in the pseudo-hymn of 13.4 will find a new lease of life amid the outpouring of the other bowls; in this way, the diabolical litany of chapter 13 enjoys yet another extension.

Two utterances by a 'loud voice'[49] frame the bowls septet. Although not explicitly identified, the fact that it comes from the Temple (16.1) or even the throne (16.17) would seem to indicate that God is speaking – for when words come from the Temple, 'it is the Lord' (Isa 66.6):

Then I heard a loud voice from the temple telling the seven angels,
Go and pour out on the earth the seven bowls of the wrath of God!

(16.1)

It is God himself who authorises and sets in motion the bowl judgements, just as it is he who will declare them to be over in 16.17. Before we hear the renewed blasphemies which these judgments elicit from the hard-hearted, an angel in charge of the waters affected by the third bowl in the series once more offers God worship, welcoming the righteous nature of these judgments:

> You are just, O Holy One, the Is and the Was,
> For you have judged these things!
> Because they shed the blood of saints and prophets,
> You have given them blood to drink.
> It is what they deserve!   (16.5-6)

In both its form and content this doxology particularly (though not exclusively) recalls the song of 15.3-4,[50] for God's holiness and righteousness are at the heart of them both. As before (in 11.17), so again here God is no longer the Coming One; now, however, he is the 'Holy One', unlike 1.4,8 and 4.8. Furthermore, the payback by means of which those who have spilt blood must drink blood, mirroring the polluted waters of 16.3-4, is itself parallel to the wrath that requites wrath in 11.18. An antiphonal response is given:

> *And I heard the altar respond,*[51]
> Yes, O Lord God, the Almighty,
> Your judgments are true and just!   (16.7)

Again, the link to the hymn of 15.3-4 is explicit since both have the same pair of adjectives for describing God's ways. As again in 19.2, here God's judgments are meant. The voice speaking from the altar in 16.7 cannot be identified with certainty, although by analogy with 6.9 it is plausible to take it as the voice of believers praying.

The reaction of the monsters' slaves to the punishments resulting from these bowl plagues is very different. As happened when the sixth trumpet sounded (9.20-21), they again formulate blasphemy against God, only this time, in triplicate (16.9,11,21). There had been solemn warnings, on two occasions, of the need to give God glory in view of his impending judgment (14.7; 15.4), but in persisting with their blasphemies these stubborn human beings serve a reminder to those whose hard hearts could not be converted by the previous judgments, when the trumpets sounded.[52] Blasphemy was said to be characteristic of the first monster (13.5-6), so by their repeated blasphemies its diehard followers resemble it more and more.[53] It is highly likely that their triple blasphemy betokens a hardening of similar sort to that shown by the Pharaoh of Egypt; and now, as then, increased hardening meets with a tougher response from God's justice. The picture is shaped by a liturgical ritual whereby the angels come solemnly from the throne and out of the Temple to pour out their bowls of wrath (16.1,17).

The events glimpsed at the outpouring of the last-but-one bowl are especially alarming. Three unclean spirits appear and, at their instigation, preparations are made to assemble for war 'on the great day of God the Almighty' (16.14). Then comes a statement reminiscent of 14.13, marked by abruptness, with no mention of a voice uttering anything, or of an order to write anything down. A warning already heard in the oracle to Sardis (in 3.3) and familiar, from Gospel traditions, as a word of Jesus is here combined with Revelation's third beatitude before a detail borrowed from the oracle to Laodicea provides further extension (3.18):

> See, I am coming like a thief!
> Blessed is the one who stays awake and is clothed,
> Not going about naked and exposed to shame.   (16.15)

As in 14.13, so again here it is appropriate to identify the speaker of these words as the Risen One.[54] Doubtless, this was how Revelation was heard by the first recipients present in worship. This is another instance of their Lord intervening, in dramatic fashion, to address them before the seventh bowl is poured out.[55] No less dramatic – one word in the Greek and in the perfect tense – is the anonymous heavenly declaration which accompanies this final bowl and provides commentary upon it:

> *A loud voice came out of the temple, from the throne, saying,*
> It is done!   (16.17)

After this declaration comes a cataclysm of unprecedented violence (16.18-21), culminating in a terrible plague of hail, together with one last blasphemy (16.21). Does this mean that the last judgment has now finally arrived?[56] Or should we recall the parallel cry of Jesus on the cross (Jn 19.30), and with it the johannine perspective whereby the victory of his death is seen as beginning (at the very least) the process that will one day lead to both the completion of God's judgment and salvation?[57] For Revelation, as well, the death of Christ is the great reality which precedes everything else that takes place (1.5,6, *etc.*); it should therefore come as no surprise to us to hear 'it is done!' repeated, in 21.6, in context both of the fulfilment of promised blessings (21.6-7) and of a reminder that the second death awaits those who have not repented (21.8).

Revelation 17

> *Then one of the seven angels who had the seven bowls came and said to me,*
> Come, I will show you the judgment of the great whore . . .
>
> *So he carried me away in the Spirit into a wilderness, and I saw a woman*
> *Sitting on a scarlet beast that was full of blasphemous names . . .*
> *Holding in her hand a golden cup full of abominations . . .*

And on her forehead was written a name, 'Mystery', 'Babylon the great',
'Mother of whores and of earth's abominations . . .'
Drunk with the blood of the saints and the blood of the witnesses to Jesus.
When I saw her, I was greatly amazed. But the angel said to me,
Why are you so amazed? I will tell you the mystery . . .
The inhabitants of the earth, whose names have not been written
In the book of life from the foundation of the world,
Will be amazed when they see the monster,
Because it was and is not and is to come back.
This calls for a mind that has wisdom . . .   (17.1-9)

The last chapter in part two of this book will provide us with an opportunity to study in close detail the characterisation of this astonishing woman. For the moment, the essence of 17.1-9 (as just presented) entails us noticing both her traits of anti-worship and her close association with the monster. In correspondence with the blasphemous names of the monster, which like the dragon is a usurper of God's prerogatives, her own name reveals her rebellion against God and highlights the corruption she foments. In sum, hers is the name of someone not registered in the Lamb's book, like 'earth's inhabitants' (17.8). The obscenities or 'abominations' in her bowl, synonymous with spiritual prostitution, doubtless refer to everything which disgusted the prophets about idolatry. To drink from this bowl is to communicate, not in the redeeming blood of the Messiah, but in the persecutions which spill the blood of his witnesses.

Revelation 18.1–19.10

The wave ridden by the anti-hymn of 13.4 now reaches the literary gem that is Rev 18.1-24. We will have to delve farther into this text in Part Two of this book (in chapter 6). For now, we will approach it from the angle of the three parallel laments, with their similar codas, which become audible to our ears in 18.9-10, 18.11*ff* and 18.17*ff*; we will also look at it in conjunction with 19.1-10.[58] The three groups that raise funereal chants on the subject of 'Babylon' are matched by three others – 'saints', 'apostles' and 'prophets' – who sing the praises of God (18.20) before dissolving into an immense heavenly company, which takes over the task of sustaining the contrast (19.1a): the victory hymn they sing strongly resembles the song already heard in 7.9, on the lips of the human throng on earth.

In other words, 18.1–19.10 as a unit is governed by the same logic of antithesis which, in earlier scenes, has already placed the adoration of God and the Lamb in counterpoint to the idolatrous worship of the monsters. Three earthly laments[59] from the mouths of kings, merchants and seafarers (18.9-19) – apparently inspired by the triple lamentation over Tyre found in Ezek 27 – are answered by three heavenly hallelujahs (19.1,3,6), in such a way that the anti-liturgy's swan-song (chapter 18) receives its answer from the final hymn in which Revelation brings to a climax the acclamation of the Lamb (chapter 19). Let us now come down to details.

1) Revelation 18.2-3

Straightaway we should notice how insincere is the mourning raised by
the three funereal songs of chapter 18. On earth, nobody really weeps for
'Babylon'. The tone is set by the shout of derision from the 'mighty voice'
in 18.2-3, an angelic cry which picks up the diction of Isaiah's prophetic
oracle against Babylon (Isa 21.9), briefly alluded to in 14.8, and turns it into
a lament heavy with sarcasm instead:[60]

> Fallen, fallen is Babylon the Great!
> She has become a dwelling place of demons,
> A haunt of every foul and hateful bird,
> A haunt of every foul and hateful beast.
> For all the nations have drunk of the wine of the wrath of her fornication,
> And the kings of the earth have committed fornication with her,
> And the merchants of the earth have grown rich from the power of
> her luxury.   (18.2-3)

2) Revelation 18.4-8

Although the preceding proclamation is addressed to the whole earth
(18.1), there is no way the people of God will join in a lament of the
fact that so haughty a city as this has got her just deserts (18.7); after all,
the very chalice from which she must drink a double portion (18.6; *cf.*
17.4) is the one which God filled and gave to her (14.10; 16.19)[61] as just
retribution for her sins without number. Here is what is heard in the first
instance:

> Come out from her midst, my people,
> So that you do not take part in her sins,
> And so that you do not share in her plagues!
> For her sins are heaped high as heaven,
> And God has remembered her iniquities.
>
> Render to her as she herself has rendered,
> And repay her double for her misdeeds!
> In the cup she mixed
> Mix her a double draught!
> As she glorified herself and lived luxuriously,
> So give her a like measure of torment and grief!
>
> Since in her heart she says, 'I rule as a queen;
> I am no widow, and I will never see grief,'
> Therefore in a single day
> Her plagues will come – pestilence and mourning and famine –
> And she will be burned with fire;
> For mighty is the Lord God who judges her!   (18.4-8)

From the start, our ear is attuned in such a way as to detect an absence of authenticity in the three laments that follow. Consequently, readers should not take at face value every word of lamentation for a far-off city, invisible throughout and destroyed offstage. Mourning this fate is not what matters; making sure not to share it, does!

It is true that the kings, merchants and seafarers do mourn the fall of 'Babylon' – the debauchery which the kings had known with her, for instance, or the commercial gain made possible by her luxuries (18.3), are no more – but their motivations remain suspect. Out of 'self-interested caution',[62] these former allies of 'Babylon' (17.16-17) choose to sever their pact of solidarity with her, preferring to abandon her to her fate and to watch her crumble from a safe distance (18.10,15). The desolation of the whore, as inspired by the treacherous monster (17.16), takes form and shape in the flight from her of these kings, traders and sailors, in apparent fulfilment of the imperatives in 18.5-8. In keeping their distance these allies are behaving like people who have had prior warning, much as members of the people of God who were exhorted, just previously (in 18.4), to flee the city (cf. Isa 52.11; Jer 51.45).

3) Revelation 18.9-19

The three parallel laments form a unit. Here it is, together with their narrative envelope which, as always, is set in italics:

> *And the kings of the earth . . . will weep and wail over her when they see the smoke of her burning; they will stand far off, in fear of her torment, and say,*
> Alas! Alas!
> The great city, Babylon, the mighty city!
> For in one hour your judgment has come!
>
> *And the merchants of the earth weep and mourn for her, since no one buys their cargo anymore . . .*
> The fruit for which your soul longed has gone from you,
> And all your dainties and your splendour are lost to you,
> Never to be found again!
>
> *The merchants of these wares, who gained wealth from her, will stand far off, in fear of her torment, weeping and mourning aloud,*
> Alas! Alas!
> The great city, clothed in fine linen, in purple and scarlet,
> Adorned with gold, with jewels, and with pearls!
> For in one hour all this wealth has been laid waste!
>
> *And all shipmasters and seafarers, sailors and all whose trade is on the sea, stood far off and as they saw the smoke of her burning, they were crying out*
> What city was like the great city?
> *And they threw dust on their heads; weeping and mourning, they were crying out,*
> Alas! Alas!

> The great city, where all who had ships at sea
> Grew rich by her wealth!
> For in one hour she has been laid waste!   (18.9-19)

The tone of this three-part mourning sequence is in reality highly ironic. It should be noted how the three laments are formulated successively in future (the kings), present (the traders) and past tenses (the seafarers).[63] This grammatical feature, so skilfully worked by the author, helps our ears to hear how hollow a ring there is to the vanity of 'Babylon'. In her boasting, she thought herself destined for a long reign: 'I rule as a queen; I am no widow, and I will never see grief' (18.7). Yet it will take only an hour, in other words a moment of time, to erase even the memory of her once she falls to pieces, as we are reminded three times (18.10,17,19). How better to stress the shortness of the time-span available, before God, to this great but rebellious city than to declare, when all is said and done, that she too was, no longer is, and will be destroyed? The weeping, whether expressed in the past, present or future – 'will weep and wail' (18.9); 'weep and mourn' (18.11); 'cried out' (18.18) – is nothing but crocodile tears, cried out of mere self-interest. The whole thing is aptly summarised by a final 'wept and mourned, crying out' (18.19).

Neither the mourning of the kings, merchants and seafarers, nor the gesture of throwing dust on their heads (18.19), can dissipate the equivocation which characterises all three laments. From the moment lamentation begins, in the first of them, the likelihood that they might be expressing genuine grief is simply ruled out. To see this we need only take a closer look at the kings who lead the mourning. Whereas the twenty-four elders reign with God on thrones (4.4) and sing the righteous acts of God whom they voluntarily adore (5.8,11,14; 7.11; 11.16; 19.4), these kings are ruled by a monster which they are constrained to worship (13.8); in their opposition to the King of kings they form an association with the whore (17.10,12), only to find themselves, in the end, singing a fallen queen (18.9).[64]

4) Revelation 18.20

It is probably the same heavenly voice as told the believers to vacate 'Babylon' (18.4) which now tells them to celebrate her fall, once this has taken place (18.20). In evident opposition to the three categories of renegade who had come out of 'Babylon', three groups now sing:

> Rejoice over her, O heaven!
> You saints and apostles and prophets!
> For God has given judgment for you, against her   (18.20)

The rejoicing of those who have been vindicated through the sentence handed down to 'Babylon' is not, however, the absolute converse of the preceding dirges. The text does not appear to warrant the conclusion that lament on earth and celebration in heaven are to be seen as standing in implacable opposition to one another. Instead, heaven's exultation is shared by the saints, apostles and prophets. We may recall other rejoicing (in 12.12) which the heavens and their inhabitants were encouraged to indulge in, and which the salvo of praise that now emanates from the multitude of 19.1*ff* seems to repeat. Thus, the same voices now celebrating the fall of the idolatrous city had already greeted in song the hurling down of the dragon!

As the trilogy from the mourners was insincere, the change of tone in 18.20 is not to be taken literally either. For although the degree of sincerity on each side is not the same, the regret of some (18.9-19) and the gratitude of others (18.20) have the same cause. For an understanding of the irony and even sarcasm with which the laments are tinged we should notice how the view adopted by our author is in continuity with his predecessors, the writing prophets, whose heir he regards himself to be. In general terms these laments show evident similarities with those whose subject was Tyre in Ezek 26.15-18 and 27.1-8,26-36. And a double woe which could have its source in Ezek 16.23 is combined with the allusion to Isa 21.9 in 18.2. In this same context, Ezekiel's very severe words about Israel – a once beautiful fiancée, turned into a revolting whore – are already spoken in what is obviously a tone of mocking derision. As for the poems of Isa 23–24 and Isa 47, Jer 50–51 & Ezek 26–27, on the subject of the cities of Babylon, Tyre and Nineveh, all are sarcastic by intention. Therefore, the introduction to the three laments of 18.9-19, for which an angel is tasked (18.1-3), appears to draw the inspiration for its mockery of the fate of 'Babylon' from various several examples of prophetic derision such as Am 5.1-3.

We should compare the contrast between the triple lament of 18.9-19 and the 'invitation to joy'[65] from the heavenly voice in 18.20 with others that we have already come across in the pages of Revelation. For example, the cry of impotence from the hordes who fell under divine judgment (6.16-17) contrasted with the praises of the 144, 000 (chapter 7), while just after the second woe was announced (11.14) heavenly voices had celebrated the establishment of God's reign. Another contrast that comes to mind is that between 14.1 and 15.3-4.[66] If we limit ourselves to the present instance, which is the final case of such antithetical parallelism, the important thing is not to interpret it in a static way, as though the text merely offered a contrast between black and white. For when the three hallelujahs trump the three laments, the result is not static but dynamic. The fact that three categories of 'earth-dwellers' who had sung their funereal songs are answered (and silenced) by the opposing praises of three categories of believers, means that former slaves of 'Babylon', separated from her as they now are, may seize an opportunity: that of receiving, via this message of judgment, a proclamation of the very Gospel which could bring their salvation.[67]

5) Revelation 18.21-24 and 19.1ff juxtaposed

The lament found in 18.22-24 is the only one with the appearances of being genuine, at least at first glance; here, almost poignantly, heaven cannot help showing regret at the demise of 'Babylon'. Yet once more, the tone of 18.21 (which is hard to sever from v. 22-24) does seem to rule out such sincerity:

> With such violence Babylon the great city will be thrown down,
> And will be found no more;
> And the sound of harpists and minstrels
> And of flautists and trumpeters
> Will be heard in you no more;
> And an artisan of any trade will be found in you no more;
> And the sound of the millstone will be heard in you no more;
> And the light of a lamp will shine in you no more;
> And the voice of bridegroom and bride
> Will be heard in you no more;
> For your merchants were the magnates of the earth,
> And all nations were deceived by your sorcery.
> And in you was found the blood of prophets and of saints,
> And of all who have been slain on earth.   (18.21-24)

However we look at it, this lament placed on the lips of the narrator (or perhaps of the angel) is to be immediately replaced by a heavenly celebration from 19.1 onwards. There is no clearer way of indicating how the two registers correspond, like heads and tails on a coin. Together they convey the double significance of a single event, to be interpreted in terms of both judgment and grace: the destruction of 'Babylon' *is* a victory for God's justice and salvation; I will come back to this in my final chapter. In similar vein, we should also note how it is precisely from heaven that New Jerusalem will descend. Nothing more will be heard of 'Babylon' (18.22), now condemned as a whore (19.2), but out of the rubble of that city built by human hands will rise, by way of replacement, God's city, New Jerusalem, the beautiful bride (21.2).

From among the very ashes of 'Babylon' the justice of the verdict just given (19.1b-3) is unequivocally acclaimed, drowning out the ambivalent songs of lament that had accompanied her fall. After a first hallelujah (19.1), then another, a multitude like the one in 7.9 takes up the refrain, though not so loudly this time (19.6, where the only variation is the absence of the adjective 'loud'). This triple hallelujah comes at the core of a hymnic finale, which offers a synthesis of the other hymns in the Book.[68] Here, Revelation transports its recipients to the pinnacle of that true praise which, if we remember, had burst forth from earth and heaven from the opening dialogue onwards; accordingly, the liturgical 'we', here, echoes another in 1.5-6 at the start (*cf.* 7.12).[69] With the twenty-four elders and four living beings reappearing and falling on their faces, 19.4 recapitulates what was characteristic of the twin worship scenarios in 4.10 and 5.8, whilst from the standpoint of the narrative taken as a whole the hymns of 19.1*ff* may be understood as echoing those of 5.8-14. The crucial thing that helps us identify this synchronic parallelism is John's tell-tale appearance in both contexts (5.4-5; 19.9-10), which happens nowhere else.

6) Revelation 19.1-10 in counterpoint with 18.1-24

Before I examine 19.1-10 in detail, here is my proposal for setting out the text in such a way as to bring out its character as dialogue:

> *After this I heard what seemed to be the loud voice of a great multitude in heaven, saying,*
> Hallelujah!
> Salvation and glory and power [be] to our God,
> For his judgments are true and just!
> He has judged the great whore
> Who corrupted the earth with her fornication,
> And he has avenged on her the blood of his servants!
> *Once more they said,*
> Hallelujah!
> The smoke goes up from her forever and ever!
>
> *And the twenty-four elders and the four living creatures*
> *Fell down and worshipped God who is seated on the throne, saying,*
> Amen! Hallelujah!
>
> *And from the throne came a voice saying,*
> Praise our God, all you his servants,
> And all who fear him, small and great.
>
> *Then I heard what seemed to be the voice of a great multitude, like the sound of many waters and like the sound of mighty thunderpeals, crying out,*
>
> Hallelujah!
> For the Lord our God the Almighty has begun to reign!
> Let us rejoice and exult and give him the glory,
> For the marriage of the Lamb has come,
> And his bride has made herself ready!
> To her it has been granted to be clothed with fine linen, bright and pure
> For the fine linen is the righteous deeds of the saints.
>
> *And the angel said to me,*
> Write this:
> Blessed are those who are invited to the marriage supper of the Lamb!
>
> *And he said to me,*
> These are true words of God.
>
> *Then I fell down at his feet to worship him, but he said to me,*
> You must not do that!
> I am a fellow servant with you
> And with your comrades

Who hold the Testimony of Jesus.
Worship God!
For the Testimony of Jesus
Is the Spirit of Prophecy!   (19.1-10)

The first voice which sings the destruction of 'Babylon' and of the satan
(19.1), is joined naturally enough by a second voice to celebrate the inauguration
of the messianic reign and the Lamb's wedding (19.6): as the manmade city
falls, a sound and light show provides an indispensable prelude to the real
spectacle in which the city made *for* humankind descends. At the same time,
this heavenly liturgy finds words for the triumph of God (as anticipated
already in other praises), thus balancing the earthly mourning which we have
just heard and converting it into a joyful welcoming of the ruin of 'Babylon'.
The loud voice (19.1) is a fitting contrast to the deathly hush that has now
descended over devastated and deserted 'Babylon' (18.22). The tone of this
vast heavenly clamour, quite different to what went before, is one which
expresses a profound feeling of gratitude at so conclusive a demonstration
of divine justice in all its integrity. As can be seen from the legal vocabulary
of 19.2 (linking back to 6.10), the verdict sought for at the opening of the
sixth seal and still expected in 11.18; 14.18; 15.4 and 16.5-6, will now at last be
handed down. One further detail here has liturgical colouring: the expression
'forever and ever' shows that the smoke of the burning city, which rises up in
perpetuity (19.3; see also 17.16,18; 18.8-9,18 earlier and *cf.* Isa 34.9-10), works
in an ironic way as a kind of incense (8.3-4; 14.11).

In the introduction to the unit 18.1–19.10 it was noted that the three
categories of 'earth-dwellers' raising their funereal chants (18.9-19) would be
answered by three exactly corresponding groups of believers singing praises.
The time has come to take a closer look, for here the laments from the kings,
merchants and seafarers, who now stand divorced from 'Babylon' at a safe
distance (18.10,15,17), receive their answer from a song composed of three
heavenly hallelujahs (19.1,3,6), sung by those who share in the Lamb's wedding
and in his new city (19.7). The way in which the various elements that make
up this text are arranged confirms that it corresponds antithetically to what
precedes. In an explicit response to the order given in 18.20, the three voices
heard in this scene strangle those of former friends of 'Babylon'. To the voice
of the vast throng (19.1-3,6) are added that of the twenty-four elders and
four living creatures, singing in unison (19.4), swelled by an anonymous voice
that comes from the throne (19.5). Their threefold character is reinforced by
additional liturgical elements: the 'salvation, glory and power' attributed to 'our
God' (19.1); the triple sound of waters and thunderpeals, orchestrated by the
multitude (19.6) and borrowed from the hymn in 14.2; and lastly, 19.7's three
exhortations, with 'let us rejoice' –another no-nonsense retort, like the one
in 12.12, to the out-of-place 'they will rejoice' in 11.10 – followed by '[let us]
exult' and by '[let us] give him glory'.

Twice, in the oracles to Churches, conquerors were promised 'white robes' to wear, or the Church was advised to don these (3.4-5,18); several times in the interim the narrative has referred to them (4.4; 6.11; 7.9,13-14; *cf.* 22.14). These garments are an image for the purification of sin, for pardon and for acquittal, since they are 'washed white . . . in the blood of the Lamb' (7.14), enabling the wearer to appear before a holy God. In the present liturgical context, they occur again, in an entirely pertinent manner. The fine linen in which 'Babylon' was dressed (18.16) and which was a commodity on sale from her (18.12), is also used to clothe the Lamb's spouse: but there is a world of difference in the epithets used, since only the bride's garment is worthy to be called 'fine linen, bright and pure' (19.8), perhaps harking back to the attire of the angels 'clad in pure and shining linen' in 15.6. The same verse also explains this contrast in their respective clothing in terms of an opposition between the saints' garments of works (*i.e.* their righteous deeds) and the misdeeds or 'iniquities' of 'Babylon' (18.5).

Revelation devotes a twin-panelled account to the fall of the whore-city and to the readying of the bride-city that will replace her, moving from the demolition of the one to the descent of the other. This narrative sequence will be given our full attention in chapter 7 below. For present purposes, I find it no exaggeration to say that this double account is fundamentally liturgical in character. I need hardly repeat how, from the moment the Book opens, we are on the Lord's Day or how, in everything seen or heard in the course of the successive visions and auditions, it is intended that believers should see God revealed to them. So from a narrative point of view, once the anti-hymns of chapter 18 have faded away the adoration of 19.1*ff* ushers in the next phase: that moment when the parenthesis of evil will be closed. By this stage the entire universe cannot help directing its worship towards God, for 'how manifest it now is that God alone saves, that only his glory matters, that no power but his triumphs.'[70] From now on it will be impossible for any bogus liturgy that celebrates a rival to God or the Lamb even to be heard or for any voice or instrument (18.22) to take up counterfeit praises. Once the final hallelujah has sounded (19.6), in acclamation of the Almighty as he enters upon his reign, even the memory of any blasphemous hymns evaporates. From this point onwards, every song of praise will celebrate the salvation, glory and triumph of God.

When the seer hears the fourth beatitude of the revelation so far, he commits the unusual *faux pas* of worshipping the spokesperson who had proclaimed it – indeed, he does this twice over (here in 19.10, then again in 22.8-9). What this double scenario underlines, in my view, is the fact that no other worship has the right to exist than that which believers, in Ephesus or Laodicea, celebrate (in principle) whenever they come together: genuine adoration of God and of the Lamb only. For Revelation, it seems that in this world it is too easy to confuse those who will one day worship God in heavenly Jerusalem (7.15; 14.3; 15.3-4; 22.3; *cf.* 11.1) with those who, entangled by their idolatry (2.14,20; 9.20), become worshippers of the dragon or the monster (13.4,8,12,15; 14.9,11; 16.2; 19.20; 20.4). This would explain why both visions where John slips up culminate in the injunction 'worship God!' Two refusals of his misplaced worship by God's messengers stress, better than one, that monsters are not to be worshipped, or even angelic servants of God: worship is for God alone.

Revelation 19.17-18

Although there is not so much as a fragment of counterfeit praise to be found in Revelation's closing scenes, nevertheless the opposition between legitimate and bogus worship does not disappear completely. It is a well-known fact that the Bible describes meals more often than it composes prayers, and at this juncture a somewhat lugubrious meal is responsible for keeping counterfeit worship and worshipping in view. We have hardly set eyes on the guests invited to the coming nuptial banquet (which the Lord's Supper anticipates, 19.9; cf. 3.20), and they have not even sat down at the table (as it were), before we are presented with the spectacle of a quite different parallel banquet altogether:

Then I saw an angel standing in the sun,
And with a loud voice he called to all the birds that fly in midheaven,
Come, gather for the great supper of God,

To eat the flesh of kings . . . captains . . . the mighty . . .
Of horses and their riders–
Flesh of all, both free and slave, both small and great.   (19.17-18)

What we see here is a macabre parody of the messianic banquet and of the sacrifice of Christ, a correspondence which fills it with meaning.[71] The idea for this picture probably owes something to the text of Ezek 39.17, which ridiculed pagan festive meals in its time.[72] As for what this incident contributes to the plot at this point, we could say that so repugnant a feast as to bring carnivorous birds flocking (19.18,21), by 'signifying desolation and death'[73], throws into relief the previous festive liturgy, which is shaped by blessings, and offers a parody of the wedding feast which the Lamb has invited believers to attend.

The antithetical parallelism which ties feast and anti-feast together relies, among other things, on an explicit correspondence between the two invitations 'to/for the feast' (19.9,17). There are two sorts of invited guest. Those attending the wedding banquet are believers persecuted for righteousness, whose exultation is founded on their Lord's invitation to sit at his victory table (19.7-8). Their participation fulfils a promise received in the worshipping assembly on the Lord's Day, at the close of the first septet: 'I will eat [the Supper] with him and he with me' (3.20). However, before delving deeper into this blessing, in its final vision, Revelation focuses on the wicked. For them, by contrast, idolatrous service of the monster will have no outcome but a false feast for vultures, a scenario whereby they are crushed in total defeat before the invincible rider (19.17-21) encountered just a moment before (19.11*ff*).

Repulsive though it may be, this scene is therefore not fundamentally different, in its narrative logic, to the one which related the inevitable end of 'Babylon' as a prelude to New Jerusalem becoming a reality. Here at the denouement of the plot nothing must any longer prevent God, in the person of the messianic rider, from making his victory consummate; this is done in the broad light of day, by legitimate elimination of all opposition to his reign with no hope of resistance. This anti-banquet should therefore be linked to sinners' free justification by grace, as symbolised by their sitting down at the banqueting table of the kingdom and prefigured in the Lord's Supper on the Lord's Day. By giving material shape to opposite outcomes this anti-banquet illustrates the sentence handed down at the last judgment to those who do not know God.

Revelation 19.20; 20.4,6

Revelation's narrative has been unmasking, and thereby cancelling out, idolatrous false worship, inspired by demons, whose hijacked liturgy had parodied Israel's hymns. In what happens next, Revelation will make only two brief references to the bogus worship of the monster and/or its image. First, there is an account of the demise both of the false prophet that had inspired it and made human beings into idolaters, and of the first monster (19.20). Second, and negatively, the resurrection takes place of those who had not taken part in it:

> [*Those who*] *had not fallen down before the beast or its image*
> *And had not received its mark on their foreheads or their hands . . .*
> *Came to life and reigned with Christ a thousand years . . .*
> Blessed and holy are those who share in the first resurrection!
> Over these the second death has no power,
> But they will be priests of God and of Christ.

This fifth beatitude in the Book is the first to mention the holiness of those who, on the strength of the salvation God has given them, carry out priestly service devoted entirely to the service of God and of the Lamb-Messiah (*cf.* 1.6).

Final glimpses of bogus worship

Once the satan-dragon and the two caricatures of a false crucified one and a monstrous false prophet have all been neutralised, no more mention is made (in chapter 21) of a counterfeit to worship of God and the Lamb, which blasphemers might offer to one who is not God through one who is no mediator. Only true worship in its perfected state now remains. Thanks to the Lamb's triumph, this has become direct communion (21.3-4) without ritual or any holy place (21.22). Yet in the series of paragraphs that make up Revelation's finale, several motifs nevertheless echo in muted fashion the memory of false worship. Such worship may have been robbed of anything to say, by this stage in the plot, yet the seer seems to stay on guard and to keep in mind the situation in which recipients of the revelation find themselves. Therefore, before taking a closer look at the genuine worship in its perfected form, which brings together heaven and earth, we should find these clues.

First, it is stated that nothing impure or linked to the corruption of the anti-city 'Babylon' (18.2) will have a place in the holy city (21.8,27; 22.15); now that darkness is no more, this has become home to the holy God (21.2-3,10; 22.19) and the God of light (cf. 1 Jn 1.5). Illumination represents one of the key images in the description of this God-given city, for it punctuates the narrative on three occasions like a liturgical refrain (cf. 21.11,23-24; 22.5).

Second, we should notice the deliverance of the nations and kings of the earth to serve God (21.24), in fulfilment of the song sung by the redeemed (15.4). There is a patent contrast here with the scenario in which earth's peoples had formerly brought their tribute to 'Babylon' (18.11-17).[74] The narrative effects a first important transposition when, instead of bringing their goods, the nations simply present themselves. In this act of bringing God their offering of glory and honour, the nations balance up and even compensate for the adoration previously offered to the monster. Only God's glory will subsist from this point on (21.11), so to him and to the Lamb go the honour already given, and received, in the course of the earlier liturgies (4.9,11; 5.12-13; 7.9-10,12; cf. 11.15; 19.6-7). However, what is new is that now, it is brought by the converted nations (21.26)!

Third, in yet another transposition the heavenly throne comes down to the earth (22.1). This detail underlines the finality of the dislocation suffered by the rival throne when it was snatched from heaven and hurled into the lake of fire after transiting through the earth and the abyss. Its abolition means that the trajectory which we have been following throughout this chapter now results in the unique and exclusive adoration of God. Forever established among human beings (22.3), God's immediacy allows believers to offer him ceaseless face-to-face worship (22.3-4); doubtless, this recalls the priestly service of 7.15,[75] where the verb is the same. The absence of any temple (as a now defunct edifice) is compensated for, in a way, by the fact that a priestly aspect now characterises the people-city, whose precious stones encrusted in the great walls (21.14,19-20) recall the high priest's breastplate.[76]

Historical detour 5:
Is the bogus worship identifiable?

It is not among my preoccupations in the present thematic study to find a historical identification for the false worship or its practitioners referred to, or warned about, by our author. Nevertheless, the textual data examined throughout the present chapter and the prophetic sub-texts to which they refer suggest that Revelation's polemics might have as their main target, not Asia's pagan idolatry and the flourishing emperor cult of the eastern Empire, but something else which this writing seeks to unmask and to bring an end. Moreover, that something is false worship, of Jewish inspiration, which Revelation regards as a parody of the genuine worship in which the Churches of Asia indulged.

At the end of my article 'Approche thématique'[77] I formulated a series of four questions which must be faced when reflecting on the historical problem of this rival worship. Here they are again unchanged, except for their being rendered into English:

a) Did members of the assemblies of Jesus in Asia, as Revelation's recipients, have to confront in their context a reading of the Jewish Scriptures which was in competition with their own, finding similar elements but using these in quite a different way, so as to give an opposing interpretation of the (hi)story they conveyed?

b) Did followers of the Lamb, in Asia, find themselves obliged to combat a rival messianism which explicitly rejected Messiah Jesus?

c) In consequence, were these believers living cheek by jowl with partisans of another vision concerning the state of the covenant uniting YHWH to his people? Furthermore, was this a version hostile to any expansion of Israel that would include Gentiles justified through their faith in Messiah Jesus?

d) Might Revelation be an energetic apologetic *for* this faith in Messiah Jesus, whose words and deeds had renewed and saved Israel, and *against* a faith inimical to it, whose worship – which, according to Revelation, has got it all wrong – is therefore ridiculed, refuted and neutralised in the course of the narration?

Back to the text: Revelation 21.1-8

It is time now to turn our attention to the climactic point which the theme I am tracing now reaches in the finale. We start with the opening section of chapter 21:

> *Then I saw a new heaven and a new earth . . .*
> *And I saw the holy city, the new Jerusalem, coming down out of heaven from God,*
> *Prepared as a bride adorned for her husband.*
> *And I heard a loud voice from the throne saying,*
> See, the home of God [is] among mortals.
> He will dwell with them as their God; they will be his peoples!
> And God himself will be with them;
> He will wipe every tear from their eyes.
> Death will be no more;
> Mourning and crying and pain will be no more,
> For the first things have passed away!

And the Seated One on the throne said,
See, I am making all things new!

Also he said,
Write this,
For these words are trustworthy and true!

Then he said to me,
It is done!
I am the Alpha and the Omega, the Beginning and the End!
To the thirsty I will give water
As a gift from the spring of the water of life!
Those who conquer will inherit these things,
And I will be their God and they will be my children.

But as for the cowardly, the faithless, the polluted, the murderers,
The fornicators, the sorcerers, the idolaters, and all liars,
Their place will be in the lake that burns with fire and sulphur,
Which is the second death!   (21.1-8)

What is striking, here, is the way everything now has a finished character to it – something which was anticipated in my earlier discussion of 7.13-17. Everything here belongs, in a sense, to a liturgy of the Word. Following the declaration of 21.3-4, apparently by an angel, God offers a revelation of himself in a series of statements, which could be equated with an announcement that declares the wedding to be underway and where it is specifically said that an intimate relationship between humanity and *Immanuel* has now been brought about. For human beings such nearness is of a kind found in worship only, even if in the newness of their eschatological life – symbolised by living water freely given (21.6; *cf.* Jn 4.14) – they now meet God in a more direct way. At this final stage there is no place for offering God a refusal in any shape or form (21.8), for from now on God is to be known in all his holiness and truth.

Revelation 21.9–22.20

The finale will be examined in three parts.

1) Revelation 21.9-27

As a passage, 21.9-27 takes 21.1-8 and sets it on a broader canvas, where several of its elements contribute to the picture of perfected worship. The angel's opening remark tells us right away that we are about to see a people:

Come, I will show you the bride,
The wife of the Lamb!   (21.9)

It is not wrong to interpret this bride-city as an assembly of worshippers, as is confirmed by other details scattered throughout the text:

He showed me the holy city Jerusalem coming down out of heaven from God . . .
The angel who talked to me had a measuring rod . . .
I saw no temple in the city
For its temple is the Lord God the Almighty and the Lamb.
And the city has no need of sun or moon to shine on it,
For the glory of God is its light, and its lamp is the Lamb.
People will bring into it the glory and the honour of the nations.
But nothing unclean will enter it, nor anyone who practises abomination or falsehood,
But only those who are written in the Lamb's book of life.

(21.10-27, extracts)

Despite the fact that this is Jerusalem in her finished state – a sanctified city, at long last, made by God – no temple is to be found there (21.22), and this fact runs counter to the general eschatological expectation of a renewed Temple (Ezek 40–48; Hag 2.9; Zech 1.16 ; 6.12-15 ; *cf. 1 Enoch* 90.28-29). This is to be explained by the resurrection of Messiah Jesus, in whom God makes himself known. His presence with his people no longer requires that a sacred space in which to meet him be set apart from the profane; since he now dwells with his people, the entire people-city has become like a temple in its communion with the Christ-Lamb. The adoration offered by this people of worshippers is called 'the glory and honour of the nations' (21.26; *cf.* v.24), since this is Revelation's way of speaking of worship of God and of the Lamb (4.9,11; 5.12-13). There may well be an implied contrast with the luxury and opulence previously associated with 'Babylon' (18.9,19).[78] Finally, for the entire biblical revelation it goes without saying that any worshipper wanting to approach God must be pure: nothing unclean (21.27) may therefore pollute what Christ, through his shed blood, has made pure (*cf.* 1 Jn 1.7).

The communion between the saints and their Lord is now perfect and in its 'liturgy from start to finish, it is new worship'.[79] The celebration to which the whole city devotes itself has a ritual and processional framework. Details are supplied, in turn, about the main thoroughfare (21.21; 22.2): a parade of nations and kings which wends its way along it (21.24), gates to this city which will never again be shut (21.25), water that comes from springs (21.6) or from a river (22.1) and lighting for which God alone is responsible (21.23; 22.5). Each of these elements evokes the Feast of Booths (*cf.* Zech 14.16-19), for which the perfected worship of New Jerusalem must be the ultimate, grandiose fulfilment.[80]

2) Revelation 22.1-5

Here is part one of the final vision, taken in two separate stages:

He showed me the river of the water of life, bright as crystal,
Flowing from the throne of God and of the Lamb
Through the middle of the street of the city.
On either side of the river is

The tree of life with its twelve kinds of fruit,
Producing its fruit each month;
And the leaves of the tree are for the healing of the nations.

(22.1-2)

According to this vision, the bride-city, enjoying the greatest possible closeness with her Lord, becomes a garden-city irrigated by living water flowing from the throne. What this means is that by his work on her behalf, the Mediator (the Lamb) has restored the communion which characterised the relationship of Adam and Eve with their God prior to the Fall – an act which is, therefore, a 'healing'. Accordingly, before the final two beatitudes of the revelation are heard, more implications need to be spelt out . . .

There will be no curse any more.[81]
The throne of God and of the Lamb will be in it,
And his servants will worship him
They will see his face, and his name will be on their foreheads.

And there will be no more night;
They need no light of lamp or sun,
For the Lord God will be their light,
And they will reign forever and ever.   (22.3-5)

Since their transgression in Eden, humanity had been living in banishment from the divine presence (Gen 3.20-24), affected by a curse that imprisoned them under the power of sin and death. Now, through the Lamb's sacrifice, with the healing and newness of life it has brought, humanity will no longer suffer this ban but have access, instead, to the glory and light of God and the Lamb in unceasing worship before the throne (*cf.* 7.15). Mention of the name on their foreheads, at this point, may suggest that their service in worship is priestly in nature; the high priest bore YHWH's name on his brow (Exod 28.36-38) and from the outset faith in Jesus Christ has entailed a vocation to be 'priests serving his God and Father' (1.6). Apart from this, affixing a new name to the new people (22.4; *cf.* 3.12; 7.3; 14.1) seals the relationship to God of those whose worship celebrates his presence and whose testimony (*cf.* 22.10) reveals him to the world. Seeing his face (22.4) is yet another metaphor for worship that has now become direct encounter.

3) Revelation 22.6-21

In its epilogue – part two of the final vision – Revelation continues to make careful use of the cultic framework put in place from the start. The implicit demand throughout has been that only one response, in heaven or on earth, can adequately reflect God's initiative in coming, in the Person of Jesus Christ, to save his people: that response is to worship him in spirit (1.10; 2.7,11,17,29; 3.6,13,22) and in truth (1.1,2; 22.6,18-20). Faced with the unveiling of God which Revelation has been conveying (and which is now complete), the only appropriate reaction is to fall face down before God, and him alone (22.9; *cf.* the seer's *faux pas* in v.8).

I am reproducing 22.6-21 here in full, before offering some comments. Since almost the whole section is couched in direct speech, this is reflected in how I set out the text:

> *And he said to me,*
> These words are trustworthy and true!
> For the Lord, the God of the spirits of the prophets,
> Has sent his angel to show his servants what must soon take place.
>
> See, I am coming soon!
> Blessed is the one who keeps the words of the prophecy of this book!
>
> *I, John, am the one who heard and saw these things. And when I heard and saw them,*
> *I fell down to worship at the feet of the angel who showed them to me; but he said to me,*
> You must not do that!
> I am a fellow servant with you
> And with your comrades the prophets,
> And with those who keep the words of this book.
> Worship God!
>
> *And he said to me,*
> Do not seal up the words of the prophecy of this book,
> For the time is near!
>
> Let the evildoer still do evil,
> And the filthy still be filthy,
> And the righteous still do right,
> And the holy still be holy!
>
> See, I am coming soon; my reward is with me,
> To repay according to everyone's work.[82]
> I am the Alpha and the Omega,
> The first and the last, the Beginning and the End!
> Blessed are those who wash their robes,
> So that they will have the right to the tree of life
> And may enter the city by the gates!
>
> Outside are the dogs and sorcerers and fornicators and murderers
> And idolaters, and everyone who loves and practises falsehood.
>
> It is I, Jesus, who sent my angel to you
> With this testimony for the churches.
> I am the Root and the Descendant of David,
> The Bright Morning Star!
> The Spirit and the bride say, 'Come'.
> And let everyone who hears say, 'Come'.

And let everyone who is thirsty come!

Let anyone who wishes take the water of life as a gift!

I solemnly warn everyone who hears the words of the prophecy of this
book:
If anyone adds to them,
God will add to that person the plagues described in this book!
If anyone takes away from the words of the book of this prophecy,
God will take away that person's share in the tree of life and in the
holy city,
Which are described in this book!

The one who testifies to these things says,
Surely I am coming soon!

Amen!
Come, Lord Jesus!

The grace of the Lord Jesus be with all the saints!   (22.6-21)

As 22.6-8 takes up once more the revelatory chain established in 1.1-2, we
come to a penultimate beatitude (22.7) very like the first one (in 1.3), before
a seventh and final one (22.14) focuses on two things which have both now
been achieved: redemption, and access to God. The first of these beatitudes
has obedience in view – something which has always been of greater value in
worship than either sacrifices or offerings (Ps 40.7-9; Jer 7.22-23) – and this
harks back to an important element of the oracles to Churches (notably to
Sardis and Philadelphia, 3.3,8,10). What are to be 'kept', here, are the 'words
of the prophecy of this book' – a phrase which is nothing less than a leitmotiv
for the whole epilogue (22.10,18,19; *cf.* v.9) – and these contain the entire
revelation that has reached the Churches. This proclamation has an urgency
about it, since the time is near (22.10). The very last beatitude (22.14) puts in a
positive way what the fifth (20.6) had already said more negatively about access
to life which God grants to those associated with the Risen Messiah. The
continually washed robes (by implication, in the blood of Christ) signify active
participation in the benefits of his death and thus, membership of the people
which has been constituted by his sacrifice. Finally, a reminder about those
who are barred from entering this people-city (22.15) provides confirmation
that the last beatitude is like the previous six, which have added their rhythm
to the ongoing worship so far: it is in reality an exhortation to take hold of
whatever blessing is being referred to, and not to miss out.

From v.16 onwards, several speakers participate in an antiphonal dialogue.
It is difficult to identify them with any degree of certainty or to apportion
to one or another of them the various pronouncements that are made (for
instance, in v.17). What we *can* say is that Jesus the Revealer (he is 'Lord
Jesus', v.21, or 'the Spirit', v.17), who has already spoken twice (22.7,12-
13), is in dialogue here with believers ('you', v.16, or 'the Bride', v.17) and

probably with their liturgist, drawn from their ranks (cf. 1.3).[83] The liturgist is doubtless the one to bring the public reading to an end – unless it is the seer himself – and this is done by saying final words of grace over the assembly before it disperses (v.21), as is reminiscent of Paul's custom.

At the close of the revelation, we are still at worship on the Lord's Day. This section in dialogue answers the inaugural dialogue in 1.3-7. The schema comprising verses 17-21 – with an invitation (v.17) warning (v.18-19), 'our Lord, come' (marana tha, v.20) and a benediction (v.21) – both develops the one found in 22.12,14-15 (affirmation-beatitude-imprecation/expulsion) and also appears to reproduce a primitive liturgy for the Lord's Supper;[84] the amen ought not to be forgotten (v.20). Every part of the worship, here, is orientated towards a coming: 'come! / come! / let . . . come' (v.17); 'surely I am coming soon!' (v.20a); '. . . come, Lord Jesus!' (v.20b). Such a 'coming' coincides, of course, with perfected adoration; it will begin once believers see God face to face, and it will never end. Yet there is another 'coming' that happens already in worship on the Lord's Day, when the Risen One and the Spirit speak to the Churches. For as the Word is heard and the bread and wine are received, the Lord comes already – just as, in his flesh, he had already come proclaiming God's reign, or laying down his life – in anticipation of his final coming when time will end.

Notes

1   C. Le Moignan, Following the Lamb. A Reading of Revelation for the New Millennium, Peterborough, Epworth, 2000, p.85. This quotation begins a very stimulating chapter entitled 'Worship: Learning to See', in which a brief presentation of Revelation's message serves as a springboard for consideration of the practice of worship in the Church and, beyond that, of service in the world.

2   In recent study, Revelation's liturgical register has come to be taken seriously. Three studies in German and three in English deserve special mention. First, those in German: S. Läuchli's article, 'Eine Gottesdienst-struktur in der Johannesoffenbarung', Theologische Zeitschrift 16, 1960, pp.359-78; the part given over to Rev in R. Deichgräber's study, Gotteshymnus und Christushymnus in der frühen Christenheit, Göttingen, Vandenhoeck und Ruprecht, 1967; and the work of K.-P. Jörns, Das hymnische Evangelium: Untersuchungen zu Aufbau, Funktion und Herkunft der hymnischen Stücke in der Johannes-offenbarung, Gütersloh, Mohn, 1971. Then, those in English: M.H. Sheperd's book, The Paschal Liturgy and the Apocalypse, London, 1960; D. Carnegie's article, 'Worthy is the Lamb: The Hymns in Revelation', in H.H. Rowden (ed.), Christ the Lord. Studies in Christology presented to Donald Guthrie, Leicester, IVP, 1982, pp. 243-56, which surveyed the state of things at the time; and lastly M.M. Thompson's contribution, 'Worship in the Book of Revelation', Ex Auditu 8, 1992, pp.45-54.

3   I have already published a preliminary study of the subject of this chapter, namely 'Pour lire l'Apocalypse de Jean', op. cit. Considerable amplification of the contents of this article provided the present chapter with a backbone. I have been able to enlarge the study here, not only through my own presentation of all the relevant texts, but in four additional ways: a) an examination of

materials previously passed over in silence, for want of space within the limits of a review article; b) a closer look at this or that aspect of the relevant theme; c) incorporation of this third theme into the overall logic of the much wider argument put forward in the present book; finally d) notes in which I dialogue with earlier exegesis, wherever it has seemed either useful or necessary to do this.

4   D. Peterson, *Engaging with God. A biblical theology of worship*, Leicester, Apollos/ IVP, 1992, p.264. Peterson's study contents itself with exploring the first half of the pair, true worship.

5   I am in fact presupposing that Revelation was originally intended for oral communication or performance by one or more liturgists in a worship setting – much as Paul envisaged for his letters. On this subject, see the article by D.L. Barr, 'The Apocalypse of John as Oral Enactment', *Interpretation* 50, 1986, pp.243-56.

6   By proposing here, in Rev 1.1-8, as elsewhere in this Book, that a plurality of voices is to be distinguished, I am leaving as an open question whether the text would be better served if spoken aloud by a single voice or by several voices in dialogue. In the latter case, it must be admitted that it would often be difficult to apportion plural roles, for want of sufficient indicators in the text on how to do this. For a very suggestive study of this question, see M. Boring, 'The Voice of Jesus in the Apocalypse of John', *Novum Testamentum* 34/4, 1992, pp.334-59. In an appendix, Boring presents 141 units of direct speech. For each of them he tries to answer two questions: Who is speaking? And, what voice does the reader-hearer actually hear? This produces plural voices but, in spite of this, Boring proposes to identify a unique voice that operates at the most fundamental level: 'in John's view the whole of Revelation is Word of God' (p.345).

7   Similarly J. Kovacs, C. Rowland and R. Callow, *Revelation: The Apocalypse of Jesus Christ*, Malden/Oxford/ Victoria, Blackwells, 2004, p.40.

8   For Peterson, *Engaging with God*, p.277, 'it is possible that the visions of the eschatological drama came to John when he was meeting with other Christians 'on the Lord's day'. Whilst this is true, we can only speculate as to exactly where and when this happened. Explicitly, John speaks only of being illuminated by the Spirit on the Lord's Day. Peterson is right, however, when he goes on to underscore why the seer put his visions into writing, namely: 'so that they could be read aloud in that context [of public worship]'.

9   For a summary of what materials the hymns are made of, see especially K.-P. Jörns, *Untersuchungen*, p. 161*ff*. Compare also, more recently, R. Morton, 'Glory to God and to the Lamb: John's Use of Jewish and Hellenistic/Roman Themes in Formatting His Theology in Revelation 4-5', *Journal for the Study of the New Testament* 83, 2001, pp.89-109. For Morton the hymns of 4.8-11 and 5.8-12, as well as those that come later, have as their *double function* to introduce what follows and summarise what went before and as their *double content* themes drawn from the Scriptures – or sometimes, the Jewish apocalypses – together with motifs borrowed from the Graeco-Roman milieu.

10   Compare A. Yarbro-Collins, *Apocalypse*, p.92.

11   The acclamation 'worthy!' belongs to the ritual which accompanied the arrival of Roman emperors; *e.g.* according to Flavius Josephus, *Jewish War*, vii.4.1, the emperor Vespasian was declared 'worthy!' at his accession in the year 70. The

liturgical pieces of chs. 4 and 5 are commonly read in parallel with the imperial cultus and seen as borrowing (and thereby subverting) the imperial accession rite or acclamation which accompanied some victory or investiture; in them is detected a retort to those rituals employed in imperial temples. Although possible, this reading nonetheless seems as improbable to me as it did over forty years ago to J. Comblin, *Christ*, p.105, when he wondered whether Rev's author would conceivably 'copy a demoniacal liturgy and direct it to Christ' (my translation).

12   Jörns, *Untersuchungen*, p.165.

13   Inelegant though it is in English, I am deliberately reproducing here the future tense (in the original) of all four verbs 'will give', 'will fall', 'will fall on their faces' and 'will cast'.

14   Similarly, S.S. Smalley, *The Revelation to John*, London, SPCK, 2005, p.123: 'With John, we enter heaven to see and hear what we now understand to be a ceaseless round of immediate, liturgical adoration; and this embraces the worship of the saints on earth'.

15   Under the old covenant, the number seven, more than any other, characterised Israel's worship and the ritual associated with it. As a result the focal point in 5.12 is not *these seven honours*, all of which the Lamb receives (where seven is taken to be the number of perfection), but rather *the Lamb himself* to whom, under the new covenant, they are to be given. I will return both to the theme of the renewed covenant and to the symbolism of the number seven in the final chapter of this book.

16   For an analysis, from a liturgical standpoint, of the end of ch. 5 in parallel with its beginning, E. Schüssler-Fiorenza may be consulted, *Revelation: Vision of a Just World*, Edinburgh, T&T Clark, 1993, p.60. She finds there four distinct stages: 1) The 'new song' (v.9-10), which corresponds to the consolation brought by the elder in v.5; 2) the angels' hymn (v.11-12), which balances the seer's tears in v.4; 3) the world's praise (v.13), which is apparently the counterpart of the silence of the cosmos in v.3; finally 4) the amen from the four living beings and the elders' adoration (v. 14), which together reply to the angel's question in v.2.

17   See for example Beale, *Revelation*, p.736.

18   For another point of view, see D.E. Aune, *The New Testament in its Literary Environment*, Philadelphia, Westminster, 1987, p.243. For Aune, the various hymns of Revelation function not in relation to any false worship – which he thinks is only mentioned in 13.4! – but only as counterparts of the ceremonies of the imperial cultus. Parallelism with the imperial cultus is also developed by J.N. Kraybill, *Imperial Cult and Commerce in John's Apocalypse*, Sheffield, Sheffield Academic Press, 1996, pp.221-22 and more recently by P. Duff, *Who Rides the Beast? Prophetic Rivalry and the Rhetoric of Crisis in the Churches of the Apocalypse*, New York, Oxford University Press, 2001, *e.g.* pp.17-18. Proposals like this, which claim to be able to decode this or that detail of Revelation against the backdrop of carefully reconstructed Graeco-Roman realities, are frequent enough. Independently of the difficulties of the historical question (for which see my introduction to this book), I am still unpersuaded that such procedures of referential decoding may legitimately or usefully be applied to an apocalypse.

19   The term generally used for this approach is its German designation *Zeitgeschichte* (the study of contemporary history). A political interpretation of Rev's cultic language and of what its hymnic materials might refer to is

suggested by E. Schüssler-Fiorenza, *Just World*, *e.g.* p.103. Taking inspiration from her work, B.K. Blount, *Can I Get A Witness? Reading Revelation Through African American Culture*, Louisville, WJK, 2005, takes the themes of political resistance farther by developing an analogy between Rev's hymns and Afro-American rap music (or indeed blues/spirituals), particularly in his final chapter, pp.91-117.

It is well known that Rev is felt to be relevant by readers who find themselves victims of oppression. Excellent examples of this are the commentaries written by two Reformed pastors. K.H. Kroon's *Der Sturz der Hure Babylon* (tr. Berlin, Alektor), 1988, had its genesis in a series of sermons preached in the Netherlands during the Nazi occupation, whilst A.A. Boesak's *Comfort and Protest: The Apocalypse from a South African Perspective*, Philadelphia, Westminster 1987, was written in the context of South African apartheid. Another example is P. Richard's *Apocalypse: A People's Commentary on the Book of Revelation* (tr. New York, Orbis), 1995; written by a South American priest-theologian, this reflects popular reading of the Bible in the Roman Catholic context. We can also compare the political tenor of several contributions to the collective volume edited by D. Rhoads, *From Every People and Nation: The Book of Revelation in Intercultural Perspective*, Minneapolis, Fortress, 2005, which brings together several cultural perspectives on Rev.

20   Athough expressed with some retinence, this is Prigent's conclusion, *Apocalypse*, pp.289-90.

21   I draw attention, here, to two recent pieces of work which have linked 7.1-17 and/or other texts from Rev to the Feast of Booths (or Tabernacles) and to reflections of it in the prophets. J.A. Draper's article 'The Heavenly Feast of Tabernacles', *Journal for the Study of the New Testament* 19, 1983, pp.133-47, reads Rev 7 as an interpretation of Zech 14, where the restored chosen people and the pilgrims who have come from the nations join together in eschatological Jerusalem. More recently, E. Reynolds, 'The Feast of Tabernacles and the Book of Revelation', *Andrews University Seminary Studies* 38, 2000, pp.245-68, succeeds by means of a cumulative argument in finding a parallel between twelve of the main elements of the Feast of Booths and the use Rev makes of the same components, especially in 7.9-17 but also in 14.1-20, 15.2-4 and ch. 21–22.

In the period separating these two contributions, the standard reference work on the question was written by H. Ulfgard, *Feast and Future: Revelation 7.9-17 and the Feast of Tabernacles*, Lund, Almqvist, 1989.

22   'It is as though there is one bar's rest for the whole orchestra and choir of heaven before they launch [in the trumpets] on the second of John's symphonic variations', Caird, *Revelation*, p.106. It is unfortunate that Aune, *Revelation 6-16* (vol. 2), p.507, calls this pause a drop in tempo which holds back the narrative action – as though this seal contained nothing at all. Quite the opposite is the case! It is worth recalling the wisdom of Father Allo, when faced in his own day with platitudinous exegesis of this sort: 'we ought not to say, here, that 'our expectations have been disappointed' . . . as though the seventh seal were only there to make up the numbers', *Apocalypse*, pp.117, 119 (my translation).

23   For different options proposed since the time of Victorinus, in the third century, see especially Smalley, *Revelation*, pp.211-12. The most thorough discussion of the silence in 8.1 remains that offered by Beale, *Revelation*, pp.446-454.

24 Beale, *idem*, by analogy, in particular with the *Book of Wisdom* 18–19, sees a silence which echoes the primordial silence that existed before creation, and a silence with which the last judgment will also be greeted as a prelude to new creation.

25 Probably we ought to see only one heavenly altar here, in which the functions of both corresponding altars in the earthly Temple are combined. In any case incense was mingled with the blood sacrifices (*cf.* the ritual of the Day of Atonement in Lev 16.11*ff*).

26 Prigent, *Apocalypse*, p.301.

27 Rev 10.1–11.13 (or 11.14) may legitimately be considered a literary unit, as in Prigent, *ibid.*, p.342, for whom it is 'a coherent entity' – on this subject now see Smalley, *Revelation*, p.253*ff*. For convenience, however, I nonetheless include 11.15-19 as part of it.

28 We will take time to examine this figure in greater detail later, from the angle of the major theme of covenant.

29 Prigent, *Apocalypse*, p.365.

30 This is how M. Carrez puts it in 'Déploiement' (my translation). Carrez notes how, following the grand liturgical moment in 7.11-13, the creatures or the elders are involved with diminishing frequency.

31 Peterson, *Engaging with God*, p.266.

32 The same statement is found on an angel's lips in 14.12.

33 Comparison may also be made with Deut 3.24; 1 Sam 26.15; Isa 40.25; 44.7; 46.5; and Mic 7.18. For a non-canonical parallel *cf.*, in the Qumran documents, *1 QH* 7.28 or again the homage made to the power of Rome's armies by Agrippa, according to Flavius Josephus, *Jewish War* ii.4.380.

34 Prigent, *Apocalypse*, p.407.

35 With several commentators we may note how *Ascension of Isaiah* 4.2-14 presents, in similar fashion, an eschatological adversary who receives adoration from the earth; the same goes for the *Sibylline Oracles* 5.33-34.

36 For Schüssler-Fiorenza, *Just World*, pp.61-62, this violent death is analogous to that of the paschal lamb (*cf.* 1 Cor 5.7; 1 Pet 1.18). It conjures up a trajectory through the world by which one people is freed from among the nations, rather as prisoners of war might be freed by an agent sent from their country of origin to redeem them from the conquerors' country. In addition, it also means that those redeemed are constituted as a kingdom of priests (1.6) who, despite their ordeals here and now, are able to recognise that God and Christ reign in power and able, also, to bear witness to this.

37 See Aune, *Revelation 6-16*, (vol. 2), p.741. Charlier, *Comprendre* (vol. 1), p.283, speaks of *external* worship in the case of 13.4, deepened to become *internalised* worship in 13.12, in what he calls '*latria* and . . . acknowledgement in the full sense' (my translation).

38 For the great majority, what is involved is the emperor cult, particularly widespread in Roman Asia, and its Asian worshippers. Some, like Bauckham, *Climax*, p.445, also factor in the pagan worship of traditional gods, remarking on how Greek cities would accept the cult of the emperor by assimilating him to those gods, on account of his power. It is eminently possible that Revelation is at least implicitly criticising the worship rendered to Caesar or to the pantheon in the cities of Asia. However, like Prigent, p.407, I prefer to locate the sharp end of the description in a polemics which, as with OT authors, is aimed at

anything which might supplant the worship of the one true God. Yet unlike Prigent, I see no reason to regard this as *politically* motivated in the narrow sense (as being linked to some particular time or precise place), for it seems preferable to detect here a criticism that is *prophetically* motivated: prophets, out of their particular historical circumstances, made a habit of aiming general criticism at human history as a whole.

39 Brütsch, *Clarté*, p.239 (my translation). For several decades of the twentieth century, this commentary, which is strictly speaking the work of a German-speaking author, had a wide readership in francophone Europe thanks to its French translation.

40 Allo, *Apocalypse*, p.216 (my translation).

41 On this point, see Schüssler-Fiorenza, *Just World*, p.88.

42 Charlier, *Comprendre* (vol. 2), p.294 (my translation).

43 Bauckham sees it this way, *Climax*, p.28.

44 Father Allo, *Apocalypse*, p.241 (my translation). Allo, like other more recent commentators, has in mind the considerable *theological* importance of the two statements, which promise happiness to believers in contrast to the punishment awaiting the monster's false worshippers. What interests me here, however, is the passage's significance for the development of the theme of worship. In this respect, the complete absence, among commentators I have read, of any consideration of this matter is somewhat surprising.

45 Various voices in Rev remain unidentifiable (*cf.* 10.4; 11.12; 14.2; 18.4). An attempt to identify the speaker in the present instance is sometimes made, with varying degrees of probability. On an analogy with the tandem formed by the Risen One and the Spirit speaking in the oracles to Churches, the anonymous voice with whom the Spirit agrees, here, might well belong to Messiah Jesus – as suggested for example by H.R. van de Kamp, *Openbaring. Profetie vanaf Patmos*, Kampen, Kok, 2000, p.347.

46 For what follows I am happy to acknowledge my debt both to Bauckham, *Climax*, pp.301-06, and to Schüssler-Fiorenza, *Just World*, pp.91-92.

47 A number of commentators pay attention to the various Old Testament accents which come to be heard in the song of Rev 15; see for example Mounce, *Revelation*, pp.285-88.

48 Exod 15.11 may be compared, for example, to Pss 6.4; 15.1; Isa 40.25; Mic 7.18.

49 This is actually the only occurrence of the expression 'loud voice' where the adjective precedes the verb (although the same happens for 'mighty voice' in 18.2). For the previous uses of 'loud voice' – usually for angels – see 5.2; 6.10 (the souls' one voice); 7.2; 11.15 (in the plural); and 14.7,9,15. In the rest of the Book, see 19.17; 21.3.

50 See, for example, Smalley, *Revelation*, p.402. For Prigent, *Apocalypse*, p.361, the hymn of 16.5-6 is 'the heavenly and angelic counterpart' of the previous one.

51 What is heard is expressed in the genitive, best translated 'from the altar'. If translated, as here, 'I heard the altar respond' then the altar is personified. An alternative way of reading the genitive would be, 'I heard someone respond from the altar'.

52 This exegesis can already be seen in L. Cerfaux and J. Cambier, *L'Apocalypse de St. Jean lue aux chrétiens*, Paris, Cerf, 1955, p.141.

53 For Caird, Revelation, p.202, 'they have wholly taken on the character of the false god they serve'.

54   In similar vein see, for example, Smalley, *Revelation*, p.411, who contemporises
     Caird's approach.

55   Caird reads it this way, *Revelation*, p.208, against Lohmeyer. Ever since Theodore
     Beza, exegetes of Rev have regarded 16.15 as a touchup job, which (so the
     Reformer thought) is not quite where it belongs. For a sober assessment of
     discussion and the contrary conclusion that this utterance 'fits very well' where
     it is, see Prigent, *Apocalypse*, p.473.

56   For one who agrees see Hendriksen, *More Than Conquerors*, pp.164-65, who
     underlines the scene's air of finality and completion.

57   I am following Smalley here, *Revelation*, p.413. As this commentator reminds us
     later (p.540-1), 'throughout Revelation, the salvation and judgement of God
     belong together'.

58   For whilst the words 'after this', in 19.1, signal as they have on a number of
     occasions the start of a new scene (*cf.* 4.1; 7.1,9; 15.5; 18.1), this does not mean
     that the scene in question should be separated off from the foregoing one.

59   Some analyses of this chapter do not limit the number of laments to three.
     The most suggestive of these is that of W. Shea, 'Revelation 5 and 19 as literary
     reciprocals', *Andrews University Seminary Studies* 22, 1984, pp.249-57. Whilst
     noting how three groups lead the mourning in ch. 18, Shea argues for a series
     of seven chiastically- arranged hymns, based on their form and their contents. I
     still find a tri-partite division to be preferable.

60   It is interesting to discover that Revelation's other eight angelic discourses all
     have the same form as 18.1-3 (7.2-3; 10.1-7; 14.6-7; 14.8; 14.9-11; 14.14-16;
     14.18-20; 19.17-18). For a good discussion, see Aune, *Revelation 17-22* (vol. 3),
     p.976*ff.*

61   Thus, Charlier brings the two together, *Comprendre* (vol. 2), p.105.

62   This is how Brütsch puts it, *Clarté*, p.297 (my translation).

63   I am indebted to Charlier, *Comprendre* (vol. 2), p.107, for having made me think
     about this combination of past, present and future. It is to be deplored that
     translations often do not reflect with full accuracy either this movement from
     future to past via the present, or the aorists and one imperfect of the past
     tenses in the original. Accordingly, I have amended the NRSV rendering above,
     translating 'were crying out' in 18.14-15.

64   Similarly Resseguie, *Revelation Unsealed*, p.69.

65   This is how Prévost puts it, *Apocalypse*, p.143 (my translation).

66   See once again Prévost, *idem*.

67   On this question Roloff, *Revelation*, pp.207-208, may be consulted.

68   At this point I am following Ellul's proposal, *Architecture*, pp.266-68, with which I
     agree.

69   There is a good discussion of Rev 19.1-8 by G. Kennel, *Frühchristliche
     Hymnen? Gattungs-kritische Studien zur Frage nach den Liedern der frühen Christenheit*,
     Neukirchen-Vluyn, Neukirchener Verlag, 1995, pp.256-64.

70   Brütsch, *Clarté*, p.304 (my translation).

71   Among several commentators who take this line, I may mention M.A. Wilcock,
     I Saw Heaven Opened, Leicester, IVP, 1984, p.185.

72   This is Aune's suggestion, *Revelation 7-17* (vol. 3), p.1063. The same author (p.1064)
     also sees, in this meal, a parody of the messianic banquet in Jewish tradition.

73   Prévost, *Apocalypse*, p.152 (my translation).

74   Thus, for example, Fekkes, *Visionary Antecedents*, pp.270-71.

75 Not 7.1 which was suggested (by a typographical error) in my article 'Approche thématique', p.61. Also see Beale, *Revelation*, p.1113.

76 Compare Exod 28.17-20; 39.10-12 and Ezek 28.13. On this point, Prigent offers the following conclusion, *Apocalypse*, p.620: 'Our author . . . [describes] the new Jerusalem . . . and sees in this the fulfilment of the prophecies that he finds in the composition of the high-priest's pectoral: the 12 precious stones that are set in its . . . symbolise the 12 tribes . . . the people of the 12 tribes are indeed the Church, a people of priests (Rev 5.10) built on the foundation of the 12 apostles. Thus the priestly calling that is central in Israel finds its ultimate fulfilment'. For more detail, see his full discussion, pp.616-20.

77 *Op. cit.*, p.63.

78 Smalley, *Revelation*, p.558.

79 Charlier, *Comprendre* (vol. 2), p.242 (my translation).

80 This linkage was already suggested by J. Comblin, 'La liturgie de la Nouvelle Jérusalem (Apoc. 21.1– 22.5)', *Ephemerides Theologicae Lovanienses*, 1953, pp.5-40. For McKelvey, *New Temple*, p.163*ff*, the influence exerted by the Feast of Booths can be detected in each of the seven liturgies which punctuate ch. 4–20 of Rev (4.2-11; 5.8-14; 7.9-17; 11.15-9; 14.1-5; 15.2-4 and 19.1-8). See also my own discussion of 7.9-17 earlier and the relevant note.

81 This is to be preferred to the NRSV translation, 'nothing accursed will be found there any more', which obscures specific allusion to the edenic curse.

82 The NRSV's syntax, here (22.12) – where repay, although transitive, has no object – is inexplicably odd. 'To repay everyone according to their work', which would do justice to the Greek, is the obvious correction.

83 For some additional remarks concerning this section, see the discussion I devote to it at the close of the next chapter (whose standpoint is that of the major theme of true proclamation).

84 On this subject, see Prigent's convincing discussion, *Apocalypse*, pp.502-3, in which he sets Rev 22.17-21 in parallel with 1 Cor 16.20*ff* and with a dialogical text from the *Didachè* (*Did.* 10.6). Prigent concludes summarily (p.653), 'the book opens with a liturgical dialogue (Rev 1:4-8), its first great vision has as its object heavenly worship (Rev 4 and 5), every one of its pages contains numerous allusions to celebrations (prayers, hymns, various acts of worship), and finally it ends by paraphrasing a Eucharistic liturgy.'

Conclusion to Part One

The themes investigated in the three chapters of Part One work together in a three-part harmony whose character is predominantly theological.

We have been concerned, first of all, with *theology and christology*, with what is peculiar to God in his otherness above and beyond the confines of the created world (chapter 1). Then our focus was *theodicy*, whereby God in his supremacy (*i.e.*, his sovereignty, lordship and victory) is architect of his creation, ruler over the universe and victor over evil (chapter 2). Lastly, we concentrated on *liturgy* or *worship*, since the God who reveals himself to human beings in Jesus Christ is the One who is to be worshipped and served (chapter 3).

Put another way, we have taken an interest in everything, in Revelation, which has to do with God (his nature, will and actions) and with Jesus Christ, who shares equal status with the Father in this Book: we have seen who God and the Lamb are, in all their dignity and attributes, and what they do. Furthermore, we have paid equally close attention to the dragon and its sidekicks, who caricature them by laying claim to primacy, sovereignty and worship due only to God and the Lamb.

This systematic parodying of theological truth happens throughout the text. At its heart lies a very close antithetical correspondence linking two textual sequences: chapters 4 and 5 on the one hand and chapters 12 and 13 on the other (for which chapter 14 is an extension). This is something that is carefully prepared for by the first septet and developed still farther by chapters 15 to 22.

Part Two
Humanity Finds Itself

Introduction

At no point in Revelation have human beings been absent from the question of God which was our focus in Part One. It has simply been a matter of choice to reserve an examination of the question of humanity for the second part of this book. Now that this moment has arrived, our investigation will involve doing justice to various interlocking themes which have to do with the question of man in Revelation, in all their wealth and complexity.

Whenever human beings are viewed in relationship to God and the Lamb, humanity's story as told by Revelation has a positive thrust; but there is also a negative twist as and when they allow the dragon and monsters to enslave them.

Genuine testimony and counter-proclamation

In the first chapter, I will endeavour to present what Revelation understands as the right way for human beings to behave, as well as the Book's view of misguided human conduct. Receiving God's self-revelation as good news, then bearing witness to it joyfully, is seen to be humanity's true vocation; being taken in by a false gospel, and propagating this instead, is its caricature. For humankind, what is at stake here is true life lived free of all hindrances (thanks to God and his Messiah), or enslavement to falsehood as its substitute.

Faithful belonging and counter-allegiance

The second chapter will aim to clarify both what it is to be truly human, according to Revelation, and what this cannot be. Positively, human beings may find their *raison d'être* in faithful belonging to the Lamb, who is the true Man. Negatively, if they run blindly after a false saviour they will lose their dignity as human beings. It is humankind's prerogative to have been made and remade in the image of God and to be the beneficiary of his salvation, but all could be lost through a stubborn intention to revolt.

Bride-city and whore-city

In a third and final chapter I will examine everything which relates to the corporate entity formed by humanity whenever God is welcomed into their midst or when, on the contrary, their desire is to exclude him from their culture and civilisation altogether. This will feature a welcome for the God who has come to dwell among human beings, but also rejection when human beings seek to build an infernal city where God is not to be found.

At least implicitly, the chapters that follow will take up the issues raised in the three previous ones (in part one) and so formulate three two-fold questions: who is God and how should human beings – made in his image – then live? What has God done to alter, permanently, his broken image in human beings? And how do human beings and God approach one another?

4. Genuine testimony and counter-proclamation

*'In the plot of Revelation . . . a scenario is created where the Lamb's faithful
followers, obedient to the Word of God, are continually pitted against an enemy
wielding lying counter-propaganda'* (G. Campbell).[1]

In Revelation, God reveals himself; we have studied the Book's specifically
theological materials in Part One. In light of God's self-revelation,
humankind undergoes corresponding self-discovery; we therefore turn
now, in Part Two, to a complementary exploration of Revelation's main
anthropological subject matter.

Revelation depicts human beings by presenting two opposing peoples
characterised by their differing responses to the revelation they receive.
In the two chapters which follow, we will consider first (in chapter 5) the
antithetical identities of the Lamb's followers and the monsters' adherents.
We will then (in chapter 6) concentrate on the various women, cities and
corresponding women-cities which either give concrete shape to God's
dwelling place with humanity or else encapsulate, in a contrasting way, the
hellish place where God is not. First of all, however, in the present chapter
we will study the Book's characterisation of humankind as diffuser of a
revelation which has been received and assimilated. Or more precisely,
our investigation will take as its focus the major theme of true and false
proclamation, genuine testimony or counter-propaganda, truth and
falsehood.

A revelation of Jesus Christ comes from God and is communicated to
John (1.2-3), and at its heart there is a message destined for the Churches.
Its recipients, through their faithful response, become spokespersons for the
prophetic witness they have received.[2] Anchored in the introduction (1.1-8)
and in the opening vision-audition (1.9-20), this theme is fleshed out in four
complementary ways as the plot unfolds: firstly, by the successive visions and
especially auditions which are narrated; secondly, by diverse proclamations
that are made and particularly via the oracles sent to the seven Churches
(2.1–3.22) or by the witness of the two figures in chapter 11; thirdly,
through revelatory signs that occur at crucial junctures in the development
of the plot; and finally, by means of certain devices which facilitate readers'
understanding or interpretation of everything that happens, especially of
whatever God may say or do, where at any given moment the issue at stake
is always that of truth.

Along a trajectory where true and false declarations alternate, everything which comes about at the positive pole of this thematic plotline will become the object of careful parody at its negative end. Although the issue of truth becomes more sharply focused with every occasion when Good News[3] is unveiled, received, assimilated and transmitted, at every point there is risk of counterfeiting and a danger that the Gospel might be stifled by plausible proposals and mouth-watering propaganda, and truth buried under lies. The true prophet will speak, in authentic pronouncements backed up by accompanying signs; but there will also be illusory and misleading counter-signals from false witnesses and false prophets. All this and much more will be encountered in a plot that makes considerable use of deceptive appearances as a way of highlighting the reality and truth which they conceal.

In the scenario which Revelation develops, the Lamb's faithful ones, who obey his Word, run the great risk of falling for deceitful counter-propaganda that is taken at face value by virtually everybody else. If they are not to succumb to it, believers will have to listen up, keeping their eyes peeled and their wits about them. For today's readers, as for the original recipients (Roman Asia's Christians, in the first instance), there is much to learn by identifying with the experience of the characters in the Book and the dilemmas they face; for the challenge of tackling the problems of existence, today's readers may be armed with what their ears have heard, their eyes have seen and their wisdom has gleaned here.

A sketch of Revelation 1.1–3.22

Jesus Christ the Faithful Witness (1.5) acts as guarantor for revealed truth from the outset. It is he who orders John to write (1.11,19) and it is his testimony, intended for the Churches, that may be likened to a sharp word-sword (1.16). The opening septet determines all that follows and in the case of just one Church (Pergamum, 2.12,16) this metaphor is underlined twice; it will be recalled twice more, in a balancing way, in the christological vision which encompasses Revelation's closing scenes (19.15,21). Every vision in the Book without exception, in fact, is prefaced by a word of divine origin whose role is to make explicit the vision's meaning. Accordingly, it is vitally important that interpreters recognise 1.12 as crucial: the very first thing John *sees* is, quite literally, the voice that speaks to him. This makes the revealed Word itself the object of his vision, strictly speaking, which is confirmed by the expression 'I saw . . . in the vision' (in 9.17).

A revelatory chain is established for ensuring the transmission to the receiving Churches, of this message with divine origins. The chain contains seven links in all: God; the Spirit – or the seven spirits or sevenfold Spirit; Jesus Christ; angels; John; the officiating reader or liturgist; and finally the recipients.[4] In this connection, 1.4-5 is of special interest, since it places the Spirit between God and Christ. The importance of this text can scarcely be overstated. It gives advance notice of the joint role which the Risen One and the Spirit will together assume in the septet of oracles to Churches, where their co-operation will be underlined repeatedly by a double refrain. Oracle by oracle, Christ generates the message to the Church as he commands the seer to write it and then dictates it, as it were ('write: thus says…', 2.1, *etc.*). Throughout the septet it is also Christ's lips alone which announce the promise to the victor or repeatedly declare 'I know' or 'I will give' (*cf.* 2.7, *etc.*). The Spirit's task, meanwhile, is to recapitulate everything and to enunciate, to every Church in turn, the same injunction: 'let whoever has ears hear what the Spirit is saying …' (2.7, *etc.*).[5] In between these invariable beginnings (when Messiah speaks) or stereotyped endings (where the Spirit calls for vigilance) is sandwiched the body of each oracle, which is put together in identical fashion.

The dynamic whereby the Risen One and the Spirit participate together in a joint act of communication represents a crucial presupposition for the theme we are exploring here. They collaborate in the revealing of a message of divine origin and authority to the intended recipients and their joint working constitutes the *reality* for which a strict *parody* is offered when another duo – comprising the bogus risen one and the pseudo-spirit (13.1-18) – collaborates in the service of diabolical propaganda. We will examine this more closely in due course. For the moment it is enough to note how, in the third oracle to Pergamum, readers are already brought face to face with an infamous duo – acting as forerunners – formed by Balak and Balaam (2.14); they are taken over from Israel's history and represent a preliminary sketch for the tandem of false revealers that will eventually burst on the scene in chapter 13.

Revelation 1

We ought not, however, to play down John's place in the revelatory chain: the significance of the seer's role as spokesperson and secretary (1.2,4,9-10; *cf.* 22.8,18), indeed as chief recipient, we might say, of the message which Christ wishes to communicate to those who are his (1.1) means that he is not its weakest link! Nevertheless, the seer does not put himself forward as the author of his message; instead, its ultimate source of inspiration lies in God, the risen Jesus and the sevenfold Spirit in combination. As a result, in the septet of oracles to Churches the seer disappears behind the Messiah. Each communication begins by repeating this or that element of the titles or detailed description applied to the Risen One in 1.12-20 and this serves as a reminder that the oracle proceeds directly from the mouth of Christ the Revealer (1.1-2) who, in every case, has perfect knowledge of the situation of the Church in question (2.2, *etc.*). John's involvement remains implicit, of course, since the same Spirit who speaks to the Churches (2.7, *etc.*) had taken hold of him (1.10); nevertheless, whereas the Risen One and the Spirit speak, the seer, for his part, stays discreetly in the wings. His apocalypse is most certainly 'written proof of God's Truth among everyone [who receives it]',[6] to which the addition (or subtraction) of anything would be a crime of dire consequence (1.18; cf. 22.18-19). Yet in spite of this, Asia's Christians are to meet not with John but with the Risen One in person, assembled as his Church on the Lord's Day.

Four prominent indicators, all easily spotted in the text, underscore the dignity of believers as recipients of revelation. First, there is John's insistence that being a seer does not make him any less one of their number: he is both a servant (1.1) and a 'brother', as far as shared Christian experience goes (1.9). Secondly, an inaugural beatitude (1.3) future reward is promised for those believing hearers who will respond to his words by heeding and obeying his prophecy. Thirdly, believers are explicitly designated to be addressees of the revelation by the imperatives of 1.11, which govern the writing down and dispatching of the verbal testimony. Fourthly, the fact that the secret of the seven stars and seven lamp stands is explained to them confirms how it is their privilege to be in receipt of a message authorised by God himself.[7]

The effect of such details is to prepare the members of the Churches, in advance, for responsibly sharing the Testimony of Jesus (1.2,9) – Good News that is meant to be visible to 'every eye' or all people (1.7). The universal scope of this revelation is borne out by an initially obscure detail which will become clear farther on. The Risen One's voice is compared, in 1.15, to the 'noise of great waters': this simile is only clarified much later when, in 17.15, there comes the explanation that 'the waters you have seen are peoples, crowds, nations and languages'.[8] Thus it is being assumed from the start that Revelation conveys a message of universal relevance, and this is also reflected in the seven-part structure of a set of oracles addressed to the sevenfold, symbolically complete Church. The premise is that this all-embracing proclamation is positive in nature; it is this fact which will enable readers to recognise for what it is, in due course, a rival campaign whose characteristic will be big talk and blasphemies (13.5; cf. 13.14). As we will discover in more detail later, the goal of this conflicting enterprise will be to lead earth-dwellers astray (13.3,7-8,12ff) by means of universal claims whose scope is calculated to imitate the prior revelation.

Revelation 2.1–3.22

As a unit, the seven oracles to Churches expand upon the theme, rooted in chapter 1, of a divine revelation transmitted to Churches whose task it will then be to make it the object of their own witness. Together, these oracles form seven proclamations in one – 'all the Churches will know . . .', as we read in the central message (2.23) – and therefore they have cumulative force. Their mixture of approval and hard-hitting critique, based on positive or negative findings by the Risen One, helps create a to-and-fro movement between the good to be pursued and the evil to be shunned. This movement back and forth portrays the equivocal nature of the human condition, setting out the ethical challenge posed for Christians by life in this world. The decisive aspect, here, is the perfect awareness of each Church's situation which Messiah possesses and shows. One refrain, with some variation, punctuates all seven dispatches and it is first heard in the opening message to Ephesus: 'I know your deeds' (2.2, *etc.*). Linked to this there is a focus, from the very start, on the Sunday encounter with the Lord when believers' hearts are searched by the preached Word and their intentions brought to light. This helps recipients see not only that the revelation is addressed to them but, more crucially, that it comes to them *just as they are*: as such, it concerns them intimately.

At the heart of this first septet, Revelation begins weaving together the contrary strands of what is true and what is false. Discerning which is which is a task for the aware, who have ears to hear (2.7, *etc.*) – a trait reminiscent of the attentive hearer whom the Jesus of the Gospels sought out (*e.g.* Mt 13.9). Amid the dilemmas that arise in Revelation, not least in chapter 13, the need for such discernment will often resurface: 13.9, 'let whoever has ears listen up'; 13.10, 'perseverance is needed here'; 13.18, 'wisdom is needed here'; 14.12, 'perseverance is needed here'; 17.9, 'a mind with wisdom is needed here'. The message to the Church at Philadelphia highlights, as a particularly vital aspect, the idea of persevering on the right road; indispensable for knowing what this means is Jesus's exemplary life, as the Pauline tradition would concur: 2 Th 3.5 invites readers to aim at the perseverance of Christ, whilst Heb 12.2 concentrates on the One who 'endured the cross'.

Exercising discernment entails being able to spot, then spurn, whatever is false. There are pseudo-apostles, stigmatised as 'liars' (2.2) and no doubt identifiable by their lack of valid apostolic credentials (*cf.* 2 Cor 12.12), present in the Churches, along with several other groups of impostors. The hateful actions of 'Nicolaitans' (2.6) who show up in Ephesus are replicated in the form of equivalent doctrine known at Pergamum (2.15); 'Jezebel', who calls herself a prophetess (2.20) and who commands a following (2.22-23), is assimilated in no uncertain terms to the false prophet figure of Balaam, from Israel's past, whose 'teaching' some at Pergamum espouse (2.14). To the self-proclaimed apostles in Ephesus may be added Smyrna's 'so-called Jews' (2.9), whose words amount to no more than 'blasphemies', or their counterparts in Philadelphia (3.9) of whom it is expressly said 'they are liars' – all of them gathered in their 'synagogues of the satan'; at Sardis, it is implicit that most members of the community have soiled their clothes (*cf.* 3.4). Over against all these followers of falsehood stands the lone figure of Antipas. In describing him as 'my faithful witness, who was put to death among you' (2.13), the text seems to evoke the lot of the *true* prophet who bears witness and has to suffer for it: this may be a reference to Messiah Jesus himself, given that 'the Testimony of Jesus is the Spirit of Prophecy' (19.10).

It will be appropriate to return to the character called Jezebel of Thyatira in the last chapter of this part of the book, devoted to Revelation's feminine and urban imagery (chapter 6). For the present, however, it is worth taking a closer look at the traits which make her a false prophetess. Even though the biblical writings consider prophecy to be a defining element of the

believing community, it remains a problematic entity to the extent that it
is open to fabrication. Jesus's apocalyptic discourse in Matthew comes to
mind, with its threefold statement that false prophets or false messiahs
will emerge and lead many astray (Mt 24.5,11,24). For its presentation
of 'Jezebel', Revelation takes up the logic of Dt 13, where incitement to
worship other gods and so to imitate the practices of pagan nations is said
to be a mark of false prophecy; the same problem is also dealt with in Dt
18 and Jer 19. 'Jezebel's' actions are characterised, by the Risen One, as
leading his servants astray 'into self-prostitution and the eating of meat
devoted to idols' (2.20); elsewhere, the verb 'leading astray' is used for the
activity of the satan, its side-kicks and also 'Babylon' (12.9; 13.14; 18.23;
19.20; 20.3; 20.8; 20.10). In sum, the role of 'Jezebel' at this point is that
of a rival, falsely prophetic voice of similar stamp to the false prophecy of
the monster and its agent (chapter 13; *cf.* 19.20) – which is precisely why
she is to be repudiated (2.20).

It should be stressed that in Revelation truth and lies confront one another
inside the Churches, not outside them: it is there, from the seer's standpoint,
that Christ's Word, reinforced by the Spirit, runs the risk of not being heard.
Thus, toleration of falsehood alongside truth is pinpointed in several of
the congregations; it has the upper hand in Sardis or Laodicea and is more
or less influential in Pergamum and Thyatira. In Smyrna, believers valiantly
hold out against it, but even here, the devil has declared war on them in
his three characteristic guises of *agent provocateur*, prosecuting counsel and
father of all lies (2.10). As for Philadelphia, the followers of Jesus there are
protected by their steadfast attention to the truth (3.10).

In sum, the Word of God vies together with whatever other words
purport to speak truth for the ear of the faithful who may sometimes be
unable to distinguish which is the true Word: making shipwreck of their
faith is therefore a real possibility everywhere. The consequence of this
would be their failure to hear Christ confess their name before his Father
(3.5, apparently reflecting traditions of Jesus's words, *cf.* Mt 10.32/Lk 12.8),
or put another way their name being blotted out of the book of life (*cf.*,
in the Old Testament, Ex 32.32-33; Ps 69.28-29 where only the names of
those who are loyal to the end are indelible, 3.5); this register will feature
again later, several times (13.8, 17.8, 20.12,15; 21.27). In emulation of the
Confessor *par excellence*, who had appeared before Pontius Pilate (1 Tim
6.13), his loyal followers in their turn will have to confess the truth of their
faith on the witness-stand of the world (2.13; 6.9; 11.7; 12.11,17; 17.6; 20.4).

Christ alone is the *really* Faithful Witness (*cf.* 1.5), 'the one who is true'
(3.7). So it is hardly fortuitous that the Risen One should make himself
known, in the final oracle, as 'the Amen' (*cf.* Isa 65.16), the 'Faithful and
True Witness' (3.14): these terms emphasise his reliability and the truth of
his testimony (*cf.* Ps 89.37; Prov 14.5,25; Isa 8.2). But in the very place where
the Risen One knocks at the door (3.20), other communications are to be

heard. Messiah may have perfect knowledge of the state of his Church; she alas proves not to be so discerning, unaware as she is of being 'wretched, pitiful, poor, blind and naked' (3.17). In the name of the One who, as True Wisdom, reproves and corrects his fragile, feeble Church in such precarious circumstances, our author has therefore conceived a quite precise rhetorical strategy. Through caricature of what is genuine by what is counterfeit, his narrative will heap ridicule on the powerful piece of deception which has enthralled the Church, aiming thereby to shake out of their self-satisfaction the most blind or deaf of believers, galvanising them into making the right choices.

Revelation 4.1–5.14 . . .

Although the theme we are analysing at present undergoes only slight development in the diptych that is 4.1–5.14, a number of relevant issues nonetheless receive further clarification. In the Lamb with seven eyes and seven spirits (5.6) we meet the one whose job it will be to disclose God's purposes. We are explicitly told that what is *seen* (5.1-2,6,11) is inseparable from what is *heard* ('I saw and I heard', 5.11; *cf.* 6.1,5-6,7-8), because the audition expounds the vision.[9] This is indispensable orientation for readers who will soon face deceitful sights and sounds that need unmasking (13.9*ff*,18; 17.9). Finally, this is the very text by which we are granted access to the central space where the seer's ears and eyes are opened by revelation: here we are in the heavenly throne-room (4.2) where, as in the synagogue, the scroll is unrolled and read (5.1*ff*); once the fifth seal is broken (6.9), we will even catch sight of 'the altar' (whose definite article belies the fact that it has not so far been seen!), apparently identical to the altar of prayer and incense in 8.3*ff.*

. . . and the ramifications of it

Very soon, the dragon will attempt to intrude as a rival revealer with its own 'power…, throne and great authority' (13.2). This serpent-satan was originally a part of the heavenly council (Job 1.6-12; 2.1-7; Zech 3.1-5), where it had played the part of accusing counsel; but now it has been expelled from the divine presence (12.10) and thrown down to earth (12.13) and it will not manage, by its machinations, to overturn the guilty verdict which led to this fate. Nor will the flood of words it can inspire (13.6*ff*) ever be deposited in any sort of rival book of destiny[10]: the transmission and appropriation of authentic knowledge only is what the seals of chapters 6 to 8 symbolise and mark out. They attest to the fact that what is from God is God's alone, that only he has the secret of what he does and that, when the Lamb opens the seals, he alone will divulge this mystery and thereby consolidate his power. To God's rival and his henchmen will be permitted only a fleeting word that has been disqualified ahead of time and will not even be given a hearing until true testimony has already been spoken (11.7).

Revelation 6.9-11

In this cameo, faithful witnesses manifest traits that are as precise as they are noteworthy: they are described as having been 'immolated because of the Word of God and the Testimony of Jesus they had borne' (6.9). When they ask, 'how long?' (6.10; *cf.* 15.3; 16.5,7; 19.2), their request binds them to the martyr-witnesses of the old covenant.[11] As purveyors of God's Word and witnesses to Jesus Christ their task is identical with the one allotted to John the seer at the outset (1.2), a task carried out from Patmos for his 'brothers'. Indeed, in 1.9 there is a very similar expression, 'because of the Word of God and the Testimony of Jesus'. However, these witnesses have also given their lives, just as Antipas had done (2.13): now 'souls', they have been sacrificed exactly like the Lamb (5.6) who broke open the seals. The coincidence between their fate and his confers upon them a dignity reminiscent of his, whilst their exemplary testimony, which others will take up after them, depends upon the One declared in the opening revelatory chain to be the Faithful Witness (1.5).

Finally, their white tunics (6.11) allow us to relate these martyrs to those who will be associated with the blood of the Lamb in 7.14. The 'great tribulation' through which the latter must pass is simply one instance of 'tribulation… in Jesus' (1.9) with which every true witness is necessarily confronted (2.10); the care the Lamb gives them (7.17) together with the promises which the final vision will take up again (21.3-4; 22.3-5) are the compensatory benediction that makes up for their pains. All in all these martyrs in 6.9-11, like the 'blessed ones' of 7.9*ff*, anticipate the fuller characterisation which has been reserved for the two witnesses in 11.3-12. It is not impossible that their prayer and the response it requires are what drive the remainder of Revelation's plot, which unfolds in the period of time separating their plea for justice, here, from the final satisfaction they will obtain in the end.[12]

Revelation 11.1-13

We have already noted how the responsibility of bearing prophetic testimony is given, in chapter 11, to two witnesses. Up to the moment they are killed (11.7), their ministry meshes with that of witnesses under the old covenant (11.5-6), which had a clearly defined requirement of double or multiple witness (Num 35.30; Dt 17.6; 19.15). Thus, Moses testified before Pharaoh, with the plagues (*cf.* 15.1*ff*) providing material accompaniment for a word and witness directed against those who would not listen to God. Elijah also bore witness before Jezebel, with fire and a rainless sky as his corroborating signs. Moreover, according to Lk 10.1 it was Jesus's own practice to dispatch his disciples and spokespersons two by two. In the present context the two olive trees (betokening Israel, Zech 4.2-3 ; *cf.* 11.14) – olive oil, like God's Word, providing light, comfort and medicine – or alternatively, two lamp stands (standing for the Church, 11.4),[13] share Messiah's fate by undergoing death and desecration right where he had suffered and been crucified (11.8). There are four additional ways in which the description of their lot closely parallels his:

a)   They have a message of universal scope intended for humanity as a whole (11.9-10) – the counterpart of which, in exaggerated form, will be the wholesale duping of human beings by evil (12.9);

b)   They, too, will undergo resurrection (11.11),[14] a healing for which the monster will produce its own caricature (13.3,12,14);

c)   They will have their own ascension in a cloud (11.12): vague though the echoes deliberately seem to be at this point, reference both to Elijah's removal (2 Ki 2.11) and also to Jesus's ascension (Lk 24.51 and Ac 1.9) remains plausible;

d)   Their testimony bears some fruit, producing partial repentance (11.13) – which is an obvious improvement on the total hardening of 9.20.[15]

Through this parallelism, the witnesses become participants in Christ's victory, for their testimony to him corresponds to his own sworn statements as the Faithful Witness (1.5; 3.14) who keeps steadfast until death and even triumphs over it (5.6-14). Their ultimate justification and glorification, as pictured here (11.11-12), become somewhat intriguing when one ponders a parallel found in the traditions of the sayings of Jesus: had he not told his seventy-two disciples (sent out two by two), as they returned from their mission, that nothing would cause them harm (Lk 10.19)?[16]

Revelation 12

Significant elements of this chapter carry the plot forward to the point at which, in chapter 13, a veritable parody of true witness begins to emerge. For example the destiny of the male child (12.5*ff*), with a second reference to Ps 2.8-9 (*cf.* 2.26-27), looks forward to the triumph of the King of kings over the kings of the earth (17.14). Among Messiah's royal functions is his right to execute God's eschatological judgment; accordingly the allusion to the accuser's fall (12.10) may be understood as Michael's legal triumph over him, in anticipation of another victory won by the Faithful Witness against his enemies (19.11) in ratification of the verdict of his cross. This also explains why the victory of the other witnesses, on earth, can be proleptically presented here as being already complete (12.11): there can be no hope of future success for their adversary's stubborn attempts to arraign them in a mock trial, now that the satan's role as accusing counsel in heaven is no more (12.10). Described as keeping the commandments of God and possessing the Testimony of Jesus (12.17), these witnesses join the other martyr-witnesses of 6.9-11, 7.9*ff* and 11.3-12 and so complete Revelation's characterisation of Christ's witnessing followers. They have all died and triumphed in the same way as Messiah their master. His past victory at Calvary finds renewed expression in their successes, and this is so before the devil makes war on them.

Whilst every witness must still reckon with the threat of imprisonment or sword, the foregoing considerations surely carry great weight with readers. True, the serpent-devil-satan does 'lead the whole inhabited earth astray' (12.9); but if God no longer heeds its council, all it can offer is a pale parody of believers' advocate with the Father. This satan, with its angelic retinue, has been combated and defeated, hurled down from heaven to stalk the earth in pursuit of the woman and her children (12.13*ff*) and to lurk by the sea (12.18). All of which means that for the period when witnesses testify, and in a theatre of operations confined to land and sea, its continuing stratagems (12.12) are merely trying to pass off as victory its crushing defeat. Ever since the triumph of the cross, believers only have to do with a defending counsel (*cf.* 1 Jn 2.1-2); so it follows that when a stay of execution is later granted to the great deceiver, allowing it to enthral for a time the vast majority of earth-dwellers, this will not be the last word on the subject.

Revelation 13.11-18

Nor does the final say belong to the elaborate hoax recounted in chapter 13, which it is time to study in detail. In order are to grasp the extent to which chapter 13 provides a double caricature of the prophetic witness borne by Jesus, as Faithful Witness, and by his followers, we need to bear constantly in mind all that we have so far uncovered in the present chapter. By integrating what has gone before our eyes will see, in what transpires, 'bogus witnesses, phoney proclamation and fake miracles performed by false prophets'.[17] This is an anti-plot within the plot, a kind of retort to the revealing, handing on and speaking forth of God's truth which the Book as a whole addresses. In this mini-plot, things happen in such a way as to disclose, in the midst of the ambiguous world we live in, anti-witness subtly presented as true witness by anti-god forces using a clever smokescreen. The issues of daily living are rarely clear-cut; at stake, therefore, is the quest for what is true, along with the ability to recognise it when we see it.

In persuading human beings to worship the first monster, the second is doing the job of a false prophet (*cf.* 16.13; 19.20; 20.10) by spreading confusion. To see the parodic value of everything it is, says and does, we need only consider for a moment the monkey business detectable from its two horns. In Part One, we already took note of how the second monster's horns constitute an unbreakable link with the first, providing an obvious second caricature of the Lamb. Now, however, we must recognise how the horns also point to something new which the developing picture of the second monster will carefully depict. These are deliberately deceptive horns, in the same way as rapacious wolves may be disguised as sheep (in Jesus's well-known simile, Mt 7.15); this becomes clear once its dragon-like voice is mentioned and all ambiguity is dispelled. The horns are to be interpreted as clear marks of opposition to the Word (*cf.* 1 Jn 2.18,22 and 4.3, as in 2 Jn 7, where there is a parallel expectation that a false prophet will arise). The narrative, at this point, is establishing an antithetical relationship between the satanic propagandist, on the one hand, and those who speak for God on the other, namely the Faithful Witness and those to whom he delegates his testimony. This recalls the opposition between Messiah and false messiahs (Mt 24.11,24), since Messiah is the Prophet (Dt 18.15; cf. Jn 6.14; Ac 3.22). The two horns also ape true testimony (11.13) since the monster speaks like the dragon. Thus, lamb-ram's horns and dragon's voice together make up a clever amalgam[18] which the other characters do not spot but in which discerning readers are supposed to detect a fundamental contradiction.

The monster's speech and actions also betray a send-up of apostolic preaching and activity. In mimicking the ministry and authority of those who represent the Risen One's successors (13.12a), it counterfeits the accredited witness they bear to his resurrection (13.12b) and parodies the reign of God to which their signs and wonders testify (13.13):[19] whatever *their* apostolic ministry means for God's kingdom is faked by the second monster's deeds and words, on behalf of its pseudo-messianic substitute. As we have already seen in Part One, this also makes the monster a parody of the Holy Spirit since its activities in relation to the anti-christ function exactly as the Spirit's role connects to Messiah's in God's economy.[20] We may now explore the extent to which the concerted actions of the two allies of 13.1-18 – the risen impostor and the pseudo-spirit – are a simulation of the joint mantle assumed by Christ and the Spirit in the seven oracles to the Churches.

If we take, as our starting-point, the notion of a phoney paraclete (for the true One, cf. Jn 14.16-27), it becomes clear that the impressive activism of the second monster (13.12-16) is not merely symptomatic of its devotion to the first monster's cause (and to that of the dragon): it is, in every respect, the energetic anti-ministry of a thoroughly pseudo-spirit.[21] To understand the concrete effect which the monster aims to have upon human beings, it is sufficient to compare it to the Spirit of God whose work it obviously tries to counterfeit. Prophetic inspiration by the Spirit, more exactly, is what is being parodied here.[22] The second monster, a false prophet, does its work in the sight of the first (13.12,14), exactly as true prophets do before the Lord of the earth (11.4); and just as the prophetic testimony of the latter is accompanied by miracles (11.6), so the monster also uses signs to back up its message (13.13-14) in a way reminiscent of Elijah's ministry (1 Kgs 18.38).

Thus, over against the incarnate Word of God and the Spirit in his helping role, Revelation presents the reader with a powerful antagonist whose actions give form and content to counter-propaganda, that is to lies.[23] The second monster is an anti-spirit sparking off signs and breathing out a life-giving spirit of sorts (13.15); equally it is a pseudo-prophet *par excellence*, using its miracles (13.13-14) to reinforce the propaganda spewed out by the image it causes to speak (13.15) and succeeding in setting up an alternative community, albeit made up only of slaves.[24] Generally, interpreters explain this success in terms of Asia Minor's imperial cult, whose prominence at that historical period it is deemed to reflect.[25] Whatever the truth of this extrapolation, as it stands Revelation's narrative is here portraying a project aimed at rivalling the preaching of the Gospel and at equalling its degree of influence over human beings.

The second monster is falsehood personified. The discrepancy between appearances and reality in its speech contributes enormously to its characterisation as the antithesis of the Word of God and of the prophetic Testimony of Jesus.[26] We may note, in the first place, how it speaks in support of the sea monster in whose presence it stands; this detail is emphasised (13.12,14; cf. 19.20) as an implicit contrast is drawn with the place where true prophecy is given. Whether in Elijah's case (1 Ki 17.1; 18.15) or where the two prophetic figures of Zech 4.14 are concerned, that place is God's very presence, where his authority is recognised and his will expressed. The plain fact is that in all it undertakes this monster has the delegated authority of the first, to which it submits. Accordingly, one cannot help but see how this imitates delegation by the Risen One of his authority to his witnesses, as expressed in the Gospel commission of Mt 28.18-20.

The land monster's objective is to have earth-dwellers superstitiously worshipping the first monster with the healed wound (13.12), making them fall down before something pseudo-crucified and artificially resurrected. Caricature of the Christian proclamation of the Crucified and Risen One could hardly be clearer than here in this propagandist's spin. Signs and wonders of divine inspiration (Heb 2.4) substantiate and validate genuine apostolic preaching; previously, for Jesus's message of the kingdom of God as presented by the Gospels, this had already been the case. Yet according to the Bible, miracles are not unequivocal; they have always been liable to imitation (Ex 7.11; Deut 13.1). For Jesus (Mk 13.22 and par.), as for his apostles (2 Th 2.9-10), such imitation provides the tell-tale sign of a false messiah or a pseudo-prophet.[27] Nevertheless, just as the truth of Good News may be corroborated by the liberating actions that accompany it, so also the illusory nature of lying propaganda[28] comes to light whenever it is seen only to result in the enslavement of those who believe it. Whereas John's Gospel confines itself to describing 'signs' performed by Jesus himself, Revelation for its part recounts the 'constant attempts to imitate God and the Lamb which are attributed . . . to the demon . . . [as] the diabolical counterparts of the signs of Jesus'.[29]

The earth-dwellers are coerced by the monster's word and by its dominion (13.12). All without exception witness the show, as heavenly fire is brought to earth, yet nobody can spot the trickery of this. For us as readers, of course, knowing as we do the relevant warnings of Moses or Jesus, the real significance of this mimicry is apparent; it is a false imitation of the actions of true prophet-witnesses (11.5) such as, for example, Antipas (2.13), the slain witnesses of 6.9-11 or of course Elijah, the great prophet of the old covenant (1 Ki 18.38; 2 Ki 1.10). In the same way as Elijah had called fire from heaven, 'the [monster's] spectacular wonders are supposed to prove that man, like Prometheus, has stolen heaven's fire'.[30] As informed spectators, we realise just how much this monster matches expectations of a false Elijah preparing the way for a false messiah. But the characters themselves are taken in by this farce, branded as they are by the monster (as 19.20 will make clear); to them the second monster really does seem to be the skilful and convincing initiator of worship of the first, at least until real fire of divine origin finally falls (20.9) and at last they discover the hoax. A further aspect to the bogus fire is its likely allusion to true Pentecostal fire (Ac 2.3-4), to the very sign which attended the giving of the Spirit and anticipated the true prophetic witness that Peter and the others would bear.

Another look at 11.1-13

13.14 stresses the deceitful character of these signs. In conformity with the satan's activity as the epitome of one who leads others astray (12.9), they are essentially designed to mislead, just as Jezebel's prophecy was (2.20), and are therefore equivalent to pseudo-miracles.[31] The collusion of the two monsters in practising distraction and deceit through such signs is underlined by the repetition of the detail that the actions of the second monster are authorised by the first. The result is a parody of the two witnesses of chapter 11[32] who stand before the Lord of all the earth (11.4) and who devour their enemies with the fire of true testimony that comes from their mouths (11.5). Here, it is vital that we recall the point at which the monster first emerged. This was in the story of the two witnesses (11.7), whom it combated, defeated and killed before inflicting upon them the curse of non-burial. The question arises, why would the monster make this first, premature appearance out of the abyss? The answer, in my judgment, is that as readers we are being encouraged to see from the start how ineffective the monster will prove to be. For once it has done its worst, the witnesses are simply restored to life and ascend to heaven (11.11-12). For all that the monster 'will wage war against them, conquer them and kill them' (11.7), we soon realise that this victory is only apparent, nothing more. So, when the very same terms are used, in 13.7, for describing its campaign against the 'saints' – it 'will wage war against them and conquer them'[33] – we are able to interpret this seemingly triumphant new effort at counterfeiting their testimony and impressing the earth-dwellers, in light of the inconclusive attack previously launched upon the prophet-witnesses whom God had authorised and sent (11.3). Frontal assaults may now have given way to more furtive simulation, but otherwise nothing has changed and the spectator looking on ought not to be hoodwinked.

Some consideration should also be given to the team that the monsters form. Having suggested earlier that the duo of Balak and Balaam (in 2.14) was a preliminary sketch for it, I would now add that inspiration for the working tandem of monsters also comes from the collaboration of the two witnesses in chapter 11. Indeed, it is their story which is imitated and subverted by means of a counter-project modelled on it. Unaided at first, the monster emerging from the abyss (11.7) had temporarily reduced them to silence, first censuring them and then killing them. Now it engages the help of an assistant. The prophetic ministry of the true witnesses, who are an identical and undifferentiated pair in the text, thus calls forth a rival, dual counter-testimony which tries to pass itself off as true. The monsters therefore relay one another in distinct but inseparable roles and are described, as is so characteristic of Revelation, with a mixture of resemblance to and differentiation from their models. Everything the second monster does (13.12-17) amounts to an extension of the activities of the first and the indissoluble link between them is confirmed when the first one reappears in 13.15, reified as a statue.

Revelation 13.11-18 (continued)

The animated effigy of the first monster deserves our full attention at this point, able not just to speak but also to kill.[34] The wherewithal for understanding its significance is provided by several inner-textual correlations. The first of these is its capacity, through the influence of its helper, to kill those who do not bear the first monster's mark or worship it (13.15); this force for destruction is inversely parallel to the salvation of those who acclaim Jesus and bear his seal (7.2ff; 9.4). Then, secondly, there is the life-giving spirit of divine origin which revives the prophet-witnesses killed by the monster (11.11); it corresponds antithetically to the hellish and death-dealing life-breath that animates this image (cf. Ezek 37.10). Thirdly, there are also the 'hate-filled threats of excommunication and death'[35] spewed out by the talking effigy; its words of denunciation and destruction are above all false or counter-witness, parodying what is true, which bite back at the vivifying Testimony of Jesus and of his disciples. Fourthly, the second monster's actions in their entirety are anti-prophetic in nature; their intent is to entice and coerce human beings, reduced to terrorised idolaters before our eyes in 13.16-17, to worship the dragon and its representative in the very way foreseen by Dt 13.1-3, in warning against false prophets who lead people astray. And fifthly and lastly, this descent into idolatry allows the reader to exercise wisdom (13.18) in the face of what has been a complicated hoax dissimulating a false gospel: have not God's true worshippers, in obedience to his Word, always refused idolatry in whatever shape or form (cf. Dt. 3.6,11,15)?

Revelation 14

Beginning in 14.1, deceitful appearances finally give way to reality; what had seemed to be real (in the whole sequence 12.1–13.18) now turns out to have no substance, as truth returns to mock the appearances that had tried to fake it:[36] our author simply will not give falsehood the last word! Two literary devices combine, here, to ensure that no spectator of the monstrous goings-on witnessed so far can be under any illusion as to what they are. First, the text actively presupposes that readers possess, since the start of Revelation, inside knowledge and an awareness of the inspiration and content of *genuine* Testimony of Jesus together with the issues it raises and the goals it addresses. It is in our capacity to exercise judgment as readers that we may test, and so unmask, whatever is false in the parody of authentic prophetic proclamation which we have just seen played out – however carefully camouflaged it may have been. Perhaps, however, we have been too impressionable and allowed our critical awareness to slip amidst those disturbing, falsehood-ridden visions and auditions; what now renews our capacity to see and to hear, therefore, is another device: a complete change of picture. Up to and including chapter 11, everything to do with the issue of true proclamation had been giving advance warning that falsehood would eventually burst forth. By way of recapitulation, a second vision of the truth here in chapter 14 now confirms how it had done so, this time after the fact.[37]

In 14.5 comes a detail of capital importance: the redeemed have no falsehood in them. The very criterion which will permit or disallow inclusion in the book of life and enjoyment of eternal life with God (21.27; 22.15) is precisely that of one's relationship to falsehood; this had been the expectation of the prophet Zephaniah when expressing his hope for the benefit of Israel's remnant (Zeph 3.13).[38] Now, as we watch we see a company alongside the Lamb on Mt. Zion who are characterised by their rejection of all of the anti-christ's lies. Like the suffering servant free of all falsehood (Isa 53.9, also cited by 1 Pet 2.22), the Lamb's followers will neither believe lies nor tell lies – another way of saying that they will not indulge in the worship of false gods. The integrity and genuineness of those sealed by the Lamb is in radical contrast to the treachery and deceit of the monsters and their adherents. The true Good News sounds forth (14.6), drowning out all substitutes; 'eternal gospel', it is marvellous news intended for the nations (*cf.* Ac 17.29-31; Rom 2.16) which, occurring where it does, brackets out any other short-lived, so-called gospel.

By its deception the propaganda monster had first fooled virtually all earth-dwellers, then forced them into idolatry upon pain of death (13.12-13,16). Now, however, its slavish propaganda finds its answer in really Good News; aimed at the whole of humanity (14.6), this Gospel proclamation shouts down the ostensibly irresistible call to idolatrous false worship, inviting people instead to honour and bring glory to the Judge of all the earth (14.7). Whereas the dragon's associates had sought to coerce human beings into bowing down to bogus divinities, in total contrast this 'eternal gospel' exhorts them to fear the creator God, rendering to him the glory erroneously given to the monster.

The threefold, indivisible angelic proclamation[39] in 14.7*ff* counters and then replaces the monster's false testimony (13.15,17). At the same time, it is inversely parallel to the three woes pronounced by the three angels in chapters 8 and 9.[40] A positive message (14.7) which calls for the sort of repentance already seen in 11.13 is followed by two seemingly negative

pronouncements which foretell the fall of 'Babylon' (14.8) and foresee how
the monster's followers will incur a fate worse than the one with which their
master had threatened them (14.9-11). In reality, however, 'Babylon's' fall
is also Good News since its removal is, after all, a piece of essential site-
clearance to make way for a new build: New Jerusalem.

As a result, undue stress should not be laid on the negative-positive
contrast within this group of three angelic declarations. There is, in fact,
only one message here and its twin aspects of grace and judgment are
two sides of the same coin. When the third angel proclaims God's wrath
as something which genuine repentance can always forestall – something
conditional, therefore, and not merely theoretical or formal – this message
actually has positive value since it holds out real hope.[41] If a contrast is
to be noted, then surely it is between the redeemed who are acquitted
and the monster-worshippers who are condemned, or between Word and
propaganda. Armed with their singular Good News (14.6*ff*), these angelic
messengers also contrast with the propaganda monsters and correspond
negatively to the three woe-angels (8.13; then 9.1*ff*; 9.13*ff*; 11.14-15), as well
as harking back positively to the prophet-witnesses of chapter 11 whose
combined speech was just as indivisible as theirs.[42] This way of reading the
angelic proclamations is corroborated by 14.12-13, where the tone of the
final word uttered by a heavenly voice is one of consolation (14.13a) and
where the Spirit speaking to the Churches reinforces what is said (14.13b; *cf.*
2.7, *etc.*). An exhortation to persevere, obey and be faithful prefaces all this
(14.12), for these are the qualities that will prevent God's people from being
deceived or from suffering a sorry fate.[43]

Revelation 15.3-4

In the previous chapter, we already examined this hymn to truth. It rejoices
at the successful testimony which no one has been able to resist and at the
resulting worship that it has inspired among the pagan nations. There follows
the opening of the heavenly Temple which reveals 'the Tent of Testimony's
Holy Place' (15.5) not seen in the parallel vision of 11.19. A similar expression
is found in Num 9.15 and, indeed, 130 times in all in the Septuagint version
of the Pentateuch; 'Tent of Testimony' can translate either of two Hebrew
expressions: 'Tent of Assembly' or else 'Tent of Testimony'.[44] But the really
significant thing, for our text here, is the use of *marturion* in place of *marturia*
– a feature unique in the entire Johannine corpus of texts. 'Proof' may be
what is meant here, that is, legal evidence which attests to the faithfulness
or else infidelity of the covenant people.[45] Alternatively, the term might
conceivably denote the copy of the Decalogue itself, placed in the Ark (Ex
16.34, *etc.*)[46] – a 'Word' completed by the Testimony of (or to) Jesus to which,
in Revelation, every other instance of the verb *martureô* or the noun *marturia*
refers. Alongside witness to the Gospel, whose goal is the conversion of all
humanity (15.4), the final plagues (15.6; 16.1*ff*) testify, in their own way, to a

judgment that will befall all those who do not respond to the message: like any declaration God might make, all his judgments are 'true and just' (16.7)

Revelation 16.13-18

Now the pendulum of contrast swings rapidly back as the three angels give way before our eyes to three unclean spirits coming 'out of the dragon's jaws, the monster's jaws and the false-prophet's jaws' (16.13). This triple spewing out of curses highlights various earlier incidents, when the dragon disgorged floods of water (in 12.15), the sea monster vomited blasphemies (13.6), the land monster belched forth threats to enforce the worship of its partner (13.12) or the animated effigy spat out its deadly utterances (13.15). As counterparts to the three angels,[47] these unclean spirits (16.14,16) certainly prove effective and succeed in binding the earth in their spell. Accordingly, the narrative introduces a cautionary note at this point (16.15) and rings an alarm-bell in the ear of listeners who hear again an earlier warning given to the Church of Sardis (3.3), to whom watchfulness had been strongly recommended (3.2), as indeed to Laodicea (3.18).

This prophetic word of warning echoes words of Jesus from the Gospels, where a tone of urgency may be detected upon his lips (as in Mk 13.15-16), or he is heard to warn of the emergence of an unexpected thief (Lk 12.39) or else exhorts his disciples to remain watchful (Mt 24.43). It is almost as if such words are condensed here and turned into direct speech: 'look, I'm coming like a thief.' Previously (in 14.13), the Lamb had interjected a word of blessing, following upon another word specifically designed to strengthen any whose resistance was in danger from terrible distress[48] and who might go on to betray their faith (13.9-10). In the unfolding plot, we are almost at the point where treason will find its embodiment in the shape of the whore (17.1ff). For now, the Enthroned One speaks a final word concerning what is past; this word – *gegonan* ('it is done!', 16.17) – is a solemn declaration, to be repeated later (in 21.6), and a word which offers the only valid guarantee possible in the face of the roller-coaster ride soon to come. Powerful and extensive special effects accompany this pronouncement, proving it to be an unprecedented divine intervention in the world (16.18), the magnitude of which is greater even than what transpired around the same throne in 4.5.

Revelation 17.1–18.24

This diptych comprises a first panel which depicts the whore mounted on the scarlet monster (17.1-17) and another showing Babylon-the-whore (17.18–18.24). It represents a significant escalation in the conflict which pits truth and falsehood, life-giving Word and deadly propaganda, against one another. Accordingly, this is one place where Revelation's frequent recourse to antithetical conditioning of its major themes is most powerfully felt. In 17.6 'saints' or 'witnesses' pay in their own blood: the two designations are in apposition here and their equivalence is a very clear indication of how the theme of proclamation being charted in the present chapter is simply not to be separated from that of identity and belonging (which will concern us next). In light of 16.6 just previously (and of 18.24 and 19.2 farther on), *martus* (witness) must apply to God's people or to one of its members in the capacity of a witness, in the judicial sense of someone who is heard to give their evidence in court.[49] Jesus himself fulfils this role (1.5; 3.14), as do the two witnesses in 11.3*ff* or (in all likelihood) as did Antipas, who signed his statement with his own blood (2.13).

As the Evangelist could ask his reader to interpret and understand the startling 'abomination of desolation' (Mk 13.14), so here a measure of intelligence enlightened by wisdom would not go amiss (17.9). The seer is disorientated and shocked when he sets eyes on the blood-drunk whore; perhaps he is even entranced by such deceptive appearances of great power. The two angels (17.1 and 18.1) both convey and comment on a vision which becomes, as it unfolds, an astonishing caricature of Jerusalem-the-bride, called Babylon-the-whore. Here, an urban metaphor is used to visualise how a Church would look were she to fall into apostasy and betray the very Good News entrusted to her. By painting for yesterday or today's believer such a nightmarish picture, Revelation is seeking to insure that unfaithfulness of this sort never comes about.[50]

The command of 18.4 appears to be similarly motivated: God orders his people to abandon 'Babylon' to the sentence brought on by her sins and the plagues that cause her ruin (18.4-5). Here, John takes up the prophetic oracles against ancient Babylon (*e.g.* Isa 46–48 and Jer 50–51), especially those texts in which God's people are told to flee the city (Jer 51.45 and Isa 48.20). In the last of these, the command is hailed as a piece of Good News since, for God's old covenant people, Babylon's fall must mean salvation and restoration. The notion of the punishment fitting the crime[51] is respected, in my judgment, in the imperative to 'rejoice over her' (18.20), for this invitation to be joyful is born not out of malice but from the fact that justice is done to the one who rejoices; it is helpful to compare 12.12, which is another case of rejoicing at a verdict. Whereas 'acts of injustice' (18.5) characterise 'Babylon', the divine judgments she calls down upon her head 'are true and just' (19.2). The testimony of the true witnesses has triumphed in court; now justice is being done to compensate the blood they have spilt.

Revelation 19.11-21

Despite the obviously military terminology employed, the scene in 19.11-21 does not cease to evoke a courtroom atmosphere. Just such a combination of the judicial and the martial is familiar from Joel's valley of decision (Jl 3.1-16). Of course, the scenario in Rev 12.7-12 has already set in a courtroom a war of words in which Michael, acting as defence counsel, has taken on the outgoing prosecutor (the satan). The sub-text remains that of truth engaged in a battle with falsehood. Disciples who have heard and drawn life from an incisive Word face up to unbelievers whom this very same Word, which they reject, will 'kill' (19.21); there is a double outcome because the preaching of the Gospel produces acquittal for some and a sentence of 'death' for others (cf. Jn 16.8ff).[52]

The sea monster and false prophet tried to mimic Christ's victory and the Spirit's inspired testimony, but it was all in vain: now they are to be incarcerated, thus putting an end to their bogus miracles and their power to coerce. These events are prepared for in 19.9-10, a bridging passage which links the hymn of 19.1-8 to the present scene. Four related issues are now clarified: the need for revelation to be passed on, as shown by the renewed order 'write!' (cf. 1.11,19; 14.13; and later 21.5); the importance of keeping a faithful, written record of the true words spoken by Messiah, as stressed by the triple repetition of 'he said to me'(cf. the voice that addressed the seer in 1.12); the fact that every believer is a bearer and transmitter of the 'Testimony of Jesus' (cf. 6.9); and finally, an explicit indication that 'witness' and 'prophet' are equivalent terms (we may also note how 'brother witnesses' here will be called 'brother-prophets' in 22.9).

If we bear these points in mind, it becomes immediately clear why the rider is called 'faithful and true': as was shown to the Church at Laodicea (3.14), he is the authentic Witness who may be completely trusted. Insistence on his trustworthiness at this juncture brings to a climax an entire sequence which began in 14.1-5 and 14.6-20; there, whatever the highs and lows of the plot, believers maintained their perseverance in the truth in the face of lies. Then in the interim, we must not forget how celebration of the triumph of witness to the Gospel (in 15.3-4) gave way to a temporary revival of the enemy's fortunes through the activities of the three foul spirits and the blood-drunk whore – at least until their irrevocable defeat, as notified by the verdict of 19.2.

In the scene beginning in 19.11, the seer addresses hearers who are meant to have forgotten nothing of the struggle going on, in the story so far, between the true and the false. First of all, in the oracles to Churches, we discovered the false doctrine of Balaam or the Nicolaitans (in Pergamum or Ephesus), the seductive false prophecy of 'Jezebel' (at Thyatira), with its alleged access to the 'deep things' of the satan, and the lies put about by the 'synagogue of the satan' (in both Smyrna and Philadelphia). Then, in 6.9-11 or 7.9ff, there were the trials of the martyr-witnesses, while in chapter 11 it was the fate of the two witnesses, similar to that of their crucified master, which made a particular impression. Above all, in 12.1–13.18 the faithful Witness borne by Jesus and his followers underwent a carefully prepared, monstrous parody – a sight as grandiose as it was confusing – in the form of the second monster (phoney witness and fake prophet) and of all those taken in by its lying propaganda.

In short, up to this point in the plot various pied pipers have led people astray. Yet over against them all there now stands the rider of 19.11, who is an incarnation of the genuine Messiah (*cf*. Ps 2.9).[53] Just like the new David glimpsed in Isa 11.3-4, his Word is true: the sharp sword issuing from his mouth is the proof. He is none other than the one who had chastened and then consoled the Church at Laodicea (3.14*ff*), whom the Church at Philadelphia had come to know as the True One (3.7) and who, from Revelation's first page onwards, has been declared to be faithful (1.5). It is not difficult to follow the logic of his characterisation in the present context. The two-edged sword coming out of his mouth (19.15) – 'sharp' in 1.16 and 2.12, unqualified in 2.16, 6.8 or 19.21– aptly symbolises the authentic testimony that we would expect one known as the 'Word of God' (19.13) to give.[54] It also makes sense that he should carry out judgment, in the form of a universal anti-banquet (19.17-18), upon those who were deaf to his word.

Similar logic is still in play when we read, in turn, of the destruction of the land monster and false prophet, whose lies had deceived human beings (19.19-20), and then of how the ultimate adversary – a 'dragon', whatever name may be used for it – undergoes temporary arrest (20.2-3) en route to its final demise (20.10): at last, truth has triumphed. This means that the ostensibly universal category of the 'damned', in 19.18, is in fact deconstructed by the fate of these champions of lies and by what follows. Now that these monsters have been permanently neutralised, in the visions of a restored heaven and earth (chapter 21–22) the focus will soon shift to the innumerable 'saved' who have patently been set free from their shackles

Revelation 21–22

As the threshold of Revelation's finale looms into view, readers are expecting our chosen thematic trajectory to produce a certain outcome: a just verdict for the 'saints' who have suffered or been slaughtered for their testimony. This is precisely the meaning of rising to new life and reigning with Christ: a fitting outcome that vindicates all who shouldered the responsibility of faithful Witness to the death when they opted to resist the monster. Right to the end, however, the plot holds everything in a rhetorical tension. We see this when God, who had spoken in 1.8 (and probably again in 16.1,17, as the one behind the 'loud voice'),[55] apparently utters the 'certain and true' words of re-creation which deliver, finally, the expected inheritance for conquerors (21.7). Accompanying this declaration there is a word of solemn warning, first heard in 21.8 and then repeated at the end of the expansion that is 21.9-27. From the start, throughout the story and still at the end, Revelation still assumes that believers will always need encouragement, until their last breath, to renew and reaffirm their commitment. The assurance that their salvation is approaching must never make them fall asleep!

Moreover, so pervasive an influence has the logic of antithesis had upon the Book's composition that here at its climax – just when the promises to the victors find their fulfilment, – we still encounter the remnants of an anti-message whose role, in the final visions, is to maintain to the very end a contrast between Gospel and propaganda, authentic testimony and deceitful falsehoods. If any proof of this were needed, two vice lists provide it (*cf.* 1 Cor 6.9-11). Each of them – both a detailed version (21.8) and a summary (21.27) – is completed with a reference to lies. This is not merely the worst of the vices; it is also the sum of all the rest: John's Gospel, where 'truth' is so central, comes readily to mind and especially the moment (in Jn 8.44) when the devil is dubbed father of lies and liar extraordinary. As a final rhetorical flourish Rev 22.15 supplies an exclusion order, which again puts falsehood at the end; the idea of 'perpetrating falsehood' might this time have us recall its opposite – 'promoting truth' – in Jn 3.21. We may conclude that Revelation never tires in its double depiction, with on the one hand faithful Witness by Messiah and his followers and on the other, the counter-project carried on by the dragon, its lackeys and the earth-dwellers. The problem of falsehood has been warned about at various points (see 2.2; 3.9; 14.5) and is kept to the fore right to the end, as the Book labours to prevent any more people from abandoning true faith and from associating with the monster and its diabolical lies.

End of message: Revelation 22.6-22

As we complete our study of the theme of true and false proclamation in Revelation, several elements of Rev 22.6*ff* must be taken into account. The first point to note is an inner-textual one: 22.6 both quotes and adapts 1.1 at the start of the Book, repeating verbatim the explicit reason for the revelation ('to show his servants what must very soon take place') in a new context where reference is made, exactly as in the opening one, to God sending 'his angel'. Every piece of unveiling so far has involved an angel, so it is entirely appropriate that another should be the final speaker to give explanations to the seer in 22.6.[56]

At the start, a revelatory chain had identified and established the partners for the antiphonal dialogue (1.3-8) and for the revelation itself transmitted by John to the Churches (in 2.1–3.22). Our second point entails noticing how this chain is virtually reconstituted here, to include God, as the ultimate source of the revelation; his 'servants', who are its addressees (22.6, carried over from the vision of 22.1-5); the angel (22.6); and two further key link-witnesses in the chain, Jesus and John (1.1), who come forward to speak in 22.7 and 22.8 respectively. What now takes place is a final liturgical dialogue which corresponds to that of the opening sequence, although it is much more elaborate in nature. When Jesus seemingly interrupts John, with the interjection 'I am coming right away' (22.7), this directly picks up his words in 2.16 and 3.11 and echoes the 'soon' of 1.1. This means that we are back where we started, for all that was to be revealed has now been so. If there is anything that still needs to be underlined at this stage, it is the quality of the revelation that has been received and the responsibility carried by those who have become its spokespersons.

The angel, meanwhile, repeats something heard not long before and quotes exactly what the Enthroned One had said (*cf.* 21.5). This is final confirmation that these words are 'faithful' (or 'dependable') and 'true', like the Witness-Revealer of oracle seven to Laodicea (3.14) or the Messiah-Word of God (19.11) with his piercing, sword-like word (19.15); the angel of 19.9 had already underscored the second of these characteristics of the revelation (its truth). Two further issues are also addressed: the intrinsic quality of this revelation; and the way it ought to be received and then handed on. Regarding the first there is the claim that all the preceding vision-auditions are reliable and truthful: this is of strategic importance here at the Book's close. In respect of the second, Revelation here combines its only use of 'I've heard [everything]' (in 22.8) with its seventeenth and final use of 'I've seen/I saw': this indicates that there is quite simply no more to be seen – John has both seen and heard it all. Oral/aural communication of a revelation given by God and by the Lamb is now coming to an end and the message takes written form, as was anticipated from the start (1.11,19; 2.1, *etc.*): as a prophetic book it must be respected and protected, even as its message is to be obeyed and propagated (22.7,9-10,18-19).

The solemnity of the revelatory event itself, along with the authority of the testimony it has served to communicate, are accentuated in two additional ways. The first of these is John's inappropriate behaviour, when he succumbs for the second time to the temptation to fall at the angel's feet (22.8; *cf.* 19.10). The second is the reproof engendered by his renewed mistake, whereby the angel's role is clarified as being no different to that of any other worshipper of the only God – be they prophet, seer, or simply believers to whom the revelation is sent (22.9). For all those enlightened by its unveiling, the hour of faithful Witness is now about to strike; that is why future obedience to the words of the Book they have received will be tantamount to keeping faithfully the Testimony of Jesus it contains (19.10).[57]

The last-but-one beatitude of 22.7 recalls the very first in the series of seven (*cf.* 1.3). In between, readers have received ample enlightenment concerning the immense dignity and joy involved in the calling to be a witness in the footsteps of the Faithful Witness, Jesus Christ; now they may take comfort from the fact that provision has been made for keeping the Book's message continually accessible and useful (22.10). At the same time, the jolts experienced during the plot have made it equally clear that responsibility to witness remains constant; this is flagged up once more by the exhortation of 22.11 and the warning of 22.12, recalling 16.15. In this manner, words of reassurance are held in tension with words of caution right to the end of the revelation. A final beatitude focuses on Christ's redemption (22.14; *cf.* 7.14), but even here the restoration of humanity which it produces is antithetically counterbalanced by the solemn exclusion order of 22.15.[58]

At first sight it would appear that the 'Lord Jesus' has the last revelatory
Word, for he is the one responsible for the message addressed to the Churches
(22.16) and he is able both to attest to the exactness of what has been
communicated and to vouch for the truth of the testimony given (22.18,20a).
However, John as prophet may also be involved: some take the seer to be the
speaker in 22.18-20, by analogy with 1.2.[59] Yet *marturô egô* ('I myself attest')
in 22.18 does suggest Jesus, who is without much doubt the speaker for the
Book's other similar occurrences of *ego* (1.8,17; 2.23; 3.9,19; 21.6; 22.13,16).
There remains a third, attractive possibility for explaining this ambiguous 'I
myself': here at the climax of a revelation duly received and shared – when
all is said and done – perhaps John as prophet has no qualms in allowing his
own testimony to merge with that of his Lord. If so, he is quoting Jesus in the
first person much as Old Testament prophets, in their role as spokespersons,
had dared to speak for YHWH despite the strident voices that opposed them.

Notes

1   G. Campbell, 'True and False Proclamation in the Book of Revelation', *Irish
    Biblical Studies* 25, 2003/2, p.63. The substance of the present chapter, at an
    earlier stage of its development, provided the inspiration for this article and its
    sequel in the same journal (2003/3, pp.106-20).
2   There is an exhaustive study of the 'Testimony of Jesus' (1.2,9; 12.17; 19.10;
    20.4), from the twin angles of Jesus as witness (together with those belonging to
    him, who continue his testimony) and of John as seer (along with the recipients
    of his prophecy and book), in H. Roose, *'Das Zeugnis Jesu.' Seine Bedeutung für
    die Christologie, Eschatologie und Prophetie in der Offenbarung des Johannes*, Tübingen/
    Basle, Francke Verlag, 2000.
3   In this chapter, where we are studying Revelation's depiction of true and false
    gospels, Good News and (true) Gospel are systematically capitalised, by analogy
    with the Witness or Word of the Revealer, Messiah Jesus. This helps bring
    out the Book's emphasis upon God's self-revelation as bringing liberation for
    human beings from enslavement to all falsehood.
4   *Contra* L.L. Thompson, *Revelation*, p.178, who only finds six: 'God-Jesus-angels-
    John-reader-hearer'. Thompson, here, has simply overlooked the programmatic
    significance of 1.4-5, which situates the Spirit between the Eternal One and
    Christ the Faithful Witness.
5   We may compare Ellul, *Architecture*, p.132-33, who says: 'everything is at one
    and the same time testimony concerning Jesus Christ [objective testimony] and
    prophecy by the Spirit [who personifies the Word, which everyone is called
    upon to appropriate]' (my translation).
6   Ellul, *ibid.*, p.207 (my translation).
7   For his part Thompson, *Revelation*, p.179, also notes indicators three and four.
8   I am indebted to E. Corsini, *Apocalypse*, p.87, for having alerted me to the linkage
    between 1.15 and 17.15.
9   As Sweet, *Revelation*, rightly points out at this juncture. On the same subject
    Bauckham, *Climax*, p.185, notes that John *sees* the Lamb, the dragon and the whore
    (as visualised metaphorical figures) and in this way helps his readers 'see' them, too.

10   Exegetes have often given their attention to the interesting question of what, precisely, is meant by the scroll 'written on the outside and the inside' (5.1). Ellul, *Architecture*, pp.152-53, for example rules out no fewer than seven possibilities before settling for an eighth. He is worth summarising here: 1) a *Testament* – this first option will nevertheless be defended as most likely in the final part of this book when we turn, finally, to the theme of covenant; 2) the *Bible*, held out as it were to the Church and kept open; 3) the *book of creation*, with the obvious drawback that Genesis has no twin; 4) the *book of destiny*, when in fact 'fate' is what God, in Jesus Christ, does away with; 5) a *book about Christ*, but surely this is what Gospels are; 6) the *book of the Church* (yet this is what chs. 1–3 were); lastly 7) the *book of the saved* – in which case, where is the list of their names? For Ellul 'this can only be the book of what humanity is called by its father to be and to do, and also to become . . . both [8] the book of humanity and of the history of humanity' (my translation).

11   Several OT texts offer helpful comparisons: Psalms 6, 13, 35, 74, 80, 89, 90 and 94, together with certain prophetic texts (Isa 6.11; Jer 47.6; Hab 1.2; and Zech 1.12) – see Caird, *Revelation*, p.84.

12   For a study of 6.9-11 and its outworking in the rest of Revelation, see the *relevance theory* approach of S. Pattemore, *The People of God in the Apocalypse. Discourse, structure and exegesis*, Cambridge, Cambridge University Press, 2004, ch. 4 'Souls under the altar – a martyr ecclesiology', pp.68-116. For Pattemore, four passages in particular echo 6.9-11 in the later narrative, *i.e.* 12.10-12, 16.5-7, 19.1-2 and 20.3-4.

13   Commentaries on Revelation explore the wealth of possible allusion represented by these two witnesses. One of the earliest, written by Primasius, saw here the Church preaching and prophesying in the two covenant dispensations. The French *Traduction Œcuménique de la Bible* follows this line, seeing the witnesses as representative of the Church in recapitulation of the testimony both of Moses (v.6) and of Christ who died and was raised in Jerusalem (v.7-12). For a survey of the critical issues, a thorough examination of the passage and discussion of the part 11.1-13 plays in the rolling out of the three woes (and in ch. 4–22 as a whole), it remains profitable to read C.H. Giblin, 'Revelation 11.1-13: Its Form, Function, and Contextual Integration', *New Testament Studies* 30, 1984, pp.433-59. For him, 11.1-13 sheds light on the main preoccupations of prophetic ministry, namely judgment, salvation and the need for repentance (p.454).

      My own interpretation of the role played in the plot by the two witnesses will become clear below, when their story is lined up against that of its parody: another communicative tandem formed by the two monsters.

14   See Pattemore, *People of God*, p.164: 'The death of the witnesses… is patterned on the death of Christ their Lord… the same is true of the resurrection of the witnesses, which contains strong evocations of the gospel resurrection narratives'.

15   Some interpreters read the 'great fear' of the survivors (11.11) in a positive way: for Bauckham, *Climax*, p.280, it is no less than the means of their salvation (11.13), a positive fear which testifies to true repentance and worship of God arising in a pagan world symbolised by the great city; what judgment alone could not achieve (9.20-21), the witnesses' testimony manages to accomplish. Beale, *Revelation*, pp.597-607, defends with skill a different exegesis which reads the fear negatively; this represents the majority view. My own evaluation of the debate will be found in Part Three of this book, where I consider the witnesses in relation to the theme of covenant.

16 On this same point, see Schüssler-Fiorenza, *Just World*, p.78.

17 G. Campbell, 'True and False Proclamation' (part 2), p.109. These counterfeit 'signs' are always in the plural (13.14; 16.14; 19.20); by contrast a 'sign' in the singular always refers to what John sees in a vision (12.1,3; 15.1). For more on these signs see Prigent, *Apocalypse*, pp.375-76, who views all of them as monochrome.

18 Compare Brütsch, *Clarté*, who is also citing at this point Adrienne von Speyr, *Apokalypse*, Einsiedeln, 1950, p.432.

19 The Book of Acts offers several parallels for the three aspects of apostolic ministry mocked by the monster; on this, see Wall, *Revelation*, p.172, who lists: (i) Ac 1.1-11; (ii) Ac 2.22-36; (iii) Ac 2.14-21, 5.12 and 15.4,12.

20 Beasley-Murray, *Revelation*, p.207, taking M. Rissi's work as his basis, suggests that this parallel construction may be deliberate and could be seen as a re-using of OT prophetic and apocalyptic traditions as well as a recasting of more contemporary ones in light of current events and of God's revelation and redemption in Christ.

21 For an excellent summary of this point of view, see D. Ford, *Crisis!* (vol. 2), pp.571-72.

22 Prigent, *Apocalypse*, p.415 (esp. n.2), agrees that certain actions of the Spirit are referred to in this text. Other interpreters, such as J. Roloff, *Revelation*, p.161, prefer to read it not as a parody of the Holy Spirit as such but of prophecy in the Church and of witness upon earth to Christ's royalty.

23 Ellul, *Architecture*, pp.94-95, has the right idea when he says that the second monster's great weapon is the word, that is its propaganda – a weapon which complements the sword of temporal power and which coerces people to worship that power.

24 On this, compare Schüssler-Fiorenza, *Just World*, p.85.

25 On the basis that this success appears to have an institutional aspect, exegetes have worked on its possible derivations in the history of Roman Asia. Thus the signs might suggest the so-called 'miracles' concocted as part of the imperial cult, or else the officiating priesthood responsible for them. For more on this see Bauckham, *Climax*, p.446, who takes up the work of S.J. Scherrer, especially 'Signs and Wonders in the Imperial Cult : A New Look at a Roman Religious Institution in the Light of Rev 13.13-15', *Journal of Biblical Literature* 103, 1984, pp.599-610. Allo, *Apocalypse*, p.210, had already wondered if the historical basis might not be provided by the charlatanism of the priests and of pagan wonder-workers.

26 Prigent, *Apocalypse*, p.416, finds in this contrast a 'symmetrical opposition' between 'Christian prophecy which consists of being a witness to Christ here on earth, in the midst of a hostile world (Rev 11) . . . [and] this false prophecy whose purpose is to subordinate everything to the worship of the beast'.

27 For anti-christ traditions outside the NT canon, we may compare *Ascension of Isaiah* 4.5ff; *4 Ezra* 5.4ff; and *Sibylline Oracles* 3.63ff. Prigent, *ibid.*, p.418, also refers to the *Apocalypse of Elijah*.

28 Compare Roloff, *Revelation*, pp.162-65.

29 Prigent, *Apocalypse*, p.376.

30 Brütsch, *Clarté*, p.229 (my translation). There is no doubt some influence here from Swete, *Apocalypse*, p.169, for whom the fire accompanying the monster-cult was meant to offer a divine pseudo-guarantee to everybody watching.

31 It matters little, here, whether it is the miracles themselves that are bogus or whether it is the monster performing them that is the fraud.

32 Readers of French will find a succinct comparison between the two witnesses who act in tandem and the anti-duo of monsters which ape them in my article 'Procédé' p.510.

33 The collective interpretation which Prévost, *Apocalypse*, p.101, gives to the two witnesses is based upon the striking parallelism between 11.7 and 13.7.

34 More often than not, exegesis concerns itself here with finding the historical referent behind the text which this image might refer to. Thus one reads frequently about statues erected in honour of the emperor, able by means of various tricks to move or to utter oracles.

35 Brütsch, *Clarté*, p.230.

36 M.E. Boring, *Revelation*, Louisville, John Knox Press, 1989, p.168, offers a convincing analysis of 14.1-20 in terms of a contrast between truth, as found in the Lamb, and mock salvation as provided by the beast.

37 In a twofold anticipation of the final denouement, 14.1-5 prefigures that eschatological salvation which will come down from God, whilst 14.6-20 foreshadows the divine judgment which will deliver its final verdict upon human pretensions.

38 Mounce, *Revelation*, p.268.

39 Similarly Ellul, *Architecture*, p.186.

40 Compare Schüssler-Fiorenza, *Just World*, p.89, who construes the angels' combined good news, calling people to worship the living God, as a complement to the woes.

41 I share the view of Prévost, *Apocalypse*, p.117, that the three angelic pronouncements constitute one single piece of good news.

42 For this equivalence between the angels and the witnesses, I am following Bauckham, *Climax*, p.286.

43 According to Beasley-Murray, *Revelation*, p.226, this exhortation spurs the Church on to resistance (14.12), whereas the objective of the beatitude (in 14.13) is to bring consolation.

44 For a detailed discussion see Aune, *Revelation 6-16* (vol. 2), pp.877-78, who understands the genitive 'of the tent' in 15.5 as a genitive of apposition: 'the Temple, *that is* the Tent of Testimony'. This was already I.T. Beckwith's view, *The Apocalypse of John*, New York, Macmillan, 1919, and Beale, *Revelation*, p.801, subscribes to it in his turn.

45 See also Beale, *ibid.*, p.802, for whom 'the tabernacle witnesses . . . to judgment, introduced in Rev 15:5 as the source of the following bowl plagues'.

46 As Beale thinks, *idem*.

47 Father Allo, *Apocalypse*, p.259, already suggested this correspondence, taking the demons to be working for the dragon even as the angels worked for Christ.

48 In the opinion of Schüssler-Fiorenza, *Just World*, p.94, the 'rhetoric of judgment' inspiring the process of symbolisation carried on in Revelation is directed towards producing an ethics of resistance, whilst simultaneously reassuring and encouraging the reader.

49 Contra Harrington, Revelation, p.172, in whose opinion 17.6 is the only place in Rev where martus means martyr. I prefer to follow A.A. Trites, 'Martuv and Martyrdom in the Apocalypse', Novum Testamentum 16, 1973, pp.72-80, for whom the vocabulary in question – 'witness/testimony' (marturia, marturion),

'to witness/testify' (martureô) and 'witness' (the person, martus) – does not yet have the later nuance of martyr and martyrdom. Instead, its connotation is legal, like twenty or so other words in Revelation whose interpretative horizon is provided by Jesus's death as Faithful Witness in an act of self-sacrifice which functions as a pattern to be followed, to death if necessary.

50 Picking up on P. Minear, *I Saw a New Earth, An Introduction to the Visions of the Apocalypse*, Washington, Corpus Books, 1968, p.211, D. Ford, *Crisis!* (vol. 3), p.667, takes the biting rhetoric of the metaphors of infidelity (a whore to parody the Church, Babylon as a caricature of New Jerusalem, the monster as a parody of the Lamb) to be a warning to the Church against betraying the Gospel. This makes John the successor of great prophets like Isaiah, Jeremiah or Ezekiel – all of them sent to Israel because of apostasy.

51 The original text of Rev 18.6-7 is problematic and so is its translation, due to the paradoxical way it combines a punishment to fit the crime (on the like for like principle of the *lex talionis*) with twofold retribution. A good solution is suggested by M.J. Kline, 'Double Trouble', *Journal of the Evangelical Theological Society* 32, 1989, pp.171-80, which involves interpreting the uses of the Hebrew verb normally translated as 'pay him back twofold' as connoting like-for-like equivalence.

52 We may compare Rowland, *Revelation*, p.146, who says (thinking of Jn 16.8*ff*): 'It is Jesus's words recalled by the Spirit which assist in the conviction of the world of sin, righteousness and judgement . . . and are the cornerstone of the indictment against a world that prefers darkness to light'.

53 In the *Apocalypse of Baruch* 40.1-3, as well, Messiah is a judge whilst in the *Book of Wisdom* 18.14-15 the Word of God is presented as the exterminator who had acted at Passover.

54 For a fuller discussion, see the following chapter where, in particular, the question of just what 'death' is inflicted by this sword will be examined.

55 Thus, Mounce, *Revelation*, p.384.

56 Corsini, *Apocalypse*, p.415, helpfully reminds us that as in the case of 'Babylon' and New Jerusalem (17.1*ff*; 21.9*ff*), so here the angel is testifying to the truth of the revelation given and bearing the responsibility of making it known. Perhaps then the angel of 22.6, the earlier one in 21.9 and (logically) the first angel of 1.1 are all one and the same, as E. Delebecque certainly thought, *L'Apocalypse de Jean*, Paris, Mame, 1992, pp.159, 260.

57 For this equivalence, see Prigent, *Apocalypse*, p.491.

58 On this, see also Beasley-Murray, *Revelation*, p.339.

59 Such is Kraft's view, *Offenbarung*, at this point in his commentary.

5. Faithful belonging and counter-allegiance

'Earth-dwellers and heaven-dwellers are indistinguishable, except by their loyalties, commitments and ultimate destination' (J. L. Resseguie).[1]

There are two rival camps in John's Revelation: the faithful followers of the Lamb, on the one hand, are faced by an apostate horde that dances to the monster's tune on the other. As we plot another thematic trajectory through the text, it will be my aim to investigate this double characterisation.[2]

Rival identities in brief

From the septet of oracles to Churches onwards, readers of Revelation become progressively acquainted with a people belonging to God as well as with their caricature. Readers are invited to identify with the little flock faithful to the Lamb. As the Book's plot develops, these disciples of the Lamb, marked out by a seal of recognition and divine protection, will have to resist the powerful tide of a counter-movement that sweeps virtually all of humanity along with it towards idolatry. By their righteous acts the Lamb's followers must therefore swim against a fast-flowing stream of earth-dwellers who bear a mark, engage in activities, display loyalty and move towards a destiny which is in every case the inverted parallel of their own. This diametric opposition is most clearly visible in the juxtaposed contrasting scenes of 13.1-18 and 14.1-5. Only at the denouement will the battle for allegiance be resolved, once God's faithful ones enter fully into their inheritance in the New Jerusalem.

Revelation's depiction of the triumph of the Creator God over the satan and of the Redeemer Lamb over the two monsters is the necessary prerequisite for understanding how this conflict of human identities is played out. Thus, the 'tribulation' or 'suffering' (*thlipsis*) which the Lamb's faithful must endure in their life of faith and their battle with evil (1.9) mirrors the struggle already undertaken by Jesus before them, in his life and death. To resist and to win through, they too need the perseverance (*hypomonê*, 1.9b) or faithfulness under trial that Jesus the Faithful Witness showed in his life and testimony. One thinks of the parallel Pauline tradition, with a reference to 'Christ's perseverance' in 2 Th 3.5, or to his 'obedience' in Heb 5.7-10 and (later in the same writing) to the idea of running with perseverance and the race of faith (Heb 12.1-2). In the oracle to Philadelphia, the Risen Jesus speaks of the 'word of my perseverance' (3.10), while similar patient endurance or constancy is also alluded to explicitly in the messages to Ephesus or Thyatira (2.2-3,19). Perseverance will be required later of the vulnerable mother figure (in 12.4*ff*), just as it will be demanded of the saints in their battle with the monster (in 13.10). For the Lamb's disciples, unflagging perseverance is the means whereby they may endure tribulation and counter the unrelenting temptation to bow down before something that has already suffered defeat (12.8-10).

To *thlipsis* and *hypomonê* we must also add a qualifying term that unites them both, namely *basileia* (1.9), often rendered as 'kingdom'. It is through his blood-sacrifice for sin on the cross (1.4) that Messiah Jesus displays his royalty or reign; therefore, as priest-kings (according to 1.5-6), the Lamb-Messiah's followers also share this third characteristic which makes their basic identity complete. The Lamb reigns through the shedding of his blood (5.5-6), as does his alter ego the messianic rider (in 19.3), and it is by their own faithfulness under trial that his followers will win through in their turn.

From what has been said so far, it might be imagined that the Lamb's followers will be sharply distinguishable from their adversaries in Revelation's successive visions. Instead, there is no neat distinction made between an elect Church and a lost world in the Book's depiction of the elect and of the reprobate. A moment's thought accounts for this fact: have not confusion and compromise existed at the very heart of the Church from the beginning? Accordingly, the lines of demarcation are blurred and readers find the two destinies to be superimposed on one another, as for example in the expression 'earth-dwellers' (*katoikountes epi tes ges*), first encountered in the Philadelphian oracle. Although it is a neutral designation at first, it soon becomes a quasi-technical term for those who are inimical to God and to his pilgrim people with their citizenship in heaven (*cf.* Ph 3.20), those against whom the saints will pray (6.10).[3]

The 'earth-dwellers' stand in contrast to those who obey God in Jesus Christ – a people universal in scope, as suggested by the flexible expression 'from every tribe, language, people and [all] nations' (5.9, subtly varied thereafter in 7.9, 10.11, 11.9, 13.7, 14.6 and 17.15). Thus the fragile Church of the opening septet, whose lamp stand is under threat (2.5), will be expanded in the course of the narration, into a universal civilisation whose exponentially intensified light will suffice to illumine the nations (22.5). Yet robust Christian confession, accompanied by deeds of patent faithfulness (*cf.* 2.19), may at any moment – as both Jesus and Paul foresaw – give way to apostate action (2.4; *cf.* Mt 24.12; 2 Th 3.14-15/2 Tim 2.24-26). Accordingly, the narrative retains an ambiguity which will not be dispelled until the pagan nations have at last been healed and can bring their tribute into New Jerusalem, to worship God and to reign with him there (21.26; 22.2).

Revelation will close with just such a future, with the full restoration one day of God's *shalom* (as in the complete reconciliation pictured by Paul in Col 1.20). This is how the dualism of a humanity separated into two camps

– the monster's servile slaves and the Lamb's faithful servants – is finally resolved, proving not to have been such a radical solution after all. On closer examination the two alternatives of total commitment to Messiah's cause, or counter-allegiance to an anti-messiah, are found not to be watertight: the text in fact paints a world of grey where the protagonists – and by extension, the first recipients in Roman Asia, or indeed today's readers – must react to what befalls them and make their own choice between good and evil, as best they are able (22.18-19). When at last the tension is resolved at the close of the Book, what finally separates the saints from the ungodly is the differing responses of each to the Gospel; but until then, the hard road of faithfulness to the Gospel's call lends to the developing story a certain urgency throughout

Revelation 2.1–3.22

The challenge of faithfulness or loyalty, no matter what the trial, runs through this opening septet. Within the Church, there is an enemy whose proximity is unnerving. There are those, for example, who have become 'false Jews' and a 'synagogue of the satan' (2.9; 3.9) instead of constituting the Lord's synagogue (Num 16.3, LXX), like 'the Israel of God' in Paul's terminology (Gal 6.16); so-called Jews whose rival synagogue is the antithesis of the true Temple (3.9,12), they stand opposed in Smyrna or Philadelphia to the faithful who are free of all blame. Paul's criterion that a true Jew is 'one inwardly', by 'circumcision of the heart' (Rom 2.28-29), comes to mind, as does the view of the Johannine Jesus that regarding Abraham as one's ancestor does not preclude being a child of the devil (Jn 8.31-47). However, not before Rev 21.12, upon arrival in God's end-time city, will the names of the tribes of the *true Israel* actually be mentioned. In similar vein the Church at Pergamum is said to reside where the satan has also established a base (2.13); this is the very place where the difficult choice between idolatry and fidelity has to be made (2.14), with compromise as a constant threat. One day of course, the faithful hope to exchange this dwelling place, subject as it is to the usurped dominion of the satan, for another where they will be in the vicinity of the divine throne (22.1). For the sake of completeness in characterising the enemy within, mention should also be made of pseudo-apostles (2.2), those who uphold the teaching of Balaam (2.14) or the Nicolaitans (2.6,15).

The seven oracles offer an initial line drawing of the main traits by which, throughout the story, those who stay faithful to the Risen One or their adversaries will be known. We may focus first on the signifiers of belonging to Messiah Jesus. The most important of these is the 'new name' (2.17 and 3.12; 19.12; *cf.* Isa 62.2; 65.5), of those who belong to Christ or to God (3.12; *cf.* 14.1; 22.4) and who will be made victorious participants in his feast; the name implies faithful witness (2.13; 3.8) and it will be caricatured by another blasphemous appellation used to nickname the monster's slaves (13.17). Secondly, there are the white garments, whether 'clothes' (3.4-5,18; 4.4) or 'robe(s)' (6.11; 7.9,13-14; 22.14), or again the 'pure, shining linen' which stands for the 'righteous deeds of the saints' (19.8): used to clothe with righteousness Messiah and those he has delivered from sin and death, such garments are a picture of justification or even baptism (*cf.* Gal 3.27), that is, of putting on Christ (*cf.* 1 Cor 6.9-11). Here in Revelation they are a contrast to soiled clothing (3.4) or, worse still, to nakedness which betokens spiritual bankruptcy or the absence of good works (3.17). A third signifier to be noted is the 'book of life' (3.5, then 13.8; 17.8; 20.12,15; 21.7), a ledger of the elect already familiar from the Old Testament (Ex 32.32-33; Ps 69.28-29; Dn 12.1) in which no reprobate's name can be written: the names of the elect found in it figure in a solemn declaration made to the conqueror ('I will confess his name', 3.5), for which the Son of Man acknowledging his own (in Lk 12.8-9) provides a parallel. Finally, the faithful follower is also designated an 'overcomer' (2.7,11,17,26; 3.5,12,21); by analogy with Christ the victor (3.21; 5.5), the disciple also overcomes through death.[4]

The signs of an opposing identity are also evoked by the oracles, for the inroads made by unfaithfulness are observable *inside* the Churches not outside them. There are 'Jezebel's' obedient 'children' (2.23), in other words her 'converts' or 'initiates', who quite clearly contrast with Messiah's 'servants' and who imagine that divine mysteries are to be found in their knowledge of the satan's so-called *deep things* (2.24-25). In Sardis (3.1) a discrepancy is unmasked between apparent life and the actual death which this conceals: this establishes a marker for a later life-and-death game (in 13.3-4) through which the monster will bewitch the whole earth and draw it to its destruction. While the lines of battle are drawn in the world, the front-line (as it were) cuts right through the people of God who live at the heart of unfolding history. Jesus had warned his disciples against the idea of being able to serve two masters (Mt 6.24) and the Churches of Roman Asia, reflecting in this instance the people whom God has gathered together, must now come up with a decisive answer to the question: *to whom are glory, honour and power to be given?*

A fourfold phase:
Revelation 5.9; 7.9; 10.11; 11.9; 13.7; 14.6; 17.15

The Church that takes shape in Revelation's visions extends beyond the ecclesial communities of Roman Asia to those redeemed by the Lamb from humanity as a whole. This is especially clear from the phrase alluded to earlier, 'from every tribe, language, people and [all] nations' (5.9; 7.9; 10.11; 11.9; 13.7; 14.6; 17.15). Cipher for the universal Church, this expression functions as a kind of slogan for attacking the universalistic claims of the monster's empire, which craves equal scope (13.7). The phrase can describe humanity in receipt of prophecy (10.11), of good news (14.6) or it can refer to the unnumbered host of redeemed humanity assembled in God's presence (5.9; 7.9). However, on occasion it may designate humankind in its almost unanimous opposition to the two witnesses (11.9) or signify the completely hoodwinked earth (12.9). From its ultimate use as a way of denoting captive humanity gathered together (in 17.15), it emerges that a phrase tinged with so much ambiguity needs, in the last analysis, to be interpreted in context every time it appears. It is particularly interesting how its use in 13.7 is the inverted parallel of its earlier occurrence in 5.9: the universal domination of the monster caricatures the universality of the people of diverse origin who have chosen God as king (5.10, picking up on 1.6). This would seem calculated to stress to readers how faithfulness is no neutral thing but entails making an active choice for God. We will return to this fourfold formula below, following its final occurrence in 17.15.

Rival identities in Revelation 6–12

Rival forms of belonging receive fuller exploration once Messiah opens the seals and the events unleashed by this begin to happen. The breaking of the sixth seal (6.12-17) and the anticipation of the seventh (7.14-17) create a space in which we discover two literary units set carefully in an antithetical relationship. In contrast with those fleeing the judgment of 6.15, there are the righteous ones of 7.14, clad in white; chapters 8 and 9 further illustrate their fortunes as they face the idolatry that surrounds them, while a more positive rendering of the calling lived out by the Lamb's faithful followers is offered to us as spectators by the section 10.1–11.14. In this connection 11.1-2 picks up the reassuring scene in 7.1-8, where measuring the Temple signified protecting the saints, as well as anticipating an intensification of conflict when, subsequently, the Gentile nations will overrun the outer court and it is abandoned. Perhaps that is why this very compact text (11.3-13) flows in two directions, with the witnesses being killed by the monster but then restored to life by the Spirit in a scenario which fills the vast majority of 'earth-dwellers' with both joy and terror. Finally, chapter 12 develops further the fate of a protected Church – sealed in advance (chapter 7) and then measured (11.1-2) – by using the additional image of nourishment in the desert (12.6,14); even after all this, the people of God still find themselves pursued by their enemy.

The 'sealed' and the 'tattoed':
Revelation 7.1-8,9*ff*; 9.4,20-21; 14.1ff; 22.4
and 13.16-18; 14.9,11; 16.2; 19.12-13,20; 20.4 in counterpoint

Before exploring how the parallel passages 13.1-18 and 14.1-5 set two rival identities in opposition to one another, it is worth returning to the juncture when the saints are sealed. Here begins a double series of inversely parallel texts concerned with identifying and authenticating two adversarial communities: the Lamb's followers (7.1-8,9*ff*; 9.4,20-21; 14.1*ff*; 22.4) and, over against them, the monster's slaves (13.16-18; 14.9,11, 16.2; 19.12-13,20; 20.4). Whatever the differences in their respective traits the 144, 000 Israelites (7.4-8) or the vast international throng (7.9*ff*) are essentially one; together they form a single undivided company[5] of those who are servants of God (7.3), chosen for salvation. For the theme of belonging which we are investigating here, it is scarcely possible to overestimate the importance of the action of sealing God's servants on the forehead: in this sealing of the saints we have a deliberate anticipation of the mark of the monster branded or tattooed on hand or brow (13.16), which is its very parody.

Names denoting glory are applied to the Lamb and to the Father in 14.1. They will find their exact counterpart in 17.5 in the abominable name engraved on the forehead of the adulteress;[6] confirmation of this is provided by the parallelism between 'his name and his Father's name written on their foreheads' (14.1) and 'this name was written on her forehead' (17.5). In 19.12, once again Revelation's listeners hear a play on contrasting names, as the name of the messianic rider – 'name written... that no-one knows but he himself' – offers an exact parallel to the 'name written..., a mystery' of the adulteress. Not only does the noun 'mystery' in 17.5 find its clearly antithetical equivalent in the paraphrase of 19.12, but the 'secret' involved is explained in both instances; in addition, the obscenity 'mother of whores and of earth's abominations' (17.5) contrasts with the name of unequalled dignity, 'Word of God' (19.13).

Therefore, those whom God has 'sealed', as first encountered by readers in 7.3*ff* and then later in 14.1*ff*, are actually 'pre-sealed' or marked out and named in advance; this is with a view to being protected *from* something (impending trials, such as the exclusion of 9.4) but also *for* something (forthcoming witness to be given in hostile circumstances, 11.7-8). Several Pauline references spring to mind: 2 Tim 2.19 has a seal applied to God's solid foundation, called 'the Lord knows those who are his'; 2 Cor 1.22 features a 'seal of ownership' deposited by the Spirit; or in Rom 4.11 the mark of circumcision is understood as 'a seal of righteousness... by faith'. For the biblically aware reader, this initial act of sealing and protecting also calls up many others that took place in the course of salvation history: the Israelites' preservation when the angel of death passed by (Ex. 12.13,21-24); analogous marking which enabled those who had escaped Jerusalem's destruction to form a 'remnant' for rebuilding God's people (Ez. 9.4-6); or again, in Jewish literature, the angelic action of holding back the waters during the construction of Noah's Ark (*2 Bar* 6.4; *1 En* 6.6).

Bearing in mind all of these texts, it would seem that there are several nuances to being 'sealed'. These include possession and belonging, protection or guarantees as well as authentication. However, irrespective of nuance, there is one outcome for the person so sealed – confidence and assurance – and this raises a fascinating question: in this mark of ownership which the monster felt obliged to counterfeit, might Revelation's first readers have detected a reference to Christian baptism? Unlike the blood smeared on the lintels to protect the Israelites from the curse of death (Ex. 12.13), baptism did not shield the bearer from troubles brought on by belonging to Christ; instead, it constituted a cup of suffering to be drunk (Mk 10.38-39). In subapostolic literature it would rapidly come to be called a 'seal' (cf. 2 Clem 7.6; Act Thom 26) connoting, for the first Christians, protection against demons – a fact borne out by Lactantius, one of the Church Fathers (Inst Div 4.26).

Whether or not baptism was understood, in Revelation the 'seal' and its rival corresponding 'mark' signal two categories of people: God's servants on the one hand (7.2ff; 9.4; 14.1; 22.4) and the monster's children on the other (13.16ff. 14.9,11; 16.2; 19.20; 20.4). Those who display the seal and those who exhibit the rival mark each have a declared allegiance with the rival people, displaying a series of characteristics meant to counterfeit the matching traits of God's servants: 'the Devil, too, chooses his elect... loathsome parody.'[7] 'Brothers' and 'saints' are equivalent terms used to describe the Lamb's adherents and to distinguish them from the 'earth-dwellers' whom the monster manages to draw in. These latter possess a powerful rival identity whose destiny is destruction not salvation; as false worshippers, won over and bewitched by the monsters (13.3-4,8,12-14), they incarnate the "black" of demonic enslavement over against the liberating 'white' of being in Christ.

Yet to the extent that all human existence is acquainted with an ambiguous 'grey' which is experienced in the ups and downs of every day, the clarity of choices which followers of the Lamb must make becomes clouded and the gulf is narrowed that separates the Lamb's followers and the monster's worshippers into opposing camps. A good example of this sort of ambiguity is provided by the variations which Revelation employs to denote the same ambivalent period of time, counted sometimes in days and at other times in months or in times and half-times (11.2-3; 12.14; etc.). This length of time relates both to the hour of faithful witness and resistance but also, in a parallel way, to the limited time for action during which evil may make its slaves. We could also call this time 'space', a place for Christians in Roman Asia (and with them, today's readers) to exercise their freedom in a world where discernment is difficult and where, more often than not, it is hard to distinguish good choices from bad.

Before the monster-worshippers receive their grotesque tattoo (13.16-17) or rear up in opposition to Messiah's retinue, Revelation designates them as 'earth-dwellers' (13.8,12; cf. 3.10; 6.10; 8.13; 11.10; lastly 17.2,8). As we have seen, this expression has entirely negative connotations; it denotes a wicked anti-people, established as a parallel anti-community to the Church by the brand they bear. Hardly has it been constituted in chapter 13 when its very existence and claims are disputed (in 14.1-5) by those belonging to the Lamb who come forth with sealed foreheads, bearing God's very name on their brow, and give their retort to the monstrous name that marks their opponents. A similar scenario to this one may be found in Ps Sol 15.8-10.[8]

Revelation 13.1-8 and 14.1-5 in counterpoint

In this beautifully crafted double sequence, the fundamental fact to be observed is the confrontation between two mutually exclusive identity markers. In light of this, exegetes' preoccupation with decoding the monster's mark is surely a matter for some regret. For what matters here is not the identification of a supposed *referent* for this mark but quite simply, the very *notion* of the mark itself.[9] Here, as elsewhere, Revelation's constant recourse to antithetical parallelism is governed by a compositional logic which requires that there should exist, as a counterpart to veritable sealing by God, a monstrous anti-seal diabolically applied in caricature of the first. Readers are already aware, by this point, that part of humanity does not have God's seal (9.4) because of its refusal to repent (9.20-21); therefore, when a truly rival mark is dramatically applied (as here), the void is filled by something which provides a travesty of God's sealing and encroaches upon the human freedom which such protection secures (13.16-17). Thus the diabolically tattooed, unbelieving horde is characterised by a ridiculous name and an infinitely imperfect number (13.17-18) which contrast with the name of Christ and the symbolic number of those redeemed by the Lamb.

In 14.1*ff* the Lamb and his own reappear, united in close communion and in unbreakable solidarity.[10] By bursting upon the scene in deliberate opposition to the monsters and their supporters who had been occupying it, those who already have the victory from 7.4-14 return (as it were) to back up the One whose triumph represents the great pre-requisite of the entire story (5.5-14). We have just seen how the seal of God and the Lamb's name differentiate the faithful from those whom the monster has branded, and now at the start of chapter 14 we may note other contrasts that reinforce this one. Everything, here, is calculated to offer a contrast with the previous scene, in a process that could be called parodied parody: through this description, all the anti-traits of the monster's slaves are rubbed out; in their place, the narrative paints in correspondingly authentic characteristics. In place of the mimicry of those whom the monster has duped we now see emulation of the true Lamb. The Jesus of the Gospels said 'follow me' (Mk 2.14; 10.21; Lk 9.59; Jn 1.43; 21.19,23; *cf.* Mk 8.34; Jn 8.12; 10.4,27; 12.26; Jn 13.36),[11] and what – asked Augustine – is following if not imitation? Called followers or disciples (14.4), these companions of the Lamb are shown by their qualities to be all that the monster's hangers-on will never be. In principle, there can be no more confusing those who are *for* God with those *against*.

Rather than be hauled before the dragon's false lamb, the 'sealed' stand in the presence of the only true Lamb of God with 'his name and his Father's name written on their forehead' (14.1). Their name declares their allegiance, a fact which provides readers with an interpretation of the seal first met in 7.3 and which lines up symmetrically with the prior name on the brow of 13.16-17.[12] Supposedly they had been defeated (13.7), yet liberated from their enemies, these 144, 000 (*cf.* 7.4 already) now stand triumphant beside the Lamb on Mount Zion – hill of deliverance and of divine glory (Jl 2.432; *cf.* Isa 24.21-23; Mic 4.6-7) which may very well recall the mount of Jesus's crucifixion.

By contrast with the characters of chapter 13, the redeemed, here, are spotless: they are consecrated and irreproachable, and they follow the Lamb with undivided loyalty 'wherever he goes'.[13] They are also guileless, like a lamb ready for slaughter, the servant in whom no lie was found (Isa 53.7,9) or the 'remnant of Israel' (Zeph 3.13) – all of which contrasts with the 'liars' shut out of the eternal city (21.27; 22.15). As 'first fruits for God and the Lamb', which in light of Heb 9.14 and 1 Pet 1.19 would appear to be a sacrificial metaphor for Messiah's death, the Lamb's followers lead a life which has become acceptable to God (*cf.* Eph 1.4; 5.27; Col 1.22; Jude 24). Despite the almost universal dominion of the sea monster, which might have appeared uncontested, God has after all preserved a contrasting holy people: in the end, therefore, what the monsters and their minions are or do (chapter 13) proves to be of no ultimate interest, since it is ephemeral and bound to disappear.

Overall, the narrative force of the picture painted by 14.1-5 appears to me to be twofold. As the reverse image of the preceding scene (13.1-18), first, this cameo fairly shouts its answer to the foregoing spectacle of the 'earth' or 'land' dwellers in their headlong rush to idolatry. At the same time, it offers a description of redemption as it has already been obtained for the Lamb's true followers, by means of which idolatry, lust and deceit give way to faithfulness, chastity and truth (14.4-5)[14] and as their worship drowns out the servile prostration of false worshippers. Stress is laid on the destiny of the redeemed and in this fashion, the author is able to encourage recipients of his apocalypse to make the right decision, follow the Lamb wherever he goes (14.4) and, whatever may befall, reject the devil's offer and with it any other 'salvation', however inviting this might seem.

The security which characterises this scene of eternal happiness in the Lamb's presence should certainly be read in continuity with the theme of protection under enemy fire which suffuses all of 12.1–13.18; there, both 'woman' and 'offspring' found themselves cared for (that is, spirited away and nourished, 12.5-6) in a veritable *present moment* of salvation (12.10). Yet it would be wrong to think that, with this depiction of a happy scene on Mount Zion, Revelation is somehow relinquishing its rhetoric of urgency, discernible from the start, directed at those Asian Christians tempted by compromise (or at any reader who might be in a similar situation). We should not forget how the 'brothers' and 'saints' were victors (12.11), but also besieged (12.17) and even defeated on history's stage (13.7): that is precisely why perseverance was called for (13.10) in the face of evil's charms (13.14) or coercion (13.15). Therefore, as long as the dragon and its henchmen have not met with their final fate, Revelation's continuing plot will persist in pointing out how God's plan, which essentially involves the calling of a people to himself, will continually attract the mimicry of a deceitful rival project.

Revelation 14.6-20

The dilemma of believers faced with the choice either to worship the beast and its image (14.9-11) or to resist it in obedience to God (14.12-13), appears to have in part conditioned the immediate sequel in the text (14.6ff). Therefore, an 'eternal gospel', whose proclamation has universal scope, calls for a positive decision to revere God by giving him glory and falling down before him (14.7). This is how the true worshipper should behave before the Creator God, following a correct decision in response to the Good News; it is an act which neutralises all the previous imitative and idolatrous worship behaviour of the monster's adherents (13.12ff). Whereas the assistant monster had worked to force the 'earth-dwellers' into directing their worship at the first monster, now in strict contrast an angel – the first of three who will grace the scene – has the task of announcing the Gospel to all, so as to put an end to all prostration before the monster's image (13.15).

This portion of text is the latest to give clear expression to a contrast between two ways of life. The angel pronounces judgment on all the 'tattooed' who grovel before the monster (14.9); we recognise them, both because those who are here marked on brow and hand are the same as those already styled as being marked on the right hand and forehead (13.16), and because another careful linguistic ploy attunes the ear of the hearer to a subtle variation in their description, which confirms that they are the same: in both contexts two *epi* + genitive constructions in the Greek (where *epi* means 'on') are followed by *epi* + accusative, but with a twist which inverts brow and hand from one text to the other.[15] A similar expression, but this time with a double *epi* + accusative in the singular, will recur in chapter 20; there, in a positive designation applied to believers, the latter are referred to (negatively this time) as *non-tattooed* on hand and brow (20.4), which is a new and ironic way of saying 'sealed' (7.4). This play on words confirms something we have already discovered previously: 'seal' and 'mark' form a strict antithesis. It may be added that the existence of the *non-tattooed* implies something about human adherence to the monster's cause: this merely appears to be universal but is, in fact, capable of alteration!

The judgment oracle of 14.9-11 underlines the fact that turning one's back on the only true God constitutes a poor choice. It had seemed that a life of hardship leading to death awaited every non-adherent of the monster (13.15,17); this must have given real pause for thought to Revelation's first recipients concerning their commitment as disciples of the Lamb. However, where the consequences of choices are concerned, the angel now makes clear how the fate of the monster-worshippers turns out to be much worse: diabolical disturbance (however transitory) to the divine way of things, which is ultimate reality, calls for just retribution. Any Christian who would give up, at the risk of foregoing due reward (3.5), is thus warned in advance of what the true outcome of their defection would be and comforted, instead, in their choice to remain faithful and obedient. The saints' perseverance, in 14.12, picks up an idea from the passage which is its negative counterpart (13.10); for the Lamb's followers, who will be the truly happy in the end, such 'endurance' proves to be a much lower price to pay than that of apostasy.

The blindness and hardening of those who follow the anti-messiah need not be fatal, provided those involved speedily renounce their idolatry and fall down before the true God. For them, the angel's message has all the potential of a salutary warning which would direct them to make a better choice. Rather like the climax of the Sermon of the Mount we are faced, here, with the rhetoric of the two possible ways;[16] this is conveyed by a double image, with judgment viewed first in a positive manner, as an ingathering of the redeemed (14.14-16), and then negatively as a grape harvest evoking retributive justice (cf. Isa 63.2ff) and the punishment of idolaters (14.17-20).[17] This choice concerning belonging and identity, where each option leads to a corresponding reward, will remain in play for the rest of the plot: by an inner-textual reworking of 14.11, 19.3 will provide Revelation's second borrowing of the perpetual smoke found in Isaiah's oracle against Edom (Isa 34.10), while later 20.10 will once more hark back to 14.10-11.[18]

Revelation 16

Yet if those whom the monster has in its thrall are ever to change sides, the problem of their hardened hearts must be resolved. This problem actually gets worse between the sounding of the trumpets and the outpouring of the bowls, with rebelliousness against God growing in intensity; as a result, we become acquainted, in the bowls septet, with a company that is irremediably and irreducibly tied to the monster. By this point, virtually all of humanity is affected (16.2-9), in what could be dubbed a crescendo of blindness as the degree of punishment (repaying such behaviour) increases progressively from the episode of the trumpets onwards.[19] The positive response which was elicited by the witnesses' message (11.13) does not recur; instead, there is a complete absence of repentance (16.8,11,21) which testifies to the fact that there has been polarisation. Quasi-universal worship of the monster (in 15.2-4) could still , however, call forth the protest of a universal hope (cf. Isa 12.4-5) targeting the conversion of the nations along the lines of their eschatological submission to God, as advocated by the deuteronomistic version of the Song of Moses (Dt. 31.1-8; 32.44–33.29).

In consequence, the threat voiced by the angel's proclamation in 14.9-11 now begins to come about when the bowl of 16.2 is poured out, with as its first taste the ulcers afflicting the incorrigible false worshippers. Demonic powers had no sway over those whom God had sealed (9.4b); now, likewise their own slaves have no means of obtaining salvation: 'the image before which they fell down, whether enthusiastically or under duress, remains insensitive to their distress and incapable of helping them'.[20] The monster's 'mark', which is these people's badge of belonging, turns out to be the cause of their torment, for in its opposition to the protective divine 'seal' it cannot hope to save; instead, it can only reveal the true nature of its bearer and bring down an appropriate condemnation. The resulting sentence is an ulcer (alluding to one of Egypt's famous plagues) which applies a supplementary mark and betokens divine chastisement.

In what follows, various details help us tell the difference between the Lamb's 'sealed' ones and these 'earth-dwellers', who will receive their just deserts. It is as though the outpouring of the other bowls of judgment which they have to endure continues to play upon their grotesque tattoo, highlighting their real allegiance and true identity, depriving them of the very things which the Lamb's friends enjoy and afflicting them with what cannot touch believers. The water is polluted (16.4), whereas by contrast the Lamb's 'sealed' ones drink their fill through access to life-giving springs (7.16-17); there is blood to drink (16.6), since those who have spilt blood deserve all the more to drink it – they are 'worthy' but, unlike the believers in Sardis (3.4), not for good reason (so instead, they 'deserve' it); lastly, a plague not found in the Egyptian series serves as the formal counterpart to the protection promised to the faithful in 7.16, as the sun burns the ungodly (16.8) whilst the redeemed, for their part, enjoy precisely the benefit of preservation from such eventualities.

In conformity with the template of those Egyptian plagues characterised by Pharaoh's lack of repentance,[21] when bowls four, five and seven are poured out, human beings' lips frame blasphemy; this is repeated several times over with slight variations: they either 'curse the name of God' (16.9), 'curse the God of heaven' (16.11) or simply 'curse God' (16.21). Interestingly, previous or subsequent occurrences of blasphemy (as so described) typify their master the monster (13.1; 17.3) as it gives vent to explicit rage against God, God's name and God's heaven (13.5-6). Could the text better underline the fact that the impenitent blasphemers of chapter 16 are indelibly marked with an anti-seal, which causes them to share the nature and the fate of the monster that they so resemble?

Two stories in one

For God's recalcitrant enemies and for those the Lamb has redeemed, two distinct destinies now appear on the horizon. One is a coming-together of the nations, willed by God and effected by his Messiah through the inauguration of a new covenant. The other is a corresponding assembly of kings, short in duration (16.14,16) and doomed to fail totally (19.19-21). Incorporated within Revelation's theme of rival identities is a double strategy being developed in respect of its first readers; this aims to cement believers' attachment to the Lamb, but equally (if possible) to wean the monster's slaves off their tragic dependency. In the text, everything takes place in a world of grey where separation between the two camps is never complete, and this of course is exactly what any witness or disciple actually experiences. The dual rhetorical goal forewarns readers who belong to Jesus, so that they resist any temptation to jump ship, but simultaneously opens up a possible escape-route for all victims of the rival satanic project for whom the message might yet bring liberation. The aim is to confirm believers in their resolve never to veer into apostasy, while persuading the lost or the apostate to stop their headlong rush, and to backtrack.

There is so much more to Revelation's depiction of rival peoples – in covenant with God or in league with the dragon – than merely to provide one more contrast in a series of antitheses that comprise so much of the Book's decor. Ultimately, Revelation seeks to prevent its addressees, for whom appearances prove deceptive in this world, from confusing the ultimate destiny of God's people, brought together by the Crucified and Risen One, with the fate of the wicked who refuse his rule. When combined with the prior expectation of Christ's certain coming like a thief, its narrative of two differentiated destinies helps readers to get their bearings and fosters their persistence in ways of repentance and obedience (3.3). It is in this vein that a warning designed to make recipients listen up can lead on to a beatitude for whoever is paying attention (16.15), even if little hope in fact remains for those whose spiritual blindness and deafness prove incurable.

The case of the 'Kings of the Earth'
(cf. 1.5) – 16.14; 17.2,12-14,18; 18.3,9-10; 19.19-21; 21.24

The usefulness of the preceding remarks can immediately (if briefly) be verified by considering the 'kings of the earth'. In conformity with Ps 2.2, these kings are found pitted against God and his Messiah in an enemy camp (16.14; 17.2; 18.3). Similarly, ten kings later receive a kingship which coincides with the ascent of the monster to which they willingly devolve their power (17.12-13). However, these kings suffer defeat at the hands of the One who is King of kings (17.14) and then, in a complete turn-around, become the destroyers of the great city to which they had themselves been subject previously (17.18)! The allegiance of the 'kings of the earth' is found to be correspondingly tinged with ambivalence in 18.9-10, where they are seen putting distance between themselves and the great city that had been the object of their affections thus far. So begins their progressive desertion from the hellish alliance (19.19) which will eventually see them transfer their allegiance to its rival, New Jerusalem, the city into which they will ultimately bring their tribute (21.24). In their revolt against the Lord of lords and King of kings, all these kinglets with a short-lived kingship ('for an hour', 17.12) will one day find their time has run out, on the day when all God's words are fulfilled (17.17). However, it should be remembered that in any case they are all, without exception, under the sovereignty of Christ (1.5). We will return to these kings below.

Another look at a fourfold formula:
Revelation 5.9; 7.9; 10.11; 11.9; 13.7; 14.6; 17.15

In 17.14-15, the Lamb's followers rub shoulders with the great city's underlings. Co-victors with the Lamb, they are described here as 'called, chosen and faithful' (17.14); this has the effect of conforming the external mark of their faith to the inner reality of their calling and election. It should be noted that they are identical with those encountered in 14.1.[22] In a commentary provided by the interpreting angel the text then sets alongside them those who are called out from 'peoples, multitudes, nations and languages' (17.15); this is the final occurrence of the variable but always fourfold expression which, as we saw earlier, is used to denote humanity as a whole. In this case, the formula functions as a way of making explicit what was meant by the 'many waters' in 17.1. Compared to the other examples, examined previously, there are two particularities this time, namely, the placing of 'peoples' in first position and the inclusion in the list (for this time only) of 'multitudes'. As this is Revelation's final use of this elastic formula, we may now profitably review the set of seven texts where it appears (5.9; 7.9; 10.11; 11.9; 13.7; 14.6; 17.15); by so doing, we may evaluate its contribution to the play on rival identities that we have been investigating.

Although this expression is always synonymous with universality, it never recurs in identical fashion twice and this is more than simply a matter of its form. Allowing for two shifts in meaning, it has three distinct nuances in all.[23] The first is positive, when the phrase applies to the whole company of the redeemed – whether from an earthly (5.9) or heavenly (7.9) point of view. A second usage proves to be neutral, since on two occasions the expression also describes all those who are in receipt of public prophecy (10.11) or of the Gospel (14.6). The third and final nuance is negative, whilst retaining an element of ambiguity: in the relevant cases, all those who are implicated reject the witnesses' message (11.9) become the monster's slaves (13.7) or come under the woman-city's domination (17.15) – even though, in this last instance, the forthcoming destruction of 'Babylon' will actually set free the nations led astray (18.23), rendering their healing possible (22.2).

Bearing in mind these nuances, it is reasonable to conclude that the formula in question undergoes a very subtle evolution as Revelation's plot moves forward, until in 17.15 it has become ambivalent. Although this last case is an obvious caricature, with the 'multitudes' clearly aping the numerous citizens of the kingdom (5.9; 7.9; *cf.* 13.3,8 and 16.14,16),[24] it remains the case that, for these enslaved nations, there is considerable potential in the triumph of the Lamb and of his followers – such is the liberating power of the Gospel! So, ultimately this formula draws attention, in its own way, to the fact that changing sides remains a real possibility for human beings.

Revelation 18

Going over to God's side, in nick-of-time repentance, is precisely the message reinforced by the next celestial appeal which asks God's people to forsake 'Babylon' without further delay (18.4). Just like the New Testament in general, Revelation here presupposes a separation between those who belong to God and those who turn their back upon him – a differentiation that takes place in the world (and not outside it), where both believers and their adversaries must live out their lives side by side. Confirmation that this is the case is provided by the reason given for such separation: 'that you will not share in her sins [or] receive any of her plagues' (18.4). A Pauline ethical exhortation offers an interesting parallel to this prohibition on walking in sinners' ways, or sharing in an anti-communion, which can only be a ridiculous ersatz for the communion of saints: 'have nothing to do with the fruitless deeds of darkness' (Eph 5.11). Whilst it is inevitable that believers and idolaters share the same living space, what must be avoided is the former's participation in the sins of the latter, which God will remember and requite; 18.5-6 underlines this, with divine wrath functioning in a similar way to Eph 5.6.

The question arises as to whether those who were formerly staunch supporters of the 'great city' also hear the call to leave 'Babylon'. The erstwhile allies of the human city do not, in fact, yet realise that the fate which has overtaken their gilded idol (18.10,16,19; cf. 8.13) is in reality their own; what eludes *them*, however, is certainly within *our* grasp as readers. Yet an affirmative answer to the question appears justified all the same. For, as we have already established, the kings who make themselves scarce when the time is right and so put distance between themselves and the whore-city are, by their very escape changing sides in order to make common cause with the bride-city.[25] By keeping well back (18.15), or mooring at a safe distance (18.17), the merchants and mariners participate with the kings in the same typology: all are now *former* commercial associates of the 'great city'.

In the punishment of a now deserted 'Babylon', God's sovereignty is at work, for evil is here turned against evil (17.16) as only the Omnipotent One, the Judge of evil (18.8), knows how to do: 'one word from God will suffice'.[26] In a single day (18.8) or in the space of one hour's deserved chastisement (18.10,17,19), equivalent in length to her usurped reign (17.12-14), the ostentation and arrogance of 'Babylon' (18.7) which had seemed eternal are, as expected (16.17), reduced to a void[27] and the question of 18.18, 'was there ever a city like this city?'(cf. Ez. 27.32, on the subject of Tyre), now sounds terribly ironic. Accordingly, 'it is done!' in 16.17 will not, after all, fail to find an echo in 21.6: what had already put God's wrath in a nutshell (16.17) can now express equally well the kernel of his salvation (21.6) and what had served previously to announce the fall and destruction of 'Babylon' may now be used for declaring the other side of the coin; namely, how blessings will flow from the life, death and resurrection of Christ.

For the present, however, all of the human city's former allies seem to remain unenlightened; they are unaware, as yet, that in the collapse of their idol may be glimpsed a judgment pronounced not so much upon her as upon them, or that the triple woe (each of the three laments having one woe, 18.10,16,19; *cf.* 8.13) is in actual fact their own. Yet so little in Revelation's plot appears to separate the ungodly from the believers that they could one day become. Interpretation, then, ought not to empty of its pregnant ambiguity a zone which Revelation has so carefully filled with irony.

Revelation 19

The multitude in 19.6 contrasts with that other human throng ruled over by the whore, as well as with every other assembly opposed to God that has arisen in the story so far.[28] At this point, the followers of the Lamb are the object of an interesting double characterisation, which makes them both a collective entity (they are like a bride) as well as individuals (like guests at the wedding). What allows the imagery to toggle between these two is the white robe, which may be either the bridal gown or a guest's wedding garment. For those who belong to the Lamb, attending the wedding certainly signifies safe arrival at their destination after having successfully overcome various trials. There is no reason for distinguishing any longer between 'called' and 'chosen', as in Mt 22.14, because the perfect participle *keklêmenoi* ('the invited', 19.9), does not connote guests who, at the last moment, might not come, but rather means those who will not fail to take their place (in other words, who are confirmed participants).[29]

In 19.7,9, the 'wedding' and 'wedding supper' of the Lamb doubly underline what is a key event for the Lamb's own. The importance of this wedding for Revelation is far from exhausted by the perspective of a thematic of identity, which I am working from here; but even when viewed from this angle alone, no fewer than five elements of textual data – four of them found in 19.9 – contribute something to the solemnity and the vital significance of this espousal. There is, first of all, the order to write which updates those from the opening septet (1.11,19; 2.1, *etc.*); then comes the fourth beatitude of Revelation, addressed to those gathered round the feast table, in which are paraphrased the words of the guest at a banquet attended by Jesus (in Lk 14.15); thirdly, a solemn declaration is made ('these are the true words of God'); and fourthly, the repetition of 'and he said' underlines the importance of the communication John is receiving. Finally, in the following verse (19.10) additional reinforcement comes from the seer's confusion when faced with the grandeur of the scene.

The logic of the antithesis underlying so much of Revelation would lead us to expect that so great a wedding banquet, which crowns the faithfulness of some, might also give rise to a lesser imitation. Such is the case with the so-called supper of the birds of prey. Just as evoking the Lamb's feast is a way of celebrating the perfecting of God's people, so this 'great supper of God'

(19.17) lifts the curtain, for just a moment, on the way God views the rival gathering mounted by the monster for a final assault (19.19). It is no surprise that the battle itself should be devoid of narrative interest since, as a final reminder in 19.16 makes clear, we already know the identity of the winner. Only the outcome matters (19.20-21), and this is described in details that are highly significant for our theme of belonging: the two monsters –the general and the adjutant, we might say – are captured and irrevocably consigned to final perdition. It only remains for the dragon, supreme commander of the forces assembled against God, to meet its fate and the final part of its story will inevitably be told very soon (in 20.1-10).

Another look at the case of the 'Kings of the Earth'

Although this scene is principally about insuring the defeat and ensuing condemnation of the monsters, we ought not to overlook the kings and their armies, simply referred to (in 19.21) as 'the rest of them'. The lake of fire patently does not apply to them, since the narrative consigns only the sea monster and the false prophet, and later the dragon, to it. However, these kings fall by the mouth-sword wielded by the rider on the horse (19.21), synonymous with his name as 'Word of God' (*cf.* 19.13,15). Three exegetical questions remain. How, then, are we to account for the reappearance (in 21.24,26) of these 'kings of the earth', whose connotations have been negative up to this point? What is meant by their bringing tribute into New Jerusalem? In light of this, what are we to make of their apparent death by the mouth-sword here, which seems to involve no shedding of blood?

By his sword, the rider is identifiable for readers as another figure or representation for the Risen One alive for evermore (introduced in 1.1-18): the One who, by his Word, has from the start been involved in a combat fought either within the confines of the Churches themselves (see 2.12,16) or, as here, among the nations. Therefore, despite the punitive aspect of 19.21, the possibility remains that through the execution described here the sword achieves a positive effect. Two correlative texts spring to mind: from Isaiah there is the action of the Servant in regard to the nations when, by means of his sharpened sword, salvation is brought to the ends of the earth (Isa 49.2,6); and, in a Psalm which matters greatly to our author, there is the iron sceptre which succeeds in causing kings to fear the Lord (Ps 2.8-11).

In spite of these antecedents, exegetes have been prone to read Rev 19.19-21 as the carrying-out of a literal death-sentence handed down to the kings and resulting in their annihilation; often this is by analogy with another text which has to do with the wicked of the earth being struck by the 'rod' of Messiah's mouth (Isa 11.4). The kings' fate, thus the argument goes, might then be an anticipation of the 'second death' (20.6) and of judgment, whose irrevocable outcome is final separation from God in the lake of fire (20.15). In my view, this line of reasoning too quickly forgets Isa 60.10-11 and the hope it articulates concerning the destiny of those pagans whom

Israel has enlightened – a hope also expressed in many other Scriptures.[30] For Revelation envisages that in the new earth there will be enlightened nations and 'kings of the earth' to come and worship God and the Lamb in New Jerusalem (21.24-26), much as historically their predecessors had come to Solomon's capital (1 Ki 10.23-25). So even if it were the case that 19.21 narrates the perdition of all wicked kings (*cf.* 17.2,18; Isa 60.12), in parallel with the way that 20.9 in turn will relate the ultimate fate of all hostile nations, it remains exegetically rash to rule out too quickly the influence of the positive tradition we have evoked.

Revelation 20

The contrast between the approaching banquet of the Lamb and the carnivorous feast which is its caricature, carries over into another scene that also precedes the forthcoming wedding. Within it, two destinies remain in opposition to one another in a double representation of judgment. The seer first of all notices thrones presiding over a resurrection scene, in which believers receive their reward (20.4*ff*), before watching a general convocation for final judgment, which opens before the great white throne (20.11*ff*). I will examine this sequence in three stages.

1) Revelation 20.4-6

This episode, played out before the throne, has as its primary focus all those for whom God works a reversal of fortune by rendering them justice and restoring them following their sufferings. Involved in the scene are not only the martyrs 'beheaded' for 'the Testimony of Jesus and... the Word of God' but also, by extension, all who have resisted the monster and refused submission to it. (20.4). Even at this late stage in the plot the narrative continues to make use of negative terms for describing these followers of Jesus. Thus they are said not to have twin traits displayed by those who have fallen victim to the false prophet, namely, idolatrous worship and a corresponding brand or tattoo; 20.4 borrows this characterisation from 19.20 and, as we have come to expect, symmetrically inverts the two elements. Positively, however, their recompense is narrated by two aorists translatable as simple past tenses: 'they revived (came to life) and reigned with Messiah for a thousand years.' By insisting, here, upon the promise of a millennial reign – the fact is declared in 20.4, before being repeated and reinforced in 20.6 – the text underscores the protection to be enjoyed by these resurrected ones, in spite of the satan's renewed activity in a final mobilisation designed to do its worst. Full salvation has been represented earlier in Revelation through images such as the sealing of the 144, 000 (in 7.1-8) or the measuring of the Temple and its true worshippers (in 11.1-2);[31] a later example, here in chapter 20, is the *parembolē* or 'camp' of the saints (20.9) where they are safe. As a parallel and equivalent image, the millennium also offers powerful assurance of a salvation that cannot be overturned.

Yet in direct antithesis to all this, and by clever use of chiasmus, the text briefly mentions 'the rest of the dead' (20.5) or those who 'did not come to life', with the reason for their non-resurrection being that they may not participate in the millennial reign. Accordingly, the victors have a new negative qualification: they *will not be affected by* the 'second death' (20.6), for which the lake of fire will prove to be synonymous (20.14) in confirmation of knowledge that readers have actually had ever since the oracle to Smyrna (2.11). In its concentration upon those resurrected in Christ, the account here stresses the happiness of those who 'have [a] part' in the first resurrection (20.6). Here, we find the first of three contrasting uses of *meros* (literally 'part') in the course of Revelation's closing episodes which together constitute a clever literary device for sustaining a tension between the two destinies right to the end of the narrative. Between a beatitude that holds out the positive prospect of benefiting from the first resurrection (20.6, 'have [a] part in') and a last warning about the unhappy eventuality of losing one's 'part' (or 'share') in the fruit of the tree of life (22.19), the narrative inserts another negative use of *meros* in 21.8; here, by contrast, the 'part' (or 'place') allotted different categories of permanently excluded people will be in the lake of fire.

2) Revelation 20.7-10

We have already seen the kings and their armies amassed for war (in 19.19). Now, at the end of the thousand-year reign with Christ, the satan makes one last sortie with the aim of causing the nations, too, to revolt (20.7-10). This is the very point at which the story line brings to a climax the play on rival identities, throughout Revelation, which has set the Lamb's followers over against the partisans of the dragon and monsters. Readers discover a horde called 'Gog and Magog', recalling the archetypal enemy of God and his people described by Ezekiel (Ezek 38–39). Ezek 39.11-16 had already highlighted the fact that 'Gog' was a multitude and in our text there is once more a large number 'like the sand on the seashore' (20.8), as well as an attack launched upon the camp of the redeemed and against their city (20.9). Together these aspects convey the scope of the vain claims to universality and supremacy, heard repeatedly in Revelation, which are characteristic of the satanic anti-project. At this decisive juncture in the proceedings, there is something of a heightening of the struggle for universal lordship.

Readers come face to face, here, not only with a grotesque imitation of the vast company of the redeemed already seen in earlier scenes, but one which patently ridicules the entire divine plan in operation since the inception of salvation history. When Abraham's name was solemnly altered, he had received from God the promise of a posterity made up of a multitude of peoples and vast in number (Gen 17.4-6) and the same text specifies that his descendants would include both nations and kings. 'Peoples and kings' are also found in Isa 60.3 – a passage which will in fact play a key role in the denouement of Revelation's plot, in relation to the Book's keen interest in the people that God is calling together (which we have been studying here). Apparently drawing inspiration from the promise given to Abraham, Revelation arranges its own scenario in two halves, depicting mustering for war in two parallels (19.19; 20.8).[32]

Subsequent to Abraham's test at Mount Moriah, the promises made to him were renewed and it was expressly said that his descendants would be as numerous as the stars in the sky and as 'the sand of the sea' (Gen 22.17). When recounting the highs and lows of Israel's history, Scripture often uses the image of a vast throng for describing various enemy gatherings lined up against God's people: examples of this include the armies of the coalition of kings who had joined their horses and chariots in common cause to fight Joshua (Josh 11.4), the portrayal of the Midianites who had lined up against Gideon, with their innumerable camels (Jud 6.5), or again the uncountable Philistine foot soldiers ranged against Saul in 1 Sam 13.5;[33] any or all of these passages may have exercised a greater or lesser influence on the coalition of Rev 20.8-9. By its origins at the four corners of the earth and by spreading out over its entire surface, this league represents an anti-alliance *par excellence* around a standard that is the polar opposite of the one raised over Israel by God in the face of their enemies (Isa 11.14-16).

There is further reference to the Abraham cycle in 20.9, where antithetical parallelism crafts a take-off of the capture of enemy cities by the descendants of the patriarch (Gen 22.17): we watch as the saints' camp is surrounded (*cf.* Deut 23.15) and siege is laid to the 'beloved city',[34] cherished Zion (Ps 87.2) or beloved people (*cf.* Jer 11.15; 12.7). Ezekiel's prophecy also continues to function as a sub-text here, since the fire that had engulfed 'Magog' in Ezek 39.6 (*cf.* 2 Ki. 1.10,14) now descends as a fire for devouring the attackers and signalling the absolute defeat of rebellious humanity. The fire of the lake which will receive the devil as ringleader of evil (20.10) is a related image; there may well be influence from Gospel traditions, here, since in a series of parables Jesus had spoken explicitly of the 'eternal fire prepared for the devil and his angels' (*e.g.* Mt 25.41).

3) Revelation 20.11-15

With this section we move closer still to the destination both of God's redeemed people and of their adversaries. Readers have known of the existence of a 'book of life' ever since the oracle to Sardis (3.5) and Revelation now picks up this motif once more as the plot draws to its close (20.12). At both the start and end of the story, this Book stands for the destiny of those whose names are written there (3.5; *cf.*, later, 21.27); in two intervening passages governed by the logic of antithesis (13.8; 17.8), however, it has been used negatively to evoke those whose names *are not found there* and the same is true again here (20.15). Over against the *biblion* ('book') of life there are also other *biblia* ('books'), registers[35] which recount the acts of those whose names they list. The text distinguishes several such books of the dead (whose records may not be appealed) from that unique register of life by which, alone, access to eternal life is given to the elect (*cf.* 21.27), in obvious contrast to the exclusion and sentence awaiting those whose names do not appear. The 'second death' of 'the dead', accentuated by the four references to *nekroi* in 20.12-13, brings their story to a close and frees readers' attention for the bliss of those that have been granted eternal life.

Revelation 21.1-8

In the lake of fire, the vain pretentions to universal lordship of the dragon and monsters are eternally silenced and their enslavement of earth's peoples comes to an end. From now on, nothing but God's universal plan for humanity may exist, which will be fulfilled without opposition. In conformity with this plan of salvation, the 'peoples' of humanity have become the one people with whom God dwells (21.3) and now that all things have been made new (21.4), the multitude without number, first glimpsed in 7.9, blots out for ever the throng that had followed the monster. Early on in the tale of two identities, a promise had been made to Thyatira, which is now fulfilled: 'I will repay each of you according to your deeds' (2.23). Final separation from evil at last meets the expectation voiced by the faithful witnesses and victims of injustice in 6.10. In fact, every promise for conquerors expressed in the septet of oracles to Churches is realised here as the 'victor' reappears (in 21.7) and enters into possession of an inheritance which can be summed up as a Father-Son relation, in terms reminiscent of 2 Sam 7.8,14.

Revelation 21.9-27

In a development which parallels 21.1-8, the nations soon capitalise on their right to reside in New Jerusalem by bringing with them their 'glory and honour' (21.24-26). What have thus far been two separate designations (believers and nations), and two states, now at last coincide. As we have come to expect, this development is the cue for a reference to the contrary fate which, again unsurprisingly, is also twofold. Balancing the faithful victor, first, there is a description of non-victors consisting of eight elements whose worst and summary characteristic is the designation 'liars' (21.8). Then, set against the blessing of the nations, comes a reference to the non-accession of those who, according to 21.27, may be called both idolaters (2.14,20-21 seems to be in mind here) and 'liars'. In both 21.8 and 21.27 lying or deceit might refer particularly to the error of having judged the monster to be beyond compare (13.4),[36] since according to the Gospel it is only Jesus who is peerless and who truly merits the gratitude of the forgiven sinner.

Many exegetes register shock at how Revelation can still persistently warn (to the bitter end) against the eventuality of finding oneself excluded from the community of the redeemed, when the complete triumph of God's plan over the constitution of a rival people is being celebrated. In my judgment, this alleged contradiction is perfectly consonant with the pastoral strategy by which the author has sought, all along, to encourage his hearers to choose the Lamb and to follow him faithfully in the present time – in other words, to be committed to the risks entailed by faithful witness. Since what will distinguish the just from the wicked, ultimately, are simply their respective responses to the Gospel, such final words of warning are therefore quite in order (22.15): where faith is concerned, universal hope in no way rules out the careful exercise of vigilance.

The unexpected repentance of 11.13[37] and the reference to the nations' salvation in the song of the redeemed (in 15.4) are our only prior hint of the spectacular turn-around by which the nations and kings (21.24), who had previously trampled over the outer court of the Temple in the unfaithful city (11.2), now find themselves incorporated into the perfect city as a result of their conversion.[38] This event correlates with the prophetic anticipation of an eschatological pilgrimage of the nations (Isa 60.3; *cf.* the parallel in *Ps Sol* 17.34).[39] The nations and kings had been dupes of the devil and of 'Babylon'; their ability to change sides and to obtain residents' permits for God's city and the right to pay him tribute is the result of what has been fittingly called a process of 'purification and trans-valuation'.[40] Such a transformation of their fate is symbolised by the gates of the city, which never shut (21.25).

Revelation 22

Once the nations are healed (22.2), the number of God's servants united in his worship is complete. So significant is this that a final reference to the wearing, on the brow, of God and the Lamb's name (22.4) is merited. This name already signified allegiance; now it has the further connotation of communion and perhaps even immortality.[41] At last, worshippers may see God face to face, in exact fulfilment both of a beatitude of Jesus (Mt 5.8) and also of the people's sacrificial calling, as anticipated a number of times in the course of the story (1.6; 5.10; 20.6).[42] The prospect of a massive defection by wicked nations, who transfer their allegiance to God and join up with his people, gives readers of Revelation a picture of a startling turn-around which we could never have dared hope for. Such a transformation is the fruit of the costly but effective witness of disciples walking in the furrow already ploughed by the Faithful Witness himself. Should such a result surprise us? Surely not, for the series of promises given to Abraham in Genesis began and ended with a blessing directed at all the clans of the earth (Gen 12.3) and all its nations (Gen 22.18), at the coming together of nations and kings in one great company (Gen 17.4-6); several times, these same texts underscore the extreme fruitfulness of the descendants, who are as numerous as grains of sand (Gen 13.16) or the stars (Gen 15.5).

In the spectacular conversion of the nations, Revelation paints a picture of God's magnificent revenge upon the dragon and its sidekicks for the seduction of humanity, which they carried on amidst the vicissitudes of the story.[43] By recounting, at this point, how universal proclamation of the

Good News (14.6) will, in the end, be met by the faith and repentance of
a very large number – drawn from crowds of a fallen humanity estranged,
until now, from God – Revelation gives simple and forthright affirmation to
the Christian hope, according to which God's wonderful promises cannot
fail to be accomplished.

Notes

1 Resseguie, *Revelation Unsealed*, p.153.
2 I first explored Revelation's antithetical theme of belonging and rival belonging
   in two successive articles published in French, in 2004, in the journal *Théologie
   Evangélique* 3 (2004/1, pp.41-54 and 2004/2, pp.113-22).
3 Interestingly, *1QH* 8.19-36 also sets in opposition 'earth-dwellers' and 'the
   army of the saints' while *Enoch*, *2 Baruch* and *4 Ezra* also use the expression
   'earth-dwellers'. It should be noted, too, that 'land-dwellers' might be a better
   translation, since *he ge* could conceal a semitism reflecting *ha-aretz*, i.e. the land
   of Israel; R. van de Water takes this line in 'Reconsidering the Beast from the
   Sea', *NTS* 46, 2000, p.255.
4 Compare D.E. Aune, 'Following the Lamb: Discipleship in the Apocalypse', in
   R.N. Longenecker (ed.), *Patterns of Discipleship in the New Testament*, Grand Rapids/
   Cambridge, Eerdmans, 1996, p.278: 'the victory achieved by Jesus through suffering
   and death becomes a central paradigm for discipleship in the Apocalypse'.
5 I find the 144, 000 and the great multitude to be equivalent, since John first *hears*
   the number of the sealed (as 144, 000) and then *sees* the multitude: throughout
   Revelation, *hearing* is regularly required in order to understand what has just
   been *seen*. As for the debates provoked by exegesis of this text, one may still
   profit from A. Feuillet, 'Les 144,000 Israélites marqués d'un sceau', *Novum
   Testamentum* 9, 1967, pp.191-224.
6 Often decoded by the commentaries as a reference to Roman prostitutes whose
   foreheads bore their names.
7 E.-B. Allo, *Saint Jean. L'Apocalypse*, Paris, Gabalda, 1933, p.202 (my translation).
8 As noted by Prigent, *Apocalypse*, p.421, n.30.
9 Since the start of the twentieth century and subsequent to the work of A.
   Deissmann and H.B. Swete, reason was sought for Revelation's semantics and
   the question posed: why instead of *stigma* do we find another Greek word
   (*charagma*, 'mark') as a contrast to God's seal, and is not *charagma* also the term
   used to designate the imperial seal, the Caesar's own stamp applied to official
   documents (or else, the imperial head engraved on coins)? Thus, E.A. Judge,
   'The Mark of the Beast, Revelation 13.16', *Tyndale Bulletin* 42, 1991, pp.158-60,
   suggests that the first readers must have had in mind, at this point, the practice
   of cultic or commercial tattooing in the ancient world. Yet such a suggestion
   can be neither falsified nor proved. Instead of speculating about the imperial
   seal or about the branding by which this grotesque 'mark' might be explained,
   I prefer to follow G.R. Beasley-Murray, *Revelation*, London, Eerdmans, 1974,
   p.218, in deriving the meaning of the 'mark' from the role expressly given to it
   by Revelation's own internal narrative symbolism.
10 As S. Pattemore puts it, *The People of God in the Apocalypse. Discourse, structure and
   exegesis*, Cambridge, CUP, 2004, p.191, 'the story of discipleship is like the story
   of the Lamb'.

11 Almost all of these texts are dealt with by Swete, *The Apocalypse of St. John*, London, Macmillan, 1907, p.179.

12 I owe my linkage of the name on the brow to the seal (14.1 to 7.3) to I.T. Beckwith, *The Apocalypse of John*, New York, Macmillan, 1919, p.651, while my aligning of 14.1 with 13.16-17 comes from Prigent, *Apocalypse*, p.421.

13 One of three ways of characterising discipleship; on this see Aune, 'Following', pp.274-76.

14 For A. Yarbro-Collins, *Crisis and Catharsis*, Philadelphia, Westminster John Knox, 1984, pp.129-131, the description of the Lamb's companions as pure and chaste means they are priests. More recently, see also J.W. Marshall, *Parables of War. Reading John's Jewish Apocalypse*, Waterloo CDN, Wilfred Laurier University Press, 2001, p.160*ff* and pp.191-92; for Marshall, Revelation's *Sitz im Leben* is the period of the Jewish War and he assimilates the priests of 14.1*ff* to consecrated warriors ready to fight for the Lamb.

15 This clever reworking of 13.16 in 14.9 was brought to my attention by E. Delebecque, *Apocalypse*, pp.218, 222.

16 For J. Fekkes, *Visionary Antecedents*, p.194, John is addressing apostates (3.4), *i.e.* those who seek a syncretistic compromise (2.14-15,20-22) and, more generally, those in the Asian Church who are vacillating (2.24-25; 3.2-3; *cf.* 18.4).

17 In support of this positive-negative reading, see Prigent, *Apocalypse*, pp.449-53.

18 For these links, *cf.* R. J. Bauckham, *Climax*, p.28.

19 Corsini, *Apocalypse*, in his discussion of Rev 16.

20 C. Brütsch, *Clarté de l'Apocalypse*, Geneva (tr. Labor et Fides), 1955, p.264 (my translation).

21 On this topic see, for example, E. Schüssler-Fiorenza, *Just World*, p.93.

22 Similarly Prigent, *Apocalypse*, p.495.

23 R.H. Mounce, *Revelation*, p.230, also distinguishes three nuances, but his analysis is less precise: in 17.15 (he says) the expression underlines universality, whereas elsewhere it is applied either to the Church (5.9; 7.9) or else to the pagan world (10.11; 11.9; 13.7; 14.6).

24 For Bauckham, *Climax*, pp.331-32, John in this final instance of the expression draws a contrast between the nations that serve 'Babylon' and the people of God, whose suffering is caused by the city (17.6; 18.20,24).

25 R.W. Wall, *Revelation*, p.215, does not think these kings can be the same as those of 17.16. But in my opinion the kings' ambivalent attitude (in 18.9-10) renders artificial any distinction we might make between the two.

26 Prigent, *Apocalypse*, p.393.

27 On this, see the relevant comments, at this point, of M. Rissi, *Alpha und Omega: eine Deutung der Johannesoffenbarung*, Basle, Friedrich Reinhardt Verlag, 1966.

28 For J. Ellul, *L'Apocalypse: Architecture en mouvement*, Paris, Desclée, 1975, p.269, the assembly of 19.6 must be the final one, for he considers that this is the point where separation between the Church and 'other peoples' finally comes to an end. However, it should be remembered that at this stage in the intrigue, the long-awaited wedding announced as imminent has yet to occur as such; thus 19.17-18 can still present the reader with another adversarial horde (for this, see the discussion below).

29 J. Sweet, *Revelation*, London, SCM Press, 1979, p.280.

30 Two variants of this hope may be distinguished which either make pagans dependent upon Israel or else grant pagans equal status with the elect people

of God in their access to salvation. The following texts may be consulted: Pss 22.27-28; 72.8-11; 86.9; 138.4-6; Isa 2.2-4; 18.7; 45.20-24; 49.22-26; 55.5; 56.6-8; 60.1-22 (undoubtedly the most important of these texts for this part of Revelation); 66.18-21; Jer 3.17-18; Mic 4.1-4; Zeph 3:9-10; Hag 2.7-9; Zech 2.11-12 ; 8:23; 14.16-19; Dan 7.14. In the Greek version, Isa 54.15 and Am 9.12 have a similar slant. For an inventory of non-canonical Jewish writings which prolong this universalistic hope, see D.E. Aune, *Revelation 17-22*, p.1172.

31   Schüssler-Fiorenza, *Just World*, pp.107-8.

32   In the partisans of the satan, Brütsch, *Clarté*, p.337, sees a figure for rebellious humanity, great in number and in its capacity for any and all wrongdoing.

33   Here I am relying on Sweet, *Revelation*, p.291, who in his discussion of this passage brings together various discrete references to enemy hordes as numerous as grains of sand.

34   This designation can also be found in *Sirach* 24.11.

35   Prigent, *Apocalypse*, p.579, notes various apocalyptic texts where a ledger of human actions is found, providing a list of Jewish writings (whether canonical or not) in which a book of the elect occurs.

36   As E. Cothenet puts it, *Apocalypse*, pp.166-68.

37   As C. Le Moignan reminds us, *Following the Lamb*, p.111, whenever judgment falls in the course of Revelation's plot, the response is usually cursing and obstinate persistence in sin.

38   Similarly S.S. Smalley, *Revelation*, p.559, who calls them 'a converted society which has learned to serve the Lord'. Smalley also directs his reader to the start of the NT, where in Mt 2.1-12 the coming of the Magi to visit the King of the Jews could anticipate the displacement of the kings here.

39   On this topic, see Prigent, *Apocalypse*, p.622.

40   I borrow this elegant phrase from Brütsch, *Clarté*, p.374 (my translation).

41   This was the view of M. Kiddle, *Revelation*, p.444.

42   For Sweet, *Revelation*, p.312, those marked on the forehead are consecrated priests; he bases his view on instances (in Philo and Josephus) of the high priest wearing YHWH's name on his brow.

43   For a useful discussion of this very issue, see Bauckham, *Climax*, p.310*ff.*

6. Bride-city and whore-city

'John mixes his metaphors, providing a richer understanding of the church triumphant as both the dwelling place of God and the beloved of the Lamb'.[1]
(R. C. Ortlund)

The first two chapters in Part Two have already provided two opportunities for exploring Revelation's dramatisation of the story of a people and an anti-people, focusing first on the activities (chapter 4) and then on the respective identities (chapter 5) of these inversely corresponding groups. To complete our study of humanity's self-discovery in the face of God's self-revelation, this chapter will address the fickleness of humanity's response to the initiative taken by God on its behalf, closely examining the faithful and obedient 'yes' of those who live in a relationship with God in response to his love, as well as the idolatrous and rebellious 'no' of those who turn their backs on him. All this is powerfully dramatised through a cluster of feminine and urban images, used separately or in combination. Together, they constitute the most elaborate and striking example of antithetical parallelism in the whole of Revelation.[2]

A brief survey of Revelation's women-cities

Several women and several cities make their contribution to the development of this major twin theme. Among Revelation's women figures are the so-called prophetess 'Jezebel' (2.20*ff*), then the woman robed with the sun (12.1-6), the adulteress astride the monster (17.1-6) and last of all the bride (19.6-9a, 21.9-10). As for the cities, the data cover those where the Churches of Asia are to be found (2.1–3.22), Jerusalem (11.1-13), 'Babylon' (14.8, 18.1-24) and at the close of the Book, New Jerusalem (chapter 21–22). The complex women-city metaphor generates 'a double series of attributes, some of which fit a woman and others a city'[3] and these are variously alternated or combined in such a way that all these women and personified women-cities are indivisible from one another in Revelation's plot.

As a biblical concept with positive or negative overtones, the woman-city is rooted in traditional images by which Jerusalem was compared: for example, to Zion's daughter decked out for a feast (Isa 52.1-2)[4] or to a married woman forgetful of her first love (Jer 2.2,32). As happened already in prior revelation, both feminine and urban imagery are used to personify God's project of bringing humanity together in the very context where human beings, as builders of cities, have set about mounting their own such projects. He will make ready for them a Church-city – a dwelling place where they will live as conquerors and where a vast population of those he has redeemed will enjoy citizenship together. Thus, the double metaphor is a means of exhorting believers, who live out their Christian faith in the Churches and cities of Ephesus and its hinterland, to stand firm in the human city and to resist apostasy.

The fusing together[5] of feminine and urban metaphors is a configuration detectable elsewhere in ancient Jewish literature;[6] in Revelation it comes to a climax when our eyes turn towards two women-cities, Babylon-the-whore and Jerusalem-the-bride. These are correlated with one another in the course of the narrative by means of highly sophisticated antithetical parallelism, which makes the former's repudiation correspond to the latter's bridal adornment and wedding. Indeed, what gives Revelation's plot such originality is just this parodic play on the disappearance of a first woman-city to make way for another, whereby the multiple traits of the one find their strict counterpart in every characteristic of the other. Yet readers will only perceive all the multiple nuances of the spectacle in chapters 17–22, as fallen Babylon-the-whore relinquishes her place to descending Jerusalem-the-bride, if full account is taken of every woman and every personified city already encountered earlier.

Revelation 2.1–3.22

The very first model of a woman-city, in Revelation, comes in the ecclesial and urban unit formed by the seven Church-cities of Roman Asia. They may be seen as providing the initial sketch for the grand fresco of heavenly Jerusalem later on.[7] Each of the seven oracles in 2.1–3.22 is addressed to the Church in a town or city. As transmitted by John, the revelation takes the form of oracles by which prophets in the Hebraic tradition had, in their own times, proclaimed the Word of the Lord to Jerusalem or to other ancient cities. The communication delivered here to Thyatira or Ephesus or Laodicea corresponds to their oracles directed at Tyre or Babylon or Jerusalem. On Sunday morning, amid the din of these cities of Asia, the Risen One and the Spirit together – as the frame for each of the seven messages – whisper in the ear of their beloved who has forgotten her first love (2.4), using words designed to reprimand and correct her (3.19). However, there are other, seductive words which compete with this appeal. They may originate in Pergamum's pagan acropolis (2.13); in defamatory accusations made by apostates gathered in rival synagogues in Smyrna or Philadelphia (2.9; 3.9); in misleading teaching given by 'Nicolaitans' within the communities themselves (2.6,15); or, most of all, in the idolatrous propaganda of a prophetess whose speech in no way reflects the words of the God of the covenant: 'Jezebel' (2.20*ff*). All this must be countered.

The seven oracles employ various elements to establish the theme of the city as a place where God will come to meet with human beings. In Pergamum, readers discover a venue where the satan dwells and has its throne (2.13) and the description locates this metropolis of flourishing paganism at the antipodes of where God sits enthroned and has chosen to dwell, namely, in Jerusalem. In the context of the pagan sacred meals and associated debauched rites that occur there, mention is first made of idolatry and religious infidelity, with a backcloth provided by Israel's infamous straying from the path under the instigation of Balaam (2.14; cf. Num 25.1-3).

Philadelphia is a Church-city which, like Smyrna, has nothing worthy of reproach. The unlimited access which Christ grants her (3.8) compensates for the exclusion perpetrated by false Jews (3.9); a promise to the victor (3.12) prepares for entry by the gates (cf. 22.14) into the city which God is holding in reserve. Every clause in this promise points from the Church-city of the here and now, Philadelphia, to the Church-city yet to come, New Jerusalem. Although the Temple will be abolished in the finale (21.22), the promised blessing of being a pillar in the Temple will still hold good since what it refers to is permanent enjoyment of God's presence. Bearing the triple name which Messiah bestows – 'the name of my God, and the name of the city of my God . . . and my own new name' (3.12) – is a way of associating victorious believers in Philadelphia, ahead of time, with the bride of God and the Lamb of chapter 21. When Philadelphia is awarded the very appellation that will designate the coming bride-city – 'the new Jerusalem that comes down from my God out of heaven' –this Church-city in Asia is made a suburb, by anticipation, of the eschatological city: on the proviso, of course, that she holds fast to what she has (3.11).

The message from the Risen One to the Church-city of Laodicea is an oracle which both concludes and recapitulates the series of seven communications. It borrows a binary motif from the stock-in-trade of the Old Testament prophets: YHWH's marriage to his beloved people and as its foil, symbolised by the image of prostitution, that same people's idolatrous unfaithfulness. This language of conjugal infidelity provides the oracle with its image of shameful nudity, something frequently exploited previously by the prophets when denouncing the people of Israel's idolatry before their God (3.17-18; cf. Ezek 16.8,35,37; 23.10,18,29; Hos 2.11; Nah 3.5; Hab 2.15). As the only Church-city to receive no praise or recommendation whatsoever, but a series of severe reprimands, Laodicea offers a foretaste of 'Babylon' herself; or more precisely, Laodicea already functions as an anti-image for the heavenly Jerusalem that 'Babylon' (once she is transformed) will eventually become. Thus, Laodicea's alleged riches anticipate the splendour in the description of 'Babylon' in chapter 18; just as Laodicea imagines she is rich, so all the wealth of 'Babylon' will evaporate when she falls (18.17). Laodicea's urgent need of white garments (3.18) points to the replacement of the purple and scarlet of 'Babylon' by New Jerusalem's pure linen; and the pure gold which Laodicea may obtain from Christ is the very material from which the city of heavenly origin will be fashioned (21.18,21).

Should the warning given to Laodicea bring her to repentance, then what is in prospect instead is nothing less than a covenant meal in communion with Messiah, who stands already knocking at the door like a bridegroom come for his bride (3.20)! We are reminded of the coming in judgment of the Son of Man as he approaches the city gates (Mk 13.29), the need to stay watchful in order to be in a position to open the gates to the master (Lk 12.35*ff*), or again of the picture of going out to meet the Bridegroom-Messiah (Mt 25.1*ff*). Another recollection might be the fiancée hearing her beloved knocking at the door (Song 5.2-3). This promise to Laodicea will be fulfilled in New Jerusalem, when God and the Lamb come to be present definitively with redeemed humanity.

Revelation 2.18-29: 'Jezebel'

It is the fourth oracle, addressed to Thyatira, which devotes most space to feminine and urban imagery: what was surely the least important of the seven cities in first-century Roman Asia, historically speaking, is the pivotal Church-city for this septet. Both by providing decisive orientation to the thematic vector of Church-cities, and preparing for all that follows, this oracle is in fact, the principal component of the septet. The greater length of this communication, compared to the other six, is due mainly to the importance attached to 'Jezebel' (2.20-24), her 'lovers' (2.22) and her 'children' (2.23). Exegetes have been preoccupied, and still are, by the problem of identifying 'Jezebel': could this figure refer to some specific woman, a historical person perhaps known to the seer and his addressees? Were the local 'Nicolaitans' led by a woman-prophetess?[8] Was there a female rival to John the seer who, as regular or resident prophet (as it were), sought to denounce her fraudulent message and its ravaging effects?[9]

The question is, do the oracles – and thereafter, does Revelation as a whole – maintain an allusive reference (which exegetes can decode) to real persons and situations located in a historical background that may readily be reconstructed? We have already had to confront this problem in the first part of this study; as we followed thematic trajectory number two, I had to give an assessment of the frequently suggested equation: *sea-monster* = *Rome*. I will return to this later in the present chapter, once it becomes necessary to assess the significance of 'Babylon', 'Babylon the great' and the 'great city'. For the moment I will confine myself to noting that, however interesting this kind of historical questioning may be, in the case of 'Jezebel' it does not get us very far. Although nothing excludes *a priori* the possibility that there was, in Thyatira, a (false) prophetess whose message rivalled that of John, nothing allows us to affirm this either – much as nothing satisfactorily elucidates the problem of the name or case of Antipas at Pergamum (2.13). All extra-textual historical references for these literary characters simply remain opaque to us.

In my view, the textual data invite us to undertake a quite different type of questioning which consists of fully investigating the role given to this feminine character within the sole bounds of the text of Revelation. The symbolic value of the other pejorative designations used in these seven messages – Nicolaitans, synagogue of the satan, Balaam, lovers and children [of 'Jezebel'] – suggest that this name with an infamous ring to it, 'Jezebel', is used to typify[10] that which, for believers, conjures up something to be avoided at all costs. Just as Balaam had the reputation of leading Israel astray (cf. 2 Pet 2.15, Jude 11), so 'Jezebel' the pagan princess was cast in the unequivocal role of inciting idolatry (1 Kgs 16.31) and dragging along with her both king and people. By 'teaching and beguiling my servants to practise fornication and to eat food sacrificed to idols' (2.20), this 'Jezebel' leads followers astray exactly as the satan and its false prophet will (13.14; 19.20) or, more to the point, as 'Babylon' herself will ('all nations were led astray by your sorcery', 18.23).

In her prostitution and sorcery, which led to her liquidation by Jehu (2 Kgs 9.22), as well as in her assassination of the Lord's prophets (1 Kgs 18.13), biblical Jezebel contributes to the prototype for the whore 'Babylon'. Nor is it fortuitous that she should have hailed from Tyre, the courtesan-city denounced in the oracle of Isa 23 from which the presentation of 'Babylon' in chapter 18 will borrow extensively. These are indications that the judgment narrated there is anticipated here by the condemnation handed down to 'Jezebel' and her followers (2.22-23); the punishment by death that hangs over those who are unrepentantly loyal to 'Jezebel' is similar to the one that threatens associates of 'Babylon' who do not flee her sins (18.4,8). Indeed, in both cases punishment is meted out using the very same measure, 'according to your works' (2.23; 18.6).[11] In sum, what is anchored to the reference to 'Jezebel' placed here at the heart of the first septet is the whole story of how an anti-people loyal to the monster was constituted, as examined in the previous chapter.

'Jezebel' is Revelation's inaugural female figure. She therefore precedes and, if truth were told, anticipates all the others: the figure of the heavenly mother in the trumpets septet; that of the fiancée in the final visions; and between the two, the adulteress who possesses both their traits and so parodies both mother and fiancée simultaneously. 'Jezebel' is a dubious mother (2.23) in so far as her 'children' are the enemies of the associates of the infant King brought into the world by the heavenly mother (12.5). She leads others astray (2.20,24; cf. 12.9;18.23) with her adultery and prostitution (2.20-22), something that will be characteristic of the whore-city in her sham motherhood (17.1-2,5) and which is in flagrant contrast to the virginity of the other eschatological woman-city (21.2,9). Her name, 'Jezebel', brings blood to mind, which is further reflected in her own destruction (2.22-23; 17.16; cf. 2 Kgs 9.33), whereas there will be no more death in the ultimate woman-city (21.4). Lastly, eating meat offered to idols, or the drinking of saints' blood by 'Babylon' (17.6), find their counterpart in the divine food given to the fleeing woman (12.6) or to heavenly Jerusalem (21.7; 22.1-2).

Church-cities: How they fare

As a unit, the seven Church-cities of the opening septet show how ambiguous life can be for God's people, in cities made by human hands. The spiritual health-checks of the Church-cities range from a clean bill of health for some to a record of chronic illness for others, with worrying symptoms afflicting still others between these two extremes. To put this in a more explicit way, the gamut runs from the faithfulness of Smyrna or Philadelphia to the very precipice of apostasy in Laodicea, crossing en route the equivocal situations to be found in Ephesus, Pergamum and Thyatira or the near-death state that applies in Sardis. Yet whatever may be the degree of infidelity which the Risen One encounters as he walks in the midst of the lamp stands, it is always *his* Church which he visits in every place: God, through the Lamb, has opted to dwell with his people and to reveal himself to them, so it is this relationship which finds its particular expression in each Church as they all come together, city by city, to hear the prophecy read (1.3) on the Lord's Day and to lend an ear to what the Spirit is saying.

This relationship explains why, on the positive side, every Church without exception receives a promise to the 'victor' for which New Jerusalem – as the place where God dwells (21.3) and where God and people will be like Father and son (21.7) – will later bring the fulfilment. On the negative side, it also accounts for the conditional curses (wherever these are deserved) which will lead, in the ensuing narrative, to the condemnation and fall of 'Babylon'. When the time comes, 'Babylon' will empty as her throng leaves her (*cf.* 17.15); by contrast, as the former 'great city' ceases to exist (18.21), New Jerusalem will be 'made ready' (21.2) and fill up with the transformed nations that flow into her (21.24-26) from her rival.

Throughout the story that begins in Ephesus, the project for a Church-city remains essentially unaltered. The city with no temple, manufactured by God (21.22) as a place where he will dwell with humanity (21.3), constitutes a spectacular affirmation of human civilisation and enterprise. The human city is the place where the identity and allegiance of those whose citizenship is in heaven are forged (*cf.* Phil 3.20). For Asia's Church-cities, anything can happen on the road from first love (2.4) to the crowning moment of the wedding banquet (3.20): the betrothed's faithfulness can be sorely tried (2.10) and she can fall prey to seduction of the worst kind (2.20), which would be her undoing if she should succumb (2.23).

The ultimate domicile for God and humanity will be a place of intimate communion. This perfect city is glimpsed from the inaugural septet onwards (in the oracle to Philadelphia, 3.12) and then revealed in the Book's final vision. This prospect does not alter the fact that, for biblical revelation, the city of men is tinted with ambiguity from the start: a divine sanction fell in the episode of the archetypal city Babel and its tower (Gen 11.5-6). Revelation's 'Babylon',[12] a city where the monster reigns in Christ's place, is Babel's heir and so takes on the mantle of the anti-god city *par excellence*.

She develops to the full the potential for rebellion found in the Church-city of Pergamum, where the satan is said to have its throne (2.13). She even has a colony in the otherwise irreproachable Church-cities of Smyrna and Philadelphia – a detail not to be passed over lightly – where an alternative community gathers in a 'synagogue' brought together by the satan (2.9; 3.9).

Revelation 11.1-13: The 'Great City'

The theme of the 'great city', so important in the later narrative (*cf.* 16.19; 17.18; 18.10,16,18-19,21), is rooted in the oracle of 11.1-13 which combines with 14.8 to offer the first anticipatory allusions to 'Babylon the great'. In the first of these texts, three explicit references are found, suggesting that readers are somehow supposed to recognise the 'city' in question: 'Holy City', 11.2; mention of the 'great city', 11.8; an attack on this same city, 11.13. But a significant detail supplied in 11.8, specifying that this is the city 'where also their Lord was crucified', guides interpretation and obliges readers to assimilate this 'great city' to Jerusalem – in perfect congruity, of course, with the notion of a 'Holy City' and with the geography of the Temple (11.2).[13]

In fact, Jerusalem fully deserves her status as a royally 'great city' (Jer 22.8 LXX; Ps 48), populous and important as she was (Lam 1.1). Jesus calls her the 'city of the great king' (Mt 5.35). From the perspective of the prophets, in particular, this city was 'great' because God had chosen her for his dwelling place; she therefore deserved to be called 'glorious' (Ps 87.1-3). For Flavius Josephus she remained 'great', despite his defection to the Roman cause (*Jewish War* vii.1.1; 8.7); his view was shared by the Roman *quaestor* and later *praetor* Tacitus (*Hist.* 5.2). Finally, in an echo of Jer 22.8 (LXX), Jerusalem still remained 'the great city' for the *Sibylline Oracles* (*Sib. Or.* 5.154, 226, 413).

More problematic is her status in terms of holiness, for although 'holy', this city in Revelation – exactly like Jerusalem, as foreseen by Jesus (Lk 21.24) – finds herself handed over to pagan nations who trample her underfoot. Accordingly, there can be no thought that this reputedly 'holy' city might somehow escape the rule that applies in every human city, whereby good and evil must rub shoulders. At the stage the plot has now reached, with the eternal Holy City still incomplete and readers still awaiting her coming, anything 'holy' can be so only in a provisional and imperfect way. This fact is reinforced by the shame attached to the epithets used in 11.8. 'Sodom' was the high place for every vice (*cf.* Gen 19), used by the prophets as a nickname for 'Judah' (Isa 1:9-10) or for Samaria (Ezek 16.46,55) and even for Babylon (Isa 13.19): where sin is concerned, Zion was quite capable of surpassing Sodom (Lam 4.6). As for 'Egypt', the word is synonymous for the covenant people with a land of servitude, as a target of the divine wrath expressed in a variety of forms in the Exodus plagues; as well as recapitulating the plagues and woes of the first six trumpets (chapters 8–9), the violent tremors which hit the city here (11.11) also hark back to these fundamental scriptural plagues and perhaps, to the earth-shattering events that had accompanied Jesus's death and resurrection in Jerusalem (Mt 27.51; 28.2). As equivalent symbols for the decay of civilisation, Sodom and Egypt have the connotation for biblical revelation of whatever is most obviously vile or oppressive: they are, in sum, 'places of revolt... of absolute rejection . . . [and] of hatred against God'.[14]

The end-time city that will bring all peoples together will be 'holy', for she will be made by God and constitute the object of his love. Yet here in chapter 11, the city in question is by contrast the theatre for displaying the arrogance of all human empires and for showing universal human opposition to the message of the two witnesses (11.9-10). In other words, the 'great city' of chapter 11 is anything but 'holy', as she kills the prophets (we will come back to this in 18.4); indeed, this was the very charge Jesus had levelled against her (Mt 23.34-35; Lk 13.34). Ultimately, she is also anything but 'great' as she is handed over to unbelievers. When it comes down to it, the 'greatness' of Revelation's 'great city' is above all ironic, like the praise of Babylon in Dan 4.27 found on the lips of Nebuchadnezzar, the king who had beautified her. Above all else, 'great' will be her fall (14.8; 18.2,10,16,19,21)!

In a note relating to 11.1, the French *Traduction Œcuménique de la Bible* legitimately draws attention to the ambiguity of a 'holy' city that might just as aptly be dubbed 'murderous'. We ought not to be surprised by the ambivalence of a 'holy' city which, despite having a temple, is made subject to pagan domination. On the one hand, God chose Jerusalem as a place to dwell and for meeting his people (Isa 60.14); as the historical centre of the covenant, the city had long enjoyed a reputation as a city of justice and faithfulness which also supplied the terms for understanding her future destiny (Isa 1.21,26-27). However, on the other hand the same Isaiah does not hesitate for a moment to dub Jerusalem, in the same breath, both 'faithful city' and 'whore' (Isa 1.21). For the Jewish people, such ambivalence hung over Jerusalem like a bad odour, especially after her fall in the sixth century BCE, when the exiles from Jerusalem and Judah were forced, against their will, to become the founders of a Babylonian Diaspora.

The 'Great City' of Revelation 11: An anticipation

In the opening septet we saw how urban and community imagery was exploited in the course of the oracles to Church-cities in Roman Asia. We can now say that here in chapter 11, recourse to the symbol of the 'great city' enables two things to happen. First, it allows fuller exploration of the contrasting character exhibited by divine and human projects for the human city. Second, it lays a foundation for the later parodying of Jerusalem-the-bride, the divine city where humanity dwells with God, by the penultimate anti-city Babylon-the-whore. Fundamentally, the power of the image of the 'great city' in chapter 11 is to be found in its multiple layers of meaning: these exert a calculated influence on our ability to distinguish, in 'Babylon', a caricature of New Jerusalem and a deliberate contrast with the renewed

Jerusalem of the future to be revealed in the denouement. For this contrast to function properly, Revelation has to exploit the eventful story of Jerusalem throughout salvation history, up to and including the time of Jesus. A few well-chosen remarks of J. Ellul show us how this is done:

The only reason Jerusalem [is called] a place of salvation, or can prefigure heavenly Jerusalem, or can provide any sort of tenuous pictorial link to the city that God himself will create, is because that is where Jesus died . . . Jerusalem, through this death, achieves what had always been foretold of her, namely, that she would play a unique role in salvation history . . . And this underlines the ambiguous character of Jerusalem . . . she may be sanctified or chosen, but she is the city that tries to fight God and to destroy whatever he does, the city that kills the Son of God . . . both in embodying hope and exemplifying the curse, Jerusalem is the measure of all cities.[15]

The degree to which, as readers, we will be able to pick up the opposition between 'Babylon' and New Jerusalem in chapters 17–22 depends on a certain prior blending of the horizons, beginning in 11.1-13. To see how this works it is sufficient to take a closer look at two motifs: the 'great earthquake' and the consequent partial collapse of the city in 11.13. The earthquake, first of all, is an important motif in Revelation's narrative and it is introduced, as part of the sixth seal's judgment, as a 'great earthquake' in 6.12. It reappears in 8.5 as a simple 'earthquake' closely linked to the Temple (and recalling the lightning, rumblings and peals of thunder of the theophany in 4.5), occurring at the very instant when fire is taken from the incense altar and hurled onto the earth. Later, there will be two further uses for an earthquake accompanied by similar manifestations: first in 11.19, where heavy hail is added to the picture, and again in very elaborate fashion in 16.18-21 where, among other things, 'Babylon the great' is affected.

As for the second motif of a fall, both earth and heaven will suffer ultimate dislocation following the millennium (in 20.11). Before that happens however, punishment through collapse is brought about in 11.13, by the murder of the witnesses. Other episodes in the story of the 'great city' and of cities in league with her will follow. The cry 'fallen, fallen is Babylon the great!' sounds for the first time in 14.8, anticipating its reprise (like a refrain) in 18.2. Between the two, where the theme of the fall of 'Babylon' is first alluded to (before its full development later in chapter 18), there is an episode where the two designations, 'the great city' and 'Babylon the great', occur together in the same sentence (16.19). Like 11.13 previously, this same text also foretells an urban collapse whose scope will be universal this time: 'and the cities of the nations fell'.

Taking into account all the textual indicators noted so far, what proves especially enlightening is the antithetical parallelism at work between 11.13 and 16.18-21.[16] The shared elements interlink through 14.8, which serves as a relay by predicting the fall of a city called 'Babylon the great' that leads nations astray. In 11.13, a tenth of the city falls; in 16.19, however, things intensify as the great city breaks into three parts and the cities of the nations associated with her fall as well. As for 'Babylon the great', God remembers what she has done and pours out for her 'the wine-cup of the fury of his wrath' (16.19); this is a complete turn-around from when she made the nations drink 'the wine of the wrath of her fornication' (14.8)! In 11.13, the earthquake kills seven thousand but the survivors, in their fright, give glory to God; in 16.21, by contrast, an earthquake unprecedented in human history is not said explicitly to kill anybody: instead, the violent hail that accompanies it only gives rise to universal blasphemy on the lips of human beings.

By bringing together the cities of the two distinct contexts in 11.13 and 16.18-21 (with help from 14.8), these important linguistic connectors confer shared characteristics on the cities. The textual indicators have cumulative force, suggesting that the city justly nicknamed 'Babylon the great' is none other than apostate Jerusalem who assassinated the prophets, crucified the Lord and left unburied the corpses of his witnesses (11.8). As for the 'great city' whose destiny it is to fall (14.8; 16.19; 18.2), apostolic tradition has passed on the memory that for Jesus, this was precisely the fate awaiting the very Jerusalem in which he had given testimony and by which he had been rejected (Lk 21.20,24). Two things, therefore, are striking about the combined texts which contribute to the characterisation of 'Babylon' in Revelation (14.8; 16.19; 17.2-7,15-16,18; 18.2-4,6-8,16,20,24; 19.2): the cumulative effect of all these traits; and, the extent to which these characteristics fit the Jerusalem described in the Gospels and Acts, as well as the one depicted by Flavius Josephus. With the utmost care, Revelation is preparing its readers for the forthcoming elaborate characterisation of Jerusalem/Babylon-the-whore, in chapters 17 and 18, by which she will be established as the anti-type of the city of God, Jerusalem-the-bride.

Historical detour 6: Is 'Babylon' translatable by Rome?

In spite of all I have said, readers will know very well that when faced with all the data concerning 'Babylon' in Revelation, exegetes more often than not decode 'Babylon' as Rome – and do so more or less confidently. Whether first-century Rome can actually support all the weight placed upon it in this way would require verification;[17] but we should notice that it is once again the principle of decoding that governs this influential interpretation. When the text is approached in this way, 'Babylon' is taken to be a cipher for Rome, an encrypted allusion to the capital of the Empire in language which (so it is claimed) the first recipients would have found no difficulty in deciphering correctly. By insisting that, as contemporary readers, we should also employ a procedure of interpretative decoding in order to understand 'Babylon' correctly, interpreters work by analogy at this very point: since certain Jewish and Christian writings of the period are held to equate 'Babylon' with Rome – the texts put forward are *4 Ezra* 3.1-2,28-31; *2 Baruch* 10.1-3; 11.1; 67.7; and *Sibylline Oracles* 5.143,159 – and since, in 1 Pet 5.13, 'Babylon' is routinely considered to be an encoded reference to Rome, therefore in Revelation, too (it is alleged), 'Babylon' must quite obviously refer to Rome, albeit in a (barely) veiled way.

It might appear presumptuous to dare to call into question received wisdom that has been so influential. I certainly have no problem *in principle* with interpreters having recourse to decoding in specific cases – at least as a last resort. Furthermore, I would find it even less problematic to make the interpretative move of exploiting probable inter-textual links between Revelation and other relevant texts. However, interpreters need to demonstrate the hermeneutical relevance, for the exegesis of Revelation, of allegedly encoded language in other texts thought to be contemporaneous with it – which has simply not been done.[18] Since such evidence is not forthcoming, before we decide to proceed by decoding in the present instance we must first ask whether 'Babylon' (or 'Babylon the great') in Revelation are examples of encrypted language at all. My answer is 'no'. 'Babylon' is not a code word for deciphering and Revelation's implied reader has no reason for treating it as encoded language for decoding.

From my standpoint it is Revelation itself – taken as a self-contained narrative – and not another, allegedly parallel text that constitutes the primary interpretative horizon against which to set 'Babylon' in order to understand this term and all it conveys. To put this another way, interpreters intent on clarifying the meaning of 'Babylon the great' in Revelation should, in my view, rivet all their attention, as a matter of first importance, on the detail of *this* text, with its peculiar poetic and narrative features. Especially significant is its *feminine-urban imagery* from which, patently, 'Babylon' ought in no way to be separated. It transpires that this vector of meaning, which runs through the text, is precisely what prevents us from reducing 'Babylon the great' to a simple cipher, to a prosaic and platitudinous concept, to a code-word which may be decoded and translated by substituting Rome for 'Babylon'.

'Babylon the great' is in reality, and on the contrary, a complex *symbol* – better still, a *theme* – whose unfolding in Revelation is intimately linked to the Church-cities of Asia, to the 'great city' introduced in 11.8 and also to the controlling concept of the *woman-city*. Consequently, the only way to interpret 'Babylon' correctly in this text is to take *all* of these realities into account, with the wealth of related intra-textual and inter-textual reference an indispensable factor.[19] It is this very complexity which forbids all peremptory attempts to boil down such a *multi-faceted* symbol to a simple matter of translation or decoding. Theoretically speaking, a number of exegetes have now conceded the very point I am making.[20] Practically speaking, however, it is proving somewhat difficult to abide by.[21]

All this means that, from the moment we first encounter the image of the 'great city' in chapter 11, very close attention must be paid to the role it will play within Revelation's narrative. The Book's plot is rooted from the start precisely in the experience of urban Churches who meet in Asia's cities and it is not long before this feminine-urban metaphor acquires all the symbolic and multi-dimensional wealth with which Babylon-the-whore and indeed Jerusalem-the-bride enrich it. Furthermore, with regard to the inter-textual dimension of 'Babylon', only biblical amnesia (or ignorance) could explain our failure to hear the resonances of prior revelation, from which Revelation – as we have found at every step – is forever drawing elements to make up its own symbolic universe. Accordingly the woman-city Babylon-the-whore calls to mind everything the Old Testament had to say about Babylon, right from Babel onwards, and about other whore-cities besides, like Tyre (Isa 23) or Nineveh (Nah 3.1-7). Who is the whore-city *par excellence* in the Jewish Scriptures? Who gave to all the others their power and significance? *Jerusalem.* YHWH's wife by covenant (Ezek 16.8), who had forsaken him for idolatry (Ezek 16.38). Revelation's 'Babylon', caught red-handed in her covenant-breaking as was Gomer by Hosea, is Jerusalem in the thinnest of disguises.[22]

Back to the text:The 'Great City in Revelation 17.18; 18.2,8,10,16,18-19,21 (*cf.* 11.8; 14.8; 16.18-21)

We have seen how the Church-city that will reach completion in Revelation's finale, when New Jerusalem descends, started life in the cities of Roman Asia in the opening septet. In between, the project of a city where God and humanity will live together is pursued through a combination of the destinies of 'Babylon' and Jerusalem. Armed with everything that characterises the 'great city' at her first appearance (in 11.8) and with what 14.8 and 16.18-21 add to this picture, we are now in a position to examine the remaining references to the 'great city' (17.18; 18.10,16,18-19,21). The first of these texts (17.18) provides an interpretation of the vision of the whore of chapter 17 and the equivalence of feminine and urban metaphors is reiterated as it is explained to the seer how 'the woman you saw is the great city'. To the extent that the double name 'Babylon the great, mother of whores' has already confirmed the whore to be a city, it would seem that, by encouraging further reflection on what the preceding vision meant, 17.18 effects a transition to the next vision which will dwell upon the already anticipated fate of 'Babylon the great'.

A statement already heard in 14.8 acquires new volume with the angelic shout in 18.2, while 18.2-3 provides an expansion of what 14.8 had already said by way of anticipation. Another reference to the same text as before, Isa 21.9 – where Babylon's fall to the army of Cyrus is announced in Israel – is buttressed by additional elements which allude to Jer 9.10 and Isa 13.21-22; 34.11,14 as well as *Baruch* 4.35. Whether fallen (18.2) or violently hurled down (18.21), the city is called 'Babylon' three times (18.2,10,21). The 'great city' of this account becomes the object of three successive parallel laments and she is mentioned in identical fashion at the beginning of each of the three oracles of woe, spoken by the kings, merchants and seafarers respectively: 'alas, alas, the great city!' (18.10,16,19). Hurt by this triple woe, the 'great city' is also affected in four other principal ways: she is a habitation for demons (18.2), which believers must abandon (18.4); she is the target for a judgment greater even than the sum of her own wicked deeds (18.8); she is stripped of everything, where once she was sumptuously clad (18.16); and lastly, she is a desert, where previously she had been a great crossroads of commerce (18.19).

The dramatic tension surrounding her spectacular fall is accentuated by an ironic question, 'what city was like the great city?' (18.18), inspired by another question formulated in the course of a lament over Tyre in the source-prophecy of Ezek 27.32. At the opposite extreme to what is hoped for concerning New Jerusalem (as promised to Philadelphia, 3.12), the 'great city' has become the haunt of demons and a den for unclean spirits. As a city from which to flee (18.4) she is in absolute contrast to what will be 'the home of God among mortals' (21.3). Synonymous with impurity (18.2,5), she will replaced by another who has nothing to make her unclean (21.27). Before ever we encounter the numerous and precise contrasts that will set New Jerusalem in opposition to the 'Babylon' she replaces, the motif of the 'great city' adequately sets the general antithesis in place:

> On the one hand is the ideal city, illuminated by the divine presence and showered with every blessing. On the other is the impure city, a horrible lair for malignant and diabolical creatures. Here are two destinies, diametrically opposed and irreconcilable.[23]

Back to feminine imagery: Revelation 12

In due course, we will explore the antithetical correspondences which intimately connect the city of God with her caricature made by human hands. First, we must backtrack and return to the more particularly feminine aspect of our major twin theme, Revelation's women-cities. To do so we have to go back to the start of chapter 12 and to the apparition, in the vault of heaven, of something of great importance: a sign that is called 'grandiose', to which spectators are supposed to give their full attention (12.1-2). A female celestial figure is in view and she has three primary characteristics which are to be taken together as mutually interpretative, just as in Joseph's dream (Gen 37.9). She is clothed with the sun, dominates the moon and is crowned with twelve stars: as such she cuts an imposing figure and is the size of a constellation in the zodiac.[24] Veritable queen of the cosmos, she is nonetheless (paradoxically) very vulnerable, pregnant and in the throes of childbirth. Readers understand straightaway that we are looking at a mother figure and that there is about to be a birth (12.5). Yet before we see the delivery, or get to know the child she will bring into the world, the one witnessing this vision on our behalf has to confront a second celestial sign (12.3-4). This time he sees a huge dragon with the trappings of great power (ten horns) and of total lordship (seven diadems), whose appearance in heaven provokes a spectacular commotion of cosmic dimensions and causes a third of the stars to fall. Quite obviously this is a sign that corresponds to the first, serving to mark out the dragon as the woman's antagonist. So, when the dragon takes up a position for devouring the child at birth, readers are caught up in a moment of great dramatic tension!

To understand this female character properly we have to look closely at all the *dramatis personae* present in this scene and at the role allotted to each of them. The woman gives birth to her child, like Zion's daughter (Mic 4.6-10; 5.1-3) or Jerusalem (Isa 66.7-9), but the dragon is unable to carry out the destruction it had planned. Instead, the child whose destiny it is to reign over the nations (12.5; *cf.* 2.27) is snatched from its jaws, like Joash from Athaliah's clutches (2 Kgs 11.1-3), and then whisked away 'to God and to his throne'. A reference to Ps 2, at this point, means that the child who is born and who must conquer is indirectly identified with the Messiah, while his transposition to the throne inevitably makes us connect him with the Lamb. We might also wonder if God is the father of the child,[25] but the ensuing narrative does not seem to require his presence. The woman finds refuge and providential succour in an earthly desert (12.6), where she enjoys protection from the destructive plans of the dragon that has now rounded on her (12.13-14); it renews its attack and attempts to drown her, but the earth comes to her aid (12.15-16).

Everything that happens here revolves around the heavenly woman as mother of the child. Nonetheless, the woman's passivity is striking as she suffers in silence – like Messiah himself at his Passion[26] – as is her fate, which is to await and receive help from the hand of providence. This is a female figure impressively splendid and at the same time, poignantly vulnerable, cast as a victim.

The chief actor is not, in fact, the woman but the dragon, whose identity as the primordial enemy is nowhere in doubt (12.9). Itself a protagonist of heavenly origin (12.7) but now expelled from heaven (12.8-9), it is forced to restrict itself from now on to the theatre in which humanity lives and moves. When it appears, the dragon is certainly a powerful traitor (12.4), but the interlude which recounts its defeat and fall (12.7-12) describes an enemy cut down to size, unable either to prosecute or obtain its objectives. Its further attacks on the woman show how true this is (12.13*ff*), for the dragon has to find a new prey and abuse the woman's remaining descendants who follow the male child, characterised by their obedience to God and their keeping the Testimony of Jesus (12.17). There the combat breaks off, although the pause as the dragon comes to adopt a position on the sand of the seashore (12.18) does mean that some follow-up actions are in preparation.

For readers, this is essentially a scene of combat where three things happen: a child heir is attacked, but is preserved for the messianic role prepared for him by God; a woman, from whom the child is 'born', is also attacked but providentially kept safe; and the dragon attacker is itself fought and defeated, with the result that none of its stratagems for kidnapping or piracy succeeds. In essence, these are the exact events, and the protagonists and antagonist, from a fundamental biblical scenario which we ought to presuppose at this point, namely, Gen 3.15-16a. The combat, here in Revelation 12, pits against one another entities that figured in the very first phase of salvation history, in the primeval confrontation between Eve and the serpent, now set amid a decor of cosmic proportions which seems to have been borrowed from an international stellar myth found virtually everywhere in Antiquity.[27] In this combat, Revelation's recipients are themselves implicated because, by their own faithful testimony, they are associated both with the woman's descendants who are being assailed here (12.17) and with the victorious redemption achieved by the Lamb (12.11).

Historical detour 7:
Is the woman of Revelation 12 identifiable?

Can the woman against whom the dragon takes up arms be assimilated to any known historical entity? A traditional answer among Roman Catholic exegetes, although seldom put forward today,[28] is the ancient reading which would see in her 'Mary, encompassing the Church, for all of whose members she is mother'.[29] One interpretative key is provided by the fact that the text carefully underlines the woman's *lot*.[30] Does this mean, as Hippolytus of Rome already thought, that she is a personification of the Church depicted as a suffering figure? The drawback with this view is that the Church derives from Messiah, not the reverse[31] – unless we are to consider the Church to be Messiah's mother in the sense that she represents a continuation of the chosen people.[32]

But it is hard not to see in her, too, an evocation of Israel who – amidst the hazards of her history – would in due time produce the promised and expected deliverer, the one towards whom the serpent shows itself to be an implacable enemy (Gen 3.15; *cf.* Rev 12.9). This would make her the mother of the promised liberator whom the satan tries in vain to destroy, whose conquest of death as the primary victor and martyr-witness conferred on him the right to be shepherd of the nations (12.5).[33] This identification is reinforced by the resemblance between 12.2 and the description of the woman Zion who, in the midst of her labour-pains, takes flight and brings a new people to birth (Isa 66.7-9). The Isaiah Targum glosses this delivery as the birth of the messianic king, which the numerous allusions to Exodus further establish.[34] A collective interpretation of the woman, rooted in the chosen people of the Old Testament of which the Church is a continuation, therefore seems inevitable; and this brings us back to the very start of the story of Revelation's interpretation, to Victorinus.[35]

Perhaps we should conclude, on this point, that the significance of the woman in Rev 12 is broader than any of the classic historical identifications individually (Israel/Zion, the Church, Mary) or together. Rather than symbolising one people only that enjoyed a privileged relationship to God – as for example Israel under the old covenant – she appears potentially to prefigure 'humanity, in its complex and troubled relationship with God'.[36]

Perhaps this relationship is even with the entire creation, with which God makes a covenant, and as the birth of the woman's child results from this.[37] For that matter, Revelation's feminine imagery is underpinned, from start to finish, by the ambiguity of humanity's relationship to her Creator, given her capacity both for following God and for repudiating any relationship with him. There are more changes to come for the woman at the heart of the developing plot: as far as later action is concerned, the woman and mother of the present vision is the indispensable prerequisite for two further figures – both of them women-cities – who are the great whore, for which she is the antitype, and the Lamb's virgin fiancée, for which she represents the prototype.[38]

Back to the text:
The women of Revelation 12 and 17 in counterpoint

Since several elements of the description allow the link to be made between the symbolic female figure of chapter 12 and others who appear later on, it makes sense to regard these details as key elements of the narrative and to grant them a decisive influence upon its interpretation. We will therefore proceed exactly as we did for the urban imagery: the 'mystery' woman of 17.5 is the deliberately crafted antithesis[39] of the grandiose woman 'sign' in 12.1. The antithetical correspondences can best be brought out by a careful listing of all the relevant details.

a) A woman who is a mother finds herself under threat from a red dragon (12.4,13*ff*), but God provides protection for her in a place of some ambivalence (in the desert),[40] which is a safe place and a refuge where she finds nourishment (12.6,14) but also a place where she suffers attacks and where her offspring are persecuted and killed. In 17.3 another 'woman' will appear in the same location, this time with its negative connotations accentuated (accursed earth, a hideout for demons), though this may be the same woman with her spiritual condition perverted in the interim.[41] She will feed herself there on blood, riding in solidarity (or maybe in dependence) on a carbon copy of the dragon, a scarlet monster with the same seven heads and ten horns, nevertheless doomed to become its prey with no hope of rescue (17.16).

b) The woman of 12.4b-5,13 is mother firstly to Messiah, to whom she gives birth, then in 12.17 to offspring characterised by their obedience to God and their faithfulness to Jesus, for which they will suffer persecution. Her anti-image – the one called 'mother of whores' – displays a maternity of sorts which consists of getting drunk on the blood of the first woman's children (17.5-6), the saints and witnesses, and in doing the dragon's work by pursuing them (12.17). She settles down to rule over an entire human community of her own (symbolised by densely populated waters, 17.15) whose primary characteristic, by inversion, is unfaithfulness.

c)	The 'celestial finery'[42] in which the first woman is clad (sun, moon and stars, 12.1) corresponds, by a patent contrast,[43] to the get-up of her rival the streetwalker, the 'woman' dressed in purple, scarlet, jewels, precious stones and pearls (17.4). This array will be picked up again unchanged in 18.16, with the addition of fine linen (from Ezek 16.10,13) which brings her into closer conformity with the lady of the night, unfaithful Zion, who wears scarlet and is adorned with gold (Jer 4.30); this contrast is reinforced by the fact that for Jeremiah, Zion's daughter is about to bring forth her first-born (Jer 4.31).

d)	The mother of the male child suffers sustained persecution (12.13-17) but in the end, this proves to be ineffective. The whore is herself a passive victim; however, she will unfortunately find no escape from the treachery of her ally the monster.

The cumulative force of these antithetical correspondences is sufficient for spectators easily to recognise, in the creature of 17.1*ff*, an arresting contrast with the celestial woman seen previously, in counterpoint to which she is intentionally set. What establishes total contradiction between the two is the characteristic of being drunk with blood, a detail which rounds off the contrast between the woman who gives birth to the Christ and to his witnesses and the other, who kills them. In this way the work of God, as symbolised by the story of the mother of the young child, is turned around by the whore.[44] From the moment, she appears readers can identify the whore, dressed in garish colours, as the shockingly degraded version of the glorious mother clothed with the sun.

Back to 'Jezebel'

Here we should cast our minds back to the very first female character of the Book, the prophetess 'Jezebel' linked to the infamous whore-city of Tyre, because at this point the narrative is reworking and adding nuanced detail to that initial sketch, in the oracles to Churches, of an anti-community dragged into idolatry. What was already said about her in anticipation of this stage can now be briefly restated: 'Jezebel' precedes the three other women, both as the anti-type of the heavenly woman who enters the scene in the trumpets septet and also of the Lamb's wife appearing in the denouement. In addition, in the in-between phase she is the prototype of the adulteress who reproduces all her traits whilst parodying those of the mother figure and the bride. The sheer number of similarities and differences, so skilfully interlaced, testifies to the considerable literary and theological importance placed, by Revelation, on the major theme of inversely corresponding women and cities.

Revelation's 'women' and 'cities': Shared development

In literary terms, Revelation develops elaborate relationships between its women. Two symbolic women share the common characteristic of an intimacy that unites God and the Messiah-Lamb to the faithful people chosen by God. They are linked to two other counterpart female figures, whose fidelity has become compromised and whose loving intimacy has been debased into prostitution. The feminine imagery undergoes the same transpositions as those already observed in the case of the related urban imagery. To see this clearly we need only bring together 17.4 and 18.16. As happens with the city where God comes to dwell with humanity, so also the 'woman' God has chosen for his wife is an entity broken down, by the mechanism of sophisticated antithetical parallelism, into several characters who correspond closely to one another. So it is that, in between two trips to the wilderness (12.6; 17.3), the concept of 'woman' can have its positive connotations replaced by associations with evil[45] and, conversely, the whore of chapter 17 or the more complex courtesan city of chapter 18 can dissolve into their permanent replacement, the bride and Church-city of the denouement. As a result, the great whore 'offers a vivid contrast with [the description] of the mother figure in chapter twelve and with the 'bride' of succeeding chapters (19.7, 21.2; 22.17)';[46] she can serve as the anti-image of the bride in 21.9ff precisely because she is already the counterpart of the celestial woman of chapter 12.

Back to Revelation 14

Rev 14 acts as a relay for the antithetical parallelism which will pit the whore-city of chapters 17–18 against the bride-city of 21.9-21, while playing on their antecedents (both the 'Jezebel' figure and the woman in the vault of heaven). We noticed the very same phenomenon earlier, when examining the urban imagery. A first glimpse of Jerusalem's eschatological salvation comes in 14.1-5, where a fivefold typology of her inhabitants presents us with choristers singing a new hymn; a crowd 144, 000 strong: pure virgins, faithful adherents, and redeemed people. Over against this, 14.6-20 foretells and anticipates the future fall of 'Babylon' and the coming of God's judgment upon those who bear the monster's mark; the account pinpoints their drunkenness and especially their prostitution, which contrast with the chastity and fidelity of those who belong to the Lamb (14.8). From 14.6 onwards begins a sketch of the whore's traits which will become a full-colour picture later; in 19.5-10, similarly, we will catch a first glimpse of a bride who will only take the stage in 21.9ff.[47] Two further correspondences with Jerusalem are to be noted in 14.8-20: as will happen again when punishment is inflicted on 'Babylon', just chastisement is meted out to all who have been following the monster (14.10-11), which is in strict opposition to the rewarding of the righteous when New Jerusalem appears (3.12; 21.1–22.5; cf. 22.14,19). The pressing of harvested grapes 'outside the city' implies a Holy City, a detail which both harks back to the city of 11.2 and also looks forward to New Jerusalem.[48]

An overview of
The Grand 'Babylon' – 'New Jerusalem' Diptych

Certain traits that distinguish both the celestial woman and the whore seated on the monster are combined with many others to establish a fundamental contrast with the bride who will take her place later. Whether in scope or in fine detail, no other major theme of Revelation rivals the antithetical parallelism by which whore and bride are set in opposition in the closing chapters of the Book.[49] Accordingly, 'Babylon the great' becomes the object of a complex diptych of its own, whose left panel consists of a vision report (chapter 17) while the right panel is a lament (chapter 18) comprising several funereal songs that enable the story to dwell on the destiny summarily described in 16.19 and explore it in detail. This unit develops the double symbolism of the adulterous woman (17.1-7,15-16; 18.3,7) and of the whore-city (17.5,18; 18.2,4,10,16,18-19,21). Further links which reinforce its unity as a passage include the whoring of the kings (17.2; 18.3,9), whose relationship to heavenly Jerusalem will be transformed (21.24-26), the blood of the saints (17.6; 18.24) or again the burning of "Babylon" (17.16; 18.8,9,18).

The best explanation for the expansiveness of this development of the 'Babylon' theme is its detailed correlation with the following parallel section given over to New Jerusalem. These two cities in fact correspond, counterbalancing one another as two poles of a carefully wrought antithesis whose phraseology and thematic sequences are equivalent. They are very finely balanced: when it is said that John will see a whore, what he actually sees is a city pictured as a woman (17.1*ff.*); his promised vision of a bride will turn out to be a woman pictured as a city (21.9*ff*). In the sections devoted to successive visions of the two women-cities (17.1–19.10; 21.1–22.5), the phenomenon of contrastive parallelism may be observed from their symmetrical introductions onwards (17.1-3; 21.9-10) and right up to their parallel conclusions (19.9-10; 22.6-9).[50] Equivalent prophetic shouts of fulfilment immediately herald both the destruction of the one and the descent of the other ('it is done!' 16.17/21.6; *cf.* 'everything is finished' in Jn 19.30), with the effect that the second shout cancels out the first.

The influence of the Jewish Scriptures

Revelation is not doing something new when it uses women-cities as a literary conceit for personifying Israel, idolatrous nations or even humanity that gathers around Israel before undergoing transformation into a faithful people. This motif is a constant feature of covenant lawsuits brought by the Hebrew prophets against the covenant people. Another constant refrain in their writings is the expectation that one day the problem will be solved, when God's promise to dwell with his people is finally fulfilled; we might think for example of 'Immanuel' chorused by Isa 7.14; 8.8,10 and perhaps echoed, soon after, by Zech 8.23. Revelation, for its part, shares this same expectation (21.3) by having the city which was an instrument for humanity's revolt against God turn into a place of reconciliation. In so doing, the narrative borrows a series of preformed motifs from the prophets. Hosea 2 is one passage which appears solely responsible for supplying several key elements. There, Israel is variously represented a) as a wife and mother taken to court for having played the whore; b) as a repudiated woman, subsequently devastated and transformed into a desert where rejoicing or celebration will never be seen again; c) as having been abandoned by her lovers and wanting her first husband back; and lastly d) as being won back by the Lord her husband who, in a renewed engagement ceremony, shows his love and gives her a dowry of righteousness and faithfulness. All of these prophetic motifs contribute something to the characterisation of 'Babylon' or New Jerusalem and help shape a plot in which the former vanishes, to be replaced by the latter.

It would not be difficult to demonstrate the influence of other source texts upon the decor of Rev 16–22; we could start with Isa 60–66, or Ezek 16 and 23. Perhaps what springs to mind most readily, however, is Jer 3 – a chapter which sets the scene of divorce proceedings on the grounds of adultery instituted by God against the kingdom of Israel (Jer 3.8) and threatened similarly against the kingdom of Judah. The southern kingdom is accused, in turn, of playing the whore (Jer 3.1; the LXX has *porneuô*, 'commit adultery') and of defiling the land (Jer 3.1-2,9), as is clearly evident from her forehead (Jer 3.3; *cf.* Rev 17.5). Her destruction by the Assyrians (Jer 50.17) may well have been the inspiration for the motif of *Babylon that falls* (Rev 17.16; 19.2). Equally significant in the same context is the first announcement of Jerusalem's future restoration (Jer 3.11-18), an element which later oracles will develop further in chapters 30–31 and 33.

The conditional fate of Israel was contingent on the people's faithfulness or unfaithfulness. Against this backdrop, the prophets never congratulate the earthly Jerusalem familiar to them for her present purity or for her fidelity to YHWH. Instead, they repeatedly direct their thunder at her immorality, injustice and apostasy. Yet the very same prophets are often to be found giving expression to an expectation that the city will one day experience glorification, to a degree never witnessed before – even if they do not know exactly when that might be. In its own way, Revelation updates this long tradition handed on by its predecessors; for their picture of a restored, earthly Jerusalem, Revelation substitutes its own vision of a New Jerusalem that comes from and is made in heaven – a vision of things foreseen, of course, by Ezekiel but left undefined.

The narrative logic which underlies Revelation's magnificent two-panelled fresco of the economy of salvation is this: out of the rubble of 'Babylon,' a city built by human hands and a convicted prostitute (19.2) – of which, very soon, no more will be heard (18.22) – there will rise up by way of replacement God's city, New Jerusalem, as his beautiful bride (21.2). By recounting the disappearance of 'Babylon'/Jerusalem-the-whore, and the disclosure of the faithful city, Revelation appears to be turning Isa 1.21 around by showing how the whore may once again become the faithful spouse.

Babylon-the-Whore and Jerusalem-The-Bride in counterpoint

It is now my intention to gather the numerous parallels which link these two women-cities and to study them in two stages. I will begin by examining every parallel which relates to the structural or architectural arrangement of the two sections – their bare bones, so to speak. From this study of the unveiling, first of 'Babylon' and then of New Jerusalem, will emerge a better understanding of how Revelation's plot is moved towards its denouement by these two coordinated phases.

Then I will bring together the multiple antithetical connectors which link the two women-cities to one another. This will help us gauge the extent of the extraordinary unity conferred on the whole section by these links, despite the irreducible literary diversity of the actual materials which have been amalgamated in the composition of the two units.

The two units, 17.1ff and 21.9ff, in counterpoint

Foreshadowed, as we have seen, by a double reference to fulfilment (16.17; 21.6), the parallel scenes which reveal *falling Babylon* and *descending Jerusalem*[51] unfold in similar ways. Father Allo spoke of 'antithetical parallelism of the strictest and most deliberate sort between the appearance of the heavenly City and that of the worldly Babylon of chapter 17'.[52] As far as many commentators are concerned, their correspondence rests squarely on two elements: the intrusion on each occasion of an interpreting angel with a vision to disclose (17.1/21.9); and the whisking away of the seer, each time, by the Spirit (17.3a/21.10a). In fact, the structural parallelism of these chapters is very elaborate, as has already been shown elsewhere.[53]

To be more specific, the beginning and ending of both units in which we are interested (17.1ff/21.9ff) show an identical sequence, as can be substantiated by an examination of their respective introductions and conclusions.

Two symmetrical introductions and conlusions.

We may begin with the introductions:

i. In both contexts, an angel from the same group comes forth to deliver an invitation (17.1/21.9). Here, 21.9 picks up no fewer than twenty words (in the Greek) from 17.1, repeating them in the same order: 'then one of the seven angels who had the seven bowls full of the seven last plagues came and said to me, 'Come, I will show you . . .' 21.9 simply adds that the bowls are 'full of the seven last plagues'. We have, here, the longest and most significant example of inner-textual quotation of Revelation by Revelation, including an element of variation to which we have grown accustomed.

ii. On both occasions, the angel transports the seer somewhere in visionary ecstasy (17.3a/21.10a). This time five Greek words are re-used in the same order: 'in the Spirit he carried me away'. The only thing to change from one text to the other is the designated locale itself – a desert in 17.3 or a high mountain in 21.10 – but these are clearly meant to be seen as parallel theatres of action.

iii. In the first case, John sees one who is called 'whore' and 'woman' (17.1,3); in the second, he discovers her obvious counterpart, who is referred to as 'bride' and 'woman' (21.9).

iv. The associates who hobnob with the two women reinforce the parallels: one woman has a monster for her mount (17.3b) while the other has a Lamb for her spouse (21.9b). The respective sexual characteristics of both women-cities are apparently being underlined here, positively for the second of them and negatively for the first. What happens to both couples is also a matter for contrast, for the association between 'Babylon' and the monster ends in the destruction of both, while the death and resurrection of Christ have already insured the salvation of the City of God.

v.   At the close of each introduction, where the transition to the vision proper occurs (17.3b/21.10b), parallel nomenclature still binds 'Babylon' ('whore/woman-city', 17.5) to Jerusalem ('bride/woman-city', 21.10).

When we turn our attention, secondly, to the two conclusions, the same meticulously arranged parallelism emerges. It shows itself in the number and order of the component parts, as well as in the continuing tendency to refer back to the preparatory text.

vi. Twin declarations affirm the truth of the words spoken: in 19.9b we read 'these are true words of God' while 22.6 expands this slightly to make them 'trustworthy and true.'

vii. In both cases, John commits the same error, falling prostrate before the angel. 22.8 repeats, in the same order, 'I fell down at the feet of' (*cf.* 19.10a) while adding that now the seer has seen and heard everything. Again, word-for-word repetition and a 'twist' (or an element of variation) are being combined here.

viii. For these duplicate faux pas, the angel uses identical words to outlaw such misplaced worship – 'you must not do that! I am a fellow servant with you and your comrades' (19.10b/22.9a) – commanding the seer, on both occasions, to worship God only (19.10c; 22.9b). Two parallel descriptions mark out these 'comrades' (literally 'brothers') as those who 'hold the Testimony of Jesus' (19.10b) or, which is equivalent, as 'prophets, those who keep the words of this book' (22.9a). As for the angels (19.9-10; 22.6-9), they are clearly the same ones as those who appeared already in the respective introductions.

ix. Finally, there is symmetry about the affirmations made: the one in 19.10d, 'for the Testimony of Jesus is the Spirit of Prophecy', is as if expanded by the parallel passage (22.7-20). This gives the Book a fitting conclusion, in which certain assertions about prophecy, testimony and the Book itself may be taken up again.

b) Additional remarks

Several additional comments about the overall parallelism of the section can now be made. In the diptych devoted to the story of 'Babylon' (chapter 17–18) the first vignette presents us with a woman who caricatures the mother of Messiah, while the second shows us a city that parodies the one where God will be domiciled with his people. Despite a transition from woman to city in 17.18-18.2, however, the author does not forget the combined imagery. Thus the language of 17.1-6 surfaces once more in 18.3,9,16 – for example, with two references to the whore's clothing (17.4; 18.16) – whilst the whore herself reappears in 19.2.

The section which consists of an account of the punishment of 'Babylon' and of the three laments which her destruction provokes is set in a framework of parallel references to her fall (14.8; 18.2,21) and to her plight as an abandoned city (18.2,4,19,22-23a). If 'Babylon' must *fall down* and be abandoned, celestial Jerusalem as her strict counterpart will *come down* from God or, more precisely, in her God will come down to dwell with his people. Just as the fall of 'Babylon', in the corresponding vision, was something foreseen (in 14.8), so now we are given a prior glimpse (21.2) of the descending city (21.10b). Once the visions are complete, the absence of all impurity from New Jerusalem (21.27) will make for a contrast with the soiled state of 'Babylon' (18.2,9a) and emphasise the presence of God and the Lamb in the ultimate city (22.3).

c) Revelation 19.11–21.8

This textual unit is a transitional passage which links the dismembering of 'Babylon' to the festooning of New Jerusalem. For the Book as a whole, this is the last such transition to occur, since the final repudiation and removal of the idolatrous whore open the way for welcoming the true and faithful bride. Two passages, again set in perfect balance, take us from one to the other: the opening one (19.11-21) emphasises the rejection of old, rebellious humanity one last time, whilst the closing one (21.1-8) looks forward to renewed humanity reconciled to God.[54]

d) Revelation 21.9–22.5

The entire diptych that focused on 'Babylon', depicted first as a woman and then a city, is now reciprocated here by a final unit which develops the theme briefly treated in 21.1*ff.* When reading this section the same double feminine-urban imagery applies, describing New Jerusalem and the Lamb's bride.

Multiple detailed correspondences

Now that we have drawn attention to the framework which carefully crafted, inverse parallelism provides for the presentation of the two women-cities, supporting both halves of the entire edifice, it is time to assemble the numerous antithetical correlations that link the courtesan to the bride whom she caricatures. My efforts will be centred on the study of a particularly large number of characteristics which, as we will see, bind together Jerusalem-the-bride (21.9*ff*) and her caricature Babylon-the-whore (17.1*ff*). Not only does this involve noting how the bride-city, as she descends, neutralises the whore-city. It also entails keeping in mind the cumulative evidence compiled throughout this chapter, allowing it to influence what we now read. It is in the nature of the double thematic trajectory we have been pursuing that several threads woven into the fabric of the narrative should connect the women-cities: the celestial woman connects to the bride via a whore that is herself a recapitulated version of 'Jezebel'; and we are transported from Ephesus or her neighbouring cities to New Jerusalem via the slums of Jerusalem/'Babylon'.

In the paragraphs that follow I will attempt, as exhaustively as possible, to correlate the multiple correspondences which combine to help readers recognise how, in every respect, the bride-city replaces the whore-city.

Two visions, the same angel

On both occasions, the same angel from the group of bowl-angels invites the seer to come and see, then carries him off 'in the Spirit' and acts as his interpreter for the respective visions (17.1-3; 21.9-10). Each time, it is a woman-city that is seen. Having contemplated the first one, spectators are made ready for the next, as it will turn out to be equivalent in every feature. When the 'great whore who is seated on many waters' (17.1) is sent away, the corresponding event is the welcome extended to the 'bride' (as happened already in 21.2) or 'wife of the Lamb' (21.9). One sits dolled up (17.4) astride a monster, in an accursed wasteland (17.3; cf. 18.2); the other, who has adorned herself (21.2) for her consort the Lamb (21.9), comes down onto a high mountain which will become (in 22.1ff) a renewed garden-city paradise.[55]

Contrasting clothing

In opposition to her rival's get-up,[56] the bride's adornment (21.18-21), starting with jasper (God's stone, 21.11), fulfils the Churches' vocation to get ready for marriage (2.1–3.22), as recalled in 22.16. Her description takes its inspiration from Isa 54.11-12 and corresponds to the glorious attire of her heavenly bridegroom the Lamb, which is the object of acclaim in 19.7. With hindsight we can see that his dress was anticipated in the inaugural vision (1.12-20). Together with the Spirit, the bride (in 22.17) delivers an invitation to 'come': ready and perfect as she now is, she is able to call upon believers in Roman Asia to join her without delay through their faith.

The women-cities' clothing and jewellery also correspond, but here a superficial resemblance hides real antithesis.[57] The whore's gold, precious stones and pearls (17.4; 18.16) that deck her out like Tyre before her (Ezek 28.13), find their counterpart in the pure gold (21.18), precious stones (21.19) and pearls (21.21) of transformed, heavenly Jerusalem. The contrast here means that whereas one sounds her own trumpet, in self-importance (18.7), the other shines with the pure 'glory of God' (21.11,23). To be 'clothed in purple and scarlet' (17.4) is the opposite of living a righteous life, signified by the wearing of 'fine linen, bright and pure' (19.8). Accordingly, sharp-eyed readers are able to detect that the amalgam 'clothed in fine linen, in purple and scarlet (etc.)' in 18.16, is presumptuousness which fails to conceal the very injustices for which 'Babylon' will be found guilty and done away with.

Conditioning from other known cities

Readers of Revelation are assumed to be conversant with the Jewish Scriptures,[58] and Old Testament women-cities predispose us to recognising both the 'whore' Jerusalem (Isa 1.21; Ezek 16!) – not to mention analogous pagan cities like Babylon, Edom (strictly, a region), Nineveh, Samaria, Sodom or Tyre – and later, by contrast, the 'bride' Zion/Jerusalem. In actively recollecting this we are also able to understand how the one can so easily become the other, through the gain (or, contrariwise, the loss) of faithfulness. In this state of affairs the whore-city *par excellence*, and the yardstick for all the others, is Jerusalem: God's bride by covenant (Ezek 16.8), she had severed the relationship through her idolatry (Ezek 16.38). In the biblically conditioned imagination of the seer and his recipients, 'Babylon' must have evoked Jerusalem above all else. As to where to locate the origins of the idea of a *New* Jerusalem – expected since the promise made in 3.12, glimpsed in 21.2 and finally encountered in 21.10 – scenarios in which to start looking would include the repeated wooing of Jerusalem, as Hosea courted Gomer, or the indelible engraving of Zion on the palms of the hands of her Lord (Isa 49.14-16).

Holy city, abominable city

One of these women-cities, New Jerusalem – an end-time city, whose construction in no way depends on humanity – is both holy (21.2; 22.19) and chaste (21.2,9), in much the same way as the Church of Corinth when seen from Paul's standpoint (2 Cor 11.1-3). There is no vice in her (21.8,27). She has her source in God and is aglow with his glory (21.2,10-11), reflecting the divine presence and the communion she has with him (21.3-4,7b). Lastly, a mark worn on her forehead signifies that she belongs to him (22.4). By contrast the other woman-city, recognisable from the nickname visible on her brow '[Old] Babylon' (17.5; 18.10,18,21), is the man-made proto-city (Gen 11.4*ff*),[59] variously dubbed (in 17.3-6) as blasphemous, abominable, impure, adulterous (*cf.* 18.9) and drunken. She offers an invitation to share in a communion cup whose toxic beverage is a parody of the one drunk at the Supper (17.4b),[60] for she is the enemy of all who are witnesses of Jesus (17.6).

Injustice turned at last to justice

The two-panelled picture devoted to 'Babylon' is a-swim (as it were) with the blood of 'the saints and . . . the witnesses to Jesus' (17.6) or the blood of 'prophets and of saints, and of all who have been slaughtered on earth' (18.24).[61] Having such blood on her hands (*cf.* Jer 51.35) makes the whore-city guilty and seals her fate.[62] At this point, the 'Babylon' veneer is very thin indeed since, as the words of Jesus in Mt 23.30-37 remind us, it is Jerusalem who is to be incriminated (and who will fall) for having persecuted and finished off the prophets and for having innocent blood on her hands. Such unjust acts cry out for judgment. Just retribution for the spilling of blood, called for by victims since the fifth seal was opened (6.10), is first of all declared as having been made (in 18.20); then it is celebrated during the transitional liturgy ('he has avenged on her the blood of his servants', 19.2); finally, it is accomplished through the advent of the Lamb's marriage and the readying of his bride clothed entirely in justice/righteousness (19.7-8), as befits the one entitled to be known as 'city of righteousness' (Isa 1.26). In the destruction of 'Babylon' or in heavenly Jerusalem's wedding feast, the same reality is viewed, first negatively then positively. This is because the spotless bride is none other than God's unfaithful wife, transformed at last.

The defeat of death, consolation for those who suffered and the denial of shelter in the heavenly city for murderers and adulterers (21.4,8; 22.15), make for a contrast with spiritual fornication and murder in 'Babylon' (17.3b-4,6) – the crimes of which Jerusalem was once accused (Ezek 16.36-38; 23.37,45). Prostitution is characteristic of 'Babylon', for she is above all else a *porné*, a whore (17.2,4; 18.3; 19.2), and her behaviour parodies the spiritual faithfulness connoted by the 'marriage supper of the Lamb' (19.7), to which God's people had always been invited. There is a stark contrast between the wedding feast (19.9), with its accompanying draught of the water of life (21.6; 22.17), and the bitter cup (17.4) or illicit wine (17.2; 18.3) from the anti-feast, which symbolise the justice that Messiah dispenses (19.17-18).

The excluded included at last

One of the characteristics of the 'earth-dwellers' (or, 'dwellers in the land'), whom 'Babylon' has bewitched, is their identification as those 'whose names have not been written in the book of life from the foundation of the world' (17.8), whereas the only ones to make it into heavenly Jerusalem are 'those who are written in the Lamb's book of life' (21.27). While the 'great whore' holds in thrall earth's kings and inhabitants (17.2), exploiting them and compelling them to share for a time in her debauchery (17.12,16-17), the bride stands for a relation between humanity and God which is reciprocal and which brings help and comfort to the former (21.3-4). The whore covets her associates' wealth (18.14) under the illusion that peoples, multitudes, nations and languages (17.15), if not all nations (18.3,23), will be her subjects forever. Yet the bride knows that in God's project for covenant it is she who brings together all mortals in her midst (21.3) – the very ones afflicted by the trumpets (8.11; 9.6,10,15,18,20) and by the bowls (16.8-9,21[63]). This means that no longer are such human beings erring 'nations' (20.3); now, instead, they are 'his peoples' (21.3). From now on the bride-city, as a metaphor for humanity living in harmony with God and with itself (*cf.* 5.9; 14.6), is the place to which the nations and kings come, bringing all their honour with them (21.24,26; *cf.* Isa 60.11).[64] For the nations, this is a veritable 'healing' (22.2) which erases their blind trampling of the Holy City (in 11.2) and brings about the scenario to which the praise in 15.4 already looked forward, *i.e.* when 'all nations will come and worship before you.'

There are mountains and mountains

The impostor-city could be surnamed *sevenfold mountain-city*. Her description has undoubtedly been influenced by the way apocalyptic traditions habitually saw the world, in situating seven mountains on the far side of the sea that borders the inhabited earth. Her 'seven hills' (17.9) allow her to reach for the sky[65] in the hope of rivalling the one built, as Zion/Jerusalem originally was, on Mount Moriah (or, on seven hills[66]) or of imitating eschatological Zion (from 14.1), established on God's unique and traditional 'high mountain'[67] (21.10). The biblical background here is extensive: we may think of the very high mountain of Ezek 40.2, with a city rising at its summit (Ezek 43.12), or of the Lord's Temple high above all other mountains (Isa 2.2; Mic 4.1); or we may also recall the holy mountain, Zion's hill and God's footstool (Ps 99.5), God's city (Ps 48.2-3) or the place of paradise restored (Isa 11.9; 65.25).

New Babylon

New Jerusalem's architecture, which might well owe something to a sketch resembling the Pauline one found in Eph 2.19-20, 'has the same structure as ancient Babylon, with its quadrangular plan (21.16)'.[68] Several elements of the topography of ancient Babylon, as described by Herodotus, are found reflected in celestial Jerusalem: her life-giving river (22.1), which contrasts with the death-dealing torrent spewed out by the dragon but swallowed up by the earth (12.15-16), recalls the Euphrates that used to flow through Babylon (9.14; 16.12); her main square or great central thoroughfare (22.1-2) harks back to the 'street of the great city' in 11.8;[69] her foundations that rest on the apostles, bearers of the Word (21.14), ensure that the confusion that befell human languages at Babel is at last disentangled. As a city shaped like a cube, arranged as one immense Holy Place made of gold (1 Kgs 6.20) – unless her form is that of a pyramid, recalling Babylon's ziggurat, and the dimensions do also allow this (21.16) – heavenly Jerusalem far surpasses any other quadrangular city in the Near East, with a temple devoted to its god at its centre.

An empire gone, a kingdom established

The reign of 'Babylon' will cease once the yoke of her oppression is broken and she is turned into a wasteland, stripped, consumed and burned (17.16). The fire motif is used again in 18.8 where the city is declared to be a place of plague, grief and starvation. This outcome has been foreseen by God (17.17), for although 'Babylon' is under the illusion that she reigns (18.7), it will take only a day (18.8) or even the space of one hour (18.16,18) for the judgment that will bring an end to her 'empire' to be carried out. Over against this, once the Lord God's reign has become established and he has begun to reign (19.6), there will be an acquitted bride to take her place, now ready in her perfected state (21.2) and able, as a consequence, to 'reign forever and ever' (22.5). The first panel featuring the whore (17.1*ff*) is nicely rounded off, in 17.18, by a transitional detail which prepares for the second entitled 'Babylon the great' (18.1*ff*), as both the adulterous woman and the 'great city' are said to share the same thoroughly dubious reign. This equivalence between the feminine and urban, at the negative pole of the antithesis, will be mirrored positively when the bride-city (21.2,9) and true 'conqueror' (21.7) come to claim their promised inheritance.

The end for unrighteousness, a start for justification

As a foil to the haunt of demons and to the lair for unclean animals that 'Babylon' has become (18.2), we find 'the home of God' (21.3) and the 'throne of God and of the Lamb' (22.3) in the Holy City. In the transition from the now despoiled adulteress (17.16) to her expanded other self – the devastated whore-city (for 18.3, 17.2 has been reworked) – the 'impurities of [her] fornication' (17.4) metamorphose into the threefold impurity[70] of the demons, birds and beasts, which have commandeered the ruins. By the close of this account, sorcery has become the focus (18.23) just as, in 9.21, magic had already been linked to murder, adultery and theft in the behaviour of unrepentant idolaters; Isa 47.9 comes to mind, with its Babylonian magicians, as does Nah 3.4 for their counterparts in Nineveh. Impurity and sorcery will both be eliminated in the description of New Jerusalem, as magicians are specifically named among those excluded from the Holy City (21.8; 22.15), whilst purity is precisely what characterises the city (19.8) along with transcendent glory (21.11).

In order to escape condemnation with 'Babylon' (18.5-7a), whose aggregate of sins reaches nearly to heaven (18.5), there has to be a complete break with her and with her sinful ways which were punished by plagues (18.4). In times past, it had been necessary to flee Sodom (Gen 19.12-22) or Babylon (Jer 50.8; 51.6) just as, in the Gospel tradition, flight from Judaea and Jerusalem was required (Mk 13.14). Here, too, this turning away is a prerequisite for citizenship in New Jerusalem. She brings heaven to earth, granting her citizens a share of corresponding rewards (21.4) and giving them access to a promised inheritance awaiting all beneficiaries (21.5-7) and to final beatitude in a city where justice and life are eternal (22.14). Having caught our last glimpse, in 18.19, of the 'great city' present in Revelation's plot since 11.8, our eyes turn in 20.9 to her counterpart, the beloved city, who though besieged is soon liberated in anticipation of New Jerusalem.

Desolation and consolation

In 18.21-24, the angel's words and the symbolic actions that attend them, interpret the demise of 'Babylon' in terms of privations, picking up almost word for word the desolation of Jerusalem as foreseen by Jeremiah (Jer 25.10) for which New Jerusalem's blessed state will offer a contrast. 'Babylon' no longer enjoys the music or song (18.22) that makes Zion joyful (14.1-3), a state of affairs that had affected Tyre (Ezek 26.13) or more generally the earth (Isa 24.8). Whereas the Holy City is resplendent (21.11,23-25), 'Babylon' is shrouded in total darkness (18.23). Most of all, no bridegroom's song is heard in her any longer (18.23); New Jerusalem, by contrast, embodies universal celebration of the Lamb's wedding, where joy and delight burst forth between bridegroom and bride (19.7-9; 21.2; 22.17) and where nothing more will be heard of the tragic circumstances which marked the end for 'Babylon', amid mourning, weeping and distress (21.4).

Final illumination

'Babylon' had seduced the earth's kings, 'earth-dwellers' and all nations (17.2; 18.3,23); this is summed up in the charge that she had corrupted the earth with her adultery (19.2). New Jerusalem, made in heaven, offers the contrasting picture of causing the nations to walk in her dazzling light, in obvious fulfilment of the calling of the Servant (Isa 42.6; 49.6)[71] to make Israel a guide for the world's peoples (Isa 51.4; 60.3). The Churches' lamp stands (2.1–3.22) or the light-bearing witnesses (11.4) imply the sort of perpetual illumination found in the ultimate city, where their Lord enlightens the inhabitants better than sun, moon or stars ever could (21.23; 22.5). Accordingly, the bride in the final vision is brighter still than even the woman robed with heavenly sources of light (12.1).[72]

Covenant made complete

If we pause for a moment to consider the Lamb's marriage[73] (19.7,9), we may note how readers share the bridegroom's perspective, seeing the preparation (21.2) of the fiancée who, in 21.9, will become the bride and wife of the Lamb. What, we might ask, is the Lamb-Bridegroom working towards? The answer is that he is preparing a people who will belong to him forever, according to a plan brought to fruition by his triumphant death. It would be artificial to drive a wedge between the metaphor of the wedding feast and this paradoxical victory through which all competing attempts to form a rival people, by the dragon and the monsters, are foiled. The marriage of convenience between the monster and the woman (17.5,7,9) barely conceals the fact that the reign which this monstrous arrangement is supposed to bring about will self-destruct once the whore is stripped, devoured and burned – wasted, in fact, by the activity of her erstwhile partner (17.16-18). In complete contrast, for the people of the promise who have persevered, the wedding feast (as a positive image of a salvation now complete) will crown the phase of betrothal with the long-awaited arrival of the Groom. Then a pure and perfect relationship will be established between God and his people – a promise which remained unfulfilled under the old covenant. It is not hard to hear echoes, in this, of two of Jesus's parables preserved by the Gospel tradition, concerning both the wedding feast (Mt 22.2ff) and the king's son (Lk 14.16-24); the beatitude in Rev 19.9 is strangely reminiscent of the preparatory exclamation by a wedding guest in the latter parable.

Dis-creation and new world

In 19.11-17 the monster with which the whore consorted (17.3,11*ff*,17) is captured and eliminated (19.20), as part of the action undertaken by the messianic horseman. This is none other than the Lamb-Bridegroom, referred to seven times during the vision of the Holy City (21.9,22-23,27; 22.1,3). The Husband enters as a conquering king, thus preceding the arrival (in 21.2) of his fiancée, as in Ps 45. Every opponent and obstacle is removed (19.20-21; 20.2-3,10,14-15; 21.1), for they belong to those first things which have now disappeared (21.4), and with them every 'curse' related to the fallen world similarly vanishes (22.3). Conversely, an efficacious word (21.5; 22.6) brings into being the new world (21.1-7) and ushers in a new relationship between God and humanity (21.9*ff*).

Second death and eternal life

The lake of fire and sulphur (19.20; 20.10,14-15) that awaits those with no place in the city is an anti-destination: the anti-god forces are certainly thrown into it 'alive' to be tormented there 'day and night forever and ever', which is tantamount to a second death. Quite differently, celestial Jerusalem erected on top of the rubble of fallen 'Babylon' welcomes, behind her imposing walls, those who eternally live because their names are entered in the Lamb's book of life (21.27b). They benefit from the water of life as well as from the fruit of (or, a share in) the tree of life (22.2,17), for these are two ways of signifying life with God, who fills all things with his presence, and life with the Lamb (21.3,7,22; 22.3-5).

Babylon-the-Whore and Jerusalem-the-Bride: some conclusions

Now that our reading of this web of corresponding elements is finished, what is impressive is not merely the number but the cumulative value of the many, often subtle, symmetrical traits involved. We should remember how this antithetical parallelism is set in place right from the opening stretches of the feminine/urban trajectory, in the septet of oracles to the Church-cities of Asia. These cities are to be counted both with the cities of the nations, which fall with 'Jezebel' or Babylon-the-whore (16.19), and simultaneously alongside New Jerusalem, because this city of cities will cancel out all that was defective in the experimental Church-cities and bring into being everything in them that held promise. From start to finish, the logic of the major theme of the women-cities works this way.

By virtue of Messiah's death and resurrection, a down-payment of a salvation which is 'near' (1.3) and coming soon (1.1; 22.7,12,20) has already been made to the seven communities loved by a Lamb-Bridegroom who has reconciled them with the Father and made them a kingdom and priests for his service (1.5b-6). In the meantime, as they wait for its fulfilment, their whole life entails striving with the perseverance of the 'conqueror'.

Whenever they come together in worship on the Lord's Day, the prophecy procures blessing for them (1.3; 22.7) by reminding them of the benefits of the redemption Jesus has won for them (1.5b) and by replenishing those benefits continually through the Spirit (1.9-10; 2.7a, *etc.*; 17.3; 21.10). As the renewed covenant people, every time they sing the praises of the Lamb they are anticipating the face-to-face banquet still to come (21.3).

The heavenly city is nothing short of a *Babylon rediviva* as, with her every characteristic, she both neutralises the city on the Euphrates and becomes far more glorious with splendour of her own.[74] The proto-city, 'Babylon the great', had almost claimed to be divine by boasting (18.7), like ancient Babylon (Isa 47.7-8), of being an eternal city. Yet impressive though she was, this did not prevent her fall or her final disappearance after her rebellion. Her vocation is taken up by New Jerusalem, fashioned by God himself; she becomes the *ultimate* city[75] in that only she, in the end, is the truly 'great city' whose impossible dimensions (21.16-17) reflect her capacity for bringing God and humanity together forever (21.3). By replacing 'Babylon', this Jerusalem-from-above also puts an end to the revolt, tyranny and oppression of Babel or Sodom or Tyre.

At the same time, the city given by God to humanity represents the ennobling, finally, of historical Jerusalem. In history, Jerusalem had been the so-called 'Holy City', repeatedly breaking covenant through her religious infidelity. This had caused the prophets to heap constant abuse upon her and to liken her to the worst of all evil cities, her implacable enemy 'Babylon'. But the bride-city from God permanently replaces the whore-city, occupying the site left vacant by the latter's fall and ruin. The perfect city thereby fulfils the highest of callings which, until now, had repeatedly been betrayed throughout the history of God's people and of humanity.[76] Thanks to the covenant renewal achieved by Jesus, believers in Ephesus and her sister cities had received a call to join all other followers of Jesus in forming the people who God was now choosing for himself. By making an appropriate response, they could become, through faith, colonies of the one real woman-city of the future and a foretaste of New Jerusalem.

Notes

1   R.C. Ortlund, *Whoredom. God's Unfaithful Wife in Biblical Theology*, Leicester, Apollos, 1996, p.168. In relation to Rev 21.1-3,9-10, Ortlund goes on: 'the lines of expectation created by the fullness of Old Testament theology crowd into John's brief description of their final resolution'.

2   Readers interested in a somewhat fuller interaction with the secondary literature should consult my article 'Antithetical Feminine-Urban Imagery and a Tale of Two Women-Cities in the Book of Revelation', *Tyndale Bulletin* 55, 2004/1, pp.81-108. There, I sought to pay more attention to the women, cities and women-cities of Rev than they had received from exegetes up to that time, tracing as exhaustively as I could the complex interweaving of feminine imagery with urban

imagery observable in Revelation. Essentially the same material is presented again here, but with considerable reworking and with an updated bibliography.

3   Allo, *Apocalypse*, p.335 (my translation).

4   We can compare *4 Ezra* 10.25-27. For a comparative study of Jewish and Christian contemporary texts which exploited the apocalyptic transfiguration of the personified city into the traditional woman figure, see E. McE. Humphrey, *The Ladies and the Cities: Transformation and Apocalyptic Identity in Joseph and Aseneth, 4 Ezra, the Apocalypse and the Shepherd of Hermas*, Sheffield, Sheffield Academic Press, 1995.

5   See also Smalley, *Revelation*, p.536.

6   The combination of a city with a married woman is to be found in *4 Ezra* 9.38 and 10.54. *Cf.* heavenly Zion, hidden with God, in *4 Ezra* 9.52-53 and 10.49.

7   It seems to me to be vitally important that like Corsini, *Apocalypse*, pp.109-10, we posit a very close relationship between 2.1–3.22 and the picture of New Jerusalem.

8   As Prigent thinks, *Apocalypse*, p.140; for him 'the choice of a feminine figure is surely not fortuitous'. One has to ask, however, whether this choice has been dictated by the external world in which the author lives, beyond the text, or by the biblical backdrop in which 'Jezebel' is a byword for idolatry and apostasy.

9   For an example of a sociological reading which takes 'Jezebel' to have been the leader of a rival Thyatiran faction and thinks that John, in order to thwart her, resorts to a rhetoric of insinuation and exaggeration, see Duff, *Who Rides*, pp.15-16, 59. Duff, p.83*ff*, takes all Revelation's four female figures – 'Jezebel', the woman clothed with the sun, Babylon-the-whore and the bride – to be outgrowths of the opposition manifested, by John, towards some historical feminine figure, to whom the symbolic forename 'Jezebel' is given. At least Duff is to be commended for not stopping at three feminine figures in Revelation – those clad respectively in the sun, in purple and scarlet or in linen – *contra* Swete, *Apocalypse*, p.246 (as the twentieth century opened) or Harrington, *Revelation*, p.188 (as it closed), both of whom missed all that links Jezebel to these other feminine figures in the Book.

10 For a similar way of reading this, see Bauckham, *Climax*, p.377.

11 So Beale, *Revelation*, p.262.

12 On the link Babel-Babylon-New Jerusalem, see B. Malina, *The New Jerusalem in the Revelation of John: The City as Symbol of Life with God*, Collegeville, Michael Glazier, 2000. He says this: 'The first city built after the biblical flood… the first city created by human beings after the Deluge… this first city of our era of humankind . . . of the postdiluvial period . . . finds its contrast with the final city, the celestial Jerusalem' (p.70).

13 *Contra e.g.* Beale, *Revelation*, p.591, who denies any link to Jerusalem here and glosses the 'great city' of 11.8 as the wicked world. Yet a reference to historical Jerusalem is quite simply undeniable and we ought to take seriously all that it conveys. In this sense, see P.G.R. de Villiers, 'The Lord Was Crucified in Sodom and Egypt. Symbols in the Apocalypse of John', *Neotestamentica* 22, 1988, p.134; he rightly insists that 11.8 be interpreted in light of 16.19; 18.10,16,18-19,21 and especially 17.15,18.

14 Ellul, *Architecture*, p.81 (my translation).

15 *Sans feu ni lieu*, Paris, Gallimard, 1975, p.200 and pp.209-11 (my translation). Compare Brütsch, *Clarté*, p.187.

16 I am taking as read, here, the attentive study of this parallelism undertaken by Bauckham, *Climax*, pp.207-9, while factoring into it another dimension, the 'great city', which he does not include at this precise point. For his own exegesis

Bauckham declares his indebtedness to Paul Minear's article 'Ontology and Ecclesiology in the Apocalypse', *New Testament Studies* 12, 1966, pp.89-105.

17   The little non-technical commentary by A.M. Ogden, *The Avenging of the Apostles and Prophets*, Somerset, 1985, pp.435-51, devotes an appendix to the 'Babylon' issue. An exhaustive list of the attributes of this city in Revelation is to be found there, arranged by the author in synopsis with what is known of ancient Rome. What emerges very clearly is that, although Rome may share *certain* of the characteristics of 'Babylon', it is the Jerusalem of the Jewish Scriptures that possesses *every one* of her traits.

18   The well-known American exegete E. Boring, *Revelation*, pp.51-59, in fact warns against the (widespread!) error of seeing coded, dissembling language in Rev, with its implication that exegetes must turn certain interpretative keys in order to unlock the hidden meaning. For Boring, Revelation is not using propositional, objectivist language for passing on information, whereby *this* in the text (*e.g.*, such and such an image) would in reality mean *that* in its deciphered form (*i.e.*, something of historical or experiential worth). Instead, it employs symbolic discourse which is by nature both evocative and impressionist, generating tension by the fact that is always brings a surplus of meaning.

19   Like many exegetes, Prigent, for example, *Apocalypse*, p. 260, can affirm how the epithet 'great city' 'is a title reserved in the book of Revelation for Babylon'. On this point, the exegesis of the 'great city' provided by Ruiz, *Transformation, op. cit.*, pp.281-89, rightly shows itself to be more nuanced. For Ruiz, 16.19 is the pivot around which turns the movement from Babylon-the-whore to Jerusalem-the-bride. For him, the 'great city' theme develops as follows: 11.2,8,13 - Jerusalem; 14.8 - Rome; 16.9 - Jerusalem and Rome in juxtaposition; 17.5,18; 18.2 - (transition having occurred) Rome; 18.10,16,19 - assimilated to Rome; 18.21 - Rome; 20.9; 21.2; 21.10 - New Jerusalem. Although Ruiz is still disposed to see in 'Babylon the great' a cipher, *more or less*, for Rome, he does nonetheless recognise the paradigmatic or symbolic value of 'Babylon' (p.529). Accordingly, in 16.19 'the great city' must be Jerusalem (via a re-interpretation of Zech 14.3-5 involving topographical transfer – a view taken, prior to Ruiz, by A.M. Farrer, J.M. Ford and J. Sweet among others), while 'the cities of the nations' are clearly contrasted with her: first Jerusalem is struck, then the cities of the nations fall; for the fourth bowl is universal in its effects.

20   Here, for example is Schüssler-Fiorenza's protest, *Just World*, p.20: 'rather than decoding either the images and symbols of Revelation or the whole book into logical, inferential, propositional language, one needs to trace how an image or symbol *works* within the overall composition of Revelation's mythological symbolization'.

21   Boring, *Revelation*, p.179*ff*, abandons his own hermeneutical guide-rail (see above) by insisting that the great whore-city who leads earth's kings astray in ch. 17 can only be Rome – or more precisely, for Boring Rome *is* Babylon. What a curious disavowal of his own admission that the description (p.180) 'is not a matter of geography but of theology and Scripture'!

22   That is, Jerusalem-the-whore, unfaithful to her calling as the city chosen by YHWH for the locale of his self-revelation and his presence *with* his people Israel and *over against* nations, which, despite being in darkness, were nevertheless heirs to the promises made to Abraham. Her unfaithfulness expressed itself, as the OT regularly complains, in abuses practised by priests and people alike, in 'prostitution' leading to the confiscation of the benefits of sacrificial worship

in the Temple, with consequences for both Israel and the nations. Compare
M. Barker, *The Revelation of Jesus Christ*, Edinburgh, T&T Clark, 2000, ch. 18,
'Jerusalem' (pp.279-301). This author's point is of interest whether or not
one accepts her proposed reconstruction of the cult celebrated in Jerusalem's
successive Temples, or of what it led to on the evidence of Revelation's oracles.

23 Prévost, *Apocalypse*, p.140 (my translation).

24 B. Malina and J.J. Pilch, *Social-Science Commentary on the Book of Revelation*, Minneapolis,
2000, p. 155*ff* (re-using, word for word, Malina's previous work in *On the Genre
and Message of Revelation*, Peabody, Hendrickson, 1995) explain the considerable
importance of Andromeda, the pregnant woman constellation, in both the
traditions of ancient Mesopotamia and Egypt and in Graeco-Roman astronomy.
Their conclusion is that for people in Antiquity, the three feminine roles of virgin,
mother and queen could all come together in one single, celestial person.

25 This is precisely the conclusion which Aune draws, *Revelation 17-22* (vol. 3), p.676.

26 See Rowland, *Revelation*, p.103.

27 As a legacy left by the history of religions school, commentaries since at least
father Allo, *Apocalypse*, pp.167-179 (excursus xxvi), list and update various
Graeco-Roman or Middle Eastern parallels. For a recent, fairly complete
presentation of the question see Aune, *Revelation 6-16* (vol. 2), pp.667-74,
excursus 'The Combat Myth and Revelation 12'.

28 Literary and iconographical exploitation of this interpretation abounds in the
patristic and mediaeval periods. The reticence of the notes in the *TOB* to retain it
even among interpretations considered to be of 'secondary and subordinate rank' (A.
Feuillet, *L'Apocalypse – L'Etat de la question*, Paris, Desclée, 1963, p.97, my translation),
doubtless represents a desire to put an end to the excesses of mariological readings.

29 Delebecque, *Apocalypse*, p.208 (my translation).

30 Compare Prigent, *Apocalypse*, p.367: 'It is unanimously stated that [the focal
point of the piece] concerns the fate of the woman . . . One cannot dispute that
there is question of this'.

31 As Ellul remarks, *Architecture*, p.85.

32 As Preston and Hanson see it, *The Revelation of St. John the Divine*, London, SCM
Press, 1945, p.92.

33 Kiddle, *Revelation*, p.220*ff*.

34 See, for example, Beale, *Revelation*, pp.643-45, excursus 'The end-time exodus
against the background of the first exodus'.

35 Of the woman in 12.1-2, Victorinus says *'ecclesia est antiqua patrum et prophetarum
et sanctorum apostolorum . . .'* ('she is the ancient Church of the patriarchs, prophets
and holy apostles . . .').

36 Corsini, *Apocalypse*, p.224.

37 I am following Ellul here, *Architecture*, p.85.

38 For a similar point of view see Schüssler-Fiorenza, *Just World*, pp.80-81.

39 *Contra* W.W. Reader, 'Babylon als Antitypos zum himmlischen Jerusalem (14.8;
16.19; 17.1-18.24; 19.1-8)'. in *Die Stadt Gottes in der Johannesapokalypse*, Göttingen,
1971, p.267, who is too quick to minimise the importance of the parallels. Charlier,
Comprendre (vol. 2), pp.78-82, offers some interesting remarks and a little synopsis
proposing different contrasting features relating to the two women (p.81).

40 Compare Resseguie, *Revelation Unsealed*, pp.80-81. In his *Revelation of John* (*op.
cit.*), p.172, he now prefers to read the 'wilderness', as 'the spiritual home for the
believing community' in contrast to and in detachment from the great city.

41 As Corsini reads it, *Apocalypse*, p.331.

42 Charlier once more, *Comprendre* (vol. 2), p.78 (my translation).

43 Compare Cerfaux and Cambier, *Apocalypse*, p.148: 'The details of the adornment create an antithesis with the woman clothed with the sun: there all the symbols were luminous, spiritual realities; here, purple and material riches are the repugnant trappings of prostitution' (my translation).

44 For Ellul, *Architecture*, pp.199-201, the whore 'represents the exact opposite of the work accomplished by God in the Incarnation' (my translation), which 12.4 bears out. However, the evidence of 12.5 suggests that Messiah's entire work (and not merely his incarnation) is involved, up to and including his ascension.

45 See Thompson, *Revelation*, p.82, for several lucid comments on this matter.

46 Brütsch, *Clarté*, p.278 (my translation). Brütsch, here, is adopting the position of E. Lohmeyer, *Die Offenbarung des Johannes*, Tübingen, Mohr, 1970, *in loc.*

47 On this subject, see Fekkes, *Visionary Antecedents*, p.232 and note 20. This author detects the following formal parallels between the two introductions: 14.6, 19.5; 14.13, 19.9; *cf.* 14.14-20, 19.11-21.

48 Ellul, *Architecture*, p.187, reads this detail in the same way.

49 For a similar verdict on just how significant this is compare for example Boring, *Revelation*, pp.178-79, or Reader, *Stadt Gottes*, p.264.

50 Bauckham, *Climax*, pp.338-39. By way of helpful comparison for this point, compare Barr, *Tales*, p.141.

51 Compare *4 Ezra* 8.52-53; 10.49. For heavenly Jerusalem, see Gal 4.21-31 and Heb 11–13.

52 *Apocalypse, op. cit.*, p.339 (my translation).

53 C.H. Giblin, 'Structural and Thematic Correlations in the Theology of Revelation 16-22', *Biblica* 55, 1974, pp.487-504; I am indebted to him for much of this (see notably pp.489-91).

54 For a very evocative handling of 19.11–21.8, see Mealy, *Thousand Years*, pp.62-65.

55 For the picture of a garden city, the perceptive comments of Ellul, *Sans feu*, remain apt. Here is a little digest of some of them, in my own translation. 'Human beings chose her themselves . . . and receive from God the perfected handiwork they could not themselves achieve . . . humanity wanted to build the city from which God would be absent . . . but for humanity God will make the perfect city, where He is all in all'. Thus, God adopts into his purposes what humanity had invented, namely the city: 'everything these walls represented, whether suffering or hope, God adopts . . . making celestial Jerusalem the very fulfilment of what humanity hoped for . . . what happens, really, is the city's assumption . . . and her transfiguration . . . [thus] re-establishing direct communion with God . . . it is God's wish that once humanity has been re-created, humanity's great achievement should forever signify God's great achievement' (pp.250-55). And later, 'what human beings were searching for from the dawn of civilisation onwards is finally theirs when God gives to them a city which gathers up their every effort . . . when time comes to an end the promised city becomes a realised city' (pp.276-77). '[This is an] extraordinary synthesis of human achievements, adopted by God, and of the completed work of the Spirit' (p.279).

These comments may also be compared with the same author's comments in *Architecture, op. cit.*, pp.234-39.

56 On this, see Prigent, *Apocalypse*, p.595.

57 Beale, *Revelation*, pp.1118-19.

58 For quite a comprehensive list of OT references usually thought to underlie 21.1–22.20, as well as parallels with the rest of the NT, see B. Malina, *New Jerusalem*, pp.49-50.

59 For the contrast, Babel-New Jerusalem, see also Ellul, *Architecture*, p.234.

60 Pohl, *Offenbarung* (vol. 2), p.199, reads this similarly.

61 Compare Ellul, *Sans feu*, p.206: 'Once again, here, we encounter the same assimilation of Babylon and Jerusalem . . . what becomes very clear is the conjunction between Jerusalem, as the place where all the prophets must die, and Babylon, where the blood of all the prophets is to be found' (my translation).

62 Gospel tradition has preserved Jesus's denunciation of Jerusalem and his forecast of her fall: Mt 23.30-37 has, as its leitmotif, the blood of the prophets – persecuted, then killed off – and the blood of the innocent, of which the city is adjudged to be guilty. Might Revelation, at this point, not be using a form of this very tradition? On this, see J.R. Balyeat, *Babylon, The Great City of Revelation*, Sevierville, Onward Press, 1991, particularly pp.71-72.

63 Bauckham, *Theology*, p.137.

64 Compare Kraybill, *Imperial Cult*, pp.206, 211. For this author, the reference to 'all nations' has to mean more than simply restoring the Jewish capital in Palestine. New Jerusalem is a metaphor for the whole of humanity. Accordingly, the redeemed city is far from being a place for small numbers of elect people to gather, but somewhere capable of housing all of earth's peoples and more besides.

65 See also Resseguie, *Revelation Unsealed*, p.83, for whom the seven hills symbolise that archetypal human city, the Tower of Babel, which strove to lay hold on heaven and to be like God and which, as such, constitutes a striking parody of New Jerusalem coming down from heaven and set on a mountain.

66 Flavius Josephus, *Jewish War* v.5.8.

67 See Bauckham, *Theology*, p.132, and the background provided by the literature he cites *in loc.*

68 Brütsch, *Clarté*, p.363. He goes on (p.364), ' . . . a chance coincidence? Or mysterious completion for the rebellious city, brought about in the bright light of divine forgiveness?' (my translation)

69 For an interesting discussion of New Jerusalem as a creative synthesis of the Graeco-Roman city with the oriental city, see Malina, *New Jerusalem*, pp.45-47, 53.

70 Adopting the same textual variant as the 27th edition of *Nestlé-Aland*.

71 P. Poucouta, 'La mission prophétique de l'Eglise dans l'Apocalypse johannique', *Nouvelle Revue Théologique* 110, 1988, pp.47-48.

72 *Contra* Resseguie, *Revelation Unsealed*, p.145. Resseguie takes New Jerusalem to be the replacement, in the new creation, of the celestial mother visible only from the old earth (pp.143-45). As I see it, however, he is hemmed in, at this point, by a reading which is far too linear and so misses the dynamics that link anticipation and fulfilment.

73 Ugo Vanni, 'Dimension', p.121, points out that this is the first occasion in Revelation when one of the Lamb's traits is drawn from the marriage metaphor.

74 As Georgi puts it in 'Visionen', p.370.

75 Compare the perceptive analysis by Bauckham, *Theology*, pp.132-43, where New Jerusalem is studied under three aspects: *Place, people* and *divine presence*.

76 The discussion of heavenly Jerusalem offered by Sweet, *Revelation*, pp.194-96, is well worth consulting.

Conclusion to Part Two

The themes traced in the three chapters in Part Two have directed our attention to Revelation's representation of humankind, on an axis perpendicular (as it were) to the predominantly theological or Christological axis which we plotted first.

We have followed the trajectory taken by each of the three major anthropological themes involved. First of all, we examined the leitmotif of prophetic testimony to God's self-revelation in Jesus Christ, and with it the counter-proclamation which provides its caricature as the narrative develops (chapter 4). Then, we returned to an issue already partly uncovered by our exploration of the first theme, namely, the question of belonging and of identity, and saw how this impinged on the Lamb's followers and also on their adversaries, the monster's supporters (chapter 5). Lastly, we traced the development of a twin theme, linked to the two preceding ones, in which two inseparable metaphors – woman and city – were combined. Each metaphor eloquently encapsulates something of God's plans for humanity (with an appropriate response from human beings) and of a rival, satanically inspired project with its own human partner (chapter 6).

With the benefit of hindsight, we can now see how the three predominantly anthropological vectors in Part Two parallel those in Part One. In the three primarily theological trajectories followed in Part One we saw how materials, whose theme was God's person or work, were being constantly parodied; now it has emerged, in Part Two, that everything to do with resultant human behaviour, or with the anthropological realities that underlie it, receives parallel treatment. Clearly, whether Revelation is speaking of God or of human beings, in both cases the same sophisticated antithetical parallelism is being used.

Having analysed Revelation's theological and anthropological aspects under separate heads, we now need to begin working towards a synthesis. Can we catch a glimpse of how the results of our second exploration (humanity finds itself) might be integrated with those compiled in our earlier dossier (God reveals himself)?

Provisionally, as things stand, the following could be said: from a positive point of view, the transcendent God, who is Saviour, Conqueror and Object of worship (Part One), remains present and active amid the vicissitudes of history, where human beings are called to live lives in which faithfulness leaves its mark on their testimony, their belonging and their corporate living (Part Two). From a negative point of view (and conversely), wherever human beings are ready to broadcast falsehood, run after a false saviour or get involved in idolatry (Part Two), they will lack all knowledge of God, be no match for evil and lose their very identity by debasing themselves before idols (Part One).

We are not yet in a position to give a more accurate reflection of the relationship between God and human beings, as presented by Revelation: this must wait until we have laid out one last major theme – that of true covenant and of false alliances which human beings might prefer. Since the imprint on the text of Revelation left by this theme is greater than any other, it will be the sole subject of the third and final part of the present study.

Part Three
When God and Humanity Meet

Introduction

My aim, in this third and last part of the book, is to ascertain whether the conclusions to Parts One and Two are sound. This requires that we study the relations that develop, in Revelation, between God and human beings.

Broken covenant and new covenant

In the sole chapter devoted to this topic, the fundamental question I will be asking is: how may God and human beings live together? Or, phrased from the perspective of a caricature of this common life (as this shows itself in the course of the narrative), how is it that human beings so easily get such covenant wrong?

Revelation's answer is to recount the double story of the true covenant which has united God and man, and of its perverted form. The way God and human beings are related to one another, in its pages, may be expressed in the following affirmation: only in and through Jesus Christ does God come to human beings and may they go to God: the relationship between God, his Messiah Jesus and humanity is structured by a covenant; while this may have been continually flouted, it has now been finally and fully accomplished.

7. Broken covenant and new covenant

'In the Apocalypse the idea of God's close and covenant fellowship with the followers of Jesus is everywhere apparent' (S. Smalley).[1]

In this final chapter, my intention is to integrate all the major themes studied so far into one overarching theme. My proposal is this: the narrative logic for Revelation's plot draws upon one of the great constants in Old Testament literature: the theme of the fluctuating fortunes of the people of Israel's covenant with YHWH, throughout their history. The narrative dynamic of Revelation, which we have so far explored through a series of thematic runs through the text, has as its principal vector the integrative theme of covenant rift and renewal. So prevalent is this theme from one end of Revelation to the other that it merits a thorough treatment of its own. Indeed, the scope of this final chapter, by far the largest in the present book, mirrors my conviction that the major theme of broken covenant and new covenant constitutes the unifying element that binds all of Revelation's scenes and materials together into one coherent whole.

To a degree greater than in preceding chapters, I will now be exploiting Revelation's multiple allusions to the Jewish Scriptures. So rich are these allusions and so complex are the ways they are deployed in the text that, to be candid, they deserve a book in themselves.[2] However, within the limits imposed by my task here I can take – as my exegetically uncontroversial starting-point – that our author is forever harking back to prior revelation as a prerequisite of his own message.[3] In reading Revelation with this general orientation in mind, I have come to identify the major theme of covenant as providing the main trajectory for the Book's dynamic inter-textual relationship with the Old Testament and the story which its various writings tell. I hope to substantiate this in the study which follows.

By its very nature, the covenant always carries with it two things: the risk of its violation, and the prospect of its own fulfilment. Many a narrative vicissitude will separate the potentially 'blessed' recipients of 1.3 from the readers-hearers of 22.7,14 who, once everything has been ratified, are indeed most blessed;[4] the central point at issue throughout remains the implementation of the promises of the eternal covenant. So a plotline is set in motion. As it begins, the transcendent God in heaven offers his covenant to humanity on earth. Then, on earth's stage, it undergoes fluctuations as the human partner either acquiesces in this covenant or overthrows it. This generates a considerable degree of conflict, which propels the plot forwards from its beginnings through various crises. A point of resolution is finally reached when the heavenly and the earthly scenes merge, in immanence and immediacy, as God comes to join his human partner in a relationship of unprecedented closeness.

As Revelation's action unfolds, the theme of covenant is what furnishes the decor for scene after scene. At certain stages of the plot, covenant is the back-drop or the foundation for all that happens and here prominence is given to metaphors, drawn from the Jewish Scriptures, which picture God's presence with or relationship to human beings. As spectators, we find ourselves watching the rehearsal of various great episodes in the constitution or ongoing experience of the first covenant people, in scenarios that feature redemption, mediation, judgment or blessing. Examples are the plagues sent upon Egypt (or indeed the Exodus as a whole), or again the encounter with God at Sinai, not forgetting the taking of the promised land under Joshua by means of war with the Canaanites. Through these reminders from holy history, John reconnects with the writing prophets who had already had cause, before him, to meditate on the hazards involved in the story of the covenant people. Fulfilling the role of God's prosecutors over against the people, the prophets had repeatedly taken Israel to court on a charge of unfaithfulness. Yet they had also called the people back from their waywardness, pointing them to renewed covenant faithfulness and reminding them of the promises of the covenant (Jer 7.23; 11.4) or even renewing these for the present time (Jer 30.22; Ezek 36.28; 37.23,27; Zech 8.8). In its own way, Revelation continues along this marked-out path. Of course, only a full exploration of the textual data (including what we have found in previous chapters) can substantiate my contention or test its pertinence.

As an initial orientation to our subject matter, we will begin by looking at various materials which relate to the major theme of covenant as it manifests itself in Revelation. The theme comes to particular prominence in both the septet of proclamations (1.1 – 3.22) and in the finale (21.1 – 22.20) which expressly corresponds to it. While chapters 4-20 of Revelation are also relevant, these are the two contexts most liberally sprinkled with objects, places, events and issues which recall, in different ways, the story of successes and failures in the covenant relationship concluded between YHWH and Israel and of its renewal and extension through the coming of Messiah Jesus.

A survey of Revelation 1 and beyond

Right from Revelation's opening sentence (1.1-2), a story of mediation is carefully put in place. The Book has a tale to tell which originates in God's decision to communicate with his vassals or servants among human beings. The message he sends them is called a 'revelation of Jesus Christ' because it is precisely in his Messiah Jesus, Mediator of the new covenant, that God has bridged the distance separating humanity from himself. 'Like God and with God',[5] it is Messiah who makes the message known through the agency of an angel as well as through John. The seer, too, is identified as a vassal but this time in relation to Jesus.[6] The mediatorial role he plays is analogous to that of Messiah since he is both associated with the Churches, through sharing (with others) in membership, whilst at the same time enjoying the status of prophet and serving his brothers and sisters as an instrument of the divine revelation intended for them. Thus, the seer receives knowledge of what God has given to Messiah, his Revealer; consequently, the Word which God has uttered, to which John as an eyewitness will testify ('everything he saw'), is equally 'Testimony of Jesus Christ.' For Messiah is above all else the Faithful Witness (1.5) whose sworn evidence will prove decisive when the heavenly tribunal sits in the presence of the covenant's earthly partners.

This opening sequence sets out the legal framework by which God's relationship to humanity is to be structured. Through his saving death and resurrection (1.5) Jesus, as Messiah, has become guarantor for this relation. In similarly meticulous fashion, this framework will be recalled at the end of Revelation, in 22.16. There, Revelation's opening is recapitulated in condensed form, as Jesus bears witness in his own name, and there is renewed mention of the dispatch of an angel to the Churches in solemn attestation of the fact that everything in the Book is legally binding and unalterable. Then, in 22.18-20, come several legal formulae, reflecting the phraseology of Deuteronomy (*cf.* Deut 4.2 and 12.32), which append final clauses to the document; these declare it to be incapable of modification and set their seal of authenticity upon it: 'I solemnly warn everyone . . . '; 'if anyone adds to . . . , God will add . . . '; 'if anyone takes away . . . , God will take away . . . '; 'the one who testifies to these things says . . . '. This forestalls any attempt either to supplement the message or to cut it short. A double sanction is also imposed, in terms which invoke the curses that Revelation describes (22.18) and cancel the benefits it promises (22.19); this constitutes the Book's final mention, in abridged format, of the sanctions which apply to the new covenant.

Although exegetes are sometimes surprised by these formal clauses at the end of Revelation, in the logic of covenantal treaties this is nonetheless exactly where we would expect to find them. It makes no difference that, in the interim, God's project of making covenant with humanity has found spectacular fulfilment and the relationship between God and his people has been made perfect. As the heavenly bridegroom's faithful love reaches its consummation, betrothal gives way to the marriage celebration and what was still a matter of promise in the septet of oracles to Churches reaches fulfilment, as New Jerusalem descends. Every curse that would bar humanity from the tree of life is now lifted (22.3), reconciliation between Creator and creatures is achieved and, in the new state of affairs brought about by Messiah's death, God in Jesus is now God-with-them (21.3; *cf.* Mt 1.23) or 'God-with and [God]-for humanity'.[7] Revelation's conclusion fully and properly certifies all this.

Messiah's self-giving establishes the necessary conditions whereby sinful human beings can have their relationship with a holy God restored.

This is stated from chapter 1 onwards, and shows how Jesus insures the redemption of Asia's Christians, providing their status as a chosen people with its necessary foundation. As Israel had been designated a kingdom of priests and a holy nation (Exod 19.6), when YHWH was about to reveal to them the law which would structure their relationship to him, so here through a renewed covenant[8] recipients of the revelation are established by Messiah, in their turn, as 'a kingdom, priests serving his God and Father' (1.6) or, as the twenty-four elders have it in variant form, 'a kingdom and priests serving our God' (5.10).

The one who thus grants them priesthood and a reign is identified as coming on the clouds, as pierced and as the focus of lamentation (1.7). These three traits recall Dn 7.13, where the Ancient of Days makes the son of man his plenipotentiary, and Zech 12.10. The context of Zech 12.10–13.9 includes circumstances where those who speak for the Lord fall victim to violence in the house of their partners (13.6b), a situation which nevertheless leads to a prophecy of covenant renewal (13.9). For its part Revelation, here, seeks a combination of positive and negative elements to portray the concept of *possible covenant*, assuming that appropriate commitment is forthcoming. Positively, first of all, there is the praise which believers offer up to the Risen One for the blessings he has bestowed on them (1.5b-6) – praise which anticipates all other worship-centred moments in the Book. Negatively, however, there is also the warning found in 1.7, where earth's tribes mourn the Crucified One. From start to finish Revelation, in perfect alignment with Israel's experience, sees no possibility of neutrality: people are either for, or against, God, his reign and his Christ. This explains why the presentation of the Risen One in the inaugural vision is governed by the double logic of making Christ both Saviour and Judge, which both reassures and challenges believers as appropriate.[9]

The seven lamp stands in 1.12-13,20 bring to mind the seven lamps and the seven-branched golden lamp stand intended for use in the Tabernacle (Exod 25.31,37); full details for worship to be undertaken there were revealed to Moses on the occasion of covenant ratification, as told by Exodus 24. Among other things, both the position of the Risen One – amid the seven blazing lamp stands – and the way he is characterised by fire (1.12-16) link back to the revelation at the burning bush (Exod 3.2*ff*) or to the furnace that was Sinai when the covenant was concluded there (Exod 19.18-19): for the Hebrew Scriptures, God is a fire (Deut 4.24; Ps 97.3; Ezek 1.4, *etc.*). Could it be that this imposing figure is meant to remind readers of the 'prophet like [Moses]' in whom Israel, in terror of the great fire, sought their defence, or to recall God's promised spokesperson to whom they must pay heed (Deut 18.15-18)? Whether or not this is so, the declarations from God (1.8) and then from Messiah himself (1.17-18) establish the authority of the covenant's divine partners – to whom must also be added the Spirit (2.7, *etc.*) or seven spirits (1.4, *etc.*) – and thereby guarantee the authenticity of the revelation which John must write down and dispatch (1.11,19).[10] As for the human partner to the renewed covenant, in her status as recipient of the revelation, the sevenfold Church is clearly designated party or signatory to it (1.11; 2.1, *etc*.): she is pictured as a golden lamp stand, betokening encounter with God in worship (1.12,20).

Reminders of covenant

When it comes to describing a relationship which characterises the people essentially as worshippers (see chapter 3, above), Revelation will attach special significance in the course of its tale to the furnishings and ritual of worship in both Tabernacle and Temple. In line with the tradition of the great feasts which celebrate God and his faithful deeds on behalf of his people, the covenant is literally sung – beginning with the two halves of the diptych comprising chapters 4 and 5. Given that it has been renewed, it must also be sung in new ways (5.9); thus, the Song of Moses which recalled deliverance from the clutches of Pharaoh is transposed into the hymn of the Lamb: in their turn, and like Israel before them, the people of the new covenant may now put their own liberation into words (15.3). The temple where God will choose to dwell, located close to his throne, appears in 7.15 while the Holy Place, together with its altar, will reappear (*cf*. 8.5), as will the outer court (in 11.1-2) or the Ark (in 11.19). The sanctuary of the tent or Tabernacle is where action is concentrated in 15.5-8; it is a place of 'testimony', doubtless meaning that the covenant document is preserved there by the people. Once the new covenant is perfected, however, this Holy Place will dissolve, metamorphosing into a sanctuary-city-Tabernacle (21.3, combined with 21.16 and 21.22) where, from now on, those who 'Tabernacle' in the heavens (12.12) will dwell with God forever – the reference to God who 'dwells' (in Jn 1.14) comes to mind.

a) Book of Life

Dwellers with God, or friends of God, have their names in a 'book of life,' which always turns up in Revelation wherever the plot is strongly coloured by covenant. The final reference to this register of the elect will come in the finale (21.27), where it will exclude those who have no access to the blessings of the eternal covenant; mention will also be made of it previously, when the enemies from whom God has delivered his people are sentenced to the lake of fire (20.15). In between, there will be allusions to this book when earth's inhabitants are described as rushing headlong in hellish league with the monster (13.8) or when they show credulous amazement at the anti-mediator or bogus risen one (17.8). Later, this book will offer a contrast to the general ledgers to be opened at the last judgment (20.12), resulting in sentencing to the lake of fire for some (20.15). In biblical tradition, a 'book of life' occurring in a covenantal context goes back to the one referred to by Moses following the rupture of the Sinai covenant (through idolatry with the golden calf) and preceding its renewal (Exod 32.32-33). Ps 69.29 and Dn 12.1 also spring to mind, as does the register in Isa 4.3, which grants the freedom of the city of Jerusalem.

b) Beatitudes (1.3; 14.13; 16.15; 19.9; 20.6; 22.7,14)

The blessings reserved for those allies who have both heeded and put into practice the divine partner's words find expression in three of Revelation's seven beatitudes, distributed between the work's preamble (1.3) and its conclusion (22.7,14). The final sanction sums them up, by articulating as the epitome of the grace shown to them their sharing in the tree of life and in the Holy City (22.19). This correlates well with the seventh beatitude itself, in which the washed garments of the elect confer on them the right to eat the fruit of the tree and to enter the city through its open gates (22.14). The penultimate beatitude (22.7), meanwhile, recapitulates and synthesises the one that began the series (1.3), as can be seen when they are set in parallel:

> 'Blessed is the one who reads aloud the words of the prophecy, and blessed are those who hear and *who keep what is written in it*'   (1.3)

> 'Blessed is the one *who keeps the words of the prophecy of this book*' (22.7)

As a group, too, the seven beatitudes shed light on the theme of covenant since the remaining four, which punctuate the apocalyptic drama at various points, help believers tempted by apostasy or faced with rebellious crowd-pressure from earth's inhabitants to keep their eyes firmly fixed elsewhere. The second beatitude of the series ('blessed are the dead who from now on die in the Lord', 14.13) follows on the heels of a reminder that what matters for the chosen people is their perseverance in faithfulness; such a life means risking martyrdom and we should notice how the key-word 'keep' ('those who keep the commandments of God and hold fast to the faith of Jesus', 14.12) is also used here, in a context where mention is made of idolatry of the worst sort (14.9-11). The third beatitude introduces an element of reassurance in similar circumstances, when human rebellion is brought to a head by the sixth bowl (16.12*ff*); once again this is a beatitude directed to whoever 'keeps' the covenant through faithful observance ('blessed is the one who stays awake and [keeps] clothed', 16.15).

Our ears hear the fourth beatitude (19.9), at the midpoint of the series, in the midst of the transition whereby the whore is supplanted by the bride. The faithless wife, in her breaking of the covenant, is once and for all repudiated – no longer are voice of bridegroom or bride to be heard in 'Babylon' (18.23) – and her sentence is a cause for joyous celebration (19.1*ff*). Her destruction occasions this joy, which then modulates into rejoicing over the wedding that will unite the Lamb and his beloved in a covenant at long last made perfect (19.7). It is this which prompts the revealing angel to instruct John to write down a blessing capable of capturing the essence of this image in a metaphor more traditional and evocative than any other for describing that communion which God offers human beings: 'blessed are those who are invited to the marriage supper of the Lamb' (19.9).

No less than the consummation of this relationship between God and human beings is being anticipated here, as shown by the angel's solemn attestation to John that 'these are true words of God'. Similar authentication accompanies the sixth beatitude, preceded as it is by 'these words are trustworthy and true' (22.6). In both cases, the seer is caught up in the unparalleled emotion of the moment: when he falls erroneously on his face before the angel, it is as though he feels that a response appropriate to a theophany or a christophany (as in 1.17) is what is needed yet again.

We should notice, finally, how there is nothing automatic about these beatitudes, all of which presuppose commitment on the part of believers. I have already indicated the importance of the verb 'keep' in 14.12 and 16.15; right from its first use in 1.3 this term conveys the notion of taking responsibility for one's actions and of being obedient. In 2.26 the 'victor' is defined as the one who 'continues to do [literally 'keeps'] my works to the end'. It is clear from the injunction made to the Church at Sardis that 'keep' entails heeding (as in 1.3) and, where there is infidelity, this involves three things: remembering former faithfulness; repentance as a means to getting back onto the straight and narrow; and also vigilance to prevent further lapses (3.3). Accordingly, Philadelphia's faithfulness, despite her limited powers, can be adequately expressed as 'you have kept my word' (3.8), a formula which will be used again in 22.9 for describing everyone who meets the exigencies of the revelation.[11] Overall, 'keep' has the sense of faithfulness born of a relationship with God through Jesus Christ.

c) Seven: Covenant number

We have just reviewed the seven beatitudes. For Revelation's reader, the surprise is to meet the number seven over and over again, as for example when the familiar seven-branched menorah turns uniquely into a sevenfold series of lamp stands in harmony with the seven Churches (1.4,11). It is customary to interpret seven as the number which figuratively reflects fullness or perfection.[12] Greater precision becomes necessary, however, as soon as a closer look is taken at its usage in biblical texts, especially in the context of Israel's worship.

My proposal here is as follows: seven is the number which, by simple addition, denotes the *harmonious relationship between God who is three and his creation which is four*. Three is the number of divinity and, in Revelation, of its counterfeit. Four is the number for earth with its four corners and their four winds (7.1; 20.8), whose inhabitants are characterised by a fourfold formula (5.9, *etc.*), as well as for the whole earth into which the seven spirits enter four times (1.4; 3.1; 4.5; 5.6); it also provides the inspiration for New Jerusalem's four- sidedness.[13] Consequently, it is probably no fluke that Revelation's narrative on seven occasions associates God with the Lamb, the man who (as is indicated the seventh time) will occupy his throne (5.13; 6.16; 7.10; 14.4; 21.22; 22.1; 22.3).[14]

As a product of the addition of three and four, seven then is the number which symbolises the covenant uniting God and humanity,[15] especially through encounter in worship. The menorah with its seven lamps and branches, placed in front of the curtain of the Holy Place in the Tent of Meeting (Exod 25.31*ff*, 26.35), bears eloquent testimony to this. Moreover, many an event in the cultic calendar, like certain of Israel's rituals, also shows this clearly. Rites for the investiture of priests lasted for seven days (Exod 29.35) and expiatory sacrifices took another seven (Exod 29.36-37), while the bread of the presence replaced each Sabbath also stayed for seven days before the Lord (Lev 24.8). When the sin of the high priest or the people was to be expiated, the curtain of the holy place was daubed seven times with blood (Lev 4.6,17), while for purifying lepers sevenfold sprinkling with blood was necessary (or with oil for the otherwise impure, Lev 14.7,27). The firstborn of all livestock were the Lord's after seven days of life (Exod 22.29). Unleavened loaves were to be eaten on seven consecutive days (Exod 12.15). The great feasts of Passover, Pentecost and Booths were all of seven days' duration, while seven multiplied by seven days separated Passover from Pentecost. The harvest Feast of Booths, for celebrating the blessings bestowed by God in his faithfulness, took place in the seventh month and lasted for seven days (Lev 23.39/Num 29.12-34), the month itself being heralded by corresponding blasts on the trumpet (Lev 23.24/Num 29.1). Lastly, seven was the gap separating Sabbath years, or seven squared (forty-nine) the interval between Jubilee years.

Back, then, to Revelation. The beatitudes which we have already examined are not a numbered series in the text and so are unlikely to be picked up at a first reading or hearing. Nevertheless, they are one of many series of sevens carefully set into the text like so many precious stones; through increasing familiarity with the text and attention to detail, they subsequently emerge.[16] It is in relation to the Churches, if not to the spirits (1.4; they are also called flaming torches in 4.5), that the first explicit use of seven arises; thus, the narrative puts in place a numerical symbolism so frequently resorted to later on – indeed 'almost excessively so'[17] – as virtually to try readers' patience. The lamp stands and seven stars assimilated to the seven angels of the seven Churches (1.20) provide John with the opportunity to lay great stress on the number's significance at the very point where proceedings begin, when the assembled Asian Christians are about to hear proclamation of seven oracles to the Churches of the new covenant. A later example is the seven thunders in 10.3-4 which resound in a scenario where God appears; this is reminiscent of the Sinai covenant and perhaps also of Ps 29.3-9 (LXX, Ps 28), where YHWH's voice thunders out for the strengthening and blessing of his people (v.11).

The seven beatitudes are far from being the only rhetorical use of the number seven, as can be seen straightaway in the series of seven 'woes' which correspond to them (8.13; 9.12; 11.14; 12.2; 18.10,16,19). Liturgical acclamation of the Lamb with seven eyes and seven horns (5.6) is also found to contain (what else!) seven elements: power, wealth, wisdom, might, honour, glory and blessing (5.12), as happens again later in the angelic worship of 7.12 (where, for variation, wealth is replaced by thanksgiving). In the course of the judgments which separate these two bursts of praise, we also find seven categories of human beings (the kings of the earth, the magnates, the generals, the rich, the powerful, everyone who is a slave and everyone free, 6.15); like the original human couple (Gen 3.8*ff*), they are in breach of covenant and they attempt to hide from God's gaze and to flee the wrath of the Lamb unleashed by the sixth seal. This sevenfold typology of humanity is also, in itself, the seventh phenomenon referred to in 6.12-15, following upon the earthquake, the turning of the sun to darkness and the moon to blood, the falling of the stars, the rolling-up of the sky and the displacement of the mountains and islands.[18] Another instance involves God and the Lamb, who are associated with one another seven times (5.13; 6.16; 7.10; 14.4; 21.22; 22.1,3). We have already studied a final example, provided by the seven occurrences of the fourfold formula used to denote all humanity – whether reconciled to God or in breach of its contract with him (5.9, *etc.*).

In view of its symbolic importance for the place of encounter between God and humanity, we should not be surprised to find that this number, which binds God and human beings together, is also affected by the parodic conditioning common to all the themes of Revelation. Sure enough, it symbolises humanity's relationship to the demonic as well as to the divine. I need only recall here the seven heads of both the dragon and the monster (12.3; 17.3), the seven mountain-heads on which the prostitute is seated (17.9) with the seven kings (17.10), or point out how this accumulation of items numbered in sevens is an antithetical retort to 1.20, designed to underline rebellion against God and the Lamb (in the form of pseudo- or self-deification) through action of an opposite kind to the covenant-making referred to there.

d) Seven again: organising compositional principle

In addition, the number seven possesses a formal, structural role in Revelation inasmuch as it constitutes a veritable organising principle.[19] Seven scenes are played out before the heavenly throne where, as the seventh trumpet declares, God reigns over evil (11.15): the majestic inaugural scene (4.1–5.14) is followed by six more (7.9-17; 8.1-4; 11.15-18; 14.1-5; 15.2-8; 19.1-10), in all of which hymns are sung, most often as commentary on what is happening in the Book.[20] We could also mention seven signs – one of them positive, six negative – which succeed one another in the course of chapters 12-19.[21] And a sequence of seven events in 19.11–20.15, all seven introduced by 'and I saw', gives way to another – with an eighth 'I saw' as the cue – where parallel sevenfold reference to the Lamb carefully punctuates the whole section 21.9–22.5.[22]

Most significant of all are the four explicit septets, themselves linked together
by sections which, on closer examination, all break down into seven parts.
This is what gives Revelation the essence of its intricate literary structure.[23]
The subdivision of these numbered septets into four times seven parts –
with seven proclamations to the Church, then seven plagues set off by seals,
trumpets and bowls respectively (with angels sounding out, or pouring out,
the last two) – is a simply remarkable phenomenon. Quite without precedent
in the literature of the period, it goes far beyond the scope of the apocalyptic
cliché it is sometimes said to be.[24] When full account is taken of the biblical
data, Revelation's systematic recourse to such sevenfold representation can be
satisfactorily accounted for, in my view, only by reference to that covenant,
concluded by God with humanity, which is addressed in various Old Testament
documents and which, in the perspective of the New Testament, finds itself
renewed and fulfilled in Jesus Christ. The complex symbolic way in which
seven is used in Revelation is a sparkling illustration of this very phenomenon,
and even serves as its functional synonym.

It is time to conclude this opening survey. Revelation tells two contrasting
tales: a version of the story of humanity's relations with God and, from the
darker side of human history, an account of its parody through rebellion and
estrangement from him. The foregoing paragraphs are sufficient to show
how these materials give us access to the thematic heart of the Book. More
than this, they confront us with the very principle which has governed the
organisation of the complex data that make up this writing. The plot which
unfolds is powered, again and again, by complex and subtle re-reading of
the Jewish Scriptures, in which is brought to bear a new perspective provided
by events which the author takes to be their outcome and fulfilment; these
concern everything involved in the perfecting of the covenant undertaken
by the Mediator, Jesus the Messiah. As we follow a final route through all
of Revelation in the present chapter, a cumulative case will be built. The
nearer we get to the denouement of the plot, the more we will see how the
six major themes, worked over separately in Part One and Two of this study,
converge together in the double theme of covenant and of the pact from
hell which lines up against it. Explicitly or implicitly, these six will now come
together in synthesis in the third and final part of this book.

The logic of Revelation's four septets

Before turning to the seven-proclamations-in-one which make up the first
of Revelation's explicit septets (2.1–3.22), I wish to fall back on one of my
published articles, part of which provided a first sketch for the present
chapter. There, I offered an integrated reading of the four successive
septets,[25] suggesting that Revelation's septets of oracles, seals, trumpets and
bowls should be regarded as symphonic variations upon a programmatic
idea. That idea, I argued, is borrowed from one text in the Jewish Scriptures
– Leviticus 26 – which is preoccupied with a problem: the repeated violation

of the covenant by a stubbornly unrepentant people who constantly need to be brought back onto the straight and narrow. In this text, the wayward human partner is threatened with up to *four punishments* for sin, each made up of *seven blows,* as it is phrased by the fourfold refrain that gives rhythm to both the Hebrew and Greek text (Lev 26.18,21,24,27[28, LXX]):

'I will continue to punish you sevenfold for your sins'   (v.18)
(LXX 'I will punish you seven times more for your sins')

'I will continue to plague you sevenfold for your sins'   (v.21)
(LXX 'I will send you seven more plagues according to your sins')

'I myself will strike you sevenfold for your sins'   (v.24)

'I will punish you myself sevenfold for your sins'   (v.27/LXX v.28)

The figure in Rev 1.9-20 speaks with a voice like a trumpet (1.10). This trumpet not only brings about the writing of the seven messages communicated to the Churches of Roman Asia: in my judgment, it also functions like the trumpet in Lev 25.9 by touching off the entire series of judgments, as is confirmed by the double-edged sword of 1.16. In proposing that Leviticus 26 provides the pattern or model used by Revelation for developing its own series of four septets, I am seeking to give an affirmative answer to a question put by Greg Beale in the course of his discussion of the seals septet.[26]

Quite apart from the issue of the covenant and everything associated with it, it seems to me that this way of reading Revelation's basic structure – a matter of controversy even yet – offers three advantages. The first is its simplicity, since it explains the entire section formed by chapters 1–16 straightforwardly in terms of a sketch from which they were developed. The second is its reflection of the only explicit account which Revelation itself provides of the structuring of its own materials, namely, as four clearly numbered septets. The third is its ability to account for the way that things deteriorate, from one septet to the next, in exactly the aggravated fashion that characterises the levitical model. Indeed, the form, content and function of this source text are all reproduced by Revelation's four septets of four times seven judgments. Although their escalating severity is a reflection of growing rebellion, their purpose remains that of bringing to a renewed faithfulness the Church drawn from Israel and the nations. Once divinely manufactured New Jerusalem descends, the Lamb's faithful followers (or members of the Church of the Risen One) at last succeed in entering into full possession of their inheritance: the four septets relate the highs and lows on their journey. For divine faithfulness to be able to bring them safely to such blessing, their penitence and obedient faith are the prerequisites.

Revelation 2.1–3.22

It is time to give our full attention to the inaugural septet and to deepen our understanding of the seven proclamations to Churches. I will re-read these oracles in light of the Jewish Scriptures, in two stages: the first will involve studying them as a history in miniature of God's people; the second will entail explaining how their particular combination of content, form and function takes its inspiration (in my view) from covenant documents to be found among Israel's traditions.

In the course of this study, we have already noted various aspects to the composition of these seven proclamations. I now wish to add one further, decisive factor: the great interest shown by these oracles in the history of the old covenant. If we read them attentively, we can see their constant reference to the Old Testament; this is not something haphazard, but rather entails 'historical progression in the biblical allusions' by following an internal logic whose concern it is to show 'the perfection and replacement of the Old Testament economy'.[27] The messages as a whole are shaped by a double relationship of continuity and discontinuity between Old and New, between the renewed covenant that blossomed when Jesus the Mediator came and the old dispensation throughout which it had already been germinating. The first remarkable thing about this is the way that the sequence of seven proclamations, every one brimming with references to prior revelation, has drawn elements foreshadowing the new dispensation from the principal stages of historical development of the old covenant, in the order they happened. No less remarkable is the fact that this sevenfold proclamation, emanating from the Risen One, may be interpreted in an integrated way as describing one unified (hi)story: God's project in favour of humanity – salvation's story or salvation history – whose progress, through all its vicissitudes, is recounted by the Jewish Scriptures.[28]

The inter-textual dynamic which is at work will be explored in two stages. The first will involve assembling message by message, and for 2.1–3.22 as a whole, the various allusions made to episodes, themes or issues embedded in the narrative of Old Testament books. Second, I will compare the septet of oracles to certain key texts in the Jewish Scriptures whose function is to document the state of the covenant between Israel and their God; here, these solemn proclamations will be re-examined as written testimony authorised by the Messiah and Mediator of the new covenant, in whom the opening chapter of Revelation showed such interest.

a) Allusions to the old covenant people's journey

i) EPHESUS: In harking back to an abandoned first love (2.4) and to a resulting fall (2.5), as well as by mentioning the tree and garden of paradise (2.7) and hard toil (2.2), this first oracle revisits the narrative of origins (Gen 2.17–3.19) with its description of that first, tragic breakdown in relations between God and humanity and the lost innocence for which Hosea 1–2 was nostalgic.[29] The Revealer, who is the Risen One, holds the seven stars like a Creator would and walks among the lamp stands like the Lord God walked in the midst of the Garden of Eden. The threat of removal hanging over the menorah

(2.5) suggests the banishment of the man and his wife. By contrast the promise of renewed access to the tree of life[30] in the paradise of God – a picture, in early Judaism, for the rewarding of the righteous – points to its accomplishment in the end-time paradise-city where it is a central element of new covenant fulfilment (22.2,14,19), reflecting the tree of redemption testified to in apostolic preaching (Ac 5.30; 10.39; 13.29; Gal 3.13; 1 Pet 2.24).

ii)   Smyrna: In various ways, it is the time of the patriarchs and of captivity in Egypt, another 'situation . . . of persecution, poverty and hostility',[31] which are alluded to here. First, there is the 'exodus' of coming back from death to life (2.8), anticipated in episodes that occurred in the lives of Isaac (Gen 22.1-14) and especially Joseph (Gen 37.18-36; 39.20-41.45; 45.4-8). Then follows unjust imprisonment (2.10; *cf.* Gen 39.13-20) and ten days of trial, which can be understood as an allusion to the plagues in Egypt (Exod 7.14*ff*). Finally, there is a reference to 'the satan's synagogue',[32] to an apostate and a persecutor whose severed relations with the God of the covenant suggest that it can be assimilated to ancient Egypt and to its recalcitrant Pharaoh; an analogy for this will be provided in 11.8 where Jerusalem, as the one responsible for the witnesses' deaths, is nicknamed 'Sodom and Egypt'.[33]

iii)   Pergamum: Israel's sojourn in the wilderness following liberation from slavery may be detected in the reference to the place where the satan dwells (2.13; *cf.* Lev 16.10; 17.7; Deut 8.15[34]) and in the link (in 2.14-15) to two infamous instigators of Israel's wandering off into idolatry, *i.e.* Balaam – himself a 'devil', Num 22.32 LXX!) – and Balak (Num 25.1-3; 31.16).[35] The hidden manna, doubtless concealed in the Ark of the Covenant (*cf.* Heb 9.4), recalls the way God takes care of his people during her growth and constitution, while the white stone bearing a 'new name' (2.17) alludes to the badge for the covenant people (for Jacob renamed Israel), reproduced twice in the ephod worn by the high priest (Exod 28.9-12).

iv)   Thyatira: 'Jezebel' (2.20), namesake of an idolatrous queen with ancestry going back to Solomon's infamous wives (1 Kgs 11), as well as a whore and a witch (2 Kgs 9.22), is described in terms which suggest Elijah's prophecy (2 Kgs 2.21*ff*). In her is concentrated all the apostasy of the kings of Israel or Judah unfaithful to the Davidic covenant (see also 1 Kgs 16.29-34). Still other images pick up both the glory (2.19)[36] and the shame of the monarchy. Messiah is to be Son of God (2.18), a royal title, and greater than David (*cf.* Pss 2.7; 89.19-37), threatening the false prophetess and her 'children' with an affliction like the one that Israel had to endure (2.22; *cf.* 1 Kgs 17.1) and with death (2 Kgs 9.22-37; *cf.* the death of Ahab's sons, 2 Kgs 10.7, and of the false prophets, 1 Kgs 18.40). At the same time, in an allusion to the messianic and royal Psalm 2 (Ps 2.9), he promises the victor a Davidic authority over the nations which only a covenant-keeper can exercise (2.26-27; *cf.* 2 Sam 7.19; 8.1-14). Moreover, the headquarters for idolatrous undertakings actually turns out to be the royal capital itself (Jerusalem, or its equivalent Samaria), the very place where the plot against Jesus was also hatched and from which persecutions were unleashed against his first disciples.[37]

v) Sardis: The remnant which are about to die (3.2) or the few who are pure (3.4), like the warning of judgment that will occur without delay (3.3), conjure up a period of rapid decline and wholesale apostasy when not even a faithful remnant remains (*cf.* Isa 1.9; 6.13) to keep watch, while virtually everyone else is asleep (3.2). All this is reminiscent of the end of the prophetic era.[38] At the same time the exhortation to be vigilant and to make responsible use of the Word received (3.2-3) might also evoke significant wisdom traditions which appear throughout Israel's history, whose treasures are preserved in the Old Testament.[39]

vi) Philadelphia: Here, the register of speech reminds us of the prophecies of Haggai, Zechariah or Malachi and we can pick up several allusions to the period subsequent to the exile and to the issue of keeping or breaking covenant. The recipients have little strength (like the Jews who returned to Jerusalem). The gates of their city are (re)opened (3.7),[40] in likely reference to Eliakim's investiture (Isa 22.22) following an oracle spoken over faithless and careless Jerusalem. There is conflict with false Jews (3.9), recalling Ezra 4 and Neh 4, 6 and 13. There is both a promise which, according to Isa 60.14,[41] is made to the people of the new covenant, and also a warning of an imminent time of trial, universal in scope, which is to strike the land (3.10) rather as did the persecutions inflicted by Antiochus Epiphanes (*cf.* Dan 8 and 11). As for the promise to the victor, it focuses on the New Temple (by alluding to 'a column in the sanctuary of my God') and on New Jerusalem (3.12). In fact key, door, column and city all refer to an edifice and suggest the reconstruction projects undertaken in Jerusalem following the time of the exile.

vii) Laodicea: Either Israel's recent history, or even current events[42] from the period between the death of Jesus and the fall of Jerusalem, are suggested by what is sickeningly lukewarm (in 3.15), that is, the covenant people's legalism or empty formalism. Their apostasy calls down judgment: they are vomited out (3.16) in a negative reference which recalls the curse of Lev 18.25,28. More positively, this brings about the invitation to give a welcome, through timely repentance, to the Messiah who offers gold[43] tested by fire (his tried and tested Word, no doubt). He asks if he may enter, as did the Beloved in Song of Songs 5.2,[44] bringing his own self into the intimate atmosphere of the covenantal (*cf.* *I Enoch* 52.14) and Eucharistic meal (3.19-20). The blessing that attends the victor is no less than the gaining of a share in the messianic reign (*cf.* Ps 110.1[45]), inaugurated at the coming of the new covenant era.

If any of these indicators of reference to prior revelation were to be evaluated in isolation, on their own merit, doubtless greater or lesser plausibility might be attached to one or another. However, the probability that what we have here is multiple echoes of the story of how human beings have walked with God, as told by biblical revelation, is significantly increased when, in message after message, and in an order that retains the basic chronology of Israel's history, allusion is persistently made to the principal stages of that adventure of faith as it is reflected in the Law, Prophets and Writings.

It was customary for the Churches of Asia to read and relate to the Jewish Scriptures. However, these messages from their Messiah were an invitation to them to look again; to let this old story shed light on their own story by reminding them (roughly speaking) of the paths of sin and repentance trodden by Israel in times past and of the ancient covenant now renewed in and for them. In the story of all those to whom God had already revealed himself, in days gone by, binding himself to them in faithful relationship by his Word, their own experience as congregations was rooted and they could now be called to account in their own setting by the Risen One, and seek a positive outcome there. As they followed in the footsteps of Messiah Jesus they were able to conceive of their own pathway toward heavenly Jerusalem – a pathway given dramatic apocalyptic dress in the Book – as the continuation or extension of a long story which many a biblical antecedent could illustrate. Put another way, they could comprehend the work of God in Jesus Christ, and subsequently in the Church, as something reconfigured in which the relations he had already had with humanity under the old dispensation were brought to fruition: they were, in a word, Israel's heirs.[46]

Later in Revelation, the very same hermeneutic still applies. In a new synthesis of elements drawn from the Jewish Scriptures, the seer will couple the traditionally messianic picture of the mighty and victorious lion with that of a slain-but-upright Lamb (5.5-6), evoking among other things Old Testament ideas of sacrifice and reconciliation. As its unfolds, Revelation's narrative tale of the story of this Lamb and his people entails subtle and profound revisiting of the story of the people of God underway since ever God revealed himself or joined himself to human beings. In my view the organising principle in this narrative, and thus its interpretative key, is the plot-line of a covenant that is kept or broken but above all, renewed. As I see it, the twin fact that there is so much thematic material related to the covenant, and that this very material supplies both the framework and indispensable inter-linkage for the Book's other thematic vectors (which we studied earlier), is to be accounted for by an over-arching vision which governs Revelation's use of the Jewish Scriptures. In this vision, the eternal covenant[47] had pride of place and, accordingly, the death and resurrection of Messiah Jesus were viewed as the decisive final episodes in a long story of the highs and lows of YHWH's relationship to Israel and the nations.

We come, now, to our second stage. Here we must delve more deeply into the way the seven judicial findings in 2.1–3.22 are also organically linked to texts in the Jewish Scriptures which enjoy the status of covenant documents. To do this properly we must devote some preliminary paragraphs to the reasons why the oracles are as they are, or contain what they contain.

b) Documents of the renewed covenant

What we have are seven proclamations given to the sevenfold Church – to a community representative of the new covenant – which, as I will show, all share the form of *mini covenant treaties* and together make up an indivisible whole. Their function is to spell out the contractual terms of the Churches' relationship to Messiah Jesus, who is their Mediator and Revealer of the divine will. A detailed audit is done for each community, on the basis of which their conduct is judged and declared to be innocent or blameworthy. The finding is given by the One who loves them all (1.5), who is there amid the lamp stands (1.13) and whose prerogative it is, as their Sovereign, to certify beyond appeal the perfect knowledge he has of their situation as his servants: 'I know your deeds' (2.2, *etc.*).

The inventory drawn up for each of the Churches provides the mandate to declare whatever needs to be said about their behaviour. There is always a blessing for the one who perseveres and this always trumps any conditional curse expressed. The recompense promised to 'victors' (2.7,10-11,17,28; 3.3-5,12,21) as a reward for their faithfulness are said to be within the reach of even the worst offenders, assuming they repent, which means that what is threatened (2.5,16; 3.3) will only ever befall the incorrigible. Such a way of speaking reflects the conditional judgment or salvation oracles that we meet in the Jewish Scriptures and, in the same vein, calls upon covenant partners to shoulder their responsibilities. In accordance with a mechanism that serves to regulate the reciprocal faithfulness required of both partners, God faithfully shows favour to his people and the people must respond with their loyal obedience. Where such obedience and fidelity are forthcoming, there will also be rewards. The fact is that everything which is promised to these congregations in the inaugural septet will find its fulfilment in the lives of the 'victors' in the course of the final visions.[48] This, we may say, is where the plot ultimately 'goes', since this is how the covenant God will demonstrate that he faithfully keeps his promises.

The Church is the sole legal beneficiary of the covenant, and this is why the seven individual cases make up a single, tightly-structured whole. To be satisfied that we are in fact dealing with only one message, sub-divided into seven constituent parts, we need only examine the first and last communications. The inaugural oracle addressed to the first community, in Ephesus, accuses her in a representative way of having forsaken her first love (2.4). This is a charge which recalls the case of Jerusalem herself, when she was young and promised in marriage (Jer 2.2) – in other words, when she came up out of Egypt and when covenant was established with her at Sinai (Hos 2.15b-20). Now, to begin by accusing the first Church of covenant unfaithfulness is inevitably to conjure up for all seven the old-covenant image, so favoured by the prophets, of a tumultuous marriage between God and his people.[49] Similar, though more positive this time, is the prospect of a covenant meal to which all are invited, set forth in the closing proclamation to Laodicea. Because the seven-in-one messages culminate in so obvious an anticipation of the wedding banquet, which the Lord Jesus will share with a partner who has shown herself ready to receive him (3.20), this can only reassure all the Churches – beginning with nauseating Laodicea herself (3.16) – that their faithful Groom loves them all without exception (3.19).

Between the start and finish of this septet, Christ's scrutinising gaze undertakes a rigorous examination of how the covenant is progressing. When it is nearly finished he presents himself to the last Church as 'the Amen, the Faithful and True Witness, the Origin of God's creation' (3.14): he is the one in a position to assess her faithfulness. Assuming the renewal of covenant with her (and with all seven), he is also the one authorised to invite them all to the new Passover which brings together Messiah and people (3.20). There is an aspect to the way the scene is developed, or the Risen One characterised, which serves both to reinforce the sense of a detailed examination and to demonstrate to the Churches the dynamic nearness of their examiner, Christ: he stands, or walks, among the golden lamp stands or stars, holding them in his hand whilst having the power, if need be, to do away with them altogether (1.13,16,20; 2.1,5). More generally, the procedure of picking up from the inaugural vision (1.12-20), in oracle after oracle, one or more traits of the Risen One, is designed to develop our perspective on just one issue: the state of the relationship between each Church and the Messiah.[50]

Several elements present in most oracles help create and maintain the atmosphere of a covenant audit:

a)   Each Church receives a promise – for all except Smyrna or Philadelphia, in the form of a threat – concerning what Messiah's coming will mean for them (2.5,16,25; 3.3,11,20; in 2.10, too, such a coming is assumed).

b)   Accordingly, most Churches have charges levelled at them for their failings (2.4, *etc.*), making punishment a real prospect; however, the contrasting absence of such a charge for two of them makes the latter stand out.

c)   All the Churches hear the constant refrain 'whoever has ears . . .' (2.7,11,17,28; 3.6,13,22), the effect of which is to tune in the ear and awaken responsibility.

d)   Five out of seven are exhorted to repent (2.5,16,21,22; 3.3), a stance reminiscent of Deuteronomy (for example, Deut 30.1-10) and of the prophetic tradition (Joel 1.8-14; Zech 1.1-6; Isa 3.1 -4.4; Ezek 14.6; 18.30).[51]

e)   In the central oracle, Messiah describes himself as scrutiniser (2.23), which recalls YHWH's lawsuit against Judah (Jer 17.10), and this is coupled with a stress upon the power, truth and reliability of his judgments ('the sword of my mouth', 2.16; 'the True One', 3.7; 'the Amen', 3.14).

f) Various actions associated with entering into a covenant are described, like receiving a garment (3.4,5; 3.18; *cf.* 1 Sam 18.4) or a new name (2.17; 3.12 - *cf.* how the Lord renamed Abram *Abraham*, Gen 17.5; Isa 65.15).

g) Lastly, a covenant register bearing a record of participants' names is mentioned for the first time (3.5).

To assert, as we have been doing, that reference is unquestionably made to the Old Testament in this opening septet is not merely a matter of its *content*. It concerns just as much the *container* formed by the seven variously-slanted messages in 2.1–3.22, united by their common structure. We have already seen how the atmosphere that reigns throughout the septet of oracles to Churches makes it legitimate to speak of an audit of the present state of the covenant. When we now include the factor of the *form* in which these seven solemn proclamations are cast, slotting as they do into an already established legal framework, confirmation is forthcoming that I am fully justified in speaking of *mini covenant treaties*.

Certain key texts in the Jewish Scriptures function as covenant documents and the time has come to spell out the formal relationship that links these seven declarations to them. To do this I will take into account some recent work[52] which is alive to the problem of the *genre* of John's Revelation, in which the explicative category of *covenant treaty*[53] has been applied to the whole of Revelation or to one or more of its main subsections and the preoccupations and terminology characteristic of the *covenant lawsuit* or *Rîb*[54] have simultaneously been identified.

Any document whose purpose is to regulate covenant and, especially, to renew it subsequent to a rupture must begin with a preamble; in the case of the seven communications to Churches, 1.1-20 fulfils this function. By way of example, we can think of the renewal necessitated by the apostasy committed in the making and worship of the golden calf, as told in Exodus 32–34. As openers, preambles fulfil two main functions. The *second* of these is to recap on God's mighty covenant deeds – that is, his redemptive acts – undertaken on behalf of his people. This is done in context of the preamble's *first* function, which is to declare the lordship of the great king who is offering a covenant by stressing, in turn, two complementary traits: his transcendence and immanence. Transcendence emphasises the gap separating him from the vassal, who is subordinate to him, while underlining the suzerain's greatness and power; immanence, however, offers assurance of his closeness to and protection of his weaker partner.

Revelation follows this model and sets about both identifying and characterising the Suzerain and his Mediator (compare YHWH and Moses in Deut 1.1-5) from the very start. Various titles for them are provided which will be picked up again at the start of the individual messages to Churches. It is important to note how Revelation makes the identities of the Sovereign God and his plenipotentiary the Lamb coincide, elevating the latter to the same rank as the former; as a result, the seer, if not a mediator in the full sense, is at least an indispensable link in the revelatory chain. Mention of the recipients' intimacy with their Redeemer, in his nearness (1.5-6), gives way to a glorious christophany that itself inspires appropriate reverential fear (1.14-17). All seven oracles to Churches begin with their own mini preamble by taking from the grand preamble (1.1-20) one or more terms which it had already used for characterising the Risen One (3.14 is the only one not to make such a borrowing).

As *mini covenant treaties*, these proclamations share a virtually identical structure which faithfully reproduces, in summary form, all the constitutive elements of covenant documents. The opening oracle, addressed to the Church at Ephesus, puts in place a five-part template which carries over from one oracle to another, together with a frame (as I argue) comprising an address and a call to vigilance. Here is how this works in detail:

Address[55] (2.1a), *re-using the overall order to write*[56] *from 1.11,19.* To the angel of the church in Ephesus write.

i) **Preamble** (2.1b), *underlining the credibility and authority of the Lord presented in the vision in 1.10-20.*[57] [Thus says][58] he who holds the seven stars in his right hand, who walks among the seven golden lamp stands:

ii) **Historical prologue** (2.2-4,6), *rehearsing how successfully the Church has carried out her obligations toward the Lord who holds her responsible and to whom she must submit.*[59] I know your works, your toil and your patient endurance. I know that you cannot tolerate evildoers; you have tested those who claim to be apostles but are not, and have found them to be false. I also know that you are enduring patiently and bearing up for the sake of my name, and that you have not grown weary. But I have this against you,[60] that you have abandoned the love you had at first. Yet this is to your credit:[61] you hate the works of the Nicolaitans, which I also hate.

iii) **Ethical stipulations** (2.5a), *calling for rectification*[62] *and outlining required action for the recovery of covenant faithfulness.* Remember then from what you have fallen; repent, and do the works you did at first.

iv) **Sanctions** (2.5b), *specifying the requisite punishment if repentance is lacking.*[63] If not, I will come to you and remove your lamp stand from its place, unless you repent.

v) **Inheritance issues** (2.7b), *aimed at insuring the covenant is perpetuated.* To everyone who conquers, I will give[64] permission to eat from the tree of life that is in the paradise of God.

Call to vigilance (2.7a), *associating the Spirit with the Risen Lord and thereby stressing that a new covenant faithfulness is being sought.* Let anyone who has an ear listen to what the Spirit is saying to the churches.[65]

As far as the genre of these seven messages to Churches is concerned, *only* the covenant treaty – biblical cousin to the suzerainty treaties – satisfactorily accounts for the threefold features combined by these seven-pronouncements-in-one: their oracular *form,* paraenetic *function* (giving ethical injunctions) and their positive, negative or mixed *content.* If we take into account all these characteristics of form, function and content we may summarise, as follows, how the discourse and procedures of the prophetic *Rib* (used throughout the oracles septet) make of the Church of Asia Israel's heir, and set in motion Revelation's entire plot:

a)   Assembled for worship from Ephesus to Laodicea, the Church of Asia – its medley of variegated colours formed by its seven-assemblies-in-one – knows it is being examined by the risen Messiah, even as previously Israel had been under the scrutiny of the covenant God because, from the seer's viewpoint, the sevenfold Church corresponds to all Israel pictured, by the Old Testament, in various scenarios of covenant inauguration or ratification.

b)   Given that the covenantal relationship[66] which the people of Israel had with YHWH brought, from its inception, a requirement of accountability, the way the Church's faithfulness is so closely examined or the exhortations directed to her are to be explained and confirmed by her status as a covenant partner.

c)   Use of the mechanism and terminology of the lawsuit implies renewal of this covenant, for, as happened with every such event in Israel's prior history, a judicial review of the fidelity of both partners to their responsibilities results here in a considered finding, on the basis of which the future of the covenant relationship may be envisaged.

d)   By reviving the Old Testament metaphor of a nuptial relationship between YHWH and his covenant people, and whether they find in favour of the bride's innocence or establish her guilt, the oracles drive a plot which will oscillate continually – until finally resolved – between the Church's fulfilment of her vows on the one hand and her unfaithfulness to her call and election on the other.

We need now to go on to examine variations to the major theme of covenant rupture as orchestrated by the three remaining septets, payback for hardness of heart is envisaged or inducements to repent are offered. First, however, it is necessary to pause and look once more at 4.1-11 and 5.1-14 – the two crucially important panels which separate the last of the oracles from the first of the broken seals.

Revelation 4.1–5.14

Revelation's ongoing debt to the Old Testament remains clear for all to see in this diptych. Especially easy to demonstrate is the way the vision of the throne revealed to the seer, here, is rooted in Ezekiel 1, with similarities extending even to details such as the crystal sea (4.6 = Ezek 1.22). Nevertheless, it should not be forgotten that for their oracles the writing prophets were already drawing partly on prior revelation. Perfectly acquainted with this procedure, John himself makes use of it: behind Ezekiel 1 there lies Exodus 24. As a result, behind Rev 4.6 we ought to see not only a reference to Ezek 1.22 but, equally, to the mysterious sapphire platform of Exod 24.10. Other connections between the two scenes reinforce the parallelism here. Both feature entry into the presence of God: 'temple', 'tent' and 'throne' are often associated in Revelation (for example in 7.15), before merging at the end into the one presence of the enthroned God.[67] Both texts have a major or minor role for elders who represent the redeemed people (cf. Exod 24.1). Most of all, in both there is a mediator in position between God and his people – there Moses (Exod 24.3-4,8,15-18), here the Lamb – and moreover each of them takes a book, with Moses writing and reading the 'book of the covenant' (Exod 24.4,7) while its counterpart, here, is the book that only the Lamb may open. Finally, both agents carry out purification by blood, Moses through the blood of burnt offerings ('covenant' blood, Exod 24.5-6,8) and the Lamb by offering his own blood.

In 3.20, the Risen One had made reference to a door that would open and give, to a suitably responsive Church, access to a relationship with him. Now, the Lord himself opens the door to her (4.1). As heaven is revealed we glimpse the white garments, crowns and thrones of the elders anticipated in the oracles addressed to believers (2.10; 3.5,21): the location may have changed, but the logic carefully put in place by the first septet is still being pursued.[68] We may recall how, for the lawsuit brought by YHWH against his people Israel, heaven and earth were to act as witnesses to the case; this happens, for instance, in the prologue to the Song of Moses in Deut 32.1-3, whose form, content and function all displays the characteristics of the *Rîb*.[69] Through a judicial framework, the Covenant Mediator has been standing on Asian soil and solemnly addressing the Church which his death and resurrection have made into the new covenant people. Now, in parallel, the heavenly court convenes to insure that the events of redemption also have their necessary universal and cosmic dimension. The notion of a covenant lawsuit may itself have arisen out of the idea that the heavenly assembly gathered around God was, above all else, a court of justice.[70]

From one end to the other, the diptych formed by chapters 4 and 5 is pervaded by covenantal logic. We are prevented from losing sight of it for even a second by numerous elements of both the celestial decor and action; these further develop the atmosphere of covenant ratification which so dominated the oracles spoken to the congregations of Messiah Jesus in Asia. Here are the main ingredients, arranged as a series of points:

a) A throne which brings John and his reader-recipients to the heart of all things will be the backdrop for the whole plot from 4.2 to 22.1,3. At the throne, they come face to face with the covenant God who has entered his Temple (cf. Isa 6.1) to preside over an investigation whereby evidence of the good deeds of some and of the abominable activities of others will be compiled gradually by the seals, trumpets and bowls. When an anti-throne bursts forth later (13.2), only to be destroyed (16.10), we can see straightway how beautifully this dovetails with a plot depicting not only the faithful love of God towards humanity but also its caricature.

b) A rainbow (4.3), no doubt inspired by Ezek 1.28, reaches right back beyond the prophet to the sign of the covenant with Noah (Gen 9.13); I will have further cause to mention this later, once we examine Rev 10.1-11.

c) Twenty-four elders (4.4), acting covenant guarantors,[71] may evoke the authors credited with the books of the Old Covenant, if our oldest extant commentary on Revelation is correct in its interpretation.[72]

d) Four creatures, which stand as sentinels, very likely combine the two that protected the Ark of the Covenant (Exod 25.17-22) with the two others that guarded Solomon's sanctuary (2 Chr 3.10-13; 4.7-8) – a reminder that, in its essentials, the Ark replicates the suzerain's throne.

e) An echo of the *trisagion* of Isa 6.3-4, accompanied by a reference to God's almightiness (4.8), reminds readers of how a prophet typically receives, at his call, a revelation containing judgment.

f) The book in 5.1 (*cf.* Ezek 2.9–3.3) is clearly central; this is true whether or not it refers, as the Church Fathers thought, to the Old Covenant whose contents Messiah could reveal by virtue of his having fulfilled its prophecies in his person. Undeniably it is a legal document[73] – perhaps indeed a testament –[74] with the Lamb-Messiah as its testator, or again a marriage contract or even a preparatory bill of divorce for infidelity.[75] Black on white, as it were, the book is a contract whose function is that of a seven-sealed covenant record; the remarkable fourfold insistence upon the need to open it underlines its vital importance. Such a scroll as this might point to the record of proceedings to which the human covenant partner could always refer, ever since Noah (Gen 9.12).

g) The need is underlined for a truly qualified mediator (5.5), fully authorised to carry out the covenant suzerain's will. With Exodus providing the prototype for eschatological liberation of the covenant people by God's hand, the slain Lamb purchases for God, with his blood, a people drawn from all nations and made up of freedmen whom he constitutes as a kingdom of priests.[76] This Lamb-Messiah is alone worthy to open the sealed scroll: by his rising from death he gained possession of what Scripture had promised and so, as Victorinus went on to say, he is the testator who has the right to unseal his own 'testament' – the Old Testament, now accomplished and revealed. In other words, he is the executor of the will, as is shown by the three parallel series of judgments which follow his breaking open of the scroll's seals.[77]

h) The Lamb's patently messianic character emerges (5.5-6), with its basis in a re-reading of some key texts from the Jewish Scriptures (*e.g.* Gen 49.9-10; Isa 11.1-10).

i)   By shedding his own blood in death as covenant blood for the purchase of a universal people (Exod 24.4-6,8), the Lamb fulfils the original promise of the covenant concluded at Sinai (Exod 19.3-6).[78]

j)   As befits any significant redemptive act of God, a psalm of praise bursts forth (5.9; cf. Ps 98) to greet and celebrate, with a new song, the Lamb's inauguration of the renewed covenant (5.9; cf. Ps 98).[79]

In the first part of this study, we had cause to examine the dualling of worship in this two-part scene (4.8-11 and 5.8-14). Our focus, there, was the adoration offered, first to the Creator of all things (4.11) and instigator of the new covenant (4.8), and then to the Redeemer whose sacrifice (5.9) ushered in the consummation of God's reign (5.10,13). This new set of components warrants our taking another look, however. What we have uncovered here is the covenant trajectory whereby, even as a new day dawned (as it were) on human beings' creation and fall, God was beginning to call out from among them a people for himself.[80] By conferring the status of kings and priests on covenant vassals (5.10) and thereby restoring dignity to humanity, the Lamb-Redeemer through his death acquires an honour that mingles necessarily with the glory belonging to YHWH the Creator, God of the eternal covenant (5.13).

As a whole, the diptych in 4.1–5.14 takes its spectators offstage into the wings of revelation. There, we come upon a double celebration of the Creator's lordship and the Redeemer's triumph. As a scenario this forestalls all the forthcoming deception, all the subsequent ridiculous attempts to take their place, and impresses on our minds what we should never forget, namely, the perspective of the covenant God upon human history. In conformity with his eternal will, his plan of salvation will come to fruition in the fulfilment recounted by Revelation's finale (from 21.1 onwards). At that point, readers will finally set eyes on new covenant in its perfected form.

Glimpsing where the plot is going: Revelation 6.1–20.15

Nevertheless, the same readers will soon find out just how disrupted relations can be between God and humanity. This happy outcome to the apocalyptic plot is preceded by everything that separates the opening of the first seal (6.1) from the 'closure' by which all would-be claimants to God's sole sovereignty are finally dispatched to the lake of fire (20.15). Fallen human beings are inveterate sinners whose right relationship with God soon degenerates into a hellish covenant, a veritable anti-pact, which they enter into blindly with God's adversaries. For those who faithfully confess they are God's, his promises and blessings do remain decisive; earth-dwellers, however, go their own way and by choosing disobedience must undergo the plagues and curses that it incurs. The result is that objects, locations and issues connected with covenant will be parodied, throughout most of the ensuing story-line, by counterparts that strangely correspond to them. Thus by a dramatic metamorphosis God's fiancée is turned into a spiritual whore who will start running off after idols as other nations do.

Compositionally, things will come to a head at the moment when God's unfaithful people face judicial prosecution and when the still faithful remnant among them are declared to be *not guilty*. The whore-city is censured and capital punishment imposed on her, to illustrate the consequences for idolaters; but her counterpart the bride-city is cleared and reinstated, an outcome which corresponds to true believers' reward. If, as the finale dawns, a pardoned and purified Jerusalem is to be able to inherit everything that God has promised her, 'Babylon' must first be brought to justice, sentenced by a clear verdict for her sins (18.20), sent down under a curse and ultimately destroyed. Vengeance upon 'Babylon' (19.2) for her rejection of God and for the persecution and death she inflicted on those sent by him – among them Messiah himself – is a sentence which carries over to heavenly Jerusalem in the form of an acquittal and a *not guilty* status symbolised by her dress (19.8). The same verdict also triggers simultaneous bestowal of the blessings that go with her justification.

Ultimately, the whore's allies turn out to have done her no good. By contrast, full justice is obtained by the Mediator for all those whose sin he has expiated, bringing the divine plan of salvation to full accomplishment; he rightfully inherits all the honorific titles of the old covenant as a worthy Lamb or a faithful and true Witness. In the end one unfaithful people must perish so that *multiple* peoples (21.3) may take her place and enjoy God's presence, as promised since the Sinai covenant (Lev 26.11-12) and since Abraham was promised a blessing which, as envisaged, would spill over from his own offspring to benefit all of earth's peoples (Gen 22.18).

Following this quick look at what the entire section 6.1–20.15 contributes to the Book as a whole, it is now time to see in full detail how this works out from stage to stage. The first septet of oracles to Churches provides the overture to Revelation's orchestration of motifs such as hardening, covenant breaking and judgment on the one hand or repentance, reparation and reward on the other: a veritable Covenant Symphony. In the form of variations, the music heard in the three cycles of judgment that follow highlights the leitmotifs of the overture and develops the grand theme. As a series, the plagues are intended to provoke sincere repentance. For this to succeed they must unsettle those listening in such a way as to prompt their proper use of wisdom from the first series onwards. Being able to stand (6.17) entails being found in the company of the Lamb (7.1*ff*).

There is an inner logic to the three septets of seals, trumpets and bowls. It becomes visible from 6.1*ff* in the scene played out before the throne, from where curses are unleashed as the seals are opened. It is what connects each of these sections thematically to texts such as Exod 24 (the covenant ratification which followed the deliverance of the Exodus), or to recurring prophetic covenant lawsuits (Ezek 2.3*ff*, *etc.*). This is the logic of covenant sanctions,

employed to bring about the repentance of the rebellious people. One after
another, the four septets conspire to turn it into a grand fresco whose four
scenes each anticipate, in their own way, the same outcome.[81] Our task will
therefore be to demonstrate how the seals, trumpets and bowls are crossed, in
turn, by a twin thematic trajectory: that of a covenant at once magnificently
renewed by the Lamb and his friends, yet correspondingly laughed to scorn by
a whole circus of rival forces, whether human or demonic.

Revelation 6.1-17; 8.1

The music of the overture heard in the oracles now finds its first variation
in the seals septet (6.1-17; 8.1). To launch this series of seven plagues
four riders are borrowed from Zechariah's prophecy, in a context where
the Lord is about to show faithful compassion to Jerusalem as the object
of his jealous love (Zech 1.10*ff*). This is a clear reference to the logic
that governs every case of covenant rupture and restoration. Ezek 14.21
has a word of judgment, spoken against Jerusalem, which threatens four
severe punishments. Not only is this a further prophetic example of the
phenomenon observed earlier in Lev 26, but a reworking of it. Exactly
as Jesus had evoked covenant-breaking Jerusalem's wish for the hills and
mountains to fall on her and so hide her from the face of God her Judge
(Lk 23.28-30), Rev 6.16 also makes use of the same text in Hosea (Hos 10.8,
cf. v.1-3),[82] but by giving it a new context. The new covenant people must be
marked in advance with a seal of protection and belonging (7.2*ff*) which is
in parallel, and in perfect continuity, with the element of divine protection
that featured in Israel's inaugural deliverance from the plagues of Egypt.
Indeed, such sealing has its origin in the events of the first Passover.[83] This
interlude before the seventh seal of wrath is broken contains an important
detail about the angel who holds this protective seal: he ascends 'from the
rising of the sun' (7.2). From the very same spot, the kings who associate
with the dragon will come forth once the sixth bowl is poured out (16.12),
in token of the antithetical relationship in which they stand.[84]

Not until the picture painted in 21.1–22.5 will God's people of the End –
new Israel, perfected in Christ and turned outward to the nations – attain its
full strength. Here in chapter 7, however, there is an anticipation of this in a
people that recalls historical Israel, by being twelve twice over, to the power
of a thousand (7.4), and that reflects the nations in being simultaneously
innumerable, just as Zechariah had imagined it for his eschatological
pilgrimage (7.9; *cf.* Zech 2.10-12).[85] As for the vast crowd waving palm-
branches and singing praises, it seems to summon another that had taken part
in the Triumphal Entry into Jerusalem when Jesus came to inaugurate the
new covenant by spilling his blood; a detail of its dress directly associates the
crowd in Rev 7 with the Lamb whose blood was shed (7.14; *cf.* 1.5). By means
of this redemption, it can fully enjoy its status as a covenant people and enter
into the nearer presence of the God who has come to save, worshipping him

there (7.15*ff*). In these ways the renewed people is organically related to, and in perfect continuity with Israel,[86] whilst at the same time being suspended somewhere between Israel and the nations. It follows that those in Israel who do not believe in Jesus as Messiah shut themselves out, by their unbelief, from any inheritance among this renewed covenant people.[87]

Set free, this people sings the praises of the Saviour who has redeemed it, as would have happened under the old covenant (Ps 102.18-22). Then, in ministry which clearly looks forward to the vision of celestial Jerusalem, the people engage in that priestly service which 1.5-6 introduced and 5.9-10 developed. We seem to be at a point on the trajectory which echoes the Exodus, regarding the route by which Israel was constituted a covenanted people.[88] In Rev 7.15 – and this is quite remarkable – not only is there mention of unceasing worship given by the redeemed to the Lamb 'day and night within his temple', but also the promise is made that God will erect his Tabernacle among them. Simultaneously, reference is twice made to the divine throne as a place where worshippers stand and have every right to be. In our earlier discussion of the major theme of worship, we already took note of how the present scene brings to fulfilment all that had been foreshadowed in the Jewish cultic festivals, and especially the one pilgrimage festival which trumped them all, for the covenant people in the first century: the Feast of Booths.[89]

Consequently, what we have here is face-to-face worship with God, for which the true Holy Place is the locale. This idea, which draws its inspiration from the prophecy of restoration in Ezek 37.26-28, prepares for several other aspects of the final vision: 'he will tabernacle with them' (21.3); there will be no temple as such in the city (21.22) and worship will be carried on in front of the throne of God and the Lamb (22.3, 'his servants will worship him'). It is noteworthy that these are the very characteristics of the new covenant people as outlined by Peter (1 Pet 2.9), whilst purification with a view to service in worship is envisaged in Heb 9.14. It appears obvious that in breaking the seals, and so opening the book taken from God's hand, the slain-but-standing Lamb has *already* effected in principle the necessary transformation of the relationship uniting the people and God, as signified by their adoration as characterised here.

Bearing in mind the careful way in which the text lays some emphasis on the fulfilment of the worship inaugurated at Sinai, we should be attentive to two more things. First, a new covenant arrangement is to be inferred from his establishment. Secondly, the Lamb, who makes God present to human beings, is the covenant personified (21.22) to the extent that he both gives God satisfaction through the shedding of his blood (7.14) and also meets fully his people's need (7.17). From now on, those who belong to him will no longer hunger, thirst or suffer burning heat (Isa 49.10), but instead will have a Davidic shepherd (caring for Israel, Ezek 34.23; *cf.* Ps 23.2): cisterns will be empty no more (Jer 2.13); the sun or moon will no longer strike anyone (Ps 121.6); and finally, there will be neither shame nor death (Isa 25.8). What is presented here is not so different from John's Gospel, with the promise of the bread of life (*cf.* Jn 6.35) and especially the water promised by Jesus at the very same Feast of Booths (Jn 7.37- 39). In exact conformity with the statement in Jn 14.6, no one will come to the Father unless through him.

As the seventh seal is broken, we catch a fleeting glimpse of the seven trumpet-bearing angels of the next series (8.1-2). Jewish apocalyptic reserved an important role for seven archangels whose origins seem to go back to the angels of Exod 12.23 (and of Ps 78.47-48) and whose function was to execute the divine judgments served to Egypt. In Revelation, the major role generally played by angels is that of conveying to humans on earth the judgments which God has pronounced. In the present case, given that the bowl-angels will have a decidedly priestly side to them (15.6), it is easy to recall the further scenario of how Israel, with seven trumpet-blowing priests at the head, had walked seven times round the walls of Jericho on the seventh day of the campaign (Josh 6).[90] In both instances, six trumpets herald a decisive act of judgment, which God will carry out the instant the seventh is blown (*cf.* 11.19). As in Am 3.6, the trumpet gives warning of approaching judgment and deliverance; these are saving events which obtain justice for the saints, in response to their prayers (8.3), although for all that they do not provoke repentance among other human beings (9.20-21). The thunder, lightning and earthquake linked to the sounding of the trumpet (8.5), by which God breaks the silence[91] and speaks forth his judgment (*cf.* Zeph 1.7; Hab 2.20; 3.3-6; Zech 2.13), are our second reminder (*cf.* 4.5 earlier) of the scene on Mount Sinai (Exod 19.16-19), with two more still to follow (11.19; 16.18-21). In a theophany on the mountain, YHWH had come, with a trumpet blast, to constitute Israel a covenant people, sealing the partnership concluded by the gift of his law – a document whose purpose was due and proper regulation of that covenant.

It may even be that this is the very same holy mountain, onto which God came down and at the foot of which Israel was born, which makes a major contribution to what follows. As the mountain of origins, wrapped in fire, it seems to provide an orientation for interpreting the vision of 'something like a great mountain, burning with fire' (8.8) revealed by the second trumpet. Could this be the same as the 'holy mountain' which God makes his inheritance (Exod 15.17), in the sense that what is being signified here is final rupture of the Sinai covenant and its replacement by another? The destroying mountain that was Babylon was finally to be overturned (Jer 51.24-26): is a similar fate foreseen, here, for Jerusalem? In that case, should we not also think of the mountain *par excellence*, thrown into the sea, to which Jesus himself had alluded (Mt 21.21-22)? What is still to come, in Revelation, would suggest that we should: as in Zechariah's vision, where the Temple is to be rebuilt on a high mountain, the New Jerusalem of the End will come down upon a mountain and replace 'Babylon'.

Revelation 8.2–9.21

Now, another variation is played by the trumpets (8.7*ff*). This septet, whose extensive nature and central position make it the most important,[92] represents the keystone in a three-part series of developments in which John sets about recounting covenant fulfilment. Everything had begun with a trumpet (1.10, recalled in 4.1) and one trumpet in particular may have been John's main inspiration here. The text of Lev 26.14-45, with its fourfold mention of the curses that result from covenant breaking, stands in contrast to what precedes it, where the subject is those blessings that YHWH rains down upon his faithful people (Lev 26.3-13). Yet just prior to all this, sustained attention is paid to the Year of Jubilee (Lev 25.8-54), inaugurated on the Day of Atonement by a blast on the trumpet (Lev 25.9, twice). This makes the judgments carried out here tally with the seven-times-seven Sabbath blessings (Lev 25.8) and with the justice for all heralded by the Year of Jubilee. Still another possible model[93] is furnished (in Lev 23.24) by the Feast of Trumpets, when the *shofar* was repeatedly sounded on the first day of the seventh month. In either case, the justification of faithful Israel, as celebrated in her solemn feasts, goes hand in hand with the judgment pronounced upon covenant-breaking humanity.

There are two things which I cannot (and probably need not) do at this point: relate the trumpets to the preceding seals in a detailed way and use inter-textual connections for quantifying their links to Exodus or to the many places where the prophets echo this book. Readers interested in such issues may profitably consult the best commentaries on Revelation. Nevertheless, a number of remarks should be made here, beginning with the first four trumpets.

Revelation 8.2-12

It may well be that the rivers and springs turned to wormwood (8.10-11) recall the waters of Egypt made bitter (Exod 7.21, a motif picked up by Ezek 29.3-5), but in a more explicit way this event subverts the miracle that had happened at Mara en route for Sinai (Exod 15.25). That this is an image chosen for portraying covenant rupture figuratively is confirmed by the parallelism with Deut 29.18, where the man, woman, family or tribe who betrays the Lord through idolatry is taken to be a root from which wormwood sprouts. Moreover, in Jer 23.11,15 apostate priests or prophets are made to drink wormwood (*cf.* Lam 3.15,19; Am 5.7; 6.12), just as the unfaithful people previously had to do (Jer 9.13-16, 25-26). As for the star whose fall precipitates the poisoning of the waters, this is the counterpart of the true dawn star (22.16), inspired perhaps by the Babylonian morning star (Isa 14.12-15) fallen from heaven to earth; mountain and star (8.8,10) are also found in combination in *1 Enoch* 108.3-6.

To put it briefly, what is seen here is abandonment of the Lord and his covenant, and this defection embroils the people engaged in it in a fate similar to that of both Egypt and Babylon. The darkening in 8.12 once again harks back to Egypt's plagues, as indeed to the Day of YHWH (Isa 13.9-11; *cf.* 24.21-23); the same motif is re-used when recounting the judgment that falls at the very instant Messiah died to inaugurate the new covenant (Mk 15.33 and par.). As I have already pointed out sun, moon and stars – whose light has ordered everything from creation onwards (Ps 148.3-6; Job 38.31-33) – play the role of covenant witnesses. Therefore, the picture of the obscuring of these sources of light, interrupting the established cosmic order, is a sure sign that when covenant obligations are broken, judgments fall, according to the logic of covenant curses. We find this picture in a great number of OT texts (Isa 13.10-13; 24.1-6,19-23; 34.4; Jer 33.20-21,25-26; Ezek 32.6-8; Jl 2.10,30-31; 3.15-16; Am 8.9; Hab 3.6-11), as well as in Jewish tradition.

Revelation 8.13–9.21; 11.15ff

The final three trumpets, simultaneously called 'woes', bring the judgments to a head in plagues which impact directly on unsealed unbelievers (9.4) and which involve demons. A flying eagle, introduced in 4.7, heralds the plagues – in part comparable to warnings in Deut 28.49; Jer 4.13; Lam 4.19; Hos 8.1; Hab 1.8[94] – and this comes straight from the image of God as protector, faithfully caring for his people (Exod 19.4) while at the same time striking Egypt. Ever more severe plagues breaking over Pharaoh's land had convinced Israel, and certain Egyptians (Exod 12.38), that the God who had come to save was to be trusted. The leitmotif of Pharaoh's total failure to repent (Exod 7.13; 8.15,19,32; 9.7,12,35) finds a renewed echo here in the 'incredible hardening'[95] shown by those who survive the scourging, as they continue to practise idolatry (9.20-21; *cf.* the even worse reaction of human beings in 16.9,11). Meanwhile, the way Israel was fortified for imminent departure from Egypt during Passover is reflected for readers in the continually expanding vision of the sovereignty of God and the Lamb. The heightened judgments proclaimed by the sixth trumpet probably originate on the incense altar from which, in Revelation's plot, prayers rise up to God from his people (6.10-11, then 8.3-5 and 9.13). As for the clear separation of believers from unbelievers it, too, is implied in the logic of covenant, whose call for renewed faithfulness can make the rebel recalcitrant.[96]

Now we come to two important passages, one of which intervenes between the sixth and seventh trumpets while the other contains everything that takes place between the seventh trumpet and the outpouring of the bowls (11.19–14.20). There has been careful investigation of these two narrative segments more than once, in previous chapters; with the major theme of covenant in mind, I will now examine them one last time, before turning to view the fourth set of judgments (the bowls) from the same vantage point.

Revelation 10

The entrance of the angel in 10.1 provides an excellent example of how the theme of covenant between YHWH and his people makes its contribution to both the decor and action of Revelation's plot, as seen in what this angel does and says as well as in the way its traits are delineated. On seeing this angelic figure's descent from heaven Revelation's readers will think, straightaway, of analogous moments in prior revelation when God came to establish his covenant (Exod 33.9; Num 11.25; 12.5). His dress (enveloped in cloud) is a reminder of just how such a descent happened on Sinai (Exod 19.16), where the cloud accompanied the arrival of the covenant God, on the Wedding Day, to inaugurate a union with Israel his wife. As for the pillars of fire, they form part of the decor for the crossing of the wilderness (Exod 13.21, *etc.*) as well as for covenant inauguration at Sinai. The seven thunders (10.3*ff*), meanwhile, refer to the outward manifestations that accompany God's speech and self-revelation at Sinai (*cf.* Ps 29) – even if their message is mysteriously inexpressible here.

The angel's face, too bright to look at, is the face of the God of blessing (Num 6.22-27), while his legs like fiery pillars evoke God's faithful presence alongside his people throughout the Exodus. The aura or halo (or rainbow, *cf.* 4.3) around the angel's head points to the establishment of the covenant with Noah after the flood (Gen 9.12-17), when the bow was set in the sky as the sign for the everlasting covenant between God and his creation. One wonders if this might not be the angel of the covenant, identified with YHWH when he comes to his Temple in Mal 3.1. The Synoptic Gospels cite this text; by making John the Baptist the forerunner who prepares the way (according to Mal 3.1) for this angel of the covenant (Mt 11.10; Mk 1.2; *cf.* Lk 1.76), they suggest that the angel in question is Jesus. The way the angel in Rev 10 is characterised works similarly, as he shares traits both of God the Judge from the Old Testament (his coming, the rainbow, the voice, the book in his hand)[97] and of the Risen One from the opening vision, with shining face and incandescent legs (1.15-16). These traits will be examined more closely in what follows.

At this point, however, our attention ought once more to be drawn to the Lamb's strange absence from Revelation's narrative between 8.2 and 14.1. To some extent, he will be represented by the two witnesses of chapter 11 and then caricatured by the two monsters of chapter 13. However, the Messiah who took the book in chapter 5 also has his functional equivalent in the angel who similarly comes forward with a book here. As a consequence, the figure of the covenant angel, in 10.1*ff*, belongs in the same category where Revelation's various christological figures are to be kept, alongside the Risen One of the opening, the Lamb who appears from chapter 5 onwards and the messianic rider of chapter 19. Victorinus of Pettau, when the story of the interpretation of Revelation began, himself read 10.1-2 by assimilating this angel to Jesus Christ.[98]

In his hand the angel holds a 'little scroll' (10.2a,8-10) linked, one way or another, to the one held out to the Lamb by the Seated One on the throne (5.1*ff*). Since this document fills the stomach with bitterness, as underlined by the text (10.9-10), it could be a scroll bearing an accusation of adultery

(Num 5.12-31),[99] in other words of covenant breaking, for when Ezekiel had eaten a similar indigestible scroll, it had fallen to him to deliver an accusation of spiritual fornication (Ezek 3). By planting his feet on land and sea (10.2b), the angel testifies to his universal sovereignty and gives notice that his message, when viewed from the perspective of the new covenant, will be universal in both its scope and relevance. This is confirmed by the use (in 10.11) of one version of the fourfold formula for designating the whole of humanity. Then, the strong voice of the angel suggests the Lord roaring from Zion (Am 1.2; cf. 3.8) and revealing himself in the declaration to 'his servants the prophets' (10.7, paraphrasing Am 3.7) of his sovereign plan.

Following the binding of Isaac, the angel of YHWH had renewed promises of blessing for Abraham by making an oath and swearing by himself (Gen 22.15ff). As YHWH spoke in the covenant hymn of Deut 32 he raised his hand to heaven and made a solemn attestation of judgment (Deut 32.39-42).[100] Both the action and declaration of the angel here follow this pattern (10.5; cf. the angel in Dn 12.7). By raising his right hand to swear a solemn oath, he is acting as is customary whenever a covenant is either ratified or modified (Gen 14.22), faithfully reproducing both the gesture of the covenant God himself (Gen 22.16; Exod 32.13; Num 14.30; Deut 32.40; Isa 45.43; Jer 49.13; Ezek 20.5ff, Am 6.8) and also the demeanour appropriate for any believer who petitions the covenant Lord (Ps 28.2; 63.5). In addition, we may note the interesting fact that procedures relating to the law of jealousy could only be engaged when accompanied by two solemn oaths.[101]

Before we discover what the oath itself contains (10.6e-7) the narrative describes the sovereignty exercised by the Creator over the traditional covenant witnesses that are earth, sea and sky, whose active presence insures that such an oath is ratified (10.6a-d). By such a reference to the crucial role of the prophets, to whom God's mysteries were made known, their ministry is underlined as covenant guardians towards unfaithful Israel (1.7). After Easter, the ministry of witnesses to the Crucified and Risen One, including John himself, extended this prophetic service (10.8-11). Summed up in the command, 'prophesy about . . .' (10.11) – an expression already hallowed by Ezekiel's prophecy, where it is used over twenty times – this ministry implies prophesying not merely *about* those to whom the prophet is speaking, but also *against*[102] them by means of a denunciation of their rebellion against God. This being said, *against* is not to be separated from *for*, since every time the message is greeted with positive acceptance, the one who so responds to God's faithful love (as the covenant testifies) receives, as good news, the word spoken to him or her.

Revelation 11.1-14

Coming to this sequence, with the major theme we are addressing in mind, the focal point seems to be the community living under covenant, seen as a spiritual temple in which God dwells (cf. 1 Cor 3.16-17; 6.19; 2 Cor 6.16; Eph

2.21-22). A first episode finds John measuring the Temple's sanctuary, that is its Holy of Holies – with its altar of burnt offerings or perhaps its incense altar (to which only the high priest has access)[103] – and the worshippers to be found there, but not including the outer court reserved for the nations. We are told that the latter, in an apparent echo of Jesus's prediction (Lk 21.24), will trample the 'Holy City' underfoot (11.1-2): to Luke's Jerusalem corresponds the Holy City here (*cf.* Mt 4.5), while Luke's 'until the times of the Gentiles are fulfilled' finds its counterpart in '[they will trample over the Holy City] for forty-two months'. In the Holy Place, whose threshold is to be crossed only on the Day of Atonement, and specifically in front of the altar of perpetual sacrifices we are at the very heart of that space where sinful people are able to encounter the holy God, thanks to the worship of Israel which is celebrated there. To put it differently, this is the very cradle of the covenant (11.1) which unites God and his people.[104]

As a deed opposite to that of abandoning the Temple's desecrated outer court (11.2), measuring it appears to signify a partitioning and protective act,[105] which serves to guarantee life, in parallel to the action of sealing (7.4*ff*). Equally, it is a preparatory gesture which anticipates coming restoration.[106] John here is once more in the process of staging a *covenant event*, which, like every other audit, ratification or renewal that has gone before or will follow, implies the very updating of humanity's relationship to its God definitively carried out by Jesus as Messiah and Mediator. The forty-two months (11.2) of trampling might even express *covenant time*, if the period involved were to prove to be 'a sort of number for Messiah'[107] as son of David. Forty-two is the sum of the consonants of David *(dwd)* multiplied or perfected by a factor of three (3 x [*d* (4) + *w* (6) + *d* (4)] = 42); the three series of fourteen generations in which Messiah Jesus's genealogy is set out, in Mt 1.2-17, also springs to mind in this connection. As a time-span during which the drama of covenant rupture and restoration is played out, it also betokens a period equivalent to that of Israel's wilderness wanderings and to the number of times in succession that camp was struck (Num 33.5-49).[108]

What comes next points yet again to a covenant lawsuit. Two prophetic witnesses solemnly give their evidence (*marturia*, 11.7),[109] and this testimony will secure a penal verdict. Moreover, by wearing sackcloth (11.3), like Elijah (2 Kgs 1.8) or John the Baptist (Mk 1.6), they manifest their full awareness that severe judgment is about to fall (*cf.* 2 Kgs 1.8; Zech 13.4; Isa 20.2; Jon 3.6) and, accordingly, that repentance is urgently required (Isa 20.2; Zech 13.4; 2 Kgs 1.8). The duration of their service, identical to the space of time when the Holy City was being profaned, helps orientate their single testimony towards this same city, now abandoned. Their status as olive tree and lamp stand, meanwhile, which links them to Israel and to the Holy of Holies, enables them to stand 'before the Lord of the earth (or, of the land)' (11.4). The same thing is meant by measuring or abandoning (v.1-2), by conducting a lawsuit or representing the Sovereign (v.3-4): against the backdrop of a covenant long flouted but now fulfilled in perpetuity, the court sits and once more deliberates. It will deliver a judgment that is both positive and negative; a double verdict illustrated by the contrast between the protection afforded the faithful people of God (11.1) and the dispossession of the unfaithful by the nations (11.2).[110] The message from the two witnesses calls to mind the struggle of covenant mediators of old such as Moses, when covenant was cut in Egypt, or as Elijah, when a faithful remnant survived in spite of Ahab's apostasy or Jezebel's threats. Their words have overwhelming force and no other will than theirs may prevail (11.5-6). Together, they bear witness that in Jesus converge the ministries of Moses and Elijah, or the message of the Law and the Prophets.

I gave my thoughts on this text when tackling (in chapter 4) the major theme of testimony. However, at this point I wish to show how an episode recounted in the Gospel of John may also shed considerable light upon it. In the Temple, the Johannine Jesus is giving his testimony before his detractors, where he quotes Torah – 'the testimony of two witnesses is valid' (Jn 8.17; *cf.* Deut 17.6*ff*) – and establishes that his Father is the requisite second witness who will confirm his words. In a manner parallel to what is described in Rev 11, two linguistic phenomena in this pericope (Jn 8.12-20) insure that the exchange between Jesus and the Pharisees has a similarly judicial character: first, the several uses of *martureô/marturia* to signify evidence admissible in court,[111] with the implied issue of the veracity of the testimony given; and second, by way of reinforcement, the use of judicial vocabulary with *krinô/krisis*.

The striking parallelism between these two scenes goes still deeper, however. In Jn 8 there is reference to the murderous project of Jesus's opponents (Jn 8.40), fuelled by three factors: misunderstanding, a refusal to entertain the evidence which he provides and their siding with the devil (Jn 8.43*ff*). In the plot-line of Rev 11, the very same elements occur in relation to the witnesses: their words, just as unbearable as those of Jesus, torment their hearers (11.5-6,11) and drive the monster to kill them (11.7). Further, it could be said that Jesus's statement 'whoever keeps my word will never see death' (Jn 8.51), is dramatised by the congruent resurrection and ascension of the witnesses (11.11-12). Finally, Jesus escapes stoning – since the hour of his Passion has not yet come – and leaves the courts of the Temple, having so severely criticised its authorities (Jn 8.59). In Rev 11, however, the two witnesses – for whom the Crucified One is 'their Lord' (11.8) – do undergo a martyr's death, following their prophesying against the desecrated outer court, and their corpses are exposed in the city square of a now cursed Jerusalem. These parallels reinforce the observations already made in chapter 4: these twin characters[112] follow an itinerary which corresponds exactly to that of the one and only Jesus,[113] in the same way as their double – the monsters who travesty their tandem – engage in activities which assimilate them to the dragon.

These clarifications entitle us to revisit the conclusions already drawn from this passage in the course of the study of genuine testimony and its parody. It now emerges that the counterfeit testimony which so impresses earth-dwellers in Rev 13 constitutes nothing less than false witness given before the heavenly court. And as for the *pas de deux* danced, as we saw, by the two monsters, it amounts to the staging of a veritable anti-covenant which is by turns both *derisory* – since its false god is ridiculous and its idolatrous ersatz of worship no less so – and also *tragic*, given earth-dwellers' blind infatuation with this solution. Jerusalem, Holy City towards which the peoples were meant to stream in order to share in the blessings of the covenant, has become a synonym for spiritual fornication of the worst kind[114]: she kills the very last Witness sent to her (11.8). In so doing, she implicates in the spectacle both the nations (11.9) and the covenant people (11.10[115]), in a tawdry imitation of the universal blessing that this death will actually bestow, according to the Gospel.

At first sight, the sad fate of the witnesses would appear to evince some failure on the part of the God of the covenant, by analogy perhaps with the forsaking of the Crucified One in Mt 27.46/Mk 15.54. Ironically, just the opposite is the case: as happens in Ezek 37, a breath comes forth from their protector to resurrect and thereby vindicate those who have died (11.11). This means that the exposure of the corpses for three-and-a-half days (11.9), in open parody of the duration of their testimony (11.3),[116] is cancelled out by the action of God's Spirit. Such faithfulness to the covenant, in contrast to the condemnation God's enemies receive, provokes a terrified reaction in those who see it (11.11,13). I alluded earlier to the exegetical and theological debate over this 'fear', pitting those who interpret it in a positive way against those who defend a negative reading.[117] However, this argument misses the main point, which is that the day is fast approaching when truth will triumph over falsehood and faithfulness over apostasy. On that day, the prosecution of Jerusalem will have succeeded.[118] When the witnesses die, it is Messiah as Faithful Witness who concludes his testimony and gives himself as a sacrifice; and this is the precise moment when the city begins to fall (11.13).[119]

An overview of Revelation 11.15–14.20

Various scenes separate the conclusion of the second woe and the sounding of the last trumpet from the impressive entrance of the seven bowl-angels, and they have already figured prominently in earlier investigations. Now, however, the major theme of covenant will allow us to gather the data provided by this study so far and to read this entire section as the coherent whole that John meant it to be. This will involve charting four successive phases of development through which the text moves and in paying close attention to the way in which its various units interlock.

Revelation 11.15-18

This liturgical piece was examined in chapter 3. Welcoming as it does the coming of God the King, who delays no longer (11.16), it expresses the discriminating way in which the covenant Sovereign recompenses his faithful vassals (11.18), on the one hand, whilst on the other punishing by appropriate destruction 'those whom sin and idolatry have made into dead people',[120] namely the destroyers of the earth. The expression *destroying the earth* was apposite, as far as the rebellion of Babylon was concerned (Jer 51.25), and the nations were called to take up arms at the sound of the trumpet (Jer 25.27); it is equally appropriate that Revelation should allude to this at the very moment when the last trumpet rings out in acclamation of the one-and-only Sovereign of the universe (11.15), come to establish his reign. This calls to mind the faith that emerged in Israel in the midst of oppression by the wicked and when YHWH seemed slow to respond: 'the Lord is king forever and ever; the nations shall perish from his land' (Ps 9.37 LXX = Ps 10.16). Yet there is no more waiting here, as the Lord – 'the Is and the Was' (11.17) – is no longer the 'Coming One' but the very one who has now come, once and for all, in his Messiah. This is yet another indication, should we require it, that we are dealing with the eternal covenant whose entire design will be summarised in the next scene.[121] As spectators, we have been waiting since 10.7 to see the fulfilment of the prophetic gospel, the ultimate revelation of what God intends to do.

Revelation 11.19–12.18

Therefore, imminent fulfilment of the covenant is exactly what is signalled here.[122] The worship we have just witnessed has the effect of ushering both seer and readers once more into heaven and into God's Temple. Such a face-to-face encounter in the ultimate Holy of Holies is in fact quite unprecedented thus far, as is indicated by the fact that 'the ark of his covenant was seen within his temple' (11.19). Better than any other object, this covenant repository symbolises covenanted salvation, evoking the presence of the divine King among his subjects; as a sort of 'mini-temple within the Temple',[123] its vital importance is spelt out by Exod 25.10-22 or 1 Kgs 8.1-11. It had disappeared when Jerusalem was destroyed but, instead of being mourned, the Ark had become reconfigured within prophetic hopes and factored into the vision of a Jerusalem that would herself be YHWH's throne (Jer 3.16-17), as part of a covenant now extended indefinitely.[124] Such a sight of the heavenly Ark, whether from earth or in heaven, conveys nothing less than the unshakable establishment of the new covenant. The Ark symbolises a 'superlatively real, intimate, and perfect fellowship between God and His people',[125] and in fact there is confirmation in what follows that we are being given a glimpse, here, of the perfecting of the covenant that unites God and humanity. This comes first in the form of commonplace theophanic phenomena (in 11.19b),[126] to be followed by a second celestial sign – a huge one, this time – which becomes visible at the same time as the Ark (12.1), thus indicating a profound linkage between the two revelatory celestial manifestations, each of which (we are told) 'was seen'.[127]

Now is the time to make use of all the exegetical results we have already obtained concerning the plot and, more especially, the protagonists of 12.1-18. In this vitally important scene, the serpent-dragon and its angels take up arms, though in vain, against Michael and his angels. Their undoing is the paradoxical triumph of Messiah's death, a victory of redemption commemorated (as we have already seen) by the hymn in 12.10-12. The defrocked accuser, now thrown down (as is stressed repeatedly in 12.9-10,13), tries to avenge its failed attempt at stopping the messianic Son, concealing the fact that its name has been struck off the register; behaving as though it could still stand at the court bar,[128] it proceeds against the other offspring of the woman.

This story opposes the woman/mother and her son to their hellish adversary, in dramatic enactment – as I concluded earlier – of the adventure story of salvation, which began originally with antagonism in Eden and continued until the serpent was crushed[129] by the victory of Messiah, Eve/Zion's offspring whose 'birth' was in the end his death-resurrection-glorification (12.5). This great victory also extends to his 'brothers', who are themselves 'descendants' (12.10-11). We saw how the figure of the woman, a complex collective metaphor, thwarts all attempts to characterise her too narrowly: she symbolises the potential for humanity, redeemed from its fallenness in new creation,[130] to enjoy a right relationship with God.[131] If the whore and especially, false Israel,[132] debases through her idolatry the image of a humanity made for fellowship with God, then the bride – as new Israel and Church – ennobles it once more through the intimacy she enjoys as creature with Creator.

In chapter 12 'the notion of Covenant is refined and personified'[133] in the most spectacular of ways, by being draped in a beauty reminiscent of the beloved in Song of Songs (Song 6.10). It is to be extended and renewed, for nothing can stop the Mediator born under it or avert the consequences for human history of his work (12.5-6); especially significant, in this regard, is the further use made of Ps 2.8-9 (*cf.* Rev 2.26-27).[134] The final vindication of partners to the new covenant, a verdict promulgated by the warlike Messiah (19.11*ff*), rests squarely on double testimony to their innocence. Such evidence jointly comprises the blood of the ultimate expiatory sacrifice, offered by the slain Lamb, together with their own exemplary crucified life which, in him, is beyond reproach (12.11).

This justification underscores, in a positive way, what was expressed negatively by the erstwhile accuser's final exclusion from the court and, in consequence, by the dismissal of any proceedings or charges that might have been instigated (12.10c). It also dramatises, positively and negatively, what may be read elsewhere in the documents of the new covenant: how the faithful are represented by a Mediator, the one called 'an advocate with the Father, Jesus Christ the righteous' (1 Jn 2.1); and how, thanks to Messiah

Jesus, covenant partners have nothing to fear from any guilty verdict applied to them, since 'there is . . . now no condemnation'. Therefore, given that no further accusation is to be made, 'who is to condemn?' or indeed, 'who shall bring any charge against God's elect?' (Rom 8.31,33-34). Accordingly, this scene gives concrete shape to the clarion-call of the seventh trumpet and its accompanying voice (12.10a) or voices (11.15a): the satan is hurled down when the new covenant arrangements are put in place by Messiah's decisive death, variously interpreted as the definitive establishment of good (*sotêria*), an ultimate demonstration of power (*dunamis*) and the final consummation of the reign of 'our God', the covenant Lord (12.10b).

Next comes an account of the dragon's futile attack upon the woman who had successfully given birth to Messiah (12.13-18), followed by its change of tactic to wage war on the rest of her descendants (included, by association, in Messiah's one seed or *sperma*, 12.17). If we are to understand this narrative, we must read it against the backdrop of inaugurated new covenant. In this way, the secondary target for the dragon's wrath, which is the Lord's faithful vassals, is to be explained on the basis of their characterisation as 'those who keep the Commandments of God and hold the Testimony of Jesus' (12.17). The synonymous parallelism of 'commandment' and 'testimony' – occurring ten or so times during the psalm dedicated to the praise of the law (Ps 118 LXX) – is a way of describing the behaviour, as regulated by obedience to the commandments, which God expects from the partner who enjoys the advantages of his renewed covenant.[135] His servants the objects of attack because they extend the mediation achieved by Messiah Jesus, the Faithful Witness (1.5; 3.14). It is 'those who keep the Commandments of God and hold fast to the Faith/Faithfulness of Jesus', as a parallel expression in 14.12 puts it, who furnish their own proof – *pistis*, faith, can have this connotation[136] – that the covenant has indeed been definitively renewed and fulfilled.

The dragon's fury against the faithful even has the logic of an anti-covenant about it. The dragon pursues the woman as Pharaoh had Israel, long ago – sign enough that what we have here is an ultimate Exodus and a successful covenant. The river with which it hopes to engulf the people from whom Messiah had come is the exact counterpart of the waters that had dried up to let Israel pass during the Exodus! In addition, the failure of its stratagem is at the same time a reminder (*cf.* 12.11) that to share in the Testimony of the Crucified and Risen One is to join in his triumph. It is vitally important for readers, at this point, to discover this take on things; it comes just in time, as a pair of anti-messiahs are about to appear as incarnations of the woe foreseen for both the earth and the sea (*cf.* 12.12) out of which they come, and are about to bring to those whose loyalty they win nothing but the curses of a monstrous anti-covenant.

Revelation 13.1–14.5

When examining the way 13.1-18 and 14.1-5 shaped the major themes discussed previously , my aim was to study as carefully as possible the large number of intentionally parodic facets which characterise the two monsters, like the dragon whose extension they are. These very traits make them the perfect literary and theological antithesis of God, of the Lamb from his throne and of the seven spirits tied to his presence (1.4-5). We saw just how much 14.1-5 contributes to the composition of the Book as a whole, offering as it does a decisive retort to the episode in which the dragon and monsters appeared. We also explored the precise way that the characteristics of those who follow the dragon and its sidekicks mimic those of the Lamb's followers.

For the purposes of the trajectory pursued in the present chapter, it is time now to attempt to bring into play all the antithetical data already gathered for the section 13.1–14.5. Revelation's readers are meant to take a warning from the description of the two monsters, in exactly the way they were supposed to pay heed, from the start, to the messages of the first septet. This is made clear by the fact that the refrain heard from one oracle to another is reprised twice here, first at the close of the narrative about the first monster ('let anyone who has an ear listen', 13.9) and then, in a patently corresponding phrase, at the end of the description of the second one ('this calls for wisdom', 13.18[137]).

It would seem that as far as his recipients are concerned, the issue for John is always and only that of faithfulness to their calling. The repetition of other elements already encountered in the first septet confirms, for us, that their sense of responsibility is once again being addressed here: first, to live as 'saints' (13.7,10), whom Christ as Mediator unites with God, will involve for them *triumphing via an apparent failure* (13.7), as anticipated in the message to Smyrna (2.10), since it is by the *death* of the Messiah that the eternal covenant has been restored and extended to them (1.5-6, *etc.*); second, to square up to the power of the dragon and its acolytes (13.2,7,11, *etc.*) will entail, for believers, living where the satan is encamped – a fact mentioned by four oracles out of seven (2.9,13,24; 3.9); and third, to persevere in faith and faithfulness (13.10b) will mean living by the terms of the leitmotiv which is most constantly brought to mind throughout the series of words of congratulation or exhortation addressed to all the Churches (2.2-3,10,13,19,25; 3.2,8,10,15-16), as well as by the promises systematically made to 'overcomers'.

The victors there turn into the vanquished here (13.7), but we ought not to be unduly surprised by this, since we know it to be perfectly consonant with belonging faithfully to the slain Lamb (13.8b). Their defeat can only be a temporary affair because in 14.1-5 they will once more be found standing alongside the Lamb whom they follow, as associates of his resurrection and as partners of God himself.[138] Two things – their actions and their characteristic traits – distinguish them from the earth-dwellers whose servile worship of the first monster (13.8) and whose blindness (caused by the second monster, 13.14) set them up as an anti-covenant people. The dragon 'craves worship'[139] (13.4), doubtless out of envy for the act of reverence at the heart of the true covenant, which is offered up by the servants of the true God and his Christ.

Thus, the dragon's first lieutenant heaps abuse upon the fellowship enjoyed by God and by those who belong to him (13.6), with the aim of getting virtually the whole of humanity to fall into line behind its rival plan (13.7b-8a). And when the second monster manages to bewitch human beings in a parody of Elijah's miracles performed before an Israel in the thrall of Jezebel (13.13-14), this demonstrates its ambition to establish a counterfeit new covenant centred on the first monster, a false messiah with a healed sword-wound.[140] This exegesis warrants our adding a remark, on the subject of the monstrous number 666, to those already made. It means that the parodic value of this number marvellously expresses covenant rupture and its upshot, anti-covenant, and shows how perfectly it fits the compositional logic of 13.1-18 as a whole, as I have already sought to present it above.[141]

Revelation 14.6–20

After several previous examinations of 14.6-13 and 14.14-20, it was concluded that both these passages play a vital role from a literary point of view. They are anticipatory, first of all, in the sense that what the three angels or the unidentified voice say (14.6-13), or what the two harvests represent (14.14-20), are like buds which will flower later in the plot, laden as it is from the very start with so many contrasts. Or to change metaphors, just as the overture to a concerto states every leitmotiv for which the following movements will provide development, so chapter 14 sets out in programmatic fashion that which will provide the rest of Revelation with its structure. Yet these are also recapitulatory melodies which hark back to what was heard earlier. In particular, a retort is offered to the rebellion implicating the dragon, its sidekicks and their retainers that was so prominent in the narrative of chapters 12 and 13. This is done by means of a remarkable triple proclamation with universal scope (14.6); in it, a call is once more heard for the Lord of creation to be adored (14.7), the fall of rebellious 'Babylon' is simultaneously heralded (14.8) and the hour of tragic retribution and torment is sounded for the monster's allies (14.10), recognisable by the caricature of a mark that they bear and their idolatrous false worship.

The very skilful arrangement of the four messages found in 14.7-13 merits some consideration. What we find here are two declarations of impending judgment, with the second making the first explicit, within a framework provided by an invitation to share a relationship with God and by an antiphonal beatitude which looks forward to the closing dialogue with its two beatitudes (22.6ff). If we call the framework an envelope, it is franked (as it were) with a heavenly postmark – 'I saw another angel flying in mid-heaven' (14.6); 'I heard a voice from heaven' (14.13) –and proclaims the completion of an eternal gospel that will assure human beings who respond to the invitation of their happiness, justification and rest. Twice over, the same mailing confirms the corresponding sentencing of those who have preferred idolatry to a life lived for the glory of God and who must bear the consequences. Inherent in covenant obligations is the principle of *choice* (highlighted earlier), according to narrative logic clearly established from the Churches septet onwards, and this renewed balancing of curse and blessing – whether as a payback for revolt or a reward for submission – arises out of it.

Vitally important to the construction of this section is the transitional statement in 14.12. In much the same way that the repeated mention of the trappings of anti-covenant in 14.9,11 (prostration, monster, image and mark) recapitulates episodes devoted to the caricatures that are the monsters, 14.12 offers an inversely parallel definition: Revelation's view of the life that believers live under the renewed covenant. For this, 13.10b is drawn upon almost word for word and used to reinforce the emphasis already placed upon perseverance as part of the rhythm of the oracles to Churches in the first septet. In this way the faithful endurance that will insure hearers of their place alongside the Lamb (14.1,4) contrasts totally with persistence in idolatry, which can lead to judgment, and opens the way in advance for the repudiation of the unfaithful partner, 'Babylon', and for the corresponding betrothal of faithful New Jerusalem who will be her permanent replacement.

The same double logic of reward for the saints and punishment for the wicked governs 14.14-20, too. Whilst I have already pointed this out sufficiently, it remains the case that the very exegesis I am developing and defending here has met with insufficient acknowledgement from scholars, and that this (in my view) is the cause of seemingly unending pendulum swings in the specialist discussion of 14.6-20. I am arguing that the twin aspects of God's dealings towards humanity are attributable to the keeping or the breaking of his covenant – eventualities which, in turn, condition every theme developed in these chapters. Critics have hesitated between three interpretations of 14.6-20, whether favouring judgment, purely and simply,[142] an amalgam of judgment and salvation,[143] or again judgment that in the end transforms into universal salvation.[144] On the contrary, what governs this passage is the double logic of the gathering together or harvesting of the saved (a positive, salvific act) and the triage or grape harvest of the condemned (a corresponding, negative image). This is the application of a universal judgment undertaken by the Sovereign Lord in one of two ways, depending on whether his covenant has been honoured or, by contrast, flouted.[145]

Revelation 15.1–16.21

The seven bowls of plagues introduced for the first time in 15.1 constitute Rev's third variation on the model represented by the first septet. They are *eschatai* (last), and the simplest interpretation of this is to see them, in conformity with the sub-text in Lev 26, as the fourth and final series of seven judgments (Lev 26.28) provoked by stubborn covenant breaking, which brings God's wrath to its climax. Victorinus interpreted Rev 15–16 in just this way (15.1).[146] These plagues are to be thought of as ultimate and eschatological, exactly as those in Egypt were protological, or first. Wrath 'poured out' *(ekcheō*[147] + *thumos)* is a ready-made expression already found in the Septuagint, where it denotes the discharge of curses arising from God's judgment upon those who have broken his covenant or stood opposed to his people; Ezek 14.19; Jer 10.25 and Zeph 3.8 all use it this way, while Ezek 21 for example shows that on occasion *orgē* can replace *thumos*.

However, before delving deeper into the matter of the seven angels with their bowls of wrath, the narrative changes tack and depicts a worship setting where a new song to an old tune is struck up (in a manner of speaking). The theme of this hymn is God's royalty over all nations (15.3-4). The Song of Moses (Exod 15.1*ff*, *cf*. Deut 32) had tackled, in turn, God's faithfulness to his covenant in blessing his people; Israel's unfaithfulness and idolatry in the desert; the just punishments meted out by a faithful and jealous God to his unfaithful people, during the wilderness wanderings, in order to bring them back to him; and last of all, the mercy which God would show Israel in the end, while punishing their enemies. As it modulates,[148] here, into the song of the Lamb, the original song of the sea (Exod 15.1) implicitly passes on its content to a new context, where the conditions are those of the new covenant and of a deliverance far greater than that of Egypt. The righteousness and absolute faithfulness of the Almighty are revealed and from now on, his 'people' are drawn from all nations.

Whilst this is a new phase, it maintains continuity with those that preceded it. Accordingly, the scene in 15.5-8 offers a kind of condensed reference to various moments during the history of the covenant, under its old dispensation, using this distillation as a means of describing the new covenant:

a) The Tabernacle of Testimony (15.5; see Exod 38.21; Num 1.50,53; 9.15; 10.11) necessarily houses the covenant document – as may be seen from Exod 16.34; 25.16,21-22; 31.18; 32.15);

b) From Rev 1.2,9 onwards, readers become progressively aware that that this should now be assimilated to the Testimony of Messiah Jesus, in other words of the Lamb who emerges from the midst of the throne;

c) The seven angels-priests carry bowls filled with divine fury (15.6-7), however in 6.16 this very thing turned into the wrath of the Lamb, such that the blessings *and* curses of the covenant now come together in him;

d) The Temple where this scene is situated (15.5,8, twice) – a Holy Place to be found, now, in front of the throne of God and the Lamb (7.9-17) – is filled with the glory-cloud associated either with the dedication of the Tabernacle (Exod 40.34-35) and of Solomon's Temple (1 Kgs 5.12-14), or else with the imminent judgment it accompanies (as here), which in this case is about to strike unfaithful Israel/Jerusalem (Isa 6; Ezek 10).

Could it be any clearer that the bowls stand for judgments meted out in application of the covenant curses? The time for sanctions has come. Seven angels emerge from the Temple/Tabernacle of Testimony in heaven (15.5-

6); the documentary evidence[149] that proves covenant to have been broken gives them the right to pour out the bowls of divine wrath given to them in 15.7, whilst the seven plagues of 15.1,6,8 – referred to again, incidentally, in 21.9 – pick up on Lev 26.21.[150] The acquittal of the conquerors, which is their reason for celebration (15.2-4), finds a contrast and counterpart in what follows (16.1*ff*), as another verdict altogether is handed down to their persecutors, in keeping with the double logic of a covenant that people either adhere to or set aside.[151] The seven bowls containing a wrath which is the inverted parallel to that of the dragon's (12.12) 'represent the counterpart of the golden bowls filled with incense, which the living creatures and elders hold in their hands (5.8)'.[152] This is corroborated by the parallelism between the two expressions 'golden bowls full of incense' (5.8) and 'seven golden bowls full of fury', by which the judgments in the bowls of wrath are made to correspond to the prayers in the bowls of incense.[153]

Other elements that refer to an anti-covenant may usefully be listed here. There are the springs and rivers that turn to blood as the third bowl is poured out (16.4), whereas Christ's spilt blood redeems a people for God (5.9-10). There is blood drunk as a veritable anti-covenant ritual, echoing blood unjustly shed, since those who wear the monster's mark will have nothing to do with the Lamb's blood and must instead incur judgments, as their just deserts, that become a plague of blood (16.6).[154] There is the bowl which must be drunk by the monster's partisans (14.10) or indeed, by 'Babylon' (16.19), much as the wicked of the earth had to drain the bowl handed them by God the Judge (Ps 78.8-9): her bowl is connected both with the draught she had herself imposed on the nations (according to Jer 25.15) and with the anti-banquet during which the earth's kings will get drunk on saints' blood. Lastly, there is threefold blasphemy (16.9,11,21) and an obstinate refusal to repent – in ratification of the stubbornness of 9.20-21 – which together parody the acclamation of the Almighty (15.3) and the rhetorical questions asked, in 15.4, in expectancy (as in 14.7) of the universal glorification of the one holy Lord. Ironically, the story of the Exodus, when the heart of both Pharaoh and his people gradually became obdurate, is what provides the backdrop for this stubbornly rebellious behaviour.

Commentators on Revelation often draw attention to the fact that the woes introduced by the bowls are worse than those associated with the trumpets. Thus, the hail here is huge (16.21) and, as a general rule, whatever had a partial result previously (8.8-9) now has total effect (16.3). This escalation reproduces the worsening effect foreseen by the sub-text, Lev 26, as well as the actual historical experience of the Egyptian plagues. As happened in the case of the fourth trumpet, the fourth bowl strikes the sun and human beings are burnt, in obvious contrast to 7.16 where this is the very fate that the Lamb's faithful followers escape. Here is a contrast which underlines the difference between keeping covenant and breaking it, for one of the curses that typically falls on those guilty of covenant rupture is the fate of being

consumed by burning heat (Deut 32.34; *cf.* Exod 9.23); no wonder, then, that
'Babylon' will soon be burnt by fire (17.16; 18.8). The darkness separating
human beings from God's light (16.10) – a curse incurred by being found
guilty of covenant-breaking[155] – is a situation that is usually brought on by
idolatry (Jer 13.10,13) and by a refusal to receive the light that revelation
brings (Mic 3.5-6).

The drying-up of the Euphrates (16.12), allowing the kings of the Orient
to pass, conforms exactly to the prophetic expectation that Babylon should
undergo judgment (Isa 11.15; 44.27; Jer 50.38; 51.36). For Herodotus or
Xenophon, it is Cyrus who gained access to Babylon for his army, by altering
the course of the Euphrates. For the Old Testament, however, it is God alone
who dries up rivers; when he does so, it is with a view to achieving redemption
and judgment by the might of his arm, as when he intervened at the Red Sea
(Exod 14.21-22; Isa 11.15; 44.27; 50.2; 51.10). In addition, it is God who makes
an instrument of Cyrus, so that in Isaiah's way of thinking Cyrus becomes
YHWH's agent for striking Babylon and so for setting God's people free.

The frog-demons of 16.13 deceive and corrupt through the wonders
they perform (16.14). The deception in question involves divinities and idols
used, by the demons, for conning humans (*cf.* 1 Cor 8.14). In Egypt, frogs
symbolised, among other things, the goddess of resurrection; in so far as the
second monster sought to promote the fraudulent resurrection of the first,
the choice of frogs can hardly be fortuitous here. We need to remember
the Exodus plague of frogs – a sign of God's work in Egypt (*cf.* Ps 77.43-
45; Ps 104.27-30) – but even more so, the fact that Pharaoh's magicians
were able to imitate it (Exod 8.3); here, the frogs themselves have authority
to perform signs (16.14). Yet whatever their deceitful activities, these frogs
cannot elude the sovereignty of the Lord of the covenant. They *can* bring
about a final mustering for war (16.14), in anticipation of 19.19 and 20.8 and
more importantly, in reference to the prophecy of Zech 12–14. However,
supposed victory over the saints, which the nations are hoping for, changes
into the great Day of Judgment expected by Joel, when it is Messiah who
will win through (Rev 19.11-21).

Over against those whose aim is to thwart God's purposes by attempting
the extermination of the saints, stands the depiction of those who watchfully
keep their garments (16.15), and so give expression to the very quintessence
of covenant faithfulness. The idea of keeping watch is exactly what the
oracle to Sardis addressed (3.3), whilst their garb which keeps them from
knowing the shame of nudity (16.15; *cf.* Laodicea, 3.18) was an image used
by the prophets as a means of exposing idolatry of the most revolting sort
(Ezek 16.36-39;[156] 23.29; Nah 3.5; Isa 20.4): this, then, is why 'Babylon' will
be laid bare and stripped for her evil deeds (17.16). Believers, meanwhile,
will avoid this catastrophic fate because of their refusal to compromise.

As has been shown elsewhere, the final bowl in 16.17*ff* fuses together a
number of previous phases of Revelation's ongoing disclosure.[157] The bowls

reach their climax in a crescendo which also brings to a head the earlier judgments of the trumpets and seals. Now, everything has been accomplished (*gegonen*); this forms an *inclusio* with *etelesthē* in 15.1, and may even be a contrast to *tetelesthai* in Jn 19.30.[158] Absolute finality is accentuated by means of an unprecedented earthquake (16.18), in anticipation of consummate judgment in 21.6. This decisive manifestation of divine wrath brings to mind both the Sinai account (Exod 19.16-18), with its theophany and quake, and the storm theophany which Ezek 38.18-23 describes when recounting divine vengeance over Gog. This language is also reminiscent of Dn 12.1, which picks up on the terrible plague of hail in Exod 9.18,24. An earthquake like this one is expected to accompany the last judgment (Hag 2.6; Zech 14.4; *cf.* Ezek 38.19-22) as an event that entails the outpouring of the wrath of God the Judge (16.19). As was foreseen in 14.8,10 'Babylon' now falls, freeing up the 'site' she previously occupied so that God's city may now be erected upon it. Revelation's remaining chapters will hark back to her fall, recounting it in greater detail, and then go on to narrate the descent of her replacement.

Overview of Revelation 17.1–19.21

From the perspective afforded by the major themes studied in the two previous parts of this book, we have already explored the various materials in these three chapters in considerable depth. I will now attempt, in a series of stages, to merge the data from these thematic inventories and argue that covenant is the indispensable element that binds everything together throughout this whole section.

Revelation 16.19; 17.1-18

We have already considered the virtually anti-sacramental bowl of 16.19, a sort of anti-chalice for which the other bowl in 17.4b acts as a relay.[159] Now it is the whore who holds a golden bowl 'in a gesture which has the air of a demoniacal celebration of the memorial of his Passion'.[160] At both the beginning and end of the 'Babylon' diptych (chapter 17–18) it will be stated that she gets drunk 'with the blood of the saints and the blood of the witnesses to Jesus' (17.6) and that in her is to be found 'the blood of prophets and of saints, and of all who have been slaughtered on earth' (18.24); the two witnesses have already acted as core representatives of such victims. So it is a veritable anti-chalice that she drinks, full to the brim with abominations and therefore a flagrant contrast to the 'cup' accepted by Christ when he gave his blood (1.5; 5.9; 7.14). The crimes of idolatry (17.4, *porneia*) and murder (17.6) count as acts of rebellion against the covenant, as was the case when Ezekiel had long ago made accusations against Jerusalem (Ezek 16.36-38; 23.37,45). What we are dealing with here is quite clear: a caricature of God's people.

Let us now explore this anti-communion by considering the vision itself. In it, the great city is in the dress of a woman (17.18) and the place of 'Babylon' who had received a 'cup' (16.19) is now taken by the whore, who still holds one herself. The close association between this 'great whore' and various other actors in this scene is a textual phenomenon which specialist study has neglected; this is unfortunate, since it constitutes the key to understanding the action that takes place (confusing though that action may seem at first sight). Quite simply she is, in one way or another, a partner to all the other parties, be it the scarlet monster – her mount (17.3) and her associate (17.7*ff*) – or the 'many waters' of enslaved humanity (17.1,15), combined with the kings and earth-dwellers in general (17.2). This coalition is further reinforced by the twin reference to her as 'seated' both on peoples/multitudes/nations/languages (17.1, 17.15) and on heads/mountains/kings (17.9). Even the seer finds himself in a bond with her when, like the earth-dwellers bewitched by the monster's career (17.8), he cannot help but be captivated by the sight of her (17.6).

Revelation reserves for the woman-city, Babylon-the-whore, a magnificent parodic delineation, which we examined at the close of Part Two of the present book. As soon as we bring to bear, on this feminine-urban entity, the logic of a violated and re-established covenant it becomes clear that she is the anti-covenant personified. One way of describing the story Revelation tells is to present it as an account of how this now-deceased figure meets her end and how everything previously promised to her is to be legally transferred to New Jerusalem. As the transferee, New Jerusalem is established in her place as the partner to a renewed covenant which (in accordance with God's will) will now benefit all of humanity. The inspiration for this scenario of transformation may have come from Ezek 16, where the account of Israel's repeated whoring is followed by a coda (Ezek 16.59-63) in which YHWH's grand plan is recalled. Revelation's plot certainly seems to display the same logic at this point.

Babylon-the-whore has the principal part to play at the core of the group which constitutes the rebel forces, otherwise made up of the characters associated with her. Among these is the monster, whose characterisation as an explicit parody of God and the Lamb (17.8a-8b,11) has already been explored in considerable depth. The attempt to mimic divine almightiness is in vain, as is the effort to steal God's eternity; it is unsuccessful in even getting close to God, let alone being his equal. As for the vassal kings who hand over their royal prerogatives to the monster (17.17; *cf.* 17.13, which says the same thing with different words), their offer of submission to the woman-city (17.18) is a corrupted version of that royalty which only the unique Sovereign can bestow (1.5-6; 5.10). In return for their faithfulness the monster does not reward them with anything amounting to real *basileia* – kings though they may be – but instead, they are kinglets for just an hour (17.12), after which they fall victim to justice that benefits the true allies ('called, chosen and faithful') of the authentic Lord (17.14), whose counterparts they are. Lastly, the multitudes brought together by this alliance (17.15) are a caricature of the uncountable throng encountered in front of the throne and the Lamb (7.9).

This anti-confederation gathered round the woman, as an alliance of ten kings-with-no-kingdom (17.12), directly attacks the Lamb, the true Lord and King, with whom, alone, any royal status may be shared. It will be defeated (17.13-14), however, as will also happen to those mustered in 19.19 or again at the last stand of the anti-covenant forces in 20.8-9. The coalition will not survive since, as the angel explains, these disenchanted kings will simultaneously turn against the whore (17.16). As a result, this whole anti-tale amounts to nothing, with everything destined to fail. This is because their common desire to unite in opposition to the Lamb and his followers (17.13,17b) is an endeavour with no future, the accomplishment of which was placed in their hearts by God himself (17.17a).

Exegetes agree that the scenario before us is complex: in 17.6 the seer himself is amazed by what he sees and only fathoms the mystery once the interpreting angel explains it to him in detail (17.7-18)! While recent exegesis generally has resorted to a hermeneutic of correspondence, seeking to make allegedly opaque elements of this challenging text limpid through reconstructing their socio-historical background, our approach here (as elsewhere) is to assume the internal coherence of Revelation. How, therefore, are we to interpret so richly colourful a picture? It is possible to understand it, and to grasp how it influences the overall plot, through careful attention to the logic of the text. From this point of view, what we have here is quite simply *a ridiculous counterfeit of the covenant*. In light of the sovereignty of the true covenant God, the futility of this pact becomes clearly visible. No alliance forged in opposition to the Lord, to his will or to his people, can hope to evade his authority. The total failure that will result from the combined efforts of the monster, whore and kings proves that their association is as ephemeral an anti-covenant as it is a fruitless one. The 'lord' of this pseudo-pact is in reality unable to guarantee anything at all, bearing in mind the toppling already suffered in 9.1; 12.9, for example. As for the two false messiahs, reduced here to one, their comings and goings are a sham since they bring no benefit at all to their allies and will lead to nothing but perdition (17.8,11).

Revelation 18.1-24

What does the major theme of covenant contribute to the second part of the diptych, namely the scene in 18.1-24? This particular narrative is highly reminiscent of a courtroom scene, in the course of which guilt is to be determined in the case of the murder of the martyrs (18.24).[161] A parallel element links 18.20 back to 12.12, calling to mind a prior session of the covenant court in which the heavens already played their part by serving as witnesses:

> 'Rejoice then, you heavens and those who dwell in them . . . for the devil has come down to you with great wrath, because he knows that his time is short' (12.12).

'Rejoice over her, O heaven, you saints and apostles and prophets!
For God has given judgment for you against her' (18.20).

The guilt of 'Babylon' is nothing new for readers (*cf.* 14.8); what *is* new here
is the way in which the verdict is received with distress by some (18.9,15,18)
– whether sincerely or not –and with jubilation by others (18.20). This
means that 'fallen, fallen is Babylon the great' (18.2) is possessed of a doubly
ironic meaning: for those implicated in covenant breaking it is a disaster;
for others to whom it brings deliverance it constitutes a triumph. Those
who lament it are in fact deluding themselves, since it is their participation
in the misconduct of 'Babylon' (18.3) which brings judgment upon them.
Jerusalem,[162] by prostituting herself and breaking covenant, failed in her
duty towards the nations; however, when 'Babylon' is sentenced and justice
done, the saints, apostles and prophets present in court see their case won at
last and are able to rejoice at this outcome (18.20).[163]

Another new detail, here, is the fact that 'Babylon' is indicted for accumulated
sins 'heaped high as heaven'. This proves that 'Babylon' shares the characteristics
of Babel of old, which had risen in opposition to God (18.5). The patience
of the covenant God had been inexhaustible, but now it must yield to the
demands of his justice and faithfulness, as the powerful Lord and Judge gives his
judgment (18.8): 'Babylon' is cursed for failing in her obligations and for having
amassed her sins to their fullest extent; with such unfaithfulness, she has shrunk
to no more than the merest parody of Jerusalem. The curses which strike her[164]
are spoken in a series of utterances phrased as imperatives (render! repay! mix!
give! 18.6-7), endorsed by a commentary consisting of two verbs in the future
(will come; will be burned with fire, 18.8), which make these things certain. The
conviction that Babylon would be paid back for her misdeeds had in fact been
current since Jeremiah (Jer 50.15,29), whilst her just deserts find expression in
the very words of rejoicing framed by the exiles in Babylon itself (Ps 137.8).

Further details in the text substantiate our reading of it as a covenant
lawsuit.[165] The oracle against 'Babylon' brings to mind those of Isa 13.21
and Isa 47.7; her pride and presumption, which appear in the second of
these texts, are highlighted again here (Rev 18.7). Yet accentuation of the
angel's splendour (18.1) seems also to recall YHWH's coming to destroy
Jerusalem, suggesting that John also has Ezek 43.2 in mind. As for 'dwelling
place' (18.2) – a word used only here in the whole of the apostolic tradition,
although it occurs frequently in the Septuagint – the allusion is doubtless
both to the heavenly place where God has his home (*cf.* 1 Kgs 8.39,43,49;
2 Chr 30.27; Ps 32.14) and also to the place where God comes to live with
his covenant people, namely, his sanctuary (Ps 76.3).[166] Its transformation
into a haunt of demons echoes the prophecies of desolation spoken over
Jerusalem (Jer 9.11; *cf.* 21.13): detestable impurity, underlined by repetition
of the adjective 'foul', is in flat contrast to the purity of New Jerusalem
(21.27) and, as such, testifies to the abandonment of covenant.

It is against this backdrop that the call in 18.4 ('come out of her, my people') becomes fully intelligible. The context confirms that the term of address 'my people', applies to the covenant people, in a similar way to Hos 2.23. The 'coming out' referred to here could refer to the setting in motion of a covenant accompanying its establishment (Exod 4.22-23) or to its reactivation after judgment had fallen (Jer 51.44-45). In describing how the whore's sins are piled up to heaven, a borrowing is made from Deuteronomy. In this book, the faithfulness of the partner to her divine spouse (Deut 6.13; 10.20) is denoted by the term *kollaô*, meaning intimately to cleave to or have union with; but the same word also serves for the rebelliousness of spiritual fornication (Deut 28.60; 29.19), where anyone can see how covenant curses 'cleave', or stick, to the disobedient people. God's judgments against Egypt, as well as his project to deliver Israel, are set off by recollection of the people's sufferings in Egypt (Exod 2.24): here in Revelation, God's justice is brought to bear by a reminder of the sins of 'Babylon' (18.5).

It is my considered opinion that the account of the fate of 'Babylon' in our text is an elaboration of the sketch already offered by 17.16, where we saw a whore stripped, eaten and burned. It is a picture designed to shock, resembling Old Testament denunciations in which the prophets fulminated against the Jerusalem of their day for her immorality, injustice and apostasy. Her destruction has been on the cards for a long time, just as her future restoration has long been expected. What the scene presents would appear to be the public sentencing and execution, for adultery, of the woman-city 'Babylon' – by analogy with proceedings against the adulterous daughter of a priest (Lev 21.9) – as viewed, in turn, from the standpoint of each of the three groups who mourn her fate. Everything begins as a deadly draught is poured out (18.6):[167] a double draught since this is what is reserved for the human partner to the covenant (Isa 40.2; 61.7; Jer 16.18; 17.18; Zech 9.12). The action leads on to the economic dispossession of the whore-city, in retribution for her idolatry (18.11*ff*). Before letting the three laments be heard, the narrative uses two stylistic devices to hammer out the verdict of judgment by burning, namely repetition specially reinforced by alliteration of the Greek letter K: *katakauthêsetai . . . kurios ho theos ho krinas autên kai klausousin kai kopsontai ep' autên . . . ton kapnon* (18.8-9). With the angel's prophetic gesture foreshadowing a sentence still expressed as future (18.21), all is said and done and the final repudiation[168] of the partner for adultery is now complete: in consequence, the voice of no bride or groom will ever again be heard in the faithless city (18.23).

When 'Babylon' falls, her trade ceases, as evident from the list of cargoes for which no buyer is to be found (18.11-13). This description did not figure in the course of any of my previous discussions of chapter 18, so it is now time to give it the attention it deserves whilst factoring in the results obtained previously. At the head of the list, we find five items of cloth or precious materials which feature in the description both of the whore's dress in 17.4 and of the identical attire, comprising clothing and jewellery, of the great city of 18.16. As we have already seen, three of these – gold, precious stones and pearls (21.18-21) – are powerful items of caricature. The list before us provides an expansion on the characteristics of the woman-city to which we have already devoted much space.

The text of Ezek 27.2-24 furnishes the principal sub-text for the list of cargoes in Rev 18.12-13. When we compare the antecedent and its derivation, what emerges is that Revelation has reproduced the list of goods that feature in Ezekiel's oracle against Tyre, but with considerable modification. The changes would appear to make the listed articles correspond even more closely to those which typify the Temple trade,[169] including horses, chariots and slaves (18.13) that might also betray a reference to 1 Kings. The numerous horses owned by Solomon for his chariots (1 Kgs 4.26,28) were a flagrant breach of the ban found in Deut 17.16. Of course Solomon also wins the prize for being the first person, since the Exodus deliverance, to reduce the covenant people once more to slavery. Moreover, it is important to note that all this comes in a passage where the materials being transported to Jerusalem for the construction of the Temple were supplied by the king of Tyre himself.[170]

Once we incorporate into our reading of Rev 18, data relating to the major theme of covenant, we significantly heighten the plausibility of an exegesis which goes against the scholarly tide by interpreting the commercial activity referred to (in the description contained in Rev 18.12-13) as relating, not to Rome, but to Jerusalem and specifically to her Temple. We do in fact know that Jerusalem had, for a very long time, been carrying on extensive foreign trade with Athens, Sidon, Tyre, Cyprus, Babylonia, Persia, Arabia, Egypt and India, bringing wealth to large numbers of merchants. Most of this trade, whose abundance ought not to be underestimated, directly involved the Temple and the activities of the high priests.[171] In the description of the Temple (as well as of the treasures housed in it) provided by Flavius Josephus in his *Jewish War*, there is mention among other things of the gold with which it was clad, the scarlet and purple stored inside (for purposes of repair and maintenance of its gigantic curtain), together with fine linen, rare types of wood and huge quantities of spices.[172] In his vision, Revelation's seer discovers that none of this activity generated by the great centre of covenant life survives once she is declared unfit for purpose.

One final element which supports my reading of Rev 18.11-13 is negative in nature: not only will New Jerusalem not have a temple (21.22), she will not have any involvement in *trade*, since the world's great and good will simply bring all their glory to her (21.24,26). Explanation for this comes from the new covenant dispensation: no incense, cereals or animals are needed any more (18.13), now that the sacrifices have ceased; above all, there is no more slavery (18.13) for, as Paul says, if the present Jerusalem is still in this state, along with her children, 'the Jerusalem above is free' (Gal 4.25-26).

Historical detour 8:
Is an economic critique of Rome plausible?

I have already made clear how a minority, only, adopt an exegetical approach to
Rev 18.12-13 which involves reading the cargoes for merchants and associates of
'Babylon' in reference to biblical Jerusalem. A majority of interpreters detect, in
this list, an economic critique of first- century imperial Rome, as in the approach
to this text presented with some verve by Richard Bauckham.[173] For this exegete,
since Rome is the whore[174] – economically speaking, in his construal of the
metaphor – the cargoes listed in Rev 18 must logically form part of a critique of
her trade,[175] by analogy with a similarly critical attitude that may be identified in
the *Sibylline Oracles* and in other contemporary sources linked to Asia Minor.[176]
Recent commentators on Revelation tend to think he is right.[177]

Without revisiting the question of whether 'Babylon' in Revelation may
properly be assimilated to first-century Rome, all that is required for me to call
into question Bauckham's supposedly self-evident interpretation is to point
out that it is at least as plausible to take the historical reference lying behind
18.12-13 as the trade of the Temple and bazaars of Jerusalem.[178] Nevertheless,
recourse to reconstructed history beyond the text, using a hermeneutic of
correspondence, is once again the problem here, for 'it is surely typology,
not history that is the key to understanding the picture of the great city in
Revelation'.[179] This protest explains and, to my mind, justifies my own attempt
to shed light on this text by positing its coherence with the rest of the book
or exploring the explicit inter-textual links that bind this passage to the Jewish
Scriptures and, in particular, to its antecedent Ezek 27.2-24.

Back to the text: Revelation 18.21-24

This third narrative episode involving a powerful angel (18.21) implicitly
draws attention,[180] yet again, to the same issue as was highlighted by the
two previous interventions, *i.e.* the availability of a great covenant document
(5.2*ff*) to which another smaller one, associated with it, adds its contribution
(10.1*ff*). From now on, the contents of these two scrolls are revealed and
thus have been fulfilled.[181] Played out in turn by the first septet and then,
in escalating fashion, by the seals, trumpets and bowls, the series of four
parallel judgments borrowed from Leviticus now comes to an end with
the mediation and ratification of a new dispensation of the covenant. This
one has been concluded between the slain-but-standing Lamb and a people
themselves made up of those put to death on the earth (18.24) – a detail
from 6.9 picked up again here – who now find themselves to be vindicated.
YHWH is about to avenge innocent blood.

Revelation 19.1-8

We noted at the beginning of the previous section how 19.2 makes clearer
the somewhat less transparent thought of 18.20b. In fact, this account of the
judgment handed down by the heavenly court summarises no less than the

punishment incurred, according to covenantal logic, by the rebellious people, here assimilated to a great whore. Punishment befalls them, as expected (Deut 32.43), because they plunged into darkness the nations for whom they ought to provide light. At the same time, this punishment effects the justification and the compensation of the faithful vassals adversely affected by their treason. A vengeance called for from 6.10, by God's partners, has been carried out in the interim and may now, as a result, be duly celebrated (18.20; 19.2): the avenging of the blood with which 'Babylon' is stained (18.24) very closely reflects the vengeful words expressed in 2 Kgs 9.7 in condemnation of Jezebel, at the moment when a new vassal-king, Jehu, is anointed to replace the apostate Ahab. The final clause of Rev 19.2 – 'he has avenged on her the blood of his servants (or vassals)' – sums up, as it were, what is related by the Septuagint of 2 Kgs 9.7: 'from the hand of Jezebel you will require the blood of my servants the prophets and the blood of all the Lord's servants.' We should not forget how for Rev 2.20, Jezebel is a false prophetess.[182]

The act of worshipful acclamation accompanying, at this point, the promulgation of this verdict and the subsequent establishment of a now perfect and unshakable relationship to God, was examined in chapter 3 of this book. I drew three conclusions, at the time; to these it is now appropriate to add four more:

a)   As Revelation's seventh liturgical moment, this piece of adoration sets its crown upon the fulfilment of the Sovereign's promises, making the whore disappear forever and having the one whom she could only parody appear in her place.

b)   The negative aspect of judicial retribution fades with the approach of the wedding (19.7), a nuptial feast that corresponds to the hope and promise, never fulfilled under the old covenant, of a relationship of purity between God and his people.

c)   Accordingly, all attention falls on 'the righteous deeds of the saints' (19.8; *cf.* Lk 1.6; Rom 2.26): the behaviour of exonerated believers, here, renders explicit what is meant by the bride's state of readiness (19.7), since these are deeds characteristic of the God who is righteous, deeds consequently practised by those who are his faithful covenant partners.[183]

d)   Lastly, such deeds testify that their doers have a right to a legitimate place at the Lamb's feast, a place which – as the perfect *keklēmenoi* indicates – is definitively theirs.

Revelation 19.9,17-18

I will not repeat here what I have said already about inversely symmetrical banquets, with the macabre gore of 19.17 parodying the nuptial meal of 19.9. However, at the present juncture it is important that we clarify three supplementary matters.

The first thing to be said is that a feast attended only by birds already symbolised a mockery of a covenant meal in Jer 34.17-20. In accordance with the stipulations of Deut 28.25-26, corrupt covenant partners were cursed with being left unburied and exposed as prey for carrion-eaters. Thus it would seem quite logical to interpret an invitation to these birds to come and feed as symbolising broken covenant (cf. Ezek 39.17-20 and Gen 15.11); and as for the blatant accentuation of the consumption of flesh – no fewer than five times, in 19.18 – it would seem legitimate for us to call this a meal of anti-communion.[184]

The second involves noting how important the contribution made is to the narrative progression, as the denouement looms, by the supper of the Lamb that opens onto life and by this last meal which God has laid on for those sentenced to death. In combination, these two create a double metaphor covering *two* contrasting eschatological rendezvous. The first, an eschatological banquet presided over by God (cf. Isa 25.6-7; 65.13-17), brings us to the very threshold of total fulfilment, for believers, of the covenant promises. And the second, which is its polar opposite, marks the corresponding point at which the infidelity of those who have risen up against him comes to an end.[185] Taken together, the covenant meal where the bridegroom expects to sit down with his faithful betrothed, and its inverted parallel the feast of rebellion in which the repudiated adulterous woman has a share, unite to provide antithetical confirmation for readers that all is now ready and that vindication and vengeance are both about to take place (cf. 6.10-11).

The final thing is to draw out what was implicit in my previous remarks about the two contrasting meals. In Ezek 39.17-20, a contrast is already to be found between salvation for Israel and judgment for Gog and Magog. Here in Revelation, similar contrastive language is being used to describe a first eschatological meal – an everlasting wedding feast where the bride joins the Lamb – and a feast of abolition, with scavengers as participants, which will see to it that nothing remains of the whore and her sins. The first represents the ultimate covenant meal, whose delightfulness has been anticipated from the climax of the first septet onwards in 3.20 (if not right from the mention of heavenly manna in 2.17). The second is a stomach-churning, anti-eucharistic table which may be harking back to the foiled attempt to devour Christ in 12.4 or the draught of blood in 16.6,[186] and is a meal where those who eat become the eaten and where the stoop of the waiting birds (19.17,21), already glimpsed in 18.2,[187] re-uses an old metaphor for judgment linked to the covenant (as we saw earlier cf. Gen 15.11). Perhaps the inspiration for these twin scenes goes back to the teaching of Jesus himself, since Jesus had not only renewed expectation of an eschatological banquet (especially in Lk 14.15*ff*) but, in the context of God coming to reign, had also alluded to birds of prey gathering around a corpse (Mt 24.28/Lk 17.37).

Revelation 19.9-16

Having studied the wedding feast and the banquet of death, we are now in a position to return to the scenario in 19.11-16, already explored from the standpoint of both Part One and Two. My reading of this scene has already led me to view it as a decisive war waged by the messianic Word, whose result is total victory. As we look at it again from the perspective of the major theme of covenant, the two series of previous remarks can be brought together and combined with the following additional ones:

a) Messiah's appearance, here, is prepared for by the fourth and central beatitude (19.9), which almost amounts to a mini-covenant in its own right by blessing participants assured of their place (*keklêmenoi*, yet again) at the messianic banquet.

b) Solemn attestation that there is no overturning this benediction, whose words are those of God himself, makes this a statement with full juridical force or, more precisely (in this instance), a covenant stipulation.

c) John's inappropriate prostration (19.10a), although negative, nonetheless betrays the fact that a *true* encounter with the divine Word takes place here, through the agency of the serving angel: any doubt about this is dispelled when heaven opens (19.11).

d) Lastly, the framing of the command to worship God alone by two mentions of the *marturia Iêsou* has the effect of underlining the decisive quality of the words of Jesus the Witness, as evidence crowns that which was already marshalled in the successive cases mounted by the prophets under the old covenant dispensation (19.10b,c,d).

It follows from all this that the warlike rider described in 19.11 – 'Faithful and True, and in righteousness he judges and makes war' – can be none other than this Witness, Messiah Jesus. In 1.5, the work of the Messiah-Witness, as Mediator of a new covenant, is acclaimed in respect of the blood he has shed to obtain forgiveness of sins. The covenant which God offers to Israel and, by extension, the nations, has as its backdrop the problem of a relationship obviated by human sin but now restored through Messiah's work. In its own way, the scenario in 19.11-16 narrates a covenant enactment which features the very same elements. As Faithful Witness (*cf.* 1.5) he is 'Word of God', his words authenticated by his shed blood that sealed the new covenant (19.13), which makes him in judicial terms nothing short of 'God's legate'.[188]

At this point spectators see a penultimate opening of heaven. Through a series of such openings, which began in 4.1, we have already been granted access to the heavenly Temple (11.19) and to the Tent of Testimony (15.5) and something similar will happen one last time in 20.11*ff.* Having such access to heaven means being present in the heavenly court, in person, for its deliberations. The present scene brings to an end the revelation of the curses – not forgetting a few blessings! – which was sparked off by the opening of the seals, before being extended and deepened when the trumpets sounded or the bowls were poured out.

Now the sword falls. By a form of narrative suspense, this is what we have been waiting for since the opening vision of the Risen One (1.16) or since further mention of a sword in the course of the oracles both to Pergamum (2.12,16) and, implicitly at least, to Thyatira (2.23). Now final condemnation strikes, for 'Babylon' is no more and the judgment in question is about to befall the monsters and the dragon itself.[189] Final justification is also declared at this point, because this judgment – which cannot be appealed – will make sure that, during the course of the vision of the renewal of all things (21.1*ff*), everything which had been anticipated in the new covenant song of 5.9-10 will indeed find its fulfilment. Later, I will examine the eschatological realisation of the covenant rendered possible by the verdict delivered at this final great Assize.

Revelation 20.1-10

I have already put forward a number of exegetical strategies for dealing with this challenging chapter and it seems to me that the major theme of covenant, whether defaulted on or adhered to, now brings further clarification. The one that is bound for a thousand years and identified by the use of various anti-titles (20.2) is the cursed serpent of Gen 3, linked inescapably –from humanity's beginnings onwards – to both the Fall and the curse. Although the curse weighs heavily on all of sinful humanity, the Crucified and Risen One through his sacrifice has annulled it, so fulfilling the proto-evangel of Gen 3.15; proof of this outcome will materialise as restored access to the tree of life. In symmetrical fashion this part of Revelation recapitulates the action of chapter 12, where Messiah had conquered the dragon; he now finishes off this already thrown-down and defeated adversary, sending it irrevocably to the abyss and then to the lake of fire.

Further judgment is narrated here (20.4) with an account of how the work of Christ destroys evil at its root, crushing all resistance and any anti-covenant: the monsters are no more (19.20) and all that remains, for a while longer at least (until 20.10 settles things), is the old original enemy. The binding of the accursed dragon and the reign of the blessed, the Lamb's faithful ones, are equivalent since the latter's exaltation and the former's put down are both punctuated by the same refrain: 'for a thousand years.'

How are we to understand *krima* (20.4)? It has been taken to mean the fulfilment of the destiny of any faithful Christian who is called to become a judge: this would make the faithful martyrs who 'came to life and reigned' the same as those who sat on thrones.[190] In my view however, the term is a legal one here and means *a favourable verdict*, in other words, a verdict of acquittal or justification.[191] What then, exactly, would be the justice meted out here? It involves the complete implementation of the promises made by a faithful God, in line with his servants' hope. Death is, for human beings, the last enemy (and not the satan, 20.14!) since, from start to finish, it has been the curse of their fallen condition; but now, under the arrangements of the renewed covenant (20.4,6), death must disappear and be replaced by eternal life shared with the Risen One. Having renewed access, in this way, to the tree of life, presupposes the quashing of the original sentence of death brought about, in Eden, by primal disobedience and the rupturing of relations between Creator and creature which was its outcome. Thus, the narrative of this early rupture, at the start of Genesis, finds its answering call in the account of final restoration provided at the denouement of Revelation. I will come back to this later.

Revelation 20.11-15

Bearing these points in mind, we see that the scene now played out before the great white throne exhibits a similarly universal character. A number of details combine to make this a depiction of what is to all intents and purposes an ultimate covenant audit. Here are the relevant data:

a) The flight of earth and heaven (20.11), in other words of the original creation, makes the word of judgment, here, at least as weighty as another one spoken at the dawn of human history, when all things were created; their disappearance marks the end of the old covenant dispensation, which they traditionally witnessed, and allows for their re-creation once the moment for instituting the new covenant has come (21.1).

b) *All* the undifferentiated dead are present, the great with the small (20.12), as an expression found already in 11.18 is used again (though, as we might expect, with its two parts inverted) and all stand upright, presumably to hear the verdict concerning them as and when it is given.

c) The phrase 'books were opened' (20.12) picks up on the problem of the book needing to be opened (5.1*ff*), then opened (6.1–8.1), and also on the little open book (10.2,8-10). The clause 'another book was opened, the book of life' harks back to the declaration made to the Church at Sardis (3.5) and to the two reminders (in 13.8 and 17.8) that this is the book which confirms one's participation in the covenant. By its repetition here (20.12,15) – before its last appearance in the finale (21.27) – a tight bond is created between the punitive aspect of this judgment scene and its positive corollary, the redemptive work of the Lamb 'slain from before the foundation of the world.' It is his redemption of faithful covenant partners that gives this book both its title and its contents.

d) In this way, a double covenant trajectory is maintained from start to finish, with curses leading to a guilty verdict and blessings producing an acquittal.[192] Exactly as justification and punitive action were carefully set against one another in 11.18, so here two inversely parallel things are recounted:

    i) First, in accordance with the expectation voiced in 6.10, there is final punishment (20.15) for those whose acts provide proof (20.12-13) that they are not numbered among the faithful; this is traditional (Ps 28.4) and was foreseen as early as the oracle to Thyatira (2.23).

ii) Second, there is description of everything concerning the promised reward for those elected to salvation (21.1*ff*) which, while it is already implicit in 20.11-15, will be made explicit in 21.27 (*cf.* 3.5).[193]

e) With 'the dead were judged according to their works', the responsibility of everyone who appears for this judgment of individuals (20.13) lines up with the one which was choroused from the start throughout the opening septet, 'I know your works' (2.2, *etc.*); since human beings bear God's image, every child of Adam is responsible and therefore, accountable.

f) The death of death (20.14), as a new order is instituted, reminds us of the Mediator's own death as 'First-Born from among the dead' (1.5), a death that sounded death's death-knell and wrought the victory long-awaited by the prophets (Isa 25.8; Hos 13.14). This recalls the eschatological abolition of death, as referred to in 1 Cor 15.26 or in 2 Tim 1.10's anticipation of the same event, since by his 'epiphany' Messiah Jesus had already been established as the One 'who abolished death and brought life and immortality to light'.

Perhaps the arrival which causes earth and heaven to flee *is* Messiah Jesus's death.[194] Whether or not this is the case, 20.15 is certainly a key moment. Whilst other sessions of the heavenly court have been recounted earlier, this scene elevates to its highest point a curve, tracing the developing state of relations between God and his people, which has been rising from the inaugural septet onwards. As confirmed by the data already collated, what we have here is essentially the court in final session, engaged in examining the state of the relationship between humanity and their God.[195] Up to this point, forces have been set in opposition to God, the Lamb and those who belong to them; now that these have all been destroyed, the parenthesis is finally closed on an anti-covenant which sought to parody any and every aspect of God's project. Nothing can now caricature the advent of a perfected covenant and so a natural transition to a new heaven and new earth comes about.[196] Nothing can get in the way of that which is painted by the final picture, namely, the accomplishment of a perfect *shalom* which brings God and humanity together forever.

Revelation 21.1–22.20

It is time to augment the results from my previous discussions of this finale with detailed consideration of the conditioning[197] it receives from the major theme of a now perfected covenant. What this new state of affairs means is the banishment, forever, of all estrangement from the relations between God and his people. At this point, it could justly be said that parody is now itself to be parodied!

Revelation 21.1-8

'I am making all things new' says God (21.5) and so it is no surprise to find that, from 21.1 onwards, it is *newness* which characterises the consummation of God's reign and the complete realisation of the covenant.[198] Several brief comments about this newness are in order here. The first is that it is newness in the sense of *Easter*,[199] because the renewal of the everlasting covenant is effected through Messiah Jesus's work as the Redeemer slain before the foundation of the world (13.8). In Pauline perspective, as well, the cross of the Risen One is where God's plan to reconcile all things on earth and in heaven to himself was accomplished (Col 1.20). The second remark is that the newness of the renewed heavens and earth (21.1*ff*) is distilled down, as it were, into a one-of-a-kind city where the heavenly and the earthly are fused together and where it no longer makes sense to distinguish God's transcendence from his immanence.[200] Here, newness is very close in meaning to eternity and at this point, as at many others, Revelation's perspective is like that of Isaiah: speaking to his people Jacob/Israel, or Zion – first among all of earth's nations (Deut 28.1) – the God of the covenant who founded the earth and stretched out the heavens from the very beginning (Isa 48.12-13; 51.16) points to a future time when new heavens and a new earth would be perfected (Isa 65.17) and New Jerusalem created (Isa 65.18). This is the characteristic language used, in the Jewish Scriptures, for describing God's plan to bring about the salvation of his people.[201]

Therefore, at the heart of this definitive newness, new creation and new covenant coincide: the very first aspect of the new heaven and new earth (21.1) is new covenant.[202] In the Church which is drawn from all peoples and has now been made perfect, it is not only Israel but also the nations who have God's ancient promises as their inheritance. The particular and the universal come together[203] in the new era inaugurated by the sacrifice of Jesus as Mediator of the new covenant. The life of the new people of God drawn from Israel and the nations is lived, Sunday by Sunday, to the rhythm of the hearing of his Word and of communion in the body of his Son; this life will be made perfect at his final return. Meanwhile, worship is the context in which this outcome is reflected, as is clear enough from Revelation's worship framework, permeated as it is by the mechanisms of covenant. As the Word is heard on the Lord's Day an audit takes place, in which accents both of grace and judgment become audible. Through their worship, believers give contemporary shape to the faithfulness of their God in time past and also to his people's constancy in response to this. Assuming they repent and start over, they may look forward to a blessed future, a future celebrated by anticipation in the present time through a liturgical 'today'.[204]

The God of the renewed covenant, in this vision, has been called 'absolute Newness, with whom total communion is established'.[205] Indeed, by coming to dwell with redeemed humanity from now on (21.3), God brings to completion the plan which all prior revelation had been anticipating. As an idea, final perfection is yet another link back to the long prophetic tradition. It seems clear that John is recalling his predecessor Ezekiel who had chosen for a climax to his own vision the city which God and his people would share, bearing the name *Adonai-Shamma*, YHWH is there (Ezek 48.35).[206] Thus, the end-time city is entirely Tabernacle, entirely temple, perfectly realising all the potential for creating harmonious covenant which both of these had possessed (for example, Lev 26.11-12; Ezek 37.26-28). Made by God's own hand and given truly as his gift, she corresponds to everything that the covenant people had been longing for (*cf.* Gal 4.22-31; Eph 2.19; Phil 3.20; Heb 11.10,16; 12.22-23).

The counterpart for this organic linkage between creation and covenant is found in the relationship between anti-covenant and dis-creation, reflected in Revelation much as in the Jewish Scriptures. In a sequence of prophetic words where Jeremiah (in Jer 4) acts as spokesperson for the Lord before the covenant people Israel-Judah-Jerusalem and their leaders, the prophet hears the daughter of Zion's lament. He looks and sees a woman-city (Jer 4.29-31), dressed like the whore-city of Revelation: as a city she lies devastated, abandoned and deserted; as a woman she is spurned and killed by her lovers. Yet Jeremiah also sees, simultaneously, the earth laid to waste and in mourning, empty and formless as at the dawn of creation (Gen 1.2; *cf.* Isa 34.11) and the heavens enshrouded in darkness (Jer 4.23-28). It is easy to see how the end suffered by Babylon-the-whore in Revelation is modelled on these antecedents: the mother of all earthquakes accompanies her fall (16.18*ff*) as she is stripped and liquidated by her former allies (17.16) and turned into a wilderness in the space of one hour (18.19). After the repeated ravages of the seals, trumpets and bowls which have been tearing earth, sea, sun, moon and stars apart (6.12-14, *etc.*), this disaster crowns everything. 2 Pet 3.10-13 would appear to make an analogous correlation between the old covenant, for which renewal is anticipated, and the establishment of a new heaven and earth in a transformation preceded by the break-up of the 'elements' (*cf.* Gal 4.3,9; Col 2.8,20; Heb 5.12).[207]

As full and final reconciliation is achieved, there comes a solemn statement (21.3) which takes over a refrain from the Jewish Scriptures relating to the reciprocal nature of covenant. One thinks especially of Ezek 37.23,27 and 36.28, but also of the establishing of the covenant (Exod 19.5; 20.1) and of other prophetic re-runs of this same event (Jer 31.33; Ezek 36.28; Hos 1.6- 8; 2.24-25). To what is mentioned in 21.3 is then added a similar promise, in the future tense, which is declared to be the full and legally assured inheritance of readers who, by inheriting 'all things' (21.7), are deemed 'conquerors'.

These final promises have immense significance, for several reasons. First, because they make renewed use of a key aspect of the promises made to Abraham or again, to David: the concept of a covenant heir, whose use here brings to a climax the whole trajectory of covenant fulfilment running through Revelation.[208] Second, and more significant still, is the fact that just when Revelation seems steeped in the Old Testament to saturation point, almost quoting it formally, the author is yet again availing of the fundamental text Lev 26[209] (among others) and specifically that part of it which concerns the covenant blessings. From the start readers have grown accustomed to a narrative procedure whereby prior revelation is constantly alluded to; here, the connections with Lev 26 are relatively direct ones: following a promise to uphold the covenant –'I will establish my covenant with you' (Lev 26.9, LXX) – there comes a passage which may helpfully be set in parallel with Rev 21.3,7:

'I will make my home among you and my soul will not be averse to you; and I will walk among you and I will be your God and you will be my people. I am YHWH your God'.   (Lev 26.11-13a)[210]

'See, the home of God is among mortals. He will dwell with them as their God; they will be his peoples, and God himself will be with them'.   (21.3)

'I will be their God and they will be my children'.   (21.7)

By declaring that he will 'make his home' (21.3; cf. 7.15; 12.12; 13.6; 15.5), God is at long last bringing his relationship with his people to perfection and universalising it, in terms reminiscent of Zech 2.14-15. At the very moment when final redemption approaches for Israel, whose consolation will be that God will dwell with his people as promised, the covenant is enlarged to encompass within this same people, and within the scope of their salvation, the nations who come to YHWH.[211] That Lev 26 remains Revelation's subtext at this juncture is confirmed by several details: whereas Lev 26.5b-8 (cf. Gen 17.7-8, comparable to it) promises a victory over wild beasts and enemies, Revelation makes a once-only use of klêronomeô (inherit) to declare the promise of 21.7 to be the inheritance of conquerors – much as does Isa 55.1-3, where precisely the everlasting covenant is at stake.[212] The water of life (21.6) and the trees and their fruit (22.2) are in parallel with the rain, trees and their fruit promised in Lev 26.4; peace, security and rest in Lev 26.5-6 are reflected in Rev 21 in the absence of death or mourning, crying or pain (21.4); and most of all, the inclusion of a curse pronounced upon covenant rebels (21.8) is a distillation of the woes decreed in what follows in Lev 26, i.e. in the very scenario which has so inspired our author for the structuring of his own work.

Although God's purpose has been victorious and the plans of every rival horde have come to nothing, 21.8 maintains the double logic whereby covenant blessings are in every case accompanied by the curses that covenant violation would produce: once more eight opposites to the benefits summarised in 21.6-7 are enumerated, attitudes which constitute hypothetical examples of how the breaking of covenant obligations,[213] by failure to show appropriate obedience, would disrupt full communion with God through his Messiah.[214] If this text (and later both 21.27 and 22.15) are reminders of what would happen should the contract binding God to

redeemed humanity ever be broken, clearly their purpose is to sustain to the
very end Revelation's rhetorical exigency that no believer should ever settle
for self-satisfaction. The duty to keep oneself separate from all impurity
is a leitmotiv of Israel's belonging to a holy God: exactly as under the old
covenant dispensation, communion with the Lord comes at this price (Deut
23.14), as the prophets had occasion to underline (Ezek 44.6-9). Following
both Jesus and Paul (in 1 Cor 6.9-11), Revelation in turn assumes that
restored Zion-Jerusalem will behave as a faithful covenant partner under the
new covenant (cf. Isa 52.1).

Revelation 21.9-27

At this point the wide-angle lens is replaced by a zoom lens (21.9), with
one last appearance of an angel implicated in the carrying out of God's
judgments (17.1ff; 18.1,21; 19.17; 20.1; 21.9) and acting in the role of
interpreter to the seer. It has been thought that this signifies an organic link
between judgment and grace, whether, under the new covenant or in the old
economy;[215] however, it is rather the covenant ally's need for a revelation of
the will of the superior covenant partner, as a thing to be respected, which
is entailed by the presence of a mediating angel. The Holy City also has
angels emblazoned on its twelve gates (21.12),[216] as part of a description
(21.12-14; cf. expansion on 21.14 in 21.19-21) where the number twelve (4 x
3), never caricatured in Revelation,[217] becomes the focus along with twenty-
four (12 + 12).[218] As in other texts where seven proves to be composite (4
+ 3), the number twenty-four stands here for the addition of the tribes of
Israel and of the apostles. It has already been used for the enthroned elders
in 4.4 and it calls to mind other realities of the old economy in the Davidic
period as well, such as the orders of priests in the service of the Temple (1
Chr 24.3-19), its twenty-four orders of levitical singers (1 Chr 25.6-31) or its
doorkeepers (1 Chr 26.17-19). I doubt if we must choose between any of
these; it is probably sufficient, for present purposes, to speak of *new covenant
mathematics* where what matters is to show continuity with the old while
figuring a new universalising of covenant introduced by Messiah's sacrifice.

There are also signs of covenant renewal visible in the architecture itself:
if the tribes of Israel are like gates that create openings in the city walls
and allow access to it (21.12), then the apostles are like the foundations on
which it rests (21.14). We are dealing, here, with new Israel[219] and so 'the
city represents Covenant now made perfect and all-embracing'.[220] Although
Revelation specialists have a lot to say about the missing Temple (21.22),
quite *why* it is absent has not been sufficiently grasped. For the city's part,
God is her 'temple' from now on; for God's part, he looks on the city in the
same way.[221] Thus the space left empty (as it were) in heavenly Jerusalem, in
which no sanctuary will be built, testifies to the immediacy of relationship
that exists between the new covenant people and their God. This state of
affairs may only be accessed through relationship with the Lamb. Previously,

God drew near to humanity in encounter through the sacrifices of the Jerusalem Temple; but now incarnation has made his Messiah to be God's definitive Holy of Holies among human beings, rendering superfluous any concrete edifice which might be supposed to contain his presence. Therefore, '[Temple] worship, priesthood, sacrifices, rituals, religion or any sort of mediation are no more, since that time is now past'.[222] In other words, 'the more the covenant approaches perfection, the closer God comes'.[223]

By insisting on God's presence, chapter 21 is able to underscore several of the responsibilities he carries as faithful covenant suzerain. A case in point is the image of measuring. Measurement of the city and especially its imposing ramparts (21.15-17) signifies that its protection and security are taken care of, in conformity with what God's allies may expect from their Sovereign: thanks to his perfect presence among them, the people may live their lives in inviolable security.[224] Since the covenant is operative at the intersection of the reality of God with the world of human beings, a perfected covenant will deliver an effective encounter between these two horizons, and their harmonisation. Accordingly, the renewal of the heavens and the earth entails the loss of anything which had previously kept them apart. God comes to join his people in a city: tall enough to reach for the sky, this city symbolically renders or figures the whole cosmos a city – as the Holy Place had once done – and in this city both Redeemer and people are happy to dwell.

Revelation 22.1-5

In this city, where the one throne of God and the Lamb is to be found, the Mediator makes the covenant God immediately present (22.3). There is another consequence to be drawn from this: God's covenant friends enjoy a state of bliss,[225] which may be characterised positively as a 'healing' that benefits the nations (22.2) and negatively as the complete removal of the curse (*katathema*, 22.3). This happiness is the result of having one's name registered in the Lamb's book of life (21.27), that is, of being a party to the new covenant sealed in his blood (*cf.* 1.5) which, in itself, is also a 'healing' (*cf.* 5.9). These twin elements of healing and cancelled curse, are mutually interpretative[226] since healing comes from the leaves of the very tree to which access had been forbidden. While he remained unable to access the tree of life, Adam could not live forever (Gen 3.22,24); but now that the inhabitants of the paradisal city enjoy its twelve harvests, month by month (22.2), this means that humanity once again has eternal life with God and that such life is faithfully provided by him. Adam the sinner was accursed and expelled from God's garden (Gen 3.16-22) but in Jesus Christ, his sentence of banishment is converted into an everlasting entry permit.[227]

In the context of definitive replacement of an anti-covenant by a perfected covenant, it is not beyond the bounds of possibility that *katathema* might also carry the connotation of *herem* (ban). In the case of holy war, this kept back for God the entire booty of victory and meant that the covenant people were forbidden to enter into covenant with those they had defeated (Deut 7.2). A curse applied to any violation of this ban, as in the well-known case of Achan (Josh 7.1). So when those who are 'shut out' (in 21.8,27 and 22.15) are totally destroyed or expelled from the Holy City, these are forms of excommunication from the covenant people[228] and stand as the antithesis of communion enjoyed by the true members of the covenant community (21.3,7).

Seeing God face-to-face (22.4) is a privilege which had been denied Moses (Exod 33.20*ff*), even though his own countenance had been transfigured through encounter with the divine presence (Exod 34.29*ff*). Nonetheless, this very privilege had been the object of the famous blessing in Num 6.25-27 and for David, had been his hope (Ps 17.15) and the object of his prayers (Ps 27.4). Lastly, Jesus had promised this very face-to-face encounter as a blessing of his reign (Mt 5.8), leading the apostles Paul and John to expect it as the perfected product of a relationship with God of which those joined to Christ had already been given a foretaste (1 Cor 13.12; 2 Cor 3.18; *cf.* 1 Jn 3.2). In the case of Revelation, similarly, seeing God's face and bearing his name – or to put it differently, knowing God and belonging to him – means sharing in the triumph of the Sovereign God, the victory won at Messiah's cross over the powers that had held human beings in thrall and branded them with their mark. Now, nothing in the whole universe will be able to drive a wedge between God and his people or prevent him uniting them to him in perfect communion. By their conversion, the nations no longer worship the monster nor stand opposed to the reign of God: they escape being the object of the curse and, now that God's will is at last done on earth as in heaven, he binds himself in covenant to them and enables the potential within humanity as a whole finally to be accomplished.[229] The nations joyfully bring their wealth to God, whilst the living water of the divine presence irrigates and heals the world.[230] This is a fulfilment of the original purpose of creation, as well as a magnificent crowning moment for the story of the progress of the covenant.

Revelation 22.6-20

In spite of all that has just been said, to the very end Revelation retains a tension created by the logic of antithesis that has been in operation throughout. Time and again, this mechanism has meant that various forces of evil found in the Book have parodied God's way of engaging with humanity, caricaturing with servile and idolatrous behaviour the right and good response of humanity. If proof were required that this is still the case, the final two beatitudes in the series of seven (22.7,14) provide it by persisting with a rhetoric which has not relaxed its grip on readers for a moment.[231] In between these two (in 22.11) comes the very last mention of 'that double attitude of human decision and of submission to a supernatural power, whether diabolical or divine'.[232] The final beatitude, which focuses on dress (*cf.* 19.8) and erases all memory of soiled garments (3.4),[233] is backed up by one last warning (22.15).[234] The implication is: woe to anybody who, by not washing their garments, should rule themselves out of receiving God's salvation forever (*cf.* 20.15; 21.8,27). For nothing is automatic: there is a choice to be made, a decision to be taken. Faithful members of the covenant, by sticking to their principles, are to be distinguished from the wicked by the very fact that they welcome with open arms the grace given to them in Jesus Christ. Otherwise, 'to compromise and to behave like worshippers of the beast would mean to have one's name deleted from the book of life and to receive nothing from judgment but its sentence of guilt'.[235]

It has to be admitted that large numbers of commentators express astonishment at what they perceive to be the unyielding and even vindictive tone of this conclusion, as though the descent of New Jerusalem had not really sorted things out in any definitive sense. Yet as I have been endeavouring to show, this way of talking is perfectly in line with Revelation's rhetorical thrust and with the corresponding ethical demands being made (as we have so often seen). Indeed, the difficulty felt by certain exegetes turns out to be without substance once sufficient account is taken of the legal character of this section. The clauses of 22.18-19 in fact correspond to the forensic language used at the start of the Book.[236] In a manner similar to what is intended in a text like Deut 4.2,[237] they prohibit any addition or subtraction – regarded as moves characteristic of false prophecy (*cf.* Deut 13.1-5) – and they serve to round off the covenant charter with a reminder of the sanctions integral to that contract. The two verses summarise Revelation's legal status as a legislative code. This is reminiscent of Deuteronomy, where statements like those in Rev 22.18-19 arise in three contexts: warnings against idolatry (Deut 4.1-2; 12.32; 29.19-21; *cf.* Rev 21.8,27; 22.15), promised reward – in terms of the blessing of life 'in the land' (Deut 4.1; 12.28-29; *cf.* Rev 22.14,17*ff*) – or use of the language of plagues to describe punishment for unfaithfulness (Deut 19.21; *cf.* Rev 22.18).[238] In sum, the warnings in 22.18-19 are addressed to the Church as a community in the same way as those in Deuteronomy had once applied to the old covenant people.[239]

The rewards referred to in 22.12-20 correspond to the promises to victors which punctuated the septet of oracles to Churches. For those in covenant with a faithful God, what has now been brought to completion by the Mediator's work does not alter the fact that promised blessings forever remain conditional ones. Covenant carries within it a profoundly reciprocal logic whereby the gratitude shown by the elect, in joyful submission to the one who has chosen them in his grace, constitutes the required and expected response. Yet in the revelation of divine benevolence toward human beings which is found in Israel's Scriptures, the fickleness of human response is visible throughout. As a result, believers under the renewed covenant ought always to acknowledge the real and present danger of their sliding into unfaithfulness and disobedience. Finding new relevance, for its own time, in texts which had regulated the old covenant dispensation, Revelation provides a reminder to its readers of curses which would surely affect covenant vassals even now, were they to backslide. So as well as emphasising the joy of knowing God thanks to what Messiah Jesus has done, our author never ceases to lay parallel stress on the obligations and responsibilities incumbent on faithful covenant partners, in their relationship to God, under the new covenant sealed in the blood of the Lamb.

Notes

1 S. Smalley, *Revelation, op. cit.,* p.294.

2 See, in particular, the following contributions: S. Moyise, *Old Testament, op. cit.;* G.K. Beale, *John's Use of the Old Testament in Revelation,* Sheffield, Sheffield Academic Press, 1998; I. Paul, 'The Use of the Old Testament in Revelation 12', in S. Moyise (ed.), *The Old Testament in the New Testament,* Sheffield, Sheffield Academic Press, 2000, pp.256-76; S. Moyise, *The Old Testament in the New. An Introduction,* New York/London, Continuum, 2001, ch. 9 'The Old Testament in Revelation', pp.117-127; J. Paulien, 'Criteria and the Assessment of Allusions to the Old Testament in the Book of Revelation', in S. Moyise (ed.), *Studies in the Book of Revelation,* T&T Clark, Edinburgh/New York, 2001, pp.113-29.

3 P. Prigent says something similar in a recent article 'L'Interprétation de l'Apocalypse en débat', *Etudes Théologiques et Religieuses* 75, 2000, pp.189-210: 'the author of Revelation constantly draws nourishment from the Bible, from its language and from its images'.

4 Compare R. D. Davis, *The Heavenly Court Judgment of Revelation* 4-5, Lanham/ London, University Press of America, 1992, pp.213-14, 228, 230.

5 A. Paul, *Jésus Christ,* p.259.

6 Compare F. Bovon, 'John's Self-presentation in Revelation 1:9-10', *Catholic Biblical Quarterly* 62, 2000, pp.699-700.

7 As Ellul so nicely puts it, *Architecture,* p.115.

8 On this point, compare J.E. Leonard, *Come Out of Her My People,* Arlington Heights, Laudemont Press, 1991, p.29.

9 Thus, for example, C. Koester, *Revelation,* p.51.

10 Beale, 'The Interpretative Problem of Rev 1:19', *Novum Testamentum* 34/4, 1992, p.385, reads 1.10-11 as a delegation of authority which the Risen One's credentials (1.12-18) solemnise, taking 1.19 to be the repetition of a mandate which 4.1-2; 10.1-11; 17.1-3; and 21.9-10 will further renew.

11 See C. Koester, *Revelation,* pp.46-47; although he does not use the word *covenant* as such, Koester does give a perfect description of covenantal issues. For P. Söllner, *Jerusalem, die hochgebaute Stadt. Eschatologisches und Himmlisches Jerusalem im Frühjudentum und im frühen Christentum,* Tübingen/Basle, Francke Verlag, 1998, p.254, the seven beatitudes as a group are linked to the covenant renewal brought about by the advent of eschatological Jerusalem. For a rhetorical analysis of the seven beatitudes, see L.L. Johns, 'The Lamb in the Rhetorical Program of the Apocalypse of John', *SBL 1998 Seminar Papers,* Atlanta, 1998, pp.765-66.

12 For example (however, with no explanation), J.M. Ford, Revelation, p.376; points to *1 Enoch* 21.3-6, 61.11. For the role played by the number seven in Revelation together with a survey of its usage in the NT, in apocalyptic and in Judaism, as well as in the Ancient Near East, see further: 1) K.H. Rengstorf, 'ἑπτά',

in G.W. Bromiley (tr.), Theological Dictionary of the New Testament (vol. 2), Grand Rapids, Eerdmans, 1964, pp.627-35. Although it is not his main thrust, this author nonetheless accounts for Sabbath and for seven-day-long festivals in terms of an ordering of every aspect of the people's relationship with their God. 2) E.D. Schmitz, ἐπτά/ἐπτάκις, in C. Brown (ed.), New International Dictionary of New Testament Theology (vol. 2), Carlisle/Grand Rapids, Paternoster/Eerdmans, 1986, pp.690-92. For this author, 'seven' in Revelation signifies God's activity towards his Church but also that of forces which oppose him. For my part, in the present chapter, this is what I call covenant and anti-covenant.

13 For still other correlations, see once more Resseguie, *Revelation Unsealed*, pp.53-54.

14 I am indebted to Resseguie, *ibid.*, p.132, for having already grouped these seven texts together and commented on them.

15 Similarly, Leonard, *Come Out*, p.31.

16 This phenomenon can hardly be fortuitous. In my opinion, it must reflect the more or less deliberate intention of the author to underline the importance of this symbolism. Later in this chapter, I will give priority to those instances where there is explicit numbering by seven, *i.e.* the septets.

17 A. Paul, *Jésus-Christ*, p.250. This author notes the curious absence of the 'seven heavens' which, in apocalypticism, normally function as so many successive levels through which celestial travellers must move. The redundancy of seven heavens is doubtless to be explained by the unique heaven of Revelation, which 21.1 declares to be 'new'. Similar logic means that Rev 1–3 does not present seven disparate Churches, as such, but rather one Church declined in sevenfold ways.

18 See J.M. Ford, *Revelation*, p.112. In this author's work, we can compare the seven stages, starting in 17.1, which she proposes for the fall of 'Babylon' (pp.47-48).

19 As Paul puts it, *Jésus-Christ*, p.250, 'its astonishing recurrence makes a particular contribution to the organisation and the signposting of the book as a whole' (my translation).

20 Compare K. Gamber, *Zur Symbolik der Apokalypse*, Regensburg, Pustet, 1987, p.50. I am grateful to Aune, *Revelation* 1-5 (vol. 1), xcvii-xcviii, for having alerted me to the fact that there are seven such crucial moments.

21 On this point, see J.M. Ford, *Revelation*, p.195.

22 Charlier, *Comprendre* (vol. 2), p.138*ff.*

23 The suggestion has been made that we should see a total of seven septets of visions, each consisting of seven elements. So, for example, C. Brown, editor of NIDNTT, who appends to the article by Schmitz, 'ἐπτά/ἐπτάκις', op. cit., a note on the formal role played by seven in the Book (pp.691-92) and who suggests a correspondence between the seven visions he sets out and the seven days of creation (according to Gen 1). For a nuanced structuring of Rev into seven parts, see especially Beale, Revelation, p.136 and his discussion in loc. Beale avoids claiming that there are numbered schemas within sections which are not explicitly septets (as for example 12.1–14.20). His proposal, in summary form, is as follows: 1.9-3.22 and then 21.9–22.20 function as visions 1 and 7 and form an inclusio; within this framework 4.1–21.8 may be subdivided into five parts, where there is influence from five parallel visions in Dan chs. 2,7,8,9 and 10–12, namely the three septets of seals, trumpets and bowls plus the conflict visions (12.1–14.20) and the final judgment of God's enemies (17.1–21.8). Finally, 1.1-8 represents the introduction and 22.6-20 the conclusion.

24 Missing the significance of seven in Revelation means failing to find an adequate explanation for its use. Thus, D. E. Aune, for instance (*Revelation*), does think that the septets constitute the Book's main interpretative problem but takes the elaborate use of the number seven as a structuring principle to be no more than a fine example of a commonplace in apocalyptic literary tradition, and one for which he thinks *4 Ezra* and *2 Baruch* provide sufficient parallels. This verdict does no justice to what is demanded by the textual data themselves.

25 G. Campbell, 'Findings, Seals, Trumpets and Bowls: Variations upon the Theme of Covenant Rupture and Restoration in the Book of Revelation', *Westminster Theological Journal* 66, 2004, pp.71-96. For reasons of space the article in question had to confine itself to a study of Rev 1–16, in dialogue with the work of exegetes of Revelation, and be content to make only essential points. The present chapter will now not only take full account of ch. 17–22 as well, but give consideration to *all* the pertinent data from Rev 1–16 besides.

26 Beale, *Revelation*, p.373. His question is: 'could it also be that the four judgments of Leviticus, which are each summarised figuratively as consisting of seven punishments, serve as the model for the four sets of seven judgments that so dominate the Apocalypse?' For Beale the seven thunders of 10.3-4 could be one of the four sevens; he takes up the discussion again later in a passage devoted to the bowls (p.803). Compare D. Chilton, *The Days of Vengeance*, Fort Worth, Dominion Press, 1987, pp.16-17,89. J.M. Ford, *Revelation*, p.282, commits herself to a similar hypothesis whereby the first of the four sets of judgments is the seals; this makes the fourth the fall of the whore, in which the 'fury' of Lev 26.28 reaches a climax, with Lev 26.27-33 as the text out of which are developed the woes associated with the seven figures that 'fall' (between 18.1 and 20.10). Whilst there is no denying the 'fury' of ch. 17–20, by that point in the plot all the judgments have taken place and the time has come for irrevocable divorce and (re)marriage. As for her identification of the seven figures, which entails a certain amount of regrouping, it proves unconvincing. The textual data are better explained if it is the bowls which bring to a head the series of four *explicit* judgments, as I will endeavour to show.

27 Corsini, *Apocalypse*, p.105.

28 In what follows, I am especially indebted to the work of R. Sutton, *That You May Prosper: Dominion Through Covenant*, Fort Worth, Institute for Christian Economics, 1987, as well as the commentaries by Chilton and, to a lesser extent, by Corsini. As for more scientific commentaries on Revelation which are alive to Old Testament echoes in these two chapters, see particularly those by Lohmeyer, *Offenbarung*, or by Mounce, *Revelation, in loc.*

29 So J.T. Kirby, 'The Rhetorical Situations of Revelation 1-3', *New Testament Studies* 34, 1988, p.207, n.39.

30 Oddly enough, for the majority of commentators who take their cue from Charles, *Revelation* (vol. 1), pp.54-55, this mention of the tree of life merely evokes something that symbolises immortality (*cf.* Gen 3.22), whereas in fact Revelation's resolute interest in the story of origins takes full account of that story's own breadth and depth, including the issues it raises.

31 As Corsini puts it, *Apocalypse*, p.105.

32 We encounter this synagogue of the satan in the very oracles – to Smyrna and to Philadelphia, 2.9 and 3.9 – in which each Church is praised for her fidelity in a context of apostasy. This recalls the theology of the remnant that does not

give up even though the people in general may reject the covenant. This may be compared to the later opposition between the multitudes that follow the Lamb and their parody, the slaves that run after the monster – *cf.* Friesen, *Imperial Cults*, p.192. This reference to a synagogue of the satan heaping calumny on the Church is generally interpreted, by exegetes, as a dispute that arose in Asia in John's time. With Garrow, *Revelation*, p.120, I consider it decisive that the nature of this disagreement is located in a situation where followers of Messiah Jesus and other Asian Jews were staking rival claims to be the genuine covenant people.

33 What seems to be meant is some sort of perverted Judaism held responsible for having caused the death of Jesus and later that of his disciples.

34 Unless, perhaps, what is meant is a city quite unlike what Jerusalem is (or should be), a city where God has chosen to dwell. For such a view, compare Prévost, *Apocalypse*, p.45.

35 In Num 22–24 Balaam, who hailed from Babylonia, is the one who blesses Israel. In Deut 23 he delivers a curse but God converts it into blessing. Num 31.16 does not actually state that Balak had received Balaam's advice concerning his actions, although this could be inferred (as in Philo, *Vita Mo* 1.53-55, and by Flavius Josephus, *Ant* 4.126). 2 Pet 2.15 and Jude 11 are even more critical of Balaam. For another case of a fall, *cf.* Ezek 18.30.

36 Such an enumeration of superior qualities, coalescing at some particular moment of the history of God's people, might conjure up for example David, even more so Solomon, or as a final instance perhaps the renaissance that came about under Azariah (2 Kgs 14–15).

37 For C. Tresmontant, *Apocalypse de Jean*, Paris, O.E.I.L., 1984, p.126, 'Jezebel' is a way of naming 'the highest authorities in Jerusalem'.

38 For both apostasy and the remnant see Isa 1.5-23; 6.9-13; 65.8-16; Jer 7.1-7; 9.11-16; Ezek 37.1-14; for imminent judgment, compare Isa 1.24-31; 2.12-21; 26.20-21; Jer 4.5-31; 7.12-15; 11.9-13; Mic 1.2-7; Zeph 1.

39 In Barr's eyes, *Tales*, pp.45-46, the message to Sardis is more difficult to locate at a precise juncture in Israel's history; makes an appeal for vigilance and caution in the manner of the wisdom literature.

40 Others find here an allusion to the barring of the doors of the synagogue against messianic Jews, or to the door of the kingdom and/or of heavenly Jerusalem, or even the gate to Hades.

41 It seems as though Revelation uses irony to turn around several words of Isaiah that envisage the nations' submission to Israel (Isa 45.14; 49.23; 60.14), making them into the submission of false Jews to the true Israel. So, for example, Wall, *Revelation*, p.84.

42 In a footnote, Mounce, *Revelation*, p.106, draws attention to the foundational role played by Jewish colonists in the establishment of Laodicea under Antiochus III; according to Josephus (*Ant* 12.3.4) he was instrumental in bringing 2000 Jewish families from Babylonia to Lydia and Phrygia, thus giving Laodicea its own Jewish (hi)story.

43 In Rev, everything made of gold refers, in one way or another, to God.

44 *Contra* the surprisingly categoric rejection in Mounce, *Revelation*, p.114, of any idea that Song of Songs 5.2 is being alluded to here. In fact, there is wide agreement that early Judaism (*Sirach* 3.20; rabbinic *Midrash Exodus* 33.3; rabbinic *Midrash Song* 5.2, §2; rabbinic *Pesikta de-Rab Kahana* 24.12; *Pesikta Rabbati* 15.6)

took the metaphor in Song 5.2 (of the Bridegroom knocking so as to join his betrothed) as an appeal to Israel to repent made by YHWH her 'lover'. In succession to Israel, the Church here is evidently the beloved wife.

45 See Prigent, *Apocalypse*, p.220, n.35.

46 Similarly Beale, *Use of the OT*, p. 305; *cf.* Barr, *Tales*, p.53.

47 It is uncontroversial, in biblical theology, to assert that the OT is thoroughly marked by an understanding of the relationship binding Israel to their God, or that this is expressed in terms of a covenant to which the themes of the election vocation of God's people are linked. See for example B.S. Childs, *Biblical Theology of the Old and New Testament. Theological Reflection on the Christian Bible*, Minneapolis, Fortress, 1993, ch. 6, 'Theological reflection on the Christian Bible.' In line with a certain consensus position, Childs attributes this perspective to the so-called 'deuteronomistic' editors of the Scriptures. However, he does understand their editorial work as being in profound continuity with prior tradition and so he credits it with showing respect for the way several 'melodies' contribute to one overall harmony. Childs also notices how the covenant framework or category is present everywhere. He mentions Noah or Abraham and his descendants (in Genesis); Moses at Sinai, at the heart of the Pentateuch in general and of Deuteronomy in particular; the tragic (deuteronomistic) history of Israel's disobedience to the covenant (from Joshua to 2 Kings), as well as the divine wrath this provokes; Israel's restoration through a renewed covenant which the prophets variously glimpse as betrothal (Hosea), as new covenant (Jeremiah), or as a covenant of peace (Ezekiel) or of blessing (Isaiah); and finally Daniel who, although the covenant has been broken, envisages that the faithful will be strengthened as they await their deliverance.

48 Barr, *Tales*, p.53, establishes the following correlations: *2.7* = 22.2,14; *2.11* = 20.6; *2.17* = 19.12; *2.26-28* = 20.4 (and 19.15), plus 22.16; *3.5* = 6.11, *etc.*, plus 20.15 and 21.27; *3.12* = 19.12,21.2 and, by contrast, 21.22; *3.21* = 20.4 (and 22.1). For an alternative arrangement of the correspondences, see Davis, *Heavenly Court*, p.217.

49 Kraft, *Offenbarung*, p.57, sees things similarly.

50 On this point, see also Koester, *Revelation*, p.56.

51 In both form and content, Ezek 14.3-8 offers a particularly close parallel to the oracles to Churches, especially by assigning both significance and a key role to repentance.

52 This work covers roughly a ten-year period. To the works (already cited) by D. Chilton, R.D. Davis and R. Sutton we need to add three articles: W.H. Shea, 'The Covenantal Form of the Letters to the Seven Churches', *Andrews University Seminary Studies* 21, 1983, pp.71-84, and in the same issue K.A. Strand, 'A Further Note on the Covenantal Form in the Book of Revelation', pp.251-64. The contribution of all the foregoing is anticipated in the article by J. Du Preez, 'Ancient Near Eastern Vassal Treaties and the Book of Revelation. Possible Links', *Religion in South Africa* 2/2, 1981, pp.33-43. The only major commentary on Revelation to have taken such recent research into account (specifically, Shea and Strand) is the one by Beale, *Revelation*, pp.227-28, who gives their contributions a cautious welcome.

53 This term designates a document designed for regulating the covenant between YHWH as Sovereign and Israel as his vassal, by analogy with peace treaties from the Ancient Near East. Generally speaking, such suzerainty treaties are recognised as having a six-part structure: i) preamble; ii) historical prologue;

iii) stipulations; iv) blessings and curses; v) succession arrangements; and vi) measures for safeguarding the documents. Although the sixth has no place in the oracles to Churches, at the close of Revelation the issue arises as to how the Book as a whole is properly to be used.

54 This refers to the literary shape applied to prophetic indictments which bring Israel to justice for breaking covenant obligations to YHWH. See, for example, J. Harvey, 'Le 'Rîb-Pattern', réquisitoire prophétique sur la rupture de l'alliance', *Biblica* 43, 1962, pp.172-96. For Harvey, by far the best example of the prophetic *rîb*, under the Old Covenant, is Hosea's prophecy whilst Revelation, in its turn, is a lawsuit brought by God and by his Messiah against Israel, Israel's worship and Israel's Temple.

55 Aune, *Revelation* 1-5 (vol. 1), pp.119-20, distinguishes the *adscriptio* (address) from the *superscriptio* (sender).

56 On each occasion there is 'write' but, in 1.11 'write . . . and send' covers the whole process. Beale, *Use of the OT*, p.304, finds the order to write to be natural here, since it occurs in contexts in which YHWH commends his covenant to Israel through his messengers.

57 From the point of view of rhetoric this is about reinforcing YHWH's *ethos;* according to the covenant mechanism it is his prerogative to apportion praise or reprimands.

58 This formula is characteristic of prophetic oracles.

59 The relationship is therefore hierarchical. In the entitlement of the Risen One to give an analysis of the behaviour of the congregation he is addressing, the *ethos* which he enjoys is his dignity as Covenant Mediator.

60 This expression is characteristic of the three mixed verdicts and so is used again for the oracles to Pergamum and to Thyatira (2.14 and 2.20).

61 A phrase governed by 'nevertheless' and conveying approval returns in 3.4. I am taking both statements, in their respective oracles, simply to be elements of the audit which have become displaced from the historical prologue – hence my proposal here.

62 Exceptions are the cases of Smyrna and Philadelphia, for whom the Lord has no words of reprimand; the watchword for them is, 'don't give up'. We may note how Aune, *Revelation* 1-5 (vol. I), p.122, takes 2.5-6 to be the *dispositio*; this is the most catch-all element of his formal analysis and accordingly (to my mind), its least convincing part.

63 In this case, a curse is involved. Nonetheless, blessing still remains a possibility in what is a process of ratification.

64 The same expression as in 2.17.

65 This call comes in penultimate position here (and in 2.11 and 2.17), but I place at the end in accordance with its position in four out of seven oracles (2.29; 3.6,13,22). It is an invariable formula recalling the repeated aphorism, in Jesus's parables, directed to Israel (or, to a *remnant* of Israel). On these calls to vigilance as an anticipation of the symbolic rhetoric of ch. 4–21, see especially Beale, *Use of the OT*, pp.298-317.

66 The German equivalent of this expression is *Bundesgemeinschaft*, paraphrased as *Gott-Israel-Relation* by M. Vogel in *Das Heil des Bundes. Bundestheologie im Frühjudentum und im frühen Christentum*, Tübingen/Basle, 1996, p.163. In Second Temple Judaism, Vogel identifies two parallel currents whose common objective was covenant renewal. The two alternative approaches could be summed up as

priestly-cultic on the one hand and *Torah-centred* on the other. Vogel considers Lev 26 (p.170) to be a fundamental text for the second of these currents.

67 For this point, I am indebted to A. Paul, *Jésus-Christ*, p.257.

68 As correctly argued by Koester, *Revelation*, pp.71,74.

69 On this subject, see the study by S.A. Nigosian, 'The Song of Moses (Dt. 32). A Structural Analysis', *Ephemerides theologicae Lovanienses* 72, 1996, pp.5-22.

70 As Nigosian also notes, *ibid.*, p.6, n.11. Another viewpoint prefers to connect use of the *Rîb* with sessions of courts convened at the city gate or after worship; for this see the literature to which Nigosian refers.

71 Compare, for example, *Sirach* 44–49 where there is reference to twenty-four fathers of Israel.

72 The work of Victorinus of Pettau/Poetovio. Prigent already subscribed to this idea in the first edition of his commentary, *L'Apocalypse de St. Jean*, Geneva, Labor et Fides, 1988 (*in loc.*): 'these fathers . . . of prophetic revelation are now associated with worship given to the God who lives eternally' (my translation). An alternative explanation is defended by L.W. Hurtado, 'Revelation 4-5 in the Light of Jewish Apocalyptic Analogies', *Journal for the Study of the New Testament* 25,1985, pp.111-116, and more recently by Mounce, *Revelation*: this takes the twenty-four elders to represent the elect of the new covenant and their number to be a reminder of the orders of priests and Levites according to 1 Chr 24.4-6.

73 Schüssler-Fiorenza, *Just World*, p.59, sets the book held in God's hand in parallel with the *libellus* carried by the Roman emperor. For O. Roller, 'Das Buch mit sieben Siegeln', *Zeitschrift für die neutestamentliche Wissenschaft* 26, 1937, pp.98-113, the seven-sealed scroll is a bond of entitlement. *Cf.* Mealy, *Thousand Years*, pp.66-67; although he does not explicitly mention covenantal logic or use vocabulary that would reflect it, Mealy *does* nevertheless describe how the narrative features a crucified and risen Messiah as Mediator of a new covenant dispensation.

74 *Contra* Ellul, *Architecture*, pp.152-53. As intimated above in ch. 4, note 9 (see the fuller information it gives), the first of the interpretations which Ellul rejects is the one which I am advancing.

75 On this point, see the perceptive (if hesitant!) exegesis of J.M. Ford, *Revelation*, pp.93-94. She brings to mind how *biblion* ('book' or 'scroll') is used to mean a bill of divorce in LXX Deut 24.1,3; Isa 50.1; and Jer 3.8 (with Deut 24.1-4 as its subtext); this also happens in Mt 19.7 and Mk 10.4. In all of these texts, the expression is *biblion apostasiou*, which translates the Hebrew. Given Rev's twin motif of the wife and the adulteress it would be possible to postulate, as Ford does, that a certificate of divorce permits the Lamb to repudiate unfaithful Jerusalem and marry New Jerusalem in her place. If this is so, by warning the erring wife and providing her with time to repent, the seals and trumpets put off the act of final repudiation until this is brought about by the outpouring of the bowls.

76 See E. Schüssler-Fiorenza, 'Revelation as Liberation: Apoc. 1:5f. and 5:9f.,' *Catholic Biblical Quarterly* 36, 1974, pp.228-30.

77 For Giblin, *Revelation*, p.76, the scene in 5.6-14 clarifies both the role and the unique status of the redeemer: in redeeming a universal people for God, he is the one to bring divine creation to completeness.

78 As Giblin is right to remind us, *ibid.*, p.78.

79 On the 'event,' that was the old covenant's replacement by the new, see M. Hopkins, 'The Historical Perspective of Apocalypse 1-11,' *Catholic Biblical Quarterly* 27, 1965, p.44.

80 Davis, *Heavenly Court*, p.230, for whom the covenant carried within it the potential for a re-creation, designed to bring sinful humanity back into that relationship with God which was lost at the Fall.

81 As a narrative development of the programmatic motif of the four series of judgments in Lev 26, the seals, trumpets and bowls are essentially in parallel. See A. Steinmann, 'The Tripartite Structure of the Sixth Seal, the Sixth Trumpet, and the Sixth Bowl of John's Apocalypse (Rev 6.12-7.17; 9.13-11.14; 16.12-16)', *Journal of the Evangelical Theological Society* 35, 1992, pp.69-80. He demonstrates how the *sixth* element of the seals, trumpets and bowls is parallel and, by so doing, reinforces the prior critical consensus concerning the parallelism of the *seventh* member in each series. See further D.R. Davis, 'The Relationship Between the Seals, Trumpets, and Bowls in the Book of Revelation'. *Journal of the Evangelical Theological Society* 16, 1973, pp.158-59.

82 In Jer 4.29, we find the same image, in a context where emphasis is placed upon the desire to hide from God's wrath. Beale, *Revelation*, p.400, traces all this back to Gen 3.9, where the man and the woman run and hide.

83 Ezek 9 and 14.12-23 understand this protection as applying to the faithful remnant in Israel, whereas *Psalms of Solomon* 15.6,9 – as also Rev 7 – appears to rely on Exodus and on the prophetic re-reading of that book. On this point, see Beale, *Revelation*, pp.409-10, as part of his excursus on seals (pp.409-16).

84 For this view, compare Beale, *ibid.*, p.408.

85 Also J.M. Ford, *Revelation*, p.119, for whom the washing of garments in blood could signify (among other things) one's acquiescence in covenant with YHWH.

86 Comparison may be made with P. Hirschberg, *Das eschatologische Israel. Untersuchungen zum Gottesvolkverständnis der Johannesoffenbarung*, Neukirchen-Vluyn, Neukirchener Verlag, 1999, p.304. For this writer the theme of a people of God eschatologically renewed in Jesus is to be found at the very heart of the seer's message.

87 Hirschberg, *ibid.*, p.297.

88 Beale, *Revelation*, pp.438-39, notes five elements that pick up and intensify details from Exodus: the multitude that comes out of tribulation (Exod 4.31); Israel's washed garments (Exod 19.10,14; *cf.* Lev 8.30 for the washed garments of consecrated priests); sprinkling with blood (Exod 24.8); God's promise to set up his tent; and the food, water, protection and comfort provided during the journey.

89 An annual feast whose twin functions were joyful commemoration of YHWH's faithfulness throughout the wilderness wanderings (Lev 23.42-43) and the transposition of its blessings for a sedentary situation, as translated by abundant harvests (Deut 16.13-15,17). All the key elements of this feast are picked up by Rev 7.

90 For an approach that factors in the way both Josh 6 and Num 10 were read at Qumran, Beale may be consulted, *Revelation*, p.471.

91 The place given, in Jewish tradition, to God's silence is also considered by Beale, *ibid.*, pp.448-54.

92 Charlier, *Comprendre* (vol. 1), p.203.

93 Barker, *Revelation*, p.172*ff*, alludes to parallel usage in the *War Scroll* (*QM* VII), while offering a reminder of how the warriors who accompanied Moses against Midian (Num 31.1-12) were armed not only with metallic trumpets of alarm but also with bowls taken from the sanctuary: might this be the origin of Rev's seven bowls, which also issue forth from the Holy of Holies?

94 For carnivorous birds as a figure for covenant curses (19.17-18) see Gen 15.9-12; Deut 28.26; Prov 30.17; Jer 7.33-34; 16.3-4; 19.7; 34.18-20; Ezek 39.17-20; see also Chilton, *Days*, pp.241-42.

95 Brütsch, *Clarté*, p.165.

96 Prigent's logic is different, *Apocalypse*, p.323. For Revelation's intransigent vision of things, there has to be a clear line of demarcation between 'Christians and the rest of mankind, who are nothing but pagans and idolaters.' Yet as was noticed by J.M. Ford, *Revelation*, pp.154, 9.17-21 explains the point of the trumpets as being to remind human beings of their covenant engagements. In the face of such obligations, people are either faithful or defiant.

97 Similarly, Glonner, *Bildersprache*, pp.266-67; compare Barker, *Revelation*, p.171.

98 *In Apocalypsin*, X, 1, p.88.

99 J.M. Ford, *Revelation*, pp.164-65, alludes to the rabbinic tractate *Sotah*, in which there is a description of how trial by bitter draught is to be carried out, for cases of suspected adultery, in application of the law of jealousy.

100 For Barker, *Revelation*, p.187, the figure in Deut 32.40-41 is the one most capable of explaining what is meant by Rev 10.5-7 where, once more, the sword of the covenant will soon fall.

101 For a reminder of this fact see J.M. Ford, *Revelation*, pp.164-65.

102 Similarly, Beale, *Revelation*, pp.554-55; see the literature he cites.

103 To me it seems difficult – and perhaps unnecessary – to differentiate between these two altars in the various references made to them in Rev (6.9; 8.3-5; 9.13; 11.1; 14.18; 16.17).

104 Is it the Jerusalem Temple in the literal sense of an edifice (with Charlier, *Comprendre*, vol. 1, *in loc*), or is what is meant rather its significance as the very place where Israel meets with her God? I lean towards the second solution: the Temple is supplanted by the work of Christ, who takes over all its functions; this explains why the Lamb is present in, but the Temple absent from, the ultimate city in Revelation's final vision. From 11.1 onwards a battle of rival scholarly interpretations opposes (as very much the majority choice) *the Temple in Jerusalem* – whether still in existence, or already destroyed — to another exegesis which favours *the heavenly Temple*, as adopted for example by Giblin in his published work and energetically taken up by M. Bachmann, 'Himmlisch: der 'Tempel Gottes' von Apk 11.1', *New Testament Studies* 40, 1994, pp.474-80. However, this is a false alternative, for the plot involving the Temple follows the logic of covenant renewal and fulfilment whereby God comes to dwell definitively among human beings. Thus, what is required is that Rev's early plot should simply evoke *both* the heavenly Temple *and* its earthly counterpart, in order that – at the denouement – both may disappear.

105 Prigent, *Apocalypse*, p.341: 'To measure . . . means to preserve'. J.M. Ford, *Revelation*, pp.175-77, assembles and reviews OT texts and Jewish traditions where we can find a comparable act of measuring (Ezek 40-48; Zech 2.1-6 and 12.2-3; *1 Enoch* 61.1-5; in all of these cases, Jerusalem is involved) or of analogous preserving (2 Sam 8.2b; *1 Enoch* 41.1-2) or else, of similar profanation or destruction (2 Kgs 21.13; Isa 34.11; Am 7.7-9; Lam 2.8; 2 Sam 8.2a). For a reading of Rev 10–11 that detects the influence of an apocalypse thought to be contained in Isa 24–27 see Barker, *Revelation*, p.184*ff*.

106 In Zech 2.2*ff* measuring is followed by a prophecy of Jerusalem's restoration under the protection of YHWH who wreaks his vengeance on oppressing nations, among them Babylon; *cf*. Marshall, *Parables*, p.168.

107 Charlier, *Comprendre* (vol. 1), p.246.

108 Compare Beale, *Revelation*, p.565. Like Bauckham before him, *Climax*, pp.267-73, Beale shows the decisive influence of Dn 7–12 on the way the present vision is laid out; for the figure of 42 months, or equivalent periods, Dn 7.25; 9.27; 12.7,11-12, especially, may be consulted.

109 See as well 1.9; 6.9; 12.11,17; 20.4. Speaking of *combined* evidence from *dual* witnesses is warranted by the fact that they share one mouth between two (11.5).

110 The issue of covenant faithfulness or unfaithfulness is obscured if, like Beale, *Revelation*, p.570, we simply harmonise 11.1 and 11.2 and see them as complementary. On the other hand, *contra* some commentators who still put a caesura between 11.1 and 11.2, I do take the text's compositional unity at this point to have been sufficiently proven by H. Gollinger's careful study, *Die Kirche in der Bewahrung: Eine Einführung in die Offenbarung des Johannes*, Aschaffenburg, 1973, pp.123-25.

111 Beale, *ibid.*, p.573 notes the juridical nuance carried by such vocabulary in the Johannine literature.

112 For Beale, *ibid.*, p.575, they are true prophetic twins.

113 Compare Marshall, *Parables*, pp.145-46. The two witnesses are to be understood as secondary types for Jesus, in the sense that they bear the same witness as he did. On the parallelism with Christ's career, Beale may again be consulted, *Revelation*, p.567.

114 J.M. Ford, *Revelation*, p.171, still thinking of Num 5 and of the *Sotah* tractate, wonders whether the two witnesses might not in some way represent those, as required by this rabbinic text, who must hear the court order not to frequent another man, issued on behalf of a husband to his wife suspected of adultery, or who must witness the accusation of a crime involved in such an order. This hypothesis is not unattractive, given the spiritual adultery of the chosen people as narrated by Rev here.

115 For Ford, *ibid.*, *hoi katoikoûntes epi tês gês* should be understood, in 11.10, in the narrow sense of inhabitants of the *land*, in other words *of Israel;* Chilton, *Days*, p.282, makes the same proposal. In my view, this is the correct reading at this point; the prophets famously made a priority of addressing the covenant people in order to 'torment' it.

116 Similarly, Resseguie, *Revelation Unsealed*, p.47, following C.H. Giblin, 'Recapitulation and the Literary Coherence of John's Apocalypse', *Catholic Biblical Quarterly* 56, 1994, p.93.

117 For a nicely nuanced discussion, see Beale, *Revelation*, pp.597-607. Although it cannot be summarised here, in the briefest terms Beale is not convinced by Bauckham's argument in *Climax*, pp.273-83, according to which this 'fear' is synonymous with a conversion, or by the alleged parallelism of the pair *fear-glory* in 14.7 and 15.4 (p.597). For Beale, massive conversion of the nations at the end of time, brought on by the last judgment, poses a problem theologically speaking. However, we ought to notice how this difficulty simply evaporates if Rev has in mind, for its successive judgments (including the last of them), not some ultimate rendezvous timed for the close of history but rather the logic of a covenant fulfilled by Messiah.

118 Barker, *Revelation*, p.186, is right to underline the fact that the significance of three-and-a-half (and its equivalents) is not one of length, but a matter of final (I would say, covenantal) delay *after which* Jerusalem may expect to undergo her fate.

119 So Barker, *ibid.*, p.195.

120 Charlier, *Comprendre* (vol. 1), p.259. He calls those who are rewarded 'the prophets of the two Covenants and those who heard their proclamation'.

121 My reading, at this point, is very close to that of Ellul, *Architecture*, pp.82-83.

122 For Smalley, *Revelation*, pp.294-95, the notion of a new covenant in Christ is combined with that of a new exodus, to bring the section 1.9 –11.19 to an end. He says (p.295): 'the restoration of God's people, who remain faithful to his covenant in belief and behaviour, is in view'.

123 *Ibid.*, p.261. For Victorinus at this point God's Temple is his Son (by analogy with Jn 2.19-21), while the Ark of testimony is the preaching of the gospel.

124 For Jewish expectations concerning an end-time (re-)appearance of the Ark, *cf.* 2 *Macc* 2.8. The Numbers Targum (*Rabbah* XV.10) contributes to Jewish mystical speculation on the restoration of the Ark, which it situates in the time of Messiah (as Rev also does, in its own way); on this point see also Barker, *Revelation*, p.200. For Caird, *Revelation*, p.144, the appearance of the Ark when the seven trumpets have sounded has the same function as it had at Jericho in Joshua's time: readers are meant to pick up that his namesake Jesus will give the covenant people access, once and for all, to what they have been promised and destroy all opposition in the process.

125 Hendriksen, *Conquerors*, p.133.

126 As argued, correctly, by S. Giet, *L'Apocalypse et l'Histoire*, Paris, Presses universitaires de France, 1957, p.44. Critics have not been persuaded by the general thesis propounded by Giet in this work, which involves reading the three woes as corresponding to precise episodes of the Jewish War: its author is judged to have read more into the text of Rev than may reasonably be read out of it.

127 This encourages Charlier, *Comprendre* (vol. 1), p.262, to call the woman (with only a little exaggeration) 'a new ark, and an incarnate one this time'.

128 Rowland, *Revelation*, p.103, notes how the act of ejecting the dragon from heaven guarantees God's reign and ends any proceedings against God's elect.

129 Prigent, *Apocalypse*, p.373, credits the author of Rev with the spawning of a messianic exegesis of Gen 3.15, given that nowhere in the extant writings of Second Temple Judaism is such a reading of Gen 3.15 to be found.

130 Ellul, *Architecture*, p.85, is right to see in the woman a symbol for all creation renewed, in principle, at the very moment Christ brings about reconciliation.

131 An especially clear and succinct summary of this is found in Charlier, *Comprendre* (vol. 1), p.265. 'Thus the mysterious woman, like a new Eve, heralds the appearance of a new creation; as Daughter of Zion, who manages to bring to birth more than just wind, she causes dawn to rise upon a salvation she had begun to prepare twelve centuries earlier, when she was rescued from Egypt and the wilderness' (my translation). On reference to Eve in this text C. Hauret may also be consulted, 'Eve transfigurée:de la Genèse à l'Apocalypse', *Revue d'Histoire et de Philosophie Religieuses* 3-4, 1979, pp.327-39.

132 Kiddle, *Revelation*, pp.220-25.

133 Charlier once more, *Comprendre* (vol. 1), p.262.

134 See for example Mealy, *Thousand Years*, p.69.

135 As correctly argued by Marshall, *Parables*, pp.144-45. For this author, the way 12.17 is expressed 'implies comporting oneself *according to the covenant of allegiance and practice between God and Israel* to which Jesus is, for John and his community, a paradigmatic witness . . . John understands it as incumbent upon him and upon

members of his community to stand as witnesses in the way Jesus stood as a witness to God's covenant with Israel: they are to keep the commandments of God, fulfil the practices enjoined, refrain from those prohibited, seek purity *through means provided in the covenant*.

136 On this point, Marshall, *ibid.*, p.148, has this to say: 'Jesus is for John the witness *(martus)* of the covenant or the proof *(pistis)* of the covenant, the guarantor and inaugurator of the fulfilment of God's promises and God's justice'.

137 Readers of French will find some considerations pertaining to 13.9,10b,18; 14.12; and 17.9 put forward in the course of my article 'Persévérance des saints', *op.cit.*, pp.47-49.

138 Compare Wall, *Revelation*, p.181.

139 As Brütsch puts it, *Clarté*, p.224.

140 See Mounce, *Revelation*, p.257.

141 This proposal is my own. However, what is not new is the idea that the number six be understood as the tearing in half of twelve – the number of the tribes that make up the covenant people – which is then tripled, in other words, taken to extremes. On this, *cf.* Charlier, *Comprendre* (vol. 1), p.290.

142 Thus, for example, Yarbro-Collins, *Apocalypse*, pp.102-3.

143 This is the option taken, at this point, by J.-L. d'Aragon, *The Apocalypse*, Englewood Cliffs, Prentice-Hall, 1968.

144 Caird, *Revelation*, pp.188-95, advocates this option. Although Boring, *Revelation*, p.169*ff.*, also subscribes to this reading, he does avoid falling into the triple exegetical trap by rejecting the interpretation of judgment only, or of mixed judgment and salvation, and then recommending that a balance be maintained between *the basic images* (all of which refer to a judgment) and those elements which nonetheless point to salvation. However, it should be noted that the only way to collapse these two clearly differentiated fates into universal salvation, as Boring or Caird contrive to do, is by an unwarranted deconstruction of the original aim of the text.

145 Mounce, *Revelation*, p.279, reads the grape harvest as a judicial sentence, purely and simply, whereas the harvest implies separating the wheat from the weeds (Mt 13.30) or the wheat from the chaff (Lk 3.17).

146 Referring expressly to Lev 26.28.

147 This verb has a sacrificial colouring and is used for example in Lev (LXX) to mean the pouring out of sacrificial blood – on this see Beale, *Revelation*, p.813.

148 For Beale, *ibid.*, pp.794-800, John retains the *framework* of the Song of Moses while drawing the *contents* of Rev 15.3-4 from testimony to God's character as presented by a series of OT texts (from the Psalms especially). In this he is following Bauckham, *Climax*, p.296*ff*, though (as already intimated) without going as far as to attribute to John, as Bauckham does, a *new emphasis* upon the conversion of the nations.

149 In either Rev or the whole of the Johannine literature, *marturion* is used only here. Caird, *Revelation*, p.200, notes how the focus on the Ark in 11.19 now narrows to an interest in the testimony it contains.

150 The Palestinian Targum to Lev 16, unearthed at Qumran, repeats the expression four times. Prigent, *Apocalypse, in loc.*, readily agrees that the tradition behind the seven angels carrying seven plagues comes from Lev 26. We may note the presence of the same idea of sevenfold punishment in Ps 79.12; it is v. 3 of this psalm, as noted by Beale, *Revelation*, p.803, that Rev 16.6 is alluding to. Beale

also points (p.807) to the seven angelic beings of Ezek 9.1–10.6 as possible models for John here, given that they set about those who have no protective seal from God (in the context of the Temple filled with the glory-cloud of God's presence, Ezek 10.4).

151 Similarly, Rowland, *Revelation*, p.125.

152 Allo, *Apocalypse*, p.252 (my translation). Sweet, *Revelation*, p.241, sees an analogy in the bowl that makes Israel drunk, which God places in the hands of their tormentors (Isa 51.17,22). Ellul, *Architecture*, pp.38-39, explains this ambivalence as arising from the symbolism of the cups at the Lord's Supper, already a symbol for blessing, communion and reconciliation but also for betrayal, cursing, wrath and rejection.

153 Compare Beale, *Revelation*, p.806.

154 This is how Wall takes it, *Revelation*, p.198.

155 Compare Beale, *Revelation*, pp.821-23, who notes the way several Jewish writings stress, much as does Rev 16.8-9, the dimension of spiritual punishment conveyed by the plagues of fire.

156 For an assessment of the probability of a reference to Ezek 16, especially, see Beale, *ibid.*, p.838.

157 Ruiz, *Transformation*, pp.259,62, considers that the outpouring of the bowl (16.7) implies Isa 66.1a with its theme of divine judgment, while 16.18-21 borrows a number of times from Exodus, including the Sinai narrative (Exod 9.18-26; 19.16-18, whose theophany and earthquake crop up again here) or the storm theophany from Ezek 38.18-23 (in which Gog suffers God's counterattack), all of which serves to express, in very clear terms, a manifestation of divine wrath.

158 Beale, *Revelation*, p.842.

159 In order to accentuate this Chilton, *Days*, p.389, already mentions 'chalices' in 15.7. In similar fashion Charlier, *Comprendre* (vol. 1), p.35, gives the bowls septet the title 'the world *out of* communion with God', while Ellul, *Architecture*, p.209, refers to a 'cup of reversion . . . since Babylon had made human beings commune with her power'. We should note how Ellul proposes reading the seven bowls of wrath as a form of communion with God because, as he sees it, hearing God's judgment or rebuke is to commune with him. Rather than being an exegetical conclusion, however, this is to be explained theologically as an attempt to reconcile judgment and grace. I am unable to follow him in this since the text of Revelation quite incontrovertibly refers *both* to communion and anti-communion, in accordance with the double logic of a relationship with God which may either be sustained or else irremediably broken.

160 Corsini, *Apocalypse*, p.337.

161 I am grateful to Schüssler-Fiorenza, *Just World*, p.99, for having underscored this aspect of the description. I am not, however, able to agree with her interpretation of the justification of the martyrs, in which a covenant framework plays no part at all and where 'Babylon' is assimilated to Rome.

162 And not Rome, *contra* Mounce, *op. cit.*, p.326: Jerusalem, uniquely, had this representative role.

163 Thus, the meaning of 18.20b would be that God has given *you* justice (where *you* relates to *his faithful subjects*) by turning upon her (that is, 'Babylon') the unjust sentence she had imposed on them. Charlier, *Comprendre* (vol. 2), p.113, translates the end of 18.20 like this, 'God has made her give account of the outrage [or damages] suffered by you' (my translation). As Beale suggests,

Revelation, pp.916-18, 18.20b is to be explained both in light of the martyrs' cry in 6.10 as well as by reference to 19.2, which may be considered an explanatory expansion of 18.20b.

164 Without drawing any conclusion in particular from his commentary C.S. Keener, *Revelation*, Grand Rapids, Zondervan, 2000, p.422, accepts that the lament in Rev 18.1-8 looks more like a curse.

165 For her thoughtful exegesis, I am particularly indebted, here, to J.M. Ford, *Revelation*, p.300*ff.*

166 *Ibid.*, pp.296, 301.

167 *Ibid.*, p.303. As Ford points out, the rabbinic tractate *Sanhedrin* 7.2 prescribes a death whereby a burning drink of molten lead was to be poured into the throat.

168 I. Provan, 'Foul Spirits, fornication and finance: Revelation from an Old Testament perspective', *Journal for the Study of the New Testament* 64, 1996, p.94, in dependence on the results of A.J. Beagley, *The Sitz im Leben of the Apocalypse with Particular Reference to the Role of the Church's Enemies*, New York, De Gruyter, 1987, pp.113-50. For the paragraphs that follow, relating to ch.18, I am indebted to these studies among others.

169 So J.M. Ford, *Revelation*, p.304, who reminds her readers that the listed cargoes correspond to the articles required for the Temple and its services of worship.

170 For consideration of 1 Kgs 4-5, see Provan's comments, 'Foul Spirits', pp.88, 95.

171 J. Jeremias reminds his readers of this activity in his book *Jerusalem in the Time of Jesus*, Philadelphia, Fortress, 1969, pp.31-51. For commentators on Rev who find him convincing, see J.M. Ford, *Revelation*, pp.304-5, or again Leonard, *Come Out*, pp.122-23.

172 *Jewish War* v.5.4,6; the account of the handing over of its treasures to Titus should also be consulted, in vi.8.3.

173 *Climax*, ch.10, pp.338-83. Right from the *abstract* onwards, he defends with force and conviction the view that 'the Book of Revelation is one of the fiercest attacks on Rome and one of the most effective pieces of political resistance literature from the period of the early empire'.

174 *Ibid.*, pp.343-50.

175 *Ibid.*, pp.350-71.

176 *Ibid.*, pp.378-83.

177 Such assent may be illustrated by one recent commentary (by Keener, *op. cit.*, p.428-31) and one recent journal article (by A.D. Callahan, 'Apocalypse as Critique of Political Economy. Some Notes on Revelation 18', in *Horizons in Biblical Theology* 21, 1999, pp.46-65).

178 In his time this is what A. Edersheim suggested, *The Life and Times of Jesus the Messiah* (vol. 1), McLean, MacDonald, 1886, p.116. Chilton, *Days*, p.456, refers back to this study and goes on to say that 'ancient Jewish writings enable us to identify no fewer than 118 different articles of import from foreign lands, covering more than even modern luxury has devised'.

179 Provan, 'Foul Spirits', p.99, who is explicitly critical of the reading of Rev 18 put forward by Bauckham.

180 An echo may be heard, here, of a scenario in Jer 51.63 (LXX), where the symbolic action carried out certainly does involve a scroll like those explicitly referred to in Rev 5 and 10. The total and irrevocable destruction recalls the judgment meted out to Tyre (Ezek 26.19-21 – a context still in John's mind, here), as well as the fate of Edom according to Isa 34.9-10.

181 A view taken to an extent by Beale, *Revelation*, p.919, who follows Caird, *Revelation*, pp.230-31, at this point. These authors see both of the scrolls as decrees whose fulfilment is recounted by the narrative, but not as documents whose purpose is to regulate the covenant or apply its sanctions. For a development of the point of view I am defending here, compare Chilton, *Days*, pp.460-61.

182 J.M. Ford reads things this way, too, *Revelation*, p.309.

183 Compare Beale, *Revelation*, pp.934-43, especially his discussion of 19.7-8. For another point of view that prefers 'good works', see Mealy, *Thousand Years*, p.79.

184 As Charlier says, *Comprendre* (vol. 2), p.159, 'there could be no stronger way of expressing the antithesis between those who commune with Christ and those who commune with Impurity, and so with the Satan' (my translation).

185 My way of reading this is shared by D. Ford, *Crisis!* (vol. 3), pp.688-89, who points to the same fundamental contrast.

186 For Duff, *Who Rides?*, p.104, the torrent spewed out by the dragon (12.15) also has anti-eucharistic force and offers a contrast to the water of life (7.17; 21.6; 22.1,17); the same goes, of course, for the draught of blood in 17.6.

187 Compare J.M. Ford, *Revelation*, p.324.

188 Charlier, *Comprendre* (vol. 2), p.155.

189 See Cothenet, *Apocalypse*, p.157. For J.M. Ford, *Revelation*, p.323, the sword here may have other connotations than simply the juridical one, perhaps evoking the prophetic word with its potential for bringing about what it declares, in a creative and dynamic way.

190 At this precise point, Prigent, *Apocalypse*, says there is 'no place for an accused or, for that matter, for a verdict'. For this author, 'judge' is synonymous with both 'sit on a throne' and 'reign'.

191 A favourable judgment or verdict (*krima*) is the result of the process of justice pursuing its course (*krisis*) in the same way that, by analogy, the creature (*ktisma*) is what results from the process of creation (*ktisis*). This is how Delebecque reasons, *Apocalypse*, p.248, and to me this is sound logic.

192 Similarly, R.D. Davis, *Heavenly Court*, p.214.

193 Compare Beale, *Revelation*, p.1037.

194 Corsini, *Apocalypse*, p.382*ff.*

195 Compare once more Beale, *Revelation*, p.1031.

196 See J.M. Ford, *Revelation*, p.359.

197 Compare Smalley, *Revelation*, p.579, for whom there is a covenant theology underlying all of the section 21.1–22.17. He argues that it is the figure of New Jerusalem, especially, that may be interpreted in terms of a covenant relationship with God, which his people will enjoy in the eternal state. Relationship is indeed at the heart of the metaphor for, if there are inevitably material aspects to the city (21.11-21), she is at heart a representation of a relationship or a 'special kinship' that binds God and humanity to one another.

198 On this point, compare R.D. Davis, *Heavenly Court*, p.215.

199 Corsini, *op.cit.*, pp.388-91.

200 A. Paul, *Jésus-Christ*, pp.264-66, may profitably be consulted here.

201 Chilton, *Days*, p.538.

202 As Smalley, *Revelation*, p.535, reminds us, renewed covenant is what furnishes the basis for Christian faith.

203 On this, see Bauckham, *Climax*, pp.310-13.

204 For the capacity worship possesses to transcend the limits of time, as well as for

the potential in Revelation's narrative for changing readers' perspectives, see D. Barr, *Tales,* p.174 and pp.177-80.

205 Ellul, *Architecture,* p.227.

206 M. Vogel, *Das Heil,* p.203, points out that eschatological Jerusalem symbolises the renewal of the covenant, functioning as a geographical centre for God's restored people.

207 The controversy surrounding the word *stoicheia* is familiar enough; see for example the section devoted to this by H.H. Esser in his article 'Law, custom, elements', in C. Brown (ed.), *NIDNTT* (vol. 2), Carlisle/Grand Rapids, Paternoster/Eerdmans, 1986, pp.451-53. It is sufficient for our purpose here to note the connotation of *becoming obsolete* or *being abolished* carried by these 'elements' in all the relevant texts. As in 2 Pet 3, Revelation's logic is that for newness to be established, there has to be the dissolution (*cf.* 2 Cor 5.17) of what went before.

208 In similar vein, R.D. Davis, *Heavenly Court,* p.218.

209 As mentioned in the margin of Nestlé-Aland, *in loc.*

210 A similar combination of these two eschatological promises – of God making his home with his own and establishing a relationship where he is their God and they are his people – may be found in Exod 29.45; Jer 31.33; Ezek 37.27; 43.7; Zech 2.10-11; 8.8.

211 On this point, compare M. Vogel, *Das Heil,* pp.203-4.

212 For discussion of this Isaianic echo see once more Vogel, *ibid,* p.205.

213 Leonard, *Come Out,* p.169.

214 Although he is not thinking of covenant as such at this point, Prigent, *Apocalypse,* pp.465-67, does give the list in 21.8 the general heading of idolatry and does see its thrust as primarily ethical'. He also thinks that evil's displacement by the kingdom is in view: 'that is why, he says, there has to be combat, sanction and judgment here'. Such comments only become more pertinent still once it is recognised that what is at issue, in this text, is *covenant fulfilment.*

215 Ellul, *Architecture,* p.232: 'the continuing presence of this angel very appropriately signifies the continuing reality, and even the inseparable nature, of both suffering and glory'.

216 How should this be explained? Prigent, *Apocalypse,* p.471, thinks we are no longer in a position to do so and is unconvinced by the interpretation that the reference here is to guards posted on the walls of restored Zion (Isa 62.6). This may be too hasty however. Beale, *Revelation,* p.1069 – relying on both Sweet and Mounce – does deem this a probable reference, given both the frequency with which Isa 40–66 is referred to in the finale of Rev and, above all, given the interpretation that *guards* = *angels,* as found in the two rabbinic writings *Midrash Exodus* 18.5 and *Pesikta Rabbati* 35.2. In Ezek 41, too, sculpted cherubim adorn walls and gates (41.18,20,25). In fact we can go back beyond the horticultural aspects of Ezekiel's temple, which reflect Solomon's (see 1 Kgs 6), to Gen 3.24, where it is cherubim who bar rebellious and fallen humanity from all access to the garden God gave them at the beginning. The paradisal city of Rev 21–22, its gates emblazoned with angels, would seem to re-establish in Christ the relationship that lay broken since Adam.

217 Resseguie, *Revelation Unsealed,* p.64, has spotted this.

218 Beale, *Revelation,* pp.1069-70, offers a reminder of how the precious stones of Isa 54.11-12 were interpreted representatively at Qumran as symbolising the

219 Beale, *ibid.*, p.1070; *cf.* Chilton, *Days*, p.555.

220 Charlier, *Comprendre* (vol. 2), p.225 (my translation).

221 As was well said by Farrer, *op. cit.*, p.221.

222 Charlier, *Comprendre* (vol. 2), p. 232 (my translation).

223 Brütsch, *Clarté*, p.384 (my translation), in reliance on an article by J. Comblin, 'Nouvelle Jérusalem', p.18.

224 See Beale's commentary on 21.15-17, *Revelation*, p.1072.

225 As Smalley sees it, *Revelation*, p.563, the state in question is the covenant relationship which must be characteristic of life in New Jerusalem.

226 Ellul, *Architecture*, p.243, discusses 'the transformation of the situation in Eden' and, in particular, of Adam's fate: at the time, he was condemned to death (death being, for Ellul, synonymous with fallenness, loss, absence, rupture and condemnation) but is now welcomed into an everlasting, face-to-face encounter with God.

227 I cannot improve on what Beale has to say at this point, *Revelation*, pp.1112-13: 'the curse of spiritual and physical death set on the human race by Adam in the first garden is permanently removed by the Lamb in the last garden at the time of the new creation . . . there will be no form of curse in the new Jerusalem because God's consummate, ruling presence will fill the city'.

228 According to J.M. Ford, *Revelation*, p.362, for Early Judaism the *herem* constituted the severest form of excommunication.

229 On this matter, see Bauckham, *Climax*, p.317.

230 Compare Chilton, *Days*, p.536.

231 Similarly, Schüssler-Fiorenza, *Just World*, p.115.

232 Brütsch, *Clarté*, p.387 (my translation).

233 Kiddle, *Revelation*, p.452.

234 For Roloff, *Revelation*, p.251, this 'putting outside' is to be interpreted in terms of the separation and exclusion practised at the Lord's Supper as signifying both God's judgment and God's grace. He also thinks 22.20 provides a liturgical and specifically, a eucharistic echo.

235 P. Prigent, *L'Apocalypse de St. Jean*, Geneva, Labor et Fides, 1988, p.377. Prigent's revised commentary (Eng. translation) does not reproduce in this form these closing remarks from the earlier edition. I have nevertheless chosen to retain them here (in my own translation).

236 Similarly Smalley, *Revelation*, p.583, who considers the paraenesis in 22.18-19 to be 'the obverse side of the blessing pronounced in 1.3'.

237 In 22.7b,18-19, Beale, *Use of the OT*, pp.95-98, 305, thinks there is an allusion to Deut 4.2. Caird, *Revelation*, p.287, for his part suggests some non-canonical parallels, namely the solemn warnings given by *1 Enoch* 104.10-11 and *2 Enoch* 48.7-8; Beale agrees that the first of these two texts is a true parallel, on the grounds that it does give an indication of how Deut was being interpreted in the Second Temple period.

238 I am once more indebted here to Beale for his discussion, *ibid*, pp.95-98.

239 Smalley, *Revelation*, p.584, thinks that the seer, by his threats at this point, is warning readers specifically against the lie of idol worship (exactly as Deut 4.12,29 do).

Conclusion to Part Three

At the close of Part Two of this study, I offered a provisional assessment of the combined results of Parts One and Two. From the major themes of Revelation examined there, it seemed reasonable to draw an interim conclusion which I now paraphrase as follows: *Human beings may enjoy a free and true relation to God who is wholly other, and to the Lamb, on condition that, in the various choices and commitments of their lives, they refuse idolatry with all it entails.*

How may this happen? How may believers worship the God of the Bible, in his transcendence, and enjoy close fellowship with him, in his immanence? Our study in Part Three has now supplied an answer: according to Revelation, *God offers to humankind a way of living together with him, which is structured by a covenant.*

God, who reveals himself, and humanity, which finds itself through the Word by which God addresses it, now meet one another in a way they had never met previously, and in a manner never to be bettered in the future: through the Messiah Jesus, human beings encounter God's grace and *shalom* in person. As we have traced the itinerary followed by this final major theme, we have seen emerge a logic that governs everything: the issue of covenant – in both its harmonious and horribly disfigured forms – which, like a kind of backbone, structures the antithetical arrangement of Revelation's diverse thematic materials.

Honoured alike in the breach or in the observance, this covenant has furnished Revelation's 'scriptwriter' with his lavish decor. We have seen him draw upon all its aspects, from its fixtures to its movable assets (as it were), especially in the fully updated form given it by Jesus. As for the often disconcerting happenings which occur on Revelation's stage, they too are best explained against the backdrop of the eventful history of this pact, which reaches its climax spectacularly in the grandiose vision that closes the Book.

Epilogue

A significant contribution to the literary and theological unity of Revelation is made by the complex thematic materials woven into John's Book, whether prominent major themes or diverse micro-themes and motifs. It has been my chief concern, throughout this study, to offer an integrated interpretation of this thematic whole via an analysis and synthesis of the parts. With a commitment to honouring Revelation's cohesion as a text, and using appropriate reading strategies and methodological choices (presented in the introduction), I have sought to explore under three heads a series of seven principal, convergent antithetical themes. Dialogue with more traditional diachronic approaches to the text has been carried out in the detours and footnotes. Whenever problems of interpretation have arisen in the course of study, I have favoured solutions involving the explanation of the text by the text and by the Book's sub-text (the Jewish Scriptures), rather than have recourse to external exegetical levers.

Description of Revelation's major themes, each of them cast in antithetical form, has been undertaken in three stages:

In Part One, we pursued a set of three thematic trajectories, which together reflect good news concerning the reign, power and glory shared by God and the Lamb, in all they are and do, and also set forth their caricature;

In Part Two, our focus was on human response to the divine initiative, through three further thematic itineraries – relating to the revelation, reception, assimilation and transmission of the universal gospel – which uncovered opposing responses (positive and negative) to the call to follow God and the Lamb, to belong to them and to serve them faithfully in this world;

Part Three sought to integrate all our findings by examining what I take to be the thematic hinge on which Revelation turns, namely everything that unites God and humanity in a difficult yet feasible relationship, whereby covenant determines the shape of God's presence among human beings who have been redeemed from among the nations.

With hindsight there appear to me to be two images which can help capture this thematic reading of John's Revelation. The first image pictures the seven interlaced thematic itineraries as seven streams irrigating (as it were) the text and carrying readers along with the eddies of the current into the multiple meanders of Revelation's narrative. We have had to negotiate, sometimes with difficulty, the bends and rapids of Revelation's apocalyptic plot, which is entirely shaped by the logic of antithesis, up to and including the denouement itself. It is my hope that after all these boat-trips, readers might now be ready to undertake their own exploratory journeys!

The second image hears the Book as a whole, with its three constituent parts, as though it were a symphony in three movements: *God, Humanity & Covenant*. The reading of Revelation I have proposed here has been akin to listening, in movements one and two, to the often strident dissonance of its six principal melody-lines (all of them featuring contrasts), before hearing the resolution offered by the overall harmony of the music of the last movement, as the symphonic orchestration moves with increasing intensity towards its final crescendo. Here, again, it is my hope that by the end of the concert – having heard an interpretation of the entire work – listeners might have gained an appreciation of Revelation as a whole.

* * * * *

In this epilogue, I would like to draw certain implications from my work, offering some answers to the following question: *How may John's Revelation profitably be read?* How interesting it would be to know what the repercussions were, in the lives of Revelation's first readers, of their listening to and meditating on the Book! I imagine them to have been positive in nature, for two reasons. One is the widespread presence of Christians in Asia in the early second century CE, as substantiated by historical research; the other is the very fact that Revelation has been preserved and handed down to us. Yet we know very little of what Asian believers' lives were like, whether before or after they had read Revelation, simply because we possess very few hard facts relating to the experience of the author or his first readers. At best, our critical reconstruction of society and culture, religion and politics in the ancient world can only be approximate. And one thing escapes us entirely: knowledge of the actual consequences (religious, social or political), for the congregations of Messiah Jesus in Asia Minor, of resolutely keeping the Word of God and Testimony of Jesus once the hearing of Revelation in their context had nourished their faith.

However, just because we are ignorant of what happened when Revelation was heard in its initial theatre of reception, does not mean that Revelation cannot resonate with us in our own context – quite the reverse. There was no question for John the seer, or for the members of the Church in Asia, that they must lift their eyes from the horizon of the text they had encountered in worship – worship being both a world apart and also an encounter that takes place at the heart of this world – in order to rivet their gaze once more onto the reality of their daily lives where their faith must be lived out in the ebb and flow of history. Since today's readers make the same move from hearing the text to rejoining life in this world, knowing how followers of Jesus in Roman Asia in the first century might have felt the impact, in their daily lives, of reading Revelation is less important than figuring out, for our time and place, the implications of our own reading of and meditation on this Book. If Revelation's original intent was to advance the cause of costly fidelity to Jesus among those who heard it, in and for their context – as it clearly is, from start to finish – then the challenge, for contemporary readers, remains that of responding to the Book's exigencies today.

Shouldering our responsibility as readers

In due course we will be asking what were the *means* used by Revelation's author, as he drew upon all his art and science, for capitalising on his readers' ability to understand and to respond so as to convince them to make crucial life-choices. Reflecting on this will help us see how we might become competent readers ourselves. First, however, we need to consider what objective the author was seeking to achieve. One way to formulate it might be this: *to provoke a decisive encounter with the truth revealed in Jesus Christ.* As we have seen, from the very start of the revelation communicated to the Churches of Asia, their members were hearing a proclamation of the truth about God and the Lamb and their relationship with humanity. Such a message demands a response.

From the outset, Revelation appears in principle to take for granted that its first readers adhere to good news concerning Messiah Jesus, greeting them as a royal people in the service of God who have been delivered from their sin and loved by Jesus Christ (1.5-6). However, the practical outworking of this in their life of faith seems to be partly imperilled by what is actually going on in the Churches, where the need for self-examination is emphasised. Beginning with the crucial septet of oracles to Churches, the author works hard at bringing the recipients of his prophecy to the realisation that they ought not to believe everything their eyes see or their ears hear. Every major theme explored in the Book has dealt, in one way or another, with the same basic contrast between that which (despite deceptive appearances to the contrary) is really *true* about God and humanity and that which (however authentic things may seem at first glance) turns out to be *false* on the same subject.

No one can enter the reading zone that Revelation opens up without discovering this state of affairs and being brought, through this awareness, to a place of decision. Revelation's word-pictures alert listeners' ears and spectators' eyes to *reality* and to *appearances* that emerge from this revelation of human beings and their God, thereby empowering them to make right choices. However, to choose is not easy. All kinds of disruptions bedevil the deepening of knowledge by means of truth that is properly distinguishable from falsehood. John himself – as recipient and conduit of the revelation – requires the services of an interpreting angel on occasion in order to understand certain things. Seer though he may be and compelled, in the instant when God reveals himself, to bow down, to listen and to obey (1.17-19), John remains quite capable of forgetting everything – as shown by two occasions governed by identical factors and conditions (in 19.9-10 and again in 22.8)!

From the reader's point of view, the seer's double faux pas here is especially significant. If even the prophet can stray from the path when trying to discover how to follow the Lamb faithfully and authentically in this world, then this throws into sharp relief the difficulty which even the most attentive of spectators have in truly seeing and comprehending. Choosing to obey God alone, as Lord of the covenant, obviously is and can only ever be something difficult. This important insight is gained in the very real *proximity* that readers feel towards a seer who is their imperfect guide; this calls into question a common understanding of 1.9b, which stresses the *distance* that purportedly separates John (on Patmos) from the recipients of his message (at Smyrna, Pergamum or elsewhere). On the contrary: an ostensibly reliable narrator, who can sometimes get things so badly wrong, is attractive to us as readers; and whatever problems *we* have in understanding the revelation are consequently made relative!

The bond uniting prophet and believers, as brothers and companions in their union with Jesus (1.9a), simultaneously facilitates the creation, at this early point, of a *distinction* between (on the one hand) every true witness of Jesus and (on the other) those in the Asian congregations at whom a finger is to be pointed – be they Nicolaitans (2.6), followers of the satan (2.9,24; 3.9), followers of Balaam (2.14) or of Jezebel (2.20). All alike remain misguided and misled until they repent. The programmatic inaugural septet puts into place this way of differentiating two categories of people. Nevertheless, as a division it is in fact more rhetorical than real. Distinguishing an 'us' from a 'them' in the ecclesial communities of Asia is not so much thinly-disguised name-calling of real people as a means of driving a wedge, in advance, between all those whom the ensuing plot is going to pit against one another as adversaries: the 'sealed' or the 'tattooed', faithful followers of the Lamb or blinded slaves of the monster. Believers and unbelievers will all take the stage later, in the arena of judgment and salvation, as part of an apocalyptic dramatisation of Messiah Jesus's renewal of the broken covenant. In the course of the plot, and in the face of bogus messiahs who appear, they will all have to take their stand for or against Jesus. This is Revelation's way of confronting readers, from page one, with two camps and with an unavoidable and pressing question: *With which one should I identify?*

Answering this question is both easy and difficult! Easy, in the sense that Revelation, by a skilful literary exercise, succeeds in bringing us face-to-face with two quite distinct takes on reality, achieving this on every thematic trajectory by which we have traversed the text. Using agreements and opposing traits, resemblance or difference, Revelation throughout has characterised two clearly rival causes and set in dynamic contrast two opposing teams, two conflicting ways, two diametrically opposite entities – one of which is obviously good and the other evil. Difficult, in the sense that although a surface resemblance binds these contrasting realities somewhat astonishingly together, there is a deeper dissimilarity which we need to uncover if we are to interpret things correctly.

Thus, for example, earth-dwellers regularly choose the wrong camp: they cannot see the dragon and monsters' cause for the spectacular illusion that it is, so they are blind to the fact that the first monster is only a *pseudo*-messiah, with a project that amounts to no more than an *anti*-covenant, backed up by an assistant spewing forth propaganda which is nothing less than a *false* gospel. In short, they are oblivious to the fact that, where those things that oppose God are concerned, nothing rings true – and understandably this gives readers pause for thought. By showing us this, Revelation no doubt attempts to underline, in negative fashion, something positive: the only reality that has actual existence is one where God and the human beings whom he loves may meet, in and through the Crucified and Risen One. However, the plot achieves this by depicting forces lined up against God, which recruit their own followers, exert enormous enslaving power over credulous human beings and wreak havoc even among the people God has chosen.

It would be quite unwarranted, I feel, to speak of dualism in this connection. Only God is and only God lives: outside of him are nothing but chimeras. For Revelation, as for the Old Testament writing prophets, only the truth and reality which God guarantees has real substance, even if it is always described with typically Hebraic reserve in terms of approximations (God is 'like' or 'resembles'). Anything which claims to rival God and his ways cannot exist, in and of itself, but can only be their strict negation. Nonetheless it is for readers to work things out for themselves: they must discern that the ghostly monster is a mere projection of evil which only appears to live; they must reject it every time in favour of the Lamb in whom, alone, God comes near. Yet even if, as choices go, this one seems clear, the outcome is not known in advance. In a world of appearances, where a thousand incongruities and contradictions arise, the human condition entails being suspended between the abyss and the vault of heaven, in a place where the prayers of some mix with the blasphemies of others. If those whom the sword-word of good news has set free from lying propaganda are to see and understand – or to distinguish the true from the false – they must make good use of their wisdom. Only those who remain faithful from beginning to end, through the tribulation, kingdom and constancy which all disciples of Jesus know (1.9), will manage to win through, buoyed up by the promises to the victor. To choose Jesus means to lay one's life on the line. Discipleship, as Revelation presents it, is a road just as rocky as the one to which the Evangelist Mark accustoms his readers.

It follows that readers of Revelation find no neutral space in which they might be free to take what is appealing to them, but leave the rest. This is a message that sets out to 'corner' those to whom it is sent, treating them from the start as true believers. As I have already suggested, when John the seer presents himself to his readers as their brother and companion, or as one of their own (1.1,9), he is also allying them with his own status as 'brother of the prophets' (22.9). Such a position makes him just as jealous as were the prophets for the covenant Lord and the exclusive loyalty which Israel owed him. By yoking Asia's believers to his own prophetic condition, John makes them by association the first to be 'cornered' by the fact that God judges and saves a people who are ready to belong to him one day, but just as inclined to abandon him the next.[1] Capable of faithfulness but attracted to idolatry, the members of the seven Churches are made party to the prophet's energetic pleas for God's cause by the simple act of listening to the revelation imparted to them by the seer. When the people assemble in convocation on the Lord's Day (1.10), day of grace leading to life or of condemnation leading to death, their Mediator reminds them again and again that there is a decision to be made ('this is what the One who . . . has to say . . .', 2.1, *etc.*), while the Spirit underscores this (' . . . what the Spirit is saying to the Churches', 2.7): by their choice they will either honour or repudiate their covenant responsibilities.

In such circumstances, the act of opening and reading Revelation delivers an invitation to us as contemporary readers to take our place before God and situate ourselves among the servants of Jesus Christ (1.1), electing to belong to the 'us' whose inclusive 'we' denotes his people and the object of his sacrificial love (1.5-6). Opting instead to keep our distance remains an eventuality which the plot itself envisages, but at any rate Revelation commits every reader to self-examination, obliging us to situate ourselves in relation to the Word we have received with its summons to obey. Even before we have finished reading the oracles to Churches we are being called upon as readers to get involved, to factor in our own life-story so far, and to face choices that must be made.

Revelation is a communication in story form. As we hear and read the Book, it asks questions of the way we live our lives in our own space and time – questions about how we live before God and, above all, about how we worship. As originally received, the revelation impacted its first readers or listeners as they assembled together in communal worship. Through its last Word on the slain-but-standing Lamb, on the Covenant-Person, Revelation encouraged them in the context of worship to take their place in the unfolding story of the covenant or of God's coming among Israel, according to the Scriptures. As Asia's believers joined in the praise of heaven through their encounter with the Word, so they enlisted for the task of bearing witness on earth. Today Revelation still summons its readers, wherever they are, to be in their turn worshippers and witnesses of Jesus Christ, Crucified and Risen.

Becoming competent readers

Choosing to live for Jesus Christ: this, then, is the decision which Revelation's author advocates and which is still the recommendation his writing makes to contemporary readers. But what drives the reader, from the Book itself, to take such a decision as this? In essence, two positive examples to be followed are supplied by the narrative. On the level of the apocalyptic story, first of all, we discover those who are committed disciples of a Lamb and who refuse to be worshippers of a monster. On a second level, through reading constantly between the lines to where the sub-text lies, another choice also emerges. Here, we discover members of the people of Israel who had chosen in their own time, throughout their thousand-year history (as the Scriptures testify), to live out their calling as YHWH's faithful wife and not to prostitute themselves with the seductions of idolatry. Put another way, it is with a certain degree of extravagance that Revelation's story dramatises the choice made by the faithful followers of the Lamb, against the tide, in terms of another choice already made before their time by godly Israelites, their ancestors in the faith.

As contemporary readers leave behind the context of the ancient cities of Ephesus, Smyrna or Philadelphia, but keep in mind these two exemplars, they may contemplate what it is to 'conquer', in their own time and place, where the challenges for faith have changed: what will it mean to choose to follow Jesus the Crucified and Risen One as their Lord, rather than back the wrong 'messiah'? Thus the key to readers' own faithfulness to Jesus, to be lived out in the modes of today's world, is still to be found in the characteristics of the Lamb's faithful followers or of Israel's faithful remnant that preceded them. Similarly, when Revelation's earth-dwellers (or their predecessors in salvation history) are seen to rush headlong into idolatry, today's readers may consider whether our own contemporaries in rash haste may be allowing themselves to be beguiled or enslaved by the promise of whatever so-called 'salvation' happens to come along – be it religious, economic, social or political in nature.

What was it, which enabled believers in Sardis or Thyatira, their eyes and ears opened by the revelation, to apply the insights of Revelation's narrative to what was at stake in their own life-situation? How might they have succeeded in detecting there what the seer had been disclosing about divine initiative, appropriate human response and a resulting good relationship between God and humanity – as well as any dangerous substitutes to watch out for? Two sorts of competency, it seems to me, are involved and both of them are still to be recommended to today's readers for use in attempting an analysis of their own situation. The first is a familiarity with the Jewish Scriptures, which is indispensable both for identifying the positive and negative elements of the Book's themes, arranged in antithetical parallelism, and for comprehending the message which this contrast conveys. The second competency is a readiness or willingness to frequent Revelation in a more sustained way than would be demanded by a momentary hearing or a cursory reading of the Book. It is a fact that Revelation's great literary and theological sophistication required considerable effort from its first readers and still demands the same of us.[2] Exactly what do these two kinds of competency involve? Let us take a closer look.

Revelation and the Old Testament

Of all the New Testament writings, Revelation is the one which most constantly brings precise recollection of Israel's Scriptures into play. From the literature of the Old Testament, and sometimes from other Jewish writings, Revelation borrows the majority of the positive entities which figure in the numerous uses it makes of antithetical parallelism. The same goes for the bare bones (if not the flesh) of various caricatural elements which the plot manages to set over against these positives at its negative pole. The death of Messiah Jesus on behalf of Israel but also the nations – so central, theologically speaking, to Revelation – is to be understood against the backdrop of the story of biblical Israel, to which the experience of believers in the Churches of Asia corresponded and of which their experience constituted a further extension.

John and the other members of these ecclesial communities had a characteristic disposition for reading the Scriptures as Jesus had and, especially, for viewing Jesus himself as the interpretative key for unlocking those same Scriptures. But this hermeneutical strategy does not seem to have been the only one available within the assemblies of Asia. The Jews of this province were apparently divided over the question of Messiah Jesus. It is my considered opinion that the complex data of the text are best explained if we assume the existence, in Smyrna or Philadelphia, of an implacable rivalry between two distinctive readings of what the Scriptures had to say about Israel's calling and election. As I see it, the author of Revelation is disputing and denouncing another Jewish world-view than his own – one nourished by another way of reading the same Hebrew Scriptures.[3] Revelation repeatedly goes so far as to develop a disturbing caricature of everything that was dear to the author and to the brothers and companions to whom he wrote. I suggest that, whenever this happens, the Book deliberately targets an opposing reading of Israel's Scriptures and of the state of the covenant between God and humanity to which they bore witness; in so doing it aims to mock, refute and neutralise this rival approach. In the same way that the writing prophets of the Old Testament could declare their vehement opposition to readings of the sacred writings other than their own, or other accounts of the highs and lows of the history of the chosen people, so also Revelation appears to attack a rival interpretation of the Scriptures, current at the time, which gave an altogether different rendering of the same holy history.

Revelation reads like a veritable literary and theological broadside in favour of faith in Jesus. Equally, it reads like a retort to calumny (2.9), perhaps even to persecution – if the death of Antipas is symbolical of something that really happened (2.13) – and as a call to the covenant people assembled in Asia's congregations to rally to the standard of Messiah Jesus. In our author's eyes, the covenant between YHWH and his chosen people (as spoken of by the Scriptures) can be ratified and renewed only in the

Person and through the work of the Crucified and Risen One, the slain-
but-standing Lamb. However, opposed to this view there exists a competing
vision which Revelation's author combats with all his strength.

If such a difference of opinion existed within the Jewish communities of
Asia, how is it to be explained? What exactly is at issue, and at what historical
juncture does this occur? The extent to which Revelation employs the device
of caricature might lead us to postulate the existence, in the local situation, of
a rival religio-political messianism which the Book judges, at every point, to be
'monstrous' and therefore deadly for God's people. Since wholesale changes
within ancient Judaism resulted from the Jewish War, including the eradication
of the great diversity that had characterised it in the Second Temple period,
both in Palestine and in the Dispersion,[4] the evidence of dissension points us
toward the period immediately preceding the war or to the first years of the
conflict. The existence of bitter debates within the Asian Jewish population
derives its probability from the mission already undertaken by Paul and others,
radiating out from Ephesus since the forties CE; accordingly, it is not difficult
to conceive of new tensions and changes arising in the same synagogues once
war refugees – among them followers of Jesus – flooded in from Judaea, as we
know they did in the middle sixties CE.

All of this is no more than an historical hypothesis: it requires verification,
and perhaps further modification, via historical inquiry, which at any rate
cannot be pursued here. Yet it does offer a successful explanation of the
Book's data and, in particular, of its plot. On the assumption that such
turbulence and rivalry existed among Asia's Jewish community, many
otherwise puzzling things may be satisfactorily explained. For instance, why
– in scene after scene – those faithful to the covenant are forever mixing
with renegades, and why there exist (as we have seen) bridges from one side
to the other. It also explains why the grace of God shown to the former is
so carefully contrasted with divine anger unleashed upon the latter. Again, it
accounts for why judgment brings acquittal and reward for some, while for
others there is retribution through chastisement; the contrasting images are
a communion cup on the one hand and bowls of reckoning and wrath on
the other, or a harvest that gathers in the saved and a vintage which disposes
of the condemned.

Most of all, the context of inner-Jewish controversy over the messianic
status of Jesus explains why Revelation alludes so constantly to the Scriptures:
their correct interpretation is the essential matter at stake. A re-reading of
various relevant stages in the history of Israel – times when the covenant
was broken, then restored – reveals that every renewal of the broken
covenant necessitated the overhaul of Israel. Like the New Testament in
general, Revelation insists that the covenant between YHWH and Israel was
definitively renewed by the death of Messiah Jesus on behalf of others: as a
result, Israel's limits were expanded to open the way of salvation to Gentiles.
By reading the Hebrew Scriptures in light of Jesus's ministry, Revelation's

target community understood itself as combining both Israel and the
nations and thereby taking on the role of the (re)new(ed) Israel: the Church's
inheritance of this noble calling is characterised by the sevenfold menorah
(1.12), the very symbol which bound every synagogue to the Temple at
Jerusalem.[5] In the question which the first oracle raises, as to whether a
Church's lamp stand was to be maintained or removed (2.5), we glimpse the
issue of her faithfulness or otherwise to the covenant – a matter which so
exercised the conscience of the prophets that they brought lawsuits against
apostate Israel. 'Revelation, it seems, was intended for those who knew the
Jewish Scriptures well'.[6] So much, then, for the first kind of competency.

In our present context, it would be worthwhile exploring the thorny
question of *contemporary interpretation* of the Old Testament – holy writ for
Christians, of course, but also present-day Judaism's Torah – and giving
consideration to its relationship to the New Testament. I am unable to do this
here, although I have tried to adopt a consistent position on these matters.
Nor have I made space, in these pages, for the two-sided burning question
of how the Church should relate to Israel as a political entity (established in
1948) or what might be the relationship of the contemporary Jewish state
to biblical Israel, and especially to the polymorphic Judaism of the period
before 70 CE. Nevertheless, in what I have written, canny readers will not have
missed the absence of all recourse to three things: contemporary Zionism,
which finds no foothold at all in John's Revelation; the traditional role played,
in dispensational end-time schemes, by the state of Israel through its very
existence; or any theological justification for the policies of the Jewish state or
its allies, advanced by what is called the Christian Right.

Frequenting Revelation often

What then, is to be said about readers' willingness to give Revelation their
sustained attention? Quite simply, without a constant attentiveness to the
way Revelation's narrative develops and progresses, it would not have been
possible for us to locate in the text, and draw out of it, the multiple links
between antecedents and their later developments (or, between models and
their mutations) that we have observed in the course of this study. The
results we have assembled, and the painstaking work that was involved in
obtaining them, should alert us to an important characteristic of the Book
of Revelation and to what its author wanted to achieve. In its final literary
form, the seer communicated to the Churches as a written work what he
had seen and heard, reflected on and composed. This document was not
merely to be protected from all additions or subtractions, in the customary
way (22.18-19), but also – as I said in the Introduction – to be carefully
studied. As we have seen, the first readers in meeting this requirement
needed to combine their familiarity with the Jewish Scriptures – seen as *prior
revelation* and functioning as the primitive Church's Bible and the sub-text for
its apostolic tradition – with close reading of the text of Revelation itself,[7]

whose status among them was that of *final revelation* by analogy with that which other apostolic texts in common circulation enjoyed. Brought together as a Church in Ephesus or Laodicea, believers were to steep themselves – whether by oral means and/or by textual study – in the Word as deposited in the Law and the Prophets, with the Writings, and in the apostolic witness to the Gospel, of which Revelation formed a part.

Whilst we do not know exactly what forms the primitive Church's work on these texts may have taken, whether in its worship or in other meetings, we do know our own situation. Three readings – Old Testament, Epistle and Gospel – have traditionally shaped Christian liturgy and are still practised in certain Churches. Believers today also derive encouragement not just from preaching on the Lord's Day but from Bible reading; from place to place the latter may be more or less demanding, in the form it takes, and involve devotional reading (individually or in the family) or more rigorous Bible study, whether alone or in groups. The very fact that the Book of Revelation closes the New Testament canon, and the whole Bible, suggests to me that the Church (and every believer) ought to take seriously the task of reading the particular witness it bears to God and to Christ to the testimony found in the rest of the biblical corpus.

Generally speaking, then, the first recipients of the Book of Revelation would have been able to compare its revelation with what they found already unveiled in Israel's Bible or in the apostolic testimony to Jesus. They also had another capacity, in my view, by means of which to make sense of this sort of writing and to navigate their way through its apocalyptic plot without particular difficulty. Believers in Asia might have been familiar with the Jewish apocalypses – which this Apocalypse apparently sets out to subvert[8] – or perhaps they knew, in one form or another, the so-called 'Synoptic Apocalypse' (Mt 24-25; Mk 13; Lk 17 & 21); maybe they even knew both. Whichever is the case, they would surely have been able to follow the triple movement, *affirmation* → *negation* → *reaffirmation*,[9] which is characteristic of its narrative structure. The starting-point for everything is the fact that God reigns; the happy listener to the revelation starts from here thanks to Messiah Jesus, who is worthy of the faith placed in him (1.1-5). From this beginning, the narrative goes on to recount the unsettling negation of this same reality, where the order of things becomes upset and God's plan is put in some jeopardy. Finally, everything comes back around and a resolution is reached where there can be a renewed affirmation both of every way in which God shows himself faithful to his project on behalf of humanity, and of human faith which responds to his action.

As soon as we take full account of this movement in three phases, we cannot help but notice how the anarchy of the central section which so many readers feel – caused by the breaking of the seals, the sounding of the trumpets and the pouring out of the bowls in succession – in reality has no lasting effect upon the previously established state of grace in which believers find themselves (*cf.* 1.4). The same may be said for everything that the dragon and its helpers set about doing in the interim, none of which can fall outside God's permissive will or the strict limits he has placed on it; they can never escape from their condition or their status as a paltry imitation. As it progresses, in fact, the plot gradually neutralises its own negative pole so that, by the end (chapters 21–22), the salvation alluded to at the start (1.4-6) is re-established and fully accomplished. Consequently, whatever may jump out alarmingly from the pages of Revelation in the course of the intervening episodes need not bother us any more than it did the first readers. At all times the plot is directed towards one objective, and one only, which is the confirmation (or re-establishment, if necessary) of the first recipients in their choice to place an authentic faith squarely in Jesus Christ. In pursuit of such a goal, it becomes necessary to expose any and every powerful counterfeit that may exist, heaping derision upon it and endeavouring to wean away from it anyone who might have fallen for its lies.[10]

For today's readers, the Book of Revelation keeps hard questions live: despite the good news of freedom heard in our day, might we be captive in our turn to some miserable form of idolatry that wears the garb of our own century? Such questioning has the potential to liberate us from whatever may hold us prisoner and to have us exchange our chains for 'captivity' to the Word that can set us free, through being joined to Jesus Christ by faith. According to the testimony of the Book of Revelation, Christ who is the Crucified and Risen One, and the Lord of the Church, remains the Victor. His fellow victors will inherit all the promises that faith could want, one day when God and the Lamb come at last to illuminate the city of humanity: this is the reality underlined repeatedly from the outset, in the oracles to Churches that form the opening septet. In this ultimate vision, which is also in full agreement with Paul's own preaching, we see Christ at last become all in all (*cf.* 1 Cor 15.28; Col 3.11).

Notes

1   For the prophet, this situation is irksome. Stanley Hopper calls it 'the *pathos* of the middle' (quoted by J.G. Williams, 'Irony and Lament: Clues to Prophetic Consciousness', *Semeia* 8, 1977, p.52). Later (pp.67-68), Williams recalls how God himself felt this *pathos* (owing to the contradiction between what Israel was called to be and its actual state) and how the prophet in turn, out of solidarity for this divine *pathos*, formulates a word born out of sympathy for God.

2   Both forms of competency were previously identified, in the part of section two of the *Introduction* entitled 'Reading Revelation, where do we start?'

3   Once again, see historical detour no. 5 (in ch.3) which deals with the problem of identifying the false worship.

4   For a typology of the multi-faceted nature of Judaism in the period prior to 70 CE, see F. Siegert, 'Le judaïsme au premier siècle et ses ruptures intérieures', in D. Marguerat (ed.), *Le Déchirement. Juifs et chrétiens au premier siècle*, Geneva, 1996, pp.25-65.

5   Equivalent symbolical value should be attached to the two *scrolls* (or books) found in 5.1 and 10.2.

6   G. Campbell, 'Apocalypse de Jean', *op. cit.*, p.89; *cf.* the part of section 2 of the *Introduction*, 'Reading Revelation, where do we start?' For a summary of the main ways in which Revelation makes use of the OT, see the three paragraphs in point II of the same article, entitled 'Référence aux Ecritures juives' (reference to the Jewish Scriptures).

7   When P. Duke, *Irony in the Fourth Gospel*, Atlanta, John Knox Press, 1985, pp.148-49, discusses the theatre of reception for the Fourth Gospel's irony, he could just as well have been talking about Revelation's target audience. For Duke, the Fourth Gospel implies readers who paid attention to backward allusions made to words already spoken or to forward anticipations of still unsaid things, in other words, readers able to handle its carefully crafted language and thought.

8   Could the Apocalypse be an anti-apocalypse? For more on this, see again my article 'Apocalypse de Jean', p.88.

9   On this subject see once more 'Propositions', Calloud, Delorme and Duplantier (*op. cit.*), p.367; *cf. supra* my *Introduction*, n.42.

10 For L.L. Johns, 'The Lamb', *op. cit.*, p.762, Revelation's apocalyptic vision fires the imagination of its readers and displaces their self-understanding; it does so by making use of three rhetorical devices in particular: definition, re-definition and parody. On the same point compare Barr, *Tales*, *op. cit.*, p.180, for whom Revelation affects the understanding, the psychology and the concrete actions of its readership; it effects a transformation by affording readers a new, communally-focused vision.

Bibliography

Allo, E.-B., *St. Jean, l'Apocalypse*, Paris, Gabalda, 1933, 4th edition.

Aune, D.E., 'The Influence of Roman Court Ceremonial on the Apocalypse of John', *Biblical Research* 38, 1983, pp.5-26

—— *The New Testament in its Literary Environment*, Philadelphia, Westminster, 1987

—— 'Following the Lamb: Discipleship in the Apocalypse', in R.N. Longenecker (ed.), *Patterns of Discipleship in the New Testament*, Grand Rapids/Cambridge, Eerdmans, 1996, pp.269-84

—— *Revelation 1-5*, Dallas, Word, 1997

—— *Revelation 6-16*, Nashville, Nelson, 1998

—— *Revelation 17-22*, Nashville, Nelson, 1998

Bachmann, M., 'Himmlisch: der 'Tempel Gottes' von Apk 11.1', *New Testament Studies* 40, 1994, pp.474-80

—— 'Noch ein Blick auf den ersten apokalyptischen Reiter (von Apk.6.1-2)', *New Testament Studies* 44, 1998, pp.257-78

Balyeat, J.R., *Babylon, The Great City of Revelation*, Sevierville, Onward Press, 1991

Barker, M., *The Revelation of Jesus Christ*, Edinburgh, T&T Clark, 2000

Barnett, P., 'Polemical Parallelism: Some Further Reflections on the Apocalypse', *Journal for the Study of the New Testament* 35, 1989, pp.111-20

Barr, D.L., 'The Apocalypse of John as Oral Enactment', *Interpretation* 50, 1986, pp.243-56

—— *Tales of the End. A Narrative Commentary on the Book of Revelation*, Santa Rosa, Polebridge Press, 1998

Barth, K., *Church Dogmatics* (vol. I), Edinburgh (tr. T&T Clark), 1956-69

Bartholomew, C., C.S. Evans, M. Healy and M. Rae (eds), *'Behind' the Text: History and Biblical Interpretation* (Scripture & Hermeneutics Series vol. 4), Grand Rapids/Carlisle, Zondervan/Paternoster, 2003

Bauckham, R.J., *The Theology of the Book of Revelation*, Cambridge, Cambridge University Press, 1993

—— *The Climax of Prophecy*, Edinburgh, T&T Clark, 1993

—— 'God in the Book of Revelation', *Proceedings of the Irish Biblical Association* 18, 1995, pp.40-53

—— *God Crucified: Monotheism and Christology in the New Testament*, Carlisle/Grand Rapids, Paternoster/Eerdmans, 1998

Beagley, A.J., *The Sitz im Leben of the Apocalypse with Particular Reference to the Role of the Church's Enemies*, New York, De Gruyter, 1987

Beale, G.K., *The Use of Daniel in Jewish Apocalyptic Literature and in the Revelation of John*, Lanham, University Press of America, 1984

—— 'The Interpretative Problem of Rev 1:19', *Novum Testamentum* 34/4, 1992, pp.360-87

—— *John's Use of the Old Testament in Revelation*, Sheffield, Sheffield Academic Press, 1998

—— *The Book of Revelation*, Grand Rapids/Cambridge, Eerdmans, 1999

Beasley-Murray, G.R., *The Book of Revelation*, London, Eerdmans, 1974

Beckwith, I.T., *The Apocalypse of John*, New York, MacMillan, 1919

Blount, B.K., *Can I Get A Witness? Reading Revelation Through African American Culture*, Louisville, Westminster John Knox, 2005

Böcher, O., *Das Neue Testament und die dämonischen Mächte*, Stuttgart, Katholisches Bibelwerk, 1972

Boesak, A.A., *Comfort and Protest: The Apocalypse from a South African Perspective*, Philadelphia, Westminster, 1987

Boring, M.E., *Revelation*, Louisville, John Knox Press, 1989

—— 'Narrative Christology in the Apocalypse', *Catholic Biblical Quarterly* 54/4, 1992, pp.702-23

—— 'The Voice of Jesus in the Apocalypse of John', *Novum Testamentum* 34/4, 1992, pp.334-59

Bovon, F., 'John's Self-presentation in Revelation 1:9-10', *Catholic Biblical Quarterly* 62, 2000, pp.693-700

Brütsch, C., *Clarté de l'Apocalypse*, Geneva (tr. Labor et Fides), 1955

Calloud, J., J. Delorme and J.-P. Duplantier, 'L'Apocalypse de Jean. Propositions pour une analyse structurale', in L. Monloubou (ed.), *Apocalypses et théologie de l'espérance*, Paris, Cerf, 1977

Campbell, G., 'How to say what. Story and Interpretation in the Book of Revelation', *Irish Biblical Studies* 23, 2001, pp.111-34

—— 'Un procédé de composition négligé de l'Apocalypse de Jean', *Etudes théologiques et religieuses* 77, 2002/4, pp.491-516

—— 'True and False Proclamation in the Book of Revelation' (part 1), *Irish Biblical Studies* 25, 2003/2, pp.60-73,

—— 'True and False Proclamation in the Book of Revelation' (part 2), *Irish Biblical Studies* 25, 2003/3, pp.106-20

—— 'Pour lire l'Apocalypse de Jean: l'intérêt d'une approche thématique', *Revue Réformée* 224, 2003/4, pp.43-65

—— 'Apocalypse et Extermination', *Revue Réformée* 225, 2003/5, pp.89-107

—— 'Apocalypse de Jean', in *Grand Dictionnaire de la Bible*, Le Cléon d'Andran, Excelsis, 2004, pp.87-89

—— 'Findings, Seals, Trumpets and Bowls: Variations upon the Theme of Covenant Rupture and Restoration in the Book of Revelation', *Westminster Theological Journal* 66, 2004, pp.71-96

—— 'Fidèles de l'Agneau, esclaves du monstre: identités rivales dans l'Apocalypse de Jean' (part 1), *Théologie Evangélique* 3, 2004/1, pp.41-54

—— 'Fidèles de l'Agneau, esclaves du monstre: identités rivales dans l'Apocalypse de Jean' (part 2), *Théologie Evangélique* 3, 2004/2, pp.113-22

—— 'Antithetical Feminine-Urban Imagery and a Tale of Two Women-Cities in the Book of Revelation', *Tyndale Bulletin* 55, 2004/1, pp.81-108

—— 'La royauté de Dieu, de l'Agneau et des siens dans l'Apocalypse de Jean', *Revue Réformée* 233, 2005/3, pp.44-61

—— 'Apocalypse johannique et persévérance des saints', *Revue Réformée* 236, 2006/1, pp.43-55

Caird, G.B., *The Revelation of St. John the Divine*, London, A&C Black, 1966

Callahan, A.D., 'Apocalypse as Critique of Political Economy. Some Notes on Revelation 18', in *Horizons in Biblical Theology* 21, 1999, pp.46-65

Carnegie, D.R., 'Worthy is the Lamb: The Hymns in Revelation', in H.H. Rowden (ed.), *Christ the Lord. Studies in Christology presented to Donald Guthrie*, Leicester, IVP, 1982, pp.243-56

Carrez, M., 'Le déploiement de la christologie de l'Agneau dans l'Apocalypse', *Revue d'Histoire et de Philosophie Religieuses* 79, 1999, pp.5-17

Cerfaux, L., and J. Cambier, *L'Apocalypse de St. Jean lue aux chrétiens*, Paris, Cerf, 1955

Charles, R.H., *The Revelation of St. John* (2. vols.), Edinburgh, T&T Clark, 1920

Charlier, J.-P., *Comprendre l'Apocalypse*, Paris, Cerf, 1991

Chevallier, M.-A., *L'Exégèse du Nouveau Testament. Initiation à la méthode*, Geneva, Labor et Fides, 1985

Childs, B. S., *Biblical Theology of the Old and New Testament. Theological Reflection on the Christian Bible*, Minneapolis, Fortress, 1993

Chilton, D., *The Days of Vengeance*, Fort Worth, Dominion Press, 1987

Comblin, J., 'La liturgie de la Nouvelle Jérusalem (Apoc. 21.1–22.5)', *Ephemerides Theologicae Lovanienses*, 1953, p.5-40

—— *Le Christ dans l'Apocalypse*, Paris-Tournai, Desclée, 1965

Conzelmann, H. and A. Lindemann, A. *Interpreting the New Testament: An Introduction to the Principles and Methods of N.T. Exegesis*, Peabody, Hendrickson, 1988

Corsini, E., *The Apocalypse. The perennial revelation of Jesus Christ* (Good News Study no.5), Dublin (tr. Veritas), 1983

Cothenet, E., *Le message de l'Apocalypse*, Mesnil-sur-l'Estrée, Mame/Plon, 1995

Court, J.M., *Reading the New Testament*, London, Routledge, 1997

Cuvillier, E., 'Christ ressuscité ou bête immortelle? Proclamation pascale et propagande impériale dans l'Apocalypse de Jean', in D. Marguerat & O. Mainville (dir.), *Résurrection. L'après-mort dans le monde ancien et le Nouveau Testament*, Geneva/Montreal, Labor et Fides/MediasPaul, 2001

d'Aragon, J.-L, *The Apocalypse*, Englewood Cliffs, Prentice-Hall, 1968

Davis, D.R., 'The Relationship Between the Seals, Trumpets, and Bowls in the Book of Revelation', *Journal of the Evangelical Theological Society* 16, 1973, pp.158-59

Davis, R.D., *The Heavenly Court Judgment of Revelation 4-5*, Lanham/, London, University Press of America, 1992

Deichgräber, R., *Gotteshymnus und Christushymnus in der frühen Christenheit*, Gottingue, Vandenhoeck und Ruprecht, 1967

Deissmann, A., *Light from the Ancient East*, London, (tr. Hodder and Stoughton), 1910

Delebecque, E., *L'Apocalypse de Jean*, Paris, Mame, 1992

Deutsch, C., 'Transformation of Symbols: The New Jerusalem in Rev 21.1-22.5', *Zeitschrift für die neutestamentliche Wissenschaft* 78, 1987, pp.106-26

de Villiers, P.G.R., 'The Lord Was Crucified in Sodom and Egypt. Symbols in the Apocalypse of John', *Neotestamentica* 22, 1988, pp.125-38

Draper, J.A., 'The Heavenly Feast of Tabernacles', *Journal for the Study of the New Testament* 19, 1983, pp.133-47

Duff, P., *Who Rides the Beast? Prophetic Rivalry and the Rhetoric of Crisis in the Churches of the Apocalypse*, New York, Oxford University Press, 2001

Duke, P., *Irony in the Fourth Gospel*, Atlanta, John Knox Press, 1985

Du Preez, J., 'Ancient Near Eastern Vassal Treaties and the Book of Revelation. Possible Links', *Religion in South Africa* 2/2, 1981, pp.33-43

Edersheim, A., *The Life and Times of Jesus the Messiah* (2 vols.), McLean, MacDonald, 1886

Ellul, J., *L'Apocalypse: Architecture en mouvement*, Paris, Desclée, 1975

—— *Sans feu ni lieu*, Paris, Gallimard, 1975

Esser, H.H., 'Law, custom, elements', in C. Brown (ed.), *New International Dictionary of New Testament Theology* (vol. 2), Carlisle/Grand Rapids (tr. Paternoster/Zondervan), 1986, pp.451-53

Farrer, A.M., *The Revelation of St. John the Divine*, Oxford University Press, London, 1964

Fee, G.D. (*et. al.*), *Biblical Criticism: Historical, Literary and Textual*, Grand Rapids, Zondervan, 1978

—— *New Testament Exegesis. A Handbook for Students and Pastors*, Louisville, Westminster/John Knox, 1993

Fekkes, J., *Isaiah and Prophetic Traditions in the Book of Revelation: Visionary Antecedents and Their Development*, Sheffield, JSOT Press, 1994

Feuillet, A., *L'Apocalypse – L'Etat de la question*, Paris, Desclée, 1963

—— 'Les 144,000 Israélites marqués d'un sceau', *Novum Testamentum* 9, 1967, pp.191-224

Fodor, J., *Christian Hermeneutics. Paul Ricœur and the Reconfiguring of Theology*, Oxford, Clarendon Press, 1995

Ford, D., *Crisis!* (3 vols.), Desmond Ford Publications, Newcastle, 1982

Ford, J.M., *Revelation*, Doubleday, Garden City, 1975

Frei, H., *The Eclipse of Biblical Narrative: A Study in Eighteenth and Nineteenth Century Hermeneutics*, New Haven/London, Yale University Press, 1974

Friesen, S.J., *Imperial Cults and the Apocalypse of John. Reading Revelation in the Ruins*, New York, Oxford University Press, 2001

Gamber, K., *Das Geheimnis der sieben Sterne: Zur Symbolik der Apokalypse*, Regensburg, Pustet, 1987

Garrow, A.J.P., *Revelation*, London/New York, Routledge, 1997

Georgi, D., 'Die Visionen vom himmlischen Jerusalem in Apk 21 und 22', in D. Lührmann and G. Strecker (eds), *Kirche. Festschrift für Günther Bornkamm zum 75. Geburtstag*, Tübingen, Mohr/Siebeck, 1980, pp.351-72

Giblin, C.H., 'Structural and Thematic Correlations in the Theology of Revelation 16-22', *Biblica* 55, 1974, pp.487-504

—— 'Revelation 11.1-13: Its Form, Function, and Contextual Integration', *New Testament Studies* 30, 1984, pp.433-59

—— *The Book of Revelation: The Open Book of Prophecy*, Collegeville, Liturgical Press, 1991

—— 'Recapitulation and the Literary Coherence of John's Apocalypse', *Catholic Biblical Quarterly* 56, 1994, pp.81-95

Giesen, H., 'Symbole und mythische Aussagen in der Johannesapokalypse und ihre theologische Bedeutung', in K. Kertelge (ed.), *Metaphorik und Mythos im Neuen Testament*, Freiburg/Basle/Vienna, Herder, 1990

—— *Im Dienst der Weltherrschaft Gottes und des Lammes: Die vier apokalyptischen Reiter (Offb 6.1-8)*, Stuttgart, SNTU, 1997

Giet, S., *L'Apocalypse et l'Histoire: étude historique sur l'apocalypse johannique*, Paris, Presses universitaires de France, 1957

Glonner, G., *Zur Bildersprache des Johannes von Patmos. Untersuchung der Johannesapokalypse anhand einer um Elemente der Bilderinterpretation erweiterten historisch-kritischen Methode*, Münster, Aschendorff, 1999

Gollinger, H., *Die Kirche in der Bewahrung: Eine Einführung in die Offenbarung des Johannes*, Aschaffenburg, Paul Pattloch Verlag, 1973

Grünzweig, F., *Johannesoffenbarung* (2 vols.), Neuhausen-Stuttgart, Hänssler Verlag, 1981-82

Guillemette, P. and M. Brisebois, *Introduction aux méthodes historico-critiques*, Montreal, Fides, 1987

Guthrie, G., 'Boats in the Bay. Reflections on the Use of Linguistics and Literary Analysis in Biblical Studies', in S.E. Porter & D.A. Carson, *Linguistics and the New Testament*, Sheffield, Sheffield Academic Press, 1999

Harrington, W., *Revelation*, Collegeville, Michael Glazier, 1993

Harvey, J., 'Le 'Rîb-Pattern', réquisitoire prophétique sur la rupture de l'alliance', *Biblica* 43, 1962, pp.172-96

Hauret, C., 'Eve transfigurée: de la Genèse à l'Apocalypse', *Revue d'Histoire et de Philosophie Religieuses* 3-4, 1979, pp.327-39

Hemer, C., *The Letters to the Seven Churches of Asia in their Local Setting*, Sheffield, JSOT Press, 1986

Hendriksen, W., *More Than Conquerors*, London, The Tyndale Press, 1962

Herzer, J., 'Der erste apokalyptische Reiter und der König der Könige. Ein Beitrag zur Christologie der Johannes-apokalypse', *New Testament Studies* 45, 1999, pp.230-49

Hirschberg, P., *Das eschatologische Israel. Untersuchungen zum Gottesvolkverständnis der Johannesoffenbarung*, Neukirchen-Vluyn, Neukirchener Verlag, 1999

Hopkins, M., 'The Historical Perspective of Apocalypse 1-11', *Catholic Biblical Quarterly* 27, 1965, pp.42-47

Humphrey, E.M., *The Ladies and the Cities: Transformation and Apocalyptic Identity in Joseph and Aseneth, 4 Ezra, the Apocalypse and the Shepherd of Hermas*, Sheffield, Sheffield Academic Press, 1995

Hurtado, L.W., 'Revelation 4-5 in the Light of Jewish Apocalyptic Analogies', *Journal for the Study of the New Testament* 25, 1985, pp.105-24

Jenks, G.C., *The Origins and Early Development of the Antichrist Myth*, Berlin, W. de Gruyter, 1991

Jeremias, J., *Jerusalem in the Time of Jesus*, Philadelphia, Fortress, 1969

Johns, L.L., 'The Lamb in the Rhetorical Program of the Apocalypse of John', *SBL 1998 Seminar Papers* (vol. 2), Atlanta, Scholar Press, 1998, pp.762-84

Jörns, K.-P., *Das hymnische Evangelium: Untersuchungen zu Aufbau, Funktion und Herkunft der hymnischen Stücke in der Johannes-offenbarung*, Gütersloh, Mohn, 1971

Judge, E.A., 'The Mark of the Beast, Revelation 13.16', *Tyndale Bulletin* 42, 1991, pp.158-60

Keener, C.S., *Revelation*, Grand Rapids, Zondervan, 2000

Kennel, G., *Frühchristliche Hymnen? Gattungs-kritische Studien zur Frage nach den Liedern der frühen Christenheit*, Neukirchen-Vluyn, Neukirchener Verlag, 1995

Kiddle, M., *The Revelation of St. John*, London, Hodder and Stoughton, 1940

Kirby, J.T., 'The Rhetorical Situations of Revelation 1-3', *New Testament Studies* 34, 1988, pp.197-207

Kline, M.J., 'Double Trouble', *Journal of the Evangelical Theological Society* 32, 1989, pp.171-80

Knight, J., *Revelation*, Sheffield Academic Press, Sheffield, 1999

Koester, C.R., *Revelation And The End Of All Things*, Grand Rapids/Cambridge, Eerdmans, 2001

Kovacs, J., C. Rowland and R. Callow, *Revelation: The Apocalypse of Jesus Christ*, Malden/Oxford/Victoria, Blackwells, 2004

Kraft, H., *Die Offenbarung des Johannes*, Tübingen, Mohr, 1974

Kraybill, J.N., *Imperial Cult and Commerce in John's Apocalypse*, Sheffield, Sheffield Academic Press, 1996

Kroon, K.H., *Der Sturz der Hure Babylon. Eine zeitgeschichtliche Auslegung der Johannes-Apokalypse* (tr. Berlin, Alektor),1988

Kuen, A., *Introduction au Nouveau Testament: L'Apocalypse*, St.Légier, Editions Emmaüs, 1997

Lafont, L., *L'Apocalypse de Saint Jean*, Paris, Téqui, 1975

Läuchli, S. 'Eine Gottesdienst-struktur in der Johannesoffenbarung', *Theologische Zeitschrift* 16, 1960, pp.359-78

Le Moignan, C., *Following the Lamb. A Reading of Revelation for the New Millennium*, Peterborough, Epworth, 2000

Leonard, J.E., *Come Out of Her My People*, Arlington Heights, Laudemont Press, 1991

Lohmeyer, E., *Die Offenbarung des Johannes*, Tübingen, Mohr, 1970

McKelvey, R.J., *The New Temple. The Church in the New Testament*, Oxford, Oxford University Press, 1969

Malina, B., *On the Genre and Message of Revelation*, Peabody, Hendrickson, 1995

———, *The New Jerusalem in the Revelation of John: The City as Symbol of Life with God*, Collegeville, Michael Glazier, 2000

———, and J.J. Pilch, *Social-Science Commentary on the Book of Revelation*, Minneapolis, Fortress, 2000

Marguerat, D. (ed.), *Le Déchirement. Juifs et chrétiens au premier siècle*, Geneva, Labor et Fides, 1996

Marguerat, D. and Y. Bourquin, *How to Read Bible stories: An Introduction to Narrative Criticism*, London (tr. SCM Press), 1999

———, (ed.), *Quand la Bible se raconte*, Paris, Cerf, 2003

———, A. Wénin and B. Escaffre (ed.), *Autour des récits bibliques* (Cahier Evangile 127), Paris, Cerf, 2004

———, (ed.), *La Bible en récits. L'exégèse biblique à l'heure du lecteur*, Geneva, Labor et Fides, 2005, 2nd edition

Marshall, J.W., *Parables of War. Reading John's Jewish Apocalypse* (Studies in Christianity and Judaism 10), Waterloo, Wilfred Laurier University Press, 2001

Mealy, J.W., *After the Thousand Years: Resurrection and Judgment in Revelation 20*, Sheffield, JSNTSS, 1992

Meynet, R., *Initiation à la rhétorique biblique: qui donc est le plus grand?* (2 vols.), Paris, Cerf, 1982

———, *L'analyse rhétorique. Une nouvelle méthode pour comprendre la Bible*, Paris, Cerf, 1989

———, *Lire la Bible*, Paris, Flammarion, 2003

Miller, K., 'The Nuptial Eschatology of Revelation 19-22', *Catholic Biblical Quarterly* 60, 1998, pp.301-18

Minear, P., 'Ontology and Ecclesiology in the Apocalypse', *New Testament Studies* 12, 1966, pp.89-105

———, *I Saw a New Earth. An Introduction to the Visions of the Apocalypse*, Washington, Corpus Books, 1968

Morton, R., 'Glory to God and to the Lamb: John's Use of Jewish and Hellenistic/ Roman Themes in Formatting His Theology in Revelation 4-5', *Journal for the Study of the New Testament* 83, 2001, pp.89-109

Mounce, R.H., *The Book of Revelation*, Grand Rapids, Eerdmans, 1998, 2nd edition

Moyise, S., *The Old Testament in the Book of Revelation*, Sheffield, Sheffield Academic Press, 1995

———, *The Old Testament in the New. An Introduction*, New York/London, Continuum, 2001

Müller, H.P., *Formgeschichtliche Untersuchungen zu Apok.4f*, Heidelberg, unpublished dissertation, 1962

Murphy, F.J., *Fallen is Babylon: The Revelation to John*, Harrisburg, Morehouse, 1998

Mussner, F., '"Weltherrschaft" als eschatologisches Thema der Johannes-apokalypse', in E. Grässer and O. Merk, *Glaube und Eschatologie: Festschrift W.G. Kümmel*, Tübingen, Mohr, 1985

Neef, H.-D., *Gottes himmlischer Thronrat. Hintergrund und Bedeutung von sôd JHWH im Alten Testament*, Stuttgart, Calwer, 1994

Neudorfer, H.-W. and E. J. Schnabel (ed.), *Das Studium des Neuen Testaments. Eine Einführung in die Methoden der Exegese* (vol. 1), Wuppertal, R. Brockhaus, 2000

Nigosian, S.A., 'The Song of Moses (Dt. 32). A Structural Analysis', *Ephemerides theologicae Lovanienses* 72, 1996, pp.5-22

Niles, D.T., *As Seeing the Invisible*, New York, Harper, 1961

Ogden, A.M., *The Avenging of the Apostles and Prophets*, Somerset, Ogden Publications, 1985

Ortlund, R.C., *Whoredom. God's Unfaithful Wife in Biblical Theology*, Leicester, Apollos, 1996

Pattemore, S., *The People of God in the Apocalypse. Discourse, structure and exegesis*, Cambridge, Cambridge University Press, 2004

Paul, A., *Jésus-Christ, la rupture: Essai sur la naissance du christianisme*, Paris, Bayard, 2001

Paul, I., 'The Use of the Old Testament in Revelation 12', in S. Moyise (ed.), *The Old Testament in the New Testament*, Sheffield, Sheffield Academic Press, 2000, pp.256-76

Paulien, J., 'Criteria and the Assessment of Allusions to the Old Testament in the Book of Revelation', in S. Moyise (ed.), *Studies in the Book of Revelation*, T&T Clark, Edinburgh/New York, 2001, pp.113-29

Peterson, D., *Engaging with God: A biblical theology of worship*, Apollos (IVP), Leicester, 1992

Philonenko, M., 'Une voix sortit du trône qui disait . . . (Apocalypse 19,5a)', *Revue d'Histoire et de Philosophie Religieuses* 79, 1999, pp.83-89

Pohl, A., *Die Offenbarung des Johannes* (2 vols.), Wuppertal, Brockhaus, 1983

Poirier, J.C., 'The First Rider', *New Testament Studies* 45, 1999, pp.257-62

Poucouta, P., 'La mission prophétique de l'Eglise dans l'Apocalypse johannique', *Nouvelle Revue Théologique* 110, 1988, pp.38-57

Poythress, V.S., 'Counterfeiting in the Book of Revelation as a Perspective on Non-Christian culture', *Journal of the Evangelical Theological Society* 40, 1997, pp.411-12

Preston, R.H. and A.T. Hanson, *The Revelation of St. John the Divine*, London, SCM Press, 1945

Prévost, J.-P., *L'Apocalypse*, Paris, Bayard, 1995

Prigent, P., *L'Apocalypse de St. Jean*, Geneva, Labor et Fides, 1988

——, *L'Apocalypse de St. Jean*, Geneva, Labor et Fides, 2000, 2nd edition

——, 'L'Interprétation de l'Apocalypse en débat', *Etudes Théologiques et Religieuses* 75, 2000, pp.189-210

Provan, I., 'Foul Spirits, fornication and finance: Revelation from an Old Testament perspective', *Journal for the Study of the New Testament* 64, 1996, pp.81-100

Reader, W.W., *Die Stadt Gottes in der Johannesapokalypse*, Göttingen, 1971

Rengstorf, K.H., "ἑπτά", in G.W. Bromiley, *Theological Dictionary of the New Testament* (vol. 2), Grand Rapids (tr. Eerdmans), 1964, pp.627-35

Resseguie, J.L., *Revelation Unsealed. A Narrative-Critical Approach to John's Apocalypse*, Leiden/Boston/Cologne, Brill, 1998

——, *Narrative Criticism of the New Testament*, Grand Rapids, Baker, 2005

——, *The Revelation of John. A Narrative Commentary*, Grand Rapids, Baker Academic, 2009

Reynolds, E., 'The Feast of Tabernacles and the Book of Revelation', *Andrews University Seminary Studies* 38, 2000, pp.245-68

Rhoads, D., *From Every People and Nation: The Book of Revelation in Intercultural Perspective*, Minneapolis, Fortress, 2005

Richard, P., *Apocalypse: A People's Commentary on the Book of Revelation* (tr. New York, Orbis), 1995

Ricœur, P., *Interpretation Theory: Discourse and the Surplus of Meaning*, Fort Worth, Texas Christian University Press, 1976

——, 'Philosophies Critiques de l'Histoire: Recherche, Explication, Ecriture', in G. Floistad (ed.), *Philosophical Problems Today I*, Dordrecht, Kluwer Academic Press, 1994

——, *La Mémoire, l'Histoire, l'Oubli*, Paris, Seuil, 2000

Rissi, M., *Was ist und was geschehen soll danach. Die Zeit und Geschichts-auffassung der Offenbarung des Johannes*, Zurich/Stuttgart, Zwingli Verlag, 1965

——, *Alpha und Omega: eine Deutung der Johannesoffenbarung*, Basle, Friedrich Reinhardt Verlag, 1966

Ritt, H., *Offenbarung des Johannes*, Würzburg, Echter Verlag, 1986

Roller, O., 'Das Buch mit sieben Siegeln', *Zeitschrift für die neutestamentliche Wissenschaft* 26, 1937, pp.98-113

Roloff, J., *The Revelation to John*, Minneapolis, Augsburg Fortress, 1993

——, 'Neuschöpfung in der Offenbarung des Johannes', in *Schöpfung und Neuschöpfung*, Neukirchen-Vluyn, Neukirchener Verlag, 1990

Roose, H., '"*Das Zeugnis Jesu.*" *Seine Bedeutung für die Christologie, Eschatologie und Prophetie in der Offenbarung des Johannes'*, Tübingen/Basle, Francke Verlag, 2000

Rowland, C., *Revelation*, London, Methodist Publishing House, 1993

Ruiz, J.-P., *Ezekiel in the Apocalypse: The Transformation of Prophetic Language in Revelation 16.17-19.10*, Frankfurt, Peter Lang, 1989

Scherrer, S.J., 'Signs and Wonders in the Imperial Cult: A New Look at a Roman Religious Institution in the Light of Rev 13.13-15', *Journal of Biblical Literature* 103, 1984, pp.599-610

Schlatter, A., *Die Offenbarung des Johannes*, Stuttgart, Calwer, 1910

Schmitz, E.D., 'ἑπτά / ἑπτάκις' in C. Brown (ed.), *New International Dictionary of New Testament Theology* (vol. 2), Carlisle/Grand Rapids (tr. Paternoster/Zondervan), 1986, pp.690-92

Schüssler-Fiorenza, E., 'Revelation as Liberation: Apoc. 1:5f. and 5:9f.', *Catholic Biblical Quarterly* 36, 1974, pp.228-30

——, *The Book of Revelation: Justice and Judgment*, Philadelphia, Fortress, 1985

——, *Revelation: Vision of a Just World*, Edinburgh, T&T Clark, 1993

Shea, W.H., 'The Covenantal Form of the Letters to the Seven Churches', *Andrews University Seminary Studies* 21, 1983, p.71-84

——, 'Revelation 5 and 19 as literary reciprocals', *Andrews University Seminary Studies* 22, 1984, pp.249-57

——, 'The Parallel Literary Structure of Revelation 12 and 20', *Andrews University Seminary Studies* 23, 1985, pp.37-54

Sheperd, M.H., *The Paschal Liturgy and the Apocalypse*, Richmond/London, John Knox, 1960

Skehan, P., 'King of kings, Lord of lords (Apoc.19.16)', *Catholic Biblical Quarterly* 10, 1948, p.398

Slater, T.B., 'On the Social Setting of the Revelation to John', *New Testament Studies* 44, 1998, pp.232-56

Smalley, S.S., *The Revelation to John*, London, SPCK, 2005

Söllner, P., *Jerusalem, die hochgebaute Stadt. Eschatologisches und Himmlisches Jerusalem im Frühjudentum und im frühen Christentum*, Tübingen/Basle, Francke Verlag, 1998

Stauffer, E., *Die Theologie des Neuen Testaments*, Stuttgart, Kohlhammer, 1948

—— *Christ and the Caesars*, London (tr. SCM Press), 1955

Steinmann, A., 'The Tripartite Structure of the Sixth Seal, the Sixth Trumpet, and the Sixth Bowl of John's Apocalypse (Rev 6.12-7.17; 9.13-11.14; 16.12-16)', *Journal of the Evangelical Theological Society* 35, 1992, pp.69-80

Stemberger, G., *Le symbolisme du bien et du mal selon saint Jean*, Paris, Seuil, 1970

Strand, K.A., 'Chiasmic Structure and Some Motifs in the Book of Revelation', *Andrews University Seminary Studies* 16, 1978, pp.401-8

———, 'A Further Note on the Covenantal Form in the Book of Revelation', *Andrews University Seminary Studies* 21, 1983, pp.251-64

———, '"Overcomer": A Study in the Macrodynamic of Theme Development in the Book of Revelation', *Andrews University Seminary Studies* 28, 1990, pp.237-54

Sutton, R., *That You May Prosper: Dominion Through Covenant*, Fort Worth, Institute for Christian Economics, 1987

Sweet, J., *Revelation*, London, SCM Press, 1979

Swete, H.B., *The Apocalypse of St. John*, London, MacMillan, 1907

Thompson, L.L., *The Book of Revelation: Apocalypse and Empire*, Oxford/New York, Oxford University Press, 1990

———, 'Mapping an Apocalyptic World', in J. Scott and P. Simpson-Housley (eds), *Sacred Places and Profane Spaces. Essays in the Geographics of Judaism, Christianity and Islam*, Westport, Greenwood Press,1991

Thompson, M.M., 'Worship in the Book of Revelation', *Ex Auditu* 8, 1992, pp.45-54

Thüsing, W., 'Die theologische Mitte der Weltgerichtsvisionen in der Johannesapokalypse', *Trierer Theologische Zeitschrift* 77, 1968, pp.1-16

———, 'Die Vision des 'Neuen Jerusalem' (Apk 21,1-22,5) als Verheissung und Gottesverkündigung', *Trierer Theologische Zeitschrift* 77, 1968, pp.17-34

Trites, A.A., 'μάρτυς and Martyrdom in the Apocalypse', *Novum Testamentum* 16, 1973, pp.72-80

Tresmontant, C., *Apocalypse de Jean*, Paris, O.E.I.L., 1984

Trummer, P., *Aufsätze zum Neuen Testament*, Graz, Eigenverlag, 1987

Ulfgard, H., *Feast and Future: Revelation 7.9-17 and the Feast of Tabernacles*, Lund, Almqvist, 1989

Ulland, H., *Die Vision als Radikaliserung der Wirklichkeit in der Apokalypse des Johannes*, Tübingen/Basle, Francke Verlag, 1997

van de Kamp, H.R., *Openbaring. Profetie vanaf Patmos*, Kampen, Kok, 2000

van de Water, R., 'Reconsidering the Beast from the Sea (Rev 13:1)', *New Testament Studies* 46, 2000, pp.245-61

Vanni, U., 'La dimension christologique de la Jérusalem nouvelle', *Revue d'Histoire et de Philosophie Religieuses* 79, 1999, pp.119-33

van Unnik, W.C., '"Worthy is the Lamb' - the background of Apoc 5', in *Mélanges Bida Rigaux*, Gembloux, Duculot, 1970

Vogel, M., *Das Heil des Bundes. Bundestheologie im Frühjudentum und im frühen Christentum*, Tübingen/Basle, Francke Verlag, 1996

Vouga, F., *Geschichte des frühen Christentums*, Tübingen/Basle, Francke Verlag, 1994

Wall, R.W., *Revelation*, Peabody, Hendrickson, 1991

Watson, F., *Text and Truth. Redefining Biblical Theology*, Edinburgh, T&T Clark, 1997

———, *Text, Church and World. Biblical Interpretation in Theological Perspective*, London/New York, Continuum, 2004

Wilcock, M.A., *I Saw Heaven Opened*, Leicester, IVP, 1984

Williams, J.G., 'Irony and Lament: Clues to Prophetic Consciousness', *Semeia* 8, 1977, p.52

Yarbro-Collins, A., *The Apocalypse*, Dublin/Wilmington, Michael Glazier, 1979

———, *Crisis and Catharsis: The Power of the Apocalypse*, Philadelphia, Westminster John Knox, 1984

Index of Revelation passages

Index of other biblical references

Index of references to ancient literature

Thematic Index

Elements belonging to the negative pole of antithetical pairs studied in the course of this book have usually been allocated their own separate entries here: examples are adversary or monsters. However, within entries whose topic reflects a positive pole, the identifier ↔ signifies a relevant negative or contrasting theme: Thus, for example, worship • genuine, legitimate or true w. ↔ false or rival w. In order to avoid undue repetition within entries, further uses of the key topic/term are abbreviated (thus, in the previous example, w. for worship).

Author Index

Lightning Source UK Ltd.
Milton Keynes UK
UKOW040015040812

197046UK00002B/60/P